REVIEW OF RESEARCH

CONTRIBUTORS

GAIL P. BAXTER
KING BEACH
JENNIFER BERNE
LLOYD BOND
JOHN D. BRANSFORD
MARILYN COCHRAN-SMITH
ANNE HAAS DYSON
CAROLINE GIPPS
ROBERT GLASER
JOHN HATTIE
KENNETH R. HOWE
RICHARD M. JAEGER
GLORIA J. LADSON-BILLINGS
SUSAN L. LYTLE
MICHELE S. MOSES
JAMES W. PELLEGRINO
WILLIAM J. REESE
DANIEL L. SCHWARTZ
SUZANNE M. WILSON

IN EDUCATION

24 1999

ASGHAR IRAN-NEJAD
UNIVERSITY OF ALABAMA

P. DAVID PEARSON
MICHIGAN STATE UNIVERSITY

EDITORS

PUBLISHED BY THE
AMERICAN EDUCATIONAL RESEARCH ASSOCIATION
1230 Seventeenth Street, NW
Washington, DC 20036-3078

Copyright © 1999
American Educational Research Association
Library of Congress
Catalog Card No.—72-89719
Printed in the United States of America
ISBN 0-935302-24-7
ISSN 0091-732-X

Contents

Foreword

At the dawn of a millennial century, this volume of *Review of Research in Education* was designed to take a broad look at the field of educational research. As a sequel to Volume 23, the present volume continued a journey already in progress. Planning for the two volumes began in parallel at the same advisory board meeting in September 1996. Our goal for the two volumes was to work toward a gestalt, and hopefully balanced, representation of some of the field's major assumptions, themes, topics, approaches, and perspectives. Volume 23 was designed with eight chapters within the broad theme of the social organization of learning. We left the 1996 meeting with a tentative set of topics for Volume 24 as well, and had a few months to reflect before regrouping in February 1997 in Chicago. Two days of brainstorming produced the current structure and outline for Volume 24.

The turn of a millennial century offers a unique opportunity to reflect on the past and to anticipate future courses of action. For Volume 24 we asked ourselves again what past and future issues our profession should be addressing at this time. Toward the end of the first day of the 1997 meeting, we had reached consensus on three broad issues—transfer, teacher learning, and assessment—that would constitute the core of the volume. We were struck by how consistently each issue called out for multiple perspectives, although in each case a somewhat different set. For the issue of transfer, a trifurcation of cognitive, sociocultural, and critical lenses emerged. We had a somewhat different set for teacher learning, focusing on knowledge of profession, learner diversity, and practice. For assessment, the lenses were cognitive, sociocultural, and technical.

So our first decision was to address these three topics, each from three perspectives. These nine chapters alone, as meaty and multifaceted as they would be, would not suffice for a turn of the millennium volume—something was missing, and that was the broad perspective on educational inquiry. As we pored over the many brainstorming sheets of paper on the walls around us, two more topics presented themselves as candidates for the lead chapters: the history of the impact of educational research on practice and the ethics of educational research. They were the perfect missing pieces to complement the first nine in providing a broad look across the field of educational inquiry.

The second day of the meeting produced a large slate of potential authors and consulting editors. As we headed for the airport in the early afternoon, still dizzy and overwhelmed by the intensity, speed, and excitement of more than a dozen brainstorming hours, we were content that we were off to a good start. And now we are at the finish—a long time coming, but well worth the effort.

The design of Volume 24 challenged the authors, along with their consultants, to create a timely and engaging rendering of their topic for the occasion. Authors were to think about their topics in a different way, more as reflections than as compendiums. Rather than aiming for an exhaustive and meticulously woven tapestry of facts, the reviews were to be conceptually rich renditions of the past, while still allowing future-oriented readings of the field. The audience of *RRE* was made explicit to the authors—colleagues, graduate students, and educational practitioners in the wide range of disciplines and fields in the world of educational research. The volume was to fill such roles as a set of readings for a graduate course, a guide for an individual quest on a particular topic, or a road map for research and development, among others. As the authors crafted their chapters, they kept in mind these thoughts about audience and purpose.

Each author was encouraged to incorporate a retrospective-prospective format in whatever manner seemed to fit the topic. Each chapter was to be grounded in the scholarly literature on the topic, but also was to address epistemological issues—how we know what we know, what counts as knowledge, what counts as evidence, or how the researcher influences knowledge production. Mindful of the need for conceptual richness and depth, we asked authors to incorporate, where appropriate, theories of mind, analytic tools of inquiry (ways of framing questions, data collection approaches, and rhetorical traditions of reporting research), issues of policy, plurality of approaches and constituencies, and practice. All chapters were to be crafted in a way that might extend knowledge and understanding beyond its current boundaries. No small task!

The consulting editors served as a resource to authors, general editors, and the organization, rather than reviewers in the traditional sense. Authors and consulting editors could choose to stay involved for ongoing interaction throughout the process of developing the chapter or to provide focused feedback at the outline, rough draft, and final draft stages. Most of the authors shared outlines in the spring of 1998, first drafts in the summer, and final drafts by the late fall. Chapters went into production in the spring of 1999.

In the process, our greatest assets were the people who helped us negotiate the issues and topics that fill the two volumes for which we were responsible: the colleagues who gave us good advice about whom to invite as members of our Editorial Advisory Board; Editorial Advisory Board members who shared their creativity and clear thinking about the topics, authors, and consulting editors for each volume; and, of course, the authors and consulting editors who made it happen.

Asghar Iran-Nejad
P. David Pearson
Editors

Introduction

Welcome to the Threshold of a New Science of Education

ASGHAR IRAN-NEJAD
University of Alabama

P. DAVID PEARSON
Michigan State University

The Volume at a Glance

As we page through the chapters of this volume, the dominant emotion we feel is pride in having been at least remotely involved in their creation. The chapters are rich in coverage, depth, originality, and clarity. Perhaps the most salient theme across the set of chapters is the relationship between research and practice. One cannot help but sense throughout our preternatural commitment to solve this—as yet—inexorable problem.

The research-practice relationship is the explicit topic of Chapter 1, William J. Reese's "What History Teaches About the Impact of Educational Research on Practice." Reese offers a highly readable demonstration of how the research-practice connection, although elusive in its historical manifestation, has been intimately tied to the very identity of the field of education as a science, and has cogently characterized its hitherto more common growing pains and its as yet rarely decisive accomplishments. In Chapter 2, Kenneth Howe and Michele Moses address a different aspect of the relationship between research and practice. They offer an engaging analysis of the foundational perspectives and operating principles that govern traditional and contemporary approaches to the ethical dilemmas inherent in educational research, including how these dovetail with federal regulations and the AERA code of research ethics.

According to Lagemann (1997), one of the early "powerful insights" of the twentieth century was "the discovery that teaching had to be geared toward encouraging a transfer of learning if insights derived from studying one subject were to be recognized and applied within another (Judd, 1915; Schulman & Quinlan, 1996)" (p. 8). Our next three chapters deal with this practical aspect of educational research. In Chapter 3, John Bransford and Daniel Schwartz look at learning transfer through the lens of its measurement. Prevailing theories divide learning transfer into two separate steps, each of which is complete within its own realm. In the first step, the learning situation tends to exclude transfer considerations by importing and completing a predetermined learning product within its bounds. The learner, then, is assumed to hand carry this finished product for direct application to the transfer (mainly testing) situation. There, measures of transfer position the learner to engage, like a member of a court jury, in "sequestered" problem solving barred from any action that might promote new learning. In doing so, conventional learning excludes the very kind of knowledge on which learning transfer thrives, namely, contextual knowledge. Bransford and Schwartz demonstrate how broadening the scope of transfer tests to include the learner's preparation for future learning can solve many of the problems facing transfer researchers by allowing learners to engage in their own explorations and discoveries.

In Chapter 4, King Beach delves even deeper into the assumptions governing prevailing research on transfer. His conclusion is that the traditional concept of transfer has outlived its usefulness. Therefore, he goes on to demonstrate how viewing the phenomena of transfer through the new lens of consequential transitions can solve many of the theoretical and methodological barriers facing transfer researchers.

In chapter 5, Anne Dyson shows how the traditional research on transfer has created the problem of transfer by positioning education the wrong way around. As a result, Dyson argues, transfer researchers and their fellow technical practitioners have separated themselves, by means of the stone wall of incommensurability, from the real world, in which transfer is an everyday occurrence for learners. Thus, children appear, literally speaking, unruly because they live in a world that contains none of the normalizing rules so well known in the official world that education tends to create for them. Equally unruly must appear our adults' official world of the school to them. In their world, they benefit from "a diversity of resources . . . not necessarily visible . . . in [our] official worlds" (p. 145). So long as children stay on their unofficial side of the wall and clear of the official worlds of our labs and classrooms, they possess the keys to the doors of transfer that we lack. But when they cross over that wall, they are as lost in our world as we are in their world. The solution that seems as difficult as it is self-evidently critical by the end of Dyson's chapter is that educational research and practice must find ways to reposition themselves the right way around with the real world of learners.

Chapters 6, 7, and 8 witness the unfolding of the research-practice relationship in the realm of teacher learning. Making progress in practices that promote teacher learning is a Sisyphian task that can be likened to trying to reverse the downhill current while swimming upstream. In Chapter 6, Suzanne Wilson and Jennifer Berne examine how the field of professional development has moved from a segregated "incoherent and cobbled-together nonsystem" toward an integrated system of evolving communities of learners. Wilson and Berne examine the struggles, challenges, and the notable successes of these communities and remind us that in reality much more is being accomplished than has so far been possible to illuminate because of the difficulty of measuring how subtle changes in teacher knowledge and skills translate into classroom practice.

In Chapter 7, Gloria Ladson-Billings shows us how to reposition ourselves for this challenge in the context of the most uphill battles of all—education in a diverse society—by leading us through the journey in the next best way to experiencing it firsthand, namely, by telling the story of where we have been and where we could be. Ladson-Billings marks the crucial landmarks and points to innovative practices that take us in the right direction. In the end, Ladson-Billings intrigues us with the question that offers a glimpse of a challenge we will be wise to embrace: "How do we deconstruct the language of differences to allow students to move out of categories and into their full humanity?" She leaves us with the bitter taste of the conclusion, "As long as we continue to create a category of difference—teacher preparation versus teacher preparation for diverse learners—we are likely to satisfy only one group of people, those who make their living researching and writing about preparing teachers for diverse learners" (p. 244).

In Chapter 8, Marilyn Cochran-Smith and Susan Lytle lead us through yet another provocative turn in the upstream journey. They trace the boundaries of the current sources of specialized professional knowledge in the field of teacher learning. Their analysis reveals three very different conceptions of the relationship between professional knowledge and practice. One of these conceptions has been responsible for the *knowledge-for-practice* traditionally created by university researchers, corresponding to the area Schön (1987) characterized as the stone-solid hill of professional (research) knowledge. The second conception corresponds to the traditional view of acquiring *knowledge-in-practice*, reminiscent of what Schön identified as knowledge-in-action. The third conception is learning by taking an inquiry stance through participation in lifelong communities of learners responsible for the creation of *knowledge-of-practice*. The conceptions may employ similar language, tools, and goals; however, they differ fundamentally in their images of research, knowledge, teaching, practice, and development initiatives.

Chapters 9, 10, and 11 move us to a different topic and a slightly modified trifurcation. They look at assessment from a cognitive, sociocultural, and psychometric perspective. In Chapter 9, James Pellegrino, Gail Baxter, and Robert Glaser propose that assessment, cognitive psychology, and constructivism must come together. They trace the historical efforts to unite cognitive science, psychometrics, and education and demonstrate how "traditional disciplinary boundaries need to be redrawn and new disciplines defined in ways that focus a coordinated educational research and development agenda around the relationship between instruction and assessment" (pp. 345–346). In Chapter 10, Caroline Gipps traces the historical roles and functions of assessment both at the global level of the society and at the local level of the classroom. She then brings to bear the sociocultural and interpretive perspectives on these aspects to "cast new light on the power and control dynamics between pupil and teacher in the context of assessment" (p. 358). And, finally, in Chapter 11, John Hattie, Richard Jaeger, and Lloyd Bond's retrospective look at the technical traditions of assessment research reveals that traditional psychometric models have been mostly capable of handling the first one or two levels of Bloom's taxonomy of educational objectives. Prospectively, the authors stress the "need to expand our models to include higher order or deeper conceptions of learning and knowing" (p. 435).

Toward a New Science of Educational Practice

The solution to the complex problems of educational practice presented in this volume will require some careful, if unconventional, practices on the part of educational scholars. We will have to rethink the distribution of our existing knowledge and social wisdom of the field. And we may have to go against, not just beyond, the knowledge and social wisdom of the time. Understanding the dynamic structure of the current educational landscape is helpful here as well, but we need to do more. As already noted, what we face here is not only the task of swimming against the downhill current, but also managing to turn back that current as we battle it. A very different kind of conception of learning and science will be needed to do this. The new conception must provide a superlens for bringing into focus the forces that currently pull the current downhill. In education, these underlying forces are intuitively entrenched assumptions (e.g., "the smaller is the easier and the better") that work so well in the everyday world but are inapplicable to the complex world of educating people. Everyday experience has planted these assumptions deep down at the base of our intuitions beyond the reach of any ordinary knowledge and beneath the lens of awareness. The new science of education must unearth these intuitively entrenched assumptions, magnify them to make their threats to progress evident, and then transform them into forces that will turn back today's downhill currents. Before one can turn uphill the direction of a downhill current, one must reach deep down and neutralize the gravity that is pulling it downhill. For those of us who are ready and willing to witness the process, we hope the intellectual microscope of this volume will contribute to the transformation of the old into a new science of education.

References

Judd, C. H. (1915). *Psychology of high-school subjects*. Boston: Ginn.

Lagemann, E. C. (1997). Contested terrain: A history of education research in the United States, 1890–1990. *Educational Researcher, 26*, 5–17.

Schulman, L. S., & Quinlan, K. M. (1996). The comparative psychology of school subjects. In D. C. Berliner & R. C. Calfee (Eds.), *Handbook of educational psychology* (pp. 399–422). New York: Simon & Schuster Macmillan.

Chapter 1

What History Teaches About the Impact of Educational Research on Practice

WILLIAM J. REESE
University of Wisconsin–Madison

The title of this chapter is somewhat misleading, since it is uncertain whether history teaches clear "lessons" about the past. Yet, nearly everyone naturally wonders how everything has come to be, and historians for centuries have tried to describe and understand the past not just for its inherent value but also to help account for the present and perhaps to guide the future. Whether reading the daily press or interacting in their own professional worlds, professors of education commonly hear that the relationship between education-related research and changing and improving school practice is ambiguous, difficult to pinpoint, perhaps nonexistent. "Education" research has often been criticized within and outside the academy throughout the 20th century, yet how research relates to practice is a fascinating research problem of its own. Can historians shed any light on this issue?

In comparison with their writings on a host of educational topics, historians have unfortunately written very little on the relationship between research and practice. Most histories of public education, for example, do not directly address the subject, and there are far more histories of ideas about education or schools than about actual school practices. That makes the task of writing about the secondary literature difficult, given the scattered nature of the sources. But since the 1920s, a handful of writers, many of them not historians per se, have written essays, reports, and occasional books on the nature and possible influence of educational research, especially on the public schools. And in recent years, a handful of prominent, talented historians and educators, including Geraldine Joncich Clifford, Larry Cuban, and Ellen Condliffe Lagemann, have published fascinating work on aspects of the subject. By exploring some of their ideas and those of scholars in earlier decades, one can gather insights into the problem. Still, it is important to remember that the subject has not been central to the research of most historians of education, despite its evident, perhaps growing, importance today. Moreover, many scholars who conducted educational research during the past century did so for a variety of reasons, not simply because it

I would like to thank Barry Franklin, Ellen Condliffe Lagemann, B. Edward McClellan, and John Rury for their excellent criticisms of an earlier version of this chapter. I would also like to thank Carole Trone, a doctoral student at the University of Wisconsin, for her research assistance.

would probably shape policy and practice. This chapter first examines some of the earliest attempts at understanding educational research and its effects on public school practices, written mostly before the 1950s, and then turns to some of the most important historical scholarship that has appeared in recent decades.

THE EMERGENCE OF A SCIENCE OF EDUCATION

Any historical study of the relationship between educational research and practice begins for the most part in the early 20th century. During the so-called progressive era (ca. 1890–1920) the field of education, like other emerging areas of study, including the professional study of history, was swept along by new intellectual currents that emphasized the power of science and laboratory methods; the period witnessed the rising dominance of expertise over amateurs and attempts at discovering truth through objective, systematic methods of inquiry (Lagemann, 1997; Novick, 1988). Symbolized best by the survey method and expressed most visibly in the public schools in various intelligence and achievement tests, new "scientific" approaches quickly dominated education research. As academics within newly formed departments or schools of education in the emerging university system and in various educational research bureaus struggled to give their labors scientific legitimacy, a single best way to study the manifold problems of teaching and learning quickly defeated alternative approaches, although never completely (Lagemann, 1989). The lure of "science" was powerful in Western intellectual circles and became the dominant approach to educational inquiry until the late decades of this century.

Buried on library shelves one can, however, find various attempts to survey the progress and nature of educational research—its origins, approaches, and possible ties to public school practice—that were published in the first half of this century. Nearly all rightly examined the powerful influence that psychology (rather than philosophy, history, or other disciplines) had in shaping the dominant norms of "educational science," the foundations of educational research. As many historians have noted, the progressive era was the great age of scientific management in business as well as in the schools, and most early chroniclers of the evolution of education research applauded these developments. As corporations supplanted small businesses to become the heart of a growing industrial economy, schools became increasingly consolidated, standardized, removed from lay control, and professionalized. This was well symbolized through numerous interconnected changes: the turn-of-the-century collapse of ward representation on large urban school boards, the rise of social elites to positions of dominance on small boards elected at large, and the rising power of superintendents, who helped bring the gospel of science to the classroom and most parts of the educational experience. Most influential at first in the cities, where industry concentrated, providing useful models for the champions of educational administration and science, these consolidating trends ultimately would reshape the nature and structure of schooling throughout the nation. The spread of towns and cities brought with it new ways of organizing and administering the public school system, models that ultimately spread to the countryside (Fuller, 1982; Tyack, 1974).

Exactly which ideals shaped educational research in the emerging decades of the 20th century, and what impact did they seem to have on practice? In books, journal articles, conference reports, and other publications before the 1950s, a number of scholars and educators tried to assess these issues, especially the rise of research methods in education. Research publications on every conceivable aspect of education and schooling began to proliferate after 1900, so a survey of general trends can describe and assess only a selective though important segment of this writing. There were innumerable studies of school finance, building construction, teacher pay, school board size, various school tests, and other basic facets of formal education. The school survey became a common means by which to attempt to measure change carefully and objectively, promoting the idea that science and systematic investigation would inevitably lead to social reform and educational improvement (Lagemann, 1997, p. 6).

A useful starting point in examining earlier understandings of the linkages between research and practice includes an essay by J. Cayce Morrison, who was the assistant commissioner for research for the State Education Department in New York. The essay nicely illustrates major themes in educational analysis common throughout the first half of this century. Morrison published it in 1945 in the yearbook of the National Society for the Study of Education, long a prestigious publication from the University of Chicago and itself a sign of the spread of knowledge about education. Written when ideas about ''planning'' were in the air during the New Deal, the essay tried to reconstruct the history of educational research and to account for its enormous expansion. Like so many educators involved in research, Morrison did not doubt that it had a direct tie to practice, although, as shown later, he thought much research was useless. The war and economic depression, he believed, would nevertheless make research even more important in policy-making. ''Education for the years ahead must be characterized by more rigorous thinking, bold experimentation, and scientific appraisal,'' Morrison claimed on the opening page of his essay. ''A resume of the problems confronting education is appropriate to a consideration of the role research will play in the impending reconstruction of education'' (Morrison, 1945, p. 238).

Without question, since the early 20th century educators such as Morrison had believed that ''research is basic to the formulation of educational policy'' (Morrison, 1945, p. 240). Equally without question, research studies in education had exploded since ''scientific'' methods gained popularity in many academic fields in the early 1900s. As opposed to the case in the 19th century, when the study of education was mostly the province of amateurs and those without graduate training (just being conceived and institutionalized late in the century), research now occurred in multiple sites: in research bureaus within urban school systems, in special divisions within state departments of public instruction, and at many universities, especially at prestigious private schools such as Teachers

College, Columbia, and at the larger state universities. Specialized periodicals published at the local, state, and national levels that explored virtually all educational phenomena (including research) abounded. Morrison noted that *Review of Educational Research,* the child of the American Educational Research Association (AERA), first appeared in 1931 and reflected this great passion for inquiry. "A single issue of the *Review,*" he emphasized, "usually lists from five hundred to a thousand separate researches. The great majority of these have appeared in print—magazine articles, doctor's dissertations, official bulletins and reports, chapters or contributions to yearbooks, and other professional publications" (Morrison, 1945, p. 243).

Education research had come of age. Quantity was not synonymous with quality, unfortunately, even though Morrison nevertheless emphasized that scientific ideals of research had clearly advanced educational inquiry. By the early 20th century, educational study boomed, inspired by the pioneering work of Joseph Mayer Rice, a pediatrician-turned-muckraker who called for more scientific studies of education, and it was especially promoted by Edward L. Thorndike, the rising academic star at Teachers College, Columbia University, who helped make psychology the most important stimulus to empirical and scientific research in education (Cremin, 1961, pp. 3–8, 110–115; Lagemann, 1989). Along with other university-based researchers, Thorndike and his followers popularized the use of statistics and social science models, leading to countless studies of school achievement, failure rates, dropouts, and other investigations amenable to scientific analysis. Simultaneously, the early influence of European developments in research was evident. For example, American educators and social scientists adapted Alfred Binet's work with exceptional children in France and pioneered in the use of ability grouping, group intelligence tests, and then an array of achievement tests, soon common in the schools. Faith in the power of science to understand reality and then provide the guidance to manage and improve the future was widespread in the early 20th century. While acceptance of the validity of many of these assumptions would weaken late in the century, there was then considerable hope in the promise of objective, empirically based inquiry. Testing, the best studied example of the influence of science in the schools, became the most visible example of the ties between research and practice by the 1920s (Brown, 1992; Chapman, 1988; Sokol, 1987).

In 1910, the first school survey (in Boise, Idaho) began and heralded a movement that would sweep across the educational landscape, another example of the powerful hold of science upon the minds of leading educators in the progressive era (Caswell, 1929, p. 5). First individual educators, initially often state bureaucrats, and then small teams of researchers under the guidance of university-based education professors, conducted the surveys, which were usually instigated by local school boards, superintendents, civic groups, or some combination of the above to study the local scene and make recommendations for improvement. These surveys numbered in the thousands and were common not just in schools but in industry by the 1920s. Other examples of the proliferation of research could be seen in the establishment of research bureaus in some of the larger city school systems and in many state departments of public instruction. Again, education research leaped forward rapidly, inspired by a powerful faith in applying science to age-old pedagogical problems. There was no doubting the excitement and hopefulness of reformers, social scientists, and educators during these years. The survey of the Cleveland schools during World War I was massive, numbering more than a dozen volumes; its size was unusual but not its emphasis on statistical data and its presentation of numerous charts and graphs and facts and figures to help guide the policymaker (Caswell, 1929, p. 5; Morrison, 1945, pp. 238–265).

Morrison's useful historical survey of the rise of "scientific" educational research was, like many earlier and subsequent studies, somewhat vague on the actual impact that research had on public school practices. Following in the steps of Thorndike, he seemed convinced that many scholars had transformed contemporary understanding of "individual differences among children," and one could point to the rise of the testing movement in its various expressions as proof that research had decisively shaped practice (Morrison, 1945, p. 242). Morrison accurately noted, furthermore, that "a period of intensive study and experimentation with the curriculum" emerged between 1920 and 1940. "Marked progress," he claimed, "was made in adapting the content and method of instruction to the abilities and needs of individuals; and in making the processes of education harmonize with the purposes of democracy" (Morrison, 1945, p. 239). He could not really prove that the ties between research and practice were ones of cause and effect, and in fact he undercut his own assumption by repeatedly claiming that education research was often "superficial and futile," as he said at one point in describing most research studies before 1925 (Morrison, 1945, p. 242). Even when he noted the long lists of publications in *Review of Educational Research*, he concluded that most scholarship examined

the minutiae of educational problems. Much of it is little more than descriptive recording of status or progress—not infrequently indifferent description. Some of it is little more than superficial analysis of trends of opinion, attitude, or practice. Some of it advances scarcely beyond the counting stage. This is too wide a gap between research at its best and much of its practice in education. (Morrison, 1945, p. 243)

Morrison reminded his readers that education, unlike industry, did not really have that many full-time researchers. At the universities, even the prestigious ones, faculty engaged in educational research on the side. They frequently had demanding teaching loads and other professional obligations, and they were dependent on outside contracts to conduct surveys of local schools or on foundation grants that similarly funded such projects or other forms of educational inquiry. Here and there, at Iowa's Child Welfare Research Station, or in various projects at Teachers College, admirable work was done, but most education research was fragmentary, incomplete, often ill conceived, badly executed, and poorly written (see also Cravens, 1993). Unlike the work of scientists in industry, research in education was usually the product of the "lone" researcher, not a team of analysts dedicated to solving problems or studying phenomena that were replicable in the laboratory (Morrison, 1945, p. 253). No classroom was exactly like another, and most education research was thus very limited in its influence. Morrison continually emphasized that a central dilemma was the very nature of the "research community." In research bureaus in small cities, for example, the staff typically included "one professional worker, sometimes with one professional assistant, a stenographer and one or more clerks. Frequently the research function is combined with some other such as statistics, instruction, curriculum, or guidance" (Morrison, 1945, p. 256). Like their counterparts at the university, where they had trained, educational researchers there completed yet more empirical studies, which continued to multiply. Morrison concluded his essay by invoking the professional's now-ritualistic plea for more money for more researchers while carefully warning about creeping "federal" control of the schools (Morrison, 1945, p. 253).

Morrison's often insightful analysis of the nature of research is illustrative of the sorts of studies done within the educational scholarly community before the 1950s. The author was not trained as a historian, but he was curious about the dramatic rise of educational science, especially the obvious impact that psychology in particular and social science in general had on educational research methods. And he was convinced that with more research funds, more applications of the scientific method (usually deemed synonymous with quantitative methods), and more scholars engaged in study, the reconstruction of education and improvement in schools would follow. Yet, Morrison quite openly said that most existing research was weak and ineffectual. So while scientific testing seemed influential in terms of practice, the precise ways in which research shaped practice were not really explored very carefully or thoroughly.

To put Morrison's writing in context, one must recall the low status accorded education research at most universities in the early 20th century. Morrison liberally quoted Abraham Flexner's observations in his well-known book *Universities*, published in 1930 (Morrison, 1945, p. 245). Flexner, who had helped popularize changes in modern medical education earlier in the century, was horrified at what passed for educational and social science research. He believed that the American university was in a state of decline, thanks to the hiring of weak academics such as educationists and sociologists, who confused their trivial pursuits with serious research. Education research, Flexner pointed out, usually was little more than the mere gathering of information, using (and misusing) limited research tools like questionnaires and surveys and then equating the process with serious scientific study. Much education writing, he argued, was jargon laden and littered with meaningless graphs and curves, percentages and standard deviations, which masked the lack of knowledge or scientific method underlying the enterprise. "A very large part of the literature now emanating from departments of sociology, departments of education, social science committees, and educational commissions is absolutely without significance and without inspirational value," Flexner had concluded. "It is mainly superficial; its subjects are trivial; as a rule of thumb nothing is added to the results reached by the rule of thumb or the conclusions which would be reached by ordinary common sense'' (Flexner, 1930, p. 127).

Morrison basically agreed with Flexner, though as an administrator of research within a state department of education, he ultimately believed that a better day would dawn. While accepting criticisms of the weakness of educational research and remaining somewhat vague on the actual power of research to change practice, Morrison stood in a long and crowded line of educators who believed that the scientific study of education would ultimately prove a veritable boon to the nation and its schools (Tyack & Hansot, 1982, pp. 105–128). Since the 1920s, nearly all of the prominent writings on educational research had emphasized the power of "science" in inquiry and pointed to the obvious impact that school surveys, psychological testing, and related studies had had on educational practice and businesslike efficiency in the schools. Like Morrison, writing near midcentury, scholars since the 1920s had exuded the period's faith in the power of a fact-oriented science to offer definitive, objective knowledge, which in the long run would lead to educational progress. Despite a spirited reaction in the 1920s by some scholars and public intellectuals against the misuses of intelligence testing, faith in science was largely unquestioned, criticized by only a handful of professional educators who resisted the reduction of research to fact-finding empirical science (Lagemann, 1997). During the same period, historians such as Carl Becker and Charles Beard also criticized their peers for assuming that an objective past could be known, but it would take some decades before their views grew more popular among professionals.

In retrospect, one can see that the need to create a coherent narrative and explanation of the rise of educational science was essential in the shaping of a larger community of researchers. Nearly every field of study coming of age in the progressive era competed for influence; each had to make its claim to legitimacy, and the scientific basis for educational improvement and management was a powerful congealing element in the still low-status professions (Tyack & Hansot, 1982, pp. 129–152). Professionalizing fields of study such as history, which would struggle to define itself either as a humanistic or social science discipline throughout the century, similarly tried at the turn of the century to embrace the idea that they too could be regarded as a science, objective in appraisals of the past (Novick, 1988). At stake was the question of who would have power over professional development, amateurs or experts, and what procedures, methods, and philosophies would guide legitimate research.

In 1929, Hollis Leland Caswell published one of the best appraisals of his era on the evolution of school surveys, and he typically revealed the widespread, positive image of science in his day. Caswell understood that the educator's fascination with science was no accident; he cited a report by the Russell Sage Foundation demonstrating the existence of nearly 3,000 surveys already in print on innumerable subjects, sponsored not only by school systems but also by foundations, corporations, and other interests (Caswell, 1929, p. 3). The metaphors he (and most of his contemporary educators) employed to describe the intellectual climate of the times are revealing. Studying the rising popularity of city school surveys, Caswell said they were part of the larger "scientific spirit" that guided scholarship, vital to the search for "objective" truth and reliable knowledge. "Essentially the survey method is a part of the movement which is basing human thought and conduct on facts objectively measured, rather than on the assertion of authority." Whether in studies of religion, business, schools, or municipal government, "the demand has been for facts." To know the facts helped pave the way to social improvement; educators understandably wanted to forge the "connecting link between research and action." To conduct school surveys was simply a way "to secure facts as a basis for action" (Caswell, 1929, pp. 3–4, 21).

Caswell astutely noted that the survey movement was integrally bound to the larger changes influencing modern education, especially in urban school systems. Surveys were guides to action but also provided other clues to social change. Surveys were the tools of newly empowered experts such as urban superintendents, whose rise to power at the turn of the century led to the building of hierarchical chains of professional commands within expanding bureaucratic fiefdoms. Rule of thumb methods of assessing children at school gave way to a barrage of specialized tests, measurements, and instruments, as science revealed itself in educational jargon and mysterious new tools of evaluation. The Ayres spelling scale, the Hillegas composition scale, the Courtis arithmetic scale, and the Thorndike handwriting scale—these and other products of scientific research were essential to the modern educator though perhaps bewildering to ordinary people (Caswell, 1929, pp. 96–97). Educators had entered a brave new world of questionnaires, IQ and achievement tests, records and files, as statistical measures reduced the complexities of teaching and learning to more precise numbers, percentages, and marks (Tyack, 1974). Caswell interpreted this accurately as part of the larger movement of a world where the distance between expert and layperson had widened—officially all in the name of better schools for America's children. Surveys, he realized, were fads, and their proponents sometimes exaggerated their value (Caswell, 1929, p. 5). But they ultimately held the promise of connecting research and practice, though he admitted (like Morrison later) that few scholars had in fact studied precisely how research actually promoted change.

It seems somewhat surprising that educators who studied the foundations of educational science in the first half of the century so casually assumed that research inexorably led to changing policy and practice. Yet, the faith that the two were somehow inextricably linked was strong throughout these decades, even if there were occasional admissions about the low quality of research generally. In 1938, Charles H. Judd, who had helped champion surveys and scientific research as a leader in the education department at the University of Chicago, published a useful analysis of school surveys, still the dominant interest for chroniclers of the history of the field. Judd's essay, like so many in this period, affirmed that educational research before 1900 was primarily in the hands of amateurs, including the famous school reformers Horace Mann and Henry

Barnard (Judd, 1938, p. 9; Travers, 1983, chap. 1). It was somewhat anachronistic to call these men (both trained in the law, not pedagogy) researchers, but Judd rightly pointed out that both had conducted some fact-finding studies of local schools: Mann had promoted citywide tests in Boston in 1845, and Barnard had published innumerable empirical studies on the process and character of educational development. Barnard and other school reformers had also visited schools abroad, hoping to rally fellow citizens behind a particular innovation by their sometimes glowing accounts of educational practices in Europe. Judd typically assumed that this had influence on educational policy in the 19th century, but he avoided explaining how and seemed unaware that reformers were often dismissed by elected officials for suggesting that, say, the Prussian model of state centralized power was appropriate in republican America (Kaestle, 1983, p. 187).

Judd then proceeded to chronicle the ascendance of Joseph Mayer Rice, Edward L. Thorndike, and other prophets of educational science, emphasizing how faith in the "impartial judgment" of outside experts became commonplace in school policy in the early 1900s (Judd, 1938, p. 12). Surveys were assumed to have had a substantial impact on schools—precisely how was left unexplored. Did surveys confirm what local reformers wanted to hear in the first place, before they invited the outside experts to town (Tyack & Hansot, 1982, pp. 160–167)? Did "research" on local conditions really matter, and in what ways?

Judd admitted that it was in fact difficult to summarize the overall nature or effects of surveys, since they existed in such bewilderingly large numbers and since no one had ever actually tried to read them all, or many of them. Like other scholars, he more effectively proved that research had exploded in the 20th century than explained exactly what difference it meant in terms of practice. By the 1930s, education research had already gained a reputation for its low quality and doubtful utility outside the educational research community; moreover, research proliferated on so many different facets of schooling that the failure to evaluate its effects is not particularly surprising.

In 1939, Douglas Scates, a prominent student of educational research, helped explain why in an article published in *Review of Educational Research*. Scates, who would continue to publish essays on the importance of school surveys in the 1950s, observed that research in education was a diffuse enterprise. Since 1867, when it was formed "to collect information," the U.S. Office of Education had published reams of bulletins, articles, and facts and statistics on the schools. Various states had research bureaus on education, and so did an expanding number of universities. Testing departments and others dedicated to vocational education and job counseling existed on many campuses and within larger consolidated school systems. Students wrote master's and dissertation theses on education, adding to the mounting pile of educational research. And while quantitative measurements fed an apparently insatiable quest for hard facts, Scates seemed only to affirm that education research was ever growing, whatever its meaning, value, or influence. "Research is larger than statistical work; it is something more than testing," he assured his readers as he concluded his essay. "It is a continuous fact-finding, exploring, investigating service applicable to all aspects of education—administration, business management, finance, schoolbuilding, transportation, curriculum, instruction, and psychological and sociological principles" (Scates, 1939, pp. 576, 590; Scates, 1950, pp. 1126–1133).

Throughout these decades, other education scholars interested in the history of their field routinely described the rising popularity and embrace of scientific norms, which meant an emphasis on the gathering of facts and accumulating empirical evidence. Books and articles, papers and invited addresses, would continue to document the rise of an educational research community dedicated to finding objective truths that when known were assumed to lead ultimately to changes and improvements in the schools. Scholars explored the research activities, budgets, and mission of city research bureaus, state departments of public instruction, and philanthropic organizations, as well as the work of university professors and professional organizations like the National Education Association, the Progressive Education Association, and the Social Science Research Council, among the innumerable groups that sponsored "research" on teaching, learning, and other facets of education and schooling (Good, 1939; Liu, 1945; Scates, 1950). The fascination with school surveys did not abate, since they were the most publicized forms of scientific work in the schools, the subject of newspaper headlines as experts came to town to bring modern science to bear on local problems. A detailed study of 12 city research bureaus in 1945 concluded that research was a foundation for school improvement, which depended on "objective inquiry" (Liu, 1945, chap. 7). As J. Cayce Morrison predicted in that same year: "Looking to the future, education will be characterized by more rigorous thinking, bold experimentation, and scientific appraisal. To attain these characteristics, educational leadership will draw more and more on research" (1945, p. 265).

HISTORIANS AND RESEARCH ON THE IMPACT OF RESEARCH

In the past 30 years, increasing numbers of historians of education have been attracted in a broad sense to the question of how educational research shaped school policies and practices in the past. Since educators even today have considerable difficulty pinpointing the influence of research on contemporary schools, it is not surprising that historians face some arduous, sometimes insurmountable hurdles when studying the problem in previous decades. Usually histories are based on written records, which exist in infinite variety, both qualitative and quantitative, but few of these records provide direct evidence of how research shapes practice. As H. Stuart Hughes wrote a generation ago of the general plight of historians, often there is "silence in the historical record. The result is a vast unevenness in what the historian has to work on, an *embarras de richesse* combined with and canceled out by the most distressing lacaunae" (1964, p. 93).

Scholarship by writers such as Geraldine Joncich Clifford, Larry Cuban, Ellen Condliffe Lagemann, and others contains wonderful insights into the nature and role of research in the past, helping to fill important gaps in our knowledge. But there is an obvious need for book-length historical studies of educational research and practice similar to the work of educational psychologist Robert Travers, whose comprehensive analysis of the role of his field stands alone as a starting point for all readers (Travers, 1983). More and more historians are interested in the policy implications of their work, and increased numbers of scholars, inspired by the writers just mentioned, have turned their sights on ways in which research and practice interconnected (Ravitch & Vinovskis, 1995). As more scholars try to reconstruct the history of teaching and classroom experiences—a daunting task, given the nature of the source materials—we will gain a better understanding of the interconnections between ideas and action, research and practice (Finkelstein, 1989; Rousmaniere et al., 1997). But nothing like a comprehensive understanding of the overall problem seems likely to appear on the horizon anytime soon.

It all looked simpler to the generation that helped found "educational science." In 1938, Charles H. Judd confidently predicted that the proliferation of surveys would provide later chroniclers with a clearer sense of what really happened in the past.

The writers on the history of education heretofore found it necessary to depend on the writings of educational reformers and on scattered and meager data as the basis for their statements. In the future the survey reports will make possible a far more detailed treatment of school practices for this period than has ever been possible for any earlier period. (Judd, 1938, p. 18)

Yet, the reports did not speak for themselves any more than other sources used by scholars to understand America's educational past. Much more is still known about what educational reformers said than about what teachers did, about proposals for change than about the realities of everyday classroom experiences, about what research showed than about what actually characterized the lives of children and teachers.

It is imperative to remember that educational research has not been exclusively focused on practice, the main concern of this chapter. Many scholars of education in the past studied, analyzed, and debated educational issues without focusing directly on the ties between research and practice or accepting the once fashionable norm of objectivity. Moreover, ongoing debates about the possibility of reconstructing the past accurately have followed the widespread abandonment of the notion of "objectivity" within the historical profession. While much useful empirical evidence lies buried in sources in archives and on library shelves, historians have largely dispensed with the once popular idea that there is a science of history, that the facts speak for themselves, or that the facts speak unambiguously. Also, as Hughes argued, historians face a mountain of documents on the past, but they are often silent on issues of most contemporary interest. In addition, some postmodern writers, who have influenced some but not most historians, go so far as to suggest that historians are so enmeshed in their own language and literary conventions that their histories say more about their politics and discursive style than any supposed "past." Despite all of these matters of epistemology, source materials, and changing philosophical viewpoints, many scholars continue to believe that they can legitimately reconstruct the past and that their work is not synonymous with fiction (Appleby, Hunt, & Jacob, 1994; Southgate, 1996). And a number continue to try to make sense of the ties between education research and practice, whatever the epistemological objections or practical obstacles.

Perhaps the most impressive article written by a historian during the past generation on the subject of research and practice appeared in 1973 in the *Second Handbook of Research on Teaching*. However unexciting the title may appear— "A History of the Impact of Research on Teaching"—historian Geraldine Joncich Clifford provided readers with an incredibly well-researched and thoughtful essay on a notoriously difficult subject. Clifford had already written the standard biography of Edward L. Thorndike, and her mastery of the history of his influence on educational science was evident throughout the essay (Joncich, 1968). Moreover, she advanced ideas that had become more tenable by the 1960s but would have been heretical for most education scholars of earlier generations. A minority of education professors had often publicly stated that research had minimal impact on practice, but those numbers now swelled. To prove that research had a particular impact on teaching, Clifford wrote succinctly, was "a near impossibility" (Clifford, 1973, p. 3). In fact, educators seemed much better at blaming or praising a particular school practice than actually providing incontrovertible evidence about it. By the 1960s, educators increasingly doubted that the accumulation of research necessarily made a huge difference in school practice. Rumor, anecdote, and the like had often informed educational thinking and substituted for analysis even when science was more in professional vogue (Clifford, 1973, pp. 3–4). Clifford's essay, like Morrison's in 1945, is a useful point of illumination showing how different generations of scholars tried to understand the interconnections between research and practice.

As Clifford makes clear, most historians traditionally wrote about the history of ideas, not school practices. The two might be conflated but were hardly synonymous. How could one make useful claims about the impact of research on teaching? The problems were daunting. Given the existence of the most decentralized system of mass education in the Western world, researchers of American classrooms, for example, had understandable difficulty knowing what was typical, which subject was informed by what specific piece (if any) of research, or whether or not teachers taught as they were taught more than as some researchers desired. Did teachers, superintendents, and educators working in the schools read much research, think about its implications, and try to act upon it? Clifford surveyed an incredible array of sources to document that, while previous generations of education researchers often assumed research influenced practice, this was nearly impossible to prove.

The proliferation of research had not usually produced useful or practical knowledge. In reading, the most studied subject area, about 4,000 studies existed by 1960, and they hardly settled the matter of which of the two leading approaches worked best (Clifford, 1973, p. 5). Did teachers and administrators simply hear what they wanted to believe when they heard about a new "finding"? Did even professionals in a position to shape "policy" know much about research? Surveys in the 1960s showed that superintendents were not particularly aware of much research or its possible role in school improvement. Often research studies were fragmentary, limited in appeal, poorly written, and not even reported in teacher magazines, which were not necessarily read by most practitioners anyway. Throughout the 1960s, "action research"—oriented toward the spread of democracy and progressive practices—was not necessarily research based, and ideological fashion would continue to shape educational programs and research as much as anything else (Clifford, 1973, pp. 5, 21–22).

Many of the perennial problems an earlier generation of scholars had bemoaned continued to undermine the value of education research after World War II. Few studies were replicated, most researchers still labored part time, and many of them wrote an article or two at most and were never heard from again, a sign of democracy but also weakness in the research community. Clifford thus cites William Brownell's study of arithmetic research in 1950, which "showed that 615 of 778 authors never reported more than one study, and only 53 persons reported more than three each" (Clifford, 1973, pp. 23, 197). AERA, despite its name, claimed in a survey in 1968 that most of its members were not fully invested in research. In fact, the editor of *Review of Educational Research*, echoing ideas heard earlier in the century, said that 90% of published education research should have been rejected (Clifford, 1973, p. 23). Much of what was called education "research" was ideologically driven or based on opinion, supposition, or personal experience, and it was rarely replicable.

Skepticism about the nature of education research remained powerful after the 1960s. Historian William R. Johnson, in an analysis of the Holmes and Carnegie reforms in teacher education, noted in 1987 that throughout the 20th century education research remained of low status, viewed with suspicion within and outside the academy and mostly ignored or rejected by classroom teachers. He cited Benjamin Bloom's assertion in 1966 that, of the 70,000 studies reported in *Educational Researcher* during the previous 25 years, only 70 had any real import. Which 70 would be a matter of debate, too, but the proliferation of educational research had not seemed to settle many basic controversies (Johnson, 1987, p. 229). Like Clifford, Johnson was critical of the noticeable gap between researchers and practitioners, which an earlier generation more confidently assumed would be bridged as knowledge flowed from the laboratory and ivory tower downward to inform everyday practice and experience.

By 1992, scholars writing in the *Encyclopedia of Educational Research*, an AERA publication, could simply state that "research only intermittently had direct influence upon policy." While many factors shaped policy-making, "research had little effect" (Weiss & Vickers, 1992, p. 1093). Researchers moved in one direction, practitioners in another, and it often seemed as if never the twain would meet. Whatever the potential benefits of research for the practitioner, it remained unclear whether much "significant knowledge" even existed "to transmit" to the policymaker (Weiss & Vickers, 1992, p. 1098). Before the 1950s, educators more confidently assumed that with more research an increased amount of improved knowledge would appear, but our generation seems more sober and self-critical in its judgments of quality and suspicious of the heady optimism that doers of education science previously exuded.

During the past generation, the continued debunking of the value or impact of research by the public and skepticism by many scholars has naturally helped lead scholars such as Clifford, Johnson, and others to reflect upon what light history can shed on the problem. The progressive era assumptions about the value of scientific models in educational research have eroded since World War II, and the pressures and attractions of being relevant have motivated many historians to turn their attention to numerous issues related to educational policy and practice in the 20th century. Again, there is not a huge or coherent literature by historians on how research shapes practice, yet a number of scholars have written insightful books and articles on aspects of the subject. More will undoubtedly appear in the coming years.

Consider, for example, the deservedly well-known work of Larry Cuban, especially *How Teachers Taught: Constancy and Change in American Classrooms, 1880–1990*, which appeared in a second edition in 1993. While it is not primarily a study of the relationship between research and teaching, the volume has many valuable insights into the tensions between the two. *How Teachers Taught* is the most comprehensive history of teaching in print: It imaginatively tries to not only reconstruct the changing theories about teaching since 1890 but, to the degree possible, determine what actually transpired in the classroom. In this way, it is part of the larger attempt over the past generation to write more social history. Like anyone doing historical research, Cuban is faced with the problem of finding useful primary sources. The most ordinary of experiences for children in the 20th century included going to school, but finding direct evidence on how teachers taught them (never mind what they learned) is no simple matter. Unlike a modern ethnographer who can at least revisit classrooms and reinterview informants, the historian is restricted by what written or other records exist; much of what actually went on in classrooms is often shrouded in mystery given the lack of suitable sources. Like most subjects in educational history, the history of teaching is still largely about the history of ideas—of what teachers were supposed to teach and how—rather than about the realities of classrooms. By examining photographs, reading various written sources, and unearthing relevant knowledge from innumerable sources, Cuban explores the phenomena of "constancy and change" in the classroom—what remained the same or did not—over a long time span, itself a rare achievement for historians (Cuban, 1993).

Throughout the century, all sorts of ideas emanated from different places, including the university, on how teachers should teach, what they should teach, and how their labors would be evaluated. Some of this was based on research, but much of it was not, the product of reform sentiments by various individuals and groups who sometimes were driven by ideology (child centeredness, back to the basics, etc.) more than anything else. As Cuban demonstrates, definite changes occurred overall in the nature of teaching in the 20th century, as he reemphasized in the preface to the second edition of his book (Cuban, 1993, pp. xvii–xix). While most high schools remained more teacher centered in terms of pedagogy, elementary schools increasingly moved toward more student-centered instruction, not always and everywhere, but increasingly so. How this occurred was not especially the result of "research," whose actual impact is often difficult to pinpoint. Smaller class sizes today, relative to the early 20th century, resulted from agitation by teachers' unions and educational professionals, not especially because "research" was powerful in the decision making. A book that explores the tensions between policy pronouncements and actual school practice, *How Teachers Taught* helps explain how policies themselves are a mixture of ideological belief and political passion, occasionally informed by study and research.

Much writing on the history of education has been oriented around the idea of "reform" (Berube, 1994; Reese, 1986, 1998; Tyack, 1974; Tyack & Cuban, 1995). An ill-defined term (like "research"), reform exists in the eyes of the beholder, but the label has been so commonly used as a synonym for all sorts of efforts at school improvement that it is difficult to dispense with. Nearly everyone who has tried to change something in the schools has worn the label or had it placed on them. Shelves of books in the library deal with how an array of reformers in different periods tried to improve school practices; many of them deal at least incidentally with the subject of research and its ties to educational practice. The richest trove of books on the subject centers on the early 20th century, especially on the testing movement and related reforms. There are numerous books and articles on the creation and social uses of IQ and other school tests; biographies of Lewis Terman, Thorndike, and other advocates of educational science; and books on reforms such as guidance and counseling, the junior high school, and vocational education (Horn, 1989; Minton, 1988; Sokol, 1987). Some deal in part with the connections between research and practice, but the majority of books on school reform generally deal with politics, ideology, and issues of gender, race, and social class. In fact, most of the important reform movements of the 20th century—such as vocational education—were based not primarily on research but on political ideology, initiated by capital and particular professional educators and often initially resisted by organized labor (Wirth, 1971). In an insightful history of special educational programs and curricula in the 20th century, Barry M. Franklin describes the complicated role of psychological, medical, and educational research in the shaping of particular classroom practices (Franklin, 1994).

The best single volume on the history of reform in the 20th century is by David B. Tyack and Larry Cuban, *Tinkering Toward Utopia: A Century of Public School Reform* (Tyack & Cuban, 1995). The authors of numerous books on different aspects of school reform movements in American history, Tyack and Cuban provide a succinct analysis of the varied nature of reform movements over the last century. Concerned with analyzing why certain reforms resonated with teachers and survived, while others did not, the authors provide some helpful clues on the relatively minor role that research played in the reform process. Many reforms, as other scholars pointed out, did not gain power as a result of "research," a term that, according to Clifford, is sometimes vague enough to be meaningless. For example, the kindergarten first emerged in the 19th century and reflected the values of romantic reformers and other enthusiasts whose religious and spiritual values were perhaps decisive in shaping their world view and educational ideals. When the first public playgrounds were established in St. Louis in the 1870s, they were created because of strong support by Germans on the school board, enthusiasm from the superintendent (a leading student of German idealist philosophy), and a belief (resurrected in the 1960s) that early schooling could improve the morals and academic achievement of the urban poor (Troen, 1975, chap. 5). Tyack and Cuban point out that those trying to change (not always improve) the schools can include textbook salespersons, politicians, professional altruists, and teachers, the latter often ignoring when they can ideas from the experts that seem utopian, muddle-headed, or just plain impractical. Sometimes teachers in the past took reforms hatched in universities and quietly labeled them dead on arrival; at other times, certain reforms took hold, slowly becoming adapted to everyday practice (Tyack & Cuban, 1995).

Readers interested in historical work on the overall nature of education research also now have the insightful research of Ellen Condliffe Lagemann. In 1989, she published a well-conceived essay in the *History of Education Quarterly* titled "The Plural Worlds of Educational Research." In it she explored the broad history of research in education while focusing on why the traditions of educational science promoted by Thorndike triumphed, whereas those of Dewey and other academics proved less influential (Lagemann, 1989). This was a notable attempt to understand the roads not taken in educational research and the losses thereby incurred. Lagemann built upon and extended this work in a recent article, emphasizing the continuing gaps between researchers and practitioners and the barriers that still exist between education scholars and those in the arts and sciences. The essay is the best yet written on the history of educational science and research traditions in American education (Lagemann, 1997). Together these essays begin to raise among historians broader questions about the nature of educational research, a harbinger, it is hoped, of a growing body of scholarship.

While a host of articles and books by historians on numerous subjects address, usually indirectly, the issue of how research has affected practice, the topic is obviously massive and intimidating to most historians. For that reason, we will have to be content for now as scholars chip away at areas of research that answer part of the problem. There is some reason to be hopeful. Scholars such as Barbara Finkelstein, Kate Rousmaniere, and others continue to explore the history of classrooms, which inevitably (at least for the 20th century) opens up the question of whether research has made a decided difference in teaching, the curriculum, and so forth (Finkelstein, 1989; Rousmaniere et al., 1997). Historians influenced

by Cuban and the many who continue to explore teaching and classroom pedagogy, and others interested in the many school reform movements of the 20th
century, will also shed light upon the issue. And, finally, the growing interest in
policy studies among a core of historians such as Maris Vinovskis, Diane Ravitch,
and many others will undoubtedly add to our knowledge about the relative
influence of research on educational change (Ravitch & Vinovskis, 1995). As
historians begin to explore in greater detail the last half century of public education, we will also benefit from their understandings of how research may have
influenced various dimensions of the lives of teachers and children at school.

There is obviously no simple way to review historical studies on the question
of how research shaped practice. The historians discussed in the last section of
this essay obviously have tackled important dimensions of the question. And
many historians, writing books and articles on various elements of education and
schooling, will continue to offer helpful insights on the question, however indirectly in many cases. Trying to see how ideas shape action is an old problem in
intellectual and social history, as Clifford reminded us. Finding the sources that
directly prove influence or cause and effect is never easy, no matter what the
historical project. Like those writers who came before them, contemporary scholars will continue to face the difficult task of finding evidence that Clio, the muse
of history, often preserves for herself and shares with others only reluctantly.

REFERENCES

Appleby, L., Hunt, L., & Jacob, M. (1994). *Telling the truth about history.* New York:
    Norton.
Berube, M. R. (1994). *American school reform: Progressive, equity, and excellence move-
    ments, 1883–1993.* Westport, CT: Praeger.
Brown, J. (1992). *The definition of a profession: The authority of metaphor in the history
    of intelligence testing, 1890–1930.* Princeton, NJ: Princeton University Press.
Caswell, R. L. (1929). *City school surveys: An interpretation and appraisal.* New York:
    Bureau of Publications, Teachers College, Columbia University.
Chapman, P. (1988). *Schools as sorters: Lewis M. Terman, applied psychology, and the
    intelligence testing movement, 1890–1930.* New York: New York University Press.
Clifford, G. J. (1973). A history of the impact of research on teaching. In R. M. W. Travers
    (Ed.), *Second handbook of research on teaching* (pp. 1–46). Chicago: Rand McNally.
Cravens, H. (1993). *Before Head Start: The Iowa Station & America's children.* Chapel
    Hill: University of North Carolina Press.
Cremin, L. A. (1961). *The transformation of the school: Progressivism in American
    education, 1876–1957.* New York: Vintage Books.
Cuban, L. (1993). *How teachers taught: Constancy and change in American classrooms,
    1880–1990* (2nd ed.). New York: Teachers College Press.
Finkelstein, B. (1989). *Governing the young: Teacher behavior in popular primary schools
    in the nineteenth-century United States.* New York: Falmer Press.
Flexner, A. (1930). *Universities: American, English, German.* New York: Oxford Univer-
    sity Press.
Franklin, B. M. (1994). *From 'backwardness' to 'at-risk': Childhood learning difficulties
    and the contradictions of school reform.* Albany: State University of New York Press.
Fuller, E. W. (1982). *The old country school: The story of rural education in the Middle
    West.* Chicago: University of Chicago Press.

Good, C. V. (1939). Organized research in education: Foundations, commissions, and committees. *Review of Educational Research, 9,* 569–575.

Horn, M. (1989). *Before it's too late: The child guidance movement in the United States, 1922–1945.* Philadelphia: Temple University Press.

Hughes, H. S. (1964). *History as art and as science: Twin vistas on the past.* New York: Harper & Row.

Johnson, W. R. (1987). Empowering practitioners: Holmes, Carnegie, and the lessons of history. *History of Education Quarterly, 27,* 221–240.

Joncich, G. (1968). *The sane positivist: A biography of Edward L. Thorndike.* Middletown, CT: Wesleyan University Press.

Judd, C. H. (1938). The contributions of school surveys. In G. M. Whipple (Ed.), *The thirty-seventh yearbook of the National Society for the Study of Education, Part II: The scientific movement in education* (pp. 9–20). Bloomington, IL: Public School Publishing.

Kaestle, C. F. (1983). *Pillars of the republic: Common schools and American society, 1780–1860.* New York: Hill & Wang.

Lagemann, E. C. (1989). The plural worlds of educational research. *History of Education Quarterly, 29,* 183–214.

Lagemann, E. C. (1997). Contested terrain: A history of education research in the United States, 1890–1990. *Educational Researcher, 26,* 5–17.

Liu, B. A. (1945). *Educational research in major American cities.* Morningside Heights, NY: King's Crown Press.

Minton, H. L. (1988). *Lewis M. Terman: Pioneer in psychological testing.* New York: New York University Press.

Morrison, J. C. (1945). The role of research in educational reconstruction. In N. B. Henry (Ed.), *The forty-fourth yearbook of the National Society for the Study of Education* (pp. 238–265). Chicago: University of Chicago Press.

Novick, P. (1988). *That noble dream: The 'objectivity question' and the American historical profession.* Cambridge, England: Cambridge University Press.

Ravitch, D., & Vinovskis, M. (Eds.). (1995). *Learning from the past: What history teaches us about school reform.* Baltimore: Johns Hopkins University Press.

Reese, W. J. (1986). *Power and the promise of school reform: Grassroots movements during the Progressive Era.* Boston: Routledge & Kegan Paul.

Reese, W. J. (Ed.). (1998). *Hoosier schools: Past & present.* Bloomington: Indiana University Press.

Rousmaniere, K., Dehli, K., & de Coninck-Smith, N. (Eds.). (1997). *Discipline, moral regulation, and schooling: A social history.* New York: Garland.

Scates, D. E. (1939). Organized research in education: National, state, city, and university bureaus of research. *Review of Educational Research, 9,* 576–590.

Scates, D. E. (1950). School surveys. In W. S. Monroe (Ed.), *Encyclopedia of educational research* (pp. 1126–1133). New York: Macmillan.

Sokol, M. (Ed.). (1987). *Psychological testing and American society.* New Brunswick, NJ: Rutgers University Press.

Southgate, B. (1996). *History: What & why? Ancient, modern, and postmodern perspectives.* London: Routledge.

Travers, R. M. W. (1983). *How research has changed American schools: A history from 1840 to the present.* Kalamazoo, MI: Mythos Press.

Troen, S. W. (1975). *The public and the schools: Shaping the St. Louis system, 1838–1920.* Columbia: University of Missouri Press.

Tyack, D. B. (1974). *The one best system: A history of American urban education.* Cambridge, MA: Harvard University Press.

Tyack, D., & Cuban, L. (1995). *Tinkering toward utopia: A century of public school reform.* Cambridge, MA: Harvard University Press.

Tyack, D. B., & Hansot, E. (1982). *Managers of virtue: Public school leadership in America, 1820–1980*. New York: Basic Books.

Weiss, C. H., & Vickers, M. (1992). Research, impact on educational policy. In M. C. Alkin (Ed.), *Encyclopedia of educational research* (Vol. 3, pp. 1093–1099). New York: Macmillan.

Wirth, A. G. (1971). *Education in the technological society: The vocational-liberal studies controversy in the early twentieth century*. Scranton, PA: Intext Educational Publishers.

Manuscript received July 2, 1998
Accepted December 15, 1998

Chapter 2

Ethics in Educational Research

KENNETH R. HOWE AND MICHELE S. MOSES
University of Colorado at Boulder

The ethics of social and educational research has been significantly complicated over the last several decades as a consequence of the "interpretive turn" and the ever-increasing use of qualitative research methods that have accompanied it. In this chapter, we identify what came before and after the interpretive turn with the *traditional* and *contemporary* approaches to research ethics, respectively. The distinction is a heuristic one. We do not mean to suggest that the interpretive turn occurred at any precise point in time or that it has completely won out. In this vein, the traditional approach is no doubt still in currency.

Embedded in the distinction between traditional and contemporary approaches is another between the protection of research participants ("research subjects" in the traditional vocabulary) and research misconduct. This, too, is a heuristic distinction, because it involves significant overlaps. In particular, research misconduct largely subsumes the protection of research participants. Nonetheless, it is a distinction that has the virtue of familiarity, since it parallels the way federal regulations and universities divide the issues in research ethics.

We should observe here at the outset that medical research has been at the forefront of the ethics of research involving humans, both with respect to the development of vocabularies and frameworks and with respect to the formulation of federal policy. Social research in general and educational research in particular have generally followed this lead. We do not make this observation to suggest that social and educational researchers have remained on the sidelines, simply applying the precepts of medical ethics. On the contrary, as we shall see, for at least some theorists an adequate approach to the ethics of social and educational research requires significantly modifying the vocabularies and frameworks that have come down to them through the ethics of medical research. We make this observation instead to apprise readers of why we borrow so heavily from sources outside education and to alert them to an important part of the history of the ethics of educational research.

THE TRADITIONAL APPROACH

The "traditional approach" draws a rather sharp line between the "prescriptive" (moral-political) component of social research and the "descriptive" (scientific-methodological) component (Beauchamp et al., 1982). It divides questions concerning the morals and politics of social scientific studies from questions

21

concerning their scientific merits and pursues them relatively independently. Indeed, not keeping these domains separated is often considered the mark of biased social research and advocacy.

In our discussion of the traditional view, we follow suit and separate the ethics of social research from broader political and methodological issues. We save raising questions about this maneuver for our discussion of the "contemporary approach."

Protection of Research Participants

Protecting individual autonomy has long been a central principle in Western moral-political thought. That it should also occupy a central place in Western thought about the ethics of research, particularly research involving human participants, should thus come as no surprise. The traditional controversy about autonomy has been cast in terms of Kantian versus utilitarian ethical frameworks. The Kantian (also nonconsequentialist or deontological) framework employs *categorical* ethical principles, the most general of which is the following: "Always treat persons as ends in themselves and never solely as means." In this framework, individual autonomy is fundamental, since respecting autonomy is tantamount to treating individuals as ends in themselves. By contrast, the utilitarian (also consequentialist or teleological) framework employs *hypothetical* ethical principles that are subsidiary to the uniform goal of maximizing the balance of benefits over harms. Thus, "always treat persons as ends" is subject to the condition "*if* this maximizes benefits." In this framework, autonomy is instrumental; respecting it must serve the overall utilitarian goal.

Utilitarian reasoning is widely criticized for sanctioning unacceptable moral conclusions in both theory and practice. In theory, one can imagine a society in which benefit is defined as what gives people pleasure and in which fights to the death among enslaved combatants serve to maximize the total balance of pleasure over pain—a society in which, by summing the pleasure experienced by the spectators and subtracting the pain experienced by the combatants, the total value would be higher than if the practice were prohibited. In practice, certain biomedical research (e.g., the Tuskegee study of the progression of untreated syphilis in African-American men [Jones, 1993]), as well as social research (e.g., Milgram's [1974] studies of obedience), receives its sanction from utilitarian reasoning when it is defended on the grounds that the harm done to research participants in the short term is outweighed by the long-term benefit of the knowledge produced.

To be sure, these are research practices that many (perhaps all) utilitarian theorists would condemn. Arguably, however, it is only by adopting rule utilitarianism and providing utilitarian reasons for following moral rules independent of the calculation of specific benefit-harm ratios—that is, only by providing utilitarian reasons for eschewing utilitarian reasoning in specific cases—that the unacceptable moral conclusions that follow from a thoroughgoing application of utilitarian reasoning can be blocked.

Venturing deeply enough into moral philosophy to fully develop this point would take us too far afield from the task at hand. We thus adopt the more modest tasks of examining the most outstanding difficulty for utilitarianism in the context of research involving human participants and then showing how, whatever the ultimate theoretical foundations might be, the principles employed to govern the treatment of research participants are de facto Kantian.

The most outstanding difficulty for utilitarianism is specifying the benefits and harms that are to go into its calculations. Not only are people likely to disagree about what these are. An important corollary is that all morally relevant considerations must be cast in terms of benefits and harms, in which, for instance, the harms done to slaves who must fight to the death are put on the same scale as the benefits that accrue to those who enjoy watching such a spectacle. Otherwise, utilitarian calculations would not be possible.

MacIntyre contends that confinement to utilitarian benefits-harms calculations eliminates two additional kinds of morally relevant considerations in the context of social research: "wrongs" and "moral harms" (1982). Take the famous (or infamous) Tearoom Trade study. Keeping his identity as a researcher secret, Laud Humphreys assumed the role of a lookout, a "watchqueen," in public restrooms as men engaged in homosexual acts. Arguably, the balance of benefits over harms in this study was positive, if not for the men actually involved in the study, then for gay men overall. (There has been much actual discussion along these lines, and Humphreys saw himself as producing overall beneficial effects by reducing homophobic stereotyping [see, for example, Beauchamp et al., 1982].) But restricting the relevant considerations to benefits and harms circumscribes the analysis in a way that excludes the question of whether deceiving these men did them a moral wrong, independent of the calculation of overall harms and benefits. It may be argued that Humphreys's deception of these men disregarded their dignity and their agency, and, in general, treated them as mere means for achieving other persons' ends. The response that treating persons as mere means is just one kind of harm to be entered into the benefit-harm calculation misses the point of the objection and begs the question in favor of utilitarianism's premise that all morally relevant considerations can be put on the same scale.

The Tearoom Trade example may also be used to illustrate the issue of "moral harms," the other morally relevant consideration eliminated by confinement to utilitarian benefit-harm calculations. According to MacIntyre, "Moral harm is inflicted on someone when some course of action produces in that person a greater propensity to commit wrongs" (1982, p. 178). It is a plausible conjecture that, as a result of Humphreys's study, the men involved in it were made more cynical and distrustful and more inclined to treat others as mere means to pursuing their own ends. (The Tuskegee study provides a more dramatic example and one for which "moral harms" have been documented [Haworth, 1997].)

If inflicting moral harm is something that social research ought to avoid, then the justification for doing so has to be sought beyond utilitarian benefits-harms calculations. Moral harms cannot be routinely plugged into utilitarian benefit-harm calculations; rather, avoiding them places a fundamental constraint on the use to which such calculations can be put. This is true for moral wrongs as well because they involve the rights to self-determination and privacy, rights that, in Dworkin's (1978) suggestive phraseology, "trump" utilitarian calculations.

As mentioned earlier, there is a version of utilitarianism that putatively avoids the kinds of criticisms just advanced, namely rule utilitarianism. Kelman (1982), a self-described rule utilitarian, provides a good example of such a view applied specifically to the ethics of social research.

The benefit that Kelman ultimately seeks to maximize is the "fulfillment of human potentialities" (1982, p. 41). He concedes, however, the extreme difficulty involved in determining whether this applies in specific circumstances and, for this reason, rejects *act utilitarianism*. He goes on to use "consistency with human dignity" as his criterion for moral evaluation (1982, p. 42), which he subsequently identifies (in language almost straight from Kant) with treating "individuals as ends in themselves, rather than as means to some extraneous ends" (1982, p. 43). In a related vein, under the rubric of "wider social values" (1982, p. 46), Kelman embraces the idea that social research should avoid engendering "diffuse harm," the "reduction of private space," and the "erosion of trust."

The parallel between Kelman's and MacIntyre's views is striking. Corresponding to MacIntyre's admonition to avoid "moral wrongs," we have Kelman's admonition to treat persons as "ends in themselves"; corresponding to MacIntyre's admonition to avoid "moral harms," we have Kelman's to avoid "diffuse harms." In both cases, confinement to utilitarian benefit-harm calculations is viewed as morally inadequate. If moral justification is to be ultimately utilitarian, to ultimately fall under the rule of benefit-harm calculations, then it is not only individually defined benefits and harms that must be taken into account but also benefits or harms to the moral health of the human community overall.

This should explain why we would say that thinking about the ethical treatment of participants in social research is de facto Kantian: There is rather widespread agreement that whatever the ultimate justification for moral conclusions regarding the treatment of research participants might be, certain ethical principles should constrain the manner in which researchers may treat research participants in meeting the traditional utilitarian goals of advancing knowledge and otherwise benefitting society.

Informed consent is the most central of such ethical principles, and it is prominent in federal regulations governing social research. The basic idea is that it is up to research participants to weigh the risks and benefits associated with participating in a research project and up to them to then decide whether to take part. And they can do this only if they are informed about and understand what their participation in the research involves. In this way, their autonomy is protected in a way it was not in the Tuskegee, Tearoom Trade, and Milgram studies. Informed consent is de facto Kantian because refusal to participate on the part of research participants is binding, even if their refusal results in a failure to maximize presumed benefits.

It should be observed that the doctrine of informed consent, as explicated in the Code of Federal Regulations for the Protection of Human Subjects (45 CFR 46, 1991, as amended), is not so permissive as to sanction any research in which humans agree to participate. Special protections are provided to "vulnerable populations" of various kinds (for example, children and prisoners) who are too immature or in too compromised a position to make a truly autonomous decision. Furthermore, researchers must seek a just distribution of the burdens of participating in social research over different populations. Finally, proposed research projects may also be blocked if they are so methodologically flawed as to provide little or no promise of generating credible findings, rendering any potential risks or harms too great.

Privacy is the second central principle in the traditional conception of the ethical treatment of social research participants, in addition to autonomy. The two vehicles for protecting it are anonymity (not gathering identity-specific data) and confidentiality (not revealing identity-specific data). The relationships among autonomy and informed consent, on the one hand, and privacy, confidentiality, and anonymity, on the other, are varied and complex.

In one form of analysis, privacy is a kind of autonomy. For example, in the celebrated *Roe v. Wade* decision (1973) and the precedent on which it depended, *Griswold v. Connecticut* (1964), the right to privacy was invoked as equivalent to protecting the autonomy of individuals regarding abortion and birth control, respectively. In a related way, autonomy has also been advanced as the justification for protecting the privacy of medical records, school records, and social research data, on the grounds that the release of such information can restrict the options available to those about whom it is released. For example, depending on the circumstances, the release of medical records could reduce a person's employment opportunities, the release of school records could label a child and thereby restrict his or her life options, and the release of social science data could cause someone to be deported.

In a second form of analysis, privacy has an intrinsic value tied to human dignity and security and distinct from its relationship to autonomy (e.g., Beauchamp et al., 1982). According to Arthur Caplan, "Privacy is a basic human need. Without privacy, it is not possible to develop or maintain a sense of self or personhood." Thus, the attempt to derive privacy from autonomy puts "the cart before the proverbial horse" (Caplan, 1982, p. 320). Save the limiting case of not choosing to be observed, the value of privacy may have little or no connection to self-determination. It is the value of having "private space" (e.g., Kelman, 1982), of being free from surveillance, from looking over one's shoulder, from humiliation and embarrassment, and the like, that privacy protects. Consider the reason one would not want to be observed by strangers going to the toilet or engaging in sex.

As it turns out, the requirement of informed consent diminishes the importance of determining which analysis of privacy is the correct one, and in which contexts. For part of the informed consent process is describing to participants just what the risks to their privacy might be and what measures will be taken to ensure anonymity or confidentiality. In this way, how important privacy might be, and why, largely devolves to individuals' exercise of autonomy.

Research Misconduct

While the issue of research misconduct encompasses both the treatment of research participants and fraudulent or deceptive practices of research and reporting, this section focuses primarily on the latter. Even when having no direct effect on research participants, research misconduct nonetheless wrongs others within the research community and damages the research enterprise overall. Thus, in this section, we explore issues of research misconduct among researchers. We begin with a discussion of the general nature of the scholarly endeavor that frames how to think about research misconduct. We then examine plagiarism and data fabrication/misrepresentation. We end with a few observations about how pressures facing contemporary researchers may contribute to research misconduct.

The Scholarly Endeavor

Scientists and researchers have long been regarded as the "seekers of truth" (LaFollette, 1994a, p. 261). Accordingly, the scholarly endeavor focuses on producing new knowledge and understanding. The concepts of trust and accountability are central to the research enterprise, as, ideally, knowledge and truth, rather than wealth and power, are sought (LaFollette, 1994a). Educational researchers, in particular, often hope that the new knowledge they produce will contribute to the improvement of educational practices and policies, as well as better treatment of students.

So, just how widespread is the problem of research misconduct, and how do researchers perceive their responsibility to combat it? A 1988 survey of professional scientists defined research fraud as falsifying data, reporting results incorrectly, and plagiarizing. When asked whether they had *direct* knowledge of research misconduct, 19% said that they did (LaFollette, 1994b). Although by no means comprehensive, these results suggest that research misconduct is more widespread than commonly thought. Yet, *The Academic's Handbook*, a recent publication intended to clarify issues of conduct for those working in academia, spends a scant eight pages on "the responsible conduct of academic research," of which a main section centers on avoiding "bad manners" (Vesilind, 1995, p. 105). This type of cursory treatment of research ethics underscores what Goodstein calls the "myth of the noble scientist" (1991, p. 515).

It is true that in the vast scheme of scholarly research through the years, there have been relatively few documented cases of researchers who knowingly engaged in misconduct. Still, there are a handful of famous cases, mainly from the 1970s and 1980s, that stand out, such as the Alsabti and Soman plagiarism cases and the Darsee data fabrication case (described later). Not only were they the impetus for the much-increased federal and local oversight of scientific and social scientific research processes and practices, but they have stayed on the minds of today's researchers. In many instances, they are emotional reminders of how researchers can lose their integrity even in the search for knowledge and truth. These incidents of misconduct compromise the integrity not only of the researchers involved but of the entire research community (Chubin, 1985). Misconduct and dishonesty by some researchers reflect poorly on all, especially in the eyes of the government and the public.

What, then, constitutes misconduct within scholarly research? A narrow interpretation defines research misconduct as intentional deceit and falsification of research, plagiarism, and misinterpretation or misrepresentation of results (Steneck, 1994). Broader definitions also include inappropriate collaborations, inappropriate faculty-graduate student relations, denying knowledge of dishonest research practices by another, and conflicting interests with funding agencies.

This much is uncontested: True misconduct must be distinguished from honest mistakes, shoddy work, and real disagreements about results or interpretations (Steneck, 1994). The outstanding problem here, of course, is determining the actual knowledge and intent of the researcher.

Also uncontested (although perhaps less so) is that harms that are intrinsic to research should be distinguished from harms that are extrinsic (Warwick, 1982). For example, using deception as part of the research technique is intrinsic to the research process, and researchers are in control and should therefore be held morally responsible for the harms that are caused by the research. Extrinsic harms, on the other hand, are not part of the research process that is controlled by the researcher. If someone uses research findings for unethical aims that could not have been foreseen by the researcher, the researcher is not morally responsible. Determining the knowledge and intent of the researcher is once again problematic, because it is possible that the researcher could foresee negative and unethical uses for her or his research findings and yet continue the research in spite of— or, worse, because of—those reasons. In that type of case, researchers should not be able to evade moral responsibility for the uses to which their research is put. Certain research on race could fall into this category, such as using IQ data to establish certain races as inferior or superior.

Donald Warwick (1982) proposes a taxonomy of harms attending research misconduct useful for broadening our discussion. He categorizes such harms into three main areas: (a) harms to research participants, (b) harms to society, and (c) harms to researchers and the research professions. We have already discussed ethical issues concerning research participants. Included under possible harms to society are the development of public cynicism and/or mistrust of academic research processes and the perpetuation of stereotypes or adverse images of certain societal groups. Increased public mistrust of scholarly work negatively affects the public perception of researchers and their activities, as well as the possibilities for funding and support of important research endeavors. One current example of the fallout from serious misconduct is that, in the United States after the Tuskegee deception, the federal government now needs to offer strong incentives for people of color to participate in federally sponsored health research

(Haworth, 1997). As for the harms to researchers and the research professions, Warwick cites the development of a deceptive, manipulative attitude toward others; increased restrictions on research activities; and lowered overall quality of research.

Plagiarism

Instances of plagiarism are perhaps the most common of all research misconduct, in any field. Plagiarism can take different forms: copying another researcher's work verbatim, which is the most blatant form; using intellectual property without the express permission of the owner of those ideas; or lifting substantial portions of another's work without any citation of that author. While it often may be obvious when someone actually copies the work of another, what makes plagiarism especially complicated to contend with is that it is often very difficult to locate the exact origins of ideas. Two prominent cases from the biomedical sciences, the Alsabti case and the Soman case, illustrate these issues.

Elias Alsabti came to the United States in 1977 from Jordan to pursue postgraduate medical education. He was hired by a cancer research laboratory within Temple University's medical school, where he supposedly did cancer research. He ended up publishing more than 60 articles within 2 years of his arrival in the United States, some of which appeared in prestigious journals such as the *Journal of Cancer Research and Clinical Oncology* (Broad, 1980a). However, as he moved from one lab to another, his work became suspect, until he finally was accused publicly of severe plagiarism and of making up the names of various listed coauthors. For example, one article by Alsabti published in a European journal was found to have been copied almost word for word from a 2-year-old article in a Japanese journal. As the investigation of Alsabti continued, it was found that he never even had received a medical degree in Jordan (Broad, 1980a). This incident shook the world of medical research and publishing. People wondered how so many fraudulent articles could have slipped by the screening review systems. Apparently, even those who had noticed something fishy with Alsabti's work did not have him investigated. Rather, they just terminated him, which gave him the opportunity to move to other research laboratories and continue his plagiarism (Broad & Wade, 1982).

Another prominent case occurred at around the same time. In 1979, a National Institutes of Health (NIH) medical researcher accused two Yale medical researchers of plagiarizing a manuscript that she had submitted to the *New England Journal of Medicine*. She had been asked to review a paper submitted for publication by Philip Felig, vice-chair of Yale's Department of Medicine, and his junior coauthor, Vijay Soman. The NIH researcher, Helena Rodbard, recognized the data and a portion of the writing as her own (Broad, 1980b). Concerned about priority of publication, she contacted the dean of the Yale University School of Medicine, who responded by asking the researchers whether they had conducted the study on which their paper was based. Felig and Soman said yes, and once he saw their data sheets, he considered the matter closed. His high respect for senior researcher Felig allowed him to give the benefit of the doubt. Still, Rodbard pushed for further investigation and was eventually satisfied. It turned out that Felig had not been supervising Soman very closely and Soman had actually used Rodbard's study as his own, plagiarized her writing and that of others, and fudged some of his own data (Broad, 1980b).

After these two sensational misconduct cases, it became apparent that the traditional system of self-regulation was not working. In the Soman case, Rodbard had brought up the ethical questions only because of a competitive threat to her work. Moreover, the investigation took an inordinate amount of time because she had no ethics board to which to turn. Instead, she had to appeal to a dean who happened to be a close colleague of one of the alleged plagiarizers (Broad, 1980b). The result of these incidents was not only that the researchers involved were penalized (even Rodbard soured to a career in research); the research community as a whole faced increased scrutiny. Most specifically, the government looked to increase its role in the oversight of research conduct (Broad, 1980c).

Data Fabrication/Misrepresentation

In addition to the research misconduct issues surrounding authorship and plagiarism, issues of the integrity of data are also salient ethical matters. For both quantitative and qualitative research studies, the integrity of the research is determined by the authenticity of data, proper data representation, and political issues surrounding research findings.

When data are fabricated and peer reviewers do not catch on, it is clear that something is amiss in the system of scholarly publication. John Darsee was a Harvard University cardiologist who published more than 100 articles between 1978 and 1982 based on fabricated data (Chubin, 1985). When Harvard officials were first notified of the suspicion of Darsee's misconduct, they did not notify anyone at NIH, his funding agency. Instead, it was seen as an isolated incident, and Darsee was given the benefit of the doubt and allowed to continue his work in the Cardiac Research Laboratory, although an offer of an assistant professorship was rescinded (Chubin, 1985; Greene et al., 1985). The officials did not want to ruin Darsee's life or the reputation of their lab. It was not until NIH itself questioned some of Darsee's submitted data that an investigation occurred. The investigation showed a clear pattern of fabricated data over a 4-year period (Broad & Wade, 1982).

Different from pure fabrication, the misrepresentation of data includes "massaging" data to favor a preferred hypothesis or outcome or omitting relevant sources present in the literature. Cyril Burt, a prominent British psychologist, was accused after his death of misrepresenting his data on identical twins who were raised apart as well as completely fabricating some of the data (Chubin, 1985). Whether or not Burt actually engaged in research misconduct remains contested; prominent scholars fall on both sides of the debate (Hattie, 1991). Burt's defenders, such as J. Philippe Rushton (1994) and Robert Joynson (1994), say that the main reason that Burt has been accused of misconduct is racial politics. According to Rushton, Burt's findings oppose what he terms "genetic equalitarianism" (1994, p. 40). Rushton's own psychological research on cranial size differences by race and sex and their relation to IQ is also quite controversial. Burt's critics claim that he must have fabricated data because he could not have found so many cases of identical twins who were raised apart; he misrepresented the data so that they would fit with his predetermined theories (Joynson, 1994).

So-called advocacy research, which places the researcher in the role of advocate for some view or another, is a frequent target of criticism. The ethical issues here are extremely tricky, and, most recently, Charles Murray and Richard Herrnstein, authors of *The Bell Curve* (1994), have been accused of this type of unethical advocacy research (Strosnider, 1997). Some scholars believe that by using race as something more than a socially constructed label, researchers like Murray and Herrnstein play into a culture of racism (Anderson, 1992). Neil Gilbert (1994) has criticized advocacy research on any side of the political spectrum as eroding research standards and abusing statistics, especially in social research.

What is perhaps most difficult to ascertain in many of these cases is the issue of intentionality. When there is clear evidence of data fabrication, as finally with Darsee, unethical conduct is clear. However, data fabrication is difficult to prove, especially when confidentiality issues arise. There are few checks on researchers within the research process. Data misrepresentation is even harder to prove. It is very tricky to distinguish for certain between willful misinterpretation of data and shoddy or incompetent research practice. In addition, the politics of certain types of research and research findings make ethical judgments very complicated indeed.

Pressures on Researchers

What might compel some researchers to engage in unethical research behaviors, particularly when the potential harm to the research community and themselves is severe? Daryl Chubin (1985) identifies seven causes of research misconduct: "psychopathy, unbridled ambition, pressure for publication, competition for federal support, the 'lab-chief' system, failings of the 'peer-review system,' and lack of replication and sheer sloppiness" (p. 177). Excluding psychopathy, these can be reclassified into four more general causes: researcher-researcher competition, funding conflicts, publication pressure, and abuse of power.

First, competition among researchers has stiffened immensely in recent years. This is due to, in part, the dearth of academic positions, especially tenure-track positions at top-notch research institutions. It is interesting to note that the most sensational cases of research misconduct have come from top-level institutions such as Yale University (Soman) and Harvard University (Darsee).

Second, there is also a notable increase in competition for research funding, prompting conflicts of interest associated with increasing funding for higher education from private industry (Burgess, 1989). How much does a funding agency's agenda affect research practice and publication? A 1996 study of top biology and medicine journals found that in approximately one third of the articles sampled, the lead author(s) had some sort of conflict of interest. The conflict was usually a financial one, for example, holding investments in a company connected to the research in some way (Cho, 1997). Another recent investigation revealed that 98% of research studies that were funded by the pharmaceutical industry found new drug therapies to be more effective than the current drug, whereas 79% of studies that were not funded by the pharmaceutical industry found the new drug to be more effective. All of these studies were published in peer-reviewed biomedical journals (Cho, 1997).

Third, the long-standing pressure to "publish or perish" within academia continues to put strain on young researchers. The top-level research institutions require numerous publications as a condition of tenure. Consider Alsabti, a junior researcher. When asked why he engaged in such misconduct and fraud, he blamed the pressure to move up within academia. He said that his "actions . . . were done in the midst of significant pressure to publish these data as fast as possible so as to obtain priority" (Broad, 1980b, p. 39). According to Alsabti, the cutthroat research atmosphere had compelled him into fraud. For Felig's part, although it was found that he had not been aware of Soman's unethical behavior, he made sure that, as a senior researcher, his name appeared on Soman's papers even when he was not involved in the research project. Certainly, an interest in adding to his list of publications played into Felig's ethical negligence.

Finally, the various pressures just mentioned can also lead to abuse of power. One prominent example from the biomedical research community is the Baltimore case at the Massachusetts Institute of Technology (MIT). In 1988, David Baltimore, a Nobel-prize-winning biologist and director of a laboratory at MIT, was indirectly accused of data misrepresentation because the evidence presented in an article by Baltimore and five other colleagues did not support the conclusions drawn (Goodstein, 1991). The primary researcher and author of the article was Thereza Imanishi-Kari, the director of another laboratory at MIT. Baltimore's role was as senior scientist; it was Imanishi-Kari's lab team who did the primary work for this particular paper. Baltimore's lab team was collaborating with Imanishi-Kari's on a larger project from which the research in question came. After repeated denials from both Baltimore and Imanishi-Kari, the Office of Research Integrity's Commission on Research Integrity found that Imanishi-Kari had indeed falsified data to help support research findings that were published in the journal *Cell*. Much later, in 1996, Imanishi-Kari won her appeal to the Department of Health and Human Services' Integrity Adjudications Panel, when they decided that the Office of Research Integrity had never adequately proven its charges of intentional data falsification (Kevles, 1998).

What makes this case fall under the abuse of power category is that it was two junior scholars, postdoctoral fellow Margot O'Toole and graduate student Charles Maplethorpe, who first questioned the Imanishi-Kari/Baltimore research. There were two other graduate students in the laboratory who also suspected data falsification, but when O'Toole brought the accusations, they refused to support her because they feared jeopardizing their degrees (LaFollette, 1994a).

It turns out that their fear was justified; O'Toole has accused both Baltimore and Imanishi-Kari, as well as other senior scientists who became involved with the controversy, of damaging her reputation and making it very difficult for her to obtain a position in academe. She insists that it was her position as a junior scientist that made her first hesitate to make official accusations, but when she finally did, she was fired from her post in the MIT lab and later from her position as a research professor at Tufts University (O'Toole, 1991).

Faculty-student relations are very complex. While in some sense they are often collegial, there is always an imbalance of power and often a dependent relationship (Penslar, 1995). In social and educational research, where the "lab-chief" system is less prevalent than in biomedical research, the general problem of the imbalance of power among graduate students and professors nonetheless remains a constant source of ethical worries.

THE CONTEMPORARY APPROACH

The traditional approach to research ethics finds its roots in experimental and quasi-experimental, so-called "quantitative," research methodology, still the gold standard in medical research and the methodology traditionally predominant in the social sciences and education. Thus, the burgeoning of so-called "qualitative" research methodologies over the past several decades poses a potential challenge to the adequacy of the traditional approach. To be sure, the challenge is not new—field researchers have long contended with it—but it is more prominent, pressing, and pervasive than it once was. The advent of federal regulations is one stimulus. New and revitalized perspectives in moral theory that question the centrality of autonomy—communitarianism, care theory, and postmodernism, for instance—are another.

The "interpretive turn" in social research is implicated in both of these developments. Rabinow and Sullivan (1987) coined this phrase to describe the epistemological shift in the mid- and late 20th century away from positivism and toward hermeneutics. Given the interpretivist perspective, beliefs, attitudes, customs, identities—virtually everything that makes humans what they are—are created and exist only within social relationships, relationships in which language use looms large. No neutral scientific language, à la positivism, exists with which to describe social life wholly from the outside, as it were. Instead, social life is "dialogical," as Charles Taylor (1994) puts it, and thus the methodology of social research must be so as well: It must seek out and listen carefully to "voices" embedded in their social context to gain a true understanding of what people are saying and why they do what they do. And dialogue itself has consequences: Beliefs, culture norms, and the like are not just there, waiting to be uncovered, but are negotiated and "constructed" via the interactions among researchers and those they study.

The implications of this methodological-cum-epistemological shift in social research ethics may be divided into two general areas: *fundamental perspectives* and *operating principles*. The former refers to the broad moral-political frameworks that undergird social and educational research; the latter involves the more specific principles used to govern and evaluate social and educational research vis-à-vis ethics.

Fundamental Perspectives

The interpretive perspective jettisons the positivistic fact-value distinction and, along with it, the idea that social and educational researchers can confine themselves to *neutral descriptions* and effective *means* toward "technical control" (Fay, 1975). Rather, *value-laden descriptions* and *ends* are always pertinent and always intertwined. Because each are part and parcel of social science research, the researcher has no way to avoid moral-political commitments by placing ethics and politics in one compartment and scientific merit in another. As stated by MacIntyre:

> The social sciences are moral sciences. That is, not only do social scientists explore a human universe centrally constituted by a variety of obediences to and breaches of, conformities to and rebellions against, a host of rules, taboos, ideals, and beliefs about goods, virtues, and vices . . . *their own explorations of that universe are no different in this respect from any other form of human activity.* (1982, p. 175, italics added)

This general stance is one that a variety of contemporary perspectives converge on: In addition to communitarianism, care theory, and postmodernism, already mentioned, critical theory and contemporary liberalism may be added to the list. Nonetheless, these perspectives can diverge quite dramatically, and, although we will eventually draw them together again around several points of agreement, it is worth briefly describing where their differences lie. (We do not deny there may be other ways of distinguishing perspectives. For instance, feminism is perhaps conspicuous in its absence. But feminism cuts across the five perspectives. Furthermore, Noddings's care theory is one kind of feminist perspective we explicitly address.)

Communitarianism

Communitarianism locates morality within a given community and its shared norms and "practices" (MacIntyre, 1981). Accordingly, what is conceived as the morally good life has to be known from the inside and varies from one community (or culture) to another. Because social and educational research cuts across communities that may differ from the social researcher's own, ensuring the ethical treatment of research participants who are members of such communities is doubly problematic. Not only are the normal problems involved in protecting autonomy potentially complicated by a lack of mutual understanding; a commitment to the fundamental values that undergird social research may not be shared.

For example, certain communities do not place a high value on individual autonomy (the Amish perhaps being the most well-known case). As such, it is not up to individual community members to give their informed consent to have social researchers peering into the social life of the community, for it is not always *theirs* to give. The community may reject the way of explaining and rendering community life transparent associated with social science and may not want its practices understood and portrayed in these terms. True, an individual community member who agreed to participate in developing such a portrayal might be viewed as a rogue who was wronging the community, but the social researcher could not avoid the charge that it was he or she who was the true instigator of such an "act of aggression" (MacIntyre, 1982, p. 179). The social researcher has no wholly neutral position from which to conduct research. "The danger" in believing otherwise, according to MacIntyre, "is that what is taken to be culturally neutral by the [social researcher] may be merely what his or her own culture takes to be culturally neutral" (1982, pp. 183–184).

The ethical predicament for social and educational researchers raised here is close to the one historically raised under the anthropological concept of "cultural relativism." The difference is that it may now be recognized as a pervasive problem that applies to the broad range of "qualitative" social and educational research conducted across a broad range of cultural contexts and groups, not only exotic ones.

Care Theory

Care theory is a close cousin of communitarianism insofar as both emphasize concrete circumstances and specific demands on individuals ("the view from here") over ideal circumstances and the demands placed on individuals by abstract principles ("the view from nowhere") (Nagel, 1986). On the other hand, care theory embraces, if not a culturally neutral ideal, one that nonetheless is to be applied across cultural encounters; for Noddings (1984), caring is the ethical universal.

Noddings (1986) applies the ethics of care specifically to educational research. Her first thesis is that the relationship between researchers and participants ought to exemplify caring, particularly trust and mutual respect; her second thesis broadens the first so as to apply to the educational research enterprise as a whole. According to Noddings, the choice of research questions and the overall conduct of the research ought to be based on their potential to contribute to caring school communities. Educational research should not be conducted on the basis of mere intellectual curiosity; much less should it be conducted in a way that is likely to be harmful to individual students or groups of students or destructive of school communities. Educational research should be "*for* teaching," Noddings says, not simply "*on* teaching" (1986, p. 506). Ignoring these concerns renders the traditional emphasis on autonomy and privacy incomplete at best.

Postmodernism

Postmodernism shares the premise found in communitarianism and care theory that social and educational research cannot, first, isolate the descriptive component of social research from its moral component and, second, ensure the ethical treatment of research participants by obtaining their informed consent and protecting their privacy. But the postmodernist critique is more radical. Whereas communitarianism and care theory identify dangers with and lacunas in the traditional conception, postmodernism questions the very existence of the integral selves on which the traditional conception is based.

In the postmodern analysis, individuals are not capable of freely directing their own lives; rather, they are always enmeshed in and shaped by relationships of knowledge/power. These "regimes of truth," as labeled by Foucault, serve to "normalize" individual selves and render them acquiescent and "useful" vis-à-vis the institutions of modern society (Foucault, 1970). Traditional forms of social and educational research foist such regimes of truth on participants, however masked the nature of their activity might be. When practiced unreflectively, these forms of research create a situation in which, far from fostering autonomy or even respecting it, social and educational researchers are accomplices in social domination.

Given a "strong" version of this thesis (Benhabib, 1995), postmodernism, ironically it would seem, can provide little or no guidance about what direction social and educational research should take to avoid domination. If there are no criteria of truth, justice, and reason independent of the perspective of a given regime of truth and the position of power researchers occupy within it, then there are no criteria for distinguishing *abuses* of power from its (unavoidable) *uses* (see also Burbules & Rice's, 1991, characterization of "anti-modernism").

In educational research, postmodernism typically takes a less extreme, or "weak," form. As Stronach and MacLure (1997) put it, a "positive reading" is required. The basic idea is that researchers must be alert to the often subtle asymmetrical relationships of power that threaten to oppress participants. Accordingly, participants must take a much more active role than they have traditionally in shaping the research process and in challenging its methods and findings as it unfolds. In general, educational researchers should be much more suspicious than they typically are of the idea that educational research is per se a progressive force. Not unrelated to this, the validity of the findings of educational research cannot be divorced from how it treats relationships of power (e.g., Lather, 1991, 1994).

Critical Theory

The sine qua non of critical theory is its characterization of and opposition to "technical control" as the primary or only role for social and educational research (e.g., Fay, 1975). Technical control is closely associated with positivist social research; it is the goal educational research adopts when it proceeds by bracketing moral and political ends and investigating only the means of achieving them. The current testing/accountability movement launched by *A Nation at Risk* (National Commission on Excellence in Education, 1983) is illustrative. First, the end, economic competitiveness, is bracketed and left to politicians and policymakers (presumably, it is unimpeachable). Second, coming up with effective means in the form of testing/accountability regimens is left to the expert researchers. Finally, research-sanctioned testing regimens are then put in place with little or no input from those most affected: teachers, students, and parents.

The means-ends bifurcation (a particular instance of the broader fact-value bifurcation) is open to at least three criticisms. First, means are relative to ends. Adopting the end of economic competitiveness ipso facto restricts the range of relevant means to those associated with achieving it. Accordingly, such means are laden with the end (read: value) of promoting economic competitiveness. Furthermore, whether something is a means or an end typically depends on its place in a longer chain of means and ends. For example, achievement in math and science is an end relative to instruction but a means relative to economic competitiveness.

Second, means themselves are subject to value constraints, even relative to some end. If it could be shown that an effective means for improving economic competitiveness is putting all "at-risk" students in forced labor camps, we trust that no one would seriously entertain such a policy. Unfortunately, the general point this example illustrates often gets lost when dealing with less obvious examples of morally suspect means—talent tracking, for instance.

Third, and most fundamentally, positivist technical control is irremediably undemocratic. Presupposing the ends of those with the power to formulate them, and then employing expert researchers to investigate the means to effect such ends, engenders technocracy rather than democracy. Genuine democracy requires that participation be respected as an end in itself. Social and educational research in service of democracy requires that no end or ends be settled on ahead of time, prior to and independent of the investigation of means. Rather, dialogue about both should be free, open, inclusive, and "undistorted," to use Habermasian language, by imbalances of power and by confining social science to the role of controlling social life. From the perspective of critical theory, an additional and fundamental role of social science is (should be) emancipation.

Contemporary Liberal Theory

Liberalism has been one of the primary targets of the four perspectives just described, particularly its utilitarian strand. Utilitarianism generalizes a certain conception of individual rationality (maximize benefits over harms) to the level of ethics and social policy (maximize benefits over harms in the aggregate) (e.g., Rawls, 1971). It is vulnerable at both levels. First, the view of rationality presupposed is not shared across groups and, worse, is not a particularly desirable one in any case. Second, extending the principle of utility maximization to the level of ethics and policy can result in wronging people in the way previously described by MacIntyre (1982). Finally, in the practice of social and educational research, the principle of utility maximization tends to work in tandem with the goal of technical control.

Utilitarianism was the major strand of liberalism until the appearance of John Rawls's *A Theory of Justice* in 1971, which has since been the point of departure for liberal thinking. The kind of "liberal-egalitarian" view (e.g., Kymlicka, 1990) that Rawls formulated constrains the principle of maximizing utility in the name of justice. That is, not only aggregate utility is morally relevant. How utility (benefit) is distributed is paramount: Stated most generally, Rawls's principle of justice is that distributions (or redistributions) should tend toward equality. Although providing an advance over utilitarianism, Rawls's theory has nonetheless been criticized for making several of the same general mistakes, including (a) presupposing a certain Western (and male) conception of rationality (i.e., maximize utility within constraints) and (b) conceiving of policy-making on the model of technical control (merely operating with different principles than utilitarianism).

The most general difficulty is liberal-egalitarianism's commitment to the "distributivist paradigm" (Young, 1990). The basic criticism is that liberalism defines and identifies the disadvantaged and then goes about the task of compensation. Compensation takes the form of various social welfare programs, including educational ones. Insofar as those targeted for compensation have been excluded from participation, what counts as rational and good is foisted upon them, and they are the pawns of technical control. And compensation, so called, can come at a cost. Consider a sexist curriculum in which girls fare poorly relative to boys. It is hardly a benefit to girls to compensate them so that they, too, can become sexist.

Contemporary liberal-egalitarians have taken these difficulties seriously and have proffered remedies aimed at preserving the viability of liberalism. The general strategy is to tilt liberalism's emphasis on equality away from the distribution of predetermined goods and toward participation in determining what those goods should be. As stated by Kymlicka:

It only makes sense to invite people to participate in politics (or for people to accept that invitation) if they are treated as equals. . . . And that is incompatible with defining people in terms of roles they did not shape or endorse. (1991, p. 89)

The "participatory paradigm" (Howe, 1995) exemplified in Kymlicka's admonition is much more attuned to the "interpretive turn" in social and educational research than the "distributivist paradigm." It fits with a model of research in which justice and equality are sought not only in the distribution of predetermined goods but also in the status and voice of research participants.

The five perspectives we have portrayed differ in the ways we have indicated and, no doubt, in further ways we have not developed. We do not wish to deny that these differences can be deep, perhaps even irreconcilable. Still, there are several shared themes across these perspectives regarding the ethics of social and educational research.

First, as we have indicated, there is a strong tendency in what we call the "traditional view" to distinguish the "descriptive" (scientific-methodological) component of social research from the "prescriptive" (moral-political) component. Each of the five alternative perspectives denies that social and educational research can be (ought to be) divided up in this way. On the contrary, social and educational research is (ought to be) framed by self-consciously chosen moral-political ends, for example, fostering caring communities or fostering equality and justice.

It follows that all social and educational research is *advocacy* research, by its very nature, and it is thus no criticism of a given study that it adopts some moral-political perspective. Criticism arises instead with respect to just what that moral-political perspective is as well as the consequences of framing research in terms of it. This casts a different light on research like Murray and Herrnstein's (1994) *The Bell Curve*. The problem is not that they are engaged in advocacy research in virtue of making policy recommendations. The problem is with the moral-political basis of such recommendations, combined with the consequences of their recommendations and their claim that they are simply following science where it leads.

Second, and related especially to this last point, the research questions deemed worth asking are circumscribed by the moral-political framework in which they are couched. Educational researchers might (and many no doubt do) ostensibly conduct research *on* teaching rather than *for* teaching, to use Noddings's (1986) distinction once again. But rather than getting rid of the question of what research might be *for*, they are merely closing their eyes to it. Any research that is used at all is used *for* something, and the range of uses is limited from the outset by how the research is conceived and designed.

Third, social and educational research ought to have points of contact with the insiders' perspectives, with their "voices." In this way, the moral-political aims of social and educational research affect its methodology. Interpretive, or "qualitative," methods are best suited for getting at what these voices have to say and what they mean.

Finally, and dovetailing with each of the preceding three observations, contemporary perspectives militate against the race, gender, and class biases that have historically plagued social and educational research—forms of bias that grow out of the assumed premise that the attitudes, beliefs, and reasoning of mainstream White males are the norm against which all other social groups must be measured (Stanfield, 1993).

We have seen a shift from social and educational research that asks how diverse groups are either similar to or different from mainstream groups to research concerned with finding out about those diverse groups in their own right. A prominent example of such a contemporary perspective is Carol Gilligan's (1982) landmark study of girls' and young women's psychological development. In it, her findings and discussion challenge the developmental theories of psychological researchers, such as Lawrence Kohlberg, who excluded female voices from their research studies, yet generalized their findings to both males and females. This type of sex bias resulted, in Kohlberg's case, in a tendency to label women as deficient in moral development. In the attempt to fit women into a theory of moral development that came out of research conducted exclusively on male participants, women were being held unjustly to a male standard of development.

As the contemporary approach to research ethics has evolved in recent years, there have been cases similar to the Kohlberg-Gilligan studies that have involved bias not only against females but against people of color and the poor and working classes as well. In one such case within educational research, anthropologists John Ogbu and María Matute-Bianchi (1986) address the issue of school failure among students of color. By citing various sociocultural factors that contribute to less than optimal school environments for students of color, they confront theories that tend to place all responsibility (and blame) for such failure on the shoulders of the student of color. In doing so, they challenge a dominant view within educational research that, since school "works" for most White students, students of color must deserve the blame for their school disappointments.

One more example is relevant here. Consider ethnographer Paul Willis's 1977 study of working-class male youth in England. Through his research, Willis attempts to shed light on what goes on in school for these young "lads." He discovers a culture of resistance against school knowledge and success that had developed among the young working-class lads. Through their rebellion, they were sabotaging their own chances at educational opportunities to get out of the working class. This finding challenged the more accepted theory that poor and working-class students were merely being manipulated by an education system intent on reproducing their social class roles.

Through these examples from current research, we see that the influence of contemporary perspectives has caused researchers to examine things in new ways. This has led researchers to ask different questions and use different methods in finding the answers.

Operating Principles

The distinction between research ethics in the sense of operating principles and in the broader, fundamental sense is not hard and fast. What questions are worth asking and how researchers are to conduct themselves in the process of answering them cannot be divorced from the overarching aims that research seeks to achieve, one of the fundamental premises of the "contemporary approach." Nonetheless, there exists a "looseness of fit" between operating principles and competing perspectives, such that reasonable agreement on what constitutes ethical conduct is (or should be) possible in the face of broader theoretical disagreements. Bearing in mind, then, that broader ethical obligations associated with broader moral-political perspectives are always lurking in the background, there remain general ethical implications of the interpretive (qualitative) turn in educational research that may be best understood in terms of the methodological nitty-gritty of "techniques and procedures" (a description that owes to Smith & Heshusius, 1986).

Protection of Research Participants

The techniques and procedures of interpretivist research possess two features that experimental and quasi-experimental research lack (at least to a relatively significant degree): intimacy and open-endedness (Howe & Dougherty, 1993; see Wax, 1982, for a similar analysis). The features of intimacy and open-endedness significantly complicate protecting participants' autonomy and privacy and complicate the researcher's moral life as well.

Interpretive (qualitative) research is *intimate* insofar as it reduces the distance between researchers and participants in the conduct of social research. Indeed, the growing preference for the term *participants*—who take an active role in "constructing social meanings"—over *subjects*—who passively receive "treatments"—testifies to the changed conception of relationships among human beings engaged in social research that has attended the interpretive (qualitative) turn. The face-to-face interactions associated with the pervasive techniques of interviewing and participant observation are in stark contrast to the kind of interactions required to prepare "subjects" for a treatment.

Interpretive research is *open-ended* insofar as the questions and persons to which interviewing and participant observation may lead can only be roughly determined at the outset. This, too, is in stark contrast to the relatively circumscribed arena of questions and participants that characterizes experimental and quasi-experimental research.

What intimacy and open-endedness mean for researchers employing qualitative techniques and procedures is that they are (whether they want or intend to or not) likely to discover secrets and lies as well as oppressive relationships. These discoveries may put research participants at risk in ways that they had not consented to and that the researcher had not anticipated. These discoveries may also put researchers in the position of having to decide whether they have an ethical responsibility to maintain the confidentiality of participants or to expose them, as well as having to decide whether to intervene in some way in oppressive relationships (see, e.g., Dennis, 1993; Roman, 1993).

Researchers employing experimental and quasi-experimental techniques and procedures can face the same problems. For instance, information can simply fall into their laps in the process of explaining a protocol and recruiting participants, a treatment may prove so obviously effective (or harmful) that the trial should be stopped, and so forth. Still, the odds of facing unforeseen ethical problems are surely much higher for interpretive researchers. Generally speaking, then, interpretive research is more ethically uncharted, and thus more ethically hazardous, than experimental and quasi-experimental research. Once begun, it requires more vigilant ethical reflection and monitoring for that reason.

Some interpretive researchers have recoiled at this suggestion, on the grounds that the current ways of thinking about and monitoring the ethics of social research are rooted in the experimentalist tradition and are therefore inappropriate for interpretivist research (e.g., Lincoln, 1990; Murphy & Johannsen, 1990; Wax,

1982). Wax, who is exemplary of this view, contends that informed consent "is both too much and too little" to require of interpretivist research ("fieldwork," to be precise):

Informed consent is *too much* . . . in requesting formal and explicit consent to observe that which is intended to be observed and appreciated. Formal and explicit consent also appears overscrupulous and disruptive in the case of many of the casual conversations that are intrinsic to good fieldwork, where respondents (informants) are equal partners to interchange, under no duress to participate, and free either to express themselves or to withdraw into silence. On the other hand, informed consent is *too little* because fieldworkers so often require much more than consent; they need active assistance from their hosts, including a level of research cooperation that frequently amounts to colleagueship. (1982, p. 44)

Wax seems to go in two incompatible directions. When he claims that informed consent requires too much, he focuses on how it can be a nuisance and obstruct social research. He goes so far as to defend deceptive (covert) research, research in which the requirement of informed consent is suspended, on explicitly utilitarian grounds: "On a utilitarian basis, we can contend the wrongs incurred by the practice of covert fieldwork may be far outweighed by the social benefit" (p. 41). That it might be more difficult and more of a nuisance to obtain informed consent in interpretive research provides no principled reason for not doing so. It is hard to see Wax's argument as anything other than special pleading on behalf of interpretive research. Experimentalists can offer the same kind of utilitarian arguments for deception.

When Wax claims that informed consent requires too little, he is, in fact, getting at something that distinguishes interpretivist from experimentalist research. The mechanism of informed consent grew out of the kind of imbalance of power associated with the experimentalist tradition in which the researchers versus subjects distinction implies "subjection" on the part of the latter. "Informed consent," says Wax,

is a troublesome misconstrual of . . . field relationships because the field process is progressive and relationships are continually being negotiated, so that, if the research is going well, the fieldworker is admitted to successively deeper levels of responsibility together with being required to share communal intimacies. (1982, p. 45)

According to Wax, the relationship between researchers and participants should exemplify "parity" and "reciprocity," and "where there is parity and reciprocity, the ethical quality of the relationship has progressed far beyond the requirements of 'informed consent'" (1982, p. 46).

This analysis is correct as far as it goes: Certain features of interpretivist research—"intimacy" and "open-endedness," to use our vocabulary—distinguish it from experimentalist research and render informed consent more problematic. But it does not follow from this that the requirement of informed consent ought to be jettisoned in the case of interpretivist research. In this vein, the way Wax pooh-poohs the notion that research participants might feel under pressure to cooperate gives one pause, particularly in light of the close relationships he thinks should be established.

Wax construes informed consent as a one-shot, all-or-none event, the model that fits biomedical and experimentalist social research. But this is not the only form it might take. The underlying rationale for informed consent, after all, is the protection of autonomy and, in the way described previously, privacy. The one-shot approach to informed consent fails to provide these protections in light of the special features of interpretivist research, namely, its intimacy and open-endedness. But informed consent may be reconceived so that it better takes these features into account. In this vein, interpretivist researchers themselves have proposed construing informed consent on the model of an ongoing "dialogue" (e.g., Smith, 1990) and have suggested periodic reaffirmations of consent (e.g., Cornett & Chase, 1989) as the procedural embodiment of this notion.

Yvonna Lincoln (1990) provides a more radical and far-reaching critique of the traditional emphasis on the protection of autonomy and privacy than the kind provided by Wax. Central to Lincoln's view is the fundamental gap she perceives between the logical- and post-positivistic "epistemologies" that allegedly under-gird the traditional regulations and the phenomenological/constructivist "philoso-phies" appropriate for interpretivist ("qualitative") research. One of the more dubious of Lincoln's conclusions is that informed consent is less, not more, problematic in the case of interpretivist research. Because its aim is to portray the "multiple social constructions that individuals hold," anything short of complete openness on the part of researchers does not make sense for well-executed interpretivist ("phenomenological and constructivist") research. As Lincoln sees things, it makes sense only for positivist-oriented researchers, who seek to con-verge on a "'real' reality 'out there'" independent of individuals' constructions (1990, p. 280).

Lincoln takes a similarly dismissive stance toward the principle of privacy. The following summary points capture the substance as well as the tone of her position:

First, privacy, confidentiality, and anonymity regulations were written under assumptions ["logical positivism and postpositivism"] that are ill suited to qualitative and/or phenomenological, constructiv-ist philosophies; second, from some small preliminary studies, we now understand that respondents may be willing to give up strict privacy and anonymity rights for the larger right to act with agency in participating in the research efforts as full, cooperating agents in their own destinies; third, we . . . must trade the role of detached observer for that of professional participant. But, clearly, the issue is far more complex than simply fretting about privacy, anonymity, and confidentiality. (1990, p. 280)

The general view Lincoln advances is that the traditional emphasis on autonomy and privacy is grounded in positivism. But positivism is *"inadequate* and, indeed, *misleading* for human inquiry" (1990, p. 279), according to her. Because interpre-tive researchers have repudiated positivism's quest for reality in favor of a quest for the meanings individuals construct, they seek to grant "coequal power" (1990, p. 279) to participants and have no reason to ever be anything but fully forthcoming with them.

Lincoln's analysis is more than a little problematic. Consider her second summary point: "Respondents may be willing to give up strict privacy and anonymity rights for the larger right to act with agency in participating in the research efforts." Well, they *may* be, but apparently it is they who decide. And they decide, give their informed consent, under the conditions of uncertainty associated with the open-ended nature of interpretivist research. Nothing Lincoln says removes this uncertainty or the ethical hazard it creates.

More generally, Lincoln's view is remarkably oblivious to the kinds of ethical quandaries in which interpretivist researchers can find themselves. Take the issue of researchers being less than forthcoming, or even deceptive, with participants. In fact, many objects of social research, including schools, do not exemplify equality among actors. Being open can serve to reinforce such inequality where those in power move to protect their positions. As we observed before, interpretivist researchers can discover oppressive relationships they had not anticipated at the outset (e.g., an abusive teacher, a racially based tracking scheme, a sexist curriculum). What to do about these discoveries is often arguable, and often depends on the particulars. But this much is clear: Researchers cannot automatically get off the hook by distancing themselves from positivism and pushing on with the construction of meanings. As Dennis remarks regarding his use of participant observation to study race, it is sometimes necessary to "choose sides":

Fieldwork is often fraught with informational and emotional land mines between which and around which the researcher must maneuver ... when issues involve racial justice, for instance, there is no question but that the researcher should be on the side of the excluded and oppressed. (1993, pp. 68–69)

It should be observed here that one need not fall back on utilitarian reasoning to defend being less than open or deceptive where asymmetrical and oppressive power relationships characterize institutions and practices, the kind of defense Wax offers in regard to deceptive ("covert") field research in the following:

If we regard the focus of inquiry as an entire social situation, and if we take the elite (or the gatekeepers) on whom much of the research is focused to be but one element of the situation, then, on a utilitarian basis, we can contend the wrongs incurred by the practice of covert fieldwork may be far outweighed by the social benefit of exposure and analysis. (1982, p. 41)

We saw earlier the sort of abuse utilitarian reasoning is liable to (e.g., justifying the infamous Tuskegee research). But instead of arguing this way, one may argue in a nonutilitarian way by ranking the wrongs in question. In particular, one may argue that oppression is a wrong that should be eliminated and is a greater wrong, especially when children are its victims, than the wrong done to the oppressors (the "gatekeepers") by deceiving them.

Short of having to "choose sides," interpretivist researchers are constantly faced with less dramatic reasons for refraining from being fully forthcoming with research participants. For example, in order to gain access to the voices of older Chicana women, Elisa Facio explains how she had to initially play up her role as a volunteer in the seniors' center that was the site of her research. That she was a student and, furthermore, was doing research were revealed later in the course of her research. Facio believed that the culture and social histories of these women required this kind of procedure, and citing Punch (1986), she observed that participant observation "always involves impression management," including "alleviating suspicion." Nonetheless, she confessed to feeling "uncomfortable with the deceit and dissembling," as she put it, that "are part of the research role" (1993, p. 85).

Was Facio's incremental approach to consent ethically defensible? We think it was. But saying this does not provide social and educational research with any rule that will apply in all cases. What to do in specific cases is very often not going to be an easy call, and misgivings like Facio's often cannot be eliminated. To further complicate matters, in addition to differing concrete circumstances, differences in fundamental frameworks can also contribute to ethical complexity. Contra Lincoln, whatever benefits the interpretive (qualitative) turn has brought, an ethically simpler life for researchers is quite clearly not among them.

Research Misconduct

This leads to a further kind of ethical complexity engendered by the interpretive (qualitative) turn in social and educational research: how to report results. We include this issue under the heading of research misconduct because it involves the possible misrepresentation of data and possible researcher incompetence and because, for the most part, it is one step removed from the face-to-face interactions with participants that are central to issues falling under the rubric of the protection of research participants. Of course, the line between research misconduct and the protection of research participants vis-à-vis reporting results is a fuzzy one, all the more so for the "contemporary approach," which generally blurs the traditional dividing lines.

As before, experimentalist (quantitative) researchers can face some of the same difficulties as interpretivist (qualitative) researchers in writing their reports. But also as before, they are more numerous and more acute for the latter. The general source of the difficulties is the "thick description" that characterizes interpretive research. Because such descriptions are judged for accuracy, at least in part, by how well they square with the insider's or "emic" perspective, researchers must negotiate or "construct" these descriptions in collaboration with research participants. (Compare negotiating statistical analyses with participants.) This raises the questions of who owns the data (e.g., Noddings, 1986) and how the data may be used subsequently (e.g., Johnson, 1982), as well as the question of how much power participants should have to challenge, edit, and change written reports. Except by adopting the extreme of providing participants either absolute power or none, crafting a defensible report is a thorny ethical problem.

Thick description in reporting also complicates the protection of privacy. In contrast to survey researchers, for instance, interpretive researchers can rarely (never?) provide anonymity to research participants. Instead, they must rely on maintaining confidentiality as the means to protect privacy. The possibility sometimes exists, however remotely, that researchers could be required by a court to reveal their sources. This is a possibility to which research participants, especially "vulnerable populations" (e.g., undocumented immigrants), should be alerted.

A more pervasive threat to privacy posed by reports is that the real sites and individuals described in such reports might be identified. Various techniques to protect confidentiality, for example, the use of pseudonyms, are typically employed to mask identities, but these techniques can fail (e.g., Johnson, 1982). And it is doubtful whether a more rigorous application of techniques to protect confidentiality can eliminate this problem. Population, physical geography, economic base, class stratification, and so forth all go into understanding a community; habits, attitudes, language, physical bearing, and so forth all go into understanding social life within it. These are the very kinds of things that, when reported, lead to breaches of confidentiality (see, e.g., Johnson, 1982). Unfortunately, suppressing them can only come at the cost of forgoing the value of thick description.

Breaches of confidentiality are not generally a problem unless a negative picture is painted by a report of a community or some of its members. Part of the remedy is thus engaging participants in dialogue about the contents of reports in the way described previously. But this is only a partial remedy and will work only sometimes. A negative picture might be called for. For instance, suppose a community (or school) and its leaders can be characterized as profoundly racist and sexist. Shouldn't such findings be reported in the interests of those who are being oppressed, at the site in question and elsewhere?

Of course, researchers must be extremely careful and deliberate about rendering such judgments, but this much is clear: The problem cannot be eliminated by casting reports in wholly *objective* (read: sterile and value-neutral) language (one reading of Johnson, 1982, and a common proposal). As description moves toward being more objective in this sense, it simultaneously moves toward "thin" description. Compare "Girls alternate between being bored and intimidated in the typical classroom discussion" with "Girls participate less than boys in the typical classroom discussion." The first description is thicker than the second and is less objective only in the sense that it requires different (and admittedly more) evidence to substantiate. On the other hand, it is also at least one step closer to understanding what is going on and one step closer to informing what actions might be taken to improve girls' school experience. Description and evaluation are generally related in this way in social and educational research (e.g., House & Howe, 1999; Rorty, 1982, chap. 11; Scriven, 1969). The key is thus not to eliminate the evaluative component from descriptions in social and educational research, since this just dilutes them and compromises their usefulness. The key is to get the descriptions right.

EDUCATIONAL RESEARCH AND FEDERAL REGULATIONS

In this section, we focus on the federal regulations that formally apply to educational research, references to which have been sprinkled among our previous, more philosophical analyses. We also expand the discussion, raising some issues for the first time (e.g., the special ethical problems associated with student researchers). Once again, we entertain the issues under the two general categories of the protection of research participants and research misconduct.

Protection of Research Participants

Educational research has historically enjoyed a special status with respect to formal ethical oversight because a significant portion of it is singled out for "exempt" status in the Code of Federal Regulations for the Protection of Human Subjects (45 CFR 46). Determining precisely which educational research projects should qualify as exempt has always been a source of conflict, potential as well as real, between educational researchers and the university institutional review boards (IRBs) responsible for interpreting and applying the federal regulations. However, this source of conflict has become more pronounced over the last several decades, as the face of educational research has been changed by the "interpretive turn" and the ever-increasing use of qualitative methods. Because of the intimate and open-ended features of qualitative methods (discussed earlier), their increased prominence within educational research raises difficult ethical issues with which educational researchers must grapple. These features also provide the impetus for taking a closer look at the general rationale and criteria for affording educational research a special status vis-à-vis IRB review.

Preliminary to our analysis, however, we first make a few remarks about IRB oversight of educational research. The idea that such oversight is warranted is by no means universally shared among educational researchers and is itself a source of controversy.

Many educational researchers challenge IRB oversight on the grounds that it is researchers, not members of IRBs, who possess the specialized knowledge and experience needed to appreciate the ethical nuances associated with different research methods and different research contexts. They charge IRBs of, among other things, obstructing academic freedom, obstructing the free pursuit of knowledge, and being especially hostile toward qualitative research (e.g., Murphy & Johannsen, 1990). Accordingly, these researchers question the legitimacy of IRBs looking over their shoulders and demanding they fill out the designated forms.

This is an overreaction. In the first place, the portrait of researchers assumed is a bit unrealistic. Although moral abominations in social research are rare, other pressures—for instance, pressures to "publish or perish"—are real and ubiquitous, and one need not be a bad person to be tempted to cut ethical corners in response to them, especially if cutting corners is the norm. Furthermore, one need not be a bad person to be unaware of ethical worries that others are able to detect, particularly others who have a good deal of experience with the pertinent issues.

This portrait also misconstrues the nature of ethics, inasmuch as it involves what ethicist Robert Veatch (1977) labels the "fallacy of generalized expertise." For example, just as physicians qua physicians have no special expertise regarding whether a woman should accept a slightly greater risk of death from breast cancer by opting for radiation therapy over a mutilating and debilitating mastectomy, educational researchers qua educational researchers have no special expertise regarding whether parents should be given the opportunity to refuse to have their children involved in a given educational research project. Indeed, given their aims and interests, physicians and educational researchers are probably in the *worst* position to make these judgments. It is for this reason that 45 CFR 46 requires IRBs to be staffed by persons who represent a range of perspectives and interests, including at least one member of the community who is not affiliated with the university and at least one member whose chief interests are nonscientific (e.g., clergy, lawyer, or ethicist).

In the second place, although IRBs are often overly bureaucratic and discharge their duties in a rather perfunctory manner that takes too lightly the ethical complexities involved (Christakis, 1988; Dougherty & Howe, 1990), they are the only formal mechanism in the United States for overseeing social research (McCarthy, 1983). The shortcomings in the practices exemplified by IRBs are insufficient to abandon or radically change this oversight tool. The alternative of no policing or self-policing has proven to have worse consequences, on balance, than those associated with the institution of IRBs. Furthermore, remedies for these shortcomings are not altogether lacking (for example, Silva and Sorrell, 1988, suggest ways for IRBs to enhance informed consent by focusing on the process of consent rather than the wording of the consent form). Finally, IRBs can serve an important educational function. In our experience (which we suspect reflects what is generally true), the IRB is the chief, and often only, locus of reflection and debate about the ethics of social research.

Interpretation of Special Exemptions for Educational Research

Paragraph 46.101(b)(1) of 45 CFR 46 singles out the following kinds of educational research as "exempt" from its requirements:

Research conducted in established or commonly accepted educational settings involving *normal educational practices* such as (i) research on regular and special educational instructional strategies, or (ii) research on the effectiveness of or the comparison among instructional techniques, curricula or classroom management methods. (italics added)

This provision potentially includes a large part of educational research but is so vaguely worded as to leave much room for competing interpretations among educational researchers and local IRBs. In view of the inherent vagueness of this provision, it is useful to begin with a brief examination of its history and rationale.

The first policies set up for the protection of research participants were done with a primary focus on biomedical research, which had already shown itself to be potentially harmful to the participants involved. At that time, in the early 1960s, research in the social sciences was not believed to be hazardous to those involved because it did not include any "invasive" procedures. However, as the National Institutes of Health and then the Department of Health and Human Services became involved, the initial guidelines were seen as more and more problematic. Thus, in the 1970s a national commission was set up for the protection of human participants that thoroughly reviewed policies for the social sciences, including education. With essentially the same model as that addressing medical research, the idea of an independent review board and the emphasis on the need for informed consent prevailed in the new policies on social research.

The commission made provisions in its final recommendations to allow some discretion on the part of IRBs to reduce the burden placed on them. Specifically, a series of thresholds were developed that defined three levels of review: exempt (no IRB review), expedited (review by a representative of the IRB), and full IRB review. The commission also reduced the burden placed on IRBs by giving prospective research participants, through the vehicle of informed consent, a significant role in determining the worth and moral acceptability of research projects for which they are recruited. (Partly because of this, the issue of informed consent has become of paramount concern for research in the social sciences.)

The commission believed that educational research, in particular, required less stringent oversight than other varieties of social research, both because the risks were perceived as slight and because district- and school-based procedures were believed to already exist to screen and guide research. Thus, the commission believed that the area of educational research was one place where the IRB's role could be minimized, especially since it believed that mechanisms of accountability for educational research were already in place at the local level. Accordingly, it crafted 45 CFR 46 so as to provide explicit exemptions for educational research.

The commission, nonetheless, mandated in 45 CFR 46 that some sort of administrative review (e.g., by department or college) would take place in every case of research involving human participants. As a consequence, the apparent wide latitude afforded educational research was significantly narrowed by many universities as they went about the task of articulating the purview and responsibilities of their IRBs. In particular, IRBs typically do not permit educational researchers to decide for themselves whether their research is exempt from the 45 CFR 46 regulations. In many universities, "exempt" has come to mean exempt from certain requirements and full committee review, not exempt from IRB oversight altogether.

That IRBs, not educational researchers, are responsible for determining when educational research qualifies as exempt from the normal requirements of 45 CFR 46 engenders potential conflicts between educational researchers and IRBs. Taking the responsibility for determining what educational research satisfies the exemptions in 45 CFR 46 out of the hands of educational researchers and placing it in the hands of IRBs makes the latter the arbiter of key questions such as what constitutes "normal educational practice." This is problematic for educational researchers because IRBs are composed mostly of university faculty who have little knowledge of the workings of public schools.

We share the concern of other educational researchers about whether the typical IRB is composed of individuals who are in a good position to determine when educational research should qualify as exempt (i.e., qualify as "normal educational practice"). In our view, there is an answer to the question of how to make such a determination that stops short of the extremes of permitting educational researchers to decide for themselves, on the one hand, or of placing the decision exclusively in the hands of IRBs, on the other. Our suggestion is the simple and straightforward one to formally include school people in the review process, particularly regarding the judgment of what is to count as "normal educational practice" (Dougherty & Howe, 1990).

Accommodation of Qualitative Research Methods

It should be borne in mind that the special exemptions for educational research were formulated prior to the advent of qualitative methods in educational research and were justified on the grounds that educational research is extremely low risk and does not substantially deviate from practices routinely conducted by schools themselves for the purposes of evaluating and improving curricula, testing, and teaching methods. When educational research departs from this model to take a close look at social structure and to establish an intimate relationship with participants, there is no justification for providing it with greater latitude than other social research merely because it has to do with education, is conducted in schools, or is conducted by educational researchers.

Viewed in another way, the advent of more intimate and open-ended methods in educational research creates a distinction between educational research as conceived in 45 CFR 46 and what might be termed *social research on education.* The latter variety includes much of qualitative research and is educational research only by virtue of its topics and settings, not its aims and methods. This kind of educational research is thus indistinguishable from the aims and methods that might be employed by other researchers, particularly fieldwork sociologists and anthropologists, working in other contexts. Accordingly, it should receive no especially liberal treatment with respect to the protection of research participants.

To be sure, the issue of informed consent is especially tangled and contested where qualitative methods are involved. But, consistent with our previous arguments, we reject the suggestion (e.g., by Lincoln, 1990; Murphy & Johannsen, 1990) that because they were initially designed primarily for biomedical and experimental research, the informed consent requirements of 45 CFR 46 are inappropriate for qualitative research. Informed consent is central to research ethics per se, not to any particular kind of research method: It is the principle that seeks to ensure that human beings retain control over their lives and that they are enabled to judge for themselves what risks are worth taking for the purpose of furthering scientific knowledge.

Oversight of Student Research Practicums

As qualitative methods in educational research have proliferated, so have undergraduate and graduate courses that teach their use. Such courses often take the form of practicums, in which students try out and practice the qualitative techniques. Just as the advent of qualitative methods in educational research prompts closer scrutiny of the question of what kinds of educational research should qualify as exempt, their introduction into courses prompts closer scrutiny of the question of whether such student research should fall within the purview of IRBs.

The 45 CFR 46 regulations do not explicitly refer to research practicums. Instead, they apply to university "research," which they define as "a systematic investigation designed to develop or contribute to generalizable knowledge." Given that most research that is required as part of a course is variously perceived as no more than a "trial run," a "pilot study," or "getting one's hands a little dirty" (Dougherty & Howe, 1990)—and, in particular, not as an attempt to contribute to generalizable knowledge—it would seem that it should not fall within the scope of the regulations.

Although the appeal to the criterion of whether an activity "contributes to generalizable knowledge" is certainly germane to its ethical dimensions—for example, it is related to the intent of an activity and to whether information about individuals might become public—it is quite insensitive to the ethical dimensions of the interactions between persons, particularly the intimate ones associated with qualitative methods. Furthermore, given the nature of such interactions, one can reasonably ask whether neophytes, just learning to interact with research participants, might require more oversight, rather than less, than experienced researchers.

In this connection, our preceding observations about the potential for increased ethical difficulties associated with qualitative research—particularly its intimacy and open-endedness—apply a fortiori to student research in courses. There simply is no defense for the kind of policy common among university IRBs (Dougherty & Howe, 1990) in which the ethical standards and procedures governing studies done by the most inexperienced members of a research community are lax (or nonexistent) in comparison with those governing its more experienced members. (Compare medical students' interactions with patients.)

On the other hand, it does not necessarily follow that student research in courses should be subject to the very same review procedures as faculty research, in which each and every student activity must be submitted to the IRB. Instead, a sensible policy is one that is not overly cumbersome in regard to the protections it provides for human participants. In our view, a workable alternative places responsibility on course instructors to judge when a student activity is exempt and when it should be submitted to the IRB. Such a policy provides some oversight but avoids the absurdity that research that would be reviewed by the full IRB if conducted by a faculty member escapes such review if conducted by a student. On the other hand, it also avoids burdening students and instructors with preparing, and IRBs with reviewing, numerous virtually risk-free exercises (e.g., passive observation of public behavior) whose function is merely to provide students with practice in applying data collection techniques.

In addition to being ethically sound, this kind of policy also has a desirable educational spin-off. In the process of complying with its requirements, instructors and students alike must familiarize themselves with the ethical requirements of research involving human participants, particularly regarding the different levels of review associated with different kinds of research activities. Such issues typically receive too little attention, and too late. (Students often don't give ethics a thought until they learn they must have their dissertation proposals approved by the IRB.)

Insofar as more sophisticated and ethically complex research requires normal IRB review, this policy will no doubt inhibit instructors from encouraging and students from conducting such research. But this is not a bad thing, for students just learning to conduct research involving human participants are the least prepared to successfully grapple with ethically complex situations that arise in the course of planning and carrying it out.

Research Misconduct

Until quite recently, the general consensus between research communities within higher education and the federal government was that scientific and social scientific researchers, including educational researchers, did not need regulations to ensure ethical conduct. Rather, there was an implicit ethical code that called for professional self-regulation and honesty in one's research conduct and data reporting. Misconduct was thought to be a rare event (Steneck, 1984). Research communities enjoyed considerable autonomy in directing the conduct of research (LaFollette, 1994a). As Deborah Cameron and her colleagues put it, "All social researchers are expected to take seriously the ethical questions their activities raise" (Cameron, Frazer, Harvey, Rampton, & Richardson, 1993, p. 82). In the cases in which research turned out to be fraudulent in some way, it was presumed that members of the community would sanction their own.

This presumption was not borne out. As research institutions grew, competition between scholars stiffened, and the pressure to produce new scholarship and procure funding intensified. With the increased competition came more frequent and visible cases of research misconduct. Official regulations on the conduct of scientific and social scientific research soon followed (Price, 1994; Steneck, 1994). While ethical conduct concerning research participants had been monitored more closely (especially in the wake of the Tuskegee debacle), scrutiny of research misconduct concerning data collection and representation and the originality of research ideas and writing has been more recent. Most documented cases of research fraud and misconduct have come from the biomedical research community. Of the 26 cases of serious misconduct reported between 1980 and 1987, 21 were biomedical research cases (Goodstein, 1991). Sensational cases of misconduct in social research have arisen more often around the issue of deceptive research practices, such as Milgram's obedience experiments in the 1960s and Humphreys's Tearoom Trade study in the 1970s. Thus, the medical and scientific communities were the first to prompt worries about research misconduct and to take the lead in formulating specific regulations. Social and educational research communities have been catching up.

As a result of the aforementioned prominent cases of research misconduct, both the federal government and institutions of higher education were prompted to begin overseeing more closely the conduct of research. These cases challenged the system of self-regulation that had been in place and remained largely unquestioned until the 1970s. Thus began the present era of government oversight of research and the proliferation of ethical codes and institutional review boards—an era, according to David Goodstein, marked by confusion "because, except in the most extreme cases, no general agreement exists on what constitutes fraud or serious misconduct in science" (1991, p. 505).

In 1981, the United States House of Representatives' Subcommittee on Investigations and Oversight of the Committee on Science and Technology, chaired by Albert Gore, conducted hearings on fraud in biomedical research. The hearings were a direct reaction to the previously discussed Alsabti and Soman fraud cases (Steneck, 1984). Interestingly, the Darsee case (also previously discussed) surfaced a few weeks after the hearings. In testimony to the subcommittee, Philip Handler, then president of the National Academy of Sciences, said that the members of the subcommittee had no business meddling in issues of scientific research because they could not possibly understand the issues (Goodstein, 1991). Congress, of course, thought that their oversight was indeed proper, since much research was supported by agencies of the federal government and the public. And Congress had precedence on their side. For example, in 1966, the United States surgeon general established regulations covering federally funded scientific and social scientific research with human participants (Pattullo, 1982). It was other types of unethical research practices that had not received formal attention. While the 1981 congressional hearings did not result in any formal legislation, they did find that research institutions of higher education generally did not have policies in place concerning research misconduct and how to handle it and that researchers seemed reluctant to investigate charges of possible misconduct (Greene et al., 1985). The message came through loud and clear that allegations of research fraud and misconduct needed to be dealt with quickly, through formal institutional mechanisms (LaFollette, 1994a).

Not long thereafter, major professional associations such as the Association of American Medical Colleges (AAMC) and the Association of American Universities (AAU) began to develop ethical regulations to explicitly govern the conduct of their members. The AAMC was the first to issue a report on ethics, "The Maintenance of High Ethical Standards in the Conduct of Research," and in 1983, AAU's Committee on the Integrity of Research came out with recommendations encouraging intellectual honesty and discouraging a success-obsessed mentality (Steneck, 1984). Soon, too, there were detailed federal ethical regulations in place that governed all types of research misconduct, including plagiarism and fraud, as well as the treatment of research participants. Congress had passed a statute—the Health Research Extension Act of 1985—requiring any institutions seeking federal funding for research to have formal policies in place against scientific fraud (Price, 1994). The University of Michigan, Harvard, Stanford,

Yale, and Emory were among the first institutions of higher education to begin the process of formalizing ethical codes and procedures (Steneck, 1984). In fact, by the middle of 1983, 80% of all medical schools had begun establishing rules for investigating research misconduct (Chubin, 1985).

Major organizations such as NIH (in 1988) and the National Science Foundation (in 1989) published their own formal regulations on scientific research misconduct in the *Federal Register*. NIH had established the Office of Scientific Integrity and stipulated that research proposals from institutions without formal regulations on scientific misconduct would not be accepted (Goodstein, 1991).

Although the movement toward increased ethical regulation of research stemmed from the biomedical sciences, it strongly affected those in the social science and educational research communities as well. The federal government, via the Health Research Extension Act of 1985, imposed regulations stipulating that all applications for research funding and sponsorship from both the biomedical and behavioral sciences had to include a plan for examining allegations of research misconduct. In addition, institutions of higher education became responsible for promptly reporting any research misconduct to the federal government (LaFollette, 1994a; Steneck, 1994). These federal regulations, in combination with institutional policies on research misconduct, affect educational research in the same way they affect social research in general. Unlike the federal regulations that protect human research participants, the government outlines no provisions that specifically concern educational research.

In addition to the federal regulations, the social science research community as a whole and the educational research community in particular have established their own ethical codes to govern the research conduct of their members. We move now to a discussion of the major educational research professional organization, the American Educational Research Association (AERA), and its code of research ethics.

The AERA Code of Research Ethics

Professional ethical codes have existed at least since the Hippocratic oath of ancient Greece. In general, such codes express the creed of a given group of professionals and, unlike governmental regulations, do not have the force of law.

Nowadays, professional groups typically include a great diversity of individuals with varying viewpoints on controversial issues. In order to win broad acceptance, professional ethical codes must be exceedingly general. Thus, they provide little specific guidance regarding what to do in concrete cases of ethical perplexity. Nonetheless, professional ethical codes have considerable value, since they highlight the special duties and dangers associated with different kinds of professional activities. For example, physicians worry about unnecessary medical procedures; nurses, about protecting patients' interests without usurping physicians' legitimate authority; and journalists, about purveying false and damaging stories. The value to a profession of the initial process of clarifying and codifying ethical principles is that it explicates and clarifies ethical fundamentals; the ongoing value of an ethical code is that it serves as a reminder for veteran members of a profession and as a starting point for its initiates.

Codes of ethical conduct for social and educational researchers are a relatively recent development. Among social research organizations, the American Psychological Association was the first, in the late 1940s, to establish an ethical code for its members. The major anthropological and sociological associations followed suit in the years to come (Hamnett et al., 1984). Just as Alsabti and Soman were watershed cases in biomedical research misconduct, the Milgram and Humphreys cases were critical for social research. The most visible ethical concern has been with the treatment of research participants (issues of harm, respect for persons, and confidentiality) rather than with issues of plagiarism or data fabrication and misrepresentation. However, the increasing amount of qualitative research more recently has highlighted the issue of data misrepresentation.

Protection of Human Research Participants

Within educational research in particular, the main objective of the current American Educational Research Association (AERA) ethical standards is "to remind us, as educational researchers, that we should strive to protect these [children and other vulnerable] populations, and to maintain the integrity of our research, or our research community, and of all those with whom we have professional relations" (AERA, 1992, p. 1). The standards follow the federal code of regulations. It is important, within educational research, to highlight the protection of vulnerable populations, as the AERA standards do. Six guiding ethical standards were adopted by AERA; the second, "Research Populations, Educational Institutions, and the Public," deals mainly with the protection of research participants. The emphasis is on respecting the rights and dignity of research populations.

According to this second guiding standard, educational researchers are to take special care to properly inform their research participants—and, when appropriate, the participants' parents or guardians—of the possible risks and consequences of the research. Here, the standards emphasize the need for informed consent. Recently, educational research has been affected by federal regulations regarding the protection of students' rights. This has underscored the need for parental consent regarding research in schools (Hecht, 1996).

The standards openly discourage the use of deception in research. While deception is not strictly prohibited, its use should be avoided or, at the very least, minimized. Researchers are also warned to be careful not to exploit research participants for personal gain in any way. Both honesty and communication are highlighted as essential to the research process. In addition, the standards stress the importance of privacy and confidentiality. Educational researchers are expected to protect the privacy of research participants and data as much as is possible.

Research Misconduct

The AERA code has clear standards regarding researchers' responsibilities to the field of education. Two of the guiding standards directly involve how the proper conduct and improper conduct of research affect the field of education. These standards are "Responsibilities to the Field" and "Intellectual Ownership."

The standards regarding researchers' responsibilities to the field focus on researcher behavior and how inappropriate conduct could negatively affect the public standing of the field and its future research endeavors. Most important, these responsibilities stipulate that "educational researchers must not fabricate, falsify, or misrepresent authorship, evidence, data, findings, or conclusions" (AERA, 1992, p. 2). They should also monitor the uses of their research to avoid its use for any fraudulent purposes.

Regarding issues of authorship, the section on intellectual ownership centers on making sure that credit for research contributions goes where it is properly due. Both plagiarism and assuming credit for research to which one did not contribute in a significant creative way are prohibited. In a related vein, researchers are to be wary of any undue influence from government or other sponsoring agencies regarding the conduct of the research, its findings, or the reporting of it.

Traditional and Contemporary Aspects of the AERA Standards

The AERA standards are broad enough to include various research methods. They address concerns from both the traditional and contemporary approaches, with perhaps a slight slant toward the contemporary approach.

First, the standards emphasize traditional issues of informed consent, privacy, and protection of the autonomy of individual research participants. In addition, a theme throughout the standards is communication, especially between the (powerful) researcher and the research participants. This seems to fit in well with the contemporary approach to research ethics because it deemphasizes the researcher's technical control and seeks to empower research participants. Similarly, researchers are encouraged to make their research reports and their practical implications as accessible to the general public as possible.

The foreword to the standards highlights the nature of educational research as involving the improvement of people's lives and contributions to the educational process. Under the "Responsibilities to the Field" standard, researchers are called on to be well informed about many different forms and methods of research. Although it is not mentioned directly here, it seems that this is a nod to the increasing prevalence of research methods other than the experimental and quasi-experimental types. Overall, the AERA standards call on educational researchers to be sensitive to power issues involving their co-researchers, research participants, and research sites and to be aware of the social consequences of their research.

CONCLUSION

In this chapter, we have endeavored to cover quite a bit of ground regarding the traditional and contemporary approaches to research ethics, paying special attention to issues important for educational research. With recent increases in the use of so-called "qualitative" research methods in addition to experimental and quasi-experimental "quantitative" methods, some different ethical issues have arisen for researchers. As such, educational researchers need to stay abreast of the current ethical imperatives associated with various research methods.

That is not to say that only qualitative studies now deserve stringent ethical scrutiny or that current quantitative studies are all ethically problem free. Instead, both quantitative and qualitative research warrant strict scrutiny, and researchers need to be aware that particular research methods bring certain ethical issues to the fore.

Educational research is always *advocacy* research inasmuch as it unavoidably advances some moral-political perspective. This is especially important for educational researchers to bear in mind because educational research so often deals with vulnerable student populations, and research results often have a direct impact on students' schooling experiences and educational opportunities. In addition to abiding by federal, institutional, and AERA codes of ethics, to be truly ethical, educational researchers must be prepared to defend what their research is *for*.

REFERENCES

American Educational Research Association. (1992). *American Educational Research Association ethical standards*. Washington, DC: American Educational Research Association.

Anderson, J. A. (1992). On the ethics of research in a socially constructed reality. *Journal of Broadcasting & Electronic Media, 36,* 353–357.

Beauchamp, T. L., Faden, R. R., Wallace, R. J., & Walters, L. (1982). Introduction. In T. Beauchamp, R. Faden, R. Wallace, & L. Walters (Eds.), *Ethical issues in social science research* (pp. 3–39). Baltimore: Johns Hopkins University Press.

Benhabib, S. (1995). Feminism and postmodernism. In L. Nicholson (Ed.), *Feminist contentions* (pp. 17–34). New York: Routledge.

Broad, W. J. (1980a). Would-be academician pirates papers. *Science, 208,* 1438–1440.

Broad, W. J. (1980b). Imbroglio at Yale (I): Emergence of a fraud. *Science, 210,* 38–41.

Broad, W. J. (1980c). Imbroglio at Yale (II): A top job lost. *Science, 210,* 171–173.

Broad, W., & Wade, N. (1982). *Betrayers of the truth.* New York: Simon & Schuster.

Burbules, N., & Rice, S. (1991). Dialogue across difference: Continuing the conversation. *Harvard Educational Review, 61,* 396–416.

Burgess, R. G. (Ed.). (1989). *The ethics of educational research* (Vol. 8). New York: Falmer Press.

Cameron, D., Frazer, E., Harvey, P., Rampton, B., & Richardson, K. (1993). Ethics, advocacy and empowerment: Issues of method in researching language. *Language and Communication, 13,* 81–94.

Caplan, A. (1982). On privacy and confidentiality in social science research. In T. Beauchamp, R. Faden, R. Wallace, & L. Walters (Eds.), *Ethical issues in social science research* (pp. 315–328). Baltimore: Johns Hopkins University Press.

Cho, M. K. (1997, August 1). Secrecy and financial conflicts in university-industry research must get closer scrutiny. *Chronicle of Higher Education,* p. B4.

Christakis, N. (1988). Should IRB's monitor research more strictly? *IRB: A Review of Human Subjects Research, 10*(2), 8–9.

Chubin, D. E. (1985). Misconduct in research: An issue of science policy and practice. *Minerva, 23,* 175–202.

Code of Federal Regulations for the Protection of Human Subjects, 45 CFR 46 (1991, as amended).

Cornett, J., & Chase, S. (1989, March). *The analysis of teacher thinking and the problem of ethics: Reflections of a case study participant and a naturalistic researcher.* Paper presented at the annual meeting of the American Educational Research Association, San Francisco.

Dennis, R. (1993). Participant observations. In J. Stanfield & R. Dennis (Eds.), *Race and ethnicity in research methods* (pp. 53–74). Newbury Park, CA: Sage.

Dougherty, K., & Howe, K. (1990). *Policy regarding educational research: Report to the Subcommittee on Educational Research of the Human Research Committee.* Unpublished manuscript.

Dworkin, R. (1978). *Taking rights seriously.* Cambridge, MA: Harvard University Press.

Facio, E. (1993). Ethnography as personal experience. In J. Stanfield & R. Dennis (Eds.), *Race and ethnicity in research methods* (pp. 74–91). Newbury Park, CA: Sage.

Fay, B. (1975). *Social theory and political practice.* Birkenhead, England: George Allen & Unwin.

Foucault, M. (1970). *Discipline and punish: The birth of the prison.* New York: Vintage Books.

Gilbert, N. (1994). Miscounting social ills. *Society, 31*(3), 18–26.

Gilligan, C. (1982). *In a different voice: Psychological theory and women's development.* Cambridge, MA: Harvard University Press.

Goodstein, D. (1991). Scientific fraud. *American Scholar, 60,* 505–515.

Greene, P. J., Durch, J. S., Horwitz, W., & Hooper, V. S. (1985). Policies for responding to allegations of fraud in research. *Minerva, 23,* 203–215.

Griswold v. Connecticut, 381 U.S. 479, 507 (1964).

Hamnett, M. P., Porter, D. J., Singh, A., & Kumar, K. (1984). *Ethics, politics, and international social science research: From critique to praxis.* Honolulu: University of Hawaii Press.

Hattie, J. (1991). The Burt controversy. *Alberta Journal of Educational Research, 37,* 259–275.

Haworth, K. (1997, May 30). Clinton starts efforts to recruit minority volunteers for federal research projects. *Chronicle of Higher Education,* p. A39.

Hecht, J. B. (1996, April). *Educational research, research ethics and federal policy: An update.* Paper presented at the annual meeting of the American Educational Research Association, New York City.

House, E., & Howe, K. (1999). *Values in evaluation and social research.* Thousand Oaks, CA: Sage.

Howe, K. (1995). Democracy, justice and action research: Some theoretical developments. *Educational Action Research, 3,* 347–349.

Howe, K., & Dougherty, K. (1993). Ethics, IRB's, and the changing face of educational research. *Educational Researcher, 22*(9), 16–21.

Johnson, C. (1982). Risks in the publication of fieldwork. In J. Sieber (Ed.), *The ethics of social research: Fieldwork, regulation, and publication* (pp. 71–92). New York: Springer-Verlag.

Jones, J. H. (1993). *Bad blood: The Tuskegee syphilis experiment.* New York: Free Press.

Joynson, R. B. (1994). Fallible judgments. *Society, 31*(3), 45–52.

Kelman, H. (1982). Ethical issues in different social science methods. In T. Beauchamp, R. Faden, R. Wallace, & L. Walters (Eds.), *Ethical issues in social science research* (pp. 40–100). Baltimore: Johns Hopkins University Press.

Kevles, D. (1998). *The Baltimore case: A trial of politics, science, and character.* New York: Norton.

Kymlicka, W. (1990). *Contemporary political theory: An introduction.* New York: Oxford University Press.

Kymlicka, W. (1991). *Liberalism, community and culture.* New York: Oxford University Press.

LaFollette, M. C. (1994a). The politics of research misconduct: Congressional oversight, universities, and science. *Journal of Higher Education, 65,* 261–285.

LaFollette, M. C. (1994b). Research misconduct. *Society, 31*(3), 6–10.

Lather, P. (1991). *Getting smart: Feminist research and pedagogy with/in postmodernism.* New York: Routledge.

Lather, P. (1994). Fertile obsession: Validity after poststructuralism. In A. Gitlin (Ed.), *Power and method: Political activism and educational research* (pp. 36–60). New York: Routledge.

Lincoln, Y. (1990). Toward a categorical imperative for qualitative research. In E. Eisner & A. Peshkin (Eds.), *Qualitative inquiry in educational research: The continuing debate* (pp. 277–295). New York: Teachers College Press.

Lincoln, Y. S., & Denzin, N. K. (Eds.). (1994). *Handbook of qualitative research.* Beverly Hills, CA: Sage.

MacIntyre, A. (1981). *After virtue.* Notre Dame, IN: University of Notre Dame Press.

MacIntyre, A. (1982). Risk, harm, and benefit assessments as instruments of moral evaluation. In T. Beauchamp, R. Faden, R. Wallace, & L. Walters (Eds.), *Ethical issues in social science research* (pp. 175–192). Baltimore: Johns Hopkins University Press.

McCarthy, C. (1983). Experiences with boards and commissions concerned with research ethics in the U.S. In K. Berg & K. Tranoy (Eds.), *Research ethics.* New York: Alan R. Liss.

Milgram, S. (1974). *Obedience to authority.* New York: Harper & Row.

Murphy, M., & Johannsen, A. (1990). Ethical obligations and federal regulations in ethnographic research and anthropological education. *Human Organization, 49,* 127–134.

Murray, C., & Herrnstein, R. (1994). *The bell curve.* New York: Free Press.

Nagel, T. (1986). *The view from nowhere.* New York: Oxford University Press.

National Commission on Excellence in Education. (1983). *A nation at risk.* Washington, DC: U.S. Government Printing Office.

Noddings, N. (1984). *Caring: A feminine approach to ethics and moral education.* Berkeley: University of California Press.

Noddings, N. (1986). Fidelity in teaching, teacher education, and research on teaching. *Harvard Educational Review, 56,* 496–510.

Ogbu, J. U., & Matute-Bianchi, M. E. (1986). Understanding sociocultural factors: Knowledge, identity, and school adjustment. In *Beyond language: Social and cultural factors in schooling language minority students* (pp. 73–142). Sacramento: Bilingual Educational Office, California State Department of Education.

O'Toole, M. (1991). The whistle-blower and the train wreck. *New York Times,* p. A29.

Pattullo, E. L. (1982). Modesty is the best policy: The federal role in social research. In T. L. Beauchamp, R. R. Faden, R. J. Wallace, & L. Walters (Eds.), *Ethical issues in social science research* (pp. 373–390). Baltimore: Johns Hopkins University Press.

Penslar, R. L. (Ed.). (1995). *Research ethics: Cases and materials.* Bloomington: Indiana University Press.

Price, A. R. (1994). Definitions and boundaries of research misconduct: Perspectives from a federal government viewpoint. *Journal of Higher Education, 65,* 287–297.

Punch, M. (1986). *The politics and ethics of fieldwork.* Beverly Hills, CA: Sage.

Rabinow, P., & Sullivan, W. (1987). The interpretive turn: Emergence of an approach. In P. Rabinow & W. Sullivan (Eds.), *Interpretive social science* (pp. 1–21). Los Angeles: University of California Press.

Rawls, J. (1971). *A theory of justice.* Cambridge, MA: Belmont Press.

Roe v. Wade, 410 U.S. 113 (1973).

Roman, L. (1993). Double exposure: The politics of feminist materialist ethnography. *Educational Theory, 43*, 279–308.

Rorty, R. (1982). *Consequences of pragmatism.* Minneapolis: University of Minnesota Press.

Rushton, J. P. (1994). Victim of a scientific hoax. *Society, 31*(3), 40–44.

Scriven, M. (1969). Logical positivism and the behavioral sciences. In P. Achenstein & S. Barker (Eds.), *The legacy of logical positivism.* Baltimore: Johns Hopkins University Press.

Silva, M., & Sorrell, J. (1988). Enhancing comprehension of information for informed consent: A review of empirical research. *IRB: A Review of Human Subjects Research, 10*(1), 1–5.

Smith, J., & Heshusius, L. (1986). Closing down the conversation: The end of the quantitative-qualitative debate among educational researchers. *Educational Researcher, 15*(1), 4–12.

Smith, L. M. (1990). Ethics of qualitative field research: An individual perspective. In E. W. Eisner & A. Peshkin (Eds.), *Qualitative inquiry in education: The continuing debate.* New York: Teachers College Press.

Stanfield, J. (1993). Epistemological considerations. In J. Stanfield & R. Dennis (Eds.), *Race and ethnicity in research methods* (pp. 53–74). Newbury Park, CA: Sage.

Steneck, N. H. (1984). Commentary: The university and research ethics. *Science, Technology, and Human Values, 9*(4), 6–15.

Steneck, N. H. (1994). Research universities and scientific misconduct: History, policies, and the future. *Journal of Higher Education, 65*, 311–329.

Stronach, I., & MacLure, M. (1997). *Educational research undone: The postmodern embrace.* Philadelphia: Open University Press.

Strosnider, K. (1997, September 19). A new reply to "The bell curve." *Chronicle of Higher Education*, p. A12.

Taylor, C. (1994). The politics of recognition. In A. Gutmann (Ed.), *Multiculturalism: Examining the politics of recognition* (pp. 25–74). Princeton, NJ: Princeton University Press.

Veatch, R. (1977). *Case studies in medical ethics.* Cambridge, MA: Harvard University Press.

Vesilind, P. A. (1995). The responsible conduct of academic research. In A. L. DeNeef & C. D. Goodwin (Eds.), *The academic's handbook* (2nd ed., pp. 104–111). Durham, NC: Duke University Press.

Warwick, D. P. (1982). Types of harm in social research. In T. L. Beauchamp, R. R. Faden, R. J. Wallace, & L. Walters (Eds.), *Ethical issues in social science research* (pp. 101–124). Baltimore: Johns Hopkins University Press.

Wax, M. (1982). Research reciprocity rather than informed consent in fieldwork. In J. Sieber (Ed.), *The ethics of social research: Fieldwork, regulation, and publication* (pp. 33–48). New York: Springer-Verlag.

Willis, P. (1977). *Learning to labor: How working class kids get working class jobs.* New York: Columbia University Press.

Young, I. M. (1990). *Justice and the politics of difference.* Princeton, NJ: Princeton University Press.

Manuscript received May 10, 1998
Accepted August 20, 1998

Chapter 3

Rethinking Transfer: A Simple Proposal With Multiple Implications

JOHN D. BRANSFORD AND DANIEL L. SCHWARTZ
Vanderbilt University

A belief in transfer lies at the heart of our educational system. Most educators want learning activities to have positive effects that extend beyond the exact conditions of initial learning. They are hopeful that students will show evidence of transfer in a variety of situations: from one problem to another within a course, from one course to another, from one school year to the next, and from their years in school to their years in the workplace. Beliefs about transfer often accompany the claim that it is better to "educate" people broadly than simply to "train" them to perform particular tasks (e.g., Broudy, 1977).

In this chapter, we discuss research on transfer from both a retrospective and a prospective perspective. What has past transfer research taught us that is especially important for education? What might research on transfer look like in the future? Our discussion of past research is brief, not because it is unimportant but because of space limitations and the fact that our primary emphasis is on the future. We argue that prevailing theories and methods of measuring transfer are limited in scope; we propose an alternative that complements and extends current approaches; and we sketch this alternative's implications for education.

Our discussion is organized into five sections. First, we briefly summarize some of the key findings from the literature on transfer—both the successes and the disappointments. Second, we contrast the "traditional" view of transfer with an alternative that emphasizes the ability to learn during transfer. Third, we discuss mechanisms for transfer that emphasize Broudy's analysis of "knowing with" (which he adds to the more familiar replicative "knowing that" and applicative "knowing how"). Fourth, we show how our alternate view of transfer affects assumptions about what is valuable for students to learn. Finally, we show

Funding for studies described in this chapter was provided by grants from the Office of Educational Research and Improvement (R305F960090) and the National Science Foundation (The Challenge Zone: ESI-9618248; Center for Innovative Learning Technologies: CDA-9720384). We greatly appreciate their support but emphasize that the views expressed herein are those of the authors and not of the granting agency. We are very grateful to Carl Bereiter, Asghar (Ali) Iran-Nejad, and David Pearson for excellent comments and suggestions. In addition, we thank our colleagues Kay Burgess, Xiaodong Lin, and Sean Brophy for graciously allowing us to discuss some of their yet-to-be-published data. We also thank the members of the Cognition and Technology Group at Vanderbilt who provided invaluable feedback on our work.

how our view encourages a dynamic (rather than static) approach to assessment that can provide new insights into what it means to learn.

RESEARCH ON TRANSFER: ECSTASIES AND AGONIES

One of the most important benefits of research on transfer is the window it provides on the value of different kinds of learning experiences. A particular learning experience may look good or poor depending on the testing context (e.g., Morris, Bransford, & Franks, 1977). Different kinds of learning experiences can look equivalent given tests of memory yet look quite different on tests of transfer (see Figure 1). Measures of transfer provide an especially important way to evaluate educational success.

In this section, we briefly summarize contributions from research on transfer that are particularly relevant to education. We then discuss some of the disenchantments with the transfer literature.

Contributions From Research on Transfer

Thorndike and his colleagues were among the first to use transfer tests to examine assumptions about the benefits of learning experiences (e.g., Thorndike & Woodworth, 1901). One goal of their research was to challenge the doctrine of "formal discipline" that was prevalent at the turn of the 20th century. Practice was assumed to have general effects; for example, people were assumed to increase their "general skills of learning and attention" by learning Latin or other taxing subject matters. Discussions of assumptions about formal discipline date back to the Greeks (see Mann, 1979). Challenging these assumptions, Thorndike's work showed that even though people may do well on a test of the specific content they have practiced, they will not necessarily transfer that learning to a new situation.

Thorndike and colleagues' studies raised serious questions about the fruitfulness of designing learning environments based on assumptions of formal discipline. Rather than developing some type of "mental muscle" that affected a wide range of performances, people seemed to learn things that were very specific. As Thorndike and Woodworth (1901) stated:

The mind is . . . a machine for making particular reactions to particular situations. It works in great detail, adapting itself to the special data of which it has had experience. . . . Improvement in any single mental function rarely brings about equal improvement in any other function, no matter how similar, for the working of every mental function group is conditioned by the nature of the data of each particular case. (pp. 249–250)

Thorndike and his colleagues helped establish an important tradition of examining assumptions about learning and transfer through rigorous experimental research. During the past century, researchers have discovered a number of important principles about the conditions of learning that enhance and impede transfer. We briefly discuss some of the findings that are particularly relevant

FIGURE 1
Examples of Studies Showing That Transfer Tests Can Be More Sensitive Measures of Different Learning Experiences Than Memory Tests

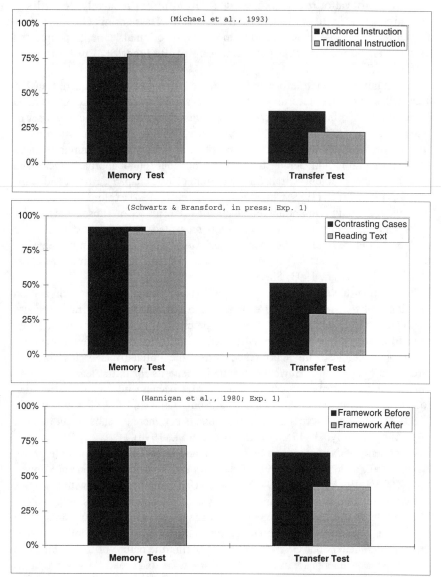

to education (more extended discussions can be found in Anderson, Reder, & Simon, 1997; Detterman & Sternberg, 1993; and Lee, 1998).

One important finding from research is that effective transfer requires a sufficient degree of original learning. Although this seems obvious, a number of claims about "transfer failure" have been traced to inadequate opportunities for people to learn in the first place (e.g., see Klahr & Carver, 1988; Lee, 1998; Lee & Pennington, 1993; Littlefield et al., 1988). The degree to which learning has made the retrieval of relevant knowledge "effortful" or relatively "effortless" also affects transfer (e.g., Beck & McKeown, 1983; Hasselbring, Goin, & Bransford, 1987, 1988). Without attention to degree of original learning, people can erroneously conclude that potentially helpful educational programs are ineffective.

The manner in which information is learned also affects subsequent transfer. Judd's classic studies of learning to throw darts at underwater targets demonstrated the value of learning with understanding rather than simply mimicking a set of fixed procedures (cf. Judd, 1908). Wertheimer (1959) compared instruction that focused on a computational versus conceptual approach to determining the area of parallelograms and demonstrated how the conceptual approach facilitated transfer to new problems. Bransford and Stein (1993, chap. 7), Brown and Kane (1988), and Chi et al. (1989; Chi, Slotta, & deLeeuw, 1994) explored how learning with understanding is important for enhancing performance on subsequent transfer tasks. Studies also show that information presented in the context of solving problems is more likely to be spontaneously used than information presented in the form of simple facts (e.g., Adams et al., 1988; Lockhart, Lamon, & Gick, 1988; Michael et al., 1993; Sherwood et al., 1987).

Researchers have also explored the effects of using concrete examples on learning and transfer. Concrete examples can enhance initial learning because they can be elaborated and help students appreciate the relevance of new information. In addition, learning potentially confusable concepts in different contexts can protect people from interference during the initial trials of learning (cf. Bransford et al., 1990). However, despite its benefits for initial learning, overly contextualized information can impede transfer because information is too tied to its original context (e.g., Bjork & Richardson-Klahaven, 1989; Gick & Holyoak, 1980). Presenting concepts in multiple contexts can increase subsequent transfer (e.g., Gick & Holyoak, 1983; cf. Bransford et al., 1990).

Proponents of case-based, problem-based, and project-based learning (e.g., see Barron et al., 1998; Barrows, 1985; Cognition and Technology Group at Vanderbilt [CTGV], 1997; Hmelo, 1994; Williams, 1992) attempt to deal with problems of overcontextualization in a number of ways, including presenting similar materials in multiple contexts, having students engage in "what if" problem solving that prompts them to think about the qualitative effects of varying particular problem parameters (CTGV, 1997), and changing the nature of the problems to ones in which students are asked to invent solutions to a broad class of problems rather than simply attempt to solve only a single problem (e.g., Bransford et al., 1999; CTGV, in press). Viewing problem environments from multiple perspectives also increases the flexibility with which people can deal with new sets of events (e.g., Bransford et al., 1990; Spiro et al., 1987).

Related to issues of overcontextualization is the issue of helping people represent problems and solutions at appropriate levels of abstraction. Appropriate problem representations increase positive transfer and decrease the probability of negative transfer (for discussions of negative transfer, see Chen & Daehler, 1989; Luchins, 1942; Singley & Anderson, 1989). For example, students solving CTGV's Jasper adventure "The Big Splash" learn to use statistical information to create a complex business plan (see CTGV, 1997). Ultimately, they need to realize that their solution works well for "fixed cost" problems but not for those in which costs are not fixed. Without this more general understanding, they apply their knowledge in the wrong settings. Informative studies about helping students create effective problem representations for transfer include Singley and Anderson (1989) and Novick (1988).

An emphasis on metacognition (e.g., Brown, 1978; Flavell, 1976)—on helping students monitor, reflect upon, and improve their strategies for learning and problem solving—has also been shown to increase transfer. Examples include learning in the areas of science (e.g., Lin et al., 1995; White & Fredrickson, 1998), mathematics (e.g., CTGV, 1994; Schoenfeld, 1985), computer programming (Bielaczyc et al., 1995), and literacy (e.g., Palincsar & Brown, 1984; Pressley & Afflerbach, 1995). Research also suggests that metacognitive activities such as comprehension monitoring have strong knowledge requirements; they are not general skills that people learn "once and for all." For example, without well-differentiated knowledge of the performance requirements of a particular task (e.g., monitoring a river for water quality), people cannot accurately assess whether they are prepared to perform that task (e.g., see Vye et al., 1989).

Disenchantments With the Transfer Literature

Even the preceding brief review illustrates that research has provided some fundamental insights into the kinds of learning experiences that promote transfer. Nevertheless, there is also considerable disenchantment with the transfer literature. One set of criticisms comes from proponents of "situative cognition" who argue that cognitive theorists need to redefine their approach to transfer (see especially Greeno, 1997; Lave, 1988). Even within the cognitive tradition, researchers have worried that transfer is too hard to find—that there are too many examples of transfer failure. The title of a recent book, *Transfer on Trial*, illustrates this point (Detterman & Sternberg, 1993). In the volume's introductory chapter, Detterman presents "the case for the prosecution" and provides the following analysis of the transfer literature:

First, most studies fail to find transfer. Second, those studies claiming transfer can only be said to have found transfer by the most generous of criteria and would not meet the classical definition of transfer [defined by Detterman as "the degree to which a behavior will be repeated in a new situation"; p. 4]. . . . In short, from studies that claim to show transfer and that don't show transfer, there is no evidence to contradict Thorndike's general conclusions: Transfer is rare, and its likelihood of occurrence is directly related to the similarity between two situations. (p. 15)

Not all theorists are as pessimistic about transfer as is Detterman (e.g., see the other contributors to Detterman & Sternberg, 1993). Nevertheless, there are enough examples of transfer failure to consider positive transfer to be at least a relatively rare event according to the criterion of repeated behavior.

Broudy (1977) also discusses the difficulty of consistently finding evidence of transfer. His focus is on evidence of the benefits of formal education for future thinking and problem solving:

Ever since formal schooling was established, it has been assumed that knowledge acquired in school would be used to enhance the quality of human life. The investment in schools was supposed to yield a return in the form of greater adequacy in occupational, civic, and personal development. (p. 2)

Broudy notes that people rapidly forget the facts that they learned in school, as might be measured by tests of "replicative knowing." He also concedes that most people have difficulty applying their knowledge in order to solve new problems, or what he calls "applicative knowing." He concludes that school is a failure based on replicative and applicative tests of learning. But, as discussed later, Broudy's conclusion is not that transfer is rare. Instead, his work points to the need to rethink our ideas of what it means to learn and to know and how we evaluate educational experiences.

In line with Broudy, we argue for the need to reconsider some of the prevalent beliefs about what constitutes a valuable demonstration of transfer. Our thesis is that evidence of transfer is often difficult to find because we tend to think about it from a perspective that blinds us to its presence. Prevailing theories and methods of measuring transfer work well for studying full-blown expertise, but they represent too blunt an instrument for studying the smaller changes in learning that lead to the development of expertise. New theories and measures of transfer are required.

As an illustration, consider a set of studies conducted by Kay Burgess, Sean Brophy, and the present authors. In one study, we asked fifth graders and college students to create a statewide recovery plan to protect bald eagles from the threat of extinction. Our goal was to investigate the degree to which their general educational experiences prepared them for this novel task; none of the students had explicitly studied eagle recovery plans.

The plans generated by both groups missed the mark widely. The college students' writing and spelling skills were better than those of the fifth graders, but none of the college students mentioned the need to worry about baby eagles imprinting on the humans who fed them, about creating tall hacking towers so that fledgling eagles would imprint on the territory that they would eventually call home, and about a host of other important variables. In short, none of the students generated a recovery plan that was even close to being adequate. On the basis of these findings, one might claim that neither the fifth graders' nor the college students' general educational experiences prepared them adequately for transfer.

However, by another measure of transfer, the differences between the age groups were striking. We asked the students to generate questions about important issues they would research in order to design effective recovery plans for eagles (see the Appendix). The fifth graders tended to focus on features of individual eagles (e.g., How big are they? What do they eat?). In contrast, the college students were much more likely to focus on issues of interdependence between the eagles and their habitats. They asked questions such as "What type of ecosystem supports eagles?" (reflecting an appreciation of interdependence), "What about predators of eagles and eagle babies?" (also reflecting interdependence), "Are today's threats like the initial threats to eagles?" (reflecting an appreciation of history and change), and "What different kinds of specialists are needed for different recovery areas?" (reflecting an appreciation of a possible need for multiple solutions). Because they had not studied eagles directly, the college students were presumably generating questions framed by other aspects of biology that they had learned. So, by this alternative form of transfer test, it would appear that the college students had learned general considerations that would presumably help shape their future learning if they chose to pursue this topic (Scardamalia & Bereiter, 1992). In this regard, one would call their prior learning experiences a success.

In the discussion to follow, we explore what we consider the "traditional" view of transfer and contrast it with an alternative view that has important implications for educational research and practice. The alternative we propose is not something that we have invented—it too exists in the literature. However, the contrast between it and the "traditional" view has not been emphasized as much as it might be, and the implications for educational practice have not been explicitly explored.

TWO VIEWS OF TRANSFER

Central to traditional approaches to transfer is a dominant methodology that asks whether people can apply something they have learned to a new problem or situation. Thorndike and colleagues' classic studies of transfer used this paradigm. For example, in Thorndike and Woodworth (1901), participants took a pretest on judging the area of rectangles and then were given opportunities to improve their performance through practice plus feedback. Following this learning task, participants were tested on the related task of estimating the areas of circles and triangles. Transfer was assessed by the degree to which learning skill *A* (estimating the area of squares) influenced skill *B* (estimating the area of circles or triangles). Thorndike and Woodworth found little evidence of transfer in this setting and argued that the "ability to estimate area" was not a general skill.

Gick and Holyoak's (1980, 1983) work on analogical transfer provides a modern-day example of a similar paradigm for studying transfer. Participants in their studies first received information about a problem and a solution, such as "the general and the fortress problem." They then received a second problem (Duncker's [1945] irradiation problem) that could be solved by analogy to the first problem. Depending on the conditions of the experiment, participants either did or did not show evidence of applying what they had learned about the general's solution to solve the irradiation problem. In many instances, there was a surprising failure to transfer spontaneously from one problem to the next. Many other researchers use a similar paradigm of initial learning followed by problem solving (e.g., Adams et al., 1988; Bassok, 1990; Brown & Kane, 1988; Chen & Daehler, 1989; Lockhart, Lamon, & Gick, 1988; Nisbett, Fong, Lehman, & Cheng, 1987; Novick, 1988; Perfetto, Bransford, & Franks, 1983; Reed, Ernst, & Banerji, 1974; Thorndike & Woodworth, 1901; Wertheimer, 1959).

A striking feature of the research studies just noted is that they all use a final transfer task that involves what we call "sequestered problem solving" (SPS). Just as juries are often sequestered in order to protect them from possible exposure to "contaminating" information, subjects in experiments are sequestered during tests of transfer. There are no opportunities for them to demonstrate their abilities to learn to solve new problems by seeking help from other resources such as texts or colleagues or by trying things out, receiving feedback, and getting opportunities to revise. Accompanying the SPS paradigm is a theory that characterizes transfer as the ability to directly apply one's previous learning to a new setting or problem (we call this the direct application [DA] theory of transfer). Our thesis is that the SPS methodology and the accompanying DA theory of transfer are responsible for much of the pessimism about evidence of transfer.

An alternative to SPS methodology and DA theory is a view that acknowledges the validity of these perspectives but also broadens the conception of transfer by including an emphasis on people's "preparation for future learning" (PFL). Here the focus shifts to assessments of people's abilities to learn in knowledge-rich environments. When organizations hire new employees, they do not expect them to have learned everything they need for successful adaptation. They want people who can learn, and they expect them to make use of resources (e.g., texts, computer programs, colleagues) to facilitate this learning. The better prepared they are for future learning, the greater the transfer (in terms of speed and/or quality of new learning).

As an illustration of transfer as PFL, imagine elementary education majors who graduate and become classroom teachers for the first time. By the standard DA definition of transfer, the test of transfer would be whether the beginning teachers, without coaching, can apply to the classroom the methods they learned in school. As noted earlier, this is an important concern, yet it is only one part of the larger story. The larger story involves whether the novice teachers have been prepared to learn from their new experiences, including their abilities to structure their environments in ways that lead to successful learning (e.g., arrange for peer coaching). There is no preliminary education or training that can make these people experts; it can only place them on a trajectory toward expertise.

A focus on transfer from the perspective of its effects on new learning is not an idea that is unique to us; the idea has been discussed and studied by many theorists (e.g., Bereiter, 1990; Bereiter & Scardamalia, 1993; Glaser & Chi, 1988; Gott et al., 1992; Greeno, Smith, & Moore, 1993; Lee, 1998; Lee & Pennington, 1993; Singley & Anderson, 1989; Spiro et. al, 1987; Wineburg, 1998). Nevertheless, as we worked on this chapter, we realized that our thoughts about the two perspectives were not well differentiated; we switched from one view to the other without realizing the shift in our thinking. We have come to believe that this lack of differentiation is not unique to us and that it is worthwhile to contrast these two views of transfer explicitly because they have different implications for educational practice.

One important difference is that the PFL perspective helps us notice evidence of positive transfer that is often hidden in the traditional SPS paradigm. Studies in the area of skill acquisition illustrate this point. Researchers such as Singley and Anderson (1989) have asked how experience with one set of skills (e.g., learning a text editor) affects people's abilities to learn a second set of related skills (e.g., a second text editor). These studies used what we are calling a PFL paradigm; the focus was on students' abilities to learn the second program as a function of their previous experiences. Data indicate that the benefits of previous experiences with a text editor did not reveal themselves immediately. The researchers found much greater evidence of transfer on the second day than on the first. One-shot SPS tests of transfer are often too weak to detect effects such as these.

As we describe later in the section on assessment, the ideal assessment from a PFL perspective is to directly explore people's abilities to learn new information and relate their learning to previous experiences (e.g., see Brown, Bransford, Ferrara, & Campione, 1983; Bruer, 1993; Singley & Anderson, 1989). However, more standard SPS tasks can sometimes be reinterpreted from a PFL perspective. The PFL perspective helps counter the tendency of SPS methodologies and DA theories to focus primarily on deficiencies in problem solving when novice learners are compared with experts. In the study on eagles described earlier, the SPS assessment revealed how far the fifth-grade and college students were from developing an adequate eagle recovery plan, and it invited the inference that the students' K–12 experiences had not prepared them for this kind of transfer. From the PFL perspective, one looks for evidence of initial learning trajectories. So, rather than an evaluation of whether people can generate a finished product, the focus shifts to whether they are prepared to learn to solve new problems. For example, one determinant of the course of future learning is the questions people ask about a topic, because these questions shape their learning goals (e.g., see Barrows, 1985; Bereiter & Scardamalia, 1989; Hmelo, 1994). In the eagle experiment, the PFL perspective yielded a deeper appreciation of how the college students' K–12 experiences had prepared them to learn.

TRANSFER AND "KNOWING WITH"

A PFL view of transfer fits nicely with Broudy's (1977) arguments about different types of knowing. Broudy argues that we must go beyond the "knowing that" (replicative knowledge) and the "knowing how" (applicative knowledge) that jointly constitute the characteristic focus of DA theories. People also "know with" their previously acquired concepts and experiences. "Knowing with" refers to the fact that the educated person "thinks, perceives and judges with everything that he has studied in school, even though he cannot recall these learnings on demand'' (p. 12). By ''knowing with'' our cumulative set of knowledge and experiences, we perceive, interpret, and judge situations based on our past experiences. ''Knowing with'' is compatible with Plato's analogy between knowledge and the sun; learning illuminates a situation without reproducing that situation.

Broudy argues that ''knowing with'' takes place through several different mechanisms. One is ''associative,'' which includes an activation of nonlogical relationships based on contiguity, resemblance, frequency, and other features discussed by associationist theorists. A second mechanism involves an interpretive function that affects how people categorize, classify, predict, and infer. Broudy argues that this interpretative function of ''knowing with'' is different from either a replicative or applicative use of knowledge:

Interpretation, although essential to application, does not by itself yield any technology which can cause change. And although the interpretation of the situation invariably involves some use of a previous experience, it cannot be reduced to a simple replication of that experience. (p. 11)

Broudy emphasizes that much of the knowledge that supports ''knowing with'' is tacit and may be unavailable for recall except in its most skeletal form.

The concept of bacterial infection as learned in biology can operate even if only a skeletal notion of the theory and the facts supporting it can be recalled. Yet, we are told of cultures in which such a concept would not be part of the interpretive schemata. (p. 12)

The absence of an idea of bacterial infection should have a strong effect on the nature of the hypotheses that people entertain in order to explain various illnesses, and hence it would affect their abilities to learn more about causes of illness through further research and study. This is similar to the findings from the eagle study discussed earlier, which showed that the college students, but not the fifth graders, began with ideas such as ''interdependence'' that influenced their learning goals for researching eagle recovery plans.

Perceptual Learning and "Knowing With"

Research on perceptual learning provides a good illustration of what it means to ''know with'' our experiences (e.g., Garner, 1974; Gibson & Gibson, 1955). Perceptual learning theorists point toward the importance of contrasting cases, such as glasses of wine side by side, as guides to noticing and differentiation. One is unlikely to be able to remember each of the contrasting cases, and experience with a set of cases will not necessarily allow one to induce principles that guide unaided problem solving. Nevertheless, experiences with contrasting cases can affect what one notices about subsequent events and how one interprets them, and this in turn can affect the formulation of new hypotheses and learning goals.

Garner (1974) provides a powerful illustration of the role of contrasting cases in noticing. He asks readers to look at a stimulus such as Figure 2 (we have

FIGURE 2
How Would You Describe This Figure?

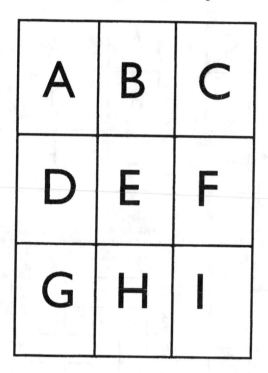

adapted his demonstration to new figures) and then asks "How would you describe the figure?" Most people describe it as a grid with letters. Some may describe it as a set of lines.

The demonstration continues by considering the same figure (we label it the "standard" figure) in the context illustrated in Figure 3. This time the standard is in the context of another figure. Now features such as the size, shape, and symmetry of the grid and its rectangles become relevant. When people see the standard in isolation, they generally fail to mention anything about the size, shape, or symmetry of the grid.

We can continue the demonstration by considering the standard in a new context as in Figure 4. Now features such as font, number of grid entries, and "indexing" scheme become relevant.

Garner notes that one could continue to make contrasts indefinitely so that additional features become salient—features such as the thickness of the lines, the fact that the lines are solid rather than broken, and the color of the ink. Garner's conclusion from his demonstration is that a single stimulus is defined in the context of a "field" of alternatives. In Broudy's (1977) terms, this field

FIGURE 3
The Standard Figure in the Context of a Second Figure

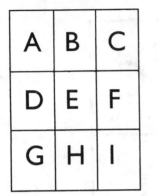

FIGURE 4
Putting the Standard in Different Contexts Reveals Different Features

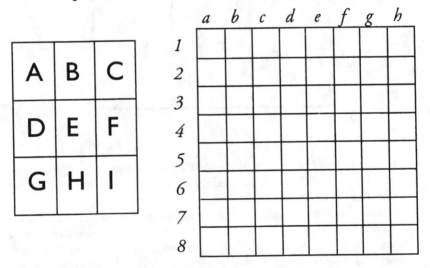

becomes something that we "know with"; it affects what we notice about subsequent events.

The field that people "know with" is not limited to perceptual alternatives. Changes in our ability to "know with" are also affected by the interpretations that we "know" the cases with in the first place. As an illustration, consider the set of grids shown in Figure 5. Each differs from the others, but it is difficult to know which features are most important.

What can be learned from Figure 5 is affected by additional interpretive knowledge that helps people develop learning questions. In the present case, for

FIGURE 5
Which Grid Would You Choose and Why?

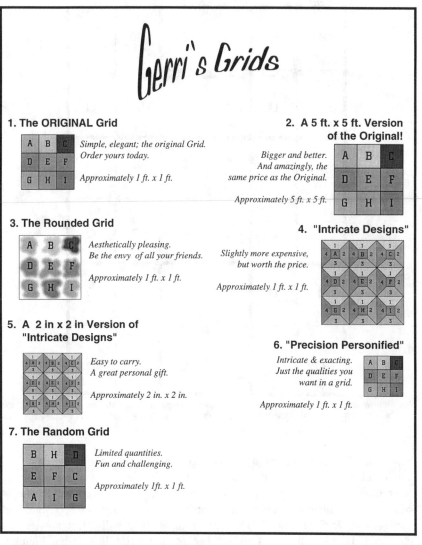

example, assume that the grids represent possible designs for the backs of T-shirts used to facilitate backscratching (Bransford et al., 1999). Given this information, it becomes possible to think about which features would be useful and which would not: Is the grid shaped correctly? Are the squares the right size? Does the design have an easy indexing scheme so that people can remember where to tell other people to scratch their shirts?

By comparing the grids in the context of a meaningful framework, people might improve in their ability to remember the individual cases. But even after

FIGURE 6
"Knowing With" Prior Experience

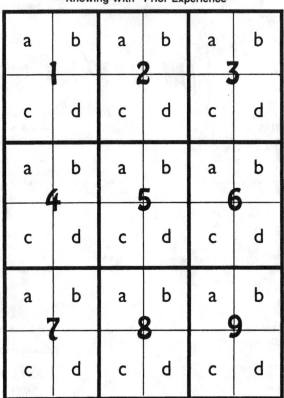

Note. After studying the previous backscratcher grids, people can evaluate the new features of this backscratcher grid even though the features are not "common elements" from the previous grids.

these individual cases are most likely forgotten, people can still "know with" their learning experiences, and this will affect subsequent processing. The learning experiences "set the stage" for further noticing, and their effects cannot be reduced to the mere replication of a particular experience per se (Bransford, Franks, Vye, & Sherwood, 1971). For example, they will affect how people interpret and think about the "transfer" backscratcher grid illustrated in Figure 6. Even though there are elements in this grid that are different from the original grids, and even though people's memories for the original grids may be poor, they can notice these elements and formulate goals for determining whether or not they are good features.

deGroot's (1965) conclusions from his classic studies of chess masters provide another example that is consistent with the concept of "knowing with":

We know that increasing experience and knowledge in a specific field (chess, for instance) has the effect that things (properties, etc.) which, at earlier stages, had to be abstracted, or even inferred are

FIGURE 7
Differentiated Knowledge Helps Experts Appreciate Properties That Novices Often Miss

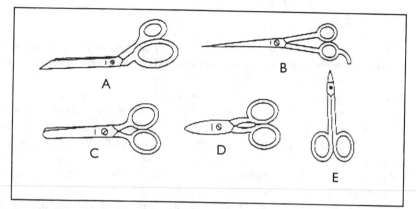

Note. Adapted from "A Sketch of a Cognitive Approach to Comprehension," by J. D. Bransford and N. S. McCarrell, in *Cognition and the Symbolic Processes*, edited by W. Weimer and D. S. Palermo, 1974, Hillsdale, NJ: Lawrence Erlbaum Associates, Inc. Copyright 1974 by Lawrence Erlbaum Associates, Inc.

apt to be immediately perceived at later stages. To a rather large extent, abstraction is replaced by perception, but we do not know much about how this works, nor where the borderline lies. As an effect of this replacement, a so-called "given" problem situation is not really given since it is seen differently by an expert than it is perceived by an inexperienced person. (pp. 33–34)

How Contrasting Cases Set the Stage for Future Learning

A study conducted by the present authors shows how experiences with contrasting cases set the stage for learning new information (Schwartz & Bransford, 1998). The primary motivation for the study arose from the observation that novices in courses often miss important ideas because their knowledge is not as well differentiated as that of the experts (e.g., in a textbook) who explain various concepts. Imagine, for example, attempting to understand the statement "The dressmaker used the scissors to cut the cloth for the dress." This statement is probably easily understood by most people; they can imagine a person using a pair of scissors to cut some cloth. However, what is their concept of the dressmaker's scissors? A scissors expert will have a much more differentiated concept of scissors than most casual comprehenders (see Figure 7). As opposed to novices, for example, experts would know which features to look for when purchasing new scissors for a dressmaker.

As another example of the importance of well-differentiated knowledge structures, consider novices who attempt to comprehend the following: "The developmental psychologist showed first graders, fifth graders, and college students a set of 30 pictures and found that their memory for the pictures was equivalent."

Novices can understand this statement at some level, but chances are that their understanding of "memory" will be relatively undifferentiated. In contrast, an expert will assume that this experiment involved recognition memory rather than free or cued recall, unless however, the 30 pictures were chosen to map very explicitly into a domain of organized knowledge in which the children were experts (e.g., see Chi, 1976; Lindberg, 1980). In short, the expert can construct a number of well-differentiated scenarios whereas the novice understands only superficially. (Schwartz & Bransford, 1998, p. 479)

The goal of our studies was to explore ways to help college students understand memory concepts (e.g., a schema). We knew from previous experiences that students often understood memory concepts only superficially and that attempts to simply explain all of the details of memory theories often did not remedy the situation. The hypothesis that drove our work was that students needed to develop a well-differentiated appreciation for the psychological phenomena explained by memory theories. We thought that an excellent way for them to do this was by analyzing simplified data sets from classic experiments and noting the patterns that emerged from the contrasting experimental conditions. In short, we used the "contrasting cases" methodology of the perceptual learning theorists (described earlier). We did not expect that the analysis of contrasting cases would, by itself, be useful. Students needed an explanation for the patterns of data they discovered, and it seemed unlikely that they could generate one without help from an expert. Therefore, our hypothesis was that the analysis of contrasting cases would better prepare the students for future learning from an expert. In Broudy's terms, the analysis of contrasting cases should provide a basis for "knowing with" when students hear or read the explanation of an expert.

Our experiments compared the effects of reading about memory experiments and theories versus actively analyzing sets of contrasting cases relevant to memory. Students in the contrasting cases condition worked with simplified data sets from original experiments. For example, they were given a sheet of paper that described the methods of an experiment in which subjects were asked to recall, with or without a delay, text passages that described typical events, and they received (simplified) data from groups of hypothetical subjects. Their task was to "discover" the important patterns in the data. Students in the other condition wrote a multipage summary of a textbook chapter. The chapter described the results of the experiments that the contrasting cases group analyzed, and it also provided the theoretical description of the results. We believed that opportunities to actively analyze contrasting cases of real data would help novice students develop differentiated knowledge of memory phenomena.

As noted earlier, our assumption was not that the analysis of contrasting data sets would, by itself, lead to deep understanding. Instead, we assumed that the use of contrasting cases would better prepare students to learn new information than would the activity of summarizing the text. As a means of examining this assumption, the new learning experience took the form of a lecture on memory theories and experiments. The lecture was heard by, and relevant to, both the "summary" group and the contrasting cases group. We also included a condition in which students analyzed the contrasting cases a second time, instead of hearing the lecture. This way, we could assess the degree to which the contrasting cases students actually learned from the lecture.

FIGURE 8
Contrasting Cases Prepared Students to Learn From a Lecture as Measured by a Subsequent SPS Transfer Test

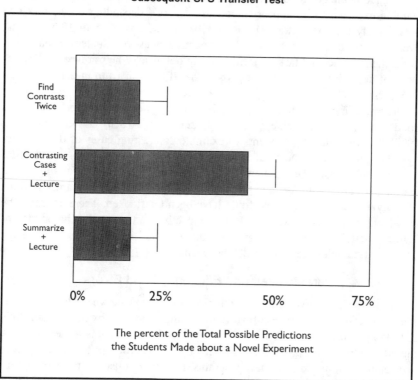

The percent of the Total Possible Predictions
the Students Made about a Novel Experiment

Data strongly supported the assumption that contrasting cases better prepared students for future learning (see Figure 8). Students received a final prediction task that presented them with a new memory experiment and asked them to make predictions about the likely outcomes. Students in the "summarize plus lecture" group did not do nearly as well as students in the "contrasting cases plus lecture" condition. Equally important, the students who received experiences with contrasting cases (the "find contrast twice" group) but never heard the clarifying lecture did very poorly on the prediction task. The act of analyzing the cases prepared the students to learn from the lecture—it created a set of experiences that enriched subsequent learning. But the opportunity for further learning was needed. For those students who had not received an opportunity to hear the expert's lecture, the advantages of the contrasting case activities were not revealed.

NEW PERSPECTIVES ON QUALITY OF LEARNING

The most important characteristic of a PFL approach to transfer is not that it makes us feel better as educators because evidence for transfer is now more visible. Instead, the PFL approach is important because it provides a framework for evaluating the quality of particular kinds of learning experiences. A particular learning experience can appear "good" or "poor" depending on the task one is eventually asked to perform (Bransford, Franks, Morris, & Stein, 1979; Morris, Bransford, & Franks, 1977). The PFL perspective focuses on "extended learning" rather than on one-shot task performances. In doing so, it helps reveal the importance of activities and experiences whose benefits are hard to measure from an SPS perspective.

The preceding study that taught students about memory concepts provides a good example of the value of the PFL perspective (Schwartz & Bransford, 1998). Opportunities for students to examine contrasting cases of data did not by themselves affect the final transfer (prediction) task, which was an SPS assessment. Instead, these pattern-finding activities set the stage for subsequent learning from a lecture. Without this subsequent opportunity to learn, the value of analyzing contrasting cases would have been overlooked. There appear to be additional situations in which a PFL perspective can show the importance of learning activities whose strengths are not revealed in many kinds of testing contexts. Examples are discussed subsequently.

Perspectives on "Efficiency" and Errors

The PFL perspective draws attention to differences between short-term and long-term efficiency. Studies of word processing conducted by Sander and Richard (1997) represent a case in point. They found that attempts to help students understand the conceptual organization of a word-processing program led to accelerated abilities to learn new programs. However, it usually takes more time to introduce students to conceptual ideas than to have them simply focus on a particular set of skills or solution procedures. If the assessment task is how well people perform on the task they are taught, the conceptual method seems to be second best because it is not as efficient. But when assessment focuses on instructional procedures designed to prepare people for future learning, the perceived quality of the two methods reverses. Spiro and colleagues (1987) have argued that optimal learning experiences can be quite different depending on the characteristics of the knowledge domain the students are likely to encounter in the future. In today's world, it is likely that the word-processing programs that people use will change over time; thus, it seems wise to prepare them for change.

The PFL perspective can also help clarify the advantages of additional teaching techniques that appear inefficient from other perspectives. For example, consider efforts to compare the benefits of (a) beginning lessons by first having students generate their own, perhaps incorrect, thoughts about phenomena and (b) simply telling students the correct answers. Examples might include attempts to have students begin an instructional sequence by first generating their own experiment to test a certain idea (Bransford et al., 1990) or creating their own formula for capturing the variance of statistical distributions (Schwartz & Moore, 1998). Since novices will often generate ideas that are incorrect, they must eventually be guided toward more fruitful ways of thinking. Why not "cut to the chase" and present the correct ideas right from the start?

The PFL perspective suggests a number of reasons for first having students generate their own ideas about phenomena. One of the most important is that it provides an opportunity for students to contrast their own thinking with that of others, including experts in an area. This sets the stage for appreciating the critical features of the new information that is presented to them—analogous to the perceptual examples from Garner (1974) discussed earlier. For example, students who first generated their own thoughts on how to design an experiment to test a particular idea expressed appreciation about the elegance of the experiments discussed in an article that was then assigned to them (Bransford et al., 1990). In contrast, students who were simply assigned the article did not have the advantage of experiencing how the article helped clarify their own thinking. As a result, they treated the article simply as a set of facts to be learned.

Schwartz and Moore (1998) illustrate a similar example in the domain of statistics. The idea is that students are better prepared to appreciate the formula for standard deviation if they are first given opportunities to differentiate the elements of variability that the formula has to account for. To help differentiate these elements, students are shown an initial pair of distributions, say {2, 4, 6, 8, 10} and {4, 5, 6, 7, 8}. The experimenters point out that the two sets have a similarity, and they ask the students to note that there is a single number for each set that helps determine this similarity: the average. This single number is easier to keep in mind and communicate than the total distribution.

The experimenters then ask students to come up with a method for determining a single number for each set that could capture what is different (i.e., the variability). After students invent their own methods (often a range formula), they receive a new pair of distributions, say {2, 4, 6, 8, 10} and {2, 2, 10, 10}, and determine whether their formula works for this set as well. If it does not, they should fix it. This continues for several cycles in which students generate a formula and then try to apply it to new distributions that highlight new quantitative properties (e.g., dispersion or sample size). At the end of these exercises, students may be shown the variability formula used by experts. The question of interest is, How do these exploratory activities prepare students to understand the variance formula in ways that go beyond teaching the formula from the start?

Initial results from the studies (Moore & Schwartz, 1998) suggest that even though the students generated faulty formulas, these experiences helped the students become aware of the quantitative properties of distributions that a formula should take into account. This set the stage for noticing critical features of experts' formulas, for example, that they yield a smaller number for smaller variances (many of the students' self-generated formulas had done the opposite), that they elegantly solve the problem of set size, and so forth. As a consequence, students in the "generate first" group were much better able to appreciate the strengths and weaknesses of different nonstandard formulas for capturing variance (e.g., a formula that summed the deviations from the median instead of the mean). In contrast, students who had been directly taught the standard formula (with no previous attempts to generate their own thoughts) simply declared that the non-standard formulas were ''wrong.'' They were not as prepared as the other students to learn about the expert formula. In Broudy's terms, they had a less well-differentiated ''field'' for ''knowing with.''

Perspectives on Negative Transfer and "Letting Go"

The preceding instructional procedures can also help accomplish another goal, namely, to let people experience how the seemingly ''intuitive'' or ''obvious'' ideas that they initially generate can appear suspect when subjected to closer scrutiny. This is important because adapting to new situations (transfer) often involves ''letting go'' of previously held ideas and behaviors. This is very different from assuming that transfer represents ''the degree to which a behavior will be repeated in a new situation'' (Detterman, 1993, p. 4). In many cases, repeating an old behavior in a new setting produces what has been labeled ''negative transfer.'' Luchins's (1942) classic studies of filling water jars illustrate this point nicely. When given a transfer task, participants in these experiments repeated a complex set of water-pouring strategies despite the fact that the task permitted a simple, efficient response. Land, inventor of the Polaroid Land camera, coined a colorful definition of ''insight'' that highlights the importance of ''letting go'' of previous assumptions and strategies rather than simply repeating them. He defined insight as ''the sudden cessation of stupidity'' (Land, 1982). Toulmin (1972) also emphasized the importance of well-reasoned changes in one's beliefs and assumptions:

A person demonstrates his (or her) rationality, not by a commitment to a fixed set, stereotyped procedures, or immutable concepts, but by the manner in which and the occasions on which, he (she) changes those ideas and procedures. (p. v)

Educational environments that are designed from a PFL perspective emphasize the importance of encouraging attitudes and habits of mind that prepare people to resist making old responses by simply assimilating new information to their existing concepts or schemas. Instead, effective learners learn to look critically at their current knowledge and beliefs (e.g., Novick, 1988).

Our colleagues Kay Burgess and Xiaodong Lin have documented the effects of an overreliance on assimilation. They created catalogs of items that one might purchase for an eagle recovery plan. Some of the items were bogus and would not work. Fifth and sixth graders were given the catalogs along with resources they could use to help make their catalog selections. Most were overconfident of their competence for this task. They simply used their everyday intuitions as human beings and made decisions (which tended to be wrong) without consulting any resources. For example, they chose the option of hand-raising baby eagles because the babies would ''feel like orphans'' if they put them in an isolated incubator. (The problem with hand-raising eagles is that the babies would imprint on humans.) In contrast, a science expert who had no knowledge of eagle recovery took a totally different approach. She knew that she needed more information and used the contrasting catalog items to formulate learning goals that guided her search through the resources available for the study. She exhibited adaptive expertise (Hatano & Inagaki, 1986).

Wineburg (1998) provides an additional example of the importance of overcoming the tendency to simply assimilate. He studied a historian who was asked to analyze a set of history documents that focused on a topic outside his area of specialization. At first, the historian resolved puzzling contradictions in the documents by using his existing knowledge of present-day culture. Eventually, he came to the conclusion that he did not have enough historical knowledge about the situation to make an informed judgment, so he devised learning goals and carried them out. After opportunities to learn, the historian did as well at analyzing the history documents as an expert who specialized in that area. In contrast, college students presented with the same documents tended to use their intuitive everyday knowledge and generated erroneous conclusions (Wineburg & Fournier, 1994). They failed to question their existing assumptions and, ultimately, failed to take advantage of new opportunities to learn.

People's mental models of what it means to be successful appear to affect their abilities to "let go" of previous beliefs and become effective learners. Elsewhere (CTGV, 1997), we have discussed the impediments to learning that are caused by people who have a (usually tacit) mental model that being "accomplished" or "an expert" means that they should know all of the answers. A healthy alternative is one that celebrates being an "accomplished novice" who is proud of his or her accomplishments but realizes that he or she is still a novice with respect to most that is knowable and, hence, actively seeks new learning opportunities. The effects of finished—expert versus accomplished—novice models are difficult to show from an SPS perspective. However, they should be revealed from a PFL perspective when people, for example, are given opportunities to collaborate and they naturally demonstrate their (un)willingness to listen and learn.

The multiply embedded social settings within which people's lives unfold have a powerful effect on the degree to which they are supported in letting go of older ideas and practices and attempting new ones. Our colleague Xiaodong Lin (1999) studied a Hong Kong mathematics teacher who agreed to try a new (for her) instructional approach in her mathematics classroom: She structured a week's worth of lessons around a Jasper problem-solving adventure (see CTGV, 1997) that had been translated into Chinese (Lin et al., 1995). The changes the teacher had to make in her teaching practices were extensive, but she and her students ultimately were successful in creating a learning experience that was satisfying to all of them.

The teacher's reflections on her experiences demonstrate the powerful impact of the social contexts in which she was embedded. First, she noted that her teaching performance was evaluated by both students and their parents, so she had to be very mindful of their opinions. Second, she noted that the principal and the parents were very positive about innovations that had the potential to prepare students to better adapt to the fast-changing world of Hong Kong. This support for innovative risk taking was crucial in convincing the teacher to accept the challenge of implementing Jasper in her classroom. The teacher also noted that her school was not a "top tier" school, and thus there were constant attempts to find an edge by taking risks and trying new programs. This made the invitation to experiment with Jasper a positive opportunity rather than too much of a risk. Despite all of this support, the teacher still proceeded very cautiously and reflectively; she assembled daily written feedback from the children and studied it prior to the subsequent day's activities. By systematically noting students' current understandings and questions, she was able to adjust her teaching in ways that ultimately led to success. Overall, the teacher had acquired a set of knowledge, beliefs, and strategies that allowed her to adapt to new technologies.

Perspectives on the Active Nature of Transfer

The act of critically examining one's current beliefs and strategies is related to another important feature of the PFL perspective, namely, its focus on the active nature of transfer. The learning environments in which people must eventually operate are not necessarily "given" (Pea, 1987). As deGroot (1965) observed with respect to chess and as the Garner examples demonstrate, people's perception of the givens of a situation depends on what they have at their disposal to know with. Thus, the individual's knowledge actively constitutes the perceivable situation.

People can also change the situation itself. They can modify their environments by changing them physically, by seeking resources (including other people), by marshaling support for new ideas, and so forth. Rather than simply viewing transfer as the mapping of old understandings and practices onto a given situation, the PFL perspective emphasizes that people can actively change the given situation into something that is more compatible with their current state and goals.

An interesting example of this comes from research in robotics (Hammond, Fasciano, Fu, & Converse, 1996). Robots are being taught to stabilize their environments to simplify their tasks. For example, kitchen robots make sure that the refrigerator is full, and they put the briefcase next to the door so that it will not be forgotten. More generally, people actively adapt their environments to suit their needs. For example, they will modify the positions of utensils and dry goods when they go to a new kitchen. This new kitchen does not have to be exactly like their old one (e.g., the kitchen might have a different number of drawers). People accommodate their old schemes to the new kitchen, and they adapt the kitchen to their old schemes and "personal" strengths. Actively controlling the environment seems especially important with regard to future learning, yet it is something that is typically outside the realm of SPS tests and DA models of transfer.

An important way in which learners interact with their environments is by creating situations that allow them to "bump up against the world" in order to test their thinking. If things do not work, effective learners revise. The importance of these kinds of "test your mettle" opportunities is illustrated by research on our Jasper problem-solving series (CTGV, 1997). In some of our more recent work, we have begun to ask students to create "smart tools" that allow them to solve a wide variety of problems (e.g., graphs and tables; Bransford et al., 1999). In this context, we have created "embedded teaching scenes" (see CTGV, 1997) and additional materials that provide models for smart tools that students can adapt in a "just-in-time" fashion. If the effectiveness of this instructional approach is evaluated in a typical one-shot SPS paradigm, it looks weak and problematic.

For example, in one study with middle school students, more than half of the students chose the wrong smart tools, and most used the embedded teaching models inappropriately. However, the students' performances changed quite dramatically once they received an opportunity to test the mettle of their tools and revise their thinking. After only one such experience, the percentage of correct choices of smart tools (along with the ability to explain choices) jumped from less than 40% to more than 80%. Opportunities to receive feedback and improve one's work have been shown to help students increase their appreciation of the revision process (e.g., Schwartz, Lin, Brophy, & Bransford, 1999). Additional research indicates that experiences such as these strongly increase the likelihood that students will spontaneously invent their own tools to control novel problems in their environment (Schwartz, 1993).

An especially important aspect of active transfer involves people's willingness to seek others' ideas and perspectives. Helping people seek multiple viewpoints about issues may be one of the most important ways to prepare them for future learning. Physicist David Boehm points out the value, and emotional turmoil, involved in seeking others' opinions; his description refers to a scientist (in this case, a male scientist) being confronted by conflicting opinions:

His first reaction is often of violent disturbance, as views that are very dear are questioned or thrown to the ground. Nevertheless, if he will "stay with it" rather than escape into anger and unjustified rejection of contrary ideas, he will discover that this disturbance is very beneficial. For now he becomes aware of the assumptive character of a great many previously unquestioned features of his own thinking. This does not mean that he will reject these assumptions in favor of those of other people. Rather, what is needed is the conscious criticism of one's own metaphysics, leading to changes where appropriate and ultimately, to the continual creation of new and different kinds.

The need for people to actively seek others' perspectives is also central to Lagemann's (1997) insightful discussion of the history of education research during the past century. She shows how this history can be viewed as a fight among different professional groups (e.g., measurement experts, learning theorists, school administrators, teachers' unions) for jurisdiction over the domain of education. She directly links possibilities for future learning to the need for collaboration across professions:

What all this suggests, I think, is that professionalization has been a barrier to the effective linking of knowledge and action in education. . . . Possibilities for the future will depend on understanding and surmounting the constraints of professionalization in order to develop more truly equal, genuinely respectful, and effectively collaborative relationships among the groups most directly involved in the study and practice of education.... If new, more collegial patterns of collaboration can be nourished and sustained on even a small scale and the difficult political problems of this enterprise better understood and more widely and openly discussed, it may be possible to encourage the more democratic, cross-profession, cross-discipline, cross-gender social relationships that would seem to be an indispensable precondition to effective knowledge-based reform in education. Were that to happen, there would be much to be gained. (p. 15)

Overall, one of the important lessons of the PFL perspective is that it moves "affective" and social concepts such as "tolerance for ambiguity" (Kuhn, 1962), courage spans (Wertime, 1979), persistence in the face of difficulty (Dweck, 1989), willingness to learn from others, and sensitivity to the expectations of others from the periphery toward the center of cognitive theories of learning. These factors can have a major impact on people's dispositions to learn throughout their lives. The PFL perspective emphasizes the importance of understanding the kinds of experiences that prepare people to question their own assumptions and actively seek others' opinions on issues.

Research in the area of "metacognition"—especially research on reflection and comprehension monitoring—provides information that is relevant to this question (e.g., see Brown, 1978; Flavell, 1976; Hacker et al., 1998; Pressley & Afflerbach, 1995; White & Frederickson, 1998). People who actively monitor their current levels of understanding are more likely to take active steps to improve their learning. Nevertheless, monitoring is not a "knowledge-free" skill; people whose knowledge is not well differentiated can think they understand yet fail to understand at a sufficiently deep level (see Schwartz & Bransford, 1998; Vye et al., 1989). Helping students develop well-differentiated knowledge—and helping them understand its role in self-assessment—is an important part of preparing them to learn throughout their lives.

We believe that people's preparation for future learning can be further enriched through an active examination of issues that are more frequently raised in the humanities than in the natural sciences. What are examples of "effective learners" who can serve as models for lifelong inquiry? How do we evaluate "inquiry" per se rather than evaluate only the results of one's inquiry (i.e., whether one's findings seem true or false with respect to current theory)? Issues such as these are discussed in the next section.

Perspectives on "Lived Experiences" and the Humanities

The PFL perspective may eventually help us better appreciate the value of a number of "humanistic" activities, including (a) "lived experiences" that introduce people to alternative perspectives and cultural assumptions (e.g., living in another country or participating in "alternative spring breaks" to work in Appalachia) and (b) studying the arts and humanities in order to better understand the nature of the human condition and one's place within it. From the perspective of the SPS methodology and DA theory, it is difficult to show the value of these experiences because they do not readily affect immediate problem solving. From a PFL perspective, it may become easier to conceptualize and assess their value. This, in turn, can help us better understand how to structure experiences so that people receive maximum benefits.

Consider "lived experiences" such as spending time in a different country. These experiences can function as "contrasting cases" (see our earlier discussion of Garner and others) that help people notice features of their own culture that previously were unnoticed. The experiences can prepare people to be more appreciative of others' ideas and values as they encounter them throughout their lifetime and, eventually, to actively seek others' opinions about important issues and hence accelerate their abilities to learn. However, just as experiences with a set of contrasting data cases required a summarizing lecture to help students develop a conceptual framework that eventually led to strong transfer (see our earlier discussion of the Schwartz and Bransford study), it seems highly probable that people need help thinking about their experiences and organizing them into some coherent view of the world.

This same point seems relevant to other lived experiences such as learning to play a musical instrument, learning to perform on stage, and learning to participate in organized sports activities. Some music, drama, and athletic teachers (coaches) appear to help students learn about themselves as they struggle to perform in these arenas. Other teachers seem to focus solely on the performance and provide minimal suggestions for helping students think through important issues such as their commitment to excellence; their need to be in the limelight rather than a team player; their respect for others who are not equally musical, dramatic, or athletic; their (often tacit) fears and strategies that may be hampering their progress (e.g., in sports, some people fall into the trap of "playing not to lose" rather than "playing to win"). The PFL perspective suggests that, when properly mediated, lived experiences can provide powerful resources for "knowing with" (Broudy, 1977). It also reminds us that we need a much better understanding of the kinds of "mediated reflections" that best prepare people for learning throughout life.

Many believe that lived experiences can be enriched by a study of the arts and the humanities. Broudy, for example, argues that "the study of poetry enriches the imagic store in ways that everyday experiences may not" (1977, p. 11). He contends that experiences of viewing art or reading poetry have a strong impact on "knowing with" when they are subjected to serious study and analysis. In part, this is because study of the arts and humanities provides invaluable opportunities to contrast surrogate experiences with one's own. And in part, this is because the arts and humanities offer frameworks for interpreting experiences and helping people develop a more coherent world view.

A particularly important challenge from the perspective of PFL is to explore ways to help people balance their respect for knowledge gained from areas such as science, history and literature, religion, and personal experiences. Our bet is that most people (ourselves included) do not have a well-differentiated conception of what it means "to know" when thinking about different areas of their lives. According to Broudy (1977):

The evidence for the assertions "The sun is 93 million miles from earth" and "I know my Redeemer livith" are not of the same order. The self-evidence of mathematical tautologies is not the same as that entailed by "Beauty is its own excuse." Humanistic truth of knowledge involves something other than logical or scientific validity. Perhaps it is authenticity. Authenticity is the property of being genuine, nonfake, as really issuing from the source that claims to originate it. (p. 5)

Helping people develop an appreciation of, and commitment to, an authentic pursuit of new knowledge seems particularly important for preparing them for future learning. Such pursuits usually involve a combination of humanistic and scientific/mathematical approaches and cannot be reduced to one or the other alone. Nobel Laureate Sir Peter Medawar captures this point in his discussion of the scientific method:

Like other exploratory processes, [the scientific method] can be resolved into a dialogue between fact and fancy, the actual and the possible; between what could be true and what is in fact the case. The purpose of scientific enquiry is not to compile an inventory of factual information, nor to build up a totalitarian world picture of Natural Laws in which every event that is not compulsory is forbidden. We should think of it rather as a logically particular structure of justifiable beliefs about a Possible World—a story which we invent and criticize and modify as we go along, so that it ends by being, as nearly as we can make it, a story about real life. (1982)

Broudy's emphasis on "authenticity" as a humanistic truth provides a potentially powerful focus for preparing people for future learning. The genuineness of people's inquiry is relevant in all areas: science, mathematics, history, literature, and so on. It represents a characteristic of individuals and groups that can be differentiated from less genuine endeavors such as efforts to propagate a set of ideas without regard for evidence, efforts to simply "get something finished" without worrying about quality, and efforts to take credit for work that is not one's own.

People's appreciation of authenticity in inquiry is nicely illustrated in a cross-cultural study conducted by Xiaodong Lin and her colleagues (Lin et al., 1995). Middle school students in Nashville, Tennessee, communicated electronically with students in Hong Kong about different aspects of Chinese history. The American students constructed "day in the life" scenarios that described the lives of fictitious individuals who lived during earlier times in China (e.g., during the Tzeng dynasty). The Hong Kong students (who were one grade more advanced than the Nashville students) read these stories and provided feedback about the quality of the work. The feedback often seemed harsh to the Nashville students until Lin and her colleagues implemented a simple but powerful procedure. They asked the Nashville students to accompany their work with a self-assessment of how well they had achieved particular goals such as creating stories that were interesting and accurate with respect to Chinese culture. The Hong Kong students reacted very positively to these self-assessments. For example, one group of

Hong Kong students wrote a detailed critique of a story generated by Nashville sixth graders and ended their comments with the following:

Your story was not very deep and complex. You seem to like to buy things because all of your story focused on markets of the time. However, from your self-assessment, we felt that you are willing to look into yourself for improvement and you are quite thorough about it. Overall, you guys seem to be good people.

This example illustrates the importance of different criteria for evaluating quality. One set of criteria involved evaluations of the Nashville students' stories from the perspective of story complexity (including interest) and historical accuracy. A second set of criteria focused on perceived intentions and aspirations of the authors. Even when the historical stories were weak and historical accuracy was questionable, the Hong Kong students respected the willingness of the Nashville students to reflect on their own work, criticize it, and welcome feedback. There was a strong (and we believe accurate) perception that the Nashville students were engaged in authentic inquiry rather than simply attempting to complete a task and move on. The self-assessment resulted in feedback that included many more positive comments mixed with the criticisms (see the preceding example). U.S. students in the self-assessment condition felt more of a bond with the Hong Kong students and were more likely to continue to want to work with them.

Issues related to the authenticity of inquiry may lie at the heart of debates about grading for "effort" as well as "achievement." Acknowledging the authenticity of students' inquiry seems very valuable in terms of preparing them for future learning. Redefining effort as authenticity may be useful for helping teachers rethink such acknowledgments. A serious study of the humanities—by both teachers and students—should help develop a more differentiated understanding of what authenticity might mean.

At a more general level, the idea of combining the study of the humanities with the study of mathematics and the sciences is, of course, the rationale for a liberal arts education. Ideally, people can be helped to develop a coherent, well-differentiated framework for "knowing with" that is relevant to life in general rather than specific to only one particular discipline or field.

The PFL perspective reminds us that some ways of structuring liberal arts experiences will be more useful than others, For example, it is doubtful that students develop a coherent, well-differentiated perspective for "knowing with" simply by taking a set of courses in the humanities, science, and mathematics. First, many of these courses are disconnected from one another, and hence there is no common ground for comparison and contrast. The experience is similar to viewing Figures 2–6 without the common ground supplied by the idea that these are possible designs for backscratcher T-shirts. Without this "ground" or "field," many important distinctions are missed.

A second problem with many liberal arts programs is that the experiences in many of the courses appear to resemble the summarize plus lecture condition in the Schwartz and Bransford study—the students read and summarize a text and then hear an organizing lecture. They have no opportunity to deal with specific cases that set the stage for their future learning (Figure 8 shows the effects of this type of instruction). The ideas that students are exposed to in formal courses are often not grounded (anchored) in their experiences. Understanding how to improve this situation is a major challenge for educators. The PFL perspective serves as a reminder that these issues are worth exploring. It also suggests methodologies for studying the issues. This topic is discussed subsequently.

FROM STATIC TO DYNAMIC ASSESSMENTS

The PFL perspective suggests that assessments of people's abilities can be improved by moving from static, one-shot measures of "test taking" to environments that provide opportunities for new learning. What one currently knows and believes is clearly important for future learning. Yet, SPS tests of current knowledge are indirect measures of people's abilities to learn; they do not capture the learning process itself. For example, they do not directly capture the dispositions that influence people's learning; rather, they capture only the dispositions that influence test taking (e.g., Dweck, 1989; Holt, 1964; Ng & Bereiter, 1991). Moreover, there are possible dissociations between SPS and PFL assessments. Figure 9 illustrates this possibility. It shows two people, A and B, who begin a job. On SPS tests of facts and problems deemed relevant to the job, person A scores better than B, perhaps because A had some specific, job-relevant training. Over time, however, B turns out to be the most effective learner. Similar scenarios are possible in other settings; for example, the top 10% of nation A's students may look better than nation B's on SPS tests, yet it is possible that nation B's students are more broadly prepared for future learning. The PFL perspective does not make such a prediction; rather, it simply suggests that such questions need to be asked. The PFL perspective also suggests the possibility that a dynamic assessment of a person's ability to learn over a period of a month might better predict that person's success 4 years down the line at a job or in college than a one-shot SPS test at the beginning. This is a major challenge for future research.

We attempt to illustrate the potential importance of dynamic assessment by discussing a particular problem environment that we have been exploring. Participants are presented with a challenge that involves items such as those illustrated in Figure 10. They are asked to choose the one that gives them the most and the least for their money. We have given this challenge (and others like it) to a wide range of individuals, from middle school students to adults. Their reactions to the challenges tell us a lot.

Consider first the middle school students. Most of them get the challenge wrong. They choose the items with the "biggest number" (for the best deal) and the "smallest number" (for the worst deal). Many of these students are quite confident about their answer and do not feel the need for further learning or discussion. High confidence without corresponding competence creates situations that are the furthest from being ideal.

FIGURE 9
Static Tests May Not Predict Who Will Perform Best When There Is an Opportunity
to Learn More

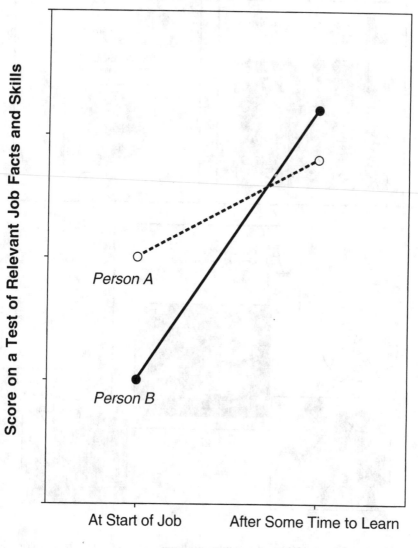

Other participants who make the wrong choices are more aware that they do not know the answer. Some, especially many of the adults (who have not been in school for some time), feel that they simply need to be reminded of the definition of terms such as diameter and circumference; others request definitional help along with a reminder of relevant geometry formulas (e.g., C = pi D). Still

FIGURE 10
Which Pizzas Give the Most and Least for the Money?

other participants (especially many middle school students) are not confident about their answers but cannot define the kinds of help they need in order to proceed. For example, one group of students engaged in an intense discussion for more than 10 minutes before a group member asked "Would it help to know what diameter means?"

To provide an example of a dynamic approach to this problem, we have begun work with several colleagues (Jan Altman, Sean Brophy, Joan Davis, Nancy Vye, Linda Zech) on computer-based environments for dynamic assessment. This work draws heavily on the dynamic assessment literature (e.g., Bransford et al., 1987; Campione & Brown, 1987; Cole & Griffin, 1987; Feuerstein, 1979; Lidz, 1987; Vygotsky, 1978). The environment is designed to assess people's preparation for learning to solve particular classes of problems. By participating in these environments, people can also learn to self-assess their readiness to learn. Our prototype is organized around a set of geometry problems similar to "Penelope's Pizza Challenge" (see Figure 10). Participants first (a) answer the challenge, (b) indicate their confidence in their answer, and (c) indicate whether they want to go on to a different kind of problem or check out resources for how to solve the pizza problem. If participants answer correctly and confidently, they receive one additional analogous problem. If they repeat their confidence and competence, they can go on to more challenging problems to solve.

The most interesting data come from people who cannot initially solve the problem. If they are wrong but confident of their answer, these data are recorded. If they are wrong and not confident (which is a much healthier pattern), these data are also recorded. Participants are then given feedback about their initial answers, for example, feedback that emphasizes the dangers of confidence with little competence and feedback that helps people appreciate the value of "problem finding" (cf. Bransford & Stein, 1993)—of discovering the existence of a problem and taking steps to fix it.

After receiving feedback, participants are provided with opportunities to access different resources that might help their learning. They can choose to seek "minimal help" (e.g., a dictionary of definitions), "intermediate help" (e.g., a brief verbal lecture about relevant information), or several levels of "extended help" that provide opportunities to see dynamic visual events (rather than hear only lectures) and to explore relationships through the use of simulations. Participants access the type of help they need and decide for themselves when they are ready to solve an analog of the original challenge problem. Once again, the program assesses their competence and confidence and offers them additional opportunities to learn the relevant information and apply it to a series of analogous problems. Over time, participants should need less and less assistance in order to solve the challenge problems. If none of the types of help work for them, they are given opportunities to assess the learning opportunities and suggest ways that they might be improved.

Our fledgling dynamic assessment environments are just being developed. They are not yet as social as we want them to be, although users can interact with virtual experts who provide guidance. Ultimately, we believe that dynamic assessment environments will yield interesting information that will be valuable to both teachers and students. Teachers who focus solely on "teaching to the test" may find that their students have difficulty assessing their own knowledge and learning on their own. Similarly, the dynamic assessment environments should help students learn about themselves as learners. And, depending on the topic, they should begin to differentiate cases in which they need simple reminders from ones in which they need opportunities for in-depth exploration. In addition, the dynamic assessment environments help students see learning positively. Students are not simply "being tested"; instead, they are assessing the adequacy of different strategies for learning, and they are using these opportunities to control their learning environments.

SUMMARY

We have proposed a way to think about transfer that is simple yet has important implications for educational practice. In addition to the more typical approach, which views transfer as the direct application (DA) of knowledge and measures it in a context of sequestered problem solving (SPS), our proposal is to view transfer from the perspective of preparation for future learning (PFL). The idea of transfer as PFL is not unique to us; many other theorists have linked transfer to learning. Nevertheless, the educational implications of different views about transfer have not been as well differentiated in the literature as they might be. Our goal in this chapter has been to more explicitly contrast the SPS and DA view from the PFL approach and show how they diverge.

We have argued that the PFL perspective reveals evidence of transfer that is easy to miss when one adopts a DA theory and its accompanying SPS methodology. The latter focus on the degree to which people can apply their previous knowledge to solve new problems. Data often show how far people are from complete solutions and give the impression that transfer is rare. In contrast, the PFL perspective focuses on evidence for useful learning trajectories. Examples include the sophistication of the questions students ask about a topic and the assumptions that are revealed in their discussions (we demonstrated this in the context of recovery plans for bald eagles). More sophisticated questions and assumptions lead to learning activities that are more likely to help people acquire the relevant expertise.

We noted that the PFL perspective fits nicely with Broudy's emphasis on "knowing with." Typical assessments of learning and transfer involve what Broudy calls the "replicative" and the "applicative" (knowing that and knowing how, respectively). "Knowing with" is different from either of these; it provides a context or "field" that guides noticing and interpretation. Perceptual learning provides an excellent example of "knowing with." As the demonstration of the "transfer backscratcher grid" showed, noticing new features is not an act of simply finding common elements between the past and present. Through contrasting cases, one develops the ability to notice finer and finer distinctions. One becomes a connoisseur of the world.

An important implication of the PFL perspective is that it can show the value of a variety of learning activities whose impact is difficult to measure from an SPS perspective. For example, a study conducted by the present authors demonstrated that opportunities to actively compare sets of contrasting data patterns were extremely helpful to students, but their usefulness did not show up unless students were given the opportunity to learn new information. We argued that students were better prepared for this learning because they had acquired a more differentiated field for "knowing with."

We discussed additional instances in which the PFL perspective suggests the value of learning activities that might seem to be a waste of time from an SPS perspective. Examples included helping people learn a particular software package versus taking the extra time to prepare them to continually learn new packages and understanding the value (from the perspective of contrasting cases and knowledge differentiation) of first having students generate their own thoughts about a topic and then comparing them with the thoughts of others, including experts.

The PFL perspective also highlights the importance of dispositions that affect future learning. Future learning frequently requires "letting go" of previous ideas, beliefs, and assumptions. Effective learners resist "easy interpretations" by simply assimilating new information into their existing schemas; they critically evaluate new information and change their views (accommodate) when necessary. We presented two examples, one involving work with eagle catalogs (Burgess & Lin, 1998) and one involving interpretations of historical texts (Wineburg, 1998). In both cases, transfer involved conceptual change rather than the persistence of previous behaviors and beliefs.

We also argued that the PFL perspective highlights the importance of allowing people to actively interact with their environments—opportunities that are rarely present in SPS environments. When people have opportunities to "bump up against the world" and receive feedback, their learning can improve quite dramatically, and the value of their previous experiences can be revealed. To illustrate this point, we noted how the use of instructional approaches such as embedded teaching (analogous to worked out examples) in our Jasper adventures (CTGV, 1997) can result in an alarming number of errors in an SPS paradigm. However, after only a single opportunity to "test their mettle" and revise, students' performances improved dramatically.

An especially significant benefit of the PFL perspective is that it may help us understand how to maximize the value of a variety of experiences (e.g., studying the humanities; participating in art, music, and sports; living in a different culture) that seem important intuitively but are difficult to assess from a DA point of view.

We concluded our discussion by noting the implications of the PFL perspective for assessment. Most assessments follow the SPS format; in Broudy's terms, they emphasize the replicative and the applicative. Using the logic of "transfer appropriate processing" (e.g., Morris, Bransford, & Franks, 1977), we argued that the activities that prepare people for static tests may be different from those that best prepare them for future learning. In conjunction with a number of colleagues, we are constructing computer-based dynamic assessment environments to explore this idea.

We finish our chapter with the observation that the DA perspective and its accompanying SPS methodology have been, and will undoubtedly continue to be, very important in the cognitive literature. The SPS paradigm provides a methodology for empirically determining the psychological similarity between different situations and showing how the criteria of similarity change depending on knowledge and other factors. By testing when people spontaneously transfer (in an SPS sense) from one situation to another, researchers can determine the psychologically common elements that cued the replication or application of an idea learned in one situation to the other. For example, it has been very instructive to see that novices often rely on surface similarities, whereas experts find deeper, less apparent structural similarities (e.g., Chi, Feltovich, & Glaser, 1981). Despite the value of the SPS methodology, it often comes with a set of unexamined assumptions about what it means to know and understand. The most important assumption is that "real transfer" involves only the direct application of previous learning; we believe that this assumption has unduly limited the field's perspective of what it means to use one's previous learning in a new situation effectively. Unassisted, direct applications of knowledge are important, but they are only part of the picture. The PFL perspective highlights the importance of helping people learn throughout their lives.

A potential danger of the PFL perspective is that it could lead to claims such as "I'm teaching for future learning, so I don't worry about mastery of content." We do not wish to encourage such claims and have emphasized that some activities prepare people for further learning better than others. For example, we have tried to show that well-differentiated knowledge is crucial for future learning (e.g., Schwartz & Bransford, 1998), and we have emphasized the importance of using dynamic assessments to measure the degree to which people's past experiences have prepared them for future learning.

Much work remains to be done to develop the kinds of computer-based dynamic assessments that we described at the end of this chapter. Teachers can do their own dynamic assessments by looking not only at students' performances on tests (which use SPS methodologies) but also at their abilities to learn new sets of materials. Are they using what they know to define learning goals? Are they carefully evaluating new information rather than simply assimilating it to existing schemas? Are they able to work collaboratively with others? Are they reaching sound conclusions based on existing evidence? Are they able to reflect on their learning processes and strategies?

People's ability to dynamically assess their preparedness for learning should itself be knowledge that transfers and helps them learn. This does not, however, mean that it is a general skill or a formal discipline (e.g., see Vye et al., 1989). In agreement with Broudy's (1977) analysis, the PFL perspective suggests that these kinds of activities arise from a well-differentiated knowledge base that students are able to "know with." The ideal scope of that knowledge appears to include the humanities as well as the often-emphasized fields of science and mathematics. The goal of helping people integrate these areas into a coherent framework for "knowing with" appears to be an important challenge to pursue.

APPENDIX
A Rough Categorization of Questions Generated by Fifth-Grade and College Students About Creating an Eagle Recovery Plan

5th-grade students

"Basic" Eagle Facts • How much do they weigh full grown? • How big are their bodies? • What is their wingspan? • How big are they? • How high do they fly? • Are they color blind? • What do they look like? • How many are there in the U.S.? • Why do you call them bald eagles?

Habitat Questions • Where do they live? • Where do you find them? • What kinds of trees do they live in?

Development Questions • How do they take care of their babies? • How many eggs do they lay at one time? • How big are their nests? • What age do they fly? • How old do they get?

Foraging Questions • How do they find food? • What do they like to eat? • How do they catch their prey?

College students

Interdependency Questions • What about predators of eagles and eagle babies? • Do other animals need to be recovered in order to recover eagles? • Why save the bald eagle versus other organisms? • What type of ecosystem supports eagles?

Survival Needs Questions • What are the eagles' daily needs? • What kinds of habitat do eagles need to live in, and is there sufficient habitat? • Are today's threats like the initial threats to eagles? • Are there different types of eagles with different needs?

Human Resource and Impact Questions • What are the laws? • What resources (financial and information) are available to support? • What are the politics of eagles? • What different kinds of specialists are needed for different recovery areas? • What facilities are needed, and transport methods? • What kind of training is necessary to handle an eagle? • What were the detrimental effects of DDT?

Goal- and Plan-Related Questions • What are the goals of current programs? • What is the ultimate goal of population recovery (how many needed)? • Why is there a belief that the population needs to be doubled? • What are the current recovery plans? • What are the eagle recovery regions and how are they working? • What are the most promising recovery methods? • How do people estimate eagle populations? • Why are some states more successful? • What can be learned from the more successful states?

REFERENCES

Adams, L., Kasserman, J., Yearwood, A., Perfetto, G., Bransford, J., & Franks, J. (1988). The effects of facts versus problem-oriented acquisition. *Memory & Cognition, 16,* 167–175.

Anderson, J. R., Reder, L. M., & Simon, H. A. (1997). Rejoinder: Situative versus cognitive perspectives: Form versus substance. *Educational Researcher, 26*(1), 18–21.

Barron, B. J., Schwartz, D. L., Vye, N. J., Moore, A., Petrosino, A., Zech, L., & Bransford, J. D. (1998). Doing with understanding: Lessons from research on problem and project-based learning. *Journal of Learning Sciences, 7,* 271–312.

Barrows, H. S. (1985). *How to design a problem-based curriculum for the preclinical years.* New York: Springer.

Bassok, M. (1990). Transfer of domain-specific problem solving procedures. *Journal of Experimental Psychology: Learning, Memory, and Cognition, 15,* 153–166.

Beck, I. L., & McKeown, M. G. (1983). Learning words well—A program to enhance vocabulary and comprehension. *Reading Teacher, 36,* 622–625.

Bereiter, C. (1990). Aspects of an educational learning theory. *Review of Educational Research, 60,* 603–624.

Bereiter, C., & Scardamalia, M. (1989). Intentional learning as a goal of instruction. In L. B. Resnick (Ed.), *Knowing, learning, and instruction: Essays in honor of Robert Glaser* (pp. 361–392). Hillsdale, NJ: Erlbaum.

Bereiter, C., & Scardamalia, M. (1993). *Surpassing ourselves: An inquiry into the nature and implications of expertise.* Chicago: Open Court.

Bielaczyc, K., Pirolli, P., & Brown, A. L. (1995). Training in self-explanation and self-regulation strategies: Investigating the effects of knowledge acquisition activities on problem solving. *Cognition and Instruction, 13,* 221–253.

Bjork, R. A., & Richardson-Klahaven, A. (1989). On the puzzling relationship between environmental context and human memory. In C. Izawa (Ed.), *Current issues in cognitive processes: The Tulane Flowerree Symposium on Cognition.* Hillsdale, NJ: Erlbaum.

Boehm, D. (1969). Further remarks on order. In C. H. Waddington (Ed.), *Towards a theoretical biology* (Vol. 2). Chicago: Aldine.

Bransford, J. D., Delclos, V., Vye, N., Burns, S., & Hasselbring, T. (1987). Approaches to dynamic assessment: Issues, data and future directions. In C. Lidz (Ed.), *Dynamic assessment: An interactional approach to evaluating learning potentials* (pp. 479–495). New York: Guilford Press.

Bransford, J. D., Franks, J. J., Morris, C. D., & Stein, B. S. (1979). Some general constraints on learning and research. In L. S. Cermak & F. I. M. Craik (Eds.), *Levels of processing and human memory* (pp. 331–354). Hillsdale, NJ: Erlbaum.

Bransford, J. D., Franks, J. J., Vye, N. J., & Sherwood, R. D. (1989). New approaches to instruction: Because wisdom can't be told. In S. Vosniadou & A. Ortony (Eds.), *Similarity and analogical reasoning* (pp. 470–497). New York: Cambridge University Press.

Bransford, J. D., & McCarrell, N. S. (1974). A sketch of cognitive approach to comprehension. In W. B. Weimer & D. S. Palermo (Eds.), *Cognition and the symbolic processes* (pp. 299–303). Hillsdale, NJ: Erlbaum.

Bransford, J. D., & Stein, B. S. (1993). *The IDEAL problem solver* (2nd ed.). New York: Freeman.

Bransford, J. D., Vye, N., Kinzer, C., & Risko, V. (1990). Teaching thinking and content knowledge: Toward an integrated approach. In B. F. Jones & L. Idol (Eds.), *Dimensions of thinking and cognitive instruction: Implications for educational reform* (Vol. 1, pp. 381–413). Hillsdale, NJ: Erlbaum.

Bransford, J. D., Zech, L., Schwartz, D., Barron, B., & Vye, N. (1999). Designs for environments that invite and sustain mathematical thinking. In P. Cobb (Ed.), *Symbolizing, communicating, and mathematizing: Perspectives on discourse, tools, and instructional design* (pp. 275–324). Mahwah, NJ: Erlbaum.

Broudy, H. S. (1977). Types of knowledge and purposes of education. In R. C. Anderson, R. J. Spiro, & W. E. Montague (Eds.), *Schooling and the acquisition of knowledge* (pp. 1–17). Hillsdale, NJ: Erlbaum.

Brown, A. L. (1978). Knowing when, where, and how to remember: A problem of metacognition. In R. Glaser (Ed.), *Advances in instructional psychology* (Vol. 1, pp. 77–165). Hillsdale, NJ: Erlbaum.

Brown, A. L., Bransford, J. D., Ferrara, R. A., & Campione, J. C. (1983). Learning, remembering and understanding. In J. H. Flavell & E. M. Markman (Eds.), *Carmichael's manual of child psychology* (Vol. 1). New York: Wiley.

Brown, A. L., & Kane, M. J. (1988). Preschool children can learn to transfer: Learning to learn and learning from example. *Cognitive Psychology, 20,* 493–523.

Bruer, J. T. (1993). *Schools for thought.* Cambridge, MA: MIT Press.

Burgess, K., & Lin, X. (1998). *Study of adaptive and non-adaptive expertise.* Unpublished manuscript, Vanderbilt University.

Campione, J. C., & Brown, A. L. (1987). Linking dynamic assessment with school achievement. In C. S. Lidz (Ed.), *Dynamic assessment: An interactional approach to evaluating learning potential* (pp. 82–114). New York: Guilford Press.

Chen, Z., & Daehler, M. W. (1989). Positive and negative transfer in analogical problem solving by 6-year-old children. *Cognitive Development, 4,* 327–344.

Chi, M. T. H. (1976). Short-term memory limitation in children: Capacity or processing deficits? *Memory & Cognition, 4,* 559–572.

Chi, M. T. H., Bassok, M., Lewis, M., Reimann, M., & Glaser, R. (1989). Self-explanations: How students study and use examples in learning to solve problems. *Cognitive Science, 13,* 145–182.

Chi, M. T. H, deLeeuw, N., Chiu, M., & LaVancher, C. (1994). Eliciting self-explanations improves understanding. *Cognitive Science, 18,* 439–477.

Chi, M. T. H., Feltovich, P. J., & Glaser, R. (1981). Categorization and representation of physics problems by experts and novices. *Cognitive Science, 5,* 121–152.

Chi, M. T. H., Slotta, J. D., & deLeeuw, N. (1994). From things to processes: A theory of conceptual change for learning science concepts. *Learning and Instruction, 4,* 27–43.

Cognition and Technology Group at Vanderbilt. (1994). From visual word problems to learning communities: Changing conceptions of cognitive research. In K. McGilly (Ed.), *Classroom lessons: Integrating cognitive theory and classroom practice* (pp. 157–200). Cambridge, MA: MIT Press.

Cognition and Technology Group at Vanderbilt. (1997). *The Jasper project: Lessons in curriculum, instruction, assessment, and professional development.* Mahwah, NJ: Erlbaum.

Cognition and Technology Group at Vanderbilt. (in press). The Jasper series: A design experiment in complex, mathematical problem-solving. In J. Hawkins & A. Collins (Eds.), *Design experiments: Integrating technologies into schools.* New York: Cambridge University Press.

Cole, M., & Griffin, P. (Eds.). (1987). *Contextual factors in education.* Madison: Wisconsin Center for Education Research.

deGroot, A. D. (1965). *Thought and choice in chess.* The Hague: Mouton.

Detterman, D. L. (1993). The case for the prosecution: Transfer as epiphenomenon. In D. K. Detterman & R. J. Sternberg (Eds.), *Transfer on trial: Intelligence, cognition, and instruction.* Norwood, NJ: Ablex.

Detterman, D. K., & Sternberg, R. J. (Eds.). (1993). *Transfer on trial: Intelligence, cognition, and instruction.* Norwood, NJ: Ablex.

Duncker, K. (1945). On problem-solving. *Psychological Monographs, 58*(5, Whole No. 270).

Dweck, C. S. (1989). Motivation. In A. Lesgold & R. Glaser (Eds.), *Foundations for a psychology of education* (pp. 87–136). Hillsdale, NJ: Erlbaum.

Feuerstein, R. (1979). *The dynamic assessment of retarded performers: The learning potential assessment device, theory, instruments, and techniques.* Baltimore: University Park Press.

Flavell, J. C. (1976). Metacognitive aspects of problem solving. In L. B. Resnick (Ed.), *The nature of intelligence.* Hillsdale, NJ: Erlbaum.

Garner, W. R. (1974). *The processing of information and structure.* Potomac, MD: Erlbaum.

Gibson, J. J., & Gibson, E. J. (1955). Perceptual learning: Differentiation or enrichment. *Psychological Review, 62,* 32–51.

Gick, M. L., & Holyoak, K. J. (1980). Analogical problem solving. *Cognitive Psychology, 12,* 306–355.

Gick, M. L., & Holyoak, K. J. (1983). Schema induction and analogical transfer. *Cognitive Psychology, 15,* 1–38.

Glaser, R., & Chi, M. T. H. (1988). Introduction: What is it to be an expert? In M. T. H. Chi, R. Glaser, & M. J. Farr (Eds.), *The nature of expertise* (pp. xxix–xxxvi). Hillsdale, NJ: Erlbaum.

Gott, S. P., Hall, E. P., Pokorny, R. A., Dibble, E., & Glaser, R. (1993). A naturalistic study of transfer: Adaptive expertise in technical domains. In D. K. Detterman & R. J. Sternberg (Eds.), *Transfer on trial: Intelligence, cognition, and instruction* (pp. 258–288). Norwood, NJ: Ablex.

Greeno, J. G. (1997). Response: On claims that answer the wrong questions. *Educational Researcher, 26*(1), 5–17.

Greeno, J. G., Smith, D. R., & Moore, J. L. (1993). Transfer of situated learning. In D. K. Detterman & R. J. Sternberg (Eds.), *Transfer on trial: Intelligence, cognition, and instruction.* Norwood, NJ: Ablex.

Hacker, D., Dunlosky, J., & Graesser, A. C. (Eds.). (1998). *Metacognition in educational theory and practice.* Mahwah, NJ: Erlbaum.

Hammond, K. J., Fasciano, M. J., Fu, D. D., & Converse, T. (1996). Actualized intelligence: Case-based agency in practice. *Applied Cognitive Psychology, 10,* S73–S83.

Hasselbring, T., Goin, L., & Bransford, J. (1987). Effective mathematics instruction: Developing automaticity. *Teaching Exceptional Children, 19*(3), 30–33.

Hasselbring, T., Goin, L., & Bransford, J. D. (1988). Developing math automaticity in learning handicapped children: The role of computerized drill and practice. *Focus on Exceptional Children, 20*(6), 1–7.

Hatano, G., & Inagaki, K. (1986). Two courses of expertise. In H. Stevenson, H. Azuma, & K. Hakuta (Eds.), *Child development and education in Japan.* New York: Freeman.

Hmelo, C. E. (1994). *Development of independent learning and thinking: A study of medical problem solving and problem-based learning.* Unpublished doctoral dissertation, Vanderbilt University.

Holt, J. (1964). *How children fail.* New York: Dell.

Judd, C. H. (1908). The relation of special training to general intelligence. *Educational Review, 36,* 28–42.

Klahr, D., & Carver, S. M. (1988). Cognitive objectives in a LOGO debugging curriculum: Instruction, learning, and transfer. *Cognitive Psychology, 20,* 362–404.

Kuhn, T. S. (1962). *The structure of scientific revolutions.* Chicago: University of Chicago Press.

Land, E. H. (1982). Creativity and the ideal framework. In G. I. Nierenberg (Ed.), *The art of creative thinking.* New York: Simon & Schuster.

Lagemann, E. C. (1997). Contested terrain: A history of education research in the United States, 1890–1990. *Educational Researcher, 26*(9), 5–17.

Lave, J. (1988). *Cognition in practice: Mind, mathematics, and culture in everyday life.* Cambridge, England: Cambridge University Press.

Lee, A. Y. (1998). Transfer as a measure of intellectual functioning. In S. Soraci & W. J. McIlvane (Eds.), *Perspectives on fundamental processes in intellectual functioning: A survey of research approaches* (Vol. 1, pp. 351–366). Stamford, CT: Ablex.

Lee, A. Y., & Pennington, N. (1993). Learning computer programming: A route to general reasoning skills? In C. R. Cook, J. C. Scholtz, & J. C. Spohrer (Eds.), *Empirical studies of programmers: Fifth workshop* (pp. 113–136). Norwood, NJ: Ablex.

Lidz, C. S. (Ed.). (1987). *Dynamic assessment: An interactional approach to evaluating learning potential.* New York: Guilford Press.

Lin, X. D., Bransford, J. D., Kantor, R., Hmelo, C., Hickey, D., Secules, T., Goldman, S. R., & Petrosino, A. (1995). Instructional design and the development of learning communities: An invitation to a dialogue. *Educational Technology, 35*(5), 53–63.

Lindberg, M. (1980). The role of knowledge structures in the ontogeny of learning. *Journal of Experimental Child Psychology, 30,* 401–410.

Littlefield, J., Delclos, V., Lever, S., Clayton, K., Bransford, J., & Franks, J. (1988). Learning logo: Method of teaching, transfer of general skills, and attitudes toward school and computers. In R. E. Mayer (Ed.), *Teaching and learning computer programming* (pp. 111–135). Hillsdale, NJ: Erlbaum.

Lockhart, R. S., Lamon, M., & Gick, M. L. (1988). Conceptual transfer in simple insight problems. *Memory & Cognition, 16,* 36–44.

Luchins, A. S. (1942). Mechanization in problem solving. *Psychological Monographs, 54*(6, Whole No. 248).

Mann, L. (1979). *On the trail of process: A historical perspective on cognitive processes and their training.* New York: Grune & Stratton.

Medawar, P. (1982). *Plato's republic.* Oxford, England: Oxford University Press.

Michael, A. L., Klee, T., Bransford, J. D., & Warren, S. (1993). The transition from theory to therapy: Test of two instructional methods. *Applied Cognitive Psychology, 7,* 139–154.

Moore, J. L., & Schwartz, D. L. (1998). On learning the relationship between quantitative properties and symbolic representations. In *Proceedings of the International Conference of the Learning Sciences* (pp. 209–214). Mahwah, NJ: Erlbaum.

Morris, C. D., Bransford, J. D., & Franks, J. J. (1977). Levels of processing versus transfer appropriate processing. *Journal of Verbal Learning and Verbal Behavior, 16,* 519–533.

Ng, E., & Bereiter, C. (1991). Three levels of goal orientation in learning. *Journal of the Learning Sciences, 1,* 243–271.

Nisbett, R. E., Fong, G. T., Lehman, D. R., & Cheng, P. W. (1987). Teaching reasoning. *Science, 238,* 625–630.

Novick, L. (1988). Analogical transfer, problem similarity, and expertise. *Journal of Experimental Psychology: Learning, Memory, and Cognition, 14,* 510–520.

Palincsar, A. S., & Brown, A. L. (1984). Reciprocal teaching of comprehension-fostering and comprehension-monitoring activities. *Cognition and Instruction, 1,* 117–175.

Pea, R. (1987). Socializing the knowledge transfer problem. *International Journal of Educational Research, 11,* 38–62.

Perfetto, G. A., Bransford, J. D., & Franks, J. J. (1983). Constraints on access in a problem solving context. *Memory & Cognition, 11,* 24–31.

Pressley, M., & Afflerbach, P. (1995). *Verbal protocols of reading: The nature of constructively responsive reading.* Hillsdale, NJ: Erlbaum.

Reed, S. K., Ernst, G. W., & Banerji, R. (1974). The role of analogy in transfer between similar problem states. *Cognitive Psychology, 6,* 436–450.

Sander, E., & Richard, J. (1997). Analogical transfer as guided by an abstraction process: The case of learning by doing in text editing. *Journal of Experimental Psychology: Learning, Memory, and Cognition, 23,* 1459–1483.

Scardamalia, M., & Bereiter, C. (1992). Text-based and knowledge-based questioning by children. *Cognition and Instruction, 9,* 177–199.

Schoenfeld, A. H. (1985). *Mathematical problem solving.* Orlando, FL: Academic Press.

Schwartz, D. L. (1993). The construction and analogical transfer of symbolic visualizations. *Journal of Research in Science Teaching, 30,* 1309–1325.

Schwartz, D. L., & Bransford, J. D. (1998). A time for telling. *Cognition and Instruction, 16,* 475–522.

Schwartz, D. L., Lin, X. D., Brophy, S., & Bransford, J. D. (1999). Toward the development of flexibly adaptive instructional design. In C. Reigeluth (Ed.), *Instructional-design theories and models: A new paradigm of instructional theory* (pp. 183–213). Mahwah, NJ: Erlbaum.

Schwartz, D. L., & Moore, J. L. (1998). On the role of mathematics in explaining the material world: Mental models for proportional reasoning. *Cognitive Science, 22,* 471–516.

Sherwood, R., Kinzer, C., Bransford, J., & Franks, J. (1987). Some benefits of creating macro-contexts for science instruction: Initial findings. *Journal of Research in Science Teaching, 24,* 417–435.

Singley, K., & Anderson, J. R. (1989). *The transfer of cognitive skills.* Cambridge, MA: Harvard University Press.

Spiro, R. J., Vispoel, W. P., Schmitz, J. G., Samarapungavan, A., & Boerger, A. E. (1987). Knowledge acquisition for application: Cognitive flexibility and transfer in complex content domains. In B. K. Britton & S. M. Glynn (Eds.), *Executive control processes.* Hillsdale, NJ: Erlbaum.

Thorndike, E. L., & Woodworth, R. S. (1901). The influence of improvement in one mental function upon the efficacy of other functions. *Psychological Review, 8,* 247–261.

Toulmin, S. (1972). *Human understanding: Vol. 1. The collective use and evolution of concepts.* Princeton, NJ: Princeton University Press.

Vye, N., Bransford, J., Furman, L., Barron, B., Montavon, E., Young, M., Van Haneghan, J., & Barron, L. (1989, April). *An analysis of students' mathematical problem solving in real world settings.* Paper presented at the annual meeting of the American Educational Research Association, San Francisco.

Vygotsky, L. S. (1978). *Mind in society: The development of higher psychological processes.* Cambridge, MA: Harvard University Press.

Wertheimer, M. (1959). *Productive thinking.* New York: Harper & Row.

Wertime, R. (1979). Students' problems and courage spans. In J. Lockhead & J. Clements (Eds.), *Cognitive process instruction.* Philadelphia: Franklin Institute Press.

White, B. C., & Fredrickson, J. (1998). Inquiry, modeling, and metacognition: Making science accessible to all students. *Cognition and Instruction, 16,* 39–66.

Williams, S. M. (1992). Putting case-based instruction into context: Examples from legal and medical education. *Journal of the Learning Sciences, 2,* 367–427.

Wineburg, S. (1998). Reading Abraham Lincoln: An expert/expert study in the interpretation of historical texts. *Cognitive Science, 22,* 319–346.

Wineburg, S. S., & Fournier, J. E. (1994). Contextualized thinking in history. In M. Carretero & J. F. Voss (Eds.), *Cognitive and instructional processes in history and the social sciences* (pp. 285–308). Hillsdale, NJ: Erlbaum.

Manuscript received July 23, 1998
Accepted December 15, 1998

Chapter 4

Consequential Transitions: A Sociocultural Expedition Beyond Transfer in Education

KING BEACH
Michigan State University

I would normally avoid using a standard English dictionary definition to begin an intelligent conversation about almost anything, let alone introduce an entire chapter with one. However, our everyday use of the term *transfer* has a powerful metaphorical bearing on how we, as educators and social scientists who also happen to lead everyday lives, think about learning transfer. The *American Heritage Dictionary* (1976) defines transfer as follows.

transfer (trăns-fûr′, trăns′fer) v. -ferred, -ferring, -fers. —*tr.* 1. To convey or shift from one person or place to another. 2. To make over the possession or legal title of to another. 3. To convey (a drawing, pattern, mural, or design) from one surface to another. —*intr.* 1. To move oneself, as from one location, job, or school to another. 2. To change from one airplane, bus, or other carrier to another.

Transfer involves the movement of a person, a transaction, or an object from one place and time to another in our daily lives. As a construct in educational psychology, it refers to the appearance of a person carrying the product of learning from one task, problem, situation, or institution to another. It is here that the metaphor begins to break down. Transfer is distinguished from run-of-the-mill learning by virtue of its distinct tasks and situations, yet it does not include the genesis of tasks and situations as a part of the process. Transfer is necessarily a part of our moment-to-moment lives, yet seems difficult to study and even more difficult to foster intentionally. This irony is not lost on Shweder (1980), who notes that the "everyday mind accomplishes a very difficult task. It looks out at [the] behavioral world of complex, context-dependent interaction effects and insubstantial correlations among events, yet it perceives continuities, neat clusters, and simple regularities" (p. 77).

However, the important educational issues and phenomena that underlie transfer do not dissipate with the metaphor or with irony. This chapter is an expedition

---

I am grateful to Asghar (Ali) Iran-Nejad and David Pearson for their patience and helpful comments; to my consulting editors, James Greeno and Yrjo Engeström, for their excellent suggestions; and to present and past members of the Transitions Research Group at Michigan State University for sharing in the labor and excitement of this expedition.

of sorts: to move beyond the transfer metaphor in understanding how we experience continuity and transformation in becoming someone or something new—a student, a machinist, a bartender, a shopkeeper, or a teacher—and how these consequential transitions may be a macrocosm of how we learn new tasks and problems.

SETTING OUT: TWO CLASSIC PHILOSOPHICAL STANCES ON TRANSFER

The concept of learning transfer has a psychological history that extends from American and European social movements for universal public education up through the triad of chapters in this volume of *Review of Research in Education* (Bransford & Schwartz, Beach, Dyson). The issues underlying transfer have a far longer and deeper philosophical history, extending back to Plato's philosophical dialogue *Meno* (1961) and to Dignaga's 5th-century system of Buddhist logic, or *Pramana.*

The problem of how individuals come to have knowledge, yet experience continuity across time and contexts led Plato to the conclusion that ideas are necessarily innate, to be uncovered through experiences with a world that cannot be directly apprehended. Individuals carry continuity with them, as opposed to continuity being located in the world. Thus, the individual and world are separated in Plato's account. Early Buddhist scholars such as Dignaga and Nagarjuna struggled with a similar problem but with a different outcome (Thurman, 1984). They formulated a concept of dependent origination to explain our experiences of continuity. Rather than locating knowledge within the individual, as did Plato, or in its opposite, the world, dependent origination allowed continuity in knowledge and identity to result from an interdependence of different systems of phenomena, such as persons and social contexts. Thus, our experiences of continuity across time and context are a function of neither the individual nor the context but of their dialectical relation (Dudjom Rinpoche, 1991). Twentieth-century intellectual work in the biological sciences (Maturana & Varela, 1980), social sciences (Herbst, 1995; Rommetveit, 1990), and philosophy (Ilyenkov, 1977; Tolman, 1991) gives Western currency to a variety of dialectical means for understanding people's experiences of continuity.

Although both stances have classic philosophical legitimacy as well as currency, most research on learning transfer and efforts at educational facilitation refract some form of Plato's solution to the continuity of knowledge, whether by opposing it in behaviorist associations built up from the environment; embracing it with an emphasis on individual psychological processes such as representational generalization, analogy, and the derivation of schemas (Dansereau, 1995; Hayes & Simon, 1977; Pressley, 1995; Singley & Anderson, 1989); or acknowledging both through a form of interaction between ontologically separate persons and environments (Salomon & Perkins, 1989, 1998). Historically, studies of transfer have located agency and explanation for the process along a Cartesian plane that cleaves individuals and social contexts. Individual agency is assumed to have little to do with the creation of social contexts supporting transfer, just as changes in contexts are presumed to have little to do with how individuals learn and develop across them.

This is a particular theoretical and philosophical stance toward the phenomenon of transfer. Other stances are possible. Refractions of the Platonic stance are particularly powerful, however, because they are affirmed by the structure of many aspects of our education system (Beach, 1994). For example, basic skills instruction and critical thinking skills curricula are designed to help individuals acquire, carry, and apply general skills in new situations. Vocational education programs are structured to resemble aspects of their target work settings, as isomorphs, so as to facilitate transfer. Packer (in press) takes this point a step further and argues that existing conceptions of transfer and our schools both draw on a political and ideological position that is dominant in American society, one that reflects a functionalist epistemology in which progress is marked by adaptation to and acceptance of existing social conditions (e.g., William James's philosophical doctrine that considers mental phenomena as a system of functions geared to adapting the organism to the environment).

One alternative stance toward transfer phenomena understands continuity and transformation in learning as an ongoing relation between changing individuals and changing social contexts. Individual and contextual agency for transfer are not ontologically independent of one another. At the same time, the role of individuals is not reduced to that of social context, nor is the role of the social context reduced to a group of individuals. To paraphrase Cole (1996), our distinctiveness as humans lies in our ability to modify our world through the construction of cultural artifacts in texts, technologies, symbols, and signs, along with our corresponding ability to reconstruct the modifications in subsequent generations through our schools, families, communities, and work. We thus transform our own learning and development. This stance is consistent with a number of learning and developmental perspectives: cultural-historical activity theory (Cole, 1996; Davydov, 1990; Engeström, Engeström, & Kärkkäinen, 1995; John-Steiner, Mehan, & Mahn, 1998; Leont'ev, 1978; Moll, 1992; Vygotsky, 1987; Wertsch, 1998), situated learning (Brown, Collins, & Duguid, 1989; Greeno, Smith, & Moore, 1993; Kirshner & Whitson, 1997), sociogenetic development (Kindermann & Valsiner, 1995; Valsiner, 1994), and discursive psychology (Gee, 1992; Harré & Gillett, 1994; Shotter, 1993). These perspectives, along with the related works of Jean Lave (1988), Barbara Rogoff (1990), Geoff Saxe (1991), and Rick Shweder (1991), share the notion that learning, development, and education are inherently cultural as well as personal enterprises, and, by extension, so is the phenomenon of transfer. It is on this basis that these perspectives will collectively be referred to as "sociocultural," although we should keep in mind that there are also many productive differences among them. The term *sociocultural* has been used by some as an alternative to cultural-historical activity theory, to deemphasize the historical analysis of social and psychological development. This is not my intention. Rather, sociocultural is used here to refer to a cluster of theories that share a premise that learners and social organizations exist in recursive relation to one another.

Ultimately, the purpose of this chapter is to offer a reconceptualization of transfer as consequential transition among social activities, and to illustrate the concept's viability with studies from our ongoing program of research (Beach, 1993, 1995a, 1995b, 1997, in press-a–d; Beach & Vyas, 1998; Gover, in press; Hungwe, 1999; Hungwe & Beach, 1995; Reineke, in press; Saito & Beach, in press). It is a reconceptualization that is consistent with the second philosophical stance, a Buddhist ontology of experience, the experience of continuity and transformation across social contexts that emerges from changing relations between persons and contexts.

Given the two rather different philosophical stances toward the nature of transfer, their differential representation in studies of transfer, and the continued centrality of transfer issues to education, we need to think carefully about where we have come from and what we have learned using the transfer metaphor before setting out anew. The following three sections of this chapter are therefore devoted to examining the historical relation between the concept of transfer and education, deconstructing an obstacle to progress in thinking about transfer, and analyzing the shortcomings of the transfer metaphor. These sections serve as the basis for how transfer is reconceptualized along sociocultural lines in the remainder of the chapter.

The brief historical analysis that follows is motivated by the need to see our way beyond where we are now. More extensive historical accounts of learning transfer have been written by others and need not be repeated here (Hilgard, 1996; Lagemann, 1988; Shulman & Quinlan, 1996).

MAPPING THE TERRITORY: A MOTIVATED HISTORY OF TRANSFER IN AMERICAN EDUCATION

Efforts at expanding and reforming American public education early in this century made learning transfer the central issue taken up by a fledgling educational psychology. Major figures in American education and psychology during the period 1890 to 1940—Edward L. Thorndike, John Dewey, Charles Hubbard Judd, William James—saw the facilitation of learning transfer as central to the future success of American education, although they strongly differed in their opinions about what transfer was and how it could be supported through schooling. By this time, American schools were no longer tailored purely to the elite or to the trades, where transfer was seen as less of an issue. Public schools were to serve all youth, and therefore education was to prepare them for citizenship along with all forms of livelihood. Thus, public education needed to be concerned with the portability of learning, knowledge, and skills in ways that it had never been before—portability to an indeterminate set of future activities located in families, communities, and workplaces. Age-based classrooms and school subject divisions that emerged with public education also generated concerns about learning transfer between subjects and grades in the schools.

E. L. Thorndike's view of transfer (Thorndike & Woodworth, 1901) was an empirical response to the law of mental discipline's "mind as muscle" metaphor. Thorndike championed transfer as a function of identical elements between tasks, locating agency for transfer in the structuring of the tasks rather than in a generic exercising of the mind through study. C. H. Judd (1915) took a contrasting approach to transfer, plying both sides of the Cartesian plane between person and environment and arguing for a concept of transfer mediated by gestalt-like mental generalizations derived from the structuring of the environment. Judd's work differs not only from Thorndike's behaviorism but also from some cognitive approaches to transfer that emphasize the mental aspects of representational processes (Greeno, Smith, & Moore, 1993). John Dewey (1916) criticized the appropriateness of both views of learning transfer for shaping a progressive public education, arguing for a form of "transfer" that emphasized the importance of meaning making, flexibility, and the role of institutions beyond the school in its facilitation. Dewey believed that

even the schools were insufficiently broad contexts for educational reform and research. Schools were not separate institutions; they were in and of the surrounding social order. One had to discover ways to increase educational efficiency via the creation of social systems in which teaching and learning could be pursued across a variety of institutions, in and out of school. (Shulman & Quinlan, 1996, p. 403)

The scientific functionalism of Thorndike's educational psychology dovetailed with the functionalist epistemology of a public education tasked with preparing all students to be productive members of a society viewed as static, neutral, and hermitic. Thorndike won, and Dewey and Judd lost in terms of their influence within educational psychology (see Packer, in press, for a more detailed account). For a period of time Dewey also lost authority within the larger educational community, despite the early progressive educational critiques against the creation of a science of education, of which Thorndike and Judd were strong proponents (Cremin, 1961).

GETTING SIDETRACKED: OBSTACLES TO MAKING BETTER SENSE OF TRANSFER

A major obstacle to moving forward in our thinking about transfer has been a series of arguments that vacillate between binary oppositions: cognitive versus social processes, mental versus environmental agency, intentional versus spontaneous elicitation, generalization versus situational specificity, epiphenomenon versus explanation (Cox, 1997). Some accounts attempt to mediate by suggesting that transfer encompasses both poles of one or more of these oppositions, but ultimately contribute to the obstacle by not providing a conceptual means for uniting them or moving beyond them. The intertwining of transfer with the history of American public education partially explains how this obstacle has been maintained.

Constructs that offload agency and explanation for the phenomenon into the head or onto the environment afford an ongoing but unresolvable debate about the relative contributions of both. Suggestions that agency for transfer exists in both simply sidestep the issue without accompanying new theory, new units of analysis, and new means of facilitation to bridge or dissolve personal and social agency in transfer. The ongoing but repetitive nature of the debate is maintained, in part, by its refraction through educational ideologies and programs designed to facilitate, for example, the formation of general cognitive representations and processes for critical thinking, or the creation of authentic understandings by using real-world tasks in the classroom.

Until recently, the strong association of mental cognitive constructs with the phenomenon of transfer (as opposed to the more content-driven cognitivism of J. Bruner, J. Piaget, H. Werner, E. J. Gibson, and others) has contributed to the obstacle. The strength of this relation has been such that criticisms of the viability of these constructs have been responded to by some as an attack on the phenomenon itself. This has resulted in inaccurate claims that those who find the cognitive construct inadequate must therefore believe that transfer does not occur (Anderson, Reder, & Simon, 1996, 1997). Greeno (1997) points to this as a category error that collapses theoretical constructs and the phenomena we seek to understand. Sociocultural critiques also contributed to this obstacle by providing pointed criticism of cognitive research on transfer (Laboratory for Comparative Human Cognition, 1986; Lave, 1988; Rogoff & Gardner, 1984) while generating research mainly on the intricacies of learning and development *within* single social practices, and thus largely avoided issues of transfer (Beach, 1997). This combined action de facto ceded the phenomenon of transfer to a single theoretical perspective.

Long-standing debates that split the agency for transfer between persons and environments, the reification of this divide in various education programs, a category error that confounds a particular theoretical stance toward transfer with the broader phenomenon, and a focus on within-practice analyses by sociocultural researchers combined to divert us from exploring better ways to understand and support learner continuity and transformation across institutions, local practices, problems, and tasks. This chapter is one attempt to move back on track, and toward a conception of transfer that is consistent with the dialectical concept of dependent origination, and with the sociocultural premise that learners and social organizations exist in a mutually constitutive relation to one another.

MARKING THE CREVASSES: AN ANALYSIS OF THE TRANSFER METAPHOR

Back on track, our expedition beyond the metaphor of transfer benefits from grounding in the lessons of extant theory and educational research that use the transfer metaphor. The larger purpose is not to critique particular lines of transfer research, something that has been done ably and repeatedly elsewhere (Beach, in press-a; Cobb & Bowers, in press; Cox, 1997; Greeno, 1997; Gruber, Law, Mandl, & Renkl, 1996; Guberman & Greenfield, 1991; Kirshner & Whitson, 1997; Laboratory for Comparative Human Cognition, 1986; Lave, 1988; Lobato,

1996; Pea, 1987; Rogoff & Gardner, 1984), but to set a new course for the entire endeavor. Our preparation to cover new ground includes marking the location of difficulties in studies using the transfer metaphor. The process allows us to learn from the difficulties and thus, it is hoped, avoid most of them. This is particularly important because part of our expedition involves an expanded notion of the phenomenon we have sought to understand as transfer.

Most efforts at defining, studying, and supporting transfer in education over the past three decades have involved a form of cognitivism that emphasizes mental representations, schemas, strategies, and models. However, many of the shortcomings of the metaphor are not, strictly speaking, unique to cognitivism. Hence, they will not automatically disappear upon offering an alternative conceptualization. They run deeper in our cultural consciousness than academic psychology and are embedded within our folk notions of teaching, classroom learning, and the role of schooling in society (Bruner, 1996). Thus, we need to identify and understand these problems in order to progress. It is in this vein that six key areas of difficulty associated with the constructs and metaphor of transfer are identified subsequently.

Transfer defines a narrow and isolated aspect of learning. Transfer is variously defined as

the effect that knowledge that was learned in a previous situation (task A) [has] on learning or performance in a new situation (task B). (Mayer & Whitrock, 1996, p. 48)

the degree to which a behavior will be repeated in a new situation. (Detterman, 1993, p. 2)

prior learning affecting new learning or performance [in which the new learning or performance] can differ from original learning in terms of the tasks involved (as when students apply what they have learned on practice problems to solving a new problem), and/or the context involved (as when students apply their classroom learning to performing tasks at home or work). (Marini & Genereux, 1995, p. 2)

The common thread among these definitions is that the products of learning from one task or situation influence learning on a later task or situation. An analysis of a person learning something on a second task (B) after having learned something during a prior task (A) contains five possible relations between the old and new learning. These possibilities are not mutually exclusive.

Possibility 1: Some learning occurs prior to A and B but is excluded from learning on both because it is not seen as relevant.

Possibility 2: Some learning occurs prior to A and B and is used in learning A and B because it is seen as relevant to both.

Possibility 3: Some learning occurs prior to A and B but is used only in learning B because it is seen as relevant to B and not A.

Possibility 4: Some learning occurs on A but is not used in learning B because it is seen as irrelevant to B.

Possibility 5: Some learning that occurs only on A is used during learning on B because it is seen as relevant to B.

Of these five potentially coexisting relations between old and new learning, only the fifth counts as transfer. Transfer is a very narrow band of all that potentially goes on in learning task B. Furthermore, it exists in conceptual isolation from the other possibilities. An expanded definition of what counts as transfer in educational research is needed.

Transfer has an agency problem. Most current accounts of learning transfer attribute cause or agency for the process to the abstraction and representation of knowledge by individual minds, and also to the similarities between routinely encountered socially organized units such as tasks, practices, and institutions. This dual attribution of agency also appears in what Salomon and Perkins (1989) distinguish as the "low and high roads of transfer." While current accounts of transfer acknowledge that both forms of agency provide impetus for the process, they are generally assumed to operate together as an interaction. The individual's psychological processes of abstraction and representation interact with the shared features of tasks to produce learning transfer. Interaction describes a relation between the two forms of agency, perhaps even a causal one. However, interaction cannot explain how the two forms of agency affect each other to produce transfer.

An analogy may be useful here. A beginning cyclist comes to understand that speed and balance interact to allow her to ride smoothly. After many bumps and bruises, she also learns that the greater her speed, the easier it is to balance and therefore arrive at her intended destination. Understanding this as an interaction does not mean that she understands how her increased speed helps her balance to reach her goal. It only tells her that it does. Similarly, demonstrating that individual psychological processes interact with task features to produce varying degrees of transfer does not provide an account of how these two forms of agency produce transfer. Providing a more viable account of agency or causation in transfer should highlight new possibilities for its study, and for how we might support it through instruction.

Transfer is no different than "just plain learning." The transfer metaphor requires that transfer differ from our usual day-to-day learning in some way. Analytic and pedagogical advantages to focusing our efforts on transfer exist only if transfer is understood as different from "just plain learning" in an important way. Some current accounts distinguish between learning and transfer by suggesting that learning is relatively effortless and occurs across very similar problems, whereas transfer is conscious and effortful and occurs across quite different problems (Salomon & Perkins, 1989). A second distinction, related to the first, is that transfer involves the application or use of prior learning products—knowledge and skill—in learning a new problem, but does not include learning as part of the transfer process. Neither presents a particularly compelling case for distinguishing transfer from just plain learning. This moved Detterman (1993) to deem transfer an epiphenomenon that explains nothing about learning and can better be explained by more elementary cognitive processes. An analytically useful and practically important distinction needs to be made between transfer and just plain learning if the concept is to help us understand learning continuity and transformation across multiple tasks and situations.

Transfer environments are assumed to be static. The transfer metaphor suggests that persons carry knowledge and skill from one task or situation to another. Changes in the tasks or situations do not fit well with the metaphor. Most current notions of transfer presuppose that the tasks across which transfer occur remain unchanged during transfer. Although the transferring individual may create analogical bridges (Gentner & Gentner, 1983) or abstract schemas (Gick & Holyoak, 1983; Reed, 1993) that address both tasks, changing the structure of the tasks would be out of bounds. The processes of researchers and teachers making tasks not too similar, yet not too different, are also excluded from consideration as part of transfer. Rather, the task relations produced by their efforts are said to affect transfer. A similar logic applied at the level of institutions would exclude changes in the family, the school, or the workplace from consideration as part of transfer processes between them.

One effect of this logic is an overemphasis on the role of the individual learner as reproducer of existing relations between fixed tasks. A corollary effect is the exclusion from transfer of those who construct tasks or collectively and historically change relations between institutions. Often, changes in tasks and situations do not occur within the same time frame or at the same rate as changes for the individual learner. Studies that use the learner as the sole temporal point of reference for studying and facilitating transfer are methodologically unable to include the genesis and dynamics of tasks and situations. A model that includes the creation and interlinking of tasks and situations as well as the continuity and transformation of individuals is needed.

Transfer assumes a "launch" model of person-environment relations. The transfer metaphor assumes what Kindermann and Skinner (1992) have called a launch model of person-environment relations.

The causal process represented by this model is analogous to a catapult, in which the initial forces of the contextual antecedent are the major determinants of the shape of the curve of the outcome. Phenomena for which launch models may be useful representations are those that are open to influence from the environment at one point and subsequently become "sealed off." (pp. 166–167)

The launch model has it that the initial task or situation through which a person learns largely determines what the person will do in a new task or situation that, unlike the first, does not alter the course of the individual's learning. It implies that earlier learning determines the trajectory of later learning because later environmental influence on learning is minimal. This is consistent with transfer as the application of prior products of learning, and with instructional efforts aimed at the creation of general schemes and strategies for transfer (e.g., Dansereau, 1995; Singley, 1995). It is also consistent with the rhetoric of the American school-to-work transition movement. Schools are where learning occurs, and failure in the workplace is largely a function of inadequate learning in school (Secretary's Commission on Achieving Necessary Skills, 1991). This affords an abdication of responsibility for supporting learning in the workplace.

The transfer metaphor suggests that when prior task-based learning is well applied to a new task, the learning that takes place when encountering the new task is minimal. However, there is no a priori reason to assume that later tasks and situations are "sealed off" from their influence on learning, whereas tasks and situations encountered earlier are highly influential. We need to adopt a model of person-environment relations that acknowledges the possibility, if not the certainty, that earlier learning contexts do not inoculate the person against learning in a new context. This may be possible only if we move away from the metaphor and associated constructs of transfer.

Transfer is difficult to intentionally facilitate. Learning transfer seems to occur on a daily basis throughout our lives, yet attempts at intentional facilitation are highly effortful and are often unsuccessful (Beach, 1993; Greeno, 1997; Lave, 1988; Mayer & Whitrock, 1996; Salomon & Perkins, 1989). The difference in the frequency of occurrence between intentionally facilitated transfer and transfer occurring without facilitation is sufficient to warrant concern. Scanty evidence that perfecting instructional instantiations of the transfer metaphor will resolve the discrepancy to any significant degree gives cause to reconsider the viability of the metaphor and associated psychological constructs.

Studies of learners moving across institutions suggest that the metaphor and accompanying constructs are at least partly responsible for the apparent difficulty in intentionally facilitating transfer. The difficulties may lie in the narrow definition of transfer as a phenomenon and in how we conceive of intentional facilitation. Generalization, or continuity and transformation, that has not been facilitated through instruction or the careful design of tasks is rarely studied. When it has been, the transfer metaphor was not invoked, presumably because it was orthogonal to understanding the processes involved in generalization between school and work (Beach, 1993; Saxe, 1991), home and school (Lareau, 1989), and school and community (Eckert, 1989; Heath, 1990).

LIGHTENING OUR LOAD: LEAVING THE TRANSFER METAPHOR BEHIND

These difficulties are serious enough that we believe the transfer metaphor and associated psychological constructs should be left behind in favor of a metaphor and set of concepts that broaden our vision of generalization across changing forms of social organization. In leaving the transfer metaphor behind, though, we need to attend to two simplifying assumptions that originate with it. These assumptions distinguish task-to-task transfer from transfer between larger forms of social organization, and intentional from unintentional transfer. Although simplification is always necessary for analysis, these simplifying distinctions need to be reconsidered as different levels of analysis, and as general and special cases, rather than as independent forms of transfer.

The law of mental discipline was concerned with a broad form of transfer. Exercising the mind in one discipline or domain was believed to generalize to many others. With the critiques of formal discipline by Thorndike and Judd, empirical concerns about transfer shifted to the level of specific tasks and problems. Thorndike suggested that learning transfer could be effectively facilitated only at the local level of the task. Although Judd claimed that transfer could occur more broadly (e.g., it may occur across the disciplines), his approach to facilitation was also located within the task or problem. Here we see an important distinction between the process of transfer and the process of facilitation. Transfer among tasks and problems was assumed to be a microcosm of the larger educational concern: the portability of knowledge and skills across grades, subject matter, and ultimately beyond the school to families, communities, and workplaces. Yet, facilitation was seen to be a very local instructional process.

Most research on transfer continues in this vein today, examining transfer between tasks (Holyoak & Koh, 1987), problems (Mayer, 1992), and well-defined local domains (Bransford, Goldman, & Vye, 1991). Others have acknowledged the larger issue at stake by studying transfer between larger socially organized situations (Beach, 1995; Hungwe, 1999; Nunes, Carraher, & Schilemann, 1993; Reineke, in press; Saxe, 1991) but have not directly taken up issues of facilitation (an exception to this is Martin, Shirley, & McGinnis, 1988). Given that it is generalization across the broader domains of human experience with which education is ultimately concerned, analyses of local attempts at facilitation across tasks and problems need to be understood within an interpretive framework that encompasses relations between larger social practices and institutions (Cole, 1996; Lemke, 1997). It may also be that relations between larger forms of social organization are a fruitful starting point for understanding local attempts at facilitating generalization across tasks and problems.

A simple count of studies of transfer could convince us that transfer necessarily involves some intention to do so by the person doing the transferring and/or others who may assist in the process (Pressley, 1995; Reed, 1993). Most research efforts have focused on intentional transfer. Yet, common sense dictates that transfer most frequently occurs without anyone thinking about how to apply prior learning or reason by analogy on a new problem or situation. In other words, it generally occurs without any intention to do so on the part of the person transferring or those assisting. In fact, Detterman (1993) argues that true transfer is, by definition, spontaneous rather than provoked by a teacher, peer, parent, or coworker. Thus, it makes sense to consider intentional attempts to generalize knowledge, skills, and identities as special cases of a larger set of phenomena that generally do not involve conscious reflection on how to apply prior learning in new situations. It may also be that unintentional generalization is a useful starting point for understanding ways to intentionally facilitate generalization.

MOVING FORWARD: A SOCIOCULTURAL VIEW OF GENERALIZATION AS CONSEQUENTIAL TRANSITION

Any sociocultural reconceptualization of transfer should be true to the premise that underlies all sociocultural approaches to learning and development: that learners and social organizations exist in a recursive and mutually constitutive relation to one another across time. In being true to this premise and to the underlying philosophical stance that our experiences of continuity and transformation across time and social situations are a function of neither the individual nor the situation, but rather of their relation, it becomes possible to move beyond the transfer metaphor and its associated constructs.

Expanding the Phenomenon of Concern

The process of placing boundaries on educational phenomena is never fully independent of the processes by which we create constructs to study the phenomena. Yet, as we can see from the history of transfer research, the danger of losing analytic power by confounding our conceptual tools with the phenomenon we are trying to understand is quite real. I therefore sketch the outlines of the set of phenomena we are seeking to understand as generalization. The sketch encompasses but goes beyond what has historically been studied as transfer. Then I propose a construct—consequential transition—that can be used to more explicitly characterize and study the generalization.

Generalization, defined as the continuity and transformation of knowledge, skill, and identity across various forms of social organization, involves multiple interrelated processes rather than a single general procedure. A similar point is made by Cox (1997) in his developmental-historical analysis of transfer, suggesting that even early Gestalt notions questioned the existence of a general procedure for transfer. Generalization as we are interested in it consists of a set of interrelated social and psychological processes and therefore requires multiple levels of explanation and educational facilitation.

The decontextualization of mediational means (Wertsch, 1985), or the formation of symbols and concepts at ever increasing distances from particular contexts and referents (Hatano & Inagaki, 1992), does not provide a sufficient basis for understanding the transformative aspects of knowledge, skill, and identity generalization. Recent ''thick descriptions'' of children learning science and math (Carraher & Schilemann, in press; Nemirovsky, in press) propose forms of generalization that do not involve a distancing from the particulars of the social world. Davydov (1990) argues from the position of dialectical materialism that curriculums and teaching should support generalization that moves toward an integration of the diverse aspects of a concept and reveals the interconnected nature of its different aspects. Movements toward abstract concepts that reveal common properties in a class of things or phenomena are seen as impoverished descriptions of reality (Falmagne, 1995). Van Oers's (1998) analysis of children's play activity in a classroom shoe store provides a wonderful description of how generalization can be obtained without decontextualization, by the embedding of contexts in other contexts.

This process is called an activity of *continuous progressive recontextualizing*. The development toward more abstract forms of activities is one of the results of continuous progressive recontextualizing. On the basis of our observations, we have reason to assume that it is certainly not typically characterized by decontextualization or disembeddedness. Rather, the important thing was the possibility for the actors to create a new sign-based context related to their previous activities that made their new activity meaningful. (p. 141)

The forms of generalization that concern us are never distanced or decontextualized in their relation to various forms of social organization. They are not located within the developing individual, nor can they simply be reduced to changes in social activities. Rather, these forms of generalization are located in the changing relation between persons and activities (Beach, 1995b; Beach, in press-d; Lemke, 1997).

Generalization at the intersection of persons and activities cannot happen without systems of artifacts, symbolic objects that are created with human intent (cf. Cole, 1996). Whitson's (1997) Peircean analysis of a case of inappropriate transfer, Walkerdine's description of students' mathematical mastery (1998), Lemke's (1997) interconnected ecosocial systems, Evans's (in press) reanalysis of Noss and Hoyles's (1996) study of "banking maths," and my studies of adults becoming bartenders (1993) and Nepali students becoming shopkeepers (Beach, 1995a, 1995b) all emphasize the centrality of symbols, technologies, and texts, or systems of artifacts, in creating continuities and transformations through social situations. The processes of generalization and systems of artifacts weave together changing individuals and social organizations in such a way that the person experiences becoming someone or something new, similar to Dewey's (1916) notion of development as "becoming." Thus, the experiences of continuity and transformation are important to, reflected on, and struggled with by individuals participating in multiple social activities: playing, studying, working, parenting, loving, and so on. Insofar as many of these experiences are life transforming, they have a developmental nature to them along with some notion of *telos* or progress. The developmental constitution of the phenomenon has also been noted by Saxe (1989, 1991).

Experiences such as learning algebra after years of studying arithmetic, becoming a machinist, founding a community organization, teaching one's firstborn to walk, an elementary school class writing a letter to a local newspaper, collaborating with NASA scientists on a classroom project via the Internet, making the transition from student to teacher, and negotiating one's identity as an African American between home and the school are all potential examples of the sort of generalization we are concerned with. Each of these experiences can involve transformation, the construction of new knowledge, identities, ways of knowing, and new positionings of oneself in the world. They are consequential for the individual and are developmental in nature, located in the changing relations between individuals and social activities. The relations involve the genesis and maintenance of systems of artifacts and all that is embodied through them, including knowledge, skill, and identity. The forms of generalization that concern us go far beyond learning transfer, but cover an educational terrain that has been reduced metaphorically to the carrying and application of knowledge across tasks.

Transfer as Consequential Transition

At its core, the concept of consequential transition involves a developmental change in the relation between an individual and one or more social activities. A change in relation can occur though a change in the individual, the activity, or both. Transitions are consequential when they are consciously reflected on, often struggled with, and the eventual outcome changes one's sense of self and social positioning. A college student becoming a teacher, a worker trying to adapt to a management-reorganized job, a middle school student doing well in math for the first time in his life, and high school students taking part-time work in fast food restaurants are all potential examples of transitions that are consequential both for the individual and for the particular social organization. Etienne Wenger's outstanding volume on communities of practice and the negotiation of their boundaries speaks to a similar set of phenomena and concerns (Wenger, 1998) but emphasizes the practices themselves as a unit of reflection and analysis.

We have identified four primary types of consequential transition: lateral, collateral, encompassing, and mediational. Lateral and collateral transitions involve persons moving between preexisting social activities. Encompassing and mediational transitions have persons moving within the boundaries of a single activity or into the creation of a new activity. This typology of transitions is necessarily preliminary, but it expresses different principal forms of relational change between individuals and social activities. Each potentially involves the continuity and/or transformation of knowledge, skill, and identity embodied in the relation. Each has potentially different implications for the learner, the social organization of learning, and what means are available to facilitate the consequential transition.

Lateral Transition

Lateral transitions occur when an individual moves between two historically related activities in a single direction. Examples would include moving from school to work (e.g., a student becoming an airline pilot) and moving from one subdiscipline to another (e.g., a student taking a first course in algebra after many years of arithmetic). Participation in one activity precedes and is replaced by participation in another activity during lateral transition. Lateral transition most closely resembles classic transfer in its unidirectionality. Lateral transitions generally involve some notion of progress embedded in the particular sequence of activities and thus in the individual's movement between the activities. Often, the activity one is in lateral transition to is considered a developmental advance beyond the previous activity, which is seen as preparation for the new activity. For example, high school students saw themselves as becoming shopkeepers during their apprenticeships to shopkeepers, not as students who happened to be learning about shopkeeping (Beach, 1995b). The unidirectional notion of progress associated with lateral transitions was closely tied to explanations of how and why the students transformed their mathematical reasoning in the process of becoming shopkeepers.

Italian novelist Italo Calvino provides a lush description of a lateral transition from Tamara, a city of signs, to the surrounding countryside, previously a world of natural objects, through the eyes of Marco Polo reporting on his expeditions to Kublai Khan.

Finally the journey leads to the city of Tamara. You penetrate it along streets thick with signboards jutting from the walls. The eye does not see things but images of things that mean other things: pincers point out the tooth-drawer's house; a tankard, the tavern; halberds, the barracks; scales, the grocer's. Statues and shields depict lions, dolphins, towers, stars: a sign that something—who knows what?—has as its sign a lion or a dolphin or a tower or a star. Other signals warn of what is forbidden in a given place (to enter the alley with wagons, to urinate behind the kiosk, to fish with your pole from the bridge) and what is allowed (watering zebras, playing bowels, burning relatives' corpses). If a building has no signboard or figure, its very form and the position it occupies in the city's order suffice to indicate its function: the palace, the prison, the mint, the Pythagorean school, the brothel. The wares, too, which the vendors display on their stalls are valuable not in themselves but as signs of other things: the embroidered headband stands for elegance; the gilded palanquin, power; the volumes of Averroes, learning; the ankle bracelet, voluptuousness. Your gaze scans the streets as if they were written pages: the city says everything you must think, makes you repeat her discourse, and while you believe you are visiting Tamara you are only recording the names with which she defines herself and all her parts.

However the city may really be, beneath this thick coating of signs, whatever it may contain or conceal, you leave Tamara without having discovered it. Outside, the land stretches, empty, to the horizon; the sky opens, with speeding clouds. In the shape that chance and wind give the clouds, you are already intent on recognizing figures: a sailing ship, a hand, an elephant. (1972, p. 15)

Lave and Wenger's (1991) account of an Alcoholics Anonymous group contains the distinction between lateral transitions, which are linear and are generally seen as irreversible, and collateral transitions, which are nonlinear and highly negotiated. Becoming an alcoholic involves a massive and irreversible transformation in knowledge, skill, and identity in the eyes of AA members. However, becoming a nondrinking alcoholic generally involves much back-and-forth collateral participation in the community of drinkers as well as nondrinkers, even though becoming a nondrinking alcoholic is what constitutes progress. It is to this far more complex form of transition that I now turn.

Collateral Transition

Collateral transitions involve individuals' relatively simultaneous participation in two or more historically related activities. The notion of collaterality was first developed in the dissertation work of Reineke (1995), in which he examined children's homework as it moved between school and home (see Reineke, in press, for an expansion of this work). Examples of collateral transitions are daily movement between home and school, participating in part-time work after school, and moving between language arts and science classes during the school week. Collateral transitions occur more frequently in life than do lateral forms, but they are more difficult to understand because of their multidirectionality. Back and forth movement between activities may or may not have an explicit notion of developmental progress tied to the movement itself. As we can see from the following example, development during collateral transitions can run in opposition to societal notions of progress as often as it runs with them.

During our study of Nepali students becoming shopkeepers, we also followed shopkeepers attending adult education classes (Beach, 1995a, 1995b). Schools did not exist in their village when the shopkeepers were of school age, and hence the evening adult education class was their first participation in schooling. The shopkeepers collaterally participated in both school and work, but did not see themselves as becoming students. Instead, they attended literacy and numeracy classes to gain skills in arithmetic and written literacy that would be of use to them as shopkeepers. They were not becoming better students so much as better shopkeepers. This runs contrary to a Nepali societal notion that participation in school constitutes a form of developmental progress in and of itself.

Collateral transition did not fit with extant American notions of developmental progress in our study of high school students learning to work part time in a fast food restaurant (Beach & Vyas, 1998). Students learned nothing beyond what they already knew about math, science, and language from school. Furthermore, the skills they acquired in making sandwiches were seen as cognitively low level and low in social status by the fast food corporation. It is not surprising that this particular collateral transition between school and work does not fit our existing conceptions of development progress. Yet, our findings do suggest that high school students develop during this collateral transition. Students struggle with and develop the ability to learn in a production activity devoid of a supportive agenda for their learning, unlike schooling.

As a final illustration of collateral transition, Bowers (1996) examined third-grade students learning arithmetic during a 9-week teaching experiment in which the students constructed new ways of symbolizing the process of combining and separating quantities (see also Cobb & Bowers, in press). These students also participated in daily mathematics lessons with their regular classroom teacher, who taught standard paper-and-pencil algorithms for combining and separating quantities. Bowers found that two thirds of the students became able to use the new ways of symbolizing the process to develop numerical meanings for the column algorithm in their regular math class. However, the remaining students simply switched between instrumental uses of standard computational algorithms in their regular classroom and their constructed means of symbolizing the combination and separation of quantities in their experimental class. Thus, collateral transition consisted of the transformation of knowledge for some and mathematical code switching for others. Other examples of collateral transition can be found in studies of teachers and students drawing community-based knowledge and wisdom into their classroom literacy practices (Moll, 1992), parents and teachers co-constructing math homework with their children/students (Reineke, in press), and the relation of social class and parental involvement at home to elementary students' participation in school (Lareau, 1989).

More than any other form of transition, collateral transition raises questions about societal notions of developmental progress. These notions generally value knowledge and skill proportional to the degree to which they are seen as higher in a hierarchy of distance from their origins in particular social activities. Collateral transitions make an exclusive concentration on this vertical dimension of developmental progress problematical. Engeström (1996) eloquently describes this concern in a discourse on the novel *Borderliners* by Peter Hoeg.

Traditional developmental theories are about progress, about climbing upward on some developmental ladders. In some theories, the ladders are very well known and fixed; in others they are more locally constructed and culturally contingent. But developmental movement happens along a vertical dimension, from immaturity and incompetence toward maturity and competency. Peter, too, realizes this. . . .

The school is an instrument dedicated to elevation. It works like this. If you achieve in the way you're supposed to, time raises you up. That's why the classrooms are arranged as they are. From primary One to Three you're on the ground floor, then you move to the second floor, then the third, then to Secondary on the fourth, until at last—at the very top, in the assembly hall—you receive your certificate from Biehl. And then you can fly in the world. I've been wondering why it is so hard for them, why there are so many rules. And it occurred to me that it is because they have to keep the outside world out. Because it's not everywhere out there that raises it up. (Hoeg, 1994, p. 79, cited in Engeström, 1996)

Encompassing Transition

Encompassing transitions occur within the boundaries of a social activity that is itself changing. In the broadest sense, all social activities are changing, even if only through collective efforts to maintain the constancy of activity through rituals, routines, revivals, and rules. One form of encompassing transition is captured in Lave and Wenger's conception of legitimate peripheral participation. The activity is stable relative to the changing individual becoming a full participant in that activity. "By this we mean to draw attention to the point that learners inevitably participate in communities of practitioners and that the mastery of knowledge and skill requires newcomers to move toward full participation in the sociocultural practices of a community" (Lave & Wenger, 1991, p. 29). A second form of encompassing transition occurs when activities undergo rapid change relative to the lives of their participants. Examples are experienced teachers responding to new education reform initiatives and conventional machinists learning to run newly introduced computer-controlled machines.

Like lateral transitions, encompassing transitions generally involve a clear notion of progress, although it is associated with the direction taken by the changing activity rather than the direction of individuals moving between activities. Unlike either lateral or collateral transitions, encompassing transitions take place within a single activity with boundaries that change, albeit at different rates with different consequences relative to the individual. It should be noted that this sense of boundary is not absolute or hermitic. Rather, an activity boundary is one that can be crossed developmentally (Engeström, Engeström, & Kärkkäinen, 1995; Gutierrez, Rymes, & Larson, 1995), and through the use of boundary objects sufficiently flexible to be adapted across multiple activities (Star, 1989, 1996).

Individuals participating in encompassing transitions often experience the process as adapting to existing or changing circumstances in order to continue participation within the boundaries of the activity. Encompassing transitions can result in generational reversals in expertise and instructional roles. Younger generations of participants often assist older generations in acquiring necessary knowledge and skills and are seen as more expert. This generational reversal in roles in the face of rapid societal change was first noted by Margaret Mead in her classic ethnography, *Coming of Age in Samoa*. Many of us experience it today when we request assistance from our students, daughters, or sons in learning a particular piece of computer software.

Our research on machining activity changing with the introduction of computerized machines illustrates an encompassing transition (Beach, in press-b; Hungwe, 1999; Hungwe & Beach, 1995). Machining parts traditionally involved machinists using lathes, milling, and grinding machines that were controlled via mechanical linkages, dials, levers, and gauges. The recent introduction of computer numerical control (CNC) machines into American manufacturing also introduced symbol-based computer programs that mediate the relation between the machinist and part creation. Traditional machinists learn CNC machining by transforming prior machining knowledge and skills into the representations and organizational structures of the program code, and by adapting to the asynchronous nature of their actions that control the machines through the program. Many from the upcoming generation of machinists have not had years of mechanical machining experience prior to learning on CNC machines. Thus, the nature of becoming a machinist, their status within the machining community, and their identity as craftsmen differs from the previous generation of machinists with whom they work. Becoming a machinist at different periods in the technological transformation of machining activity illustrates the heterochronous relation of changing persons and changing activities that is characteristic of encompassing transition. Heterochronicity, or differential rates of change between persons and activities, has also been studied as a key feature in the genesis of after-school computer clubs (Nicolopoulou & Cole, 1993) and in the development of a school-based court of law (Wilcox & Beach, 1996).

Mediational Transition

Mediational transitions occur within educational activities that project or simulate involvement in an activity yet to be fully experienced. Examples of this form of transition are particularly prevalent in vocational and adult education (Beach, 1993) but can also be seen in activities as diverse as a school play store (Walkerdine, 1988), instruction in writing (Palincsar & Brown, 1984), learning the concept of area (Sayeki, Ueno, & Nagasaka, 1991), and community- and work-based apprenticeships (Lave & Wenger, 1991). Mediational transitions exist along a continuum from classroom-based activities that have ''as if'' or simulated relations to the world beyond the school, to partial or peripheral participation in the activities themselves. No matter where they are on the continuum, however, they always maintain a ''third object'' or mediating status with regard to where the participants are currently and where they are going developmentally, roughly equivalent to Vygotsky's concept of a zone of proximal development (Vygotsky,

1978). Thus, mediating transitions always embody a particular notion of developmental progress for participating individuals.

An example of mediating transition is provided in an earlier study of mine that examined how adults participating in a private vocational school learn to become bartenders (Beach, 1993). The bartending class occupied a middle position between where its students were—highly literate part-time actors, restaurant managers, graduate students—and where they were going—part- or full-time work as bartenders or supervising bartenders. Drink recipes were initially memorized from written materials, but the press to achieve speed as well as accuracy in drink mixing meant that students were assisted in shifting away from written materials toward mnemonic materials more closely associated with the mixing of the drinks themselves. The vocational school activity existed as a bridge between two other systems of activity and embodied a clear developmental agenda for its students.

These four forms of transition—lateral, collateral, encompassing, and mediational—as diverse as they may seem, share a common set of features that justify engaging them as a whole. Each potentially involves the construction of knowledge, identities, and skills, or transformation, rather than the application of something that has been acquired elsewhere. Consequential transitions therefore involve a notion of progress for the learner and are best understood as a developmental process. Each is consequential and often involves changes in identity as well as knowledge and skill. Therefore, individuals and institutions are often highly conscious of the development that is taking place, and they have particular, sometimes publicly debated, agendas for how and why it should or should not happen. Finally, consequential transition consists of changing relations between persons and social activities represented in signs, symbols, texts, and technologies or, more generally, in systems of artifacts. This not only acknowledges the recursive relation between persons and activities, but makes it the explicit object of study.

Studying Consequential Transitions

Studying and facilitating consequential transitions requires new methodology. By methodology, I do not mean the particular nuts-and-bolts methods or tools of analysis, of which we already have many at our disposal. Rather, drawing on Valsiner's broader notion of methodology (Kindermann & Valsiner, 1989; Valsiner, 1989), I use the term to refer to new ways of constructing data, thinking about designs/methods, and asking appropriate questions that relate the construct of consequential transition to the generalization phenomena we are concerned with. I take up four key aspects of a methodology for studying consequential transitions and illustrate what such a methodology "buys" us with findings from several of our research group's studies.

Developmental Coupling as a Unit for Studying Consequential Transitions

The concept of coupling comes from the work of Varela, Thompson, and Rosch and their book *The Embodied Mind* (1991; see also Maturana, 1975;

Varela, 1981). In it they draw on post-Darwinian evolutionary biology and connectionist theory to describe coevolution as a changing relationship between a species and its environment, a structural coupling of the two systems over time—not as a property of the species, the environment, or an interaction between separable systems. I think of the concept of developmental coupling in a similar manner.

A developmental coupling encompasses aspects of both changing individuals and changing social activity. The coupling itself is the primary unit of study and concern rather than the individual or the activity per se. The coupling assumes that individuals move across space, time, and changing social activities rather than being hermetically situated within an unchanging context. If a context does appear unchanging, it is because much collective effort is being put into maintaining it in place. The coupling itself transforms or develops. Its directionality and causal relations are not efficient or antecedent/consequent; rather, they are correlational or relational in nature. Finally, developmental coupling necessarily involves artifacts: objects that embody human intention and agency in some form and that extend beyond a particular individual participating in a particular social organization at a particular time (see Beach, in press-d, for a more detailed discussion). The coevolution of bees and flowers as developmental systems provides a nice analogy for thinking about the developmental coupling of persons and activities.

On the one hand, flowers attract pollinators by their food content and so must be both conspicuous and yet different from flowers of other species. On the other hand, bees gather food from flowers and so need to recognize flowers from a distance. These two broad and reciprocal constraints appear to have shaped a history of coupling in which plant features and the sensorimotor capacities of bees coevolved. It is this coupling, then, that is responsible for both the ultraviolet vision of bees and the ultraviolet reflectance patterns of flowers. Such coevolution therefore provides an excellent example of how environmental regularities are not pregiven, but are rather enacted or brought forth by a history of coupling. (Varela, Thompson, & Rosch, 1991, p. 202)

Our first illustration of developmental coupling is from the previously mentioned study of arithmetic reasoning during transitions between school and work in rural Nepal (Beach, 1995a, 1995b). It involves instances of both linear and collateral transition. The second is from a study of machinists making an encompassing transition from mechanical to computerized technology within a large American automobile manufacturer (Beach, in press-b; Hungwe, 1999; Hungwe & Beach, 1995).

From School to Work, and From Work to School in Rural Nepal

The initial purpose of the study was to understand how adolescents' and adults' arithmetic reasoning changed during transitions between school and work in a Nepali village. At the time of the study, two major societal changes in relations between school and work were under way in rural Nepal. One change involved increasing numbers of high school graduates and dropouts becoming merchants in local shops. As a high school education became less valuable in obtaining work outside of agriculture, shopkeeping became an option for those who did not want to continue with their family in subsistence agriculture. The other change consisted of increasing numbers of shopkeepers attending adult education classes. Adults had previously not attended school because schooling was outlawed in the kingdom when they had been of school age. The shopkeepers saw the classes as providing them with written forms of literacy and arithmetic that would be of benefit in their shops. These societal-level changes were simulated voluntarily at a local level by apprenticing graduating high school students to local shopkeepers, and by enrolling shopkeepers in adult education classes. Changes in arithmetic reasoning were then tracked over a period of several months as the students participated in shopkeeping and as the shopkeepers participated in schooling.

The students constructed a new form of arithmetic reasoning in their lateral transition to shopkeeping. They shifted away from using written column algorithms toward decomposition and iteration calculation strategies that included monetary and measurement structures. The students also created a previously unseen system of written notation to support these strategies. This transformation in arithmetic reasoning had its origins not in schooling or shopkeeping but, rather, in the transition process between the two activities. Power and status played a role in this transition and in the arithmetic reasoning of the students. Prior to the introduction of schooling in the village, arithmetic originating outside of school had the status of *hisaab*, or mathematics. With the introduction of schooling, *hisaab* gradually became those calculations associated with column algorithms and paper and pencil notation, relegating other forms of arithmetic to *andaji*, or estimation. The students were clearly reluctant to move away from some form of written notation, having spent a decade studying *hisaab* in school. At the same time, they clearly saw themselves as becoming someone new, a shopkeeper, and found column algorithms often unwieldy in the context of converting prices across different systems of measurement and totaling customer purchases. More than half of the students participating in the study in fact went on to become shopkeepers.

The transition for shopkeepers attending adult education classes was collateral. Shopkeepers attending the classes were doing so because they wished to expand the nature and complexity of the goods they could sell. They consequently used the adult education classes to supplement their already-existing repertoire of arithmetic strategies with written column algorithms. Shopkeepers were not on a linear trajectory to becoming students; rather, they were enhancing their economic viability as shopkeepers. A clear illustration of this in the shopkeepers' arithmetic reasoning was their rapid forgetting of the arithmetic operations signs upon completing the class. The reason for this was that operations signs are not needed for column algorithms when the practices within the activity make explicit what needs to be done with the numbers.

Lateral and collateral transitions and the particular couplings that developed between the individuals and the activities appeared quite different. They differed despite the fact that both were transitions between school and work, and both shopkeepers and students became able to deploy a variety of written and nonwritten strategies and artifacts. Therefore, neither the nature of the particular activities nor the participants' different backgrounds offer adequate explanations of these consequential transitions. Nor does an interaction between persons and activities, because it requires the two to be analytically separable though they always co-occur in life. This would create a "black box" where the recursive relation between persons and society is played out.

Although developmental coupling is a viable concept for understanding changing local relations between persons and activities, it remains only a partial explanation of consequential transition. A more macro-level explanation exists in conjunction with local ones and involves two additional methodological concepts: leading activity and heterochronicity. These are described subsequently, after first illustrating developmental coupling during an encompassing transition.

From Mechanical to Computerized Machining Activity

This illustration comes from a compendium of studies in which we followed machinists during a major encompassing transition from mechanical to computerized machining in American industry. It is a revisitation of work that was begun almost a decade ago with Laura Martin and Sylvia Scribner (Martin & Beach, 1992; Martin & Scribner, 1992).

Over the past 30 years, American machining has undergone tremendous change in response to economic pressures from abroad. One major change has been from the making of parts with mechanically controlled machines to the use of program or computer-controlled machines to cut metal, ceramics, and plastic parts. Machinists with experience (ranging from a couple of years to several decades) on mechanically controlled machines find themselves in transition because the activity in which they participate is itself transforming. We set out to study the process of transition from mechanical to computer numerical controlled machining among these machinists.

In his dissertation, Kedmon Hungwe (1999) describes a developmental coupling consisting of three components: artifact, object, and machinist's role. A change in any one or two of the three components constitutes transformation, the creation of a new relation between machinist and the activity of machining. Rather than define each component statically, I describe each as it changes during the encompassing transition from mechanical to computerized machining.

The creation and use of artifacts shifts from primary to secondary artifacts during the course of the transition. Primary artifacts bear a direct material relation to the cutting operation of the machine and to the parts being made. They consist of levers, dials, and gauges as well as the smells, sights, and sounds of tools cutting metal. They are deployed in real time with the operation of the machine. The shift to secondary artifacts in the form of written program codes means that the system of artifacts used to control the machine no longer directly draws on the structure of the machine and the cutting process for its organization (see Wartofsky, 1979, for a detailed exegesis of his concept of primary and secondary as well as tertiary artifacts: social objects that embody human intent). Programming does not operate in machine time; rather, it occurs prior to the operation of the machine, often in an office removed from the shop floor. Traditional machinists learning computerized machining struggled with apparent but not always actual similarities and differences in the organization of the two systems of artifacts.

What constitutes an "object" shifts from the actual parts produced by the machinist to a computer program that can be used to produce thousands of parts. With minor adjustments, a program can direct a machine to produce a new part that is a modification of an old one, avoiding the lengthy setup required (for each change in a part) on mechanical machines. Thus, the program controlling the machine is, in the long term, often more valuable to the company than the parts. Machinists doing programming are often concerned with the elegance and efficiency of the program as an object in its own right. While this seems quite natural for younger machinists who have learned machining largely on computerized machines, the shift in objects is difficult for highly skilled tool and die makers who may have spent 20 years on mechanical machines prior to learning computerized machining.

The third component, that of the machinist's role, is directly tied to the machinist's identity as a highly skilled craftsman. The expansion of the activity to include computerized machining split the machinist's job into operator and programmer. Machine operation consisted of setting up the machine and monitoring it during its operation. Control of the machining processes rested in the hands of the programmer. Neither operators nor programmers had total responsibility for crafting the part and experienced a resulting loss of identity as a craftsman. This was sufficiently profound for some of the more experienced machinists that they left computerized machining and returned to work with mechanical machines, despite a decrement in status, though not in pay. In contrast, younger machinists who had trained on computer-driven machines saw computerized machining as a way of increasing their status and making themselves more marketable within and beyond the company.

The consequential transition from mechanical to computerized machining was of the encompassing form. Developmental changes in the relation between machinists and machining activity took place within the confines of the activity, which was itself changing. Instances of pure continuity in knowledge, skill, and identity were rare, as were pure instances of discontinuity. Most of what we found in the transition were transformations in the relations among artifacts, objects, and role: a developmental coupling that embodied aspects of identity in addition to knowledge and skill.

Leading Activity and Heterochronicity

Consequential transitions cannot adequately be understood only at the level of local developmental couplings between persons and activities. Activities exist in relation not only to individuals but also to broader institutional, societal, and cultural forces. An activity is the nonadditive, molar unit of life for the material, corporeal subject. In a narrower sense, it is the unit of life that is mediated by mental reflection. The real function of this unit is to orient the subject in the world of objects. In other words, activity is not a reaction or aggregate of reactions, but a system with its own structure, its own internal transformations, and its own development. (Leont'ev, 1981, p. 46)

Activities such as machining, bartending, and schooling are developmental entities in their own right. Relations between various types of activity are not neutral or simply additive for individuals participating in them, however. As Leont'ev describes it, human life

is not built up mechanically . . . from separate types of activity. Some types of activity are leading ones at a given stage and are of greater significance for the individual's subsequent development, and other types are less important. Some play the main role in development and others a subsidiary one. (1981, p. 95)

For example, playing followed by schooling, working, and retirement is a sequence of leading activity categories characteristic of most European and North American societies. Each leading activity serves as preparation for the next. In some subsistence agricultural societies, the sequence of leading activities may simply be play followed by work that is highly integrated with family and community. This should not be interpreted as meaning that a given society defines a developmental sequence of activity categories that in turn fully dictate individual development. Rather, whether or not an activity is "leading" and therefore dominant in influence relative to other activities in which the person may be participating is co-determined by both the sequence of activity categories characteristic of a society and the period in an individual's history at which she or he participates in the activity (Beach, 1995a). Changes in persons, activities, and societies are heterochronous with respect to each other. This means that the general rate of change for individuals is less than that for activities, which in turn is less than that for societies. That being said, the most revealing cases of consequential transition are instances in which activities and societies change rapidly within the time span of the individuals participating in them. Heterochrony (see Hutchins, 1995, for an elaboration of the concept within distributed technological systems), or the timing of relations among persons, activities, and more macro-social processes, often determines the nature of the consequential transition and the developmental coupling.

I return to the Nepal study to illustrate how the concepts of leading activity and heterochronicity are useful for understanding consequential transitions. Two generations of villagers with radically different relations to the transition between school and work lived in the village at the time of our study. The younger generation had spent an extensive period of time in school before apprenticing to shopkeepers but had not done shopkeeping work prior to this time. The older generation had not had the opportunity to attend schools when they were of school age and had spent a minimum of 4 years working as shopkeepers before attending adult education classes. These two generations of villagers differed in their temporal relation to schooling and shopkeeping, and to broader changes in Nepali society. Heterochronicity among the villagers' lives, the activities, and the society figures prominently in our understanding of what actually happens during transitions between schooling and shopkeeping.

Students apprenticed to shopkeepers were making a lateral transition from one leading activity to another, following a school-to-work sequence characteristic of generations to come in Nepali society. However, the two activities are defined by motives that bear little relation to one another, at least in rural Nepal. The motives are learning for a credential, with learning up front as the object of the activity, and becoming a shopkeeper, with selling goods for profit up front as the object. These unrelated motives allow schooling and with it school forms of arithmetic to achieve a status disconnected from and above that of arithmetic embedded in village work activities. We have evidence that the difference in status partially explains students' reluctance to drop the more visible portion of arithmetic originating in school while learning to become shopkeepers.

On the other hand, shopkeepers enrolled in the adult education class were participating in a collateral transition between a leading activity and a nonleading activity, following a work-to-school sequence characteristic of only a couple of previous generations in Nepali society. The motive for the shopkeepers' participation in the adult education class was to acquire additional knowledge and skills that could benefit them in the running and expansion of their shops. This was reflected in their developing a flexible repertoire of arithmetic artifacts, organizations, and operations through the adult education class, in contrast to the students becoming shopkeepers.

School and work are clearly categories of leading activities in rural Nepali society. However, the period in the development of an individual or a generation of individuals at which they participate has as much to do with whether it is leading or not as the societal sequence of activities. It is in this way that activities mediate between large-scale societal change and the local coupling of individuals with activities. A similar heterochronic relation can be found in the machining study. Individuals who participated in mechanical machining prior to the introduction of computerized machining exhibited a different developmental coupling in learning of computer-controlled machines than did those who became machinists after computerized machining had become widespread in American industry.

A Horizontal Notion of Development

If we are to take seriously the notion that consequential transitions are developmental phenomena, then we must address what constitutes *telos* or progress in consequential transition. Most grand notions of human development characterize progress as movement through some form of vertical hierarchy, toward greater levels of abstraction and away from the tangibilities of our world. While genetic epistemology displays this most clearly, Vygotsky's cultural-historical theory is not an exception, a point that has also been made by Engeström (1996) and by van Oers (1998). Notions of progress are important to study and critique. They often serve as a focus for practical action and thus should be taken seriously by any developmental theory. This is rather different, however, from a theory promoting a particular notion of progress. Theories possessing a singular notion of developmental progress run the risk of having this notion wander away from being an analytic tool to become a prescription for action, a yardstick for progress, or a call for reform. This is particularly true in the education arena. If we accept the premise that a society expresses its agendas for individual progress through its institutions and activities, embedding that notion of progress in a theory of learning and development will, at best, reduce the analytic tension between the theory and the phenomenon, and thus any analytic power. At worst, it will create a measuring stick for developmental progress derived from those who hold dominant and controlling interests in that society and will silence, coerce, and stigmatize others. Thus, the concept of consequential transition needs to include notions of developmental progress without an a priori privileging of one notion over the other.

Contrasting views of what constitutes developmental progress during consequential transition clearly emerge in our study of high school students becoming part-time crew in a fast food restaurant (Beach & Vyas, 1998). It is a collateral transition between two long-associated activities: the high school and the fast food restaurant. The fast food restaurant industry is a major employer of high school–aged youth in the United States. Becoming a fast food restaurant crew member runs against extant notions of what counts as individual progress in American society. Because fast food restaurants are the largest single employer of high school students in the United States, they provide many students with their first work experience outside the home. Thus, many students who participate in school activity with learning as its defining object first encounter the need to learn in a work activity at the fast food restaurant, where production rather than learning is the object of the activity.

The United States has seen a recent increase in attention to issues of school-to-work transition. A report published in 1988 by the W. T. Grant Foundation, *The Forgotten Half: Non-College Youth in America*, pointed out that slightly more than 50% of America's youth do not attend 4-year colleges. By indicating that a majority of American youth do not fit our society's dominant model of intellectual and economic progress, the report initiated a series of heavily funded school-to-work programs designed to facilitate, sanction, and formalize an alternative pathway to personal and economic success, one that does not involve obtaining a 4-year college degree.

Fast food work is considered by the school-to-work movement only as an example of what school-to-work should not be: preparation for low-knowledge, low-skill, low-wage employment. A highly influential report issued by the U.S. Department of Labor in 1991, *What Work Requires of Schools*, describes the economic future of American society as being in "high skill, high tech, high wage, knowledge-intensive" jobs (p. 22). This rhetoric has been widely adopted by American industry and education policymakers. It has embedded in it a metaphorical marking of individual progress as proceeding upward through a hierarchy of knowledge and skill. The final section of the report is devoted to outlining a series of generic work-related skills and abilities that all students should acquire in school, independent of whether they will attend college, and independent of the particular job they may eventually acquire. This conceptualization of skills and abilities is based on assumptions of individual epistemological progress toward greater levels of abstraction and decontextualization.

The (dominant) notion of human progress in American society and, as noted earlier, in major developmental theories is upward through a hierarchy of knowledge and skills, and away from the specifics of human activities. Our research has led us to question the fruitfulness of such a singular notion of developmental progress. The collateral transition that students in our study make is between schooling, heavily invested in the dominant notion of progress, and participation in fast food restaurants, which runs counter to that notion. This provides an opportunity to examine how we might characterize couplings between individuals and activities, and relations between activities and society as developmental, though they may run counter to a dominant notion of progress.

The corporate-designed training for fast food crews consists of videotapes specific to each restaurant work station and a written mastery test completed at the end of each video. Successful completion of a test for a particular work station should be followed by training at the actual station with a more experienced member of the crew. The corporation's view of knowledge and skill is consistent with the place occupied by fast food work within the intellectual hierarchy of American jobs. In other words, it is near the bottom. Each of the training videos breaks a station job down into a series of behavioral elements and repeats the sequence three times for the viewer. For example, some of the elements in making a cheeseburger are as follows:

1. Place the heel bun and then the burger centered on the wrapper.
2. Place cheese on the burger, followed by three pickles arranged in a semicircular fashion. Use one pickle if they request "light pickles"; use four if they request heavy.
3. Squeeze on mustard and catsup starting from the outside of the burger and moving to the inside in a circular motion. If they request "heavy," your motion should be slower. If they request "light," it should be faster.

This view of knowledge and skill separates it developmentally from that which is acquired in school because it does not advance students' understanding of a particular subject matter such as math, science, or language arts. Thus, the corporate view of knowledge and skill is both consistent with the societal hierarchy of jobs and places a developmental boundary between it and schooling. However, this is not to suggest that becoming a crew member is unrelated to one's participation in school. In fact, the structure of learning activity in school has everything to do with what needs to be learned in a production activity such as fast food work.

The official training curriculum has little to do with what actually takes place in becoming a fast food crew member. Because of high turnover rates among employees, most new crew were hired to immediately fill vacant positions in the store and never saw a training video. Though some had a period of introduction that was marked as training, most started out by operating a particular station where they were needed to maintain the collective production of the crew. The activity is highly time driven and places pressure on the crew member to perform his or her job rapidly and accurately. Speed becomes more important than accuracy at times when the shortage of one particular product holds up the production of other members of the crew. This places the students in the position of needing to learn how to learn while maintaining production, something that runs counter to their participation in schooling. The students developed new means for learning while maintaining production and were assisted in this by the more experienced members of the crew who may or may not have been designated as the students' trainers. Learning to learn in a production activity was not easily and smoothly achieved by the high school students. Rather, the students struggled with creating opportunities to learn in the midst of production.

There are multiple reasons for viewing the collateral transition of youth between school and fast food work as having nothing to do with development or progress. Certainly, this is true in the vertical sense of development. Nothing new was learned about school subjects, nor were there many opportunities to use knowledge of math, science, or written literacy on the job. The corporate view is consistent with this. Knowing how many pickles and how much mustard to place on a burger is local declarative knowledge that resides at the bottom of any hierarchy of developmental progress. Furthermore, knowledge and skills gained at the restaurant are not seen as sufficiently abstract and conceptual to generalize to other more societally valued activities.

We propose an alternative conception of developmental progress that is horizontal. First ventured by Engeström (1996), horizontal development is closely tied to the concept of consequential transition as it is defined here. Horizontal development consists of the transformation or creation of a new relation between individuals and social activities, not continuities or discontinuities experienced by the participants at some points in the transition. Horizontal development is never removed or distanced from social activities. The appearance of distancing, decontextualization, or vertical development is a special case of horizontal development—one that generally involves new layers of symbolic mediation that give the appearance of generality. This is because their referents are assumed to be unchanging while new layers of mediation are added. As can be seen from our studies of machinists, however, referents shift with the addition of new layers of symbolization.

Although vertical-appearing versions of horizontal development are generally tied to dominant societal notions of human progress, this does not mean that such notions should simply be deconstructed and ignored. What, then, does it mean to "find" development in how high school students learn to learn in becoming fast food crew members? First, it means that if our society's dominant notion of progress were embedded in our theoretical framework, it would have precluded the possibility of seeing collateral transition as a form of horizontal development. Second, the fact that horizontal development does occur is consistent with a very local notion of progress bounded within fast food crew activity. It is related to other notions of developmental progress and activities, even if in opposition to them. Finally, it would be disingenuous to suggest that by showing that students are struggling to figure out how to learn in a production activity and that there is a developmental coupling, we are suggesting that there is more of value to becoming fast food crew than society acknowledges, that it is satisfying work that prepares students for future work, or that it allows workers to survive economically. It does, however, allow us to pose new questions about how horizontal development can take on the appearance of vertical progress during consequential transitions. It also allows us to move our beliefs about human progress out from behind psychological theorizing into the realm of education and society where they can be studied, critiqued, and, when deemed appropriate, altered.

A BRIEF REFLECTION ON OUR EXPEDITION

We have traveled a great distance in this chapter, beginning with the classic Buddhist philosophical concept of dependent origination. Dependent origination locates experiences of continuity and transformation in the interdependence of persons and social organizations. We discussed its relevance to current sociocultural perspectives on learning and development that share with it the premise that relations between persons and culture are recursive. We described the contrasting Platonic stance that locates epistemological continuity across space and time within the individual. The predominance of the Platonic position within American education and psychology was not just a function of shared cultural roots. The chapter's brief history of American education and transfer research showed how the needs, beliefs, and values of a growing public education movement intertwined with a fledgling scientific psychology to maintain a view of the individual as holder of knowledge, skill, and continuity, and as a perceiver of continuity in the world. That it has continued to predominate in the face of several decades of arguments across the Cartesian plane—problem isomorphisms versus abstraction/generalization strategies—is testament to this. Cognitive and sociocultural perspectives have each made their own contribution to this.

We moved on to an analysis of constructs based on the transfer metaphor. This was done to ground our journey in a full understanding of the ''soft spots'' of the transfer metaphor and its constructs: narrow definition, split agency, difficulty of facilitation, assumption of a static context, a launch model of person-environment relations, and difficulty distinguishing transfer from just plain learning. Task versus situation levels of analysis and intentional versus unintentional generalization were reconstrued as related phenomena rather than independent forms of transfer. One of the more important lessons learned was the need to discard transfer as a metaphor for what it is we are trying to understand and support.

I proposed a broadening of the phenomenon of concern to continuity and transformation in knowledge, skill, and identity across changing forms of social organization. Generalization is the shorthand term used for this broadened area of educational concern. In the present account, generalization is highly contextualized, involves multiple processes rather than a single procedure, includes changing social organizations as well as individuals, and reflects some notion of progress.

The construct of consequential transition was then introduced as a tool for understanding and facilitating this phenomenon of generalization. Consequential transition is consistent with the Buddhist philosophical concept of dependent origination and accepts the recursive nature of changing persons and social organizations. This concept of transition involves some form of consequential change in the relation between the individual and one or more social activities across time. Four forms of consequential transition—lateral, collateral, encompassing, and mediational—were illustrated through our studies. A new series of methodological tools for studying consequential transition—developmental coupling, leading activity, heterochronicity, and horizontal development—were also illustrated through our research. This leaves us moving in the direction of what all of this may mean for the practice of education.

TOWARD DISTANT SUMMITS: CONSEQUENTIAL TRANSITION IN EDUCATION

To the initial concern of how education can prepare children, adolescents, and adults to adapt to existing society, thereby maintaining some degree of continuity in collective values and beliefs, we add a second: how to prepare individuals to participate in the transformation of society. It is this second concern to which consequential transition is directed, although it necessarily presupposes the existence and legitimacy of the first. It is a concern that echoes from the writings of both Dewey and Vygotsky (Dewey, 1977; Prawat, in press; Vygotsky, 1987). Consequential transition is the conscious reflective struggle to reconstruct knowledge, skills, and identity in ways that are consequential to the individual becoming someone or something new, and in ways that contribute to the creation and metamorphosis of social activity and, ultimately, society.

Lateral and collateral transitions sanction a broader educational focus on students' participation across schools, families, workplaces, and communities. When in the student's life experiences these transitions occur, what the activities are, what the direction of the transition is between them, and how they relate to macro-level changes in society have everything to do with the development of knowledge, skill, and identity. Though consequential transitions emphasize the transformative or developmental aspects of education, they also situate the more stable-appearing reproductive aspects as a particular claim on societal values and beliefs about knowledge and skill, placing the oft-maligned "instructional delivery of subject matter'' within a set of concerns that are broader than just constructivist versus transmission models of teaching and learning.

Encompassing and mediational transitions sanction educational practices that enact change in the educational activities themselves and, thus, developmental changes in the coupling of students with activities that support learning. This may involve the expansion of classroom activities beyond the current schools and an expansion of our definition of schooling. It may involve the genesis of ''third activities'' that not only bridge the classroom with productive activities beyond but also give developmental direction to their relation. It may also involve local curricula affording student experiences in creating new systems of artifacts for particular mathematical, historical, literary, or scientific purposes: producing culture in addition to mastering that which already exists.

This is provocative stuff, and the big educational challenge does not appear to be how schools and teachers can facilitate students' transferring of knowledge and skills. In fact, as Bereiter (1995) notes, attempts to act on this challenge have ''added up to a sense that you cannot really teach people to act more intelligently, except in particular situations on particular tasks. This is a conclusion that, quite understandably, acts as a wet blanket on smoldering hopes for improving the human condition through education'' (p. 32). Our sociocultural reconceptualization of transfer as consequential transition also presents some challenges for how we do education, but, I believe, without the wet blanket.

Clearly, consequential transition happens without the intervention of teachers or schools. It happens at work and in our homes and communities. It also happens between school and these institutions. Therefore, schools need not struggle to be society's sole source of consequential transitions. Nor should we expect that all that we value in mathematics, science, history, literature, cultural understanding, and the arts can and should be invoked through consequential transition. This being said, there is much that we have yet to figure out about how schools can support students in becoming someone or something new, negotiating the boundaries of multiple and sometimes contradictory activities, and changing their participation in these activities as the activities themselves change.

The relation between changing students and social activities—their developmental coupling—is key not only to studying consequential transitions but to shaping their existence and course. If we accept that students' learning can change their relation to an activity, as can teaching, changes in curricular content, and new educational goals, then a myriad of possibilities are before us. We need to address what sorts of consequential transitions we wish to support through education, and which we choose to work against, for much that is consequential may not be what we hope for. Becoming a gang member, becoming homeless, becoming a dropout, and becoming a racist are all highly consequential transitions. The concepts of consequential transition, developmental coupling, heterochrony, and horizontal development do not allow such decisions to be hidden behind social scientific theorizing. Rather, decisions about which consequential transitions to support and which to work against need to be made ''out in the open,'' based on what we negotiate as our collective beliefs and values for our society.

There are, however, areas in which our program of theorizing and research can be of particular use as we move into the rich tradition of educational "design experiments": Cole's after-school computer clubs (Cole, 1996), Engeström's developmental work research (1993), Palincsar's reciprocal teaching (Palincsar & Brown, 1984), Moll's funds of community knowledge (Moll, 1992), Cobb's elementary math classrooms (Cobb, Gravemeijer, Yackel, McClain, & Whitenack, 1997), and Rogoff's communities of classroom practice (Rogoff, 1990).

We need to figure out how identity making, or identity craftwork as Lave (1996) describes it, can become an institutionally sanctioned part of acquiring knowledge and skills in classrooms in ways that it currently is not, but is in most other activities in which students participate. As Gover (in press) points out,

One would never think of claiming, for example, that their identity as individuals is entirely separable from the various kinds of knowledge they possess. After all, it is only by virtue of such knowledge (or its lack) that we are positioned relative to those around us. Looking at particular domains may make this more explicit. First, in the family-of-origin, one learns many things we would all recognize as basic to identity: how to talk, work, argue, play, love, and so forth. Next, qualified by the "directive force" of our own personal and cultural backgrounds (D'Andrade & Strauss, 1992, p. xi), we learn to negotiate the community's various ethnic and institutional cultures, a process synonymous with learning how to weave our identities into the larger society. Finally, in the workplace, our identity as workers is obviously tied up with what we know regarding our specific job or career. For example, one's identity as a doctor or mechanic cannot be divorced from the knowledge which allows one to assume such titles.

We need to understand how to "transfer" opportunities for learning by expanding the boundaries of school activity into culturally productive activities that are beyond its current purview and by creating new activities that mediate participation in schooling with the activities of other institutions. As Lemke (1997) describes it,

We need to extend the networks of the classroom and the school. To extend them into professional communities of practice. To extend them into the sphere of private life. To extend them into the sphere of direct political activity. To extend them into libraries and information worlds where there are no preferential barriers to crossing from one domain to another at will. To extend them into productive activities of our ecosocial system: industrial, agricultural, financial, informational. Most of all, we need to extend them outside the networks that define only masculine, heterosexual, middle-class, north-west European cultural values and historical traditions as normative and that seek to deny the already pervasive interpenetration of other networks and practices in our ecosocial systems. (p. 54)

This will not be easily accomplished, however, given the often competing or contradictory agendas of learning in school and agendas of other activities that place the achievement of consensus in a community, production on the job, or the raising of children in a family at the forefront, and where learning is organized as a partial means rather than an ultimate end.

Finally, we need to consider how to support students in learning to produce culture as well as reproduce it. In a recent article (Saito & Beach, in press), we make the point that most classroom-based problem solving works against the creation of new systems of artifacts by students and against the use of student-generated artifacts by other students. The notion that each student learns by recapitulating the entire process of solving a problem, although the problem may have been solved many times by others elsewhere, enacts the importance we place on each student reconstructing and coming to own preexisting cultural forms and functions. However, if we value the abilities that produce culture as well as reproduce it, then we need to consider how to foster students' experiences in doing so. One possibility for facilitating consequential transitions in schools involves opportunities for the longer term narrowing of distances between problems and solutions through the creation of new systems of artifacts. It also means the sharing of those artifacts with others, others who need not struggle with and relive the full history of the problem and its solution. Ultimately, this may be what makes transitions consequential.

REFERENCES

American heritage dictionary of the English language. (1976). Boston: Houghton Mifflin.

Anderson, J. R., Reder, L. M., & Simon, H. A. (1996). Situated learning and education. *Educational Researcher, 25*(4), 5–11.

Anderson, J. R., Reder, L. M., & Simon, H. A. (1997). Rejoinder: Situative versus cognitive perspectives: Form versus substance. *Educational Researcher, 26*(1), 18–21.

Beach, K. D. (1993). Becoming a bartender: The role of external memory cues in a work-directed educational activity. *Journal of Applied Cognitive Psychology, 7*, 191–204.

Beach, K. D. (1994, April). *A sociohistorical alternative to economic and cognitive transfer metaphors for understanding the transition from school to work*. Paper presented at the annual meeting of the American Educational Research Association.

Beach, K. D. (1995a). Sociocultural change, activity and individual development: Some methodological aspects. *Mind, Culture, and Activity, 2*, 277–284.

Beach, K. D. (1995b). Activity as a mediator of sociocultural change and individual development: The case of school-work transition in Nepal. *Mind, Culture, and Activity, 2*, 285–302.

Beach, K. D. (1997). Socially-organized learning and learning-organized practices [Review of Understanding practice: Perspectives on activity and context]. *Journal of Applied Cognitive Psychology, 11*, 104–105.

Beach, K. D. (in press-a). If not transfer, then what? *Journal of the Learning Sciences.*

Beach, K. D. (in press-b). Transfer as consequential transition. *Journal of the Learning Sciences.*

Beach, K. D. (in press-c). Studying recursive relations between persons and society in education. *Mind, Culture, and Activity.*

Beach, K. D. (in press-d). The concept of developmental coupling and the phenomenon of transfer. *Mind, Culture, and Activity.*

Beach, K. D., & Vyas, S. (1998). *Light pickles and heavy mustard: Horizontal development among students negotiating how to learn in a production activity*. Paper presented at the Third International Conference on Cultural Psychology and Activity Theory, Aarus, Denmark.

Bereiter, C. (1995). A dispositional view of transfer. In A. McKeough, J. Lupart, & A. Marini (Eds.), *Teaching for transfer: Fostering generalization in learning* (pp. 21–34). Mahwah, NJ: Erlbaum.

Bowers, J. (1996). *Conducting developmental research in a technology-enhanced classroom*. Unpublished doctoral dissertation, Vanderbilt University.

Bransford, J. D., Goldman, S. R., & Vye, N. J. (1991). Making a difference in people's abilities to think: Reflections on a decade of work and some hopes for the future. In L. Okagaki & R. J. Sternberg (Eds.), *Directors of development: Influences on children* (pp. 147–180). Hillsdale, NJ: Erlbaum.

Bransford, J. D., & Schwartz, D. L. (1999). Rethinking transfer: A simple proposal with multiple implications. In A. Iran-Nejad & P. D. Pearson (Eds.), *Review of research in education* (Vol. 24, pp. 61–101). Washington, DC: American Educational Research Association.

Brown, J. S., Collins, A., & Duguid, P. (1989). Situated cognition and the culture of learning. *Educational Researcher, 18*(1), 32–42.

Bruner, J. (1996). *The culture of education.* Cambridge, MA: Harvard University Press.

Calvino, I. (1972). *Invisible cities.* London: Picador.

Carraher, D., & Schilemann, A. (in press). The transfer dilemma. *Journal of the Learning Sciences.*

Cobb, P., & Bowers, J. (in press). Cognitive and situated learning perspectives in theory and practice. *Educational Researcher.*

Cobb, P., Gravemeijer, K., Yackel, E., McClain, K., & Whitenack, J. (1997). Mathematizing and symbolizing: The emergence of chains of signification in one first-grade classroom. In D. Kirshner & J. A. Whitson (Eds.), *Situated cognition: Social, semiotic, and psychological perspectives* (pp. 151–233). Mahwah, NJ: Erlbaum.

Cole, M. (1996). *Cultural psychology: A once and future discipline.* Cambridge, MA: Harvard University Press.

Cox, B. D. (1997). The rediscovery of the active learner in adaptive contexts: A developmental-historical analysis of transfer of training. *Educational Psychologist, 32*, 41–55.

Cremin, L. A. (1961). *The transformation of the school: Progressivism in American education, 1876–1957.* New York: Alfred A. Knopf.

D'Andrade, R. G., & Strauss, C. (Eds.). (1992). *Human motives and cultural models.* New York: Cambridge University Press.

Dansereau, D. F. (1995). Derived structural schemas and the transfer of knowledge. In A. McKeough, J. Lupart, & A. Marini (Eds.), *Teaching for transfer: Fostering generalization in learning* (pp. 93–122). Mahwah, NJ: Erlbaum.

Davydov, V. V. (1990). *Types of generalization in instruction: Logical and psychological problems in the structuring of school curricula* (Soviet Studies in Mathematics Education, Vol. 2). Reston, VA: National Council of Teachers of Mathematics.

Detterman, D. K. (1993). The case for the prosecution: Transfer as an epiphenomenon. In D. K. Detterman & R. J. Sternberg, *Transfer on trial: Intelligence, cognition, and instruction* (pp. 1–24). Norwood, NJ: Ablex.

Dewey, J. (1916). *Democracy and education: An introduction to the philosophy of education.* New York: Macmillan.

Dewey, J. (1977). The child and the curriculum. In J. A. Boydston (Ed.), *John Dewey: The middle works, 1899–1924* (Vol. 2, pp. 362–363). Carbondale: Southern Illinois University Press.

Dudjom Rinpoche. (1991). *The Ningma school of Tibetan Buddhism.* Boston: Wisdom.

Dyson, A. H. (1999). Transforming transfer: Unruly children, contrary texts, and the persistence of the pedagogical order. In A. Iran-Nejad & P. D. Pearson (Eds.), *Review of research in education* (Vol. 24, pp. 143–173). Washington, DC: American Educational Research Association.

Eckert, P. (1989). *Jocks and burnouts: Social categories and identity in the high school.* New York: Teachers College Press.

Engeström, Y. (1993). Developmental studies of work as a testbench of activity theory. In S. Chaiklin & J. Lave (Eds.), *Understanding practice: Perspectives on activity and context.* Cambridge, England: Cambridge University Press.

Engeström, Y. (1996). Development as breaking away and opening up: A challenge to Vygotsky and Piaget. *Swiss Journal of Psychology, 55,* 126–132.

Engeström, Y., Engeström, R., & Kärkkäinen, M. (1995). Polycontextuality and boundary crossing in expert cognition: Learning and problem solving in complex work activities. *Learning and Instruction, 5,* 319–336.

Evans, J. (in press). Building bridges: Reflections on the problem of transfer of learning in mathematics. *Educational Studies in Mathematics.*

Falmagne, R. J. (1995). The abstract and the concrete. In L. Martin, K. Nelson, & E. Tobach (Eds.), *Sociocultural psychology: Theory and practice of doing and knowing* (pp. 205–228). New York: Cambridge University Press.

Gee, J. P. (1992). *The social mind: Language, ideology, and social practice.* New York: Bergin & Garvey.

Gentner, D., & Gentner, D. R. (1983). Flowing waters or teeming crowds: Mental models of electricity. In D. Gentner & A. L. Stevens (Eds.), *Mental models* (pp. 99–129). Hillsdale, NJ: Erlbaum.

Gick, M. L., & Holyoak, K. J. (1983). Schema induction and analogical transfer. *Cognitive Psychology, 15,* 1–38.

Gover, M. (in press). Negotiating borders of self and other: Schools as sites for the construction of identity. *Mind, Culture, and Activity.*

Greeno, J. G. (1997). Response: On claims that answer the wrong questions. *Educational Researcher, 26*(1), 5–17.

Greeno, J. G., Smith, D. R., & Moore, J. L. (1993). Transfer of situated learning. In D. K. Detterman & R. J. Sternberg (Eds.), *Transfer on trial: Intelligence, cognition, and instruction* (pp. 99–127). Norwood, NJ: Ablex.

Gruber, H., Law, L., Mandl, H., & Renkl, A. (1996). Situated learning and transfer. In P. Reimann & H. Spada (Eds.), *Learning in humans and machines: Towards an interdisciplinary learning science* (pp. 168–188). Oxford, England: Pergamon Press.

Guberman, S. R., & Greenfield, P. M. (1991). Learning and transfer in everyday cognition. *Cognitive Development, 6,* 233–260.

Gutierrez, K., Rymes, B., & Larson, K. (1995). Script, counterscript, and underlife in the classroom: James Brown versus Brown v. Board of Education. *Harvard Educational Review, 65,* 445–471.

Harré, R., & Gillett, G. (1994). *The discursive mind.* Thousand Oaks, CA: Sage.

Hatano, G., & Inagaki, K. (1992). Desituating cognition through the construction of conceptual knowledge. In P. Light & G. Butterworth (Eds.), *Context and cognition: Ways of learning and knowing* (pp. 115–133). Hillsdale, NJ: Erlbaum.

Hayes, J. R., & Simon, H. A. (1977). Psychological differences among problem isomorphs. In J. Castellan, D. Pisoni, & G. Potts (Eds.), *Cognitive theory* (Vol. 2). Hillsdale, NJ: Erlbaum.

Heath, S. B. (1990). The children of Trackton's children. In J. W. Stigler, R. A. Shweder, & G. Herdt (Eds.), *Cultural psychology* (pp. 496–519). Cambridge, England: Cambridge University Press.

Herbst, D. P. (1995). What happens when we make a distinction: An elementary introduction to co-genetic logic. In T. A. Kindermann & J. Valsiner (Eds.), *Development of person-context relations* (pp. 67–79). Hillsdale, NJ: Erlbaum.

Hilgard, E. (1996). History of educational psychology. In D. C. Berliner & R. C. Calfee (Eds.), *Handbook of educational psychology* (pp. 990–1004). New York: Simon & Schuster.

Hoeg, P. (1994). *Borderliners.* New York: Farrar, Straus, & Giroux.

Holyoak, K. L., & Koh, K. (1987). Surface and structural similarity in analogical transfer. *Memory and Cognition, 15,* 332–340.

Hungwe, K. (1999). *Becoming a machinist in a changing industry.* Unpublished doctoral dissertation, Michigan State University.

Hungwe, K., & Beach, K. (1995, April). *Learning to become a machinist in a technologically changing industry.* Poster session presented at the annual meeting of the American Educational Research Association, San Francisco.

Hutchins, E. (1995). *Cognition in the wild.* Cambridge, MA: MIT Press.

Ilyenkov, E. V. (1977). *Dialectical logic.* Moscow: Progress.

John-Steiner, V., Mehan, T. M., & Mahn, H. (1998). A functional systems approach to concept development. *Mind, Culture, and Activity, 5,* 127–134.

Judd, C. H. (1915). *The psychology of high school subjects.* Boston: Ginn.

Kindermann, T., & Skinner, E. A. (1992). Modeling environmental development: Individual and contextual trajectories. In J. B. Asendorpf & J. Valsiner (Eds.), *Stability and change in development* (pp. 155–190). London: Sage.

Kindermann, T., & Valsiner, J. (1989). Research strategies in culture-inclusive developmental psychology. In J. Valsiner (Ed.), *Child development in cultural context* (pp. 13–50). Lewiston, NY: Hogrefe & Huber.

Kindermann, T. A., & Valsiner, J. (1995). Introduction: Individual development, changing contexts, and the co-construction of person-context relations in human development. In T. A. Kindermann & J. Valsiner (Eds.), *Development of person-context relations* (pp. 1–12). Hillsdale, NJ: Erlbaum.

Kirshner, D., & Whitson, J. A. (Eds.). (1997). *Situated cognition: Social, semiotic, and psychological perspectives.* Mahwah, NJ: Erlbaum.

Laboratory for Comparative Human Cognition. (1986). Culture and cognitive development. In W. Kessen (Ed.), *Manual of child psychology: History, theory, and methods* (pp. 295–356). New York: Wiley.

Lagemann, E. (1988). The plural worlds of educational research. *History of Education Quarterly, 29,* 184–214.

Lareau, A. (1989). *Home advantage.* New York: Falmer Press.

Lave, J. (1988). *Cognition in practice.* New York: Cambridge University Press.

Lave, J. (1996). Teaching, as learning, in practice. *Mind, Culture, and Activity, 3,* 149–164.

Lave, J., & Wenger, E. (1991). *Situated learning: Legitimate peripheral participation.* New York: Cambridge University Press.

Lemke, J. (1997). Cognition, context, and learning: A social semiotic perspective. In D. Kirshner & J. A. Whitson (Eds.), *Situated cognition: Social, semiotic, and psychological perspectives* (pp. 37–56). Mahwah, NJ: Erlbaum.

Leont'ev, A. N. (1978). *Activity, consciousness, and personality.* Englewood Cliffs, NJ: Prentice Hall.

Leont'ev, A. N. (1981). The problem of activity in psychology. In J. V. Wertsch (Ed.), *The concept of activity in Soviet psychology* (pp. 37–71). Armonk, NY: Sharpe.

Lobato, J. E. (1996). *Transfer reconceived: How sameness is produced in mathematical activity.* Unpublished doctoral dissertation, University of California, Berkeley.

Marini, A., & Genereux, R. (1995). The challenge of teaching for transfer. In A. McKeough, J. Lupart, & A. Marini (Eds.), *Teaching for transfer: Fostering generalization in learning* (pp. 1–20). Mahwah, NJ: Erlbaum.

Martin, L. W., & Beach, K. D. (1992). *Technical and symbolic knowledge in CNC machining: A study of technical workers of different backgrounds.* Berkeley: National Center for Research on Vocational Education, University of California.

Martin, L. W., & Scribner, S. (1992). Laboratory for cognitive studies of work: A case study of the intellectual implications of a new technology. *Teachers College Record, 92,* 582–602.

Martin, L. W., Shirley, M., & McGinnis, M. (1988). Microworlds to macroworlds: An experiment in the conceptual transfer of ecological concepts. *Children's Environments Quarterly, 5*(4), 32–38.

Maturana, H. (1975). The organization of the living: A theory of the living organization. *International Journal of Man-Machine Studies, 7,* 313–332.

Maturana, H., & Varela, F. (1980). *Autopoiesis and cognition: The realization of the living* (Boston Studies in the Philosophy of Science, Vol. 42). Dordecht, the Netherlands: Reidel.

Mayer, R. E. (1992). Teaching for transfer of problem solving skills to computer programming. In E. De Corte, M. C. Linn, & L. Verschaffel (Eds.), *Computer-based learning environments and problem solving* (pp. 193–206). Berlin: Springer-Verlag.

Mayer, R. E., & Whitrock, M. C. (1996). Problem-solving transfer. In D. C. Berliner & R. C. Calfee (Eds.), *Handbook of educational psychology* (pp. 47–62). New York: Simon & Schuster.

Moll, L. C. (1992). Funds of knowledge for teaching: Using a qualitative approach to connect homes and schools. *Theory into Practice, 31,* 132–141.

Nemirovsky, R. (in press). How does one experience become part of another? *Journal of the Learning Sciences.*

Nicolopoulou, A., & Cole, M. (1993). Generation and transmission of shared knowledge in the culture of collaborative learning: The fifth dimension, its play-world, and its institutional contexts. In E. A. Forman, N. Minick, & C. A. Stone (Eds.), *Contexts for learning* (pp. 283–314). New York: Oxford University Press.

Noss, R., & Hoyles, C. (1996). The visibility of meanings: Modeling the mathematics of banking. *International Journal for Computers in Math Learning, 1*(1), 3–30.

Nunes, T., Carraher, D. W., & Schilemann, A. D. (1993). *Street mathematics and school mathematics.* New York: Cambridge University Press.

Packer, M. (in press). The problem of transfer, and the sociocultural critique of schooling. *Journal of the Learning Sciences.*

Palincsar, A. M., & Brown, A. L. (1984). Reciprocal teaching of comprehension-fostering and comprehension-monitoring activities. *Cognition and Instruction, 1,* 117–175.

Pea, R. D. (1987). Socializing the knowledge transfer problem. *International Journal of Educational Research, 11,* 639–664.

Plato. (1961). *Meno.* Cambridge, England: Cambridge University Press.

Prawat, R. S. (in press). Cognitive theory at the crossroads: Head fitting, head splitting, or somewhere in between? *Human Development.*

Pressley, M. (1995). A transactional strategies instruction Christmas carol. In A. McKeough, J. Lupart, & A. Marini (Eds.), *Teaching for transfer: Fostering generalization in learning* (pp. 177–214). Mahwah, NJ: Erlbaum.

Reed, S. K. (1993). A schema-based theory of transfer. In D. K. Detterman & R. J. Sternberg (Eds.), *Transfer on trial: Intelligence, cognition, and instruction* (pp. 39–67). Norwood, NJ: Ablex.

Reineke, J. W. (1995). *To home and back: The influence of students' conversations on their completion of school mathematics tasks.* Unpublished doctoral dissertation, Michigan State University.

Reineke, J. W. (in press). Homework conversations: Connecting home and school. *Journal of the Learning Sciences.*

Rogoff, B. (1990). *Apprenticeship in thinking: Cognitive development in social context.* New York: Oxford University Press.

Rogoff, B., & Gardner, W. (1984). Adult guidance of cognitive development. In B. Rogoff & J. Lave (Eds.), *Everyday cognition: Its development in social context* (pp. 95–116). Cambridge, MA: Harvard University Press.

Rommetveit, R. (1990). On axiomatic features of a dialogical approach to language and mind. In I. Markova & K. Foppa (Eds.), *The dynamics of dialogue.* Hemel Hempstead, England: Harvester Press.

Saito, S., & Beach, K. D. (in press). A lesson in consequential problem solving located between a changing society and developing individuals. *Mind, Culture, and Activity.*

Salomon, G., & Perkins, D. (1989). Rocky roads to transfer: Rethinking mechanisms of a neglected phenomenon. *Educational Psychologist, 24,* 113–142.

Salomon, G., & Perkins, D. N. (1998). Individual and social aspects of learning. In P. D. Pearson & A. Iran-Nejad (Eds.), *Review of research in education* (Vol. 23, pp. 1–24). Washington, DC: American Educational Research Association.

Saxe, G. B. (1989). Transfer of learning across cultural practices. *Cognition and Instruction, 6,* 325–330.

Saxe, G. B. (1991). *Culture and cognitive development: Studies in mathematical understanding.* Hillsdale, NJ: Erlbaum.

Sayeki, Y., Ueno, N., & Nagasaka, T. (1991). Mediation as a generative mode for obtaining an area. *Learning and Instruction, 1,* 229–242.

Secretary's Commission on Achieving Necessary Skills. (1991). *What work requires of schools: A SCANS report for America 2000.* Washington, DC: U.S. Department of Labor.

Shotter, J. (1993). *Cultural politics of everyday life.* Toronto: University of Toronto Press.

Shulman, L. S., & Quinlan, K. M. (1996). The comparative psychology of school subjects. In D. C. Berliner & R. C. Calfee (Eds.), *Handbook of educational psychology* (pp. 399–422). New York: Simon & Schuster.

Shweder, R. A. (1980). Rethinking culture and personality theory: From genesis and typology to hermeneutics and dynamics (Part 3). *Ethos, 8,* 60–94.

Shweder, R. A. (1991). *Thinking through cultures: Expeditions in cultural psychology.* Cambridge, MA: Harvard University Press.

Singley, M. K. (1995). Promoting transfer through model tracing. In A. McKeough, J. Lupart, & A. Marini (Eds.), *Teaching for transfer: Fostering generalization in learning* (pp. 69–93). Mahwah, NJ: Erlbaum.

Singley, M. K., & Anderson, J. R. (1989). *The transfer of cognitive skill.* Cambridge, MA: Harvard University Press.

Star, S. L. (1989). *Regions of the mind: Brain research and the quest for scientific certainty.* Stanford, CA: Stanford University Press.

Star, S. L. (1996). Working together: Symbolic interactionism, activity theory, and information systems. In Y. Engeström & D. Middleton (Eds.), *Cognition and communication at work* (pp. 296–318). New York: Cambridge University Press.

Thorndike, E. L., & Woodworth, R. S. (1901). The influence of one mental function upon the efficiency of other functions. *Psychological Review, 8,* 247–251, 384–395, 553–564.

Thurman, R. A. F. (1984). *The central philosophy of Tibet.* Princeton, NJ: Princeton University Press.

Tolman, C. W. (1991). Critical psychology: An overview. In C. W. Tolman & W. Maiers (Eds.), *Critical psychology: Contributions to an historical science of the subject* (pp. 1–22). New York: Cambridge University Press.

Valsiner, J. (1989). *Human development and culture.* Lexington, MA: Heath.

Valsiner, J. (1994). Bidirectional cultural transmission and constructive sociogenesis. In W. D. Graaf & R. Maier (Eds.), *Sociogenesis reexamined* (pp. 47–70). New York: Springer-Verlag.

van Oers, B. (1998). The fallacy of decontextualization. *Mind, Culture, and Activity, 5,* 135–142.

Varela, F. J. (1981). Autonomy and autopoiesis. In R. Gerhard & H. Schwegler (Eds.), *Self-organizing systems: An interdisciplinary approach* (pp. 14–23). New York: Springer-Verlag.

Varela, F. J., Thompson, E., & Rosch, E. (1991). *The embodied mind: Cognitive science and human experience.* Cambridge, MA: MIT Press.

Vygotsky, L. S. (1978). *Mind in society: The development of higher psychological processes.* Cambridge, MA: Harvard University Press.

Vygotsky, L. S. (1987). *The collected works of L. S. Vygotsky: Vol. 1. Problems of general psychology* (N. Minick, Ed. and Trans.). New York: Plenum.

Walkerdine, V. (1988). *The mastery of reason.* London: Routledge.

Wartofsky, M. W. (1979). *Models.* Boston: Reidel.

Wenger, E. (1998). *Communities of practice: Learning, meaning, and identity.* New York: Cambridge University Press.

Wertsch, J. V. (1985). *Vygotsky and the social formation of mind.* Cambridge, MA: Harvard University Press.

Wertsch, J. V. (1998). *Mind as action.* New York: Oxford University Press.

Whitson, J. A. (1997). Cognition as a semiotic process: From situated mediation to critical reflective transcendence. In D. Kirshner & J. A. Whitson (Eds.), *Situated cognition: Social, semiotic, and psychological perspectives* (pp. 97–150). Mahwah, NJ: Erlbaum.

Wilcox, C., & Beach, K. D. (1996). *Order in the court: The development of a play activity and its elementary school participants.* Paper presented at the biannual meeting of the International Society for the Study of Behavioral Development, Quebec City.

W. T. Grant Foundation. (1988). *The forgotten half: Non-college youth in America.* Washington, DC: Commission on Work, Family, and Citizenship.

Manuscript received December 28, 1998
Accepted March 31, 1999

Chapter 5

Transforming Transfer: Unruly Children, Contrary Texts, and the Persistence of the Pedagogical Order

ANNE HAAS DYSON
University of California, Berkeley

I am going to mova
on Wednes day We
Are FaMaLe I got All my
sisrs AND ME

It is odd, very odd, to be writing about "transfer," given that my imagination has been preoccupied of late by young schoolchildren like 6-year-old Denise, the author of the preceding text. Denise liked to play KMEL (the local hip hop radio station) and, along with her friend Vanessa, often displayed her sense of the rhythmic rhyming style of the current youth scene. She sometimes transferred this material from her unofficial school activities to her official ones, including her daily writing workshop entries. The text shown is an entry about an upcoming family move, and those familiar lines about family and sisters were quite deliberately taken from Whoopi Goldberg in the film *Sister Act II* (Steel, Rudin, & Duke, 1994).

Although Denise and Vanessa were unique personalities, not so unique was the ease with which they transferred unofficial cultural materials to official school contexts (i.e., applied them in new ways). Cartoons, video games, recent films, and radio songs—as well as school reading materials—all were potential sources of genres, textual elements, and appealing utterances ("We are family") for child writing. In an ongoing project, I am focusing on what schoolchildren appropriate from textual practices located outside the official school world and, thus, the cultural, social, and semiotic negotiations that ensue inside the official world between and among children, teachers, and texts. In the midst of this work, then, comes an invitation to write about "transfer," and I, of course, am at least partially oriented the wrong way around.

In educational psychology circles, transfer has been set firmly within an official school frame: It involves learners' possession of the necessary intellectual

The research reported herein was supported in part by the Spencer Foundation. I would like to thank my project research assistant, Soyoung Lee, and my consulting editors, Celia Genishi and Sonia Nieto. Although I have benefitted enormously from the thoughtful support of all named, the responsibility for the findings and opinions expressed here rests solely with me.

resources, gained through a designated "learning task"; their ability and motivation to retrieve taught resources for the targeted "transfer task"; and their recognition of the *relevance* of those resources (see Marini & Genereux, 1995). In this chapter, I use my academic disorientation to offer a critical consideration and redefinition of transfer; in this redefinition, transfer involves negotiation between and among teachers and learners, as frames of reference for judging "relevant" material are themselves differentiated and expanded. A critical rethinking of transfer seems in order, since the traditional notion has not fared well in educational research, even as it has continued its dominance in educational practice.

Beginning with Thorndike at the turn of the century, researchers have found it very hard to arrange for students' transfer of knowledge and skills from the "learning" task to a related but different one. The comments of first-grade teacher Carolyn Howard-McBride are consistent with research findings:

One time a kid said to me ["How do you spell *thing*?"]. I said that it was the spelling word from last week, and [he] said, "Oh, is that the same one?" You know, there was no connection. (Dyson, 1997, p. 76)

There was no connection, that is, between one learning task (a word on a spelling list) and an application task (composing a text). In formal studies of transfer, students rarely realize that a "learning" task and a "transfer" task are similar, sometimes despite explicit experimenter cues (Detterman & Sternberg, 1993).

Given this difficulty, theorists have offered the following: accounts of learners' own construction of knowledge, task designs that aim to foster cognitive strategies (i.e., learners' ways of paying attention and of integrating knowledge and skills), and, most recently, reconceptions of knowledge and skills themselves as not individual possessions but contextualized sociocognitive actions that must be recontextualized if transfer is to occur (for discussions, see McKeough, Lupart, & Marini, 1995). And yet, despite these efforts, traditional (if not magical) notions of transfer seem to be firmly in place in many of our schools (Berliner & Biddle, 1995; Goodlad, 1984). Indeed, as Berliner and Biddle discuss, our politicians throughout the Bush and into the Clinton era have favored a view of schools as "mechanisms for pumping bits of knowledge . . . into passive students" (1995, p. 300). The latest round of public concern about child literacy has provided abundant examples, as politicians, commentators, and educators often seem to assume that if children are taught the phonics ropes, in carefully sequenced order, they will be able to apply that learning and scale any textual mountain (for a startlingly clear illustration, see Saunders, 1997).

In this chapter, I suggest one potential contributor to this persistent desire for a homogenizing pedagogic order (i.e., the one-way transmission of skills and knowledge): the persistence of the underlying ideological order (i.e., the frames of reference that guide how adults, including researchers, interpret children and judge their "normalcy" and the "relevance" of their experiential and linguistic resources). This factor, like many others orchestrated in particular sites (e.g., stretched funding, reduced expectations, alienated communities), is especially salient in schools serving low-income and minority children, children stereotyped as less academically able (Anyon, 1997; Oakes, 1985).

I begin by describing the theoretical perspectives that undergird this concern with a persisting ideological order. I then discuss selected research efforts to transform traditional notions of transfer in young children's literacy learning. I illustrate how dominant attempts to transform transfer have been limited by the homogenization of children, their "relevant" literacy resources, and "effective" learning contexts. This homogenization is particularly striking given the complex, contested worlds of contemporary classrooms, "where students and teachers increasingly inhabit different conceptual worlds and participate in different information and social networks" (Green, 1993, p. 208). I conclude with a discussion of how a rethinking of transfer might allow educators to use that classroom complexity to further children's literacy learning.

To clarify my ideas, I use classroom vignettes drawn from my research over the years on child writing, including the ongoing project featuring Denise and her peers. The overriding research goals of all three cited projects have been to understand the kinds of social, semiotic, and language resources that may figure into children's literacy learning and, just as important, the kinds of classroom dynamics that support or hinder children's ability to be judged "competent" learners. The overriding methodological approach of all projects has been a qualitative one focused on the interplay between children's participation in official and unofficial (peer-governed) school life. In their own social worlds, children reveal a diversity of resources, but those resources are not necessarily visible— or recognized—in official worlds.

All of the studied classrooms have been located, for me, in local public schools, all racially integrated ones in which African-American children have been a dominant group; many of my focal children have been African American and from low-income backgrounds (i.e., they qualify for the school lunch programs), as were Denise and other children featured herein. These studies have yielded detailed, analytic narratives about specific children in specific settings, narratives that may be compared with equally detailed accounts of other children in other settings. In this way, I hope to offer useful perspectives for conceptualizing child literacy. Thus, study conclusions do not involve any one population of children; rather, they involve my examined phenomenon, that is, the social, cultural, and ideological nature and dynamics of teaching and learning literacy in classrooms.

Ultimately, I hope this chapter, like the larger research projects upon which it draws, contributes to our collective efforts to make schooling something other than an irrelevant, disconnected experience, to make it an experience inextricably connected to, and expansive of, all children's worlds.

"STRUCTURES OF AGENCY": CONSTRUCTING RELEVANT FRAMES

In opening this essay with Denise's piece about an upcoming family move, I situated the activity (i.e., writing about transfer) within a framework (children's literacy) that makes sense to me. Having the freedom (within certain specified parameters) to make my knowledge and experiences relevant to an unexpected task allowed me to proceed—and, before too long, the concept of transfer allowed me to view my knowledge and experiences in new ways. Within the definition I am working toward herein, this expanding of perspectives, of frames of reference, is what "transfer" involves. Unfortunately, in constructing a frame that makes my experiences relevant, I am indulging in a luxury of the well positioned, one denied many children. Gaining insight into this denial requires a consideration of how researchers and children construct frames, as well as how texts mediate those constructions.

Researchers

Underlying this chapter is an interpretivist approach to research, one informed by contemporary cultural studies (Grossberg, Nelson, & Treichler, 1992). From an interpretivist perspective, researchers aim to understand some aspect of human experience (e.g., literacy teaching and learning) as it is situated within people's everyday worlds (Geertz, 1973). In classroom settings, then, researchers examine how teachers and children jointly construct the meaning of classroom activities, procedures, and materials (Erickson, 1986). Teachers' pedagogical behaviors do not cause children's learning behaviors: There is no one-way transmission of teacher or "expert" knowledge, nor is it assumed that children or "novices" interpret ostensibly the same teaching methods in the same way. Rather, teachers and children interpret each other's actions and make, what seem to them, relevant responses.

Guided by recent insights from cultural studies (e.g., Storey, 1998; Williams, 1980; Willis, 1990), interpretivist researchers may complicate their visions of active classroom participants. They may assume that participants' agency—their sense (or consciousness) of their own possibilities for action—is guided by frameworks that originate far beyond (but are deeply embedded within) the classroom walls. Ortner elaborates:

There is an insistence, as in earlier structural-determinist models, that human action is constrained by the given social and cultural order (often condensed in the term "structure"); but there is also an insistence that human action *makes* "structure"—reproduces or transforms it, or both. (1996, p. 2)

Particular frameworks for sense making (e.g., disciplinary discourses, religious or gender ones, or those of peer worlds or families) can be imagined as sets of circulating texts that, when articulated in particular settings, read out or energize certain characters in certain roles, some more powerful than others (Fiske, 1993; Foucault, 1972, 1979). Those characters make judgments about the relevant means for responding to others, given a certain context, a certain role (e.g., a researcher, a woman, a student, a peer). But those characters are not puppets; they (we) are intentional beings who may not only enact but also resist or, at least, negotiate their actions. Moreover, there are many such frameworks, and, in their interplay, spaces for the unexpected are revealed: Denise, at once an aspiring performer, a competent student, and a sister, revoiced the cinematic words of Whoopi Goldberg's singing nun in her school composition (and they both appear in this academic's text about "transfer").

One basic research goal, then, is to use particular methods of observation and analysis to understand *others'* understandings (their sense of what is happening and, therefore, what is relevant) and the processes through which they enact aspects of their daily life (like learning to write). The necessarily reflexive nature of such work has been much discussed as of late (Clifford & Marcus, 1986; Emerson, Fretz, & Shaw, 1995): Understanding others' "sense" entails differentiating and becoming aware of one's own—itself always a process, never a fait accompli. But all researchers, whatever their theoretical bent (like all human agents), act within societal frameworks.

From this point of view, then, the actions of all participants in the classroom are intertwined. All "cope" with new material, the unfamiliar, by situating it within what may be taken-for-granted frames of reference that inform action (Bruner & Haste, 1987, p. 3). Given ideological gaps in these frames (gaps related to age, social class, culture, and role, for example), those of the dominant players in particular settings (classroom, school, university) may prevail, making invisible (making nonsense of) the others' actions. Freire expressed the idea as follows: "Many persons, bound to a mechanistic view of reality, do not perceive that the concrete situation of individuals conditions their consciousness of the world, and that in turn this consciousness conditions their attitudes and their ways of dealing with reality" (1970, p. 111).

Learning Children

This perspective on research is compatible with certain sociocultural views of learning inspired by Vygotsky (1978; e.g., Rogoff, 1990; Wertsch, 1985, 1991). In these views, children are seen as social beings who develop frameworks for "making sense" by participating in the recurrent activities of everyday life (Bruner & Haste, 1987). Their learning is mediated by—is revealed and accomplished through—socially organized and often language-mediated activities (Rogoff, 1990). Although adults offer guidance of varied types (arranging the environment, modeling, guiding, informing), children themselves are active, observing, participating, at times "even demand[ing] the assistance of those around them" (Rogoff, 1990, p. 17).

Skills and understandings thus are organized by, and occur in service of, goal-directed, socially situated activities. Moreover, these activities "come packed with values about what is natural, mature, morally right, or aesthetically pleasing" (Miller & Goodnow, 1995, p. 6). These are interwoven into the background of shared activities within which language itself emerges (Bruner, 1990; Miller & Mehler, 1994). In this way, children's subjectivities (their senses of themselves and their own possibilities for action) develop along with their symbolic resources and cognitive capacities.

Over time, children's interpretations (their sense of activities' functional possibilities) change, as do the social roles (responsibilities) they assume and the means (skills and concepts) they control. If and how learners transfer particular means across activities cannot be separated from the activities themselves and how they are socially framed and arranged (Rogoff, Radziszewska, & Masiello, 1995). If learning involves more than responding appropriately to tasks' stimuli (Thorndike's view), if it involves participating appropriately in socially organized activities, then learners are dependent not only on guiding teachers but also on features of activities that make relevant their developing resources (e.g., particular goals, social relationships, cultural tools [including speech], and traditions or routines that link activities in disciplines or other organizational schemes; Rogoff, Radziszewska, & Masiello, 1995; for pedagogical examples, see Moll & Whitmore, 1993).

In this view, schooling continues the learning process begun in the home, providing cultural symbolic forms, including written language and disciplinary taxonomies and genres, that help children gain distance from, differentiate, and recontextualize their everyday experiences with and within the "scientific" discourses of school (Vygotsky, 1962). In a well-developed discussion of this process, Nelson (1996) argues that, within young children's family lives, everyday experiences are organized in family-situated narratives that are overlain with complex understandings, including, for example, discourses of "time, space, geography, religion, gender roles, biology, and the natural world" (p. 218). In school, these "overlain" understandings are differentiated, interrelated, and elaborated through instructional activities that, at least theoretically, allow children to recontextualize (transfer) skills and concepts in (to) broader frames of reference.

Ultimately, what Nelson "finds"—or hopes for, perhaps—is "a seamless weaving together of individual experience-based constructions in collaboration with others, gradually incorporating the potential of social and cultural forms" learned in school (Nelson, 1996, p. 352). Such seamless accounts, however, can only go so far in accounting for children's school experiences, which are full of gaps, loose edges, and dangling threads. Schools, as institutional contexts, are often not known for the "intersubjectivity" (the common assumptions) that provides a smooth transition between homes and classrooms. Schools are places where "different groups with distinct political, economic, and cultural visions" do not necessarily agree on which skills and concepts are neatly categorized as scientific or canonical (Apple, 1993, p. 26) and where literacy instruction in particular is "as much about ideologies, identities, and values as it is about codes and skills" (Luke, 1994, p. 9).

Unstable Texts

As sociocultural activities, literacy events are not static determiners of what and how children learn. Rather, they are ongoing accomplishments negotiated by children and other participants as they respond to each other. In this negotiating, participants decide what is salient about the activity and, therefore, how they should respond (i.e., what relevant resources they have). Their responses index— or situate the activity within—different contextual frameworks (Bauman & Briggs, 1990). For example, a child who responds to a school literature study activity with a text based on a popular video has situated that activity differently in social and cultural worlds.

As illustrated by Denise's opening text, children seem to assume or spontaneously construct links between texts and contexts that adults may consider generically very different (Dyson, 1993b, 1997; Garvey, 1990; Jenkins, 1988; Opie & Opie, 1959; Paley, 1986). Part of becoming more deliberate, more "socioideological[ly] language conscious," is to become more actively aware of language's heteroglossia and of "the necessity of having to choose" one's words, of situating oneself in a complex world of multiple frames (Bakhtin, 1981, p. 295). However, this sort of growth is required not only of children but also of adults, whose discursive ways often render social worlds and hierarchies invisible. In Williams's words,

The educational institutions are usually the main agencies of the transmission of an effective dominant culture. . . . But always the selectivity is the point; the way in which from a whole possible area of past and present, certain meanings and practices are chosen for emphasis, certain other meanings and practices are neglected and excluded . . . reinterpreted [and] diluted. (1980, p. 39)

Authors present texts in ways that are "contingent upon their being framed as embodiments of shared beliefs and understandings" (Briggs, 1996, p. 14). More particular to this essay, authors may frame discussions of "literacy development" in ways that take for granted the truth, the goodness, of a shared experience—a "we experience" (Volosinov, 1973, p. 8; see also Dyson, 1995; Genishi, 1997; Schieffelin & Cochran-Smith, 1984). The invisibility of children's frames of reference contributes to the pedagogical dominance of traditional discourse on transfer: If frames of reference are taken for granted, then dominant players in school settings may see children only as individuals who learn with varied degrees of success (Foucault, 1979); children's identities and relationships, their knowledge and skills grounded in sources other than the school (or the "proper" home), may be filtered out, and what may be left are decontextualized children who make no official sense. Accordingly, unruly children must be fixed—not situated, learned from, and guided into new realms.

"YOU CAN'T GET THERE FROM HERE!": TRANSFER AND THE LITERACY ROUTE

At one time or another the importance of each basic element of transfer—task, learner, and context— has been emphasized by educational theorists. Given that each element plays a key role in the transfer process, taking all three into account when designing instruction is most advisable. A trend in this direction, toward a more wholistic approach to achieving transfer, is apparent. (Marini & Genereux, 1995, p. 5)

In discussions of young children's literacy (and of "implications for instruction"), this general trend can be discerned, as attention has moved from tasks to learners and contexts. Shortly after the time of Thorndike (in the 1930s), "reading readiness" was thought to be a matter of the right age (about 6½ years), when a host of general skills and concepts would allow the child to learn easily. During the 1960s, however, there was a mushrooming of readiness programs with *tasks* designed to promote these skills—and fill the instructional gap between school entry and the point of maturity. This was a clear boon for publishers—and a seeming bust for children and teachers.

Researchers questioned the transfer value of these programs' tasks, which fragmented reading and writing into a host of isolated visual, auditory, and motor tasks. Nonetheless, structured reading programs for young children have become commonplace in early schooling, consisting heavily of workbooks and worksheets especially oriented toward letters and letter sounds (see Feitelson, 1988, for a discussion of readiness programs; see Stallman & Pearson, 1990, for a discussion of tests).

Despite—and, partially, in response to—these programs, by the 1970s, researchers had begun to describe *learners* who were already skilled at school entry; indeed, many could "write now, read later" (Chomsky, 1971). Researchers argued that children's literacy knowledge and know-how did not transfer from home to school contexts, because their pattern-detecting, constructivist strategies were constrained by programs that fed them one literacy bit at a time (letters, sounds, sight words), making problematic engagement with the holistic processes of reading and writing.

Furthermore, in the 1980s and 1990s, there has been much theoretical interest in the nature of learning *contexts*, in large part as a result of the influence of Vygotsky (1978). In this work, effective contexts for learning and transfer involve interaction between child apprentices and expert others; good teachers, like good mothers, interactively guide children's attention within wholistic tasks, helping them orchestrate, apply, and extend their resources (Sowers, 1985).

And yet, this movement toward "wholism" has not been smooth. Most important for this chapter, a desire for a singular route to literacy, along with a limited vision of both literacy and resources for literacy learning, has allowed many children to slip from the discursive path, the "normal" route, becoming visible only in discussions of "retention," "remediation," or "recovery" from the experience of literacy education.

From the Task to the Learner: Alphabet (Road) Blocks on the Home/School Route

Concern for the transfer potential of the proliferating readiness programs for young children was realized in dramatically different professional texts. The most influential texts describing child writers were about middle-class, European Americans—often academics' own children. And "other" children? They were a silent backdrop, having been featured in texts by psychologists who also did not want to waste time on nontransferable "readiness" tasks—but who did want to dive right into the skills thought most apt to transfer to success in the first-grade curriculum. This striking difference in textual presentations, constructed in the very beginnings of intense interest in early literacy, can be found in unstable texts that echo today. These texts have deeply tangled notions of "our" children and "yours," of "empowering" and "disempowering," of curricula that provide children from "poor" homes "head starts" in the competitive school race and, at the same time, bring others from "rich" homes to a screeching halt on a race they seemingly have already won.

In the following subsections, I highlight selected professional texts in order to illustrate this instability. These texts are primarily research-based guides rather than research reports, since it is such texts that have echoed most persistently in the literature on early written language. I should note (to be properly "reflexive" perhaps, or horribly "irrelevant," depending on one's frame of mind) that I also chose these texts because they were professionally memorable for me. I encountered the first, Bereiter and Engelmann (1966), as an education major in the late 1960s. It was my first encounter with "poverty," not as a virtue (as the village priest would have it) or as protection against being spoiled (as my mother would have it) but as a predictor of intellectual trouble. I met the other texts cited—those on invented spelling and process writing—in the 1970s, as a first-grade teacher in an urban bilingual school. I was heartened and informed by the burgeoning interest in children's writing—and startled by the texts' didactic tone (the rush to generalize), especially given the vision of the child writer being constructed, one mighty similar to the ideal child haunting Bereiter and Engelmann's text.

Before turning to these texts, however, I begin with a classroom scene featuring a 5-year-old kindergartner, Callie. This scene dramatizes the potential gaps between official frames and children's experiences, gaps that make transfer of one's resources difficult.

Missed Connections: Children and Teacher in Search of a Frame

Today, in the kindergarten, Callie's teacher has decided to try a new kind of writing task. After months of having children copy sentences from the board, complete phonics worksheets, and, more recently, fill in blanks in those sentences with optional words, Ms. Lin has decided to do "free" writing: The children can choose their own topics and invent their own spellings. Callie takes the new task in stride. She usually copies from the board—and fills in blanks—by carefully coordinating her efforts with those of the children around her. Aiming to follow her teacher's directions, she tends to double-check her actions with others (e.g., "Do we suppose to write the one [the word] that gots the G?" and "Do we gotta write [points to a word] three times?"), evidencing only a vague sense of what exactly she is copying.

In the free writing task, she tries to proceed similarly. Her usual questions about procedure will not help this time, however; there is no set procedure. Callie glances around at her peers, trying to maneuver herself to see their papers. Finally, she copies the most available bit of print: peers' displayed name cards. When she has gotten as many letters as she can, she adds others, seemingly randomly.

A quiet, familiar observer, I intervene and ask Callie what she is writing; in response, she examines her letters and seemingly notices the letters *ET*, and the resulting extraterrestrial's name (Spielberg & Kennedy, 1982) and my question seem to inspire a plan: She is going to write about another media character—King Kong, who "dropped a lady in the water." She proceeds quietly, making letters. She reads her final product to her teacher as follows:

Carragirtri [Craig] RaiKra [Keith] AigjgET [ET]
Atth [A] Riira [King] airraggttra [Pacman]
Riars [ghost] IaBKitahr [Monster] Itirt [Kong]
BADth [eat] ADDEF [Pacman]
DEFGEE [up] EFGE ET

Callie was a focal student in a study of young children's ways of interpreting common school literacy tasks (i.e., copying brief texts from the board, filling words in blanks, and, finally, "free" writing encouraging child "invention" of spelling) (Dyson, 1984). In general, the study's findings were compatible with research on transfer in young children's learning. In Wood's words, if children "do not know what is relevant to the questions asked [or the task as set] and, hence, cannot analyze and grasp what they need to take into account, if they are unsure of the experimenter's [or teacher's] motives or . . . if they assume that there is more to the problem than meets the eye," they will appear "incompetent" (Wood, 1988, p. 53; see also Donaldson, 1978).

In the observed classroom, the teacher had a carefully constructed series of learning tasks, supplemented with regular phonics lessons. She assumed that copying sentences would give children experience focusing on discrete word units, and so it seemed sensible to her to move from copying to fill-in-the-blank and free writing tasks. Ms. Lin's clear instructional path, however, was difficult to discern in the responses of her children. Callie and her peers focused not on word units but on patterns in the ways writing events unfolded, including the materials used, the series of actions followed, and the way of talking during and about the activity. If a child could not grasp the underlying logic of a task, he or she was, by default, dependent on observing the physical unfolding of tasks, and it is these procedures that were transferred from one task to the other. With the exception of children who already had a firm grasp on basic concepts of print (e.g., the stability of messages, the one-to-one correspondence between spoken and written words, the concept of "words" itself), the children's actions had little to do with composing or meaning making.

Moreover, the more Ms. Lin fragmented any one task into a set of carefully delineated steps, the more confused the children became. Consistent with a later study (Dyson, 1993b), changes in the mechanics of how tasks should be accomplished—marks that were not to be copied, unexpected blanks to be filled in—led many children astray. The children had to remember to copy or not copy, number boxes or count lines or not do so, and so on, all non-genre-related questions and all dependent on the teacher's directions, not their own decisions. The children had no familiar meaningful frame within which to make decisions about what was relevant or not, what would be effective or not, in achieving some goal.

In making a change from "filling in the blanks" to "inventing spellings," Callie's teacher reflected the discussed trend in child composing. The research spotlight had shifted, however tentatively, from the features of tasks through which skills were learned and displayed to the constructive possibilities and constraints of child mind in a print-rich environment. Nonetheless, as Callie's "King Kong" episode suggests, that shift did not necessarily resolve gaps between teacher expectations and child responses, nor did it address underlying gaps in textual and social logic and resources (e.g., a child search for social guidance vs. a teacher search for independent efforts, a reliance on known meanings and familiar signs [i.e., names] vs. a reliance on linguistic units [i.e., phonemes], a genre frame informed by dramatic media stories vs. an absence of any such frame beyond writing *something* in sentences). And, as discussed subsequently, the shift, revealed in professional texts, offered little discursive space for issues of child diversity in linguistic and sociocultural resources and of a teacher's pedagogical options for using, as well as expanding, those resources. More particularly, Callie's determination to participate, her attentiveness to other people and to print, did not seem to be useful or used; she still seemed to be slipping off the route, becoming invisible to those looking for signs of the power of child mind in literacy learning.

Readiness and the "Underskilled Child"

Ms. Lin's carefully sequenced literacy tasks (particularly before the "free" writing task) are consistent in some ways with the teaching/learning constructs undergirding Bereiter and Engelmann's program (1966). Although the original publication is more than 30 years old, it served to stimulate much useful discussion about children and literacy, and it remains a reference point in contemporary literature—a kind of metaphor for explicit instruction (e.g., Delpit, 1995; Erickson, 1986). ("Explicit for whom?" seems an important question to ask.) Consider the following excerpt from the text:

Once the alphabet has been mastered, the work focuses upon drill with spelling patterns . . . and upon the reading of sentences and stories containing such words. . . . When this stage is reached, a graduated transition is carried out from reading material presented on the chalkboard to reading from printed sheets and finally to reading from books. (p. 298)

"Books" refers to books carefully planned for practice on the aforementioned spelling patterns. In a phrase that echoes later in this chapter, the authors noted that after "five or six spelling patterns," children can have the motivational pleasure of transferring that taught knowledge to "paper work" (p. 292).

The preceding excerpt reflects a one-way transmission of knowledge and an emphasis on components of the orthographic encoding system, with little attempt to make connections to children's known ways of representing meaning (e.g., storytelling, drawing, dramatizing) or to familiar literacy "events" or "practices." The latter terms were seldom used in educational studies of the time. Still, there were clear assumptions that children from "culturally privileged homes" were interacting with and learning through and about language, including written language, and "those" children, so to speak, were ideologically opposed to "these" children under discussion. For example:

In the course of his language learning, the culturally privileged child . . . may amuse himself by playing with words that rhyme or aliterate. . . . When such a child is told that the set of characters on a sign represents the word *stop*, the statement is likely to mean something to him. . . . The child may learn the letters of the alphabet, may learn to spell his name, and be informed when he reads off the letters on a cereal box that they spell the name of the cereal. When the culturally privileged child first encounters formal reading instruction, he already has some idea of the nature of the task. (Bereiter & Engelmann, 1966, pp. 274–275)

By "the nature of the task," the authors mean the inner workings of the system, the awareness of words and the alphabetic principle. For the "culturally disadvantaged," already "behind," written language is not situated in familiar frames, as is the assumed experience for the "culturally privileged." There is no such programmatic need, because, it is assumed, there is no knowledge to be recontextualized from the everyday to school; the everyday is the problem to be overcome, not a solution to be exploited.

Although there is little concern in the Bereiter and Engelmann text with children's identities, relationships, or points of view, there is a concern that readers take care to remember that their own texts mediate relationships with adults outside their own frame of reference. Parents and the general public should be approached with great sensitivity: After defining "cultural deprivation," inferring the potential lack of language in "lower" class homes, and suggesting the need for an occasional "slap or a good shaking" for the unruly child, the authors voice concern about "damaging" newspaper accounts that are "not written properly. An article that refers to 'culturally deprived children' and describes these children as 'having practically no language' . . . is not going to serve the preschool" (p. 95). However, an audience of fellow professionals will understand.

References to the "culturally disadvantaged" are no longer professionally acceptable, although certainly the state of the current public discussion about literacy suggests the continuing popularity of the "no frills" approach for the public schools, which, in inner cities, are attended primarily by working-class and poor children from diverse cultural backgrounds. Still, the underlying ideology of the proper child (and the dualistic improper one) did not seem to be challenged so much as it disappeared in the literature about the active child learner.

Inventing Literacy and the Already Skilled Child

Callie's teacher, Ms. Lin, decided to open up her writing activity—to make it "free"—and to invite the children to invent their own spellings because of a workshop she had attended. The seeming "opening up" of the writing activity and turning the responsibility for spelling over to her children were reflective of new directions in child writing, ones heavily influenced by developmental psycholinguistics.

If traditional notions of transfer constructed a child with no life of the mind (or body) beyond the stimuli of the task at hand, traditional developmental theorists emphasized child mind—its schemas and processing possibilities and limits. It was the engaged child mind and evolving child schemas that led to sequences of learning, not particularly ordered tasks; indeed, such tasks might interfere with that evolving knowledge and know-how. Individual child differences thus could be defined in terms of (i.e., in the discourse of) each child's place in the set order of things (Walkerdine, 1984, who builds on Foucault, 1979): in child writing, in terms of the stage of production (invention) each evidenced (Chomsky, 1971; Read, 1971). To date, pedagogical texts urge teachers to observe the "natural stages" of child writing, by which they mean changes in encoding: Early strings of circles, curvy lines, and dots give way to more differentiated and alphabetic forms (Raines & Canady, 1990, p. 82; see also Temple, Nathan, Temple, & Burris, 1993).

Bissex's (1980) portrait of her son Paul as a writer (particularly as a speller) is a classic from this body of work. Although she herself cautioned against generalizing from a case study, her emphasis on independent child mind and on the child as his or her own teacher (see also Bissex, 1984) reflects well the tenor of her times, as does the kind of literate environment in the background of her text. That background does not feature institutions like day-care centers, public libraries, or churches; rather, it features a home: "Paul lived in a house that was full of print, and he frequently saw his parents reading and writing" (p. 3). Paul had his own book collection, his own wooden letters, magnetic letter set, rubber stamps, and plenty of paper, all symbolic of the material wealth of the "culturally privileged." And, as Bereiter and Engelmann would assume, one day Paul evidenced that he had, indeed, figured out the alphabetic system: A frustrated Paul, unable to get his mother's attention, used his rubber stamp letters to write RUDF ("Are you deaf?").

"Of course," his mother "put down [her] book" (not the crying baby, not the wash, but her book). As Bissex (p. 17) explains:

With no external demands for neat letter forms, proper spacing, writing on the line, conventional spelling (and apparently only moderate internal demands, plus help from the typewriter), Paul was free to determine whatever he wanted to write and then figure out how to do it. When he was faced with these demands in school a year later, his style became more restricted.

In professional texts about young children's writing, school tasks were a major source of interference in children's transfer of skills from home to school. But school could also be the site of children's first invitations to write, to orchestrate their preexistent knowledge to enter into writing. In the words of Graves, who, in the 1970s, began a highly influential project on child writing:

Writing is not delayed. No more than five minutes into any class, . . . everyone is writing, including the teacher. There are no stories, sentence starters, long discussions of what writing is all about, or exactly what to do on a page. The younger children adjust to this approach without a ripple. (1983, p. 17)

The Graves project began as a qualitative case-study research project in a White, middle-class community; it evolved into a "collaborative researcher-teacher effort which was a catalyst for change in writing instruction" (Farr,

1985, p. 15; see also Sowers, 1985). The study's major text (Graves, 1983), a pedagogical guidebook, is undergirded primarily by models of expert writing practices, but it is explicit about the constructive skills of children who "learn to write the way [they] learned to speak" (p. 184). Thus, the book offers generalizations about child writers of particular ages and grades, with illustrative examples. The following is a description of "first composing": "Children are able to compose when they know about six consonants [echoes of Bereiter and Engelmann's "six spelling patterns"]. John began composing when he wrote SSTK (This is a truck)" (p. 184).

Early school composing is thus linked to a narrow definition of academic competence (e.g., knowledge of letter names and sounds). Moreover, it is the freedom to use this knowledge that allows children to participate in school writing programs and, thereby, to produce school-valued texts—"to write about personal experiences, imaginative writing or 'all about' books" (Graves, 1983, p. 187). Furthermore, observant, knowledgeable teachers know how children write when they are on the literacy route, using their constructive skills, transferring their available knowledge. Thus, they are encouraged to approach children with a shared framework of expected literate behaviors unproblematically associated with valued child qualities (e.g., the "risk takers" and the "personal meaning makers" vs. the rigid or instructionally damaged children clutching their known words).

Children's expectations for school and literacy are assumed, as is the nature of their experiential and linguistic resources: "Children. . .want to write the first day they attend school" (Graves, 1983, p. 3). The text makes no explicit reference to children's sociocultural experiences (although there is a description of a reluctant 11-year-old writer who is the only child constructed to drop his final "g's" and "jive" with his friends). The what and how of that first writing depend on the absence of "unnecessary roadblocks" that prevent children from using their universal linguistic and cognitive processes (p. 3).

Thus, good teachers do not need pedagogical strategies recommended by previous scholars, unless their students have "problems" (Graves, 1983, p. 205). Competent children (and teachers) have no use for "key words" (Ashton-Warner, 1963), "breakthrough to literacy" charts (MacKay, Thompson, & Schaub, 1970), dictation (Clay, 1979), or "exploring with a pencil" (Clay, 1977); they do not need help with the "drastic [message] reduction" or slow process writing entails (Rosen & Rosen, 1973, p. 89). Nor do they copy words from books or seek answers to questions like "How do you spell 'Ilovemybaby'?" unless they have school-induced problems.

Summary: Two Sides of the Same Road

In this first subsection addressing transfer and the literacy route, I have considered the nature of alphabet blocks on the path from home to school. Child composing, often reduced to spelling, has been either an activity rooted in the home (and blocked by school tasks that do not allow children to transfer their written language knowledge) or an impossible activity blocked by inadequate homes that equip children with too little knowledge to transfer to school. The two points of view are ideologically similar in their dependence on particular home environments, dualistically defined—ones that waste child literacy possibilities and ones that do not.

Certainly children bring widely varying experiences with literacy use, influenced by material privilege, cultural tradition, and familial history (e.g., Heath, 1983; Purcell-Gates, 1995; Walker-Moffat, 1995). And yet, Bereiter and Engelmann's identified resources—a functional knowledge of environmental print, pleasure in rhyming, familiarity with written names—are hardly the exclusive property of the "culturally privileged" (Heath, 1983; Taylor & Dorsey-Gaines, 1988). Moreover, not all children enter school with a felt need to write, but all want to be included and valued, to participate in official and unofficial classroom life. This social desire can be a valuable resource, as can children's experiences with varied kinds of texts and kinds of composing (through play, singing, drawing, storytelling; Dyson, 1993a, 1993b, 1997).

Narrow assumptions about how children first write in school—and how adults free children to write—have remained dominant in the language arts field, as have assumptions about ideal children and the literacy route from home to school. These assumptions make visible a limited variety of linguistic and experiential resources, on the one hand, and, on the other, they seem to equate that constrained list of resources with an expanse of language and literacy possibilities. A striking illustration appeared recently in *Education Week* (Manzo, 1997, p. 24). An educator known for helpful texts on holistic literacy teaching responded to public concerns about phonics in this way:

Most kids do not need that kind of phonics instruction. . . . Kids who come to school without language experience need to have systematic phonics, but the first problem is that they haven't heard stories.

The educator could have been misquoted, but this sort of tangled statement bespeaks the difficulty of dominant literacy assumptions. Who are these children without language experience, who have never heard stories? How can one assume a connection between a particular instructional need and a particular deprived home life (a life with no evident need for language or story)? In the case of children's written language, a set of valued home experiences is evidenced by a set of competent behaviors (six consonant sounds?) in school, for which the school can assume credit, although it has not so much taught as freed children to orchestrate and apply (transfer) what they know.

The literacy route was constructed within the scholarly frames of observers with particular lenses, including a psychological lens that highlighted alphabet drill and spelling patterns, a psycholinguistic lens that highlighted children's innate phonological knowledge, and an English composition lens that seemed to take written language itself for granted and to concentrate on "drafting, revising, and publishing." What is most relevant to the adult observers—what they can apply (transfer) of their own knowledge—becomes a quality of children themselves. In Walkerdine's (1984, p. 171) words, "knowledge as a [constructed] social category is . . . marginalized in favor of knowledge as both individual production and competence."

The value of these advances in understanding is not disputed here, but the "discursive slip" (Walkerdine, 1984, p. 171) that allows particular studies in particular sites with particular children, grounded in particular research frames, to become normalizing truths about "the child" is disputed. Placed in a new situation, children neither simply "transfer" old concepts and strategies nor "invent" (or evolve) new ones; they contextualize new situations within what seem relevant frames of reference and use available means, given (as they see it) the demands or expectations of others. For Callie and her peers, it was the interactive distance between them and their teacher that seemed to be "the block"—the dead space where frames did not productively converge, where no one's world was redefined, where teacher-intended transfers did not occur (Dyson, 1993b; Genishi, 1992; Guttierez, Rymes, & Larson, 1995; Nieto, 1992; Nystrand, 1996).

From the Learner to the Context: Tenuous Scaffolds and Collapsing Bridges

Interactive contexts are key to the Vygotskian-inspired research on learning that blossomed in the 1980s. Theoretically, the focal unit in this work is not the individual and the individual's (conceptual) possessions but the individual participating in an event or activity. Thus, the emphasis is not on how children apply previous learning in new tasks but, rather, on how they assume new roles and responsibilities within ever-evolving activities (i.e., tasks within interactive events, which, when viewed as ideologically charged, are "practices"; Miller & Goodnow, 1995). Since the social dynamics of activities change with learning (i.e., individuals' relationships and expectations for each other and for the event itself change), interaction is both situated within and constitutive of contexts.

Despite—or, rather, because of—the emphasis on the inseparability of individuals and their contexts, this perspective provides new conceptual angles for considering the concept of transfer. For example, whether or not children apply (realize the relevance of) certain knowledge or know-how may vary with the "flux of social interaction" in an activity, and thus researchers may learn "what aspects of problem solving a child . . . handles with what types of support" (Rogoff, Baker-Sennett, Lacasa, & Goldsmith, 1995, p. 55). More broadly, the transfer, or recontextualization, of knowledge or skills from one activity to another requires sociocultural and ideological learning. In the words of Rogoff and her colleagues:

Research involves examining the emergent structure of activities that relate to local economic, political, and other ideological systems that link one social activity to another and thus organize learning and conditions across activity contexts. That is, children extract sociocultural knowledge by discerning variations and commonalities across activities as they attend to the ordinary, repeated practices of care givers that are systematically linked to economic and political practices. (Rogoff, Radziszewska, & Masiello, 1995, p. 129)

This point of view has clearly been evidenced in recent theoretical work on written language, in which literacy is not viewed as a set of neutral skills that can be transferred to any task once mastered. Literacy mediates social relationships and ideological values (Street, 1995). In writing, transfer or its lack involves sociocultural learning: If and how certain symbolic means or texts figure in one institutional context (i.e., family or playground) but not another (i.e., school) is a part of learning about how both literacy and social worlds work (Dyson, 1993b, 1997).

This emphasis on learning through interactive contexts both has, and has not had, a dramatic influence on the literature about young children's written language and, more particularly, about children's movement along the literacy route. Focuses on interaction itself or "scaffolding" (Wood, Bruner, & Ross, 1976), like the emphasis on constructivism, often assumed the ease of children's pathways from home to school when good teachers behaved like good mothers—they knew when to get out of the way so that children could apply their socially constructed knowledge. Focuses on sociocultural differences emphasized the need for "cultural bridges" between homes and schools, since children's attempts to transfer home "ways with words" (Heath, 1983) to school activities could meet with unhappy consequences (but see Au, 1980; Boggs, 1985).

In the following, I illustrate the contributions and limitations of scaffolds and bridges as interactive contexts for learning and transfer. I begin, once again, with a case study child, Jameel.

Missed—and Negotiated—Textual Connections

This morning an accident happened on the street outside Louise's K/1 classroom, just as the children were arriving for school. A car had rammed into the playground fence, injuring a pedestrian. Now, during the morning composing period, 6-year-old Jameel seems inspired by this dramatic scene, and also by his concern that a similar accident may have befallen his lost cat, Panther. Using familiar characters from a Dr. Seuss book, Jameel draws a cat and a hat alternately sitting on each other and, then, a cartoonlike scene in which four "speeding robbers" zoom past. "That car is rolling," says Jameel. "He he he he. That car is ro:lling!" And it is that rolling car that runs over poor Cat.

As is the regular routine in Jameel's K/1 class, when the morning work period is over, the children gather on the front rug to read their day's compositions. When it is his turn, Jameel reads the following text:

Sat on Cat. Sat on Hat.

Hat Sat on CAT.

CAT GoN. 911 for Cat [punctuation added]

When Jameel finishes, one peer, Edward, responds appreciatively, "It's like a poem." But another, Mollie, objects: "It doesn't make any sense." Just as his teacher, Louise, does when children do not understand stories *she* reads, Jameel tries to figure out exactly what *Mollie's* problem is.

Jameel: What part of it doesn't make sense? [helpfully]

Peer: It makes sense to me. You can tell with his picture.

Mollie: It doesn't make sense.

Jameel: If your mother got hit wouldn't you call 911?. . . . If a car was passing by—and then you were by the house and then a car was going past and then you got hit—I'm talking about the hat and the cat got hit.

Mollie continues to voice her view, and Louise asks the two children to talk the problem over. As they proceed on their own, each child seems to be appropriating a "teacher" role, resisting a student role.

Mollie: Read that story. . . .
Jameel: You can read all these words.
Mollie: . . . They're smashed together.
Jameel: [laughs] Don't you know [how to read]!!?! [asked with mock amazement]
Mollie isn't laughing.
Mollie: The cat goes 911?
Jameel: The *hat* goes 911. Now the telephone right here [he draws a telephone].
Mollie: Jameel, now look.
Jameel: I don't get it. She *don't* get it. I don't got no more friends. I don't got no more friends.

After Mollie leaves, Jameel complains, "Why she tell me—I did it the way I wanted it. And now they want me to do it how they want it. But it's my decision."

Jameel was a focal student in a study of K–3 children's independent composing, particularly children's social goals and the kinds of discourse traditions they used to achieve those goals (Dyson, 1993b). From the beginning of the school year, an open-ended composing time occurred during language arts, as did alphabet games and initial consonant study, spelling-pattern practice, dictation, and much reading of literature (including poetry).

Perhaps precisely because the composing period was open ended, the children tended to contextualize their enactment of that period within familiar interpretive frames not explicitly introduced by school. For example, on different occasions the focal children (in this study, all African American) used written language as they sometimes used oral language: to affiliate with peers by recounting experiences with popular media stories or listing well-known celebrities. The desired social response seemed to be "Oh yeah, I saw that [know that] too." These were not texts that lent themselves to revision, since recalling a shared experience—not explicitly providing information—was the goal.

Sometimes the children's goal *was* to teach or explain information. For Jameel, this usually happened orally (as it did when he attempted with great care to find out exactly what it was Mollie did not understand). On still other occasions, as in the Cat and Hat composing event itself, children composed artful stories to perform using their oral expressive resources. Even first graders initiated revisions of these texts, whose production entails heightened attention to linguistic elements (Bauman, 1992). Their familiarity with popular genres allowed them a "senseable" frame for manipulating the features of written texts in order to make words rhyme, phrases rhythmic, dialogue fast paced, or images funny. Given a performance goal, children might accept help from those in "collaborator" or "teacher" roles but not from those regarded as "audience," just as Jameel had no intention of accepting help from Mollie.

Louise, Jameel's teacher, found him both delightful and exasperating. Attempting to implement much-recommended "conference" routines, Louise expected

Jameel, and all of her children, to appropriate her ways of questioning them about their texts ("Does that make sense?") so that they would learn to apply these questioning strategies. And yet, Jameel, like other children, did not always play by the script.

Jameel drew on new cultural tools (writing) to enact practices he connected to his life outside the classroom, and he assumed new roles (e.g., teacher, reviser) in collaboratively constructed events, even if they were not always the ones anticipated. He was, in effect, learning. However, as discussed in the larger study (Dyson, 1993b), his teacher Louise learned too. She learned that the generic conference scaffold could not accommodate the diversity of literacy practices and relations within which the children contextualized their writing.

Moreover, she learned that, to create a bridge from familiar practices or interpretive frames to school-introduced ones, she would need to explicitly name genre practices and roles and, in this way, help children negotiate with her—and each other—the relevance of their knowledge and know-how; for example, the sense of "911 for Cat" depends on one's genre frame, as some of the children seemed to know given their comments on poetry and pictures. Finally, Louise learned to reference certain genres (like cartoons and pop songs) not included on most lists of culturally valued forms (except, perhaps, her children's).

Thus, in attempts at understanding the nature of contexts for learning and transfer in Louise's room, the conceptual tools of scaffolds and bridges do offer some explanatory guidance. Still, as discussed subsequently, in the area of child literacy, theoretical advances slip away, as ideological conceptions of the ideal child filter out the symbolic and social possibilities of the many.

Tenuous Scaffolds

In planning for her class, Louise was influenced by her own participation in staff development on conducting "writing workshops" with young children, as well as by Graves's project (1983). As Farr (1985) comments, "Writing conferences ... were the heart of the instructional approach used by the teachers" in that work (p. xi). Although not initially connected to a sociocognitive emphasis on learning or scaffolding, the pedagogical practice of conferencing came to be seen as an instance of sociocognitive co-construction.

Inspired both by a newly available book of Vygotskian theory (Vygotsky, 1978) and by research on parent-child interaction in language learning (e.g., Cross, 1975), this theoretical view emphasized how tasks are analytically enacted not through linearly isolated skills to be "blended" together but through collaborative interactions that reveal their inner workings. In Graves's words, "The same principles underlying a child's acquisition of language and behavior from its mother were occurring in teacher-child interactions during conferences" (1983, p. 271). Unlike the parent-child interaction studies, however, the emphasis was not on co-construction *during* the child's actual composing but, rather, on responding after the fact, as it were. (Perhaps for this reason, encoding tended to remain "constructed," even as knowledge of the writing process was "co-constructed.")

Within these dyadic encounters, teachers used interactive conferencing routines that revolved around "versions of *reflect* (. . . what was it [the reported experience] really like?), *expand* (what else is important to add [to your text about that experience]?), and *select* (what is *most* important?)" (Sowers, 1982, p. 87; Sowers, 1985). Educators could thus examine how children transferred what they accomplished with more expert others (their teachers) to their own independent efforts. Those efforts were viewed primarily through the lens of teachers' instructional intention, which was that the child would assume more responsibility and, thus, as Litowitz explains, become "just like me" (1993, p. 191). And this assumption of mutual identification, of sufficient common ground, is a common critique of the scaffolding metaphor for instruction, despite the usefulness of its predictable routines and contingent responses. That is, some instructional enactments of the scaffolding metaphor seemed to assume its most critical component—a relationship situated in enough common ground to allow the coordination and communication needed for that ground to expand, for the activity to evolve (Rogoff, Baker-Sennett, Lacasa, & Goldsmith, 1995; Stone, 1993). More particularly, writing conferences were designed to help the child produce a "good text," but they assumed common textual goals and shared understandings about interactional roles and responsiveness. Observers, particularly those concerned with cultural diversity and/or gender and racial equity, began to ask: What kinds of assumptions about teacher-student relationships (Delpit, 1995; Reyes, 1991; Walker, 1992) and about textual structures and functions (Gilbert, 1989; Gray, 1987; Kress, 1989) undergird the recommended talk during conferences?

Collapsing Bridges

To understand the issues of identity and relationship raised about scaffolding requires stepping back from those dyadic encounters between teachers and children and, moreover, allowing both teachers and children complex histories and roles in diverse institutions (families, classrooms, schools, communities). This stepping back has been accomplished primarily through the study of communities whose cultural practices are viewed as different in critical ways from those of school. In this literature, there is no assumption that teacher and child share key understandings about their social purpose, interactional roles, and textual values.

One of the most often cited sociocultural studies in early literacy is that of Heath (1982, 1983). As part of her ethnographic study of different southeastern communities, Heath examined cultural differences in parent-child relationships and in literacy use. As a result of her study, she argued against the assumption of "unilinear modes of development" and for curricular recognition of the "range of alternatives to ways of learning and displaying knowledge [that] characterizes all highly school-successful adults" (Heath, 1982, p. 73). For example, children in a working-class African-American community that was part of the study

already use narrative skills highly rewarded in the upper primary grades. . . . They distinguish a fictionalized story from a real-life narrative. They know that telling a story . . . suspends reality and frames an old event in a new context; it calls on audience participation to recognize the setting and participants. . . . They need _to have the mainstream or school habits presented in familiar activities with explanations related to their own habits of taking meaning_ from the environment. (p. 73)

And yet, in the early literacy literature, Heath's work seemed to become further evidence of the ineffective "informal instruction" of "other" parents. For example:

One researcher [Heath] who observed parents reading books to their children [one aspect of the study] discovered differences in the quality and quantity of informal instruction that the parents provided. Some parents asked questions similar to those that teachers ask in school. Thus, their children had experience playing school-like question and answer games. . . . Other parents asked children perfunctory questions about stories being read or did not discuss what was being read. (Anderson, Hiebert, Scott, & Wilkinson, 1985, pp. 23–24)

The niceties of sociocultural research—issues of patterns and demands, of daily living, of differences in life rhythms and routines and resources—are filtered out so that we can get to the business at hand, portraying the most efficient way for properly orienting children to the school literacy road.

Segregated off into publications on "diversity," this literature has not seemed to complicate assumptions about the efficient route to school literacy. Although the "scaffolding" concept connotes vertical progress, "cultural bridges" may connote only horizontal movement, a means for helping children move between "home" and "school" since they may need more help to get on the "right" route. Any notion of multiple paths may be antonymous, as may any notion of a literacy outcome itself furthered by (not hampered by) experiencing cultural boundaries.

Not only may documented "differences" become stigmatized, they may slip into stereotypical cultural containers. For example, in his insightful _Acts of Meaning_ (1990), Bruner discusses Peggy Miller's (1982) sociocultural research on "Black ghetto children in Baltimore [who have] . . . a special narrative environment" (p. 84); however, Miller described the children as White and working class. Gardner (1991, p. 68) comments on Heath's "predominantly poor Black community," "impoverished Whites," and "middle-class White community," but Heath describes the former two communities as working class and the mainstream teachers as both Black and White.

Despite its textual instability in the educational literature, the sociocultural perspective has been critically important in questioning assumptions about language, literacy, and learning. Jameel, for example, had discourse strategies and styles rooted in his African-American cultural heritage, including participative sense-making strategies (e.g., tropes, hyperbole, and call and response) (Foster, 1989; Heath, 1983; Smitherman, 1986).

And yet, there were many points of textual and social connection, not to mention overlap, between "home" ways and "school" ways. For example, many books in the classroom library were composed solely of rhythmic, artful language, and many were not sensible without their pictures. Moreover, Jameel used a range of discourse genres and strategies, depending on the social role he was adopting. Furthermore, Jameel and his classmates produced texts influenced by many performative genres—cartoons, superhero adventures, popular songs—that have no presence on either end of most cultural bridges for young children. Composing time tensions seemed to have to do with belonging and with friends—with issues of legitimacy ("sense"), power ("It's my decision"), and peers ("I don't got no more friends"), all issues that Bauman and Briggs (1990) argue come into play whenever texts, along with the social relationships and ideologies they mediate, are recontextualized (transferred) to new sites. Jameel could be constructed as on the "other" side of a language bridge, but it would be a bridge constructed with selective attention and molded by a language that contains the "other" too well (Comber, 1997; Rosaldo, 1989; Vasquez, Pease-Alvarez, & Shannon, 1994).

YOU CAN ONLY GET THERE FROM HERE: AVOIDING FORKS IN THE ROAD

Literacy learning is complex [given its intertwined threads of pragmatic, discursive, grammatical, and orthographic knowledge], and . . . complexity, like a drive to a large city, might begin at any one of several different starting points and be approached in any one of several different ways. (Clay, 1996, p. 203)

When children are coming to know a new physical landscape, they construct personal landmarks that connect that landscape with their familiar lives (Trimble, 1994). This marking of landmarks happens too when children get to know the symbol-strewn landscape of classrooms. "[N] spell my grandma's name [Helen]. "That one [number 8] is my brother." These sorts of comments precede children's sense of the alphabetic system, how that system works, and how people use the system in particular places, including schools.

From the perspective of this essay, children must—they have no choice—link new material (new knowledge, new requirements for action) to old material, with its familiar frames of relationships and purposes; without such linkages, they cannot approach the new with any sense of agency, with any sense at all. At the same time, old material must be recontextualized within—transferred to—new systems of relationships and uses. Such complex transformations of what is known and what can be done require collaborative constructions, as new material enters into and transforms old relational rhythms, and old material reverberates in the new.

Adults must do this too in making sense of puzzles, including the puzzling responses of children. The theoretical trend "toward a more wholistic approach" (Marini & Genereux, 1995, p. 5) in understanding learning and transfer would seem to allow the construction of richer, more sensible children. This trend has been reflected in efforts to reimagine classrooms as places for active child participants; those active children co-construct contexts for learning by joining teachers and peers on ladders, on bridges, and even in "collective" and collecting "zones of development" where they apply their familial and community "funds of knowledge'' (e.g., linguistic, economic, geographic) to academic work (e.g., Moll & Greenberg, 1990; Moll & Whitmore, 1993).

And yet, I have argued, these efforts, so theoretically powerful in chapters and books, seem unable to contain the social and cultural complexity of many urban classrooms or to probe the complexity of child literacy learning. Popular portraits seldom include young children with a complex world among other children or include young children with guiding frameworks originating outside the mediating influence of a parent or teacher's voice. Children's frames of reference and potential understandings, unarticulated but interwoven in their experiences, are filtered out—understandings of symbolic media, discourse genres, communicative strategies, in addition to potential insights into societal categories such as age, gender, and class and social themes such as collectivity and individuality (Nieto, 1994; O'Loughlin, 1992). That is, what is filtered out is potentially constitutive of exactly what the school aims to teach.

In reproductive accounts of educational institutions and their relationship to societal inequalities, the path from home to school also figures prominently (e.g., Bourdieu & Passeron, 1977; Bourdieu & Wacquant, 1992). That path is constructed, in this view, by institutional agents who are predisposed to perceive and appreciate the competence, the potential, the teachability of those children in whom they recognize themselves or the selves they would like to be. In this way, they construct and legitimize given ideologies.

The present essay is compatible to an extent with this point of view. Schools as institutions tend to offer confusing children fragments of a removed world; confused children, without sense-allowing frameworks, have no basis for deciding what is relevant when. Unofficial peer worlds may take up the slack, but their organizing structures may diverge from, rather than (at least partially) merge with, the literacy routes institutionally visible. The literature on child literacy has seldom succeeded in complicating literacy routes or in countering ideologies of the ''good child learner.''

But I am not a social theorist; I am a teacher and a literacy researcher. Although I know schooling is limited in its influence on the economic and political contexts that anchor these ideologies, I also know, or hope, that researchers aim to at least be helpful to teachers and children. To this end, I have aimed to contribute to those who suggest that scholars of classroom learning remove their bifocals, within which appear the ''mainstream'' and the ''non.'' In Genishi's (1997, p. 11) words:

There is no tidy progression and no magical way that adults have created to make children do as they're told. . . . What we adults struggle with, especially in university settings, is how to represent children fairly, how to ''read'' what they do and say in a way that doesn't distort their own purposes or ways of looking at the world.

By working to read children's ''untidiness,'' their ways of constructing sensible actions and cultural worlds, researchers may provide visions of children's social intelligence and their range of resources. Thus, these researchers may contribute to a more precise and comprehensive understanding of children's common literacy challenges (e.g., figuring out the encoding system, learning to manipulate that code for diverse purposes, learning to reflect on the effectiveness and consequences of discourse choices), variations in their application of varied literacy means (e.g., the units with which they begin to write and read, the kinds of textual forms familiar to them, the kinds of help and response they expect), and the interplay of factors that may shape those variations, including instructional conditions as well as socioeconomic and cultural circumstances and individual interests.

At the least, such efforts should complicate visions of unruly, unready children, whose numbers have increased as definitions of early competence have narrowed (Shepard, 1991); they should make newly visible the diverse social, linguistic, and cultural "roots" of literacy that yield diverse routes (Goodman, 1984, p. 103; Schieffelin & Cochran-Smith, 1984); and, moreover, they should support the efforts of successful teachers in urban schools. These teachers commonly emphasize the breadth of their teaching strategies and their efforts to involve all children in the classroom community however they can and, once involved, to extend their roles and means (for examples, see Dyson, 1997; Genishi, 1992; Ladson-Billings, 1994).

I want to close this chapter, as I began it, with visions of unruly children, whose very "untidiness"—or what Brandt (1995, p. 660) might call their ability "to work the borders between tradition and change . . . to adapt and improvise and amalgamate"—is central to their learning and application of written means.

Children on Literacy Roads

Denise is writing about her Thanksgiving Day, but she is struggling with the spelling of that holiday.
Vanessa: You don't gotta spell the whole thing, just sound it out like you can, girl. . . . 'Cause that word . . . is *long.*
Denise, however, finds the word displayed in the classroom.
Denise: "For Thanksgiving" [reading], I [writing] had, went [planning]—How do you spell *went*?
Vanessa: W— [pauses, walks to a pocket-chart word bank, and brings back *want* for her friend]
Denise: Read the back [of the card].
Vanessa: "I want a red pencil" [reading]—oh, that's *want.* [goes and retrieves another card] This has got to be it.
Denise: That's *with.*
Vanessa: Where is *went*?
Denise: I just got to sound it out! I just got to sound it out!
Denise does so and, with Vanessa's help, writes "for Thanksgiving I wet [went] to Hace hez [Chucky Cheese]." Then she adds "and I sow [saw]."
Denise: I just gotta put one thing and you know what it's gonna be!
Vanessa: My name, or your name, [and] I love you. . . .
Denise gives Vanessa her writing book so that Vanessa can write her own name.
Denise: If you sign Wenona I'm gonna be mad at you.
Vanessa: OK.

As illustrated here, Denise and her peers in Rita's classroom constructed their literacy routes by "transferring" their symbolic and social resources to the official school world; they also "transferred" new resources, developed in school, to their own social worlds ("If you sign Wenona . . ."). Initially, most children coped with the demand that they "write" by drawing, talking, and writing familiar words (e.g., family member names) and by appropriating written forms and patterns from school (when in doubt, observe and copy what others do, say [Fillmore, 1976], or write [Bussis, Chittenden, Amarel, & Klausner, 1985; Clay, 1975; Dyson, 1989; King & Rentel, 1981]).

As the year progressed, however, the children's social, cultural, and language worlds became evident in their "free" writing: They wrote sports announcements (e.g., "The Dallas Cowboys and the Arizona Cardinals in Arizona"), cartoon scenes, R&B and hip hop songs, and bits of commercials, along with science observations, social studies summaries, personal narratives, and fictional stories. Moreover, many began to transfer not simply written patterns from school but written means for participation initially modeled and guided by their teacher (ones not wholly dependent on their developing alphabetic sense). That is, their interpretations (their sense of writing's functional possibilities) changed, as did the social roles (responsibilities) they assumed and the means (skills and concepts) they controlled; their appropriations reflected their own social relationships and distinctive vernaculars, as did Vanessa's and Denise's.

This easy transferring in and out, this weaving of social worlds together, did not, however, always go so smoothly. One day, Denise and her peers Marcel (also African American) and Denny (European American) were working together on a "Freedom and Slavery" poster. The children had been studying about Harriet Tubman and the underground railroad in the context of broader discussions of what "freedom" meant to them as children. As Denise drew cotton and Denny made grass and flowers, Marcel drew a large figure who was, he said, "going out to the underground railroad in Canada."

The figure, this man on his way to Canada, looked like Arnold from the cartoon *Hey Arnold* (Snee-Oosh & Bartlett, 1996). Marcel, who liked to draw, captured precisely Arnold's sun-ray hair and his broad face. Then, concerned that "White people" were not supposed to be on the railroad, he began to add black stripes. Denny, glancing up at Marcel, voiced his own concern.

Denny: Are you still drawing Hey Arnold?
Marcel: No. I'm drawing a person walking. They have strong muscles.

Denny persists, however, and eventually Marcel responds in a firm voice, with a defiant edge: "It's Hey Arnold. It's my idea."

After that encounter, Marcel consistently referred to his drawing as "Hey Arnold," except when a grown-up (other than me) was around—when it reverted to the figure in the underground railroad. Finally, Denny complained to Rita about Marcel's identity-shifting figure. And, when all of the children came to the rug to share their posters, Rita asked them to explain their posters and, also, their experiences in "cooperating." In their turn, Denny, Marcel, and Denise quite cooperatively reported the tension they had experienced. In Marcel's words, "Denny didn't want me to draw my favorite character." Rita responded:

Well, there are two ways of looking at it [this problem]. You could say, "Well, I'm free to draw whatever I like," right? An artist and writer can draw or write whatever they like and . . . try to publish it. . . . [But] I might say, "Marcel, you are working in a group, and the assignment is to do something about your knowledge about freedom. . . ." And he might come back and say, "Well, I disagree with you. I think my idea of freedom is to be able to draw something I want to draw." There's no answer that's right or wrong.

And, on that note, the children continued to explain to each other how groups had interpreted the assignment and the points of disagreement that had surfaced.

Marcel had deemed as relevant a big, bold figure he enjoyed drawing; he was intently engaged in the task and, in his talk, revealed his efforts to compose a picture that applied some of what he learned in school: This man was on the underground railroad to Canada. When Denny named his character "Hey Arnold" and ruled it out of bounds, Marcel responded by reinforcing those bounds. Rita, however, drew the boundaries yet again, bringing in Marcel, his figure, Denny, and a larger issue at the heart of their disagreement.

Marcel's experience, along with Rita's reaction, is an allegory for the process discussed herein, one of reconceiving transfer as recontextualization and, moreover, as a negotiated transformation of *both* school and child worlds. It is children's openness to diverse social worlds and appealing voices and symbols that accounts not only for a cartoon character on the road to Canada but for a Hat that calls 911, ET sharing a page with King Kong, and a lot of sisters and me moving to Oakland. Children need help in disciplining—not obliterating—that openness, recontextualizing their knowledge, know-how, and appropriated voices in broader social, cultural, and ideological worlds. In this way, we help avoid forks in children's literacy routes and, potentially, enrich the academic landscape for all.

REFERENCES

Anderson, R., Hiebert, E., Scott, J., & Wilkinson, I. (1985). *Becoming a nation of readers.* Washington, DC: National Institute of Education.

Anyon, J. (1997). *Ghetto schooling: A political economy of urban educational reform.* New York: Teachers College Press.

Apple, M. (1993). Constructing the 'other': Rightist reconstructions of common sense. In C. McCarthy & W. Crichlow (Eds.), *Race, identity, and representation in education* (pp. 24–39). New York: Routledge.

Ashton-Warner, S. (1963). *Teacher.* New York: Simon & Schuster.

Au, K. H. (1980). Participation structures in a reading lesson with Hawaiian children: Analysis of a culturally appropriate instructional event. *Anthropology and Education Quarterly, 11,* 91–115.

Bakhtin, M. (1981). Discourse in the novel. In C. Emerson & M. Holquist (Eds.), *The dialogic imagination: Four essays by M. Bakhtin* (pp. 259–422). Austin: University of Texas Press.

Bauman, R. (Ed.). (1992). *Folklore, cultural performances, and popular entertainments: A communications-centered handbook.* New York: Oxford University Press.

Bauman, R., & Briggs, C. C. (1990). Poetics and performance as critical perspectives on language and social life. *Anthropological Review, 19,* 59–88.

Bereiter, C., & Engelmann, S. (1966). *Teaching disadvantaged children in the preschool.* Englewood Cliffs, NJ: Prentice Hall.

Berliner, D., & Biddle, B. J. (1995). *The manufactured crisis: Myths, fraud, and the attack on America's public schools.* Reading, MA: Addison-Wesley.

Bissex, G. (1980). *GYNS at wrk: A child learns to read and write.* Cambridge, MA: Harvard University Press.

Bissex, G. (1984). The child as teacher. In H. Goelman, A. A. Oberg, & F. Smith (Eds.), *Awakening to literacy* (pp. 87–101). Exeter, NH: Heinemann.

Boggs, S. (1985). *Speaking, relating, and learning: A study of Hawaiian children at home and at school.* Norwood, NJ: Ablex.

Bourdieu, P., & Passeron, J. (1977). *Reproduction in education.* London: Sage.

Bourdieu, P., & Wacquant, L. J. D. (1992). *An invitation to reflexive sociology.* Chicago: University of Chicago Press.

Brandt, D. (1995). Accumulating literacy: Writing and learning to write in the twentieth century. *College English, 57,* 649–667.

Briggs, C. (Ed.). (1996). Introduction. In *Disorderly discourse: Narrative, conflict, and inequality* (pp. 3–40). New York: Oxford University Press.

Bruner, J. (1990). *Acts of meaning.* Cambridge, MA: Harvard University Press.

Bruner, J., & Haste, H. (Eds.). (1987). *Making sense: The child's construction of the world.* New York: Methuen.

Bussis, A. M., Chittenden, E. A., Amarel, M., & Klausner, E. (1985). *Inquiry into meaning: An investigation of learning to read.* Hillsdale, NJ: Erlbaum.

Chomsky, C. (1971). Write now, read later. *Childhood Education, 47,* 296–299.

Clay, M. (1975). *What did I write?* Auckland, New Zealand: Heinemann.

Clay, M. (1977). Exploring with a pencil. *Theory into Practice, 16,* 334–341.

Clay, M. (1979). *Reading: The patterning of complex behavior.* Auckland, New Zealand: Heinemann.

Clay, M. (1996). Accommodating diversity in early literacy learning. In D. Olson & N. Torrance (Eds.), *The handbook of education and human development: New models of learning, teaching, and schooling* (pp. 202–224). Oxford, England: Basil Blackwell.

Clifford, J., & Marcus, G. (Eds.). (1986). *Writing culture: The poetics and politics of ethnography.* Berkeley: University of California Press.

Comber, B. (1997). *The problem of "background" in researching the student subject.* Unpublished manuscript, University of South Australia.

Cross, T. (1975). Mothers' speech adjustments: Contributions of selected child listener variables. In C. Snow & C. Ferguson (Eds.), *Talking to children: Language input and acquisition* (pp. 151–188). Cambridge, England: Cambridge University Press.

Delpit, L. (1995). *Other people's children: Cultural conflict in the classroom.* New York: New Press.

Detterman, K., & Sternberg, R. (Eds.). (1993). *Transfer on trial: Intelligence, cognition, and instruction.* Norwood, NJ: Ablex.

Donaldson, M. (1978). *Children's minds.* New York: Norton.

Dyson, A. H. (1984). Learning to write/learning to do school. *Research in the Teaching of English, 18,* 233–264.

Dyson, A. H. (1989). *Multiple worlds of child writers: Friends learning to write.* New York: Teachers College Press.

Dyson, A. H. (1993a). From prop to mediator: The changing role of written language in children's symbolic repertoires. In O. N. Saracho & B. Spodek (Eds.), *Language and literacy in early childhood education* (pp. 21–41). New York: Teachers College Press.

Dyson, A. H. (1993b). *Social worlds of children learning to write in an urban primary school.* New York: Teachers College Press.

Dyson, A. H. (1995). Writing children: Reinventing the development of childhood literacy. *Written Communication, 12,* 3–46.

Dyson, A. H. (1997). *Writing superheroes: Contemporary childhood, popular culture, and classroom literacy.* New York: Teachers College Press.

Dyson, A. H. (with A. Bennett et al.). (1997). *What differences does difference make?: Teacher perspectives on diversity, literacy, and the urban primary school.* Urbana, IL: National Council of Teachers of English.

Emerson, R., Fretz, R., & Shaw, L. (1995). *Writing ethnographic fieldnotes.* Chicago: University of Chicago Press.

Erickson, F. (1986). Qualitative methods in research on teaching. In M. Wittrock (Ed.), *Handbook of research on teaching* (3rd ed., pp. 119–161). Washington, DC: American Educational Research Association.

Farr, M. (1985). Introduction. In M. Farr (Ed.), *Advances in writing research: Vol. 1. Children's early writing development* (pp. vii–xxi). Norwood, NJ: Ablex.

Feitelson, D. (1988). *Facts and fads in beginning reading: A cross-language perspective.* Norwood, NJ: Ablex.

Fillmore, L. W. (1976). *The second time around: Cognitive and social strategies in second language acquisition.* Unpublished doctoral dissertation, Stanford University.

Fiske, J. (1993). *Power plays, power works.* London: Verso.

Foster, M. (1989). It's cookin' now: A performance analysis of the speech events of a Black teacher in an urban community college. *Language and Society, 18,* 1–29.

Foucault, M. (1972). *The archaeology of knowledge.* New York: Harper & Row.

Foucault, M. (1979). *Discipline and punish.* London: Allen Lane.

Freire, P. (1970). *Pedagogy of the oppressed.* New York: Continuum.

Gardner, H. (1991). *The unschooled mind: How children think and how schools should teach.* New York: Basic Books.

Garvey, C. (1990). *Play* (enlarged ed.). Cambridge, MA: Harvard University Press.

Geertz, C. (1973). *The interpretation of cultures: Selected essays.* New York: Basic Books.

Genishi, C. (Ed.). (1992). *Ways of assessing children and curriculum.* New York: Teachers College Press.

Genishi, C. (1997, April). *Representing children in educational research: Locating Asian-American children in and out of classrooms.* Paper presented at the annual meeting of the American Educational Research Association, Chicago, IL.

Gilbert, P. (1989). *Writing, schooling, and deconstruction: From voice to text in the classroom.* London: Routledge & Kegan Paul.

Goodlad, J. (1984). *A place called school.* New York: McGraw-Hill.

Goodman, Y. (1984). The development of initial literacy. In H. Goelman, A. A. Oberg, & F. Smith (Eds.), *Awakening to literacy* (pp. 102–109). Exeter, NH: Heinemann.

Graves, D. H. (1983). *Writing: Teachers and children at work.* Portsmouth, NH: Heinemann Educational Books.

Gray, B. (1987). How natural is natural language teaching? Employing wholistic methodology in the classroom. *Australian Journal of Early Childhood, 11,* 49–76.

Green, B. (1993). Literacy studies and curriculum theorizing, or, The insistence of the letter. In B. Green (Ed.), *The insistence of the letter* (pp. 195–225). London: Falmer Press.

Grossberg, L., Nelson, C., & Treichler, P. (Eds.). (1992). *Cultural studies.* New York: Routledge.

Guttierez, K., Rymes, B., & Larson, J. (1995). Script, counterscript, and underlife in the classroom: James Brown versus Brown v. Board of Education. *Harvard Educational Review, 65,* 445–471.

Heath, S. B. (1982). What no bedtime story means. *Language in Society, 11,* 49–76.

Heath, S. B. (1983). *Ways with words: Language, life and work in communities and classrooms.* Cambridge, England: Cambridge University Press.

Jenkins, H. (1988). "Going bonkers!": Children, play, and Pee-wee. *Camera Obscura, 17*, 169–193.

King, M., & Rentel, V. (1981). *How children learn to write: A longitudinal study* (Report to the National Institute of Education). Columbus: Ohio State University.

Kress, G. (1989). *Linguistic processes in sociocultural practice.* Oxford, England: Oxford University Press.

Ladson-Billings, G. (1994). *The dreamkeepers: Successful teachers of African American children.* San Francisco: Jossey-Bass.

Litowitz, B. (1993). Deconstruction in the zone of proximal development. In N. Minick, C. A. Stone, & E. A. Forman (Eds.), *Contexts for learning: Sociocultural dynamics in children's development* (pp. 184–196). New York: Oxford University Press.

Luke, A. (1994). *The social construction of literacy in the primary school.* South Melbourne: Macmillan Education.

MacKay, D., Thompson, B., & Schaub, P. (1970). *Breakthrough to literacy.* London: Longman.

Manzo, K. (1997, March 12). Study stresses role of early phonics instruction. *Education Week*, pp. 1, 24.

Marini, A., & Genereux, R. (1995). The challenge of teaching for transfer. In A. McKeough, J. Lupart, & A. Marini (Eds.), *Teaching for transfer: Fostering generalization in learning* (pp. 1–19). Mahwah, NJ: Erlbaum.

McKeough, A., Lupart, J., & Marini, A. (Eds.). (1995). *Teaching for transfer: Fostering generalization in learning.* Mahwah, NJ: Erlbaum.

Miller, P. (1982). *Amy, Wendy, and Beth: Learning to talk in South Baltimore.* Austin: University of Texas Press.

Miller, P., & Goodnow, J. J. (1995). Cultural practices: Toward an integration of culture and development. In J. J. Goodnow, P. J. Miller, & F. Kessel (Eds.), *Cultural practices as contexts for development, No. 67: New directions in child development.* San Francisco: Jossey-Bass.

Miller, P., & Mehler, R. (1994). The power of personal storytelling in families and kindergartens. In A. H. Dyson & C. Genishi (Eds.), *The need for story: Cultural diversity in classroom and community* (pp. 38–56). Urbana, IL: National Council of Teachers of English.

Moll, L., & Greenberg, J. (1990). Creating zones of possibilities: Combining social contexts for instruction. In L. C. Moll (Ed.), *Vygotsky and education* (pp. 319–348). Cambridge, England: Cambridge University Press.

Moll, L., & Whitmore, K. (1993). Vygotsky in classroom practice: Moving from individual transmission to social transaction. In E. Forman, N. Minick, & C. A. Stone (Eds.), *Contexts for learning: Sociocultural dynamics in children's development* (pp. 19–42). New York: Oxford University Press.

Nelson, K. (1996). *Language in cognitive development: The emergence of the mediated mind.* Cambridge, England: Cambridge University Press.

Nieto, S. (1992). *Affirming diversity: The sociopolitical context of multicultural education.* New York: Longman.

Nieto, S. (1994). Lessons from students on creating a chance to dream. *Harvard Educational Review, 64*, 392–426.

Nystrand, M. (with A. Gamoran, R. Kachur, & C. Prendergast). (1996). *Opening dialogue: Understanding the dynamics of language and learning in the English classroom.* New York: Teachers College Press.

Oakes, J. (1985). *Keeping track: How schools structure inequality.* New Haven, CT: Yale University Press.

O'Loughlin, M. (1992, September). *Appropriate for whom? A critique of the culture and class bias underlying developmentally appropriate practice in early childhood.* Paper presented at the Conference on Reconceptualizing Early Childhood Education: Research, Theory, and Practice, Chicago, IL.

Opie, I., & Opie, J. (1959). *The lore and language of schoolchildren.* London: Oxford University Press.

Ortner, S. (1996). *Making gender.* Boston: Beacon Press.

Paley, V. (1986). On listening to what the children say. *Harvard Educational Review, 56,* 122–131.

Purcell-Gates, V. (1995). *Other people's words: The cycle of low literacy.* Cambridge, MA: Harvard University Press.

Raines, S. C., & Canady, R. J. (1990). *The whole language kindergarten.* New York: Teachers College Press.

Read, C. (1971). Pre-school children's knowledge of English phonology. *Harvard Educational Review, 41,* 1–34.

Reyes, M. (1991). A process approach to literacy using dialogue journals and literature logs with second language learners. *Research in the Teaching of English, 25,* 291–312.

Rogoff, B. (1990). *Apprenticeship in thinking: Cognitive development in social context.* New York: Oxford University Press.

Rogoff, B., Baker-Sennett, J., Lacasa, P., & Goldsmith, D. (1995). Development through participation in sociocultural activity. In J. J. Goodnow, P. J. Miller, & F. Kessel (Eds.), *Cultural practices as contexts for development, No. 67: New directions in child development.* San Francisco: Jossey-Bass.

Rogoff, B., Radziszewska, B., & Masiello, T. (1995). Analysis of developmental processes in sociocultural activity. In L. Martin, K. Nelson, & E. Tobach (Eds.), *Sociocultural psychology: Theory and practice of doing and knowing* (pp. 125–149). New York: Cambridge University Press.

Rosaldo, R. (1989). *Culture and truth: The remaking of social analysis.* Boston: Beacon Press.

Rosen, C., & Rosen, H. (1973). *The language of primary school children.* Harmondsworth, Middlesex, England: Penguin Books.

Saunders, D. (1997, June 15). Push Bush, less mush. *Sunday San Francisco Examiner & Chronicle,* p. 9.

Schieffelin, B., & Cochran-Smith, M. (1984). Learning to read culturally: Literacy before schooling. In H. Goelman, A. A. Oberg, & F. Smith (Eds.), *Awakening to literacy* (pp. 3–23). Exeter, NH: Heinemann.

Shepard, L. (1991). Negative policies for dealing with diversity: When does assessment and diagnosis turn into sorting and segregation? In E. Hiebert (Ed.), *Literacy for a diverse society: Perspectives, practices, and policies* (pp. 279–298). New York: Teachers College Press.

Smitherman, G. (1986). *Talkin' and testifyin': The language of Black America.* Detroit: Wayne State University Press.

Snee-Oosh (Producers) & Bartlett, C. (Creator). (1996). *Hey Arnold.* Nickelodeon Network, in association with Snee-Oosh Inc.

Sowers, S. (1982). Reflect, expand, select: Three responses in the writing conference. In T. Newkirk & N. Atwell (Eds.), *Understanding writing: Ways of observing, learning, and teaching* (pp. 47–56). Chelmsford, MA: Northeast Regional Exchange.

Sowers, S. (1985). Learning to write in a workshop: A study in grades one through four. In M. F. Whiteman (Ed.), *Advances in writing research: Vol. 1. Children's early writing development* (pp. 297–342). Norwood, NJ: Ablex.

Spielberg, S. (Director), & Kennedy, K. (Producer). (1982). *E.T. The Extra Terrestrial.* Universal City, CA: Universal Pictures.

Stallman, A. C., & Pearson, P. D. (1990). In L. M. Morrow & J. K. Smith (Eds.), *Assessment for instruction in early literacy* (pp. 7–44). Englewood Cliffs, NJ: Prentice Hall.

Steel, D., Rudin, S. (Producers), & Duke, B. (Director). (1994). *Sister Act II*. Burbank, CA: Touchstone Pictures.

Stone, C. A. (1993). What is missing in the metaphor of scaffolding? In N. Minick, C. A. Stone, & E. Forman (Eds.), *Contexts for learning: Sociocultural dynamics in children's development* (pp. 169–183). New York: Oxford University Press.

Storey, J. (1998). *An introductory guide to cultural theory and popular culture* (2nd ed.). Athens: University of Georgia Press.

Street, B. (1995). *Social literacies: Critical approaches to literacy in development, ethnography, and education*. London: Longman.

Taylor, D., & Dorsey-Gaines, C. (1988). *Growing up literate: Learning from inner city families*. Portsmouth, NH: Heinemann.

Temple, C., Nathan, R., Temple, F., & Burris, N. (1993). *The beginnings of writing*. Needham Heights, MA: Allyn & Bacon.

Trimble, S. (1994). The scripture of maps, the names of trees: A child's landscape. In G. P. Nabhan & S. Trimble (Eds.), *The geography of childhood: Why children need wild places* (pp. 15–32). Boston: Beacon Press.

Vasquez, O., Pease-Alvarez, L., & Shannon, S. (1994). *Pushing boundaries: Language and culture in a Mexicano community*. New York: Cambridge University Press.

Volosinov, V. N. (1973). *Marxism and the philosophy of language* (L. Matejka & I. R. Titunik, Trans.). New York: Seminar Press.

Vygotsky, L. S. (1962). *Thought and language*. Cambridge, MA: MIT Press.

Vygotsky, L. S. (1978). *Mind in society*. Cambridge, MA: Harvard University Press.

Walker, E. S. (1992). Falling asleep and failure among African American students: Rethinking assumptions about process teaching. *Theory into Practice, 31*, 321–327.

Walkerdine, V. (1984). Developmental psychology and the child-centered pedagogy: The insertion of Piaget into early education. In J. Henrique, W. Hallway, C. Urwin, C. Venn, & V. Walkerdine (Eds.), *Changing the subject: Psychology, social regulation, and subjectivity*. London: Methuen.

Walker-Moffat, W. (1995). *The other side of the Asian American success story*. San Francisco: Jossey-Bass.

Wertsch, J. V. (1985). *Vygotsky and the social formation of mind*. Cambridge, MA: Harvard University Press.

Wertsch, J. V. (1991). *Voices of the mind: A sociocultural approach to mediated action*. Cambridge, MA: Harvard University Press.

Williams, R. (1980). *Problems in materialism and culture*. London: Verso.

Willis, P. (1990). *Common culture: Symbolic work at play in the everyday culture of the young*. Boulder, CO: Westview Press.

Wood, D. J. (1988). *How children think and learn*. Oxford, England: Basil Blackwell.

Wood, D. J., Bruner, J. S., & Ross, G. (1976). The role of tutoring in problem solving. *Journal of Child Psychology and Psychiatry, 17*, 89–100.

Manuscript received March 2, 1998
Accepted May 15, 1998

Chapter 6

Teacher Learning and the Acquisition of Professional Knowledge: An Examination of Research on Contemporary Professional Development

SUZANNE M. WILSON AND JENNIFER BERNE
Michigan State University

In the past 10 years, the calls for a commitment to teacher learning have increased exponentially, most likely from a confluence of forces. The standards movement is one such force. Calls for higher standards for teachers inevitably erupted alongside calls for higher standards for students. If students needed their education served up differently in order to meet new assessments and standards, it followed that teachers would need something new as well (e.g., Cohen & Ball, 1990). Reformers began to note that changed curriculum and testing would not directly lead to changed teaching practices. New measures of student performance would entail new ways of teaching. Professional development was touted as the ticket to reform.

Mounting efforts to increase the professionalization of teaching constitutes yet another force. Groups such as the National Council of Teachers of Mathematics (1989, 1991), the National Council of Teachers of English (1996), the National Board for Professional Teaching Standards (1989), and the Interstate Consortium of Chief State School Officers (Council of Chief State School Officers, n.d.-a, n.d.-b) have authored mission statements and subsequent standards for professional teachers and teaching. Professional teachers require professional development.

Concurrent with this call for more professional development has been a call for more research on teacher learning. Yet, what the field "knows" about teacher learning is rather puzzling. In part, this is due to the scattered and serendipitous nature of teachers' learning. Beginning teachers take methods and foundations courses in education departments and subject matter courses in discipline departments. Sometimes they work in the field, sometimes in the university. And every school experience, whether it be in elementary or middle or high school, in a college or university, has the potential for teaching them lessons about what school is, what teachers do, and how people learn. Lortie's [1975] characterization of this curriculum as the "apprenticeship of observation" has been a major

Deborah Ball, Pamela Grossman, and P. David Pearson offered helpful insights and questions about earlier versions of this chapter. The work was supported, in part, by the National Partnership for Excellence and Accountability in Teaching, the Consortium for Policy Research in Education, and the Pew Charitable Trusts. Despite the generous commentary and support of these people and organizations, the opinions remain those of the authors alone.

influence in attempts to theorize about what prospective teachers "know" about teaching before they enter the profession.

Practicing teachers participate in mandatory part-day or day-long workshops sponsored by their school district. They pursue individual learning opportunities: enrolling in master's courses, signing up for summer and weekend workshops, joining professional organizations. Some learning, no doubt, goes on in the interstices of the workday, in conversations with colleagues, passing glimpses of another teacher's classroom on the way to the photocopying machine, tips swapped in the coffee lounge, not to mention the daily experience of the classroom. While workshop opportunities have been criticized for being decontextualized and contrived, Lord (1994) notes that these other opportunities for teacher learning (while they may be more authentic) are happenstance, random, and unpredictable. In sum, teacher learning has traditionally been a patchwork of opportunities—formal and informal, mandatory and voluntary, serendipitous and planned—stitched together into a fragmented and incoherent "curriculum" (Ball & Cohen, in press).

As a field, we know very little about what teachers learn across those multiple opportunities. Teacher lore suggests that traditional in-service programs consist of outside experts with little knowledge of local conditions who present irrelevant, sometimes amusing, often boring prepackaged information (Corcoran, 1995; Little, 1989, 1994). Teacher lore goes on to argue that these experiences are irrelevant and teach teachers little (or at least little of worth). In his survey of teachers' ratings of opportunities to learn, Smylie (1989), for example, found that district-sponsored in-service workshops were on the bottom of the heap, ranked last out of 14 possibilities in terms of what teachers considered most valuable. Although most workshops are accompanied by evaluations—typically consisting of filling out a form about what was enjoyable—efforts to measure what teachers learned have not been part of typical evaluation fare. And while Smylie found that teachers ranked direct classroom experience as their most important site for learning, extensive studies of teacher learning through practice have not yet been conducted. Action research, in which teachers document and analyze their own experiences, can be seen as one important attempt to redress this problem.

Hence, across this incoherent and cobbled-together nonsystem, structured and unstructured, formal and informal, we have little sense—save the collective and negative self-reports of generations of teachers about traditional in-service programs (Gall & Renchler, 1985; Guskey, n.d.; Showers, Joyce, & Bennett, 1987)—of what exactly it is that teachers learn and by what mechanisms that learning takes place. What knowledge do teachers acquire across these experiences? How does that knowledge improve their practice? These questions are left unanswered.

CONTEMPORARY BELIEFS ABOUT EFFECTIVE PROFESSIONAL DEVELOPMENT

Despite the lack of substantial empirical evidence about what teachers learn (or do not learn) in traditional professional development activities, many educators have embraced the calls for a wholesale rejection of the traditional, replacing the old with new images of meaningful professional development. Principles for designing such work abound in the current literature. Little (1988) nominates the following features of effective staff development: (a) It ensures collaboration adequate to produce shared understanding, shared investment, thoughtful development, and a fair, rigorous test of selected ideas; (b) it requires collective participation in training and implementation; (c) it is focused on crucial problems of curriculum and instruction; (d) it is conducted often enough and long enough to ensure progressive gains in knowledge, skill, and confidence; and (e) it is congruent with and contributes to professional habits and norms of collegiality and experimentation.

Abdal-Haqq (1995, p. 1) nominates a similar set of characteristics, claiming that effective professional development

1. Is ongoing.
2. Includes training, practice, and feedback; opportunities for individual reflection and group inquiry into practice; and coaching or other follow-up procedures.
3. Is school based and embedded in teacher work.
4. Is collaborative, providing opportunities for teachers to interact with peers.
5. Focuses on student learning, which should, in part, guide assessment of its effectiveness.
6. Encourages and supports school-based and teacher initiatives.
7. Is rooted in the knowledge base for teaching.
8. Incorporates constructivist approaches to teaching and learning.
9. Recognizes teachers as professionals and adult learners.
10. Provides adequate time and follow-up support.
11. Is accessible and inclusive.

In her review of contemporary rhetoric on professional development, Ball (1994, 1996) notes a handful of prevalent "beliefs." For example, she notes that scholars currently believe that teachers' prior experience, knowledge, and beliefs factor into teacher learning:

What teachers bring to the process of learning to teach affects what they learn. Increasingly, teachers' own personal and professional histories are thought to play an important role in determining what they learn from professional development opportunities. (Ball, 1996, p. 501)

Ball goes on to argue that current rhetoric about professional development also pays close attention to the students for whom and the contexts in which teaching takes place: "The contexts in which teachers work are believed to affect what they can do." Time, reflection, and follow-up are also thought to be important: "The most effective professional development model is thought to involve follow-up activities, usually in the form of long-term support, coaching in teachers' classrooms, or ongoing interactions with colleagues" (Ball, 1996, pp. 501–502).

Other prevalent beliefs include the idea that "teacher educators and staff developers should model the approaches that they are promoting" and that teachers need to own and control their professional development:

Teacher development is considered especially productive when teachers are in charge of the agenda and determine the focus and nature of the programming offered. In the name of professional autonomy, many argue that teachers should determine the shape and course of their own development. (Ball, 1996, p. 502)

Noting the consistency across such lists, Putnam and Borko (1997) reduce the list to four essential "mantras" or "truisms":

1. Teachers should be treated as active learners who construct their own understanding.
2. Teachers should be empowered and treated as professionals.
3. Teacher education must be situated in classroom practice.
4. Teacher educators should treat teachers as they expect teachers to treat students.

These principles and beliefs seem reasonable. Yet, we know as little about what teachers learn in these kinds of forums as we do about what teachers learn in traditional staff development and in-service. Our readiness to embrace these new principles may, in fact, be rooted in a desire to escape collective bad memories of drab professional development workshops rather than in sound empirical work. But replacing our old conceptions of professional development with new makes sense only if the new ideas are held up for rigorous discussion and evaluation. New is not always right.

If preliminary examinations of these lists yield less than compelling evidence in their support, it seems logical to delve deeper into relevant research to investigate the following: What do we *know* about teacher learning? Specifically, what do we know about the *professional knowledge* teachers acquire in such experiences? To narrow our focus here, we examine the learning of practicing (not preservice) teachers. Readers interested in reviews of the literature of preservice teacher learning might examine the recent thoughtful and comprehensive work of Putnam and Borko (Borko & Putnam, 1996; Putnam & Borko, 1997), as well as that of Feiman-Nemser and her colleagues (Feiman-Nemser, 1983; Feiman-Nemser & Buchmann, 1985; Feiman-Nemser & Floden, 1986; Feiman-Nemser & Remillard, 1995).

We began our task by reading widely. Our selection was guided by three principles. First, we opted to focus on high-quality examples of professional development and elicited nominations of thoughtful work. We stipulated that each nomination had to consist of a professional development project that also had a clear commitment to conducting research. Second, as Elmore, Peterson, and McCarthy (1996) claim, understanding teacher learning includes attending to both the curriculum and the pedagogy of professional development, to *what* teachers learn and *how* teachers are taught. Thus, we selected professional development projects in which staff thought about both the what and how of teacher learning. And third, following this principle, we acknowledged that professional teaching knowledge might include, at the very least, knowledge of subject matter, of individual students, of cultural differences across groups of students, of learning, and of pedagogy (Ball & Cohen, in press; Shulman, 1986, 1987).

With these three principles in mind, the research we collected loosely fell into three "knowledge" categories: (a) opportunities to talk about (and "do") subject matter, (b) opportunities to talk about students and learning, and (c) opportunities to talk about teaching. Rather than exhaustively review literature relevant to each domain, we opted for an alternative route, describing two exemplary instances within each of these categories with an eye toward what they teach us about the acquisition of professional knowledge.

ALTERNATIVE APPROACHES TO TEACHER LEARNING OF PROFESSIONAL KNOWLEDGE

Opportunities to Talk About Subject Matter

In the Cheche Konnen Project ("search for knowledge" in Haitian Creole), Rosebery and her colleagues at TERC in Cambridge, Massachusetts (Rosebery & Ogonowski, 1996; Rosebery & Puttick, in press; Rosebery & Warren, 1998a, 1998b), have been working collaboratively with bilingual, English-as-a-second-language, and science teachers to explore how to create classroom communities of scientific practice. In Cheche Konnen, science learning is organized around students' own questions. Students pose questions, design studies, and conduct inquiries. They collect and analyze data, make conjectures, and prove (or disprove) hypotheses. The researchers found that, over the study year, students' talk changed dramatically, their scientific thinking deepened, and they knew much more about the specific topics they studied.

As a set of parallel experiences, the TERC researchers have engaged the participating teachers in a series of professional development activities. At first, the researchers used a traditional model: They invited four teachers to a summer workshop that lasted for several days, during which time the teachers were "walked through" the new curriculum. In the following year, teachers did not enact the curriculum in ways intended. And as the researchers investigated the reasons why, they discovered that the teachers had not changed their beliefs about science or science teaching, even though they had agreed to teach a radically different science curriculum. Teachers had acquired a new curriculum, a new set of teaching moves and materials, but no new knowledge about science or the teaching of science. These new curricula, when filtered through and shaped by old beliefs, turned into something more traditional than not. As Franke, Carpenter, Levi, and Fennema (1998) learned, "Engaging teachers in current reforms requires more than showing them how to implement effective practices" (p. 1).

The following summer, the researchers designed a different form of professional development. They aimed to create—among the teachers—a scientific community. The group met every other week for 2 hours after school and for 2 weeks in the summer. The seminar involved the teachers in "doing science": Teachers engaged in investigations, pursuing their questions at home and in the seminar. In the context of that work, teachers learned to "sound scientific": They struggled to adopt a scientific discourse and to own the concepts, ideas, and inquiries. The teachers worked as a community, socially constructing their understandings of snails and ecology. Over time, they began to bring their own teaching to the table for discussion and critique. The researchers note the connection between teacher learning and student learning:

We believe that the remaking of science education into a more egalitarian sense-making practice entails deep transformations of identity for teachers and students alike, transformations that empower them to think, talk, and act scientifically. (Warren & Rosebery, 1995, p. 42)

In subsequent research, Rosebery and her colleagues began searching for research methods that enabled the documentation and analysis of what teachers were learning. In one such analysis, Rosebery and Warren (1998b) look at the discourse of the group. They propose that members with different backgrounds and expertise (teachers and biologists, say) bring different discourses to the effort and that part of the group's work involves establishing shared meanings. Because the group works together over time, these shared meanings themselves are not static but ever changing:

The construction of a shared meaning does not happen in an orderly, linear progression, from implicit to explicit meaning. Rather, it has a more mobile, mutable, improvisational character as meanings are taken up and elaborated by different participants, each of whom draws on past as well as "already accepted" perspectives in the conversation. In this way, the meaning of "hypothesis," "experiment," and "control" are in motion for all the participants—researchers as well as teachers—as they work to formulate a shared understanding. (pp. 10–11)

The researchers' analysis of the group's discourse raises several significant issues about teachers' acquisition of professional knowledge. First, they note that what is learned goes well beyond words:

This stretch of talk seems to us a good example of how learning scientific meanings for particular words is not a matter of learning at the level of the words themselves but at the level of the discourse or the practice. The sense or resonance that the word "hypothesis" has is strongly a function of the contexts of its use, of the practices of which it is a part, which crucially also involve other stances or views of the world, for example, what it means to do an experiment, what it means to explain a particular behavior, what is involved in stating a hypothesis, how hypotheses function in different forms of scientific inquiry such as observation and experimentation. (Rosebery & Warren, 1998b, p. 13)

These researchers are grappling with ways to capture "knowledge" that transcend words on paper. The participants' "knowledge" of "experiment," "hypothesis," and the like appeared to change as they engaged in the scientific process. And while their "knowledge of science" could be captured in the ways they define terms, the researchers have a hunch that some significant aspects of that knowledge go beyond paper. They use the language of "stance" and "resonance" to capture something of the quality of the teachers' developing knowledge, for knowledge goes well beyond words readily recited at a spelling bee or oral examination. Knowledge entails skills, ways of talking and interacting, ways of observing and noticing things in the environment, and dispositions toward action and interpretation. The researchers noticed teachers learning things that went well beyond their capacity to define terms. But capturing that knowledge has proved difficult.

The researchers also found that the group developed a set of "canonical stories" that served as the coin of their conversational realm. Participants developed a shorthand that took the form of cases—"Jimmy's problem," "the giraffe's neck," "pepper moths"—that meant something to them but remain obscure to those of us not present. Other such cases have recently appeared in the larger national discourse on teaching and learning; Cohen's (1990) "Mrs. O." and Ball's (1993) "Shea numbers" are but two examples. That teachers' knowledge might be held in the form of such stories or cases is a hypothesis that Lee Shulman (1986) proposed, and it might well be that one way of measuring teacher knowledge within these communities would involve documenting and assessing what these stories were and what meaning they held for the teachers. Indeed, an entire line of teacher development work has arisen in the wake of that observation, with educators using developed cases to teach teachers (e.g., Shulman, 1992) and teachers writing their own cases as a means for professional development (Barnett, 1991, 1998; Barnett, Goldenstein, & Jackson, 1994; Schifter, 1996a, 1996b; Shulman, 1992; Shulman, Lotan, & Whitcomb, 1998). While such cases are meant to be disseminated and shared, the knowledge that appears in these professional development communities suggests that "case knowledge" has validity (it naturally arises in these communities of learning teachers) and potential as a research tool or site for measuring teacher knowledge.

Grossman and Wineburg (Grossman, Wineburg, & Woolworth, 1998; Thomas, Wineburg, Grossman, Myhre, & Woolworth, 1998; Wineburg & Grossman, 1998, in press) created a different model for engaging teachers with subject matter, this time in the form of a book club. In a 3-year project funded by the McDonnell Foundation, Grossman and Wineburg met monthly with a group of English and social studies teachers (the group also consisted of a smattering of student teachers, special education teachers, and English-as-a-second-language teachers). The group selected, read, and discussed fiction and history, using their discussions to create a community of teacher-learners who could then develop an integrated English–social studies curriculum. The group read broadly: Nathan McCall's *Makes You Want to Holler*, Christopher Browning's *Ordinary Men*, Robert Olin Butler's *Good Scent from a Strange Mountain*, Rian Malan's *My Traitor's Heart*, Doris Kearns Goodwin's *No Ordinary Time*.

Eventually, the group became a "community of readers." Wineburg and Grossman (in press) saw the process as enabling:

The act of reading together in a community of learners has made epistemology visible, and the act of surfacing and naming assumptions has created the conditions for self-awareness and inter-subjectivity. We don't necessarily agree any more than we did before, but our disagreements are richer and more productive. Instead of being treated as instances of individual intransigence, our discussions of different ways of reading are now understood as reasoned and legitimate differences from which we can all learn.

While they created and participated in this group, Grossman and Wineburg also conducted research. Their research questions included: What is intellectual community among teachers? How does it develop (or not develop)? How does the development of intellectual community enable teacher learning? How do teachers learn from one another? Along the way, they collected field notes; conducted individual participant interviews; used free writes, group surveys, and evaluations; and taped the group discussions. The researchers also collected data on teachers' knowledge. They had teachers read and think aloud in interviews, as well as participate in four sets of interviews that included repeated measures of teachers' professional knowledge. However, the researchers are in the midst of conducting analyses of these data, so the review here describes only the results that have already emerged, not the potential for additional results on the horizon.

Using a system of discourse analysis that they adapted to be subject matter specific, the researchers documented differences in individuals' participation. They found evidence that some teachers learned to contribute in different ways to the group discussions and that some learned to think differently about the nature of history and literature (and their relationships and differences). Over time, group members began to realize that history and English teachers read quite differently, attending to issues of warrant and evidence differently, reacting to students making personal connections to the texts differently. For instance, in history, the fact that students sometimes assume that their world view and values are identical to those of individuals from the past (called "presentism") is a problem. Assumptions of similar valuing and perspective made it difficult for students to understand actions in the past, actions predicated on and motivated by different assumptions and values. Yet, the very same "problem" in an English class can enhance reading, for putting oneself inside the experience of a character can deepen one's reading. Participants eventually learned to notice—and value—these substantive differences rather than dismissing them as merely "personality" clashes.

But what of changes in classroom practice? According to teachers' self-reports, teachers tried to create similar discussions among their students, modeled their own thinking for students, and learned to listen for differences in students' interpretations. The researchers noted some unforeseen consequences:

We also did not anticipate some of the effects our project has had on students, who see their teachers leave the classroom once a month to model what it means to be lifelong learners. Students spy copies of the project books on their teachers' desks and then hear different versions—sometimes opposing versions—of these books from different teachers. More than once our books have ended up as the subject of student book reports or even as part of the regular curriculum. When an English teacher reminded students that they were to provide a "critical evaluation," not a piece of fan mail, for their book reports, one student teased her, "Just like you Ms T, with your books for the McDonnell Project!" (Wineburg & Grossman, 1998, p. 353)

Stories such as these are both intriguing and hopeful, but the researchers acknowledge that the link to practice is the weakest one in their project (Grossman, Wineburg, & Woolworth, 1998).

Thoughtfully and carefully constructed, these professional development opportunities had meaning for participants. As we examine other forums for professional development, the patterns that begin to emerge here will echo in other research: that teachers enjoy the chance to talk about their work, that it takes time to develop a community, that teachers have very little experience engaging in a professional discourse that is public and critical of their work and the work of their colleagues. Other issues remain less clear at this point: What exactly are these teachers learning? What science do they know, or history? What kinds of knowledge and skill are they acquiring? How do researchers document that knowledge? And how is that knowledge affecting their practice? Do these groups support teachers or teaching? Is this distinction important? These are questions that haunt researchers, and we return to them later in the cross case analysis of different forms of professional development. For now, however, we turn to our next "case": teacher learning opportunities that focus teachers' attention on students and learning.

Opportunities to Talk About Students and Learning

Our second case of teacher learning involves professional development programs that have as their focus students' thinking. The first instance of such professional development is Cognitively Guided Instruction (CGI) (Carpenter, Fennema, & Franke, 1996; Carpenter, Fennema, Peterson, Chiang, & Loef, 1989; Fennema et al., 1996; Fennema & Franke, 1992; Fennema, Franke, Carpenter, & Carey, 1993; Franke, Carpenter, Levi, & Fennema, 1998; Peterson, Carpenter, & Fennema, 1989). Carpenter, Fennema, Peterson, and Carey (1988) found that teachers' knowledge of children's thinking tended to be informal and lacking in organization or coherence. These researchers then designed a professional development project that provided teachers with a classification of addition and subtraction problems and descriptions of variations in students' thinking around those problems. Subsequent generations of CGI included information about students' thinking in regard to other mathematics areas as well (Fennema, Franke, Carpenter, & Carey, 1993).

Participants learned about a framework of children's thinking, as well as about particular mathematics problems and the patterns of children's thought about those problems. Thus, teachers might leave CGI discussions with more "theoretical" knowledge of the characteristics and development of children's thinking and "particular" knowledge of problems. No prescriptions about the implications for practice were made, and teachers made their own decisions about how to use their knowledge of student thinking in their teaching.

A series of studies have investigated the impact of CGI on teachers and students. In one analysis, Carpenter, Franke, and Levi (1998) contrasted two teachers: Ms. Sanford and Ms. Cole. Ms. Sanford had learned many things from CGI, ranging from "big ideas" (e.g., that children construct their understandings) to specific strategies that children typically invent when learning to add and subtract multidigit numbers. Ms. Sanford saw her own learning in ways similar to her views of children's learning: She built her professional knowledge through experience and reflection, some of which took place out of school, most of which happened in her own classroom. Ms. Sanford left CGI with a framework for continuing her own investigations into students' thinking. And she saw that as part of her practice.

Ms. Cole learned about constructivism. She reported that CGI helped her learn how important it was to listen to children. When asked how she would continue to learn more things, Ms. Cole talked of taking more classes and rereading articles from past classes. She did not view her own teaching as a site for her continued professional development. Rather, professional knowledge was a fixed body of information that could be packaged and delivered in courses and experiences outside of classrooms. And her job, as a teacher, was to take that newly acquired knowledge and weave it into her practice.

Carpenter, Franke, and Levi (1998) note the complex interdependence of a teacher's beliefs and teaching and how beliefs shape future learning opportunities:

Ms. Sanford believed that she would learn from her students, and her classroom practices provide a context for her learning. Ms. Cole did not perceive her classroom as a place for her own learning about student thinking, and her class interactions provided relatively little opportunity for such learning. It is not clear whether teachers construct classrooms in which they can learn from students because of their beliefs about engaging in practical inquiry to better understand student thinking or whether their beliefs come from interacting and learning from their students. We suspect it is not all one way or the other. (pp. 12–13)

In another analysis, Franke, Carpenter, Levi, and Fennema (1998) observed and interviewed 22 teachers who had participated in a later version of CGI consisting of summer workshops and 2 years of field support. The researchers found that teachers—4 years later—were at different levels of development. Based on their research, they proposed four levels of teacher development.

Level 1:   A teacher at Level 1 does not believe that the students in his or her classroom can solve problems unless they have been taught how.

Level 2:   At Level 2, a shift occurs as the teacher begins to view children as bringing mathematical knowledge to learning situations.

Level 3:   The teacher at Level 3 believes it is beneficial for children to solve problems on their own because their own ways make more sense to them and the teacher wants them to understand what they are doing.

Level 4A: The teacher at Level 4A believes that children's mathematical thinking should determine the evolution of the curriculum and the ways in which the teacher interacts individually with students.

Level 4B: The teacher at Level 4B knows how the knowledge of an individual child fits in with how the child's mathematical understanding develops (Franke, Carpenter, Levi, & Fennema, 1998).

Using interviews and observations, the researchers categorized 10 of their 22 informant-teachers as being at Level 4B, 2 as being at Level 4A, 4 as being at Level 3, 6 as being at Level 2, and 1 as being at Level 1. Teachers who had reached Level 3 showed the most instability, 4 moved to Level 2 while 4 stayed at Level 3. Teachers who were at Level 4A or 4B stayed at that level with the exception of 1 Level 4B teacher who became more of a Level 3 teacher. The researchers found that while all 22 teachers reported that children's thinking was a significant part of the way they thought about instruction, the teachers varied in both the level of detail of their knowledge of children's thinking and how much emphasis they placed on children's thinking in their teaching.

Another observable difference in the teachers was the extent to which they conceptualized CGI-related knowledge as a theoretical framework or as a set of problem types. Level 3 teachers recognized that there were different problem types and used those problems in their teaching. They imported the CGI problems into their practice, modifying their practice somewhat to accommodate for more listening to students. Teachers at Levels 4A and 4B put more emphasis on CGI's conceptual framework, placing the illustrative problem types within that overarching structure. Within the larger frame, they continued to acquire and organize a great deal of specific knowledge about children. Level 3 teachers did not:

> The Level 3 teachers focused on children's abilities to solve problems in a variety of ways. They valued the children's solutions, not in terms of the specific strategy the child used but rather in terms of having the children use and share different strategies. . . . Often Level 3 teachers could not explain their students' thinking. At times they told us that they were not sure what a given student had done; other times they made general inferences about why a child had difficulty with a problem that they could not support with specific detail. (Franke, Carpenter, Levi, & Fennema, 1998, p. 15)

The researchers also detected differences in teachers' perceptions of their role vis-à-vis the development of knowledge of children's thinking. Teachers at Level 4B thought that it was both within their power and their responsibility to develop knowledge of student thinking. While the CGI research had launched them on the path of learning about children's mathematical thinking, these teachers saw their practice as a site for further inquiry—this time, their own. They were constantly testing that knowledge and engaging in practical inquiry. Teachers at Level 4A and below did not talk about learning more about children's thinking on their own. As the researchers note, "Teachers at Level 3 and Level 4A think the knowledge is critical and it is central in how they think about their teaching, but they see the knowledge as something passed on to them" (p. 19).

The researchers also found that every teacher talked of the need for community. For some, the communities were within their schools; for others, the boundaries of the community transcended school walls. In every case of teacher ongoing learning, however, teachers were engaged in learning communities that allowed them to test, discuss, revise, and retry their ideas about children's mathematical thinking and its relationship to instruction. The teacher communities had two significant features: They were self-sustaining, and the work of the group focused on students' thinking. The researchers described the change they witnessed in some teachers as "generative" as well as "self-sustaining":

> We are not proposing that children's thinking is the only avenue for teacher's growth to become generative; however, it has characteristics that provide a basis for generative growth. Children's

thinking is available to teachers in their classrooms daily. There are regularities among the strategies that children describe and principled ideas can be ascertained about these regularities. Teachers can create a way to talk with each other about both their classrooms and their students. Teachers can create communities of learning that focus on children's thinking: how their children are thinking about the mathematics, what it might mean, how they can learn more about their children's thinking and the ways they can provide opportunities for students to build on their thinking. The learning communities these teachers create include their classrooms. These communities provide a basis for teachers to engage in inquiry focused on children's mathematical thinking with their students, their colleagues, and themselves. (Franke, Carpenter, Levi, & Fennema, 1998, p. 23)

In addition to interview and observational data, CGI researchers collected data on student achievement, teacher beliefs, and teacher knowledge. Thus, researchers were able to measure and characterize teacher learning as well as student learning. The researchers found that teachers who participated in CGI taught problem solving significantly more and taught number facts and skills significantly less. The teachers used different instructional strategies, listened to students more, and believed that instruction would build on what students know. Analyses of student achievement showed that students of CGI teachers recalled number facts at a higher level, as well as exceeding students in control classrooms in problem solving and confidence (Carpenter, Fennema, Peterson, Chiang, & Loef, 1989; Fennema, Franke, Carpenter, & Carey, 1993).

Our second case of professional development that aims to engage teachers in thinking about students is very different from CGI's research-based model. The Future Teachers' Autobiography Club started as a small group of prospective teachers who met regularly with Susan Florio Ruane to read autobiographies. The group eventually grew into a professional development community for practicing teachers, and we include this case as a stimulus for considering the potential relationships between preservice teacher education and ongoing professional development.

Florio Ruane (1994) conceived the autobiography club as a way to help prospective literacy teachers learn to think about culture, language, experience, and schooling. Noting that the majority of the teaching force remains White and female and that literacy is "neither a monolithic phenomenon nor a collection of technical skills" but, rather, "a social accomplishment" highly influenced by culture and context, Florio Ruane designed the autobiography club as a means for teaching teachers about literacy and diversity, assuming that Zeichner (1993) was correct when he claimed that teacher candidates need to acquire "the desire and ability . . . to learn about the special circumstances of their own students and communities and the ability to take this kind of knowledge into account in their teaching" (p. 6).

Florio Ruane's initial goal was to help these prospective teachers "approach the teaching of literacy inside school with greater insight, imagination, and sensitivity" by having them read—and then discuss—a half a dozen autobiographies focused on literacy, including *Lost in Translation* by Eva Hoffman, Maya Angelou's *I Know Why the Caged Bird Sings*, *The Hunger of Memory* by Richard Rodriquez, and Jill Ker Conway's *The Road from Coorain*.

Six university seniors volunteered to become club members. They agreed to meet for 6 months and read six books that Florio Ruane selected. Meetings took place over dinners in her home, outside the university's institutional walls. Florio Ruane was participant and observer, collecting field notes and audiotaping conversations. Participants also wrote in "sketchbooks" and participated in interviews. There was no teacher—as such—and the group was collectively responsible for managing the discussions.

In an early report on the club's activities, Florio Ruane (1994) reported that the club became a forum for talking about books and about the teachers' lives. In a discussion of *I Know Why the Caged Bird Sings*, readers offered their own stories of personal revelation upon graduation. Their stories focused on themes including educational equality, constraints on choice, and the search for identity. Because six students shared their very different personal stories, the participants had the chance to see how there was variation even in their small group, not to mention among their own students. Florio Ruane also noted that the discussions were more like ordinary conversations than school talk:

The Club members seem to monitor other speakers very closely, keeping track of what is being discussed and what the point of it is, in part for the purpose of turn exchange. Participation is high and marked by such involvement strategies as overlapping speech, humor, personal narrative, and repetition of key words and images across turns and speakers. (p. 62)

As she analyzed their talk, Florio Ruane (1994) observed that teachers drew on several kinds of knowledge: personal or autobiographical knowledge (what happened in my school), knowledge of the book, and knowledge of other texts (books, newspapers, movies). Teachers drew most heavily on the autobiographical knowledge, rarely discussing the book directly. As Florio Ruane notes: "They seem instead to narrate personal experiences moving near to or playing upon tacitly held notions of the book's themes but, like jazz musicians playing individual variations on a well-known tune, rarely touching it directly" (p. 64).

In subsequent analyses, Florio Ruane and Julie deTar (1995) discovered that discussing autobiography is not a "benign affair." Discussions, while remaining polite and respectful, were nevertheless uncomfortable at times, requiring that the teachers take risks. Teachers did not always agree, and although wanting to respect each other's opinion, they needed also to disagree and critique peers' positions. Merging argument with conversation was no easy matter for the group, yet talking about volatile issues—equity and equality, racism—required doing just that.

As a site for research on teacher learning, these conversations offer challenges. Peer discussion and personal narrative, while appealing, are "complicated means to not well-specified ends":

Conversation is a messy, indeterminate medium for growth. Educators believe it is necessary for rich and complex thinking, yet it is hard for them to handle and even harder for researchers to understand. Thus our preference for learning that is rooted in conversation quickly outstrips our understanding of the medium and finds our ordinary methods of inquiry challenged by its variety and complexity. (Florio Ruane & deTar, 1995, p. 36)

In subsequent work, Florio Ruane has collaborated with a number of colleagues in the design and development of a master's level course in literacy that involved reading autobiographies. At the request of the students at the course's end, Florio Ruane, Raphael, Glazier, McVee, and Wallace (in press) created the Literary Circle, a voluntary book club that continues meeting and reading. As the researchers analyzed the group's interactions, their results were similar to Florio Ruane's experience with the autobiography club: Early discussions were more like "fishing expeditions" than conversations, and it took time to develop the trust and discourse norms that would enable sustained discussion. Even then, though, the group tended to avoid difficult discussions, for instance, those about race. Furthermore, discussions could appear to be personally connected while participants were nevertheless maintaining distance between themselves and the topic, group, or book. The researchers concluded that perhaps the most powerful aspect of group participation was that it enabled the development of an "intellectual identity" for the participants.

As we consider the research on teachers' learning about subject matter and teachers' learning about students, two things seem clear. Teachers enjoy talking about materials relevant to their work, be that subject matter or theories of student learning. Teachers embrace these opportunities to be intellectuals. Yet, they bring little by way of experience to professional conversations. The norms of school have taught them to be polite and nonjudgmental, and the privacy of teaching has obstructed the development of a critical dialogue about practice and ideas. Each research project finds itself struggling to support the development of such a culture.

The research also shows how difficult it is to capture teacher learning in these contexts. CGI researchers had a framework of children's thinking, and they were able to assess whether individual teachers had acquired knowledge of that framework. In the other projects, it is less clear how teacher learning would best be assessed. Are teachers to know the plot lines and characters of the books they are reading in book clubs? Are they to understand cells and their structure as they learn science? As professional development projects engage teachers in learning the subject matter, researchers need to think about the knowledge they hope teachers will acquire through these learning opportunities. While teachers may learn many additional things, stipulating a clear set of expectations for teacher learning might enable more research on the acquisition of professional knowledge.

In addition, the location of the knowledge is also unclear. As communities grow, they develop a shared knowledge, knowledge that both transcends and shapes the knowledge of individual participants. As researchers investigate teacher learning within these contexts, they struggle with how and when to capture group knowledge versus an individual's knowledge. The fact that communities, as well as individuals, acquire knowledge has implications for crafting and assessing all professional development. Consider the differences between school-based professional development and opportunities to learn that are offered outside of the school setting. School-based professional development activities develop shared knowledge and norms that directly translate into school capacity. On the other hand, it might be easier for teachers to reveal what they do not know (so that they might learn more) in contexts away from their home schools. Yet, what they learn in those other communities might not be easily transported into a school where their willingness to learn and experiment is neither understood nor supported. These issues and others will continue to challenge researchers interested in teachers' acquisition of professional knowledge. We turn now to our third case: opportunities to talk about teaching.

Opportunities to Talk About Teaching

Clearly, our categories are not discrete, since the conversations these communities of teacher-learners engage in shift easily and sensibly from talk of books to talk of how to teach the books, from talk of students to talk of how to teach those students. Our first instance of opportunities for talking about teaching highlights this quality of shifting focus: It began as a group that would discuss teaching, only to decide that—in order to understand teaching—the members first needed more knowledge of mathematics.

The Investigating Mathematics Teaching group (IMT) is a collection of seven elementary and middle school teachers and three university teacher educators at Michigan State University who have been meeting weekly since 1991 to discuss issues related to mathematics teaching (Featherstone, Pfeiffer, & Smith, 1993; Featherstone et al., n.d.; Featherstone, Smith, Beasley, Corbin, & Shank, 1995; Pfeiffer & Featherstone, n.d.; Smith & Featherstone, n.d.). During their first semester together, the group members watched and discussed videotapes and other materials associated with Deborah Ball's teaching of third graders (cf. Lampert & Ball, 1998). After the fall term, they agreed to continue meeting, but they did not want to watch tapes. Their reasons are intriguing in light of our interest in understanding teachers' acquisition of professional knowledge:

These teachers have said subsequently that they did not understand operations involving negative numbers well enough to understand the conversations of the third graders, and that watching these videotapes made them feel stupid. (Pfeiffer & Featherstone, n.d., p. 7)

The group then began discussing their own teaching, integrating talk of their classroom practices into talk of the curriculum and evaluation standards of the National Council of Teachers of Mathematics (NCTM; 1989, 1991). At the end of the school year, the group expressed an interest in continuing in the following school year. But they wanted to begin before the school year started so that they could get some help in thinking about how to socialize their students at the beginning of the year into issues associated with "doing math."

One of these sessions turned into an activity that asked teachers to work through problems designed to challenge their math skills. Throughout their work, the teachers kept track of their thoughts and reflections in journals. They recorded, for example, their frustrations with doing the problems, sometimes feeling panic when others were writing away. Using their experiences as learners, the teachers began thinking about their students and their teaching practice. "How do third graders feel when they don't get it?" the teachers began to wonder.

According to participants' self-reports, the group served several functions, not all of them involving the acquisition of professional knowledge; doing math problems and noticing how they felt, teachers began thinking about how students felt in similar circumstances. One participant just needed to be part of a group so that she could hold on to her commitment to learning and changing her practice. Having recently had a baby, she had no time to work on her practice. But every week she drove 140 miles to be a silent partner in the group's deliberations because she was afraid—literally—to lose sight of those who were. She needed to maintain the connection, reporting that she was afraid that letting those teachers who were struggling out of her sight would cause her to forget "what it looks like" to learn and change.

In one analysis of the group's interactions over time, Pfeiffer and Featherstone (n.d.) examined changes in the group's discourse. IMT members listened to tapes of previous discussions, observing shifts in their norms. Several noted that a feature of the group's discussions had become "pushing each other." As one teacher noted, "Whew, we're playing hardball, now" (p. 10). Using the work of sociolinguists such as Tannen (1989) and Gumperz (1982), the researchers analyzed participants' "conversational involvement" and found three characteristics.

First, the conversations became more sustained and focused. For example, the number of topic changes drastically changed over time. In October of 1991, there were 37 topic changes in one evening's conversation; during the following September and October, the topic changes hovered in the range between 3 and 12. Second, the talk was "passionate":

The teachers sounded emotional and animated as they described their experiences and the realities they confront daily. Their stories included strong expressions of uncertainty and frustration about how to enact the vision to which they were now personally and professionally committed. They described their concerns as pressing. (p. 18)

Third, the researchers found that the discussions exhibited an increased amount of public disclosure. When teachers began meeting, their concerns for presenting themselves as competent professionals appeared to compromise their capacity to share their problems. For teachers, who work within contexts where parents, administrators, other teachers, and students expect them to be the authority, admitting that one's practice is less than perfect is an act of vulnerability that depends on group trust and mutual respect. Trust and respect, in a profession beleaguered by consistent criticism, take time to develop.

A fourth feature was dependent on these three previous ones: the emergence of public disagreement. As the IMT teachers' conversations became longer and more sustained, focused, disclosing, and passionate, public disagreements began to emerge.

What were teachers learning in this group? It would appear that the group was developing a set of norms that allowed for professional discourse, for talk that would push thinking, perhaps even push practice. In several instances, there is evidence that teachers were learning to rethink their arguments and to evaluate their assumptions. Several participants were actively experimenting with their teaching. The authors also claim that the IMT members were learning about the enactment of mathematics reforms by engaging in their own learning in similar ways.

Our second case of opportunities to talk about teaching looks quite different and involves a qualitatively different forum: the professional network. Professional networks for teachers have gained substantial popularity in the last 15 years (Lieberman & McLaughlin, 1992; Pennell & Firestone, 1996). As they multiply, they take many forms, with no one network offering exactly the same opportunities to educators as another.

In one study of networks, Pennell and Firestone (1996) contrast the California Subject Matter Projects with the Vermont portfolio program. They interviewed teachers and teacher-leaders statewide and conducted case studies of particular sites within each of these networks. Each network envisioned accomplished teaching in similar ways: Teachers would be facilitators and guides, students would engage in real-world problems, working would be meaningful and purposeful, skills would be embedded in large problem-solving activities, students would often work collaboratively, and assessments would be ongoing and authentic. Each network also had a commitment to a "teachers-teaching-teachers" model of professional development (Pennell & Firestone, 1996, p. 53).

The researchers found that teachers' beliefs and background, social influences, and practical circumstances all shaped teachers' reactions to their experiences within the networks. As Pennell and Firestone (1996) note:

The California and Vermont network programs were most effective when teachers held beliefs that did not strongly conflict with program philosophies, some social support existed for participation and classroom change, and practical circumstances were not heavily prohibitive of participation and change. (p. 72)

It is difficult to ascertain what teachers were learning in this study, since the researchers had to rely on evaluation feedback about participants' feelings regarding networks. Such data are constraining; respondents to surveys and evaluations seldom report on what they learned but, rather, on what they thought of the enterprise.

In another study, one involving 16 educational reform networks, Lieberman and Grolnick (1996) found that the networks, while varied, shared five organizational themes. The first theme concerned the fact that each network had a purpose and direction, a goal, a cause, an interest around which the groups coalesced. For some, the goal might be the development of professional development schools;

for others, it might be the pursuit of helping schools become democratic organizations.

A second organizational theme concerned important qualitative features of the network communities. Each network was built and sustained by a constantly growing and developing community in which individuals had voice and commitment to the group, learned to collaborate, and strove for consensus. Each network entailed bringing people together for conversations; in these conversations, participants both learned and received emotional and psychological support.

A third theme that Lieberman and Grolnick noted was that each network used a range of activities to engage participants in learning and discussions. The activities varied: Electronic networking, conferences, courses and institutes, workshops, teacher research teams, and formal and informal study groups appeared across the networks. Characteristic of these activities was "time to talk." This time enabled the development of relationships that lasted long after the meeting or institute was over.

The fourth theme concerned the facilitative leadership that was essential to these networks.

> At times, facilitating networks appears to be about making phone calls, raising money, establishing connections, forming groups, finding places to meet, and brokering resources and people. However, it is also about creating "public spaces" in which educators can work together in ways that are different in quality and kind from those typical of their institutions, as well as from much that is considered standard professional development. It may be building structures that encourage a respectful dialogue between and among school and university personnel, or modeling more collaborative stances toward learning and support, enunciating important ideals . . . or leaving room for emergent goals. (p. 25)

The fifth theme Lieberman and Grolnick noted was dealing with the funding problem. Most of the networks have received considerable funding from private or corporate foundations, and continued pursuit of funding to support the networks' activities brought with it tensions (e.g., choosing names for the networks that would appeal to, not offend, potential funders and negotiating with funders their right to chart the course and content of the networks). Perhaps the most significant tension within this theme for our analysis relates to the difficulty of assessing networks' "productivity" or "impact":

> Learning in networks can be powerful, but it is often indirect—a result of new commitments and friendships, the exposure to new ideas, contacts with and observation of others' work, long-term involvement with many kinds of educators, growing cosmopolitanism and openness to ideas. This view of learning presents a measurement and evaluation problem that has not yet been solved in ways that satisfy the expectations of many funders or confirm the concrete experiences of those who view reform networks as the most appropriate forms of professional growth and learning. (Lieberman & Grolnick, 1996, p. 26)

Lieberman and Grolnick noted several tensions within the networks: negotiating between the network's overarching purposes and its daily "work," balancing outsider and insider knowledge and expertise, creating structures that allow for centralization and decentralization, dealing with the inevitable increased formalization that comes with a network's growth, and making decisions about membership, both inclusion and exclusion. As they successfully negotiate these tensions, networks provide multiple opportunities for teachers to learn.

But what do they learn? Lieberman and Grolnick offer several hypotheses. For example, networks provide educators with chances to label, articulate, and discuss their tacit knowledge. This articulation of tacitly held knowledge and beliefs about teaching and students serves to both dignify the educators' work and shape its substance. The networks did this by moving away from prescriptive models of professional development to models that involved problem solving and collective inquiry into challenging circumstances. The researchers note:

> [The networks] tried to achieve goals of participant learning and professional competence by modeling different modes of inquiry, supporting the formation of teams to create and write school-based plans for change, finding mechanisms to encourage cross-role groups to work together, focusing deeply on particular topics, and inviting the participants to help shape the agenda in their own terms. (p. 40)

The networks, given their flattened hierarchies, also provided participants with opportunities to collaborate and to take on leadership roles, both of which have the potential for leading to new learning. But the researchers close their discussion with the claim that we need to learn more about measuring networks' impact:

> Are principals more effective, are teachers teaching better, are students learning more? These are the "bottom line" questions that funders ask when they give money to support networks. Yet, as we have seen, network activity and success must be measured by understanding and tracking the connections between member involvement, learning, and active participation, as well as by observing changes in practice. Since it is always difficult to measure the relationships between cause and effect in school improvement, how can network participation and changed practice be documented to assure funders, politicians, and the public that this investment is "worthwhile"? (pp. 43–44)

A third study illuminates other dilemmas in understanding teacher learning in such networks. In an investigation conducted under the auspices of the Educational Policy and Practice Study at Michigan State University, Wilson, Lubienski, and Mattson (1996) observed the opportunities to learn mathematics that participants in the California Mathematics Projects (CMPs) experienced. While there are more than a dozen CMPs scattered across the state, many of them share a similar structure. Participating teachers apply to attend in the summer; in exchange for their attendance, they often receive a stipend and a month's worth of professional development activities designed to increase their leadership potential, as well as their knowledge of mathematics, innovative teaching practices, new materials and resources (including technology and curricula), and new policies about teaching, curriculum, and assessment.

In our research, we observed four different CMP sites, each for a week. We documented discussions and presentations and collected calendars and handouts. We interviewed participants and teacher-leaders. The range of topics was impressive: Teachers were presented with information about portfolios and performance assessments, about state policy mandates, about how to teach diverse students.

TABLE 1
Topics for Discussion at the CMP Sites

California-specific topics	National topics	CMP commitments

Curriculum developments and materials
  NSF projects
  Replacement units
    Multiplication
    Gulliver's travels
	NCTM standards
	  Curriculum
	  Teaching
	  Assessment
	New Standards Project
		Long-range goals and strategies
		
		Ongoing professional development
		
		Developing, nurturing, deploying, and sustaining teacher leadership

California Mathematics Council
  Professional development opportunities
  Renaissance Project
  Marilyn Burns
  EQUALS
	Systemic reform efforts
	NCTM activities and projects
		Making connections and facilitating collaborations in an effort to be inclusive, not exclusive
		
		A K–14 scope

CLAS development
  Timeline
  Scoring
State department policy documents
  1985 Framework
  1991 Framework
  It's Elementary
		The "gift of diversity"
		The development of a set of "common beliefs"
		  About mathematics
		  About teaching
		  About kids

Other projects Family Math		Teachers must know mathematics if they are to teach mathematics in powerful ways Projects are regionalized

Teachers worked with new calculators and technology designed as tools for innovative mathematics teaching. Participants were also offered multiple opportunities to talk about their experiences and to act as leaders for other teachers. We offered in our analysis a tentative list of the goals and commitments that we noted across the four CMPs (see Table 1).

In addition, throughout the summer sessions, teachers were also offered many opportunities to learn mathematics. In fact, we saw mathematics everywhere. At almost every turn, leaders tried to turn the group's attention to mathematical connections. The days always started with a problem and often ended with one. Leaders constantly probed participants for connections. Unlike much professional development of the past, then, subject matter—in this case, mathematics—was part and parcel of the ethos.

This is quite an accomplishment. The discourse was technical and professional: Talk of permutations and factorials filled the air, along with talk of portfolios and performance assessment, of the California Learning Assessment System and NCTM, of the California Mathematics Council and new standards. There was much to be learned about mathematics teaching and learning: reforms, research, instructional strategies, educational philosophies, pedagogical commitments.

Yet, as we looked closely for the mathematics, we saw some patterns. Mathematics was respected and constantly pointed to but seldom pushed on. Teacher-leaders worried about embarrassing participants who offered wrong answers. Opportunities to discuss underlying mathematical ideas were missed, repeatedly.

Although the set of mathematical activities and discussions we observed was diverse, sustained inquiry into mathematics was rare. The teachers and leaders mentioned mathematical concepts with frequency, but these statements and labels were rarely parsed or pursued. On the heels of many of the math activities they had participants work on, leaders often asked one of the questions we had in mind as we observed: "What's the math in this problem?" In response, participants generated lists. And the lists were filled with key mathematical concepts. The language was there, as were math activities. In spades.

For whatever reason, those spades were not turned. The ideas captured in the labels, the terms, those lists of bona fide mathematical concepts, processes, and algorithms were only rarely probed—and even then only briefly. Math activities were described and performed, the mathematics therein often listed. And the lists were accurate. But elaboration was rare, explication rarer still. We did not conclude that leaders and teachers were incapable of explicating and applying many of the concepts we heard named, but the fact that we saw very little such explication or investigation made us wonder why, and we offered our three hypotheses as a partial explanation for this phenomenon. With an agenda crammed with commitments and reforms—teach for understanding, use small groups, develop alternative assessments, and acquire vast professional knowledge among them—mathematics sometimes gets elbowed out. But it gets elbowed out for reasons that go well beyond the fullness of the reform platter. American schooling has been characterized by an anti-intellectualism that has fundamentally shaped the nature of teacher-student interactions. It seems likely that that same anti-intellectualism might seep into professional development opportunities, unless those opportunities are purposefully designed to counter that trend. Moreover, scholars have already noted that teachers are both the target and the tool of the current reforms (Cohen & Ball, 1990). Teaching cannot change without teacher commitment and leadership, yet teachers themselves have rarely had the chance to develop the mathematical knowledge on which these reforms depend. This paradox lies at the heart of the work of the California Mathematics Projects, indeed at the heart of all professional development.

COMMON THEMES IN CONTEMPORARY PROFESSIONAL DEVELOPMENT AND RESEARCH ON TEACHER LEARNING

What do professional networks all over the country have in common with science instruction in Cambridge or history and English teachers looking at books in Washington? Several themes strike us as significant. Before we begin this discussion, however, we remind readers of two things. First, we selected only highly regarded research. The efforts described here are among some of the best in the country. Second, most of the work described is long term, unfolding even as we write this chapter. Therefore, this discussion concerns what is in the literature thus far, not what is to come.

That said, we explore here several themes that run across the extant, published research on teacher acquisition of professional knowledge. First, all of the projects involved communities of learners that are redefining teaching practice. Although many of these projects started as funded professional development or research projects, most of them have continued to exist long after funding is over. Florio Ruane's and Featherstone's groups asked to continue, and the teachers who met one another in the networks kept in touch with one another, offering mutual support. This suggests to us that the participants have re-created their practice and found ways to include in their work lives time to inquire into and about teaching. As Karen, a participant in the McDonnell Project, said, "What I'm realizing is that I need to build this reading into my life" (Wineburg & Grossman, 1998, p. 353). The CGI participants, too, reconceptualized their practice, and for teachers who made it to Level 4, teaching included inquiry into students' mathematical thinking as well as instruction.

A related and second theme across these cases is the idea that teacher learning ought not be bound and *delivered* but rather *activated*. This positions the "what" of teacher knowledge in a much different place than it has been. Traditionally, professional development has been conceptualized as a dissemination activity: locate new knowledge relevant to teaching, package it in an attractive manner, and get it into the hands of teachers. Yet, the Cheche Konnen researchers found that giving teachers a new curriculum was not enough to enact the change envisioned in that curriculum. It was only when they redirected their studies to helping the teachers understand their own knowledge that, they argue, changes occurred. This observation appears to be reinforced by the findings of the CGI researchers; teachers did not necessarily transform themselves into inquirers simply because they learned about children's thinking. Thus, in addition to asking them to reconceptualize their teaching, these projects also require teachers to reconceptualize professional development.

Essentially, what these professional development projects appear to be doing when they ask teachers to become scientists or mathematics learners or book club participants is to engage them as learners in the area that their students will learn in but at a level that is more suitable to their own learning. Teachers appear to be acquiring knowledge of subject matter and of students (both specific and more general), but the knowledge they are acquiring seems broader and more diffuse than knowledge of a particular curriculum taught to children. This is true of the Literary Circle, of the McDonnell Project, of the Cheche Konnen Project, and of IMT. And while it seems clear that the knowledge teachers acquire in these projects could and should be helpful to them, it is not clear what the relationship is between that more general knowledge and the specific curricula or students that the participants encounter in their practice. However, it is important to note that Kennedy (1998), in an analysis of in-service programs, found that programs that focused on subject matter knowledge and knowledge of students were likely to "have a greater impact on student learning than are programs that focus on teaching behaviors'' (p. 10). This suggests that current professional development is, indeed, on the right track.

A third commonality is the privileging of teachers' interaction with one another. These projects appear to have similar assumptions about the pedagogy of professional development; all appear to be aiming for the development of something akin to Lord's (1994) ''critical colleagueship.'' The projects use different mechanisms for the development of that collegiality, but each project struggles with how to build trust and community while aiming for a professional discourse that includes and does not avoid critique. And it appears that the factors that shape the development of that community might vary if the professional development is conceptualized as school-based versus outside of the confines of a teacher's home school.

Other themes are more methodological. The research reported is labor intensive and qualitative, and it involves substantial commitment to examining teacher talk in interview and group conversations and teachers' classroom behaviors. Each research project struggles with ways to document teacher knowledge, and several have developed discourse analyses of group talk. Discourse analysis techniques appear to appeal to this broad array of researchers for two reasons. First, the knowledge developed in these projects is both individual and collective, and one measure of the knowledge of the community would focus on the language and norms used by the group during discussions. Second, as the Cheche Konnen researchers note, the knowledge of such groups is ''in motion,'' consistently growing and changing. Thus, part of the appeal of discourse-analytic techniques might be that they acknowledge and use that dynamic aspect of socially held knowledge rather than ignore it by presuming more static conceptions of knowledge.

Two other research-related themes concern not what we see but what we do not see often enough. Kennedy (1998), in reviewing the professional development literature in mathematics and science, found that CGI was one of the only projects that linked studies of teacher learning and knowledge to student achievement. Furthermore, CGI researchers were able to document differences in teaching behaviors as a consequence of participating in CGI. Other research on professional development and teacher learning would benefit from conceptualizing research agendas that enable similar analyses.

CGI research offers another important contrast. Despite researchers' best intentions, it is still difficult for readers to know what the participants specifically learned in many of the professional development projects discussed herein. We are persuaded that they learned to talk in groups, that they learned to critically appraise each other's practice and ideas. All participants appear to be acquiring knowledge of professional discourse and its norms. But what of subject matter or students or teaching? CGI research is the exception to this rule. Recall that the researchers had developed a framework of problem types and children's thinking. Their goal was to have teacher-participants learn that framework and use it in their practice. Over time, the researchers used a variety of means—a CGI belief instrument with a Likert scale, interviews with and observation of teachers and students, and a knowledge assessment with a repertory grid technique—to measure teachers' knowledge of the framework (Fennema, Franke, Carpenter, & Carey, 1993; Loef, 1990). Analyses across these different instruments allowed them to demonstrate and document what knowledge of children the teacher-participants had acquired. Consider a description of one teacher:

At the end of Year 2, the data from the experimental study indicated that Ms. J ranked near the top of the experimental group on knowledge of the addition/subtraction framework. More than most of the other teachers, she was able to identify the problem types, their relative difficulty, and their related solution strategies. She was able to correctly identify which problems children in her room could solve and which solution strategies they would use.

At the end of Year 4 when Ms. J's knowledge was assessed using repertory grid techniques (Loef, 1990), we gathered data that more analytically described her knowledge of the addition/subtraction framework. Her knowledge was extensive, accurate, hierarchically organized, and integrated in a complex way. She could identify problem types, even those that were written to be ambiguous so that the action words did not indicate an action in the modeling of the solution for it (Megan picked 6 apples. Tom picked 9 apples. How many apples were picked?), and she demonstrated knowledge of the complexity of children's thinking in the domain. Interwoven with Ms. J's knowledge of problem types and solutions were pedagogical concerns about the use of counters, relevance of the problem context to children, the language used in problems, choice of number size, and selection of problems for which a variety of strategies could be used.

Ms. J's knowledge was organized into two different levels: (a) global knowledge of children's solutions that involved direct modeling or counting, and (b) instantiations of modeling and counting solutions for specific problems. What drove this organization was how children think about the problems and solutions, not how adults think about the same problems. (Fennema, Franke, Carpenter, & Carey, 1993, pp. 563–564)

The description goes on, and the researchers offer other descriptions both of what the teachers knew and of how their knowledge changed (e.g., Fennema, Carpenter, Franke, & Carey, 1992). Granted, the preceding description is part of an article that focuses only on one teacher: Ms. J. Such a focus enables this careful description of what the teacher knew about children's thinking and the nature of that knowledge. Other research reviewed here has not had that luxury, for researchers must report on both the nature of the professional development (its content and pedagogy) and the processes by which the communities of learners coalesced. However, future research will need to begin offering more detailed analyses of what exactly teachers learned within those communities.

Other researchers have, in fact, started such work. For fear of overemphasizing mathematics teaching in our review, we have not described QUASAR (Quantitative Understanding: Amplifying Student Achievement and Reasoning), a large-scale middle school mathematics reform project with a rich database of teacher and student learning (Silver & Stein, 1996, 1997; Stein, Grover, & Henningsen, 1996; Stein & Lane, 1996; Stein, Silver, & Smith, in press). Other studies have been conducted by the Center for Teaching Policy and the National Partnership for Excellence and Accountability in Teaching, as well as researchers at the National Center for Improving Student Learning and Achievement in Mathematics and Science (e.g., Lehrer & Schauble, n.d.). Of course, the capacity of researchers to tie measures of teacher learning to measures of student learning is also challenged by the lack of robust and standardized measures of student learning in many fields.

CHALLENGES FACED BY PROFESSIONAL DEVELOPMENT PROJECTS AND RESEARCHERS

But we do not wish to suggest that future research on teacher acquisition of professional knowledge is simply a matter of doing what CGI researchers have done or connecting professional development to classroom teaching and student achievement. CGI researchers have been working on their project much longer than researchers involved with these other projects. And they are able to draw on relevant mathematics-related research, as well as measures of student learning, that other researchers do not have access to. Besides, we believe that such simple, straightforward solutions are not sufficient, since the research we have reviewed suggests a set of challenges inherent in contemporary efforts to document teacher learning and knowledge growth. We highlight those challenges here.

Before we launch into a discussion of the challenges, recall the larger context of professional development. As Ball and Cohen (in press) note, we have no professional development "system." Teacher learning is fragmented. Teachers patch together a lifelong curriculum of professional development in odd and assorted ways. Some teachers pursue any opportunity to learn with passion, while others attend workshops when mandates arrive in their school mailbox. Some teachers work in schools and school districts where leaders have a theory of teaching, learning, and change that drives decisions about what opportunities teachers have to learn (e.g., Elmore, 1997). Others work in contexts where little thought is given to either how teachers learn or when. The research reviewed here was conceptualized and implemented within this random, sometimes voluntary, sometimes mandated, always fragmented system. That larger context, we conjecture, is a significant factor that shapes both what happens within professional development and, therefore, what researchers are able to learn.

One challenge is rooted in the poor reputation of traditional professional development workshops. Teachers are loathe to participate in anything that smacks of 1-day workshops offered by outside "experts" who know (and care) little about the particular and specific contexts of a given school. Similarly, researchers appear hesitant to study traditional professional and staff development: Why study something that so many teachers dismiss as less than helpful?

In response to the growing sense that there are features of promising professional development (recall the lists we noted at the beginning of this review) that would lead to better professional development, many thoughtful educators are creating alternative professional learning contexts, among them the book clubs, networks, and study groups reviewed here. But little is known about the specifics entailed in systematically constructing such opportunities to learn, and so researchers interested in studying teacher learning within these new environments find themselves researching a phenomenon while they (or others) are trying to build it. Studying a phenomenon while one creates it always presents particular problems, for two distinct reasons. For one, the endeavor is complicated because one's attention must be bifocal: creating meaningful professional development and doing rigorous research. Brown (1992) discusses this problem in the context of creating and studying "design experiments," a concept coined by Collins (1992). The goal of design experiments is to create innovative learning environments and simultaneously study the behavior and cognition of the participants. But as Brown notes, such work requires a tension between attending to teaching and attending to research:

> As a design scientist, it is necessary to tease apart the major features of enticing learning environments: the role of teachers, students, and researchers; the actual contribution of curricula and computer support; methods by which distributed expertise and shared meaning are engineered, and so forth. There is a constant tension between designing an exciting classroom for happy campers and maintaining research standards of control and prediction. (p. 173)

Contemporary efforts to help teachers acquire professional knowledge share another challenge with design experiments. As Brown (1992) argues, design experiments are messy, so much so that they are a "methodological headache for traditional psychology": "Components are rarely isolatable, the whole really is more than the sum of its parts. The learning effects are not even simple interactions, but highly interdependent outcomes of a complex social and cognitive intervention" (p. 166).

Indeed, most researchers we read explicitly or implicitly referred to the messiness of this kind of research. Grossman, Wineburg, and Woolworth (1998) discuss the implications:

> Given the challenges of collecting and analyzing data on complex, longitudinal, multi-faceted projects, how do we address the issue of evidence of teacher development? How do we define learning in these contexts? Given that much of the data consists of teachers' discourse in group settings, how do we analyze discourse to investigate the learning of both individuals and the group as a whole? What timetable is appropriate for beginning to trace changes in actual classroom practice? And how can we develop analytical approaches that are rigorous yet respect the complexity of the enterprise? (pp. 1–2)

Furthermore, as these thoughtful researcher-professional development leaders construct their projects, the research base from which they can draw varies considerably. Mathematics research on children's thinking and knowledge has a depth and breadth that other fields do not yet have. CGI researchers were able to draw on a wealth of research related to children's thinking that other researchers did not have available.

And things are more complicated still. Much as we would like to, we cannot mandate learning, only attendance. All professional development programs confront this challenge; even when attendance is voluntary, teachers arrive at professional development programs with clear ideas of what kinds of "knowledge" are most helpful and relevant to their ongoing learning. New activities, new curricula, new instructional tools and tricks are welcome. Seldom do teachers come to a professional development program assuming that their views of knowledge or subject matter or students need to change. And teachers' call for new tools and techniques is a legitimate one; all of us who teach are always in need of additional "tricks of the trade."

But most professional development that aims for the acquisition of professional knowledge assumes that teachers must engage in learning that goes beyond picking up new techniques. Thus, another challenge in professional development involves bridging the chasm between what one's clients—the teachers—want and expect and one's own goals. And because one is working with adults, and their need for new techniques is genuine, most ongoing, high-quality professional development entails a constant negotiation: of content, of purpose, of control, of discourse style. Richardson (1992) calls this the "agenda-setting dilemma." Doing research in such a context is equally challenging, since there is no simple "treatment" that one administers to the subjects (here, teachers). Furthermore, there is no agreed upon test of the results. The terrain shifts, the discussions and activities take unanticipated turns. The subjects are adults; they argue, resist, walk out, demand responsiveness. They are learners entitled to voice their opinions. The McDonnell participants explain:

It is tempting for advocates of teacher community to assume it is easy for groups of teachers, not used to working with each other (sometimes actively avoiding each other) to come together and establish norms of professional civility. Our experience belies this romantic conception. Conflict is a natural process in a diverse group of 20 people—people who represent different backgrounds, subject matter training, social and political perspectives, and beliefs (sometimes diametrically opposed) of what constitutes good teaching. As outsiders in this community, we could mediate conflict in ways that were difficult for insiders to do.

Whenever researchers approach their work as participant-observers, they face the question of how to balance these two roles. As the initiators of this intervention, we served a pivotal function. Initially, the community we envisioned was to be structured around a set of professional development activities instigated by the researchers. By providing the time and space for a community to emerge, however, we were in fact asking teachers to assume a greater agency in their professional development. In some instances, the research agenda was out of sync with the level of trust the group had developed. . . .

While from the outset it was clear to all the participants that we were engaged in a research activity, aspects of that role (such as the omnipresent tape recorders) proved troubling for some members of the community. As participants we were also members of an emerging community and found ourselves increasingly aware of the fit between project activities, our expectations and the professional culture we had entered. While at times we thought it necessary to nudge the group in a direction of our interest (e.g., the research agenda), we also came to appreciate the challenges teachers face, both on a personal and organizational level, when they are asked to rethink the accepted norms and values of their professional culture. (Thomas, Wineburg, Grossman, Myhre, & Woolworth, 1998, p. x)

In this context, it is no wonder that current research is chock-full of descriptions of process: Process is the single thing that one can count on. But what teachers come to know about subject matter or teaching or children or pedagogy depends, in part, on what the project leaders and participants negotiate.

These negotiations of content and process are complicated by yet other factors, which lead us to several other challenges. One such challenge relates to Ball's point concerning a lack of a forum for discussions of teaching:

Politely refraining from critique and challenge, teachers have no forum for debating and improving their understandings. To the extent that teaching remains a smorgasbord of alternatives with no real sense of community, there is no basis for comparing or choosing from among alternatives, no basis for real and helpful debate. This lack impedes the capacity to grow. (Ball, 1994, p. 16)

We would argue that equally important is the lack of norms and expectations for such discourse. The projects reviewed here are carefully constructed, led by thoughtful researchers and teachers. Yet, almost to a study, the one consistent result is that helping teachers learn to discuss and think and talk critically about their own practice can be painful and consumes considerable energy. Groups have to move beyond politeness and "that's fine for you" to Lord's (1994) critical colleagueship. This involves developing norms, a language, trust, and a sense that change is desirable and expected, not merely possible. Ball and Cohen (in press) argue that such work requires shifting the discourse of teaching from a "rhetoric of conclusions" to a Schwabian "narrative of inquiry" that focuses on practical reasoning (Fenstermacher & Richardson, 1993), to a discussion of conjectures and possibilities rather than of definitive answers and scripts for behavior.

Research on teacher learning in these settings suffers considerably, for funding often ends just as the group learns to be critical. All many researchers can say is that the teachers learned to talk to one another, but little is reported about what they learned.

Perhaps the most formidable challenge is one endemic to all education. Learning, real learning, is hard work. You read, you think, you talk. You get something wrong, you don't understand something, you try it again. Sometimes you hit a wall in your thinking, sometimes it is just too frustrating. Yes, learning can be fun and inspiring but along the way, it usually makes us miserable. And to move forward, we often have to acknowledge that which we do not know. Ball and Cohen (in press) theorize that teacher learning requires some disequilibrium and that important teacher learning emerges only from occasions when teachers' extant assumptions are challenged: "Situating professional development in materials, teaching, and incidents that may stimulate some productive disequilibrium offers useful territory for teachers' learning." Teachers who sign up for a professional development experience expect to learn about new theories of learning or new instructional strategies. They do not expect to have their knowledge held suspect or their previous practices questioned. And admitting that you have done the wrong thing in the past or do not know the subject matter you teach is unsettling. Yet, professional development designed to help teachers acquire new professional knowledge, especially subject matter knowledge, can often involve just that.

We pause to tell a story: In a recent course that the first author was teaching for history teachers, the class had been happily reading a history about the French Revolution by Schama, *Citizens*. The students were excited; they had not had a chance to learn history in a while, and Schama's story was captivating, if complicated. For the first week, the discussion centered on examining Schama's rhetoric:

How was he making arguments? What was he trying to persuade the reader of? Energy and spirits in the class were high, discussions lively.

The next week, the discussion turned to the content of the book, and in a move familiar to all students and teachers of history, Wilson asked the students to create a time line of the events and characters in the book: Who was doing what? When? Why? The previous lively discussions died, the room was silent, and having a discussion was like pulling teeth. Several days into this, Wilson asked the group what was wrong: "I feel like I'm 16 years old again back in school, worried about a test, scared of what I don't know," one previously enthusiastic teacher said. Her eyes brimming with tears, another teacher explained, "When we were talking about what Schama was doing, I didn't have to worry about whether I understood the story. When you asked us for the time line, it felt like you were testing my knowledge. That's not why I'm here."

One might dismiss this as a clash between the teachers' expectations and Wilson's, but we believe the story is relevant to perhaps the most critical challenge to research. Learning is hard. Studies of schools—especially high schools (Cusick, 1983; McNeil, 1986; Sedlak, Wheeler, Pullin, & Cusick, 1986)—demonstrate how students bargain the hard stuff out of the curriculum. Those students are not evil, or lazy. Learning is hard. And we live in a culture that does not necessarily reward or value knowledge. Students sensibly try to make school easier and to avoid work that will bring them no immediate reward. The intellectualism of the current standards reform movement does not acknowledge this core of anti-intellectualism in American society.

As professional development takes more authentic, more substantive forms—in an effort to provide teachers with the knowledge they need to teach students—it flies in the face of the tradition of schools, not to mention the traditions of in-service and staff development. As Little (1989) noted, "The market-driven and menu-oriented character of much [traditional] staff development [left] the field vulnerable to content that [was] intellectually shallow, gimmicky, or simply wrong" (p. 178). Leaders of "new and improved" professional development are aiming for something more substantive and substantial, something more intellectually rigorous. Aware that they need to negotiate content and process with their adult learners, and equally aware of the need to attract—and keep—their voluntary attendants, professional development projects might find themselves facing attempts at similar bargaining down (or out) of content. And not because teachers are uncommitted to change. Contemporary reforms—of curriculum, of assessments, and of professional development—assume a valuing of knowledge that is not part of the current coin of the realm in American schooling. And teachers, many of whom feel beleaguered in the face of the insistent waves of criticism of the U.S. educational system, do not want to spend their free professional time admitting to what they do not know.

For researchers of teacher knowledge, this is a particular problem; to document what teachers know, one must assess knowledge. Some of those assessments might look like, or at the very least feel like, tests. Even if an assessment is done in an interview, it can still feel like an oral examination. But we have an obligation to move beyond documenting what teachers say they know, no matter how difficult the interpersonal aspects of such research may be. How do we know that teachers' "knowledge" is knowledge? As Fenstermacher (1994) asserts:

There are serious epistemological problems in identifying as knowledge that which teachers believe, imagine, intuit, sense, and reflect upon. It is not that such mental activities might not lead to knowledge; rather, it is that these mental events, once inferred or expressed, must be subjected to assessment for their epistemic merit. (p. 47)

Fenstermacher (1994) goes on:

There is much merit in believing that teachers know a great deal and in seeking to learn what they know, but that merit is corrupted and demeaned when it is implied that this knowledge is not subject to justification or cannot or should not be justified. The challenge for teacher knowledge research is not simply one of showing us that teachers think, believe, or have opinions but that they know. (p. 51)

Thus, it is to the advantage of researchers interested in documenting teacher learning to begin to immerse themselves in issues of teacher knowledge, since we presume that what teachers learn becomes a form of knowledge that they then use in their practice.

WHERE TO RESEARCH?

The activities of staff and researchers of contemporary professional development efforts seem promising, even inviting. We would like to spend our time in the company of such colleagues. Yet, it also seems an appropriate time to take stock, in an effort to yield more consistent and insightful research results. We conclude our essay with four observations.

Our first observation involves a semi-ahistorical tone in contemporary work. The researchers tell thoughtful and personal stories of their struggles to create these communities of learners and of the importance of focusing teachers' attention on students and their ideas, on subject matter worth learning. We have traditions of such work in the United States, both within and outside the boundaries of teacher education, and it would behoove all of us interested in the development of high-quality professional development to pay more attention to Duckworth's (1987) experience with teacher study groups or the tradition of child study that emerged from the Prospect School (Carroll & Carini, 1991). For those interested in understanding book clubs, reading histories of those clubs might inform the work (e.g., Gere, 1997).

Our second observation concerns the need for subject-specific investigations of teacher learning. If teachers are to acquire subject matter knowledge, and subject matter knowledge is acquired differently across disciplines, then one would anticipate disciplinary differences in professional development. Such differences are clear in this small sampling. English and history teachers read books, mathematics teachers did math problems, science teachers engaged in experiments and scientific inquiries.

Our third observation is that future research on teachers' acquisition of professional knowledge must attend to issues of teacher knowledge. Stories of teacher learning presume that teachers learn something. The "what" of teacher learning needs to be identified, conceptualized, and assessed. This will require making informed decisions about one's assumptions regarding the nature of teaching knowledge (Fenstermacher, 1994) and building models of that knowledge against which to measure teachers' acquired knowledge. This work—part empirical, part conceptual—will entail at least three parts. One involves delineating the content of teacher knowledge: What categories of knowledge should good teachers possess? In studies of good teachers, what knowledge do these teachers possess? A second line of work involves understanding more about the ways in which teaching knowledge is held and accessed. This would involve building a conception of teacher knowledge that accommodates both the CGI framework of students' mathematical thinking and the Cheche Konnen canonical stories. Third, researchers would need more understanding of how teaching knowledge enables practice. That Ms. J surprised researchers by her applications of knowledge of student thinking suggests that there is no simple and linear map between what teachers know and what they do in classrooms. Research on teacher learning and the acquisition of professional knowledge requires better conceptualization of the mechanisms by which knowledge informs practice. This does not mean prematurely closing off one's ability to rethink the nature or content of teacher knowledge, for research will, it is hoped, push the field to a more coherent and comprehensive view of the knowledge required for and of teachers.

A fourth observation concerns the comprehensiveness of research on teacher learning and the acquisition of professional knowledge. With the exception of the CGI research, few research programs currently link studies of teacher learning to teaching behavior and student achievement. Yet, the contemporary press for accountability requires that all research, even research on teachers and their learning, include some recognition of the need for student data. This is a valid criticism of past research, for even if we knew more about what teachers learned in these enterprises, we would still need to know whether their newly acquired knowledge and skill helped them be more accomplished teachers.

Our final observation entails the explanations that are offered for why teachers learn. Researchers are making an effort to both create contexts that enable teacher learning and describe what teachers learn, but little effort has been put into explaining how those contexts enable learning. Lord (1994), for example, theorizes that critical collegiality will help teachers learn by:

1. Creating and sustaining productive disequilibrium through self reflection, collegial dialogue, and on-going critique.
2. Embracing fundamental intellectual virtues. Among these are openness to new ideas, willingness to reject weak practices or flimsy reasoning when faced with countervailing evidence and sound arguments, accepting responsibility for acquiring and using relevant information in the construction of technical arguments, willingness to seek out the best ideas or the best knowledge from within the subject-matter communities, greater reliance on organized and deliberate investigations rather than learning by accident, and assuming collective responsibility for creating a professional record of teachers' research and experimentation.

3. Increasing the capacity for empathetic understanding (placing oneself in a colleague's shoes). That is, understanding a colleague's dilemma in the terms he or she understands it.
4. Developing and honing the skills and attributes associated with negotiation, improved communication, and the resolution of competing interests.
5. Increasing teachers' comfort with high levels of ambiguity and uncertainty, which will be regular features of teaching for understanding.
6. Achieving collective generativity—"knowing how to go on" (Wittgenstein, 1958) as a goal of successful inquiry and practice. (p. 193)

These are working hypotheses about the nature of teacher learning, and future research might test these hypotheses by examining the variation across and within contexts for teacher learning. Theory development for teacher learning might then strive to explain why these characteristics matter and in what ways. For example, while CGI researchers collected data on teacher knowledge, teacher behaviors, and student achievement, their analyses do not offer us explanations of why Ms. J was able to learn as much as she did or why her knowledge took the form it did in her practice. The McDonnell Project has embraced fundamental intellectual virtues, and, by all reports, the participants are happily experiencing an intellectual life. If this new intellectualism results in better teaching and higher student achievement, we would still need to know why and how. All research on teacher learning and the acquisition of professional knowledge would benefit from more systematic theorizing about the mechanisms by which teachers learn.

In conclusion, our charge was to examine the literature on teacher learning of professional knowledge (especially content knowledge). There is much good work—both development and research—currently under way in professional development, some of which we have highlighted here. There is equally good work being conducted on the nature of teacher learning and on the professional knowledge base of teaching. Our review of the literature leads us to conclude that the field is oddly discontinuous; while we were able to locate many projects that offered teachers opportunities to learn, few such projects had yet completed analyses of what professional knowledge was acquired in those communities of learners. Fewer still had explicated their theories of how teachers learned and designed research to test those theories. The future of good research on teacher learning of professional knowledge lies in our ability to weave together ideas of teacher learning, professional development, teacher knowledge, and student learning—fields that have largely operated independent of one another.

REFERENCES

Abdal-Haqq, I. (1995). *Making time for teacher professional development* (Digest 95-4). Washington, DC: ERIC Clearinghouse on Teaching and Teacher Education.

Ball, D. L. (1993). With an eye on the mathematical horizon: Dilemmas of teaching elementary school mathematics. *Elementary School Journal, 93,* 373–397.

Ball, D. L. (1994). *Developing mathematics reform: What don't we know about teacher learning—but would make good working hypotheses?* Paper presented at the Conference on Teacher Enhancement in Mathematics, K–6, Arlington, VA.

Ball, D. L. (1996). Teacher learning and the mathematics reforms: What do we think we know and what do we need to learn? *Phi Delta Kappan, 77,* 500–508.

Ball, D. L., & Cohen, D. K. (in press). Developing practice, developing practitioners: Toward a practice-based theory of professional education. In L. D. Hammond & G. Sykes (Eds.), *Teaching as the learning profession: Handbook of policy and practice.* San Francisco: Jossey-Bass.

Barnett, C. (1991). Building a case-based curriculum to enhance the pedagogical content knowledge of teachers. *Journal of Teacher Education, 42,* 263–272.

Barnett, C. (1998). Mathematics teaching cases as a catalyst for informed strategic inquiry. *Teaching and Teacher Education, 14,* 81–93.

Barnett, C., Goldenstein, D., & Jackson, B. (1994). *Mathematics teaching cases: Fractions, decimals, ratios, and percents.* Portsmouth, NH: Heinemann.

Borko, H., & Putnam, R. T. (1996). Learning to teach. In D. C. Berliner & R. C. Calfee (Eds.), *Handbook of educational psychology* (pp. 673–708). New York: Macmillan.

Brown, A. (1992). Design experiments: Theoretical and methodological challenges in creating complex interventions in classroom settings. *Journal of the Learning Sciences, 2,* 141–178.

Carpenter, T. P., Fennema, E., & Franke, M. L. (1996). Cognitively guided instruction: A knowledge base for reform in primary mathematics instruction. *Elementary School Journal, 97,* 3–20.

Carpenter, T. P., Fennema, E., Peterson, P. L., & Carey, D. (1988). Teachers' pedagogical content knowledge of students' problem solving. *Journal of Research in Mathematics Education, 19,* 385–401.

Carpenter, T. P., Fennema, E., Peterson, P. L., Chiang, C., & Loef, M. (1989). Using knowledge of children's mathematical thinking in classroom teaching: An experimental study. *American Educational Research Journal, 26,* 499–532.

Carpenter, T. P., Franke, M. L., & Levi, L. (1998, April). *Teachers' epistemological beliefs about their knowledge of children's mathematical thinking.* Paper presented at the annual meeting of the American Educational Research Association, San Diego, CA.

Carroll, D., & Carini, P. (1991). Tapping teachers' knowledge. In V. Perrone (Ed.), *Expanding student assessment.* Reston, VA: Association for Supervision and Curriculum Development.

Cohen, D. K. (1990). A revolution in one classroom: The case of Mrs. Oublier. *Educational Evaluation and Policy Analysis, 12,* 311–330.

Cohen, D. K., & Ball, D. L. (1990). Relations between policy and practice: A commentary. *Educational Evaluation and Policy Analysis, 12,* 331–338.

Collins, A. (1992). Toward a design science of education. In E. Scanlon & T. O'Shea (Eds.), *New directions in educational technology.* New York: Springer-Verlag.

Corcoran, T. C. (1995). *Transforming professional development for teachers: A guide for state policymakers.* Washington, DC: National Governors' Association.

Council of Chief State School Officers. (n.d.-a). *Model standards in mathematics for beginning teacher development: A resource for state dialogue.* Washington, DC.

Council of Chief State School Officers. (n.d.-b). *Model standards in science for beginning teacher development: A resource for state dialogue.* Washington, DC.

Cusick, P. A. (1983). *The egalitarian ideal and the American high school: Studies of three schools.* New York: Longman.

Duckworth, E. (1987). *"The having of wonderful ideas" and other essays on teaching and learning.* New York: Teachers College Press.

Elmore, R. F. (with D. Burney). (1997). *Investing in teacher learning: Staff development and instructional improvement in Community School District #2, New York City.* New York and Philadelphia: National Commission on Teaching and America's Future and Consortium for Policy Research in Education.

Elmore, R. F., Peterson, P. L., & McCarthy, S. J. (1996). *Restructuring in the classroom: Teaching, learning, and school organization.* San Francisco: Jossey-Bass.

Featherstone, H., Pfeiffer, L., & Smith, S. P. (1993). *Learning in good company: Report on a pilot study* (Research Report 93-2). East Lansing: National Center for Research on Teacher Learning, Michigan State University.

Featherstone, H., Pfeiffer, L., Smith, S. P., Beasley, K., Corbin, D., Derksen, J., Pasek, L., Shank, C., & Shears, M. (n.d.). *"Could you say more about that?" A conversation about the development of a group's investigation of mathematics teaching.* East Lansing: National Center for Research on Teacher Learning, Michigan State University.

Featherstone, H. S., Smith, S. P., Beasley, K., Corbin, D., & Shank, C. (1995). *Expanding the equation: Learning mathematics through teaching in new ways* (Research Report 95-1). East Lansing: National Center for Research on Teacher Learning, Michigan State University.

Feiman-Nemser, S. (1983). Learning to teach. In L. S. Shulman & G. Sykes (Eds.), *Handbook of teaching and policy* (pp. 150–170). New York: Longman.

Feiman-Nemser, S., & Buchmann, M. (1985). Pitfalls of experience in teacher preparation. *Teachers College Record, 87,* 49–65.

Feiman-Nemser, S., & Floden, R. E. (1986). The cultures of teaching. In M. C. Wittrock (Ed.), *Handbook of research on teaching* (3rd ed., pp. 505–526). New York: Macmillan.

Feiman-Nemser, S., & Remillard, J. (1995). Perspectives on learning to teach. In F. Murray (Ed.), *The teacher educator's handbook* (pp. 63–91). San Francisco: Jossey-Bass.

Fennema, E., Carpenter, T. P., Franke, M. L., & Carey, D. A. (1992). Learning to use children's mathematics thinking: A case study. In C. Maher & R. Davis (Eds.), *Relating schools to reality* (pp. 93–118). Needham Heights, MA: Allyn & Bacon.

Fennema, E., Carpenter, T. P., Franke, M. L., Levi, L., Jacobs, V. R., & Empson, S. B. (1996). A longitudinal study of learning to use children's thinking in mathematics instruction. *Journal for Research in Mathematics Education, 27,* 403–434.

Fennema, E., & Franke, M. L. (1992). Teachers' knowledge and its impact. In D. A. Grouws (Ed.), *Handbook of research on mathematics teaching and learning* (pp. 147–164). New York: Macmillan.

Fennema, E., Franke, M. L., Carpenter, T. P., & Carey, D. (1993). Using children's mathematical knowledge in instruction. *American Educational Research Journal, 30,* 555–583.

Fenstermacher, G. D. (1994). The knower and the known: The nature of knowledge in research on teaching. In L. Darling-Hammond (Ed.), *Review of research in education* (Vol. 20, pp. 3–56). Washington, DC: American Educational Research Association.

Fenstermacher, G. D., & Richardson, V. (1993). The elicitation and reconstruction of practical arguments in teaching. *Journal of Curriculum Studies, 25,* 101–114.

Florio Ruane, S. (1994). The Future Teachers' Autobiography Club: Preparing educators to support literacy learning in culturally diverse classrooms. *English Education, 26,* 52–66.

Florio Ruane, S., & deTar, J. (1995). Conflict and consensus in teacher candidates' discussion of ethnic autobiography. *English Education, 27,* 11–39.

Florio Ruane, S., Raphael, T. E., Glazier, J., McVee, M., & Wallace, S. (in press). Discovering culture in discussion of autobiographical literature: Transforming the education of literacy teachers. In *The annual yearbook of the National Reading Conference.* Chicago: National Reading Conference.

Franke, M. L., Carpenter, T. P., Levi, L. W., & Fennema, E. (1998, April). *Teachers as learners: Developing understanding through children's thinking.* Paper presented at the annual meeting of the American Educational Research Association, San Diego, CA.

Gall, M. D., & Renchler, R. S. (1985). *Effective staff development for teachers: A research based model.* Eugene: ERIC Clearinghouse on Educational Management, University of Oregon.

Gere, A. R. (1997). *Intimate practices: Literacy and cultural work in U.S. women's clubs, 1880–1920.* Urbana: University of Illinois Press.

Grossman, P., Wineburg, S., & Woolworth, S. (1998). *But what did we learn? Understanding changes in a community of teacher learners.* Unpublished manuscript, University of Washington.

Gumperz, J. (1982). *Discourse strategies.* New York: Cambridge University Press.

Guskey, T. R. (n.d.). *Results-oriented professional development: In search of an optimal mix of effective practices.* Unpublished manuscript, University of Kentucky.

Kennedy, M. (1998, April). *The relevance of content in inservice teacher education.* Paper presented at the annual meeting of the American Educational Research Association, San Diego, CA.

Lampert, M., & Ball, D. L. (1998). *Mathematics, teaching and multimedia: Investigations of real practice.* New York: Teachers College Press.

Lehrer, R., & Schauble, L. (n.d.). *Modeling in mathematics and science.* Unpublished manuscript, University of Wisconsin.

Lieberman, A., & Grolnick, M. (1996). Networks and reform in American education. *Teachers College Record, 98,* 7–45.

Lieberman, A., & McLaughlin, M. W. (1992). Networks for educational change: Powerful and problematic. *Phi Delta Kappan, 73,* 673–677.

Little, J. W. (1988). Seductive images and organizational realities in professional development. In A. Lieberman (Ed.), *Rethinking school improvement.* New York: Teachers College Press.

Little, J. W. (1989). District policy choices and teachers' professional development opportunities. *Educational Evaluation and Policy Analysis, 11,* 165–179.

Little, J. W. (1994). Teachers' professional development in a climate of educational reform. *Educational Evaluation and Policy Analysis, 15,* 129–151.

Loef, M. (1990). *Understanding teachers' knowledge about building instruction on children's mathematical thinking: Application of a personal construct approach.* Unpublished doctoral dissertation, University of Wisconsin–Madison.

Lord, B. (1994). Teachers' professional development: Critical colleagueship and the role of professional communities. In N. Cobb (Ed.), *The future of education: Perspectives on national standards in education* (pp. 175–204). New York: College Entrance Examination Board.

Lortie, D. C. (1975). *Schoolteacher: A sociological study of teaching.* Chicago: University of Chicago Press.

McNeil, L. (1986). *Contradictions of control: School structure and school knowledge.* Boston: Routledge & Kegan Paul.

National Board for Professional Teaching Standards. (1989). *Toward high and rigorous standards for the teaching profession: Initial policies and perspectives of the National Board for Professional Teaching Standards.* Washington, DC.

National Council of Teachers of English. (1996). *Standards for English language arts.* Urbana, IL.

National Council of Teachers of Mathematics. (1989). *Curriculum and evaluation standards for school mathematics.* Reston, VA.

National Council of Teachers of Mathematics. (1991). *Professional standards for teaching mathematics.* Reston, VA.

Pennell, J. R., & Firestone, W. A. (1996). Changing classroom practices through teacher networks: Matching program features with teacher characteristics and circumstances. *Teachers College Record, 98,* 46–76.

Peterson, P. L., Carpenter, T., & Fennema, E. (1989). Teachers' knowledge of students' knowledge in mathematics problem solving: Correlational and case analyses. *Journal of Educational Psychology, 81,* 558–569.

Pfeiffer, L. C., & Featherstone, H. J. (n.d.). *"Toto, I don't think we're in Kansas anymore": Entering the land of public disagreement in learning to teach.* East Lansing: National Center for Research on Teacher Learning, Michigan State University.

Putnam, R. T., & Borko, H. (1997). Teacher learning: Implications of the new view of cognition. In B. J. Biddle, T. L. Good, & I. F. Goodson (Eds.), *The international handbook of teachers and teaching.* Dordrecht, Netherlands: Kluwer.

Richardson, V. (1992). The agenda-setting dilemma in a constructivist staff development process. *Teaching and Teacher Education, 8,* 287–300.

Rosebery, A. S., & Ogonowski, M. S. (1996). *Valerie: Exploring the relationship between doing science and teaching science.* Portsmouth, NH: Heinemann.

Rosebery, A. S., & Puttick, G. M. (in press). Teacher professional development as situated sense-making: A case in science education. *Science Education.*

Rosebery, A. S., & Warren, B. (1998a). *Boats, balloons, and classroom video: Science teaching as inquiry.* Portsmouth, NH: Heinemann.

Rosebery, A. S., & Warren, B. (1998b, April). *Interanimation among discourses: One approach to studying learning in teacher research communities.* Paper presented at the annual meeting of the American Educational Research Association, San Diego, CA.

Schifter, D. (Ed.). (1996a). *What's happening in math class: Envisioning new practices through teacher narratives* (Vol. 1). New York: Teachers College Press.

Schifter, D. (Ed.). (1996b). *What's happening in math class: Reconstructing professional identities* (Vol. 2). New York: Teachers College Press.

Sedlak, M. W., Wheeler, C. W., Pullin, D. C., & Cusick, P. A. (1986). *Selling students short: Classroom bargains and academic reform in the American high school.* New York: Teachers College Press.

Showers, B., Joyce, B., & Bennett, B. (1987). Synthesis of research on staff development: A framework for future study and state-of-the-art analysis. *Educational Leadership, 45*(3), 77–87.

Shulman, J. (Ed.). (1992). *Case methods in teacher education.* New York: Teachers College Press.

Shulman, J., Lotan, R. A., & Whitcomb, J. A. (1998). *Groupwork in diverse classrooms: A casebook for educators.* New York: Teachers College Press.

Shulman, L. S. (1986). Those who understand: Knowledge growth in teaching. *Educational Researcher, 15,* 4–14.

Shulman, L. S. (1987). Knowledge and teaching: Foundations of the new reform. *Harvard Educational Review, 57,* 1–22.

Silver, E. A., & Stein, M. K. (1996). The QUASAR project: The "revolution of the possible" in mathematics: Instructional reform in urban middle schools. *Urban Education, 30,* 476–521.

Silver, E. A., & Stein, M. K. (1997, March). *An analysis of some factors facilitating and inhibiting mathematics reform in middle schools: Lessons from the QUASAR project.* Paper presented at the annual meeting of the American Educational Research Association, Chicago.

Smith, S. P., & Featherstone, H. (n.d.). *"He knows there's six 100s in 26?" An investigation into what it means to "do mathematics" in a teacher group.* Unpublished manuscript, Michigan State University.

Smylie, M. A. (1989). Teachers' views of the effectiveness of sources of learning to teach. *Elementary School Journal, 89,* 543–558.

Stein, M. K., Grover, B. W., & Henningsen, M. (1996). Building student capacity for mathematical thinking and reasoning: An analysis of mathematical tasks used in reform classrooms. *American Educational Research Journal, 33,* 455–488.

Stein, M. K., & Lane, S. (1996). Instructional tasks and the development of student capacity to think and reason: An analysis of the relationship between teaching and learning in a reform mathematics project. *Educational Research and Evaluation, 2,* 50–80.

Stein, M. K., Silver, E. A., & Smith, M. S. (in press). Mathematics reform and teacher development: A community of practice perspective. In J. G. Greeno & S. Goldman

(Eds.), *Thinking practices: A symposium on mathematics and science learning*. Hillsdale, NJ: Erlbaum.

Tannen, D. (1989). *Talking voices: Repetition, dialogue, and imagery in conversational discourse*. New York: Cambridge University Press.

Thomas, G., Wineburg, S. S., Grossman, P. L., Myhre, O., & Woolworth, S. (1998). In the company of teachers: An interim report on the development of a community of teacher learners. *Teaching and Teacher Education*.

Warren, B., & Rosebery, A. S. (1995). Equity in the future tense: Redefining relationships among teachers, students, and science in linguistic minority classrooms. In W. Secada, E. Fennema, & L. Adajain (Eds.), *New directions for equity in mathematics education* (pp. 298–328). New York: Cambridge University Press.

Wilson, S. M., Lubienski, S. T., & Mattson, S. (1996, April). *What happens to the mathematics: A case study of the challenges facing reform-oriented professional development*. Paper presented at the annual meeting of the American Educational Research Association, New York City.

Wineburg, S. S., & Grossman, P. L. (1998). Creating a community of learners among high school teachers. *Phi Delta Kappan, 79*, 350–353.

Wineburg, S., & Grossman, P. L. (in press). Scenes from a marriage: Some theoretical and practical implications of interdisciplinary humanities curricula in the comprehensive high school. In S. Wineburg & P. L. Grossman (Eds.), *Interdisciplinary encounters: A second look*. New York: Teachers College Press.

Zeichner, K. (1993). *Educating teachers for cultural diversity*. East Lansing: National Center for Research on Teacher Learning, Michigan State University.

Manuscript received October 10, 1998
Accepted December 20, 1998

Chapter 7

Preparing Teachers for Diverse Student Populations: A Critical Race Theory Perspective

GLORIA J. LADSON-BILLINGS
University of Wisconsin–Madison

The charge I received for this chapter was to create a synthetic review of the literatures of diversity and teacher education—no small task. A number of scholars have done work on this topic (see, for example, Dilworth, 1992; Gollnick, 1991; Gollnick, Osayande, & Levy, 1980; Grant & Secada, 1990; King, Hollins, & Hayman, 1997; Zeichner, 1992), including me (Ladson-Billings, 1995). Each of these reviews represents an effort to present a comprehensive, coherent synthesis of the extant literature on what may be termed multicultural teacher education or teacher preparation for diverse students. At least 35 journal articles specifically on "multicultural teacher education" have appeared since 1990. These articles focus primarily on preparing teachers to work with students from ethnic and racial groups other than those composed of Whites. Computer searches that include additional terms such as *diversity* and *diverse learners* produce articles that discuss preparing teachers for teaching students identified as having "special needs" and other disabilities, as well as students with gay and lesbian parents.

Grant and Secada (1990) asserted that most of the scholarship on preparing teachers for teaching diverse learners is not based on empirical studies. Furthermore, they asserted that almost none of the empirical studies point to a view of multicultural education that supports a transformative vision of society. But the task I have carved out for this chapter is not one of once again delineating studies and attesting to their worthiness. Rather, the real intellectual task of this chapter is to reframe the notions of preparing teachers for teaching diverse learners so that we might understand the "improbability" of such a task in public school systems that work actively at achieving school failure (McDermott, 1974). I propose to do such a reframing by employing a critical race theoretical perspective.

The chapter begins with a brief discussion of critical race theory (CRT), its history and major theorists. Next, I look at how diversity is constructed in education. Then the chapter examines the literature of diversity in teacher education that has been produced over the past 8 years. The chapter concludes with

I would like to thank the consulting editors, Michele Foster and Dan Liston, as well as my colleagues Carl Grant and William F. Tate for their insightful comments on various drafts of this chapter.

a look at the work of some notable scholars and exemplary programs from a critical race theory perspective.

CRITICAL RACE THEORY: A BRIEF DESCRIPTION[1]

According to Delgado (1995, p. xiii), "[CRT] sprang up in the mid-1970s with the early work of Derrick Bell and Alan Freeman, both of whom were deeply concerned over the slow pace of racial reform in the U.S." They argued that the traditional approaches of filing *amicus* briefs, conducting protests and marches, and appealing to the moral sensibilities of decent citizens produced smaller and fewer gains than in previous times. Before long, Bell and Freeman were joined by other legal scholars who shared their frustration with traditional civil rights strategies.

Critical race theory is both an outgrowth of and a separate entity from an earlier legal movement called critical legal studies (CLS). Critical legal studies is a leftist legal movement that challenged the traditional legal scholarship that focused on doctrinal and policy analysis (Gordon, 1990) in favor of a form of law that spoke to the specificity of individuals and groups in social and cultural contexts. Critical legal studies scholars also challenged the notion that "the civil rights struggle represents a long, steady march toward social transformation" (Crenshaw, 1988, p. 1334).

According to Crenshaw, "Critical [legal] scholars have attempted to analyze legal ideology and discourse as a social artifact which operates to recreate and legitimate American society" (1988, p. 1350). Scholars in the CLS movement decipher legal doctrine to expose both its internal and external inconsistencies and reveal the ways that "legal ideology has helped create, support, and legitimate America's present class structure" (p. 1350). The contribution of CLS to legal discourse is in its analysis of legitimating structures in the society. Much of the CLS ideology emanates from the work of Gramsci (1971) and depends on the Gramscian notion of "hegemony" to describe the continued legitimacy of oppressive structures in American society (Unger, 1983). However, CLS fails to provide pragmatic strategies for material and social transformation. Cornel West (1993) asserts that:

Critical legal theorists fundamentally question the dominant liberal paradigms prevalent and pervasive in American culture and society. This thorough questioning is not primarily a constructive attempt to put forward a conception of a new legal and social order. Rather, it is a pronounced disclosure of inconsistencies, incoherences, silences, and blindness of legal formalists, legal positivists, and legal realists in the liberal tradition. Critical legal studies is more a concerted attack and assault on the legitimacy and authority of pedagogical strategies in law school than a comprehensive announcement of what a credible and realizable new society and legal system would look like. (p. 196)

CLS scholars critiqued mainstream legal ideology for its portrayal of U.S. society as a meritocracy, but they failed to include racism in their critique. Thus, CRT became a logical outgrowth of the discontent of legal scholars of color.

CRT begins with the notion that racism is "normal, not aberrant, in American society" (Delgado, 1995, p. xiv), and, because it is so enmeshed in the fabric of our social order, it appears both normal and natural to people in this culture. Indeed, Bell's major premise in *Faces at the Bottom of the Well* (1992) is that racism is a permanent fixture of American life. Therefore, the strategy of those who fight for social justice is one of unmasking and exposing racism in its various permutations.

Second, CRT departs from mainstream legal scholarship by sometimes employing storytelling to "analyze the myths, presuppositions, and received wisdoms that make up the common culture about race and that invariably render blacks and other minorities one-down" (Delgado, 1995, p. xiv). According to Barnes (1990), "Critical race theorists . . . integrate their *experiential knowledge* [italics added], drawn from a shared history as 'other' with their ongoing struggles to transform a world deteriorating under the albatross of racial hegemony" (pp. 1864–1865). Thus, the experience of oppressions such as racism and sexism has important aspects for developing a CRT analytical standpoint. To the extent that Whites (or, in the case of sexism, men) experience forms of racial oppression, they, too, may develop such a standpoint. For example, the historical figure John Brown suffered aspects of racism by aligning himself closely with the cause of African-American liberation. Contemporary examples of such identification may occur when White parents adopt transracially. No longer a White family by virtue of their child(ren), they become racialized others. A third example is that of the criminal trial of O. J. Simpson. The criminal trial jury was repeatedly referred to as the "Black" jury despite the presence of a White and a Latino juror. However, in Simpson's civil trial, the majority White jury was given no such racial designation. When Whites are exempted from racial designations and become "families," "jurors," "students," "teachers," and so forth, their ability to understand and apply a CRT analytical rubric is limited. These examples often develop into stories or narratives that are deemed important among CRT scholars in that they add necessary contextual contours to the seeming "objectivity" of positivist perspectives.

A third feature of CRT is its insistence on a critique of liberalism. Crenshaw (1988) argues that the liberal perspective of the "civil rights crusade as a long, slow, but always upward pull" (p. 1334) is flawed in that it fails to understand the limits of the current legal paradigm to serve as a catalyst for social change because of its emphasis on incrementalism. CRT argues that racism requires sweeping changes, but liberalism has no mechanism for such change. Rather, liberal legal practices support the painstakingly slow process of arguing legal precedence to gain citizen rights for people of color.

Fourth, CRT argues that Whites have been the primary beneficiaries of civil rights legislation. For example, although the policy of affirmative action is under attack throughout the nation, it is a policy that has benefited Whites. A close look at the numbers reveals that the major recipients of affirmative action hiring policies have been White women (Guy-Sheftall, 1993). The logic of this argument is that many of these White women earn incomes that support households in which other Whites live—men, women, and children. Thus, White women's ability to find work ultimately benefits Whites in general.

Andrew Hacker (1992) demonstrates that even after 20 years of affirmative action, African Americans constitute only 4%–5% of the professorate. In 1991, there were 24,721 doctoral degrees awarded to U.S. citizens and noncitizens who intended to remain in the United States, and only 933, or 3.8%, of these doctorates went to African-American men and women. If every one of these individuals with newly minted doctorates went into the academy, their numbers would have a negligible effect on the proportion of African Americans in the professorate. In addition, the majority of African Americans who earn PhDs earn them in the field of education, and of that group, most of the degrees are in educational administration, where the recipients continue as school practitioners (Hacker, 1992).

CRT theorists cite this kind of empirical evidence to support their contention that civil rights legislation continues to serve the interests of Whites. A more fruitful tack, some CRT scholars argue, is to find the place where the interests of Whites and people of color intersect. This notion of "interest convergence" (Bell, 1980) was developed to explain the ways the interests of people of color can be met. Consider the way many school desegregation programs are enacted. In order to get White parents to keep their children in a school that is desegregating, school officials often offer special programs and other perks. Magnet programs, advanced classes, and after-school programs are examples of the desegregation compromise. Bell's (1980) argument is that people of color have to begin to set the terms of interest convergence rather than accept those that Whites offer.

In a recent compilation of key CRT writings (Crenshaw et al., 1995), it is pointed out that there is no "canonical set of doctrines or methodologies to which [CRT scholars] all subscribe" (p. xiii). But these scholars are unified by two common interests: understanding how a "regime of white supremacy and its subordination of people of color have been created and maintained in America" (p. xiii) and changing the bond that exists between law and racial power.

In the pursuit of these interests legal scholars, such as Patricia Williams (1987, 1991) and Derrick Bell (1980, 1992), were among the early critical race theorists whose ideas reached the general public. Some might argue that their wide appeal was the result of their abilities to tell compelling stories into which they embedded legal issues. This use of story is of particular interest to educators because of the growing popularity of narrative inquiry in the study of teaching (Carter, 1993; Connelly & Clandinin, 1990). But, merely because the research community is more receptive to story as a part of scholarly inquiry does not mean that all stories are judged as legitimate in knowledge construction and the advancement of a discipline.

Lawrence (1995) asserts that there is a tradition of storytelling in law and that litigation is highly formalized storytelling, although the stories of ordinary people, in general, have not been told or recorded in the literature of law (or any other discipline). But this failure to make it into the canons of literature or research does not make stories of ordinary people less important. The ahistorical and acontextual nature of much law and other "science" renders the voices of dispossessed and marginalized group members mute. In response, much of the scholarship of CRT focuses on the role of "voice" in bringing additional power to the legal discourses of racial justice. CRT theorists attempt to interject minority cultural viewpoints, derived from a common history of oppression, into their efforts to reconstruct a society crumbling under the burden of racial hegemony (Barnes, 1990).

Until recently, little of CRT found its way into the educational literature. Ladson-Billings and Tate (1995) broached the subject as a challenge to traditional multicultural paradigms. They argued that race continues to be salient in American society, that the nation was premised on property rights rather than human rights, and that the intersection of race and property could serve as a powerful analytical tool for explaining social and educational inequities.

Later, Tate (1997) provided a comprehensive description of CRT and its antecedents as a way to better inform the educational research community of its meaning and possible use in education. His discussion cites Calmore (1992), who identified CRT as

a form of oppositional scholarship . . . that challenges the universality of white experience/judgement as the authoritative standard that binds people of color and normatively measures, directs, controls, and regulates the terms of proper thought, expression, presentation, and behavior. As represented by legal scholars, critical race theory challenges the dominant discourses on race and racism as they relate to law. The task is to identify values and norms that have been disguised and subordinated in the law. . . . Critical race scholars . . . seek to demonstrate that [their] experiences as people of color are legitimate, appropriate, and effective bases for analyzing the legal system and racial subordination. This process is vital to . . . transformative vision. This theory-practice approach, a praxis, if you will, finds a variety of emphases among those who follow it. . . .

From this vantage, consider for a moment how law, society, and culture are texts—not so much like a literary work, but rather like the traditional black minister's citation of text as a verse or scripture that would lend authoritative support to the sermon he is about to deliver. Here, texts are not merely random stories; like scripture, they are expressions of authority, preemption, and sanction. People of color increasingly claim that these large texts of law, society, and culture must be subjected to fundamental criticisms and reinterpretation. (pp. 2161–2162)

Although CRT has been used as an analytical tool for understanding the law (particularly civil rights law), as previously noted, it has not been successfully deployed in the practical world of courts and legal cases or schools. In fact, the first public exposure CRT received proved disastrous for presidential civil rights nominee Lani Guinier. Its radical theoretical arguments were seen as a challenge to "the American way." Guinier could not be confirmed, and the president did nothing to support her nomination.

With no support for CRT in a practical legal sense, why attempt to employ such a perspective when considering multicultural teacher education? The power of such a perspective is its ability to move us out of a cycle of detailing and ranking research and programs without a systematic examination of their paradigmatic underpinnings and practical strengths. A CRT perspective on the literature is akin to applying a new prism that may provide a different vision to our notions of school failure for diverse students.

THE "PERVERSITY OF DIVERSITY": DEPRAVITY, DISADVANTAGE, AND DIVERSITY

A few years ago, one of my master's degree students completed a thesis on the "feminization of teaching" (O'Reilly, 1995). Her research included detailed life histories of two retired female teachers, one 87 years old, the other 93. The stories of the women were fascinating and richly detailed and told of life and teaching in a small midwestern town. Included in the thesis were copies of photographs the women supplied to elaborate their narratives. Both women included photos of their classes taken in the late 1940s. As I examined each photo, I noticed that each class contained a few African-American children. How was it possible for both teachers to have African-American students without making any mention of the presence of these students in their narratives?

Perhaps the teachers' failure to acknowledge the presence of the African-American children was an oversight. However, another explanation may reside in the way difference was constructed in this 1940s small town. This construction of difference is a central discursive practice for justifying our need to "prepare teachers for student diversity." Consider the rhetorical stance taken by a noted scholar in the late 1940s.

In 1948, Allison Davis delivered the Inglis Lecture to the Harvard Graduate School of Education. The lecture was titled "Social-Class Influences Upon Learning." In it Davis declared (1965):

In order to help the child learn, the teacher himself must discover the reference points from which the child starts. . . . In every so-called "lesson," the pupil always has something important to tell the teacher; he may tell her what he has already learned that either aids or obstructs the new learning the teacher seeks to instigate. The slum pupil, to cite a case, cannot learn the teacher's culture well until his teacher learns enough about the slum culture to understand what the pupil's words and learning-acts mean. (pp. 1–2)

Davis, himself an African-American social psychologist, defined difference primarily as social class difference; he was careful to distinguish between the deportment, child-rearing practices, and "mental behaviors" among middle-class "Negro" children and lower-class "Negro" children. Later, Davis became associated with researchers who created a discourse of cultural depravity and disadvantage.

In the 1960s, many social scientists and educators began examining what was termed "culturally deprived" or "culturally disadvantaged" children and youth. The major tenet underlying this perspective or paradigm was that children who were not White and middle class were somehow defective and lacking. Thus, the school's role was to *compensate* for the children's presumed lack of socialization and cultural resources. Scholars such as Bloom, Davis, and Hess (1965); Bettleheim (1965); and Ornstein and Vairo (1968) helped to shape not only a programmatic direction but also a way of thinking about social differences that remains with us to this day. Riessman's (1962) *The Culturally Deprived Child* was perhaps one of the most influential books published for teachers and other educators. Although Riessman acknowledged the problematic nature of the term *culturally deprived*, his text proceeded to position White middle-class cultural expression as the normative or correct way of being in school and society.

The federal and state school programs that emerged from the cultural deprivation/disadvantaged paradigm are too numerous to list here. However, looking at some of the major programs such as Head Start, Follow Through, and Title I, it is clear that they rest on a foundation of cultural and social inferiority. It is important that the preceding statement not be interpreted as support for the abolition of such programs. Rather, it might be used to understand why such programs produce limited success in the school setting. If we begin with the notion that some children lack "essential" qualities deemed necessary for school success, how is it that schools can correct or compensate for those missing qualities? Some of these programs have imbedded in their premises a conception of children coming from families that are inadequate, and thus the role of the school (or the state) is to remove children from such families as soon as possible to "compensate" for those perceived inadequacies.

Hollins (1990) has looked carefully at success models for African-American urban schoolchildren. Her analysis suggests that successful approaches to raising academic achievement for Black inner-city students follow one of three theoretical perspectives. The first perspective is that of remediation or acceleration without regard to students' social or cultural backgrounds. Approaches such as the Chicago Mastery Learning Program follow this perspective. The second perspective is that of resocializing urban Black children into mainstream behaviors, values, and attitudes while simultaneously teaching them basic skills. Many Head Start programs operated from this resocialization perspective. The third perspective is one that attempts to facilitate learning by building on students' own social and cultural backgrounds. The work of Au and Jordan (1981) illustrates how teachers can use students' language and culture as a bridge to school achievement. Similarly, work done in many of the Black independent schools sees students' cultural background as critical to academic success (Lee, 1994).

Hollins's work also is important for what it says about teacher preparation; that is, these perspectives also operate in the ways in which teacher education is organized and implemented. Zeichner (1991, 1993) argues that teacher education programs are premised on a variety of traditions: academic, social efficiency, developmentalist, or social reconstructionist approaches. These premises help shape the experiences that prospective teachers have in their preparation programs. The academic tradition sees the teacher as a scholar and subject matter specialist. The focus of teacher education programs based on this tradition is on adding academic discipline to the program. Such programs minimize professional education courses in favor of more "rigorous" disciplined-based study. The social efficiency tradition in teacher education focuses on the perceived power in the scientific study of teaching as a discipline. Programs such as Competency Based Teacher Education were based on measuring a fixed set of teaching skills to determine the proficiency of prospective teachers. The developmentalist tradition is rooted in the child study movement and the notion that there is a "natural order" of the development of the learner that provides the basis for determining what should be taught to both students and their teachers. Finally, the social reconstructionist tradition defines schooling and teacher education as cultural components of a movement toward a more just and equitable society. This tradition is rooted in the progressive era philosophy of social reformers like George S. Counts.

The academic tradition, much like Hollins's first perspective, focuses on increasing the academic abilities of teachers. The developmentalist approach focuses on helping teachers to resocialize students, and the social reconstructionist approach attempts to have teachers ask fundamental questions about the persistence of social inequity and what education might offer in the way of social change. Only the social efficiency approach is missing from Hollins's analysis.

Goodwin (1997) argues that teacher education's response to changing demographics, social and political action on the part of people of color, and the proliferation of scholarship regarding the teaching of the "culturally deprived/disadvantaged" was a reactive one. Thus, instead of rethinking teacher education, most programs created appendages in the form of workshops, institutes, and courses to deal with the "problem" of culturally different students. According to Goodwin, "The core of American education with its attendant white, middle class values and perspectives remained intact. Multiethnic or multicultural education was synonymous with 'minority' education. Thus, teachers, despite cultural 'training,' continued to function within a Eurocentric framework" (p. 9).

This framing of difference as a problem has a very long history in U.S. education. Cuban (1989) argues that since the beginnings of the common school in cities in the United States, there have been labels to identify those students seen as outside of the mainstream. Cuban further asserts that "the two most popular explanations for low achievement [of children who are seen as different] . . . locate the problem in the children themselves or in their families" (p. 781). The most recent label, "at risk," is another example of how particular discursive practices operate to create categories that soon function as taken-for-granted assumptions.

In 1983, the Commission on Excellence in Education published the widely circulated and cited report *A Nation at Risk*. The very clear message of this report was that the entire nation was at risk of a variety of things, including losing its competitive economic edge and paralysis of the democracy because our children were not being educated to be the kinds of citizens the nation would need to meet the demands of the coming century. The report was seen as a wake-up call to the nation and schools, in particular. It underscored how we all were in jeopardy because of the poor performance of our schools. However, within a short time, the at-risk label went from describing the nation to describing certain children. Being at risk became synonymous with being a person of color. How did this happen? How did the category become associated primarily with difference? This subtle, but significant, shift is emblematic of the way the language of difference (disadvantage, diversity) works to construct a position of inferiority even when that may not have been the initial intent. Thus, educators (K–12 as well as collegiate level) talk about teaching "at-risk" students in a vacuum (i.e., they know little of the children other than their race or ethnicity). Teachers refer to teaching in a diverse or multicultural setting when, in truth, they are teaching in predominantly African-American or Latino schools. Diversity, like cultural deprivation and the state of being at risk, is that "thing" that is other than White and middle class.

TELLING THE "PREPARING TEACHERS FOR DIVERSE LEARNERS" STORY

One of the major principles of CRT is that people's narratives and stories are important in truly understanding their experiences and how those experiences may represent confirmation or counterknowledge of the way the society works. The use of narrative as a methodological tool is gaining some currency in the social sciences (see, for example, Bateson, 1989; Connelly & Clandinin, 1990; Lawrence-Lightfoot, 1998). However, many social scientists criticize it as "unscientific" and not scholarly. This debate is not merely one of methodology, but also one of epistemology. The question of what (and who) counts as knowledge is at the center of the debate. But this chapter makes the assumption that narrative is a way of knowing that can provide valuable insights into our social world. Thus, I proceed to tell the story of preparing teachers for diverse learners.

Once upon a time there was a mythical time and place somewhere in the U.S. where all the children were just alike. They came from similarly constituted families. They spoke the same language. They held the same beliefs, values, and attitudes. When these children went to school their teachers were just like them and they imparted to them knowledge and skills that everyone had agreed upon. Everybody talked about how wonderful things were back then. "Our teachers really knew how to teach." "The children were so smart and well behaved." "We didn't have to worry about discipline and children who weren't capable." Everyone agreed that it had been a glorious era. What happened to disturb this Eden known as "Public School Way Back When (PSWBW)"?

Some say that a disastrous decision made by the nation's Nine Wise Men caused the PSWBW to crumble. In 1954 the wise men decided that "different" children should attend PSWBW with the wonderful, smart, just like us children. Some think that the wise men's ruling, *Brown v. Board of Education*, was an attempt at social engineering—for a nefarious Big Brother called "the federal government" to wrest the local control of schools from the hands of the people. However, a broader reading of this decision suggests that the Nine Wise Men understood the international context into which their decision would be read (Bell, 1980). The nation had just fought a world war for democracy and was embarking on a "cold war" with communist nations. How could the nation reconcile its commitment to democracy worldwide while maintaining several unequal tiers of citizenship at home? The Nine Wise Men proposed a mathematical solution (Tate, Ladson-Billings, & Grant, 1993) to unequal schooling. By forcing PSWBW to desegregate, the nation could prove to the world that democracy was for everyone. Needless to say, this change was not an easy one. And, today people tell stories about how that decision may have helped or hurt all kinds of people (Shujaa, 1996).

What did this change mean for teachers and how they are educated? At first, nothing changed very much in teacher preparation programs. Prior to the *Brown* decision, people involved in the intergroup movement had begun meeting to discuss how to promote interracial harmony and understanding. Efforts were focused on preparing activities, units, and intergroup gatherings for elementary and secondary schools (Banks, 1981). Later, educators began to focus on a more pluralistic approach to education (Baptiste & Baptiste, 1980) that recognized that students would be educated in more inclusive and culturally diverse classrooms. Unfortunately, this approach typically consisted of isolated cultural awareness and sensitivity workshops that reminded people of just how different the children who were not a part of PSWBW were.

By the 1960s, the entire nation was in upheaval. Not only were schools changing, but these different people were demanding "rights" in every arena of public life: housing, employment, politics. How could schools ever meet all of their demands? Increasingly, the teachers began chanting ". . . but I wasn't prepared to teach these kinds of children." The teachers' dilemma was not helped by the teacher education programs. These programs had helped to construct PSWBW, and any real attention to the educational needs of all students would expose the mythology of PSWBW; everyone would see that it was not an objective reality but a social rubric used to justify particular schooling practices. Really paying attention to the problem would mean that teachers would learn that most teacher education programs had not helped them to teach any children (Conant, 1963; Goodlad, 1990; Herbst, 1989; Sarason, Davidson, & Blatt, 1986). Teacher education suffered from low prestige and low status. It had an unclear mission and identity. It was filled with faculty disquietude, an ill-defined body of study, and program incoherence (Goodlad, 1990). Furthermore, "the constraints of misguided regulatory intrusions and lack of educational control of or influence over bureaucratically established traditional school practices" (Goodlad, 1990, p. 189) represented additional limitations to a field that was demoralized by its low prestige, lack of rewards, heavy teaching loads, and weak professional socialization (Ladson-Billings, 1995).

Seemingly, the only logical response to difference for the PSWBW adherents was to create a new and different set of rules and regulations to add on to current practices. Totally revamping the current practice would mean that something was wrong with PSWBW. Adding a course, workshop, or field experience on diversity could help instantiate the old while presenting a veneer of change.

By the early 1970s, several widespread reviews or assessments had examined multicultural teacher education (Baptiste & Baptiste, 1980; Commission on Multicultural Education, 1978). The Commission on Multicultural Education, working under the auspices of the American Association of Colleges of Teacher Education (AACTE), surveyed 786 member institutions in 1977. Four hundred forty institutions responded to the survey, which attempted to see whether the institutions had courses, a major, a minor, or departments in multicultural or bilingual education or whether some aspect of multicultural or bilingual education was included in the foundations or methods courses. According to the directory (Commission on Multicultural Education, 1978), 48 of the 50 states and the District of Columbia had at least one institution with either a multicultural education course, major, or minor or a multicultural aspect in the foundations or methods courses.

The AACTE directory was useful in demonstrating the broad sweep of multicultural teacher education, but it failed to provide readers with any sense of the quality of these programs. This directory was followed by four volumes: *Multicultural Teacher Education: Preparing Educators to Provide Educational Equity* (Baptiste, Baptiste, & Gollnick, 1980), *Multicultural Teacher Education: Case Studies of Thirteen Programs* (Gollnick, Osayande, & Levy, 1980), *Multicultural Teacher Education: An Annotated Bibliography of Selected Resources* (Lee, 1980), and *Multicultural Teacher Education: Guidelines for Implementation* (AACTE, 1980). The attempt to document the presence of multicultural teacher education programs and practices preceded the development of standards for national accreditation of multicultural teacher education.

The National Council for Accreditation of Teacher Education (NCATE), influenced by the Commission on Multicultural Education's work, began to draft standards to examine how teacher preparation programs addressed the multicultural education of its prospective teachers (Gollnick, 1991). In 1979, NCATE began requiring institutions applying for accreditation to "show evidence of planning for multicultural education in their curricula" (p. 226). By 1981, NCATE expected these institutions to implement this planned-for multicultural education.

In its 1990 revision of the accreditation standards, NCATE moved from a separate multicultural standard to integrated multicultural components involving four different standards: the standard on professional studies, the standard on field-based and clinical experiences, the standard on student admission, and the standard on faculty qualifications and assignments.

In its review of the first 59 college and university teacher education programs seeking accreditation under the new standards, NCATE found only 8 of the programs in full compliance with the multicultural education requirements. Most of the programs were deficient in the areas of student admission (54.2%) and faculty qualifications and assignments (57.6%). Forty-four percent of this group was deficient in professional studies, and 32.2% was deficient in clinical and field-based experiences. These numbers may be indicative of the resiliency of PSWBW and the desire or willingness of teacher education programs to maintain it by continuing to prepare teachers for that vision of schooling.

Later reviews of multicultural teacher education (Grant & Secada, 1990) revealed that few empirical studies exist to determine the programs' effectiveness. Zeichner (1992) provided a comprehensive review of multicultural teacher education that included both mainstream and fugitive literature. However, few of the programs he described provided systematic research or program evaluation to determine how well teachers were prepared to teach all children. Ladson-Billings's (1995) review indicated that few multicultural teacher education programs were grounded in the theoretical and conceptual principles of multicultural education. Most programs were satisfied with adding "multicultural content" rather than changing the philosophy and structure of the teacher education programs.

Since 1995, the literature on multicultural teacher education and diversity in teacher education has continued to grow. Most of the literature, similar to that cited by Grant and Secada (1990), restates the need for multicultural teacher education without providing evidence of how such an approach will improve the academic performance of all students.

While teacher educators struggled to develop preparation programs to meet the needs of a diverse student population, theorists worked toward clarifying what multicultural education for school students should include. Sleeter and Grant (1987) determined that the literature reflects five approaches to multicultural education: educating the culturally different, human relations, single group studies, multicultural education, and education that is multicultural and social reconstructionist. The final approach, education that is multicultural and social reconstructionist, was found rarely in theory or practice. However, this was the one approach endorsed by Sleeter and Grant as having the potential to change the society.

Banks (1995) detailed the history of multicultural education and offered what he termed "dimensions of multicultural education" (p. 4). The dimensions include content integration, knowledge construction, prejudice reduction, equity pedagogy, and empowering school culture. Ladson-Billings (1995) employed these dimensions as a rubric for reviewing multicultural teacher education. Of some 42 articles published between 1988 and 1992 on multicultural teacher education, none embodied all five dimensions. Twelve reflected an emphasis on content integration. Nine had an emphasis on knowledge construction. Four had an emphasis on prejudice reduction. Two focused on equity pedagogy, and two emphasized empowering school culture. Most discouraging, from a theoretical perspective, was the fact that 14 of the studies could not readily be categorized in relation to any of the dimensions.

An electronic search employing the descriptors "multicultural teacher education" and "diversity and teacher education" indicates that a variety of studies and concept papers continue to be published on preparing teachers for diverse student populations. More than 30 journal articles have been published on the topic since 1992. Publications such as *Equity & Excellence in Education,* the *Journal of Black Studies, Multicultural Education,* and the *Journal of Negro Education* have a mission devoted to issues of equitable education. However, over the past few years, a number of the "mainstream" journals have published more articles on this topic.

The *Journal of Teacher Education* published two consecutive issues with a theme of preparing teachers for diversity. Articles such as those by Boyle-Baise and Washburn (1995), McCall (1995), Shade (1995), Deering and Stanutz (1995), and Greenman and Kimmel (1995) detail programmatic efforts to focus preservice teacher preparation on multicultural education. Unfortunately, few studies exist that document widespread use of multicultural teacher education programs. Zeichner (1992) suggests that two approaches exist for preparing teachers for diverse student populations, one integrating issues of diversity throughout course work and field experiences and the other representing a subtopic or add-on to regular teacher education programs. Zeichner further asserts that "despite a clear preference for the integrated approach ... the segregated approach is clearly dominant in U.S. teacher education programs. ... There are very few teacher education programs of a permanent nature which have integrated attention to diversity throughout the curriculum'' (p. 13). Indeed, many of the programs that do integrate diversity throughout the curriculum exist as experimental programs on soft or external funds. Rarely are such programs institutionalized or incorporated into the institution's major teacher certification program.

Zeichner's findings are consistent with my assertion that there is no desire to disrupt the discourse of PSWBW in teacher preparation programs. Rather than a radical re-formation of teaching, most teacher education programs attempt to embrace the idea of diversity as long as it does not require any fundamental attack on the PSWBW structure. Zeichner did discover a set of ''key elements'' that exist in varying degrees in most teacher education programs aimed at preparing teachers for diverse students. These elements include the following:[2]

1. Admission procedures screen students on the basis of cultural sensitivity and commitment to social justice.
2. Students' sense of their own ethnic and cultural identities is developed.
3. Students examine their attitudes toward others.
4. Students are taught the dynamics of prejudice and racism and how to deal with them in the classroom.
5. Students are taught about privilege and economic oppression and the school's role in social reproduction.
6. Histories and contributions of various groups are integrated into the curriculum.
7. Characteristics of learning styles of various groups and individuals are incorporated, and the limitations of such information are assessed.
8. Sociocultural and language issues are infused into the curriculum.
9. Methods for gaining information about communities are taught.
10. A variety of ''culturally sensitive'' instructional strategies and assessment procedures are taught.
11. Success models of traditionally underserved groups are highlighted.
12. Community field experiences and/or student teaching experiences with individuals from various cultural backgrounds are a part of the practical component of the teacher education program.
13. Students experience opportunities to ''live'' or become immersed in communities of color.
14. Instruction is embedded in a group or cohort setting that provides intellectual challenge and social support.

More recently, Bennett (1995) argued for a model of preparing teachers for diversity that pays close attention to five key components: selection, understanding multiple historical perspectives, developing intercultural competence, combating racism, and teacher decision making. Each of these components is apparent in Zeichner's (1992) list of key elements just outlined. Theoretically, Bennett's model seems reasonable, and we have seen examples of teacher preparation programs that have attempted to implement aspects of the model. However, it is important to examine the way existing teacher preparation norms and folkways have occluded our abilities to institute real change.

The very first aspect of the model—prospective teacher selection—is fraught with problems. Teacher education programs are filled with prospective candidates who have no desire to teach in schools where students are from racial, ethnic, or linguistic backgrounds different from their own (Grant, 1989; Haberman, 1989). Some novice teachers find themselves in diverse classrooms where they insist they were "not prepared to teach *these* children!" Just who *these* children are and what they represent fits nicely into the discourse of PSWBW. Indeed, if we were to push such novice teachers and raise the question "Just what kind of children were you prepared to teach?" there might be a deafening silence— an unwillingness to name the imagined, idealized children. Instead, many might begin to fault their teacher education programs for inadequate preparation. The double bind that teacher preparation programs find themselves in is as follows: In their attempt to attain legitimacy, they often become more academically selective. Unfortunately, academic selectivity for a profession of low prestige and even lower reward does not allow for much flexibility in the case of admissions.

The second aspect of Bennett's model, understanding multiple historical perspectives, is a noble notion that is dependent on an assumption that students understand any historical perspective. There is little evidence that they do. What we know about students' historical thinking and the development of the history curriculum via textbooks makes it unlikely that prospective teachers come into teacher preparation with any sense of history and its impact on our current social, political, and economic situation (Booth, 1993). According to an adage I came upon, "It's not what you don't know that's the problem; rather, it's what you know that ain't so!" So it is with history (Loewen, 1995). Most students in the United States experience an American history that tells a seamless tale of triumph, conquest, and the inevitability of America as a great nation. Teacher candidates come to preparation programs with a limited understanding of the synchronic and contiguous nature of human events. During the same year that Columbus happened upon the Americas, thousands of African Muslims and Jews were expelled from Spain. Thus, Spain was poised for conquest in one part of the world while simultaneously purging itself of what it deemed "undesirables" at home. What was the role of religion in these two instances? These are ideas with which most teacher candidates are unfamiliar. Few can talk about their own histories and backgrounds with a connection to larger historical issues. The likelihood that they can develop multiple historical perspectives is widely over-shadowed by their lack of opportunity to gain more historical knowledge in most teacher education programs.

The third aspect of the model calls for developing intercultural competence among prospective teachers. Bennett uses the term *intercultural competence* to describe teachers' abilities to communicate effectively with a variety of different people. Once again, this is an admirable quality, one we hope would be embraced by all citizens in a democratic and multicultural society. However, good communication—intercultural or intracultural—requires a healthy respect for the forms and varieties of communication styles that people use to express themselves. There is scant evidence that teachers appreciate the many ways that students different from them use language and other forms of communication. Baugh (1994), Moll (1988), and Smitherman (1987) all demonstrate that language issues are intimately intertwined with issues of race and class. As Baugh argues, "One of the primary reasons that average citizens assume that nonstandard English is inferior to standard English lies in the correspondence between speech and social class. We inherit language and wealth (or poverty) from the same source, and most observant individuals find cause-and-effect relationships that often distort linguistic reality" (1994, p. 196).

The kind of intercultural competence found among the teachers described by scholars such as Delpit (1995), Foster (1997), and Ladson-Billings (1994) is devoid of the kinds of value judgments described by Baugh. But these teachers typically have had intimate experiences with communities of color and use the language themselves, not just to communicate with students but to express their own thoughts and ideas. Typical teacher education students have led monocultural, ethnically encapsulated lives that have not afforded them the opportunities to broaden their linguistic and communicative repertoires. It is unlikely that a university-based course will adequately prepare teachers to achieve this communicative facility.

Combating racism is one of the more noble goals of Bennett's model. It also is one of the more difficult to achieve. Questions of race and racism plague our society. Most Americans are offended at the notion that they could harbor racist attitudes and perceptions. However, if we are ever to confront racism in education, we must unpack and deconstruct it in teacher education (McIntosh, 1988; Rothenberg, 1988). Most prospective teachers are not racist in the sense that they overtly discriminate and oppress people of color. Rather, the kind of racism that students face from teachers is more tied to Wellman's (1977) definition of racism as "culturally sanctioned beliefs which, regardless of the intentions involved, defend the advantages whites have because of the subordinated positions of racial minorities" (p. xviii).

These benefits are manifested in a myriad of ways in teacher education. Prospective teachers are likely to be in teacher education programs filled with White, middle-class students (AACTE, 1994). These prospective teachers rarely question their experience of being prepared to teach in a segregated setting. Their preparation is likely to be directed by White, middle-class professors and instructors (AACTE, 1994). The statistics indicate that there are 489,000 full-time regular instructional faculty in the nation's colleges and universities. Seven percent, or 35,000, are in the field of education. Eighty-eight percent of the full-time education faculty is White. Eighty-one percent of this faculty is between the ages of 45 and 60 (or older). Also, of all of the fields offered in our colleges and universities, education has the highest percentage (11%) of faculty members who are classified as having no rank. This suggests that at least 4,000 instructors in schools, colleges, and departments of education (SCDEs) are itinerants and adjuncts who do not have the security of a tenure line or the responsibility of research and scholarship. While this demographic portrait does not prove that our current teacher educators are incapable of preparing teachers to teach students different from themselves, it does suggest that the teacher educators were, themselves, people who experienced PSWBW. Their own experience with diversity is likely to have been vicarious and remote.

In addition to a predominantly White (and aging) teacher education faculty, the prospective teacher population is also predominantly White (AACTE, 1994). The enrollment of SCDEs is 493,606.[3] Of these students, 86.5% (426,748) are White, 33,436 (6.8%) are African American, and 13,533 (2.7%) are Latino. The number of Asian/Pacific Islander and American Indian/Alaskan Native students enrolled in SCDEs is negligible. Thus, we have a situation where predominantly White faculty members are preparing predominantly White students to teach a growing population of public school students who are very different from them racially, ethnically, linguistically, and economically. Where are the voices to challenge the dysconscious racism (King, 1991) so prevalent among prospective teachers? Even if teacher preparation programs do include "multicultural" curricula, King (1991) argues that

merely presenting factual information about societal inequity [and human diversity] does not necessarily enable pre-service teachers to examine the beliefs and assumptions that may influence the way they interpret these facts. Moreover, with few exceptions, available multicultural resource materials for teachers presume a value commitment and readiness for multicultural teaching and antiracist education, which many students may lack initially. (p. 142)

Zimpher and Ashburn (1992) contend that "there is little evidence to date that schools, colleges, and departments of education and the programs they maintain are, or can be, a force for freeing students of their parochialism" (p. 44). Instead, they argue that teacher education programs must be reconceptualized toward diversity, and that reconceptualization must include a global curriculum, an appreciation of diversity, a belief in the value of cooperation, and a belief in the importance of a caring community.

Similarly, work by feminist teacher educators underscores the problem that our traditional teacher education paradigms have in addressing diversity, equity, and social justice. McWilliam (1994) asserts that, "in general, the culture of teacher education has shown itself to be highly resistant to new ways of conceiving knowledge," and "issues of race, class, culture, gender, and ecology will continue to be marginalized while the teacher education curriculum is located in Eurocentric and androcentric knowledges and practices" (p. 61). McWilliam urges a break with the "folkloric discourses of teacher education" (p. 48).

PROMISING PRACTICES AND THE NOBILITY OF STRUGGLE

Legal scholar Derrick Bell is considered the father of the CRT legal scholarship movement. He contends that even though racism is a permanent fixture in U.S.

society, the struggle against it remains a noble undertaking (Bell, 1992). So it may be with preparing teachers for diverse student populations. Although I have attempted to argue that the pervasive myth of PSWBW contours most of the nation's teacher education programs, we are compelled to look for break-the-mold teacher educators and teacher education programs.

This section details a necessarily limited number of teacher educators and teacher education programs for a variety of reasons. First and foremost, space is limited. Second, regardless of the method used for selecting the teacher educators or the teacher education programs, I am not able to accurately represent the universe of possibilities. Indeed, many teacher educators and teacher education programs that are noteworthy are not represented in the literature because the people who work in them are too busy working to have the time to write about them. My intent here is to present a few representations of possibilities on which I might employ a CRT perspective.

Jacqueline Jordan Irvine: Theory Driven

Jacqueline Jordan Irvine is the Charles Howard Candler Professor of Urban Education and project director of the CULTURES program at Emory University. CULTURES is an acronym for Center for Urban Learning/Teaching and Urban Research in Education and Schools. I have chosen to discuss her and her work because she is a teacher educator who has taken a theoretically rigorous approach to preparing teachers for diversity. Irvine's work (1990, 1992) explores the notion of "cultural synchronization" as a necessary mediation for bridging the interpersonal contexts of students and their teachers. Irvine places this cultural synchronization into a larger process model of achievement for African-American children that includes the societal context, the institutional context, the previously mentioned interpersonal contexts of students and teachers, and teacher and student expectations. Irvine's work combines her earlier training in quantitative methodology and her more recent skills in ethnographic methods to document the classroom practices of successful teachers whose ideas may run counter to "standard" notions of teacher excellence (Irvine & Fraser, 1998).

The Internet Web site description of her program states that its mission is "to enhance the success of elementary and middle schools in educating culturally diverse students by providing professional development to sixty teachers annually" (www.emory.edu/CULTURES). The program provides 40 clock hours of professional development to teachers in the Atlanta, Georgia, metropolitan area. The teachers are divided into cohort groups of 15. Teachers selected for the program must have at least 3 years of teaching experience, satisfactory performance ratings on state evaluations, and an application accompanied by sample lesson plans. In addition, prospective participants must have recommendations from their principal, a peer teacher, and a parent. Finally, each applicant must have an interview with the CULTURES staff.

The program is designed to expose teachers to effective teaching strategies undergirded by sound research. It also provides cultural immersion experiences, opportunities for reflective practice, visits to the classrooms of exemplary teachers, and a chance to develop action research projects. The entire program is geared toward helping teachers recognize the need for cultural synchronization to bridge the distance between home and school cultures. Irvine's theoretical work has laid a foundation for practical work in teacher professional development.

From a CRT perspective, Irvine's work illustrates the principle of interest convergence. The teachers' interests are to be more efficacious in urban classrooms. Few, if any, teachers want to feel unsuccessful. Student academic failure often is attributed to some personal or familial flaw—poverty, family structure, imagined values. For their part, students want more out of the schooling experience than repeated failure. The CRT analysis does not presume altruism, goodwill, or sincerity from teachers. Rather, teachers in urban schools are looking for ways to survive safely while avoiding the constant scorn of the public. Thus, a CRT perspective of Irvine's program would suggest that it has found a way to relieve teachers of the guilt and sense of futility of teaching in urban schools while offering urban students and their families opportunities for more effective instruction.

The CULTURES program is not aimed specifically at changing teacher attitudes toward students, even if that occurs as an ancillary benefit. Instead, this program speaks to teachers' senses of competence and professionalism. Nothing in Irvine's work suggests that she has developed a program that is designed to benefit Whites. However, the interest-convergence premise may operate as White teachers ask themselves "Of what benefit is this program to me?" If the program promises teacher effectiveness, then perhaps being able to demonstrate success with the least successful children will bring added recognition and a vehicle for professional advancement.

Marilyn Cochran-Smith: Theory Generating

Marilyn Cochran-Smith is the director of teacher education at Boston College. Previously, she taught at the University of Pennsylvania's Graduate School of Education, where she collaborated with Susan Lytle. Cochran-Smith's work is notable for her attention to issues of race and racism (Cochran-Smith, 1995a). Cochran-Smith's work with both preservice and in-service teachers focuses on the slow and often scary work of challenging teachers to examine the way race and racism colors their thinking about human possibilities. She details the painstakingly slow and careful work that must be done with teachers to deconstruct and construct a vision of teaching that better serves all students. Her work explores the ways that teacher knowledge can serve as a catalyst for different forms of research and changed practice (Cochran-Smith & Lytle, 1993). Cochran-Smith attempts to help her prospective teachers develop five perspectives that are important in confronting race and language diversity: reconsidering personal knowledge and experience, locating teaching within the culture of the school and the community, analyzing children's learning opportunities, understanding children's understanding, and constructing reconstructionist pedagogy (Cochran-Smith, 1995b).

Rather than beginning with a commitment to a particular theoretical frame, Cochran-Smith's work involves building theory from the ground up (i.e., from the work of teachers). In an impressive series of publications, Cochran-Smith has demonstrated an unwavering belief in the power of teacher knowledge to transform teaching. Cochran-Smith's work also is a good example of the use of reflection for teacher educators. Beyond lamenting the problem of preparing prospective teachers to teach all students well, Cochran-Smith (1995a) raises questions about the ability (and will) of teacher educators, themselves, to deal with difficult issues:

I worry about how we can have more open discussions about race and teaching among our own staff, many of whom have worked pleasantly together for many years, let alone among our student teachers and their cooperating teachers who know each other much less well. How can we open up to unsettling discourse of race without making people afraid to speak for fear of being naïve, offensive, or using the wrong language? Without making people of color do all the work, feeling called upon to expose themselves for the edification of others? Without eliminating conflict to the point of flatness, thus reducing the conversation to platitudes or superficial rhetoric?. . . I have become certain only of uncertainty about how and what to say, whom and what to have student teachers read and write, about who can teach whom, who can speak for or to whom, and who has the right to speak at all about the possibilities and pitfalls of promoting a discourse about race and teaching in pre-service education. (p. 546)

Instead of a prescriptive, static program of multicultural "dos and don'ts," Cochran-Smith's work is an attempt to use student teachers' own constructions of the issues of race and teaching. These constructions require students to rewrite their autobiographies or reinterpret aspects of their life stories or previous experiences. She also pushes students to "construct uncertainty" (Cochran-Smith, 1995a, p. 553). This work, according to Cochran-Smith, requires students to explore the ways in which issues of race and teaching make sense to them. She argues that "the process of constructing knowledge about race and teaching was more akin to building a new boat while sitting in the old one, surrounding by rising waters. In this kind of construction process, it is not clear how or if the old pieces can be used in the new 'boat,' and there is no blueprint for what the new one is supposed to look like" (p. 553).

Cochran-Smith's approach of helping prospective teachers make sense of their own experiences as a basis for teaching requires a radically different and daring approach to teacher preparation that relies less on received knowledge than on knowledge in the making. It is a risky but sincere effort at generating theory—a generation that must occur with each new cohort of teachers.

From a CRT perspective, Cochran-Smith's work is an excellent example of storytelling. In CRT, scholars use stories to analyze

the myths, presuppositions, and received wisdoms that make up the common culture about race and that invariably render blacks and other minorities one-down. Starting from the premise that a culture constructs social reality in ways that promote its own self-interest (or that of elite groups), [CRT scholars] set out to construct a different reality. Our social world, with its rules, practices, and assignments of prestige and power, is not fixed; rather we construct it with words, stories, and silence. (Delgado, 1995, p. xiv)

Cochran-Smith skillfully uses teachers' stories as text. As they tell their stories, there are opportunities for exploration of experiences with race and racism. The stories provide an avenue for talking about social taboos that many teacher education programs avoid. In the discourse of PSWBW, race and racism are those things "out there," disembodied and unattached to the everyday lives of the prospective teachers. Even in those teacher education programs where prospective teachers are exposed to a multicultural curriculum, students can distance themselves from historical and social reality (Ladson-Billings, 1991). Ahlquist (1991) experienced preservice classrooms where the prospective teachers claimed that racism and sexism no longer existed and that these topics were issues only because the professor raised them. Of course, these same students never questioned the fact that despite their living in one of the nation's most diverse cities, their teacher education classroom was composed of 28 White students and 2 Mexican-American students.

Cochran-Smith attempts to create a classroom atmosphere where the stories are not merely entertainment but the basis for learning. In professions such as law, medicine, business, and theology, stories are the central texts. The training of lawyers, doctors, and businesspeople revolves around cases, and what is a case if not a good story. These good stories are illustrative of important concepts, ideas, and examples that are useful for teaching and learning. CRT is designed to add different voices to the received wisdom or canon. It offers counterstories. Cochran-Smith's work helps prospective students see their stories as a legitimate starting place for the disruption of the stories that have maintained PSWBW as a dominant discourse.

Joyce King: Theory Enhancing

Joyce King is the associate vice chancellor for academic affairs and diversity programs at the University of New Orleans.[4] Although most of her work is concerned with university administration, King has continued to regularly teach a course that builds on the work she started as director of teacher education at Santa Clara University. Trained as a sociologist, King has challenged the positivist-functionalist paradigm of traditional sociology, infusing it with perspectives from Black cultural knowledge (King, 1995). Like Joyce Ladner (1973) before her, King's work examines the "links among culture, ideology, hegemony, and methodological bias in social science knowledge production" (1995, p. 268).

In a course titled "Mapping University Assets for Public Scholarship and Community Partnering," King (1998) attempts to create a synergistic, bidirectional relationship between university students and community members. While many teacher education programs introduce prospective teachers to the more voyeurlike community observations or "immersion" experiences, King's course is an attempt at a more authentic collaboration between students and their community partners. King's students need their community partners to help them understand the way the university can better serve the community. The community partners come to the university to share their expertise and learn of ways the university can better fulfill its "urban mission" by meeting community development needs.

King employs a Black studies theoretical perspective in her work with prospective teachers (King, 1997). She helps students understand that Black studies was not merely a political movement but also a paradigm that recognizes a "dialectical link between intellectual and socio-political emancipation and is ethically committed to knowledge for human freedom from the social domination of ideas as well as institutional structures" (p. 159). The generative concepts and themes used in King's social foundations course include "individualism versus collectivism"; "ideology, hegemony, and school knowledge"; and the notion that "White is a state of mind; it's even a moral choice."

As is true with Cochran-Smith, King is not concerned with providing students with fragmented pieces of information about "different" groups that keeps White identity in the center or place of normality. Her work helps prospective teachers understand their own miseducation as well as their "responsibilities as change agents" (King, 1997, p. 162). What makes King's work with prospective teachers so exciting is her ability to translate the work of critical theorists to practice-based applications for men and women learning to teach. Her work is best understood through her own words: "I introduce them to the praxis of teaching for change or transmutation experientially in a way that includes conceptualizing not only the realities of racism, poverty, and so on, but a role for themselves in the struggle against this reality" (King, 1997, p. 169).

A CRT perspective of King's work reveals threads of several CRT premises (e.g., call for context, storytelling, racism as a normal aspect of U.S. society). However, for this discussion, I focus on King's work as an example of CRT's critique of liberalism. Delgado (1995, p. 1) insists that "virtually all of Critical Race thought is marked by deep discontent with liberalism." The liberal discourse is deeply invested in the current system. It relies on the law and the structure of the system to provide equal opportunity for all.

King's work asks students to challenge the existing structure by focusing on the "need to make social-reconstructionist liberatory teaching an option for teacher education students ... who often begin their professional preparation without having ever considered the need for fundamental social change" (King, 1991, p. 134). King observed that most of her students entered her social foundations course "with limited knowledge and understanding of societal inequity. Not only [were] they ... unaware of their own ideological perspectives (or the range of alternatives they have not consciously considered), most [were] unaware of how their own subjective identities reflect an uncritical identification with the existing social order" (1991, p. 135).

Disentangling students from the liberal discourse is not an easy task. The idea of slow, steady progress, or incrementalism, is deeply ingrained in the U.S. social and political rhetoric. The traditional chronicle of U.S. history records a story of forward moving progress, no matter how slow. Issues such as voting rights for African Americans and women, school desegregation, and social desegregation of public accommodations unfolded at a very slow pace. Thus, slow but steady progress seems the "right" way. It is clearly the way of progress that most prospective teachers have come to expect. This embrace of incremental change makes marginalized groups appear to be impatient malcontents rather than citizens demanding legitimate citizen rights.

King's work with prospective teachers is designed to help them look critically at the ways they omit "any ethical judgment against the privileges white people have gained as a result of subordinating black people (and others)" (1991, p. 139). She introduces students to the critical perspective that education is not neutral—that it can and does serve a variety of political and cultural interests. Prospective teachers in King's courses often feel "disoriented" because they are forced to "struggle with the ideas, values, and social interests at the heart of the different educational and social visions which they, as teachers of the future, must either affirm, reject, or resist" (1991, p. 141).

Martin Haberman: Theory Challenging

Martin Haberman is the Distinguished Professor of Education at the University of Wisconsin–Milwaukee. The focus of his research has been to study characteristics and practices that help make some teachers successful with students and those that make others fail. Haberman (1995a) believes that the "traditional approach to training is counterproductive for future teachers in poverty schools since it leads them to perceive a substantial number—even a majority—of 'abnormal' children in every classroom" (p. 4).

Haberman's work represents an almost wholesale rejection of traditional teacher education, and he specifically targets the admission processes attendant to such programs. In an article written for *In These Times*, Haberman (1995b) asserts that our conceptions of who is best suited to be successful in urban classrooms may be very different from who might actually be able to do the job. Haberman believes that many of the students who choose elementary education as a college major "do so because (1) they 'love children' and (2) they believe they can meet the general education requirements of the school of education" (1995a, p. 31). Haberman bemoans the fact that few prospective elementary teachers have any depth of knowledge in the subjects they are expected to teach. According to Haberman, teacher education programs perpetuate a cruel hoax on teachers that leads them to believe that because they can read a teachers' guide, they can teach children how to read (or do math, or science, or social studies). The intellectual life of the teacher is rarely considered in the certification process.

Haberman sees prospective teachers' age and maturity as one part of the problem of admission into teacher education. So, in a somewhat controversial move, he has inverted the teacher education paradigm by recruiting "adults" into teaching. Many of the students who enter Haberman's urban education program are paraprofessionals who have extensive firsthand knowledge of urban communities and their residents. Haberman requires a rigorous interview process designed to test prospective teachers' persistence, willingness to protect learners and learning, ability to put ideas into action, attitudes toward "at-risk" students, professional-personal approach to students, understanding of their own fallibility, emotional and physical stamina, organizational ability, and disposition toward cultivating student effort versus innate ability.

In summary, Haberman (1995a) asserts that "completing a traditional program of teacher education as preparation for working [in today's urban classrooms] is like preparing to swim the English Channel by doing laps in the university pool. Swimming is not swimming. . . . 'Teaching is not teaching' and 'kids are not kids.' Completing your first year as a fully responsible teacher in an urban school has nothing to do with having been 'successful' in a college preparation program" (p. 2).

A CRT perspective on Haberman's work points toward the "call for context." As Delgado (1995) explains:

Most mainstream scholars embrace universalism over particularity, abstract principles and the "rule of law" over perspectivism. . . . For CRT scholars, general laws may be appropriate in some areas (such as, perhaps, trusts and estates, or highway speed limits). But political and moral discourse is not one of them. Normative discourse (as civil rights is) is highly fact sensitive—adding even one new fact can change intuition radically. (p. xv)

For Haberman, teaching in urban schools requires a very specific type of teaching. Teaching in urban schools demands a different set of skills and abilities and requires people who themselves are committed to protecting learners and learning. Haberman believes that where teaching occurs matters. His perspective is not necessarily shared by those who construct teaching standards and assessments that are supposed to fairly judge teaching performance. A CRT perspective rejects the idea that the conditions under which urban teachers and suburban teachers work can be compared in a way that is fair and equitable. The context of the urban setting creates a challenging environment—issues of limited school funding, more inexperienced and underqualified teachers, greater teacher turnover, and more students assigned to special classes and categorical programs are endemic in urban schools.

Theory driven, theory generating, theory enhancing, and theory challenging are four ways to think about the practice of teacher educators who recognize that current teacher education programs are inadequate to prepare teachers for the rigors of teaching in classrooms that do not reflect the mythology of PSWBW. These individuals represent powerful ideas and powerful practices. What they have to share contributes to a necessary literature of teacher education. However, teacher education is dependent on more than individuals. It also requires models of practice representing systemic change that departs from PSWBW. The next section details two such programs. I have selected as examples Santa Clara University and the University of Wisconsin–Madison not because they are the best or even among the best examples of preparing teachers for success with diverse students but, rather, because of my intimate knowledge of both programs. Their role in this chapter is that of institutional prototype. Certainly there are other programs throughout the country that are equal to or better than these two.[5] In some ways, Santa Clara University and the University of Wisconsin–Madison represent the range of programs, since they are so different on a variety of dimensions.

Santa Clara University: Challenging the Children of Privilege

Perennially named as one of the best liberal arts universities in the west (by *U.S. News & World Report*), Santa Clara University (SCU) is a Jesuit school located in the midst of California's Silicon Valley. Although the valley has large Latino and Asian/Pacific Islander communities, the university's approximately 8,000 students are overwhelmingly White and upper middle class. Tuition exceeds $12,000 per year, and a large percentage of the students pursue degrees in the university's highly regarded engineering and business schools.[6]

Teacher education in California occurs at the postbaccalaureate level. The fifth-year program at SCU is in the Division of Counseling Psychology and Education. It is a small program, rarely serving more than 30 to 35 students a year. In the mid-1980s, two African-American women scholars who directed and coordinated the teacher education program took advantage of the institution's expressed social justice mission in order to restructure the teacher education program. Typically regarded as a curricular "extra," social justice generally was seen as a set of activities loosely coupled with course work or ministries directed by some of the Jesuits. The director and coordinator of teacher education decided to make changes in the existing program to ensure that issues of cultural diversity and social justice were at the center of the program (King & Ladson-Billings, 1990). The current director of teacher education, Sara Garcia (1997), has extended and revised the previous work to include a focus on self-narrative inquiry.

The SCU teacher education program is designed to cultivate "informed empathy" rather than a sense of "sympathy" where well-meaning students "feel sorry for" or pity others. The program's goal is to help prospective teachers "feel with" people they regard as different from a position of knowledge and information about how both they and others come to occupy particular social positions. The catalyst for developing informed empathy is a mandatory 1-week "immersion" experience prior to the start of classes. The purpose of this experience is to place students in social settings very different from any they have experienced. Through the use of soup kitchens, homeless shelters, and other facilities designed to serve poor and dispossessed people, students are challenged to see a fuller range of the human condition and begin a yearlong questioning of social inequity. Under the current director, the immersion experience has been expanded into a "comprehensive, structured, field-based course that provides a basis for continual self-reflection and community-based experiential learning" (Garcia, 1997, pp. 150–151).

SCU uses an integrated, cohort approach to teacher education. Students begin the program together in the fall quarter, take courses together, and complete the program at the end of the spring quarter. Because of changes in the California Commission on Teacher Credentialing, SCU now offers the cross-cultural, language, and academic development teaching credential.[7] This credential requires that prospective teachers have course work that covers (a) language structure and first and second language development; (b) methodology of bilingual, English language development; and (c) culture and cultural diversity. Santa Clara was one of the few state programs that had less difficulty moving to the new certification because five of the courses in the previous credential program were directly related to issues of diversity and social justice. Those courses were social foundations of education, cross-cultural and interpersonal communication, curriculum foundations, reading in the content areas (which requires students to work one on one with a youth who is a nonreader and is awaiting adjudication of his or her case in the juvenile justice system), and a course in second language acquisition.

Another prominent theme in the SCU program is "miseducation." Although much has been written about the way children of color have been poorly served by schooling, little attention has been paid to the way our education system miseducates the children of privilege. A journal entry from a former SCU student is illustrative:

From watching this video (*Eyes on the Prize*) I realized that the [19]50s were not such a great time. There was a lot of active discrimination and prejudice. It was hard for me to believe that White people could show such hatred for Black children just because they wanted to go to school.

This student was not atypical. Many of the students had no knowledge of the history of racism, sexism, and discrimination in the United States. Some expressed anger at the way this information was "kept from them." The challenge of a program like that of SCU is to help students construct a more accurate understanding of the past without plunging them into a state of complete cynicism and distrust.

Throughout the program, students are engaged in a field-based experience. During the fall and winter quarters, students are assigned to a half-day practicum in a local public school.[8] During the spring quarter, students participate in full-day student teaching. California State Department of Education guidelines specify that at least one of these placements must occur in a community whose population is different from that of the prospective teacher's. These placements, along with the program emphases, are often a source of contention for students who see SCU as a safe haven away from and against issues of diversity, equity, and social justice.

The SCU teacher education program fully recognizes that many of its students have never attended a public school and may have narrow conceptions of what it means to be a teacher in the latter part of the 20th century. King (1997) interviewed a 10-year graduate of the program to gain some perspective on what the SCU program meant for a practicing teacher:

I was going to recreate myself—create small versions of myself—a really arrogant point of view. The program helped me to understand that the students come to schools already with their characters intact—that my job as a teacher is to take who they are and help them define themselves culturally and personally and to develop their gifts and give that to the world. . . . [In your classes] you would, without any fear, challenge people's ideas—politely, but strongly—and get us to support our ideas, get us to reconsider what we believed. I ended the year being more open-minded than I started, and I took my job as a teacher more seriously. I also realized that I had more to learn, as much as the students. (p. 167)

Beyond helping the students to become good teachers, the SCU teacher education program attempted to provoke students' thinking about what it means to be a "good" human being. Once again, a student's journal entry illustrates the program's impact:

I don't want to talk about class or lecture because something happened to me today that made me so mad, I have to write about it. The first thing I have to say though is the reason I am most angry is because I did not say anything—and I am very angry at myself. I was in the women's bathroom this morning and saw two women students come in . . . as they came in a young Hispanic student walked out of a stall, washed her hands and left. Once she left, one of the women said, "Well, I'm not going to go where the Mexican was.". . . I wanted to ask her who the hell she thought she was. . . . That was my first reaction, then about an hour later I had another reaction—I was so mad and disappointed at myself for not saying it. How are people with those attitudes going to change if people let them do it?. . . I made a promise to myself to say something the next time something like that happens. (Ladson-Billings, 1991, p. 154)

By emphasizing equity, diversity, and social justice issues, SCU has moved away from the myth of PSWBW and toward preparing students for teaching in the new millennium. Like all teacher education programs, its impact may be minimal, but at least it has constructed itself as one whose foundation is built on principled and ethical stances toward schooling all children.

From a CRT perspective, Santa Clara University relies on a critical understanding of the social science underpinnings of race and racism (as well as other forms of oppression). According to Delgado (1995, p. 157), "A number of Critical Race Theory writers have been applying the insights of social science to understand how race and racism work in our society." The challenge of preparing teachers in an environment like Santa Clara is that most of the students have benefited from the current social order and have come to see social inequity as a "natural" outgrowth of a meritocracy. The students believe that their hard work landed them in the best private K–12 schools, and attending an elite, private school like Santa Clara is to be expected. What antagonism students do express is tied to their belief that some students (of color) ought not be at the university or that affirmative action stood in the way of their getting into an even more prestigious college or university. One student remarked, "I could have gotten into Stanford if my last name was Hernandez." Remarks such as these reflect a deep-seated resentment toward social programs designed to remedy structural inequities. The SCU teacher education program tackles such issues head on, even though "white students sometimes find . . . critical, liberatory approaches threatening to their own self-concepts and identities" (King, 1991, p. 142).

The SCU program "does not neglect the dimension of power and privilege in society, nor does it ignore the role of ideology in shaping the context within which people think about daily life and the possibilities for social transformation" (King, 1991, p. 143). Thus, the emphasis on understanding race and racism is not a goal in itself but, rather, a means for helping students develop pedagogical options that disrupt racist classroom practices and structural inequities. The SCU approach attempts to move beyond offering students a "diversity" curriculum where they act as voyeurs, exploring the culture of the other. Instead, the program is aimed at destabilizing students' sense of themselves as the norm. Although race is not the only axis on which issues of inequity turn, it serves as a powerful signifier of "otherness" and difference. Race is the one social marker that almost every student has encountered, either face to face or symbolically through media, cultural, and curriculum forms. Santa Clara, unlike many teacher education programs, has made a commitment to seriously engage race and racism.

University of Wisconsin–Madison: Pushing Past the Liberal Discourse

The University of Wisconsin–Madison is a large, land-grant university serving 40,000 students. It is regarded as one of the nation's top research institutions. Its School of Education is rated among the top five for scholarly productivity and the quality of its graduates. Teacher education (specifically elementary education) is one of the university's more popular majors. Because of the high demand of the major, the Department of Curriculum and Instruction, which administers the teacher education program, has been forced to be highly selective in its admission process. Although the entire elementary education program is grounded in a philosophy of social reconstruction (Zeichner, 1991) and reflective practice (Zeichner & Liston, 1987), both size and complexity of the elementary program caused a group of faculty to reconsider how to ensure that students are well prepared to teach diverse students.[9]

Beginning in the summer of 1994, the university initiated its "Teach for Diversity" (TFD) master's with elementary teacher certification program. A key feature of TFD was its focus on attracting prospective teacher candidates who already had an expressed commitment to principles of equity, diversity, and social justice. Admission to TFD was open to students with a bachelor's degree in a major other than education. Applicants were required to have at least a 3.0 grade point average on the last 60 credits of their undergraduate degree (or post a strong score on the Graduate Record Examination) and to submit a statement of purpose and three letters of recommendation. The applicants' files were reviewed by an admissions committee composed of approximately 20 UW-Madison faculty and teachers from the local public schools.

TFD was designed as a 15-month elementary certification program where prospective teachers begin to understand what it means to teach diverse learners by starting in the community. The entire program consists of an initial summer session, fall and spring semesters, and a final summer session. The first summer experience requires a 6-week assignment in a community-based agency (e.g., neighborhood center, Salvation Army Day Camp, city-sponsored day camp, or enrichment program). In addition to spending 10–12 hours per week in the community placement, students take two courses, "Teaching and Diversity" and "Culture, Curriculum, and Learning." Students also take an 8-week seminar to process and debrief their community placement experiences.

During the fall semester, students are placed in one of three elementary schools in the district that has both a representative number of students of color and a desire to work with the university in a new way. The students are placed in their school settings for the entire academic year and are required to maintain a community service commitment. The academic year course work includes three integrated methods courses and a state-required course in inclusive schooling. During the final summer of the program, the students enroll in courses titled "School and Society" and "Child Development." These courses are taught by the university's Educational Policy Studies Department and Educational Psychology Department, respectively. In most teacher education programs, these courses are the first courses prospective teachers take. When they are completed at the end of the program, TFD students can use their experiential knowledge as a way to understand and challenge perspectives and assumptions of educational literature. During the final summer, TFD students complete and defend their master's papers.

The truncated nature of the TFD program means that a few themes are emphasized and repeated throughout the preparation year. One such theme is that schools are community entities and teachers must better understand the communities in which they teach. Another theme is that learning specific teaching "methods" is less important than learning to develop a "humanizing pedagogy" (Bartolome, 1994). A third theme is that teaching is an "unfinished" profession. The best teachers of diverse students constantly work on their practice, looking for new and better ways to enhance student learning. A fourth theme is that self-reflection is an important skill in teacher development. A theme of the entire TFD program is that everyone is a learner. The program faculty, administrators, cooperating teachers, faculty associates, and students all are part of an exciting learning experiment.

At this writing, TFD is under moratorium while the elementary education faculty of the Department of Curriculum and Instruction determine whether or not the department can afford to maintain such a program. In comparison with the ongoing elementary certification, TFD is expensive. It requires faculty members as well as graduate students to teach and supervise students. There are few evaluation data available as to its effectiveness. What is available is anecdotal and impressionistic. The attrition rate is high. In the first cohort of 21 students, 4 failed to complete the teacher certification program. Five of the students did not complete the master's paper by the end of the second summer. In the second cohort, one student withdrew after the first 4-week summer course. A second withdrew at the end of the second 4-week summer course. Three students were not permitted to student teach because of their failure to demonstrate that they were ready by the end of the fall practicum experience. The engagement of tenured (and tenure track) faculty gave the program legitimacy and authority to make tough calls about who should and should not proceed toward teacher certification.

An important feature of TFD is its engagement with practicing teachers and the school community. Some of the seminars were held on site at the school. Cooperating teachers had some say in with whom and how the prospective teachers' placements would occur. Cooperating teachers also were members of planning teams that informed the content and organization of the students' courses.

Many of the TFD students came away from the preparation year profoundly changed. The combination of exposure to "high theory" in graduate courses and the complexity of schools and communities produced some powerful learning. The TFD program attempted to destabilize students' thinking around issues of diversity. Rather than endorse the simple notions of diversity as difference without asking "Different from whom?" TFD students were presented the daunting challenge of questioning everything they believed to be true about students, teaching, and learning. One student's master's paper, titled *Exposing Biases: Diversity Framed in a Western Lens* (Van Huesen, 1996), is illustrative:

This "Western" philosophy toward education I was employing was evident in my use of psychological explanations and tests to define [my student's] "deficits," my quickness in categorizing him and deciding what "level" he should be, my ideas of what a child should be, my interpretation of his "behavior," and what I thought was a "lack" of emotion or assertiveness. (p. 1)

Certainly, not all of the students plunged into the depths of postmodern and critical theories, but enough of them engaged in the rigors of theoretical work to elicit words of praise from faculty in other departments.

A CRT perspective on the TFD program focuses on its use of context in constructing reality and the social construction of knowledge. Although many of the students wanted the program to "tell them" what to do, the faculty insisted on plunging students right back into the specific context of the community and school to which they were assigned. TFD did not pretend to have "answers" but instead a more complex way to examine problems. Simple prescriptions such as "Teachers should make home visits" were challenged in TFD seminars. What if parents don't want you in their homes? What if parents believe you are there to judge them and their parenting? Who are you to insert yourself into people's private lives? Throughout the preparation year, TFD students are asked to make meaning from their different contexts. By "telling teaching stories" (Gomez & Tabachnick, 1991), TFD students were challenged to examine teaching and students' experiences from multiple perspectives.

TFD was careful to challenge students about fixed notions of difference and diversity they may have held. In the introductory course, "Teaching and Diversity," there was an attempt to interrogate the meanings of diversity. Like Judith Butler (1991, p. 14) we wanted the students to be "permanently troubled by identity categories, [to] consider them to be invariable stumbling-blocks, and understand them, even promote them, as sites of necessary trouble." As a consequence of this kind of teaching and learning, TFD students often were "disruptive" to both their university classes and their field experience sites. The term *disruptive* is used here not to describe uncivil or rude behavior but, rather, to describe a "disturbing" presence. TFD students constantly asked questions about why things were as they were. "Why are the Chapter 1 children always being pulled out of the classroom during some of the most important instructional time?" "Why is it that only children of color are slated for categorical services?" "How is it that our discipline program is so arbitrarily applied, resulting in suspension of male children of color at twice the rate of White children?" "Why aren't the Black children learning to read?" These questions and others like them posed a threat to notions of PSWBW that existed even in some of our most "multicultural," "progressive" schools. The TFD students began to appreciate our argument that constructing the category also creates the desire to fill it.

Destabilizing prospective teachers' thinking while simultaneously preparing them to confront the rigors of urban teaching is "dangerous" work. TFD was not attempting to raise the level of uncertainty and anxiety in its students to the point where they would be ineffective in the classroom. It was trying to help them reconceptualize some of their fundamental beliefs and attitudes toward difference and diversity, even if they came into the program believing they were "liberal" or "progressive." Ultimately, TFD could not hold up under its own weight. The intellectual work of deconstructing and reconstructing teaching and teacher education took its toll on faculty. Ironically, TFD is being rethought.

CONCLUDING THOUGHTS

What does a CRT perspective tell us about the preparation of teachers for diverse student populations? In general, it suggests that such work is difficult, if not impossible. First, it suggests that teacher educators committed to preparing teachers for effective practice in diverse schools and communities are working with either small, specialized groups of like-minded prospective teachers or resistant, often hostile prospective teachers (Ahlquist, 1991). It also tells us that many programs treat issues of diversity as a necessary evil imposed by the state and/or accrediting agency. These programs relegate issues of diversity to a course, workshop, or module that students must complete for certification. Even at schools, colleges, and departments of education with well-regarded teacher preparation programs, students talk of "getting through the diversity requirement."

Examination of the literature suggests that external accrediting agencies (e.g., state departments of education, collegiate accreditation) exert little power on SCDEs to ensure that prospective teachers are prepared to teach in diverse schools and communities. This conclusion comes from a minimal level of deductive reasoning. Few SCDEs require that students seeking admission to teacher certification programs exhibit any knowledge, skills, or experiences related to diversity.[10] Many states require that prospective teachers pass basic competency tests, even though most students do not enter the professional course sequence until their junior year and should be able to read, write, and compute. However, the state does not employ a similarly watchful eye to determine prospective teachers' multicultural competence. Even though most teacher preparation programs require course work or field experiences in diverse settings, the standard for such requirements is variable. At one of the nation's more highly regarded education schools, there are no faculty of color involved in teacher preparation and no course work that directly attends to preparing teachers for diverse schools and communities.

Third, the snapshot of four teacher educators and two teacher education programs suggests that CRT can be a way to explain and understand preparing teachers for diversity that moves beyond both superficial, essentialized treatments of various cultural groups and liberal guilt and angst. The CRT perspective exposes the way that theory works in such programs. Unfortunately, too many teacher education programs have no basis in theory. Instead, teacher educators are forced to spend much of their energy trying to determine how to force some number of credit requirements into rigid time frames.

Fourth, the CRT perspective helps to ferret out the way specifically designed programs for preparing teachers for diverse student populations challenge generic models of teaching and teacher education. Rather than submit to the discourse of PSWBW, such programs and teacher educators establish themselves in opposition to the hegemony of an idealized past. Ahlquist (1991) points out that "most teacher educators never received an education that was empowering, anti-racist, problem posing, or liberatory" (p. 168). Thus, the people and programs that served as exemplars in this chapter represent a relatively small proportion of teaching and teacher education.

This chapter was an attempt at using a lens that is new to education, critical race theory, for understanding the phenomenon of preparing teachers for diverse student populations. I tried to provide enough of a foundation in CRT to ensure coherence in the subsequent arguments. From the beginning, the chapter adopted an almost schizophrenic character in which the author both challenged constructions of difference and deployed those constructions to understand school inequity. However, it was a necessary personality split, for we are, as Cochran-Smith says, "constructing a new boat while sitting in the old one."

Simply knowing what the literature says about preparing teachers for diverse student populations is unlikely to be of much use to teacher educators. What we need to know is the meaning that these teacher preparation programs make of difference, diversity, and social justice. Thus, it was important to take the reader back through a brief historical overview of the construction of the categories of difference. Next, the chapter infused the more traditional approach of reviewing extant literature with telling the "preparing teachers for diversity" story. This story (and it was important to name it as such) is a self-perpetuating one that has had a powerful influence on the ways that diversity has been constructed for teachers. Finally, the chapter concluded with a critical race theory perspective on a select group of practitioners and programs to illustrate the possibilities for challenging dominant discourses of education and educational research.

The practitioner and practice examples are not about "right" ways of preparing teachers; rather, they are about possibilities. They are about honest attempts to break with the discourse and mythology of PSWBW. Unfortunately, these profiles are not about optimism. Indeed, the power of myths (such as PSWBW) is that they can endure and have meaning far beyond their usefulness. Practitioners and practices that defy the conventional paradigm remain as showcases and oddities. The vast majority of new teachers will continue to be prepared in programs that add on multicultural education courses, workshops, or modules. Most teacher education programs will continue to accept student resistance to issues of difference, diversity, and social justice as a given.

Our tacit acceptance of student resistance may reflect our ongoing desire to believe in some mythical time when school was perfect. We may want to be able to point to the elements (or, more pointedly, the people) that destroyed that perfection. We may want to believe that this different group of students requires some extraordinary type of teaching because if we do not believe it, it calls into question all of the teaching we have endorsed heretofore.

Perhaps the real task of this chapter was not to investigate our preparation of teachers for diverse learners, but rather simply our preparation of teachers. Perhaps the service this chapter renders is to pose a new set of questions: What kinds of knowledge, skills, and abilities must today's teacher have? How are we to determine teaching excellence? Is a teacher deemed excellent in a suburban, middle-income White community able to demonstrate similar excellence in an urban, poor community? How do we educate teacher educators to meet the challenges and opportunity diversity presents? How do we deconstruct the language of difference to allow students to move out of categories and into their full humanity? As long as we continue to create a category of difference—teacher preparation versus teacher preparation for diverse learners—we are likely to satisfy only one group of people, those who make their living researching and writing about preparing teachers for diverse learners.

NOTES

[1] Portions of this section are adapted from an earlier publication (Ladson-Billings, 1998).

[2] These elements are adapted from Zeichner's (1992) special report.

[3] This is a total figure for all students enrolled in SCDEs. It includes graduates as well as undergraduates and students not seeking teacher certification.

[4] At this writing, Joyce King has just accepted a new administrative post at the City University of New York's Medgar Evers College.

[5] Many other excellent programs could have been selected here, including those at Alverno College, the University of Alaska–Fairbanks, Wichita State University, and the University of Utah, as well as Etta Hollins's work at California State University–Hayward and Washington State University.

[6] Aspects of these profiles are taken from Ladson-Billings (in press).

[7] There is also a bilingual, cross-cultural, language, and academic development teacher credential.

[8] Prior to the change in director in the mid-1980s, SCU students regularly did their practicums and student teaching in private (often church-related) schools.

[9] Several UW-Madison faculty members, including Carl Grant, Ken Zeichner, Bob Tabachnick, Mary Gomez, and Marianne Bloch, have conducted small cohort programs whose focus has been on preparing teachers for diverse classrooms. Each of these programs was developed within the existing teacher education program structure.

[10] At the University of Wisconsin–Whitewater, teacher education applicants must meet a minimal diversity requirement.

REFERENCES

Ahlquist, R. (1991). Position and imposition: Power relations in a multicultural foundations class. *Journal of Negro Education, 60,* 158–169.

American Association of Colleges of Teacher Education. (1980). *Multicultural teacher education: Guidelines for implementation.* Washington, DC.

American Association of Colleges of Teacher Education. (1994). *Briefing books.* Washington, DC.

Au, K., & Jordan, C. (1981). Teaching reading to Hawaiian children: Finding a culturally appropriate solution. In H. Trueba, G. Guthrie, & K. Au (Eds.), *Culture and the bilingual classroom: Studies in classroom ethnography* (pp. 139–152). Rowley, MA: Newbury House.

Banks, J. A. (1981). *Education in the 80's: Multiethnic education.* Washington, DC: National Education Association.

Banks, J. A. (1995). Multicultural education: Historical development, dimensions, practice. In J. A. Banks & C. M. Banks (Eds.), *Handbook of research on multicultural education* (pp. 3–24). New York: Macmillan.

Baptiste, H. P., & Baptiste, M. L. (1980). Competencies toward multiculturalism. In H. P. Baptiste, M. L. Baptiste, & D. Gollnick (Eds.), *Multicultural teacher education: Preparing educators to provide equity* (pp. 44–72). Washington, DC: AACTE Commission on Multicultural Education.

Baptiste, H. P., Baptiste, M. L., & Gollnick, D. (Eds.). (1980). *Multicultural teacher education: Preparing educators to provide equity.* Washington, DC: AACTE Commission on Multicultural Education.

Barnes, R. (1990). Race consciousness: The thematic content of racial distinctiveness in critical race scholarship. *Harvard Law Review, 103,* 1864–1871.

Bartolome, L. (1994). Beyond the methods fetish: Toward a humanizing pedagogy. *Harvard Educational Review, 64,* 173–193.

Bateson, M. C. (1989). *Composing a life.* New York: Penguin Books.

Baugh, J. (1994). New and prevailing misconceptions of African American English for logic and mathematics. In E. Hollins, J. King, & W. Hayman (Eds.), *Teaching diverse populations: Formulating a knowledge base* (pp. 191–205). Albany: State University of New York Press.

Bell, D. (1980). Brown v. Board of Education and the interest convergence dilemma. *Harvard Law Review, 93,* 518–533.

Bell, D. (1992). *Faces at the bottom of the well: The permanence of racism.* New York: Basic Books.

Bennett, C. (1995). Preparing teachers for cultural diversity and national standards of academic excellence. *Journal of Teacher Education, 46,* 259–265.

Bettleheim, B. (1965). Teaching the disadvantaged. *National Education Association Journal, 54,* 8–12.

Bloom, B., Davis, A., & Hess, R. (1965). *Comprehensive education for cultural deprivation.* Troy, MO: Holt, Rinehart & Winston.

Booth, M. (1993). Students' historical thinking and the national history curriculum in England. *Theory and Research in Social Education, 21,* 105–127.

Boyle-Baise, M., & Washburn, J. (1995). Coalescing for change: The coalition for education that is multicultural. *Journal of Teacher Education, 46,* 351–359.

Brown v. Board of Education. (1954). 347 U.S. 483.

Butler, J. (1991). Imitation and gender subordination. In D. Fuss (Ed.), *Essentially speaking: Feminism, nature, and difference* (pp. 13–31). New York: Routledge.

Calmore, J. O. (1992). Critical race theory, Archie Shepp and fire music: Securing an authentic intellectual life in a multicultural world. *Southern California Law Review, 65,* 2129–2230.

Carter, K. (1993). The place of story in the study of teaching and teacher education. *Educational Researcher, 22*(1), 5–12.

Cochran-Smith, M. (1995a). Uncertain allies: Understanding the boundaries of race and teaching. *Harvard Educational Review, 63,* 541–570.

Cochran-Smith, M. (1995b). Color blindness and basket making are not the answers: Confronting the dilemmas of race, culture, and language diversity in teacher education. *American Educational Research Journal, 32,* 493–522.

Cochran-Smith, M., & Lytle, S. (1993). *Inside/outside: Teacher research and knowledge.* New York: Teachers College Press.

Commission on Excellence in Education. (1983). *A nation at risk.* Washington, DC.

Commission on Multicultural Education. (1978). *Directory: Multicultural education programs in teacher education institutions in the United States.* Washington, DC: American Association of Colleges for Teacher Education.

Conant, J. (1963). *The education of American teachers.* New York: McGraw-Hill.

Connelly, F. M., & Clandinin, D. J. (1990). Stories of experience and narrative inquiry. *Educational Researcher, 19*(5), 2–14.

Crenshaw, K. (1988). Race, reform and retrenchment: Transformation and legitimation in anti-discrimination law. *Harvard Law Review, 101,* 1331–1387.

Crenshaw, K., Gotanda, N., Peller, G., & Thomas, K. (Eds.). (1995). *Critical race theory: The key writings that formed the movement.* New York: Free Press.

Cuban, L. (1989). The at-risk label and the problem of urban school reform. *Phi Delta Kappan, 70,* 780–784, 799–801.

Davis, A. (1965). *Social class influences upon learning.* Cambridge, MA: Harvard University Press.

Deering, T., & Stanutz, A. (1995). Pre-service field experience as a multicultural component of a teacher education program. *Journal of Teacher Education, 46,* 390–394.

Delgado, R. (Ed.). (1995). *Critical race theory: The cutting edge.* Philadelphia: Temple University Press.

Delpit, L. (1995). *Other people's children: Cultural conflict in the classroom.* New York: New Press.

Dilworth, M. (Ed.). (1992). *Diversity in teacher education: New expectations.* San Francisco: Jossey-Bass.

Foster, M. (1997). *Black teachers on teaching.* New York: Free Press.

Garcia, S. (1997). Self narrative inquiry in teacher development. In J. King, E. Hollins, & W. Hayman (Eds.), *Preparing teachers for cultural diversity* (pp. 146–155). New York: Teachers College Press.

Gollnick, D. (1991). Multicultural education: Policies and practices in teacher education. In C. Grant (Ed.), *Research and multicultural education: From the margins to the mainstream* (pp. 218–239). London: Falmer Press.

Gollnick, D., Osayande, K. I. M., & Levy, J. (1980). *Multicultural teacher education: Case studies of thirteen programs* (Vol. 2). Washington, DC: American Association of Colleges of Teacher Education.

Gomez, M. L., & Tabachnick, B. R. (1991, April). *Preparing preservice teachers to teach diverse learners.* Paper presented at the annual meeting of the American Educational Research Association, Chicago.

Goodlad, J. (1990). Better teachers for our nation's schools. *Phi Delta Kappan, 72,* 185–194.

Goodwin, A. L. (1997). Historical and contemporary perspectives on multicultural teacher education. In J. King, E. Hollins, & W. Hayman (Eds.), *Preparing teachers for cultural diversity* (pp. 5–22). New York: Teachers College Press.

Gordon, R. (1990). New developments in legal theory. In D. Kairys (Ed.), *The politics of law: A progressive critique* (pp. 413–425). New York: Panetheon Books.

Gramsci, A. (1971). *Selections from the prison notebooks* (Q. Hoare & G. N. Smith, Eds. and Trans.). New York: International Publishers.

Grant, C. A. (1989). Urban teachers: Their new colleagues and the curriculum. *Phi Delta Kappan, 70,* 764–770.

Grant, C. A., & Secada, W. (1990). Preparing teachers for diversity. In W. R. Houston, M. Haberman, & J. Sikula (Eds.), *Handbook of research on teacher education* (pp. 403–422). New York: Macmillan.

Greenman, N., & Kimmel, E. (1995). The road to multicultural education: Potholes of resistance. *Journal of Teacher Education, 46,* 360–368.

Guy-Sheftall, B. (1993, April). *Black feminist perspectives on the academy.* Paper presented at the annual meeting of the American Educational Research Association, Atlanta.

Haberman, M. (1989). More minority teachers. *Phi Delta Kappan, 70,* 771–779.

Haberman, M. (1995a). *Star teachers of children in poverty.* West Lafayette, IN: Kappa Delta Pi.

Haberman, M. (1995b, January/February). The meaning of the best and brightest in urban schools. *In These Times,* pp. 26–28.

Hacker, A. (1992). *Two nations: Black and White, separate, hostile, and unequal.* New York: Ballantine Books.

Herbst, J. (1989). *And sadly teach: Teacher education and professionalization in American culture.* Madison: University of Wisconsin Press.

Hollins, E. (1990, April). *A re-examination of what works for inner-city Black children.* Paper presented at the annual meeting of the American Educational Research Association, Boston.

Irvine, J. J. (1990). *Black students and school failure.* Westport, CT: Greenwood Press.

Irvine, J. J. (1992). Making teacher education culturally responsive. In M. Dilworth (Ed.), *Diversity in teacher education* (pp. 79–92). San Francisco: Jossey-Bass.

Irvine, J. J., & Fraser, J. W. (1998, May 13). Commentary—'Warm demanders': Do national certification standards leave room for the culturally responsive pedagogy of African American teachers? *Education Week,* pp. 42, 56.

King, J. (1991). Dysconscious racism: Ideology, identity and the miseducation of teachers. *Journal of Negro Education, 60,* 133–146.

King, J. (1995). Culture-centered knowledge: Black studies, curriculum transformation, and social action. In J. A. Banks & C. M. Banks (Eds.), *Handbook of research on multicultural education* (pp. 265–290). New York: Macmillan.

King, J. (1997). "Thank you for opening our minds": On praxis, transmutation, and Black studies in teacher development. In J. King, E. Hollins, & W. Hayman (Eds.), *Preparing teachers for cultural diversity* (pp. 156–169). New York: Teachers College Press.

King, J. (1998, April). *Teaching researchers, learning through cultural memory.* Paper presented at the annual meeting of the American Educational Research Association, San Diego, CA.

King, J., Hollins, E., & Hayman, W. (Eds.). (1997). *Preparing teachers for cultural diversity.* New York: Teachers College Press.

King, J., & Ladson-Billings, G. (1990). The teacher education challenge in elite universities: Developing critical perspectives for teaching in a democratic and multicultural society. *European Journal of Intercultural Studies, 1*(2), 15–30.

Ladner, J. (Ed.). (1973). *The death of White sociology.* New York: Vintage Books.

Ladson-Billings, G. (1991). Beyond multicultural illiteracy. *Journal of Negro Education, 60,* 147–157.

Ladson-Billings, G. (1994). *Dreamkeepers: Successful teachers of African American children.* San Francisco: Jossey-Bass.

Ladson-Billings, G. (1995). Multicultural teacher education: Research, practice, and policy. In J. A. Banks & C. M. Banks (Eds.), *Handbook of research in multicultural education* (pp. 747–759). New York: Macmillan.

Ladson-Billings, G. (1998). Just what is critical race theory and what's it doing in a "nice" field like education? *International Journal of Qualitative Studies in Education, 11,* 7–24.

Ladson-Billings, G. (in press). Preparing teachers for diversity: Historical perspectives, current trends, and future directions. In L. Darling-Hammond & G. Sykes (Eds.), *Teaching as the learning profession: Handbook of policy and practice.* San Francisco: Jossey-Bass.

Ladson-Billings, G., & Tate, W. F. (1995). Toward a critical race theory of education. *Teachers College Record, 97,* 47–68.

Lawrence, C. (1995). The word and the river: Pedagogy as scholarship and struggle. In K. Crenshaw, N. Gotanda, G. Peller, & K. Thomas (Eds.), *Critical race theory: The writings that formed the movement* (pp. 336–351). New York: Free Press.

Lawrence-Lightfoot, S. (1998). *Portraiture.* San Francisco: Jossey-Bass.

Lee, C. (1994). African centered pedagogy: Complexities and possibilities. In M. Shujaa (Ed.), *Too much schooling, too little education: A paradox of Black life in White societies* (pp. 295–318). Trenton, NJ: Africa World Press.

Lee, M. (1980). *Multicultural teacher education: An annotated bibliography of selected resources* (Vol. 3). Washington, DC: American Association of Colleges of Teacher Education.

Loewen, J. (1995). *Lies my teacher told me: Everything your American history textbook got wrong.* New York: Touchstone.

McCall, A. (1995). Constructing conceptions of multicultural teaching: Preservice teachers' life experiences and teacher education. *Journal of Teacher Education, 46,* 340–350.

McDermott, R. P. (1974). Achieving school failure. In G. Spindler (Ed.), *Education and cultural process.* New York: Holt, Rinehart & Winston.

McIntosh, P. (1988). *White privilege and male privilege: A personal account of coming to see correspondence through work in women's studies.* Wellesley, MA: Wellesley College Center for Research on Women.

McWilliam, E. (1994). *In broken images: Feminist tales for a different teacher education.* New York: Teachers College Press.

Moll, L. (1988). Some key issues in teaching Latino students. *Language Arts, 65,* 465–472.

O'Reilly, K. (1995). *For love of children: Life histories of two women teachers entering the profession from 1920–1940: Case studies of the feminization of the teaching profession.* Unpublished master's thesis, University of Wisconsin.

Ornstein, A., & Vairo, P. (1968). *How to teach disadvantaged youth.* New York: McKay.

Riessman, F. (1962). *The culturally deprived child.* New York: Harper & Row.

Rothenberg, P. (1988). Integrating the study of race, gender and class: Some preliminary observations. *Feminist Teacher, 3,* 37–42.

Sarason, S., Davidson, K., & Blatt, B. (1986). *The preparation of teachers: An unstudied problem in education* (rev. ed.). Cambridge, MA: Brookline Books.

Shade, B. (1995). Developing a multicultural focus in teacher education: One department's story. *Journal of Teacher Education, 46,* 375–380.

Shujaa, M. (Ed.). (1996). *Beyond desegregation: The politics of quality in African American education.* Thousand Oaks, CA: Corwin Press.

Sleeter, C., & Grant, C. A. (1987). An analysis of multicultural education in the United States. *Harvard Educational Review, 7,* 421–444.

Smitherman, G. (1987). Opinion: Toward a national public policy on language. *College English, 49,* 29–36.

Tate, W. F. (1997). Critical race theory and education: History, theory, and implications. In M. Apple (Ed.), *Review of research in education* (Vol. 22, pp. 191–243). Washington, DC: American Educational Research Association.

Tate, W. F., Ladson-Billings, G., & Grant, C. A. (1993). The *Brown* decision revisited: Mathematizing social problems. *Educational Policy, 7,* 255–275.

Unger, R. M. (1983). The critical legal studies movement. *Harvard Law Review, 96,* 561–675.

Van Huesen, C. (1996). *Exposing biases: Diversity framed in a Western lens.* Unpublished master's thesis, University of Wisconsin.

Wellman, D. (1977). *Portraits of White racism.* Cambridge, England: Cambridge University Press.

West, C. (1993). *Keeping faith.* New York: Routledge.

Williams, P. J. (1987). Alchemical notes: Reconstructing ideals from deconstructed rights. *Harvard Civil Rights-Civil Liberties Law Review, 22,* 401–433.

Williams, P. J. (1991). *The alchemy of race and rights: Diary of a law professor.* Cambridge, MA: Harvard University Press.

Zeichner, K. M. (1991, April). *Teacher education for social responsibility.* Paper presented at the annual meeting of the American Educational Research Association, Chicago.

Zeichner, K. M. (1992). *Educating teachers for cultural diversity.* East Lansing, MI: National Center for Research on Teacher Learning.

Zeichner, K. (1993). Traditions of practice in U.S. pre-service teacher education programs. *Teaching and Teacher Education, 9,* 1–13.

Zeichner, K. M., & Liston, D. P. (1987). Teaching student teachers to reflect. *Harvard Educational Review, 57,* 23–47.

Zimpher, N., & Ashburn, E. (1992). Countering parochialism in teacher candidates. In M. Dilworth (Ed.), *Diversity in teacher education* (pp. 40–62). San Francisco: Jossey-Bass.

Manuscript received August 5, 1998
Accepted November 5, 1998

Chapter 8

Relationships of Knowledge and Practice: Teacher Learning in Communities

MARILYN COCHRAN-SMITH
Boston College

SUSAN L. LYTLE
University of Pennsylvania

Over the last 20 years, teacher learning has become one of the most important concerns of the educational establishment. It has been more or less assumed that teachers who *know* more teach better. This "simple" idea has governed multiple efforts to improve education in the arenas of policy, research, and practice by focusing on what teachers know or need to know. In this chapter, we do not question this basic idea. Rather, we point out that within various change efforts, there are radically different views of what "knowing more" and "teaching better" mean. In other words, there are radically different conceptions of teacher learning, including varying images of knowledge; of professional practice; of the necessary and/or potential relationships that exist between the two; of the intellectual, social, and organizational contexts that support teacher learning; and of the ways teacher learning is linked to educational change and the purposes of schooling. Different conceptions of teacher learning—although not always made explicit—lead to very different ideas about how to improve teacher education and professional development, how to bring about school and curricular change, and how to assess and license teachers over the course of the professional life span.

What is most at stake in this discussion is how teachers and teacher learning—widely acknowledged as the sine qua non of every school change effort—are understood and positioned in the debate as well as how universities and other educational agencies—widely touted for their collaborative relationships—are actually organized as they conduct business with schools. This chapter provides a framework for considering various initiatives related to teacher learning that,

Preparation of this chapter was supported in part by a major grant from the Spencer Foundation. We would like to acknowledge the insightful and challenging questions and comments offered by Peter Grimmett and Ann Lieberman, consulting editors for this chapter. We are grateful for their interest and support of the issues considered here and for their long-term work in this field. We would also like to thank Robert Fecho and Jacqueline Jordan Irvine, who made very helpful suggestions about an early version of this chapter. Marguerite Connolly and Mary Kim Fries, graduate research assistants at Boston College, worked tirelessly to construct and organize the bibliography for this project. We are very grateful for their contribution.

although sometimes described in similar language and even featuring what appear to be similar methods and organizational arrangements, are actually very different in purpose and have very different consequences for the everyday lives of students and teachers.

In this chapter, we make distinctions among three prominent conceptions of teacher learning by unpacking their differing images. The first conception is what we refer to as "knowledge-*for*-practice." Here it is assumed that university-based researchers generate what is commonly referred to as formal knowledge and theory (including codifications of the so-called wisdom of practice) *for* teachers to use in order to improve practice. The second conception of teacher learning is what we think of as "knowledge-*in*-practice." From this perspective, some of the most essential knowledge for teaching is what many people call practical knowledge, or what very competent teachers know as it is embedded in practice and in teachers' reflections on practice. Here it is assumed that teachers learn when they have opportunities to probe the knowledge embedded *in* the work of expert teachers and/or to deepen their own knowledge and expertise as makers of wise judgments and designers of rich learning interactions in the classroom. The third conception of teacher learning involves what we call "knowledge-*of*-practice." Unlike the first two, this third conception cannot be understood in terms of a universe of knowledge that divides formal knowledge, on the one hand, from practical knowledge, on the other. Rather, it is assumed that the knowledge teachers need to teach well is generated when teachers treat their own classrooms and schools as sites for intentional investigation at the same time that they treat the knowledge and theory produced by others as generative material for interrogation and interpretation. In this sense, teachers learn when they generate local knowledge *of* practice by working within the contexts of inquiry communities to theorize and construct their work and to connect it to larger social, cultural, and political issues.

In the final part of this chapter, we suggest directions for thinking about teacher learning as we enter the 21st century. We do so by outlining the major dimensions of the construct *inquiry as stance*, which is based on a 3-year study of the relationships of inquiry, knowledge, and professional practice in urban inquiry communities[1] and on our experiences as university-based teachers and researchers working with student teachers and experienced teachers over the last 20 years. Derived from the knowledge-*of*-practice conception of teacher learning, we suggest that this new construct permits closer understanding of knowledge-practice relationships as well as how inquiry produces knowledge, how inquiry relates to practice, and what teachers learn from inquiry within communities. We believe that *inquiry as stance* may offer promising directions for initiatives related to preservice education, professional development, curriculum construction/recon-struction, and school and social change. This construct also helps point to some of the most interesting but difficult questions related to teacher learning and the role of communities as we enter the new century.

It may be useful here to say a few words about what this chapter is *not* intended to do. It is not intended to provide an exhaustive or comprehensive review of the literature on teacher learning, teacher knowledge, teacher research, or teacher communities. In this volume itself, there are two other chapters that explore teacher learning from different perspectives, and there are countless articles and chapters elsewhere that relate to these topics. Our intention here is to offer a way of rethinking teacher learning that is not based on the particular strategies of teacher education programs, the particular arrangements of professional or curriculum development projects, or the specific content of assessment tools. Rather, our framework for understanding teacher learning is based on the images and assumptions that underlie methods and on the educational purposes that drive various teacher learning initiatives.

Finally, it is worthwhile to note that although we have drawn on selected pieces of work that are relevant to the concepts considered here, our unit of analysis is not the individual but the underlying conception of teacher learning. Our intention in this chapter, then, is to write conceptually—to provide an analytic framework for theorizing teacher learning on the basis of fundamental ideas about how knowledge and practice are related and how teachers learn within communities and other contexts.

RETHINKING TEACHER LEARNING: THREE CONTRASTING RELATIONSHIPS

What we wish to propose in this chapter is that three significantly different conceptions of teacher learning drive many of the most prominent and widespread initiatives intended to promote teacher learning. These three conceptions derive from differing ideas about knowledge and professional practice and how these elements are related to one another in teachers' work. Although competing in fundamental ways, these three conceptions coexist in the world of educational policy, research, and practice and are invoked by differently positioned people in order to explain and justify quite different ideas and approaches to improving teaching and learning. Although they are considerably different, however, the lines between the three are not perfectly drawn, and the language that emanates from them to describe various policy initiatives for teacher learning is not mutually exclusive.

This is the case in part because there are no particular methods of teacher education and no particular organizational arrangements for improving teachers' practices or altering curriculum that follow directly or necessarily from any of the three conceptions of teacher learning. Rather, initiatives for teacher learning are driven primarily by interpretations and ideas—even if these are unexamined and tacit—and not simply by methods and practices. For example, some of the most widespread methods of preservice teacher education—mentoring, reflection, and teacher research/action research—carry multiple meanings and are connected to agendas that are quite different from one another. By the same token, some of the most prominent strategies for promoting professional development—inquiry groups, school-wide projects, coaching, and collaborations with universities—are constructed quite differently and serve very different purposes. This is possible

FIGURE 1

TEACHER LEARNING: **A CONCEPTUAL FRAMEWORK**	

KNOWLEDGE-PRACTICE RELATIONSHIP	What is understood or assumed to be the relationship of knowledge and practice? What is assumed about how "knowing more" and "teaching better" are connected?
IMAGES OF KNOWLEDGE	What knowledge are teachers assumed to need in order to "teach better"? What are the domains, sources, or forms of that knowledge? Who generates that knowledge? Who evaluates and interprets that knowledge?
IMAGES OF TEACHERS, TEACHING, AND PROFESSIONAL PRACTICE	What is assumed about the nature of the activity of teaching? What is included in the idea of "practice"? What are assumed to be the primary roles of teachers in and out of classrooms? What is the relationship of teachers' work in and out of classrooms?
IMAGES OF TEACHER LEARNING AND TEACHERS' ROLES IN EDUCATIONAL CHANGE	What is assumed about the roles teachers and teacher learning play in educational change? What are assumed to be the intellectual, social, and organizational contexts that support teacher learning? What is the role of communities, collaboratives, and/or other collectives in these?
CURRENT INITIATIVES	What are current initiatives in teacher education, professional development and/ or teacher assessment that are based on these images?

because the salient differences among the three conceptions of teacher learning reside not in the methods used to foster teacher learning but, as Figure 1 indicates, in the assumptions that underlie these methods—in the images of knowledge, practice, and teachers' roles that animate them.

In the instance of a particular method (such as reflection or structured discussions about cases of practice or networks formed in collaboration with university educators, for example), it is more important to consider what is made problematic and what is assumed when these methods are used than that they are used or that they are described in similar language. In order to get at the conception of teacher learning underlying a particular initiative, then, we would need to ask what teachers were reflecting on and for what ultimate purposes, or what counted as a case of something and how and in whose interest it was enlisted, or what inquiry groups were inquiring about and what they presumed were the ''givens'' of teaching and schooling, or whether a school-wide group or a school-university partnership operated from a shared idea about the larger intellectual and political project in which participants were engaged.

For each of the three conceptions of teacher learning we suggest, we provide a brief overview and then discuss major images. We use the term *images* to mean the central common conceptions that seem symbolic of basic attitudes and orientations to teaching and learning. Then we discuss several actual (and, in most cases, highly visible) initiatives related to teacher learning that are undergirded by each conception. Each of these initiatives, whether related to and labeled teacher education and professional development, curricular and school change, or teacher assessment and licensure, has to do with teacher learning.

As Figure 2 indicates, each of the three sections that make up the bulk of this chapter is organized as follows:

- overview of the conception of teacher learning and the knowledge-practice relationship from which it derives
- images of knowledge
- images of teachers, teaching, and professional practice
- images of teacher learning and teachers' roles in educational change
- current initiatives animated by the conception

Focusing on images is a heuristic for taking each conception apart and considering the dominant ideas and tendencies within it. Elaborating on the conceptions by describing current initiatives puts the pieces of the conception back together and reveals how each is instantiated in the complex worlds of schools and schooling. None of the initiatives we use as examples are to be considered exemplars of the conception or its embodiment as a ''pure type.'' Rather, each reflects what we understand to be the dominant ideas that animate the initiative and also reflects the unique ways these ideas are played out in particular contexts and at particular points in time. Note that, in this chapter, we devote proportionately more space to the second and third conceptions of teacher learning than to the first. We do so primarily because these tend to be instantiated in ways that are collaborative or collective and/or that feature teacher communities, which is a central interest of this chapter.

TEACHER LEARNING, CONCEPTION 1: KNOWLEDGE *FOR* PRACTICE

The first conception of teacher learning is based on an understanding of the relationship of knowledge and practice that may be thought of as knowledge-*for*-practice. One of the most prevalent conceptions of teacher learning, this first

FIGURE 2

CONCEPTIONS OF TEACHER LEARNING: 3 KNOWLEDGE-PRACTICE RELATIONSHIPS			
Knowledge-Practice Relationship	Knowledge-For-Practice	Knowledge-In-Practice	Knowledge-Of-Practice
Images of Knowledge			
Images of Teachers, Teaching, and Professional Practice			
Images of Teacher Learning and Teachers' Roles in Educational Change			
Current Initiatives in Teacher Education, Professional Development, and/or Teacher Assessment			

conception hinges on the idea that knowing more (e.g., more subject matter, more educational theory, more pedagogy, more instructional strategies) leads more or less directly to more effective practice. Here, knowledge for teaching consists primarily of what is commonly called "formal knowledge," or the general theories and research-based findings on a wide range of foundational and applied topics that together constitute the basic domains of knowledge about teaching, widely referred to by educators as "the knowledge base." These domains generally include content or subject matter knowledge as well as knowledge about the disciplinary foundations of education, human development and learners, classroom organization, pedagogy, assessment, the social and cultural contexts of teaching and schooling, and knowledge of teaching as a profession. The idea here is that competent practice reflects the state of the art; that is, highly skilled teachers have deep knowledge of their content areas and of the most effective teaching strategies for creating learning opportunities for students. Teachers learn this knowledge through various preservice and professional development experiences that provide access to the knowledge base. To improve teaching, then, teachers need to implement, translate, or otherwise put into practice the knowledge they acquire from experts outside the classroom.

Images of Knowledge

The knowledge-*for*-practice relationship depends on the assumption that the knowledge teachers need to teach well is produced primarily by university-based researchers and scholars in various disciplines. This includes subject matter knowledge, educational theories, and conceptual frameworks, as well as state-of-the-art strategies and effective practices for teaching a variety of content areas. The knowledge-*for*-practice conception is based on the premise that teaching has a "distinctive knowledge base" that, "when mastered, will provide teachers with a unique fund of knowledge (e.g., knowledge that is not pedestrian or held by people generally)" (Gardner, 1989, pp. ix–x). Furthermore, it is assumed that it is possible to be explicit about a formal knowledge base rather than relying on the conventional wisdom of common practice, which some have referred to as natural, intuitive, or normative (Gardner, 1989; Huberman, 1996; Murray, 1989). This conception of teacher learning indirectly underlies the burgeoning number of handbooks of research on teaching, learning, and schooling that are intended to codify and disseminate the bodies of knowledge that inform the profession (e.g., Banks, 1996; Flood, Jensen, Lapp, & Squire, 1991; Gardner, 1989; Murray, 1989; Richardson, in press; Sikula, 1996; Wittrock, 1986). Part of the point of constructing the formal knowledge base for teaching is to establish the "truth of educational practices as they may be derived from a theory" by determining the "correctness" of the theory, the educational practice, and the process by which the second is derived from the first (Murray, 1989, p. 7). In much of the literature of research on teaching, it is assumed that formal knowledge is generated through "studies of teaching that use conventional scientific methods, quantitative and qualitative; these methods and their accompanying designs are intended to yield a commonly accepted degree of significance, validity, generalizability, and intersubjectivity" (Fenstermacher, 1994, p. 8).

As Shulman (1987) pointed out more than a decade ago, however, the knowledge base needs to include an array of knowledge categories and sources. He argued that what was one of the most important sources of the knowledge base for teaching—the wisdom of practice—was generally missing from the literature. Of particular interest was what he called "pedagogical content knowledge," which he defined as:

that special amalgam of content and pedagogy that is uniquely the province of teachers, their own special form of professional understanding . . . it represents the blending of content and pedagogy into an understanding of how particular topics, problems, or issues are organized, represented, and adapted to the diverse interests and abilities of learners, and presented for instruction. (p. 8)

Following Shulman's suggestion, a number of researchers have attempted over the last decade to codify the practical, pedagogical wisdom of able teachers. Pedagogical content knowledge, or how teachers understand subject matter and how they transform it into classroom instruction, has thus become a central construct within the knowledge base. Two related programs of research, developed initially by researchers at Stanford University (e.g., Grossman, 1990; Shulman, 1986, 1987; Shulman & Grossman, 1987; Wilson, Shulman, & Richert, 1987) and at Michigan State University (e.g., Ball, 1990; McDiarmid, Ball, & Anderson, 1989; Wilson, 1994; Wilson, Miller, & Yerkes, 1993), have explored these areas, especially in relation to teachers' pedagogical reasoning as they transform their personal understandings of content into representations that can be taught to students (Grossman, 1990; McDiarmid & Ball, 1989; McDiarmid, Ball, & Anderson, 1989; Wilson, Shulman, & Richert, 1987). These and other programs of research have attempted to formalize what teachers need to know about their subjects as well as what they need to know in order to choose, construct, use, and evaluate representations of subject matter in ways that are teachable for diverse student populations.

The image of knowledge in this first conception of teacher learning is a familiar one. It bespeaks the educational community's quest to join the other major professions by establishing an official and formal body of knowledge that distinguishes professional educators from laypersons. In that sense, it reflects what Donmoyer (1996) calls a "fundamental faith in expertise and scientific knowledge as a source of that expertise" (p. 98). In another sense, the idea of a formal knowledge base that includes "the wisdom of practice" is somewhat perplexing. On the one hand, it seems critically important to acknowledge that excellent teachers have important knowledge, some of which may certainly be thought of in Shulman's terms as pedagogical content knowledge. However, including this knowledge in the formal knowledge base, which is the case in every major publication that attempts to organize and disseminate "the knowledge base," depends on codifying what competent teachers know using the standard methods, frameworks, and language of university-based researchers. It is not entirely clear, then, what it means for university-based researchers to codify school-based teachers' knowledge. The difficulty here may be due to the fact that Shulman's concept of pedagogical content knowledge, which has spawned a decade of important research and influenced the way most current teacher education programs are conceptualized and presented, does *not* fit neatly into a universe of knowledge types that subdivides into the categories of formal knowledge and practical knowledge (Fenstermacher, 1994). When all knowledge is divided into two parts, conceptions like Shulman's that attempt in certain ways to bridge the two become problematic. Perhaps, however, as we suggest in the final section of this chapter, the problem is with the application of the formal-practical knowledge distinction itself and *not* with notions of knowledge for teaching that are not easily subsumed by the distinction.

Images of Teachers, Teaching, and Professional Practice

Implicit in the knowledge-*for*-practice relationship is an image of practice as how, when, and what teachers do as they use the formal knowledge base in the daily work of the classroom. This includes the ways teachers organize lessons and units of study, the activities and materials teachers use for various groups of students, the sequence of content matter teachers present, the ways teachers structure lessons and classroom interactions, and the methods teachers use to assess individual and group progress. Teaching, then, is understood primarily as a process of applying received knowledge to a practical situation: Teachers implement, translate, use, adapt, and/or put into practice what they have learned of the knowledge base. As we said earlier, the assumption in this relationship is that the knowledge that makes teaching a profession comes from authorities outside of the profession itself. The image of the professional teacher is one who adeptly uses the knowledge base in daily practice. It is important to note here that from this perspective, teachers *are* regarded as knowledgeable in that they have "insights" as well as "knowledge, skills, and dispositions" (Reynolds, 1989, p. 138) that they call upon to explain phenomena and make judgments about practice. Generally speaking, however, teachers and other practitioners are not regarded as those who generate knowledge or theorize classroom practice (Lytle & Cochran-Smith, 1992; Schon, 1987).

The image of practice in this first conception of teacher learning, then, is one of knowledge *for* use—teachers are knowledge users, not generators. As Murray (1989) points out, educational theories do not necessarily lead directly to effective educational practices. Rather, teachers need to be knowledgeable about "educational practices that have proven records of accomplishment" (p. 12) and skeptical about the claims of educational theorists and researchers that are not warranted empirically. Efforts to improve practice through implementation of the knowledge base, then, are based more or less on an instrumental view of the relationship between theory/research/knowledge and practice. In discussions about teaching and the knowledge base, some acknowledge the teacher as decision maker and emphasize the importance of judgment and practical reasoning much more so than others (e.g., Donmoyer, 1996; Griffin, 1989). Feiman-Nemser and Remillard (1996), for example, suggest that many of the prominent knowledge base conceptions "leave open the question of what it means to know and use such knowledge in teaching . . . misrepresent[ing] the interactive character of teachers' knowledge and sidestep[ping] the issue of knowledge in use" (pp. 73–74). They point out the limitations of propositional knowledge as a guide to practice and insist that teachers do not use knowledge one domain at a time but rather meld knowledge from many domains as they make judgments and reason about what to do in a particular context. (This idea is further elaborated in the discussion of the second conception of teacher learning that follows.)

Images of Teacher Learning and Teachers' Roles in Educational Change

Over the last several decades, what some people refer to as a "new" image of teacher learning, or a "new model" of teacher education/professional development, has emerged (Grimmett & Neufeld, 1994; Hargreaves & Fullan, 1991; Lieberman & Miller, 1991; Little, 1993; McLaughlin, 1993). For prospective teachers, teacher learning is no longer seen as a one-time process of "teacher training" wherein undergraduates are equipped with methods in the subject areas and sent out to "practice" teaching. Similarly, for experienced teachers, teacher learning is no longer seen as a process of periodic "staff development" wherein experienced teachers are congregated to receive the latest information about the most effective teaching processes and techniques. The "new" image of teacher learning has been informed by research on how teachers think about their work (Clark & Peterson, 1986), and emphasis has shifted from what teachers do to "the knowledge teachers hold, how they organize that knowledge, and how various knowledge sources inform their teaching" (Barnes, 1989, p. 17). The general orientation of the "new" approach to teacher learning is more constructivist than transmission oriented—that is, it is recognized that both prospective and experienced teachers (like all learners) bring prior knowledge and experience to all new learning situations, which are social and specific. In addition, it is now broadly understood that teacher learning takes place over time rather than in isolated moments in time and that active learning requires opportunities to link previous knowledge with new understandings.

Very broadly speaking, this new vision of teacher education and professional development is shared by all three of the conceptions of teacher learning that we are exploring in this chapter. Just below the surface, however, this new vision looks very different, depending on underlying assumptions. In efforts animated by knowledge-*for*-practice, teacher learning centers around enhancing teachers' knowledge of subject matter, of the standards and content of the various professions, and of research-based strategies for effective teaching and classroom organization. A heavy emphasis here is on the need for teachers to learn additional and richer content information as well as new bundles of strategies and skills. Knowledge-*for*-practice emphasizes the acquisition of content area knowledge for elementary-level teachers as much as it does for secondary teachers. It also maintains clear distinctions between expert and novice teachers as well as between very competent teachers and those who, albeit experienced, simply do not know enough content or methods to teach effectively.

The assumption is that it is impossible for teachers at any level to teach students effectively and/or to meet the standards of the various subject matter professions without fundamental knowledge of the disciplines they teach. As McDiarmid (1989) points out, however, rich and deep subject matter knowledge is only the beginning. Following Shulman (1986), he argues that learning subject matter knowledge must be coupled with learning subject-specific pedagogy, particularly understanding the critical role of representation in subject matter teaching and being able to construct and evaluate appropriate representations.

There is some discussion in the literature about how prospective and experienced teachers might learn about subject matter representations—for example, by discussion and evaluation of the multiple representations of a particular concept that are generated by the participants in a particular class or seminar (McDiarmid, 1989). However, the overriding emphasis in this first conception of teacher learning is on what, not how, teachers are supposed to learn.

In a sense, then, the emphasis in teacher learning initiatives based on knowledge-*for*-practice is on helping new and experienced teachers come to know what, generally speaking, is already "known"—at least already known by university-based researchers or other outside experts. There are some obvious tensions and even contradictions in the ways this is played out in real situations. Perhaps the clearest example is the tension between *transmitting* a widely accepted pedagogical theory—like constructivist teaching, for example—*to* new and experienced teachers and, in contrast, *constructing it* along with them. Over the last few decades, as psychological and cultural theories of knowledge construction and constructivist teaching have been more fully worked out in the literature, these distinctions have become more elusive. Richardson (1997), for example, argues that constructivist teacher education derived from Piagetian psychology focuses on teaching teachers to teach in a very particular constructivist manner that is more or less already worked out. Constructivist teacher education derived from sociocultural and situated theories of learning, on the other hand, prompts teachers to understand and reconsider their own prior understandings and to do the same with their students. We would caution, of course, that there is no necessary relationship between a particular version of constructivism and a particular pedagogy of teacher education. However, Richardson's example highlights an obvious tension in knowledge-*for*-practice: The image of teacher learning that emerges from direct instruction about constructivism is quite different from the image that emerges from constructing constructivist pedagogy.

When teacher education programs or projects are animated by knowledge-*for*-practice (where there is so much emphasis on the knowledge base and on what teachers need to know of formal knowledge), there is an inevitable pull toward teaching as transmission and learning as accruing knowledge. This emphasis is exacerbated by high-stakes teacher assessments that privilege formal knowledge, particularly subject matter knowledge that is generally separated from knowledge of pedagogy and practice.

Implicit in the knowledge-*for*-practice conception is the assumption that teachers play a central role in educational change by virtue of their state-of-the-art knowledge acquired through teacher preparation and continuing professional development. Their role is to solve problems by implementing certified procedures rather than to pose problems based on their first-hand observations and experiences. This vision of educational change is primarily an individualistic one, even when it is carried out at the whole-school level. The goal is for each and every teacher to enact practices consistent with the knowledge base and with empirically certified best practices, as instantiated in the various curriculum and assessment frameworks that are implemented at local and state levels.

Current Initiatives in Teacher Learning

Many of the most widespread current initiatives for improving teacher learning are grounded in a conception of knowledge-*for*-practice. In particular, this conception drives many highly visible and highly politicized efforts to improve preservice teacher education, professional development for experienced teachers, whole-school change efforts, and national and/or state certification and licensure policies. In preservice teacher education, the most obvious example is the effort over the last 10 years to make the burgeoning codified knowledge base the centerpiece of the preservice curriculum. Part of what has motivated this effort is the belief that the curriculum of teacher education programs has been for the most part idiosyncratic and normative. Two major projects have spearheaded this effort: the production by the American Association of Colleges for Teacher Education (AACTE) of two knowledge base books (Murray, 1996; Reynolds, 1989) and the compilation of two handbooks of research on teacher education (Houston, 1990; Sikula, 1996) by the Association of Teacher Educators (ATE).

As Gardner (1989) points out in the preface to the first knowledge base book, "The basic premise of this book is that teacher education has for too long been a normative enterprise, and it is now time to become a state of the art enterprise . . . more deliberate and rational" (p. ix). The knowledge-*for*-practice idea is perhaps nowhere as clearly articulated as in the AACTE committee's statement of intent for the first knowledge base books project:

> We believed that by specifying the knowledge considered to be relevant for the beginning teacher, a basis for several second-order functions would be created, including the systematic delineation of prerequisites for obtaining that knowledge and for constructing assessment procedures to evaluate both individuals and programs in the several knowledge domains. Thus, it is intended that the *KBBT* [Knowledge Base for the Beginning Teacher] project should be helpful as one source of guidance in planning for pre-education and foundation courses, in facilitating work on the assessment of teacher knowledge, and in helping to specify standards for the accreditation of teacher preparation programs. (p. x)

The knowledge base books emphasize what teachers and teacher educators need to know. The ATE handbooks of research on teacher education echo the same premise—that compiling the knowledge base for teacher education is essential to making it more on par with other professions: "Few of the several hundred professions have as little of a consensus about a common knowledge base as does the teaching profession. . . . There is a growing consensus today about the need to move the profession of teaching in the direction of a more common knowledge base" (Sikula, 1996, p. xv).

Since the mid-1980s, the National Council for the Accreditation of Teacher Education (NCATE) has evaluated teacher preparation programs according to the extent to which they successfully incorporate into the curriculum the professional knowledge bases for teaching and learning (Christensen, 1996). As is stated succinctly in the introduction to the current standards:

> The NCATE standards are designed to encourage units to develop a coherent program of study according to the current and emerging knowledge bases in the respective fields of inquiry (e.g., science and science education). Education units must demonstrate that the knowledge bases are understood by—and can be articulated and applied by—faculty and students alike. (NCATE, 1995, p. 11)

With this heightened emphasis, the quality of teacher education programs has in large part been determined by fealty to the idea of a formal knowledge base, as constructed and disseminated not only by the professional organizations in teacher education but also by the professional organizations in each subject matter discipline or certification area (e.g., the National Council of Teachers of English for secondary English teaching, the Council on Young Children for early childhood education, the Council on Exceptional Children for special education, the National Association for Social Studies Teaching for teaching in history and the social studies, and so on).

The knowledge-*for*-practice conception also drives some of the most publicized and commercialized initiatives in professional development for experienced teachers. This conception is deeply embedded in many school-wide and school-system-wide professional development projects that use the now-common language of "best practice." Here the idea is that there are empirically verified strategies for classroom management, instruction, curriculum, and assessment that transcend differences in local contexts and hence require minimal translation by teachers for use in classrooms (Fashola & Slavin, 1998). From this perspective, it is pointed out that "best practices," identified through empirical research on high performing schools and teachers, are not necessarily the same as widespread practices, which, as some critics remind us, may be based on tradition (Gardner, 1989), idiosyncrasy (Carter, 1990), opinion (Fenstermacher, 1986), lore (North, 1987), inaccuracy (Murray, 1989), superstition (Leinhardt, 1989), and even delusion (Huberman, 1996) rather than on empirical warrant. Best practices, on the other hand, are based on empirical evidence of effectiveness. They are distinct from general theories or concepts that may imply practices that are not empirically certified and/or from which specific teaching practices are not apparent. This perspective is crystal clear in a recent issue of the journal of the American Federation of Teachers, an issue titled "Moving From Fads to What Works: Building a Research-Based Profession." Grossen's (1996) article in this issue, from which the title is taken, makes the following argument:

> The reformers who provide teachers with theories—but no evidence that they are effective and no details for how to use them—are really demanding that teachers do most of their work for them. To ask that teachers create all of their own tools and curricula is like asking doctors to invent all of their own drugs; like asking airplane pilots to build their own airplanes. When would teachers have time to do this? Engineering a highly effective instructional sequence would more than consume most teachers' private time.
>
> To be a profession is to have a professional knowledge base comprised of shared procedures and strategies that work. This may be a new idea for teachers, though it is quite old for other professions. Good teachers using well-engineered tools and detailed procedures can achieve remarkable results and—this is the good news—teachers can get these results and also have a personal life. (p. 27)

From the perspective of those who advocate for professional development based on teachers' learning of best practices, then, the most accomplished teachers are those who are most knowledgeable about these practices and who most accurately and consistently use these practices in the classroom. In many school change efforts animated by knowledge-*for*-practice, teachers are presumed to learn from ongoing training and coaching provided by officially certified "trainers" in a particular model. The preferred contexts in which this training and coaching occur are the course, workshop, or whole-school training project sponsored by a university, school district, or educational publisher. Currently, this kind of professional development also occurs as part of whole-school reform models wherein not-for-profit and, increasingly, commercial and privatized companies offer complete (not to mention extremely expensive) packages designed to transmit to teachers specific instructional strategies certified through large-scale, long-term, replicated (and replicable) empirical research (Fashola & Slavin, 1998; Grossen, 1996).

Finally, the knowledge-*for*-practice conception of teacher learning underlies most of the teacher tests that are currently required for initial teaching certification in nearly every state nationwide. Passing initial certification tests is generally part of the minimal standard for state licensure as distinct from national board certification or other advanced performance assessments, which are voluntary and intended to assess a higher level of professional experience and expertise (Roth, 1996). Initial certification tests generally assess some combination of communication and literacy skills, on the one hand, and knowledge of subject matter and pedagogy, on the other. Particularly the subject matter tests, which assess basic knowledge of, for example, American and world history, zero in on items of knowledge that are completely decontextualized from the contexts of teaching and from the needs and prior knowledge of individual learners or learning communities.

TEACHER LEARNING, CONCEPTION 2:
KNOWLEDGE *IN* PRACTICE

A second conception of teacher learning that is prominent in various initiatives to enhance what teachers know and improve classroom practice is what we call knowledge-*in*-practice. From this perspective, the emphasis is on knowledge in action: what very competent teachers know as it is expressed or embedded *in* the artistry of practice, *in* teachers' reflections on practice, *in* teachers' practical inquiries, and/or *in* teachers' narrative accounts of practice. A basic assumption here is that teaching is, to a great extent, an uncertain and spontaneous craft situated and constructed in response to the particularities of everyday life in schools and classrooms. The knowledge teachers use to teach well under these conditions is manifested in their actions and in the decisions and judgments they make in an ongoing way. This knowledge is acquired through experience and through considered and deliberative reflection about or inquiry into experience. From this perspective, which enhances and elevates the status of teachers' practical knowledge, it is assumed that teachers learn when they have opportunities to examine and reflect on the knowledge that is implicit in good practice—in the ongoing actions of expert teachers as they choose among alternative strategies, organize classroom routines, and make immediate decisions as well as set problems, frame situations, and consider/reconsider their reasoning. To improve teaching, then, teachers need opportunities to enhance, make explicit, and articulate the tacit knowledge embedded in experience and in the wise action of very competent professionals. Facilitated teacher groups, dyads composed of more and less experienced teachers, teacher communities, and other kinds of collaborative arrangements that support teachers' working together to reflect in and on practice are the major contexts for teacher learning in this relationship.

Images of Knowledge

The knowledge-*in*-practice conception of teacher learning depends on the assumption that the knowledge teachers need to teach well is embedded in the exemplary practice of experienced teachers. Rooted in a constructivist image of knowledge, this includes how outstanding teachers make judgments, how they conceptualize and describe classroom dilemmas, how they name and select aspects of classroom life for attention, and how they think about and improve their craft. The knowledge-*in*-practice conception is based on the premise, best articulated by Donald Schon (1983, 1987, 1995), that there is knowledge implicit in action and artistry—that artistry itself is a kind of knowing.

> When we go about the spontaneous, intuitive performance of the actions of everyday life, we show ourselves to be knowledgeable in a special way. Often we cannot say what we know. When we try to describe it, we find ourselves at a loss, or we produce descriptions that are obviously inappropriate. Our knowing is ordinarily tacit, implicit in our patterns of action and in our feel for the stuff with which we are dealing. It seems right to say that our knowledge is *in* our action. And similarly, the workaday life of the professional practitioner reveals, in its recognitions, judgments, and skills, a pattern of tacit knowing-in-action. (Schon, 1995, p. 29)

This view of professional knowledge breaks epistemologically with what Schon calls "technical rationality," wherein it is assumed that professionals are problem solvers, that the problems of professional practice present themselves ready made and full blown, and that they can be solved instrumentally through the application of research-based theory and technique. Instead, from the knowledge-*in*-practice perspective, it is acknowledged that competent professionals pose and construct problems out of the uncertainty and complexity of practice situations and that they make new sense of situations by connecting them to previous ones and to a variety of other information. Here, thought and action are linked, and the lines between knowledge generation and knowledge use are blurred. This view of knowledge is the basis of the claim that in order to understand and improve practice in the professions, it will take new epistemologies that are outside of the positivist paradigm, particularly what Schon (1983) has referred to as a "new epistemology of practice" (p. 69). The idea that there is knowledge *in* practice is congruent with the increasing acknowledgment in the educational community that much formal research has little bearing on the most immediate and central problems of education. Increasingly, there are serious questions about the usefulness for teaching and learning of a paradigm that divides knowledge generation from knowledge application.

Russell (1987) points out that Schon's general idea of professional knowing-in-action is closely akin to what many educational researchers refer to as "practical knowledge," a term that is regularly used to conceptualize and sort out varying perspectives on knowledge for and about teaching (Carter, 1990; Clandinin & Connelly, 1987, 1995; Fenstermacher, 1994; Hargreaves, 1996; Richardson, 1994b). Carter (1990) uses the term broadly as part of a category that refers to the knowledge teachers acquire that is directly related to classroom performance. She suggests that practical knowledge is "the knowledge teachers have of classroom situations, the practical dilemmas they face in carrying out purposeful action in these settings . . . the complexities of interactive teaching and thinking-in-action" (p. 299). Fenstermacher (1994) defines practical knowledge as "what teachers know as a result of their experience as teachers" as distinct from what they know based on research that has been produced by others for them to use. He includes here "how to do things, the right place and time to do them, or how to see and interpret events related to one's actions" (p. 12). Similarly, Richardson (1994b) suggests that there is a certain immediacy and practicality to the knowledge needs of teachers, which are not necessarily or even often met by what she calls the "law-like statements" (p. 8) of formal research. Richardson argues that practical inquiry is more likely both to respond to the immediacy of the knowledge needs teachers confront in everyday practice and to afford foundations for formal research by providing new questions and concerns.

There have been a number of interesting efforts to discuss and develop expanded views of teachers' practical knowledge (e.g., Carter, 1990; Clandinin, 1986; Clandinin & Connelly, 1987; Elbaz, 1983, 1990; Fenstermacher, 1994; Grimmett, personal communication, September 1998; Grimmett, MacKinnon, Erickson, & Riecken, 1990; Leinhardt, 1989; Munby, 1987; Richardson, 1994a; Russell, 1987; Shulman, 1986, 1987). Although these efforts share respect for the practicality of teaching, there are many meanings attached to the term *practical knowledge* and to the larger frameworks within which the idea is located. Some elaborations seek to enrich and elevate the notion of "practical knowledge" by breaking epistemologically with the idea that there is a body of formal knowledge generally applicable across school and classroom contexts. This view does not assume there is formal knowledge and there is also practical knowledge. Conceptions of practical knowledge based on an epistemological break with the knowledge-claiming conventions of formal knowledge refuse to make apologies for the practicality of teaching or to act as if practical work is somehow "less than." Rather, they explore how teachers invent knowledge in action and how they learn to make that knowledge explicit through deliberation and reflection (e.g., Clandinin, 1986; Clandinin & Connelly, 1987; Elbaz, 1983, 1990; Grimmett, personal communication, September 1998; Grimmett, MacKinnon, Erickson, & Riecken, 1990; Munby, 1987; Russell, 1987).

In contrast, other discussions of practical knowledge are deeply embedded inside an epistemology wherein the universe of knowledge types is accounted for by the distinction between formal knowledge, on the one hand, and practical knowledge, on the other (e.g., Carter, 1990; Fenstermacher, 1994; Leinhardt, 1989; Richardson, 1994a). From these perspectives, even though the possibility of "new epistemologies" of practical knowledge is considered, the knowledge-claiming conventions of traditional social science research and hence the hegemony of formal knowledge conventions are maintained (e.g., Fenstermacher, 1994; Huberman, 1996).[2]

Other differences among notions of practical knowledge hinge on the significance of social context for understanding and interpreting individual teachers' stories and on methods for determining the validity and trustworthiness of teachers' views (Grimmett, personal communication, September 1998). Some who work from the knowledge-*in*-practice conception talk about teachers' personal practical knowledge, or what Clandinin and Connelly (1995) refer to as "embodied narrative relational knowledge" (p. 3), which is "practical, experiential and shaped by a teacher's purposes and values" (Clandinin, 1986, p. 4). Here, there is an emphasis on the "landscapes" or milieu in which teachers' work is conducted; practical knowledge is understood to include "that body of convictions and meanings, conscious or unconscious, that have arisen from experience (intimate, social, and traditional) and are expressed in a person's practices" (Clandinin & Connelly, 1995, p. 7). This knowledge is conveyed in the language of story, "which is prototypical, relational among people, personal, contextual, subjective, temporal, historical, and specific" (p. 14). From this perspective, the classroom is thought of as a knowledge landscape—epistemologically different from the landscape outside the classroom.

Another image of knowledge prevalent in the knowledge-*in*-practice conception of teacher learning builds on the idea of teaching as "craft" (e.g., Grimmett & Erickson, 1988; Grimmett & MacKinnon, 1992; Grimmett, MacKinnon, Erickson, & Riecken, 1990; Leinhardt, 1989), a notion that was for a long time maligned by educational scholars as a conservative one oriented more or less to trial and error (read: "anti-intellectual") (Tom & Valli, 1990). More recently, however, the terms *craft* and *knowledge* have been coupled, changing the valence of meaning from one of experience alone to one of experience married to deliberate inquiry and reflection and thus upping (or at least attempting to up) the epistemological status of "craft." Leinhardt's ideas (1989), although often cited within a string of names of people who have developed this notion, are something of an anomaly here in that she couples "craft" and "knowledge" but includes in this conception both "deep, sensitive, location-specific knowledge of teaching" and "fragmentary, superstitious, and often inaccurate opinions" (p. 18). It seems more than a little contradictory to refer to fragments, superstitions, and inaccuracies as "knowledge," and indeed this elaboration works against the goal of elevating the status of the wisdom of practice.

Grimmett and MacKinnon (1992), on the other hand, define "craft knowledge" as an amalgam of teachers' pedagogical content knowledge (Shulman, 1987) and what they call "pedagogical learner knowledge," or "pedagogical procedural information useful in enhancing learner-focused teaching in the dailiness of classroom actions" (p. 387). They point out that craft knowledge is understood differently depending on underlying views of the educational process: conservative, progressive, or radical. Their own view takes a progressive perspective:

Craft knowledge is a particular form of morally appropriate, intelligent, and sensible know-how that is constructed by teachers holding progressive and radical educational beliefs, in the context of their lived experiences and work around issues of content-related and learner-focused pedagogy. In the final analysis, the essential validity and morality of craft knowledge reside in readers' "living" the life of particular teachers through stories, narrative, case studies, and other forms of vicarious experience. (p. 396)

Grimmett and MacKinnon's image of craft knowledge is distinct from several other ideas about practical knowledge in that it carries with it a sense of critique, a particular political perspective, and an emphasis on the formation of learners as citizens for a democratic society. From Grimmett's perspective on craft, the image of knowledge in teacher learning resonates deeply with Dewey's (1916) ideas about democratic schooling and preparing citizens for a democratic society. Grimmett (personal communication, September 1998) suggests that the art of teaching emerges out of a craft that has become "exceedingly accomplished" and enacted in ways that are "gripping, communicative, and ultimately educative" (p. 1).

Images of Teachers, Teaching, and Professional Practice

Implicit in knowledge-*in*-practice is an image of teaching as wise action in the midst of uncertain and changing situations. Schon (1987) suggests that different professions have different conventions for action, including the varying tools, media, and language they share as well as the different units or chunks of recognizable and recurring activity that make up practice. From this perspective on the profession of teaching, the words used interchangeably with teaching—artistry, craft, performance, skill—and many of the words used to describe practice—practical, concrete, procedural, specific—convey a valence of action and activity guided by teachers' judgments and ways of conceptualizing subject matter and classroom situations. Teaching, then, is understood primarily as a process of acting and thinking wisely in the immediacy of classroom life: making split-second decisions, choosing among alternative ways to convey subject matter, interacting appropriately with an array of students, and selecting and focusing on particular dimensions of classroom problems. To do this, outstanding teachers draw on the expertise of practice or, more precisely, on their previous experiences and actions as well as their reflections on those experiences.

Here the focus is on teaching as action, but this is not at all like the idea of teaching as simply technique and routine or the idea of teacher as technician. Rather, the images of teaching and professional practice implicit in knowledge-*in*-practice are linked to those of other professions that require artistry and design—architecture, psychoanalysis, musical performance, surgery—wherein differences in artistry are matters not simply of style but of the need to invent new knowledge and strategies in the face of unexpected situations. Schon (1995) likens the idea of design in professional practice to Dewey's (1916) notion of inquiry as thought intertwined with action. Schon suggests:

Deweyan inquiry is very close to the notion of *designing* in the broad sense of that term—not the activities of "design professions" such as architecture, landscape architecture, or industrial design, but the more inclusive process of making things (including representations of things to be built) under conditions of complexity and uncertainty. This broader sense of designing includes a lawyer's design of a case or legal argument, a physician's construction of a diagnosis and course of treatment, an information technologist's design of a management information system, and a teacher's construction of a lesson plan. (p. 31)

From the design or artistry perspective on practice, there is a clear emphasis on teaching as something that takes place primarily inside the classroom in the form of a performance (often a solo performance)—a teacher working with a group of students or a teacher preparing to or following up on her or his work with a group of students. In addition to a focus on action inside the classroom, there is also an image of the expert teacher, distinguishable not only from the novice but also from the teacher who, albeit very experienced, is simply not outstanding, that is, not sufficiently competent, wise, effective, or accomplished to be considered an expert.

From the perspective of knowledge-*in*-practice, it is not assumed that the knowledge that makes teaching a profession is generated exclusively or even primarily by experts who have studied about teaching and schooling from their professional locations outside of schools. Rather, it is assumed that professional expertise comes in great part from inside the teaching profession itself. In that there is knowledge *in* wise action, teachers, who are understood to be the designers and architects of that action, are also understood to be the generators of knowledge. As Richardson (1994a) points out, "The conception of teaching underlying these projects rejects the dominant notion among many educators and policy makers that the teacher is a recipient and consumer of research and practice. Rather, the teacher is seen as one who mediates ideas and constructs meaning and knowledge and acts upon them" (p. 6).

Images of Teacher Learning and Teachers' Roles in Educational Change

As we pointed out earlier in our discussion of the first conception of teacher learning, there has been a shift in thinking about teacher learning over the last several decades from an emphasis on what teachers do to what they know, what their sources of knowledge are, and how those sources influence their work in classrooms. New visions of teacher learning, acknowledging the importance of prior knowledge and of learning over time, are implicit in all three of the conceptions of teacher learning we are elaborating in this chapter. However, in efforts animated by knowledge-*in*-practice, teacher learning hinges on enhancing teachers' understandings of their own actions—that is, their own assumptions, their own reasoning and decisions, and their own inventions of new knowledge to fit unique and shifting classroom situations. This view of teacher learning is based on the idea that knowledge comes from reflection and inquiry in and on practice, or what Schon, following Dewey, calls reflection "in the crucible of action" (cited in Grimmett, 1988, p. 13). This idea is similar to what Britton (1987) means by his proposal that teaching—intrinsically—is a form of inquiry or knowledge generation and also similar to Berthoff's (1987) demur of the idea that teachers need to do more data gathering. Rather, she asserts that teachers already have all of the information they need and should instead learn to reexamine or, in her word, "RE-search" their own experiences.

In one sense, then, the emphasis in this second conception of teacher learning is somewhat similar to the first in that both imply that teachers learn to teach better by learning to construct and articulate their understandings of what, generally speaking, is already "known." But, of course, there is a critical difference between the first and the second. Knowledge-*for*-practice emphasizes teachers' learning of knowledge that is already known by someone else (i.e., outside experts and researchers who have developed formal information and theory in the various domains of the knowledge base, particularly knowledge of subject matter and of instructional strategies). The knowledge-*in*-practice conception, on the other hand, highlights teachers' learning of knowledge that is already known by expert teachers themselves albeit often known tacitly and in ways that are unable to be articulated clearly or appropriately to others.

From the perspective of knowledge-*in*-practice, both what teachers need to learn and how they need to learn it in order to teach better are clear. The "what" is practical knowledge, craft knowledge, or knowing-in-action—that is, the knowledge that is generated by competent teachers as they deal with classroom situations that are inherently indeterminate, including how decisions are made, how strategies are selected, how disparate instances are connected to one another, how subject matter is conveyed, and how new occurrences are understood and framed. The "how" is deliberation and consideration/reconsideration—that is, consciously reflecting on the flow of classroom action and invention of knowledge in action in order to take note of new situations, intentionally and introspectively examining those situations, and consciously enhancing and articulating what is tacit or implicit. This kind of learning sometimes occurs in dyadic situations (as in exchanges between an expert and a less experienced or less expert teacher) and sometimes in groups or communities (as in groups of experienced educators working together to reflect on, inquire about, and transform their experiences). Schon's (1987) early ideas about the context for this kind of professional learning focused on what he called the professional practicum, a term commonly used in preservice teacher education, although not necessarily with the nuances of meaning suggested by Schon. Schon made emphatic that a professional practicum was distinct from both learning on one's own, which offers freedom but requires each newcomer to reinvent the wheel, and apprenticeship, which offers real-world experience but is not conducive to professional initiation or education. Schon suggested that the professional practicum could be constructed to provide a sheltered learning space of sorts, not completely of the real world, which might be overwhelming to the newcomer, but a space that nonetheless approximated the world of practice.

Schon's ideas about the contexts for professional learning are, in general, quite similar to Dewey's (1904) ideas about teacher learning, more than 80 years earlier. Making a distinction between an apprenticeship model and a laboratory model of teacher education, Dewey cautioned against plunging would-be teachers too early into the real world of schools where they were forced to focus on details and outward management issues and hence likely to develop habits fixed through "blind experimentation" rather than considered deliberation:

The student adjusts his actual methods of teaching, not to the principles which he is acquiring, but to what he sees succeed and fail in an empirical way from moment to moment; to what he sees other teachers doing who are more experienced and successful in keeping order than he is; and to the injunctions and directions given him by others. In this way the controlling habits of the teacher finally get fixed with comparatively little reference to principles in the psychology, logic, and history of education. (p. 14)

Closely akin to the work of Dewey and Schon, the knowledge-*in*-practice conception of teacher learning is based on the idea that good teaching can be coached and learned (but not taught) through reflective supervision or through a process of coaching reflective teaching. These ideas are played out and elaborated in many current initiatives, as we point out subsequently. It is important to note, however, that there is a significant difference between coaching reflective practice, as Schon and Dewey suggest, and coaching as a way of experts training nonexperts to use teaching or cognitive strategies that are already worked out (e.g., Colton & Langer, 1994; Joyce, Showers, & Rohlheiser-Bennett, 1987). The latter is congruent with the knowledge-*for*-practice conception of teacher learning, while the former is congruent with knowledge-*in*-practice.

Current Initiatives in Teacher Learning

The knowledge-*in*-practice conception of teacher learning animates many current efforts to professionalize and improve teaching by foregrounding the teacher as valid knower of practical knowledge. For years now and almost universally, preservice student teachers have been placed with experienced teachers whose function is to teach by example about the practicalities of everyday life in classrooms. Increasingly, however, there has been emphasis on the need to identify "cooperating," "host," or "mentor" teachers on the basis not simply that they have experience but that they have expertise and artistry, or, put differently, because they are "master teachers" (Grant, 1997). Generally, this means that these teachers are knowledgeable about subject matter and pedagogy, knowledgeable about how to reflect on and learn from their practice, and knowledgeable about how to participate in learning situations, whether mentoring relationships, inquiry groups, or communities of reflective practitioners.

It is important to note once again, however, that it is not language, organizational context, or method that reveals the conception of teacher learning underlying a particular initiative. As we suggested earlier, this is the case because the salient differences among and across the three conceptions of teacher learning reside not in methods but in the ideas and assumptions that animate them. Thus, not every initiative that uses the language of "master teachers" or "mentors" for inexperienced teachers, whether at the preservice or induction level, is based on the knowledge-*in*-practice approach to teacher learning. Indeed, as Little (1990) has pointed out, the "mentor phenomenon" is played out quite differently in various state and local initiatives for beginning teacher induction, preservice teacher education, and professional development. When initiatives are, in fact, based on a view of knowledge-*in*-practice, the emphasis of mentoring or coaching arrangements is to help newcomers participate in dialogue with puzzling problems of practice—what some have referred to as a "new pedagogy of teacher education" (Heaton & Lampert, 1993) or "an approach to teacher education . . . rooted in the study of practice" (Lampert & Ball, 1998, p. vii).

Grounded in a view of learning as social and situational and in a view of knowledge as socially constructed, this approach conceptualizes teacher learning as "assisted performance" (Feiman-Nemser & Remillard, 1996) and focuses on how "experienced teachers can induct novices into the intellectual and practical challenges of reform-minded teaching" (Feiman-Nemser & Beasley, 1997). This approach is the basis of a number of initiatives for teachers' learning of "adventurous teaching" (Heaton & Lampert, 1993) or "teaching for understanding" (Cohen, McLaughlin, & Talbert, 1993), conceptualized as a kind of educational practice where "students and teachers acquire knowledge collaboratively, where orthodoxies of pedagogy and 'facts' are continually challenged in classroom discourse, and where conceptual (versus rote) understanding of subject matter is the goal" (McLaughlin & Talbert, 1993, p. 1). Initiatives based on this conception of teacher learning often provide social and organizational contexts for teacher education in which teachers work together in pairs, one less experienced teacher and one more experienced in the kind of constructivist classroom practice that is the target, or in small groups where several inexperienced teachers observe and reflect on the work of a more experienced one. Lampert and Ball's (1998) recent book on teaching, multimedia, and mathematics provides some of the most fully elaborated analysis of teacher education initiatives from this perspective. They describe a design for a pedagogy of teacher education that presents preservice students with various opportunities to conduct what they refer to as "pedagogical inquiry" (p. 110)—for example, reading or experiencing in a multimedia environment a more experienced teacher's records of practice and then reflecting on these records with the guidance of a teacher educator who may or may not be one and the same with the experienced teacher they have observed.

Other teacher education and professional development initiatives based on knowledge-*in*-practice start with what teachers (or would-be teachers) believe and what they are doing or trying to do in their own classrooms. These initiatives focus on helping practitioners develop their artistry by exploring problems of practice that cannot be solved by the straightforward application of established theories and by reconsidering their own assumptions and reasoning processes. In many of these initiatives, like the ones just described, the role of the facilitator, who coaches or guides a group in the process of learning how to reflect and/or to conduct inquiry on practice, is central. Grimmett and Dockendorf (in press) provide an interesting analysis of what they refer to as "the labyrinth of researching teaching"—that is, the complex dilemmas and issues that teacher research group leaders face when they attempt to "deconstruct our role as presenter in order to reconstruct our role as facilitator." From the perspectives, respectively, of a facilitator of a teacher research leaders group and a facilitator of teacher research groups themselves, Grimmett and Dockendorf explore the difficulties and possibilities of facilitators functioning not as university experts but as colleagues.

In preservice teacher education, this role is often taken on by a university-based instructor or fieldwork supervisor who teaches student teachers how to reflect on their experiences by guiding and shaping journal writing or other self-reflective activities. There are also many preservice initiatives where students are guided to be reflective and questioning about teaching and to practice their decision-making skills by considering cases of practice (e.g., Merseth, 1996; J. Shulman, 1992; J. Shulman & Colbert, 1989; Wasserman, 1993). As Wasserman (1993) points out, cases are "meant to provide pictures of life in schools, raising issues that beg for enlightened and informed examination. If, through studying these cases, teachers grow in their ability to see beyond the surface and feel ready to deal with deeper, more complete meanings, the cases will have served their purpose" (p. xiii).

In professional development initiatives based on this second conception of teacher learning, facilitators often work with groups of teachers, functioning as supportive outsiders who push others to question their own assumptions and reconsider the bases of actions or beliefs. Richardson's notion of practical inquiry (1994a) as a method of staff development (Anders & Richardson, 1994; Richardson & Hamilton, 1995), for example, is based on the idea that consultants, often from a university, work collaboratively with teachers to help them see the discrepancies between their beliefs and practices. This process of teacher learning hinges on constructing and reconstructing the "practical arguments" (Fenstermacher, 1994) that guide practice and consequently experimenting with alternative practices (Richardson, 1994a). The parallel initiative at the higher education level, often referred to as "self-study," also focuses on professional development by clarifying assumptions, recognizing discrepancies between beliefs and practices, and rethinking practices based on self-reflective analyses (e.g., Hamilton & Pinnegar, 1998a, 1998b; LaBoskey, Davies-Samway, & Garcia, 1998).

Duckworth's (1987, 1997) approach to working with experienced teachers also highlights the importance of teachers learning from each other as well as being guided by an insightful facilitator. Duckworth (1987) says the following about her own role as a person who helps teachers learn:

What I love to do is to teach teachers. I love to stir up their thoughts about how they learn; about how on earth anyone can help anyone else learn; and about what it means to know something. . . . [I love to] find out what people think about things and to find ways to get them talking about what they think; to shake up things they thought they knew. . . . I love to see the most productive of questions be born out of laughter, and the most frustrating of brick walls give way to an idea that has been there all along. (p. 122)

In each of these initiatives, the point is for teachers to consider and reconsider what they know and believe, to consider and reconsider what it means to know or believe something, and then to examine and reinvent ways of teaching that are consistent with their knowledge and beliefs.

The preceding discussion is not meant to suggest that every teacher learning initiative in preservice education or in professional development that uses strategies called "reflection," "case methods," or "inquiry" falls into this second conception of teacher learning. To the contrary, as a number of teacher educators have pointed out (Clift, Houston, & Pugach, 1990; Cochran-Smith, 1994; Grimmett, 1988; Grimmett, MacKinnon, Erickson, & Reicken, 1990; Houston & Clift, 1990; Tabachnick & Zeichner, 1991; Tom, 1985), there may well be little shared meaning about what it means to do reflection or inquiry in preservice teacher education, even though similar language is used and activities that, at least on the surface, are similar to one another are encouraged. Likewise, many critics (Anderson, Herr, & Nihlen, 1994; Cochran-Smith & Lytle, in press; Lytle, 1992; Noffke et al., 1996) have pointed out that among professional development initiatives that feature inquiry, there are as many differences as similarities. (This point is further developed in the third section of this chapter.) Rather than method or strategy, what makes the difference is the larger goal of using any of these for teacher learning as well as the images of knowledge, practice, and educational purpose to which they are attached. In teacher learning initiatives that derive from knowledge-*in*-practice, the point of using cases or reflections or inquiries is to provide the social and intellectual contexts in which prospective and experienced teachers can probe the knowledge embedded in the wise teaching decisions of others and/or can deepen their own knowledge and their own abilities to make wise decisions in the classroom.

Finally, the knowledge-*in*-practice relationship underlies some of the newer assessments of teachers' professional knowledge and skill. Designed for experienced teachers rather than beginners, the National Board for Professional Teaching Standards, for example, includes assessments of how teachers document and reflect on their own work through journal writing, videotaping, and preparation of portfolios that represent the rich range of their reflections and deliberations.

TEACHER LEARNING, CONCEPTION 3:
KNOWLEDGE *OF* PRACTICE

The third conception of teacher learning is what we refer to as knowledge-*of*-practice. From this perspective, both knowledge generation and knowledge use are regarded as inherently problematic. That is, basic questions about knowledge and teaching—what it means to generate knowledge, who generates it, what counts as knowledge and to whom, and how knowledge is used and evaluated in particular contexts—are always open to discussion. Furthermore, like the view of knowledge in the second conception of teacher learning, knowledge in this third conception is regarded as not existing separate from the knower. Rather, knowledge making is understood as a pedagogic act—constructed in the context of use, intimately connected to the knower, and, although relevant to immediate situations, also inevitably a process of theorizing. From this perspective, knowledge is not bound by the instrumental imperative that it be used in or applied to an immediate situation; it may also shape the conceptual and interpretive frameworks teachers develop to make judgments, theorize practice, and connect their efforts to larger intellectual, social, and political issues as well as to the work of other teachers, researchers, and communities. The basis of this knowledge-practice conception is that teachers across the professional life span play a central and critical role in generating knowledge of practice by making their classrooms and schools sites for inquiry, connecting their work in schools to larger issues, and taking a critical perspective on the theory and research of others. Teacher networks, inquiry communities, and other school-based collectives in which teachers and others conjoin their efforts to construct knowledge are the major contexts for teacher learning in this conception.

Unlike the first conception of teacher learning, the third does not build on the formal knowledge-practical knowledge distinction, nor does it, as the second conception does, use language that is (or is often taken to be) congruent with this distinction. That is, the knowledge-*of*-practice conception stands in contrast to the idea that there are two distinct kinds of knowledge for teaching, one that is formal, in that it is produced following the conventions of social science research, and one that is practical, in that it is produced in the activity of teaching itself. The knowledge-*of*-practice conception also differs from the first two in that it does not make the same distinctions between expert teachers, on the one hand, and novice or less competent teachers, on the other. Furthermore, in initiatives animated by the knowledge-*of*-practice conception, the idea is *not* to help teachers develop knowledge that is, in some senses, already known—either by outside experts or by expert teachers themselves.

We would like to stress that the idea behind knowledge-*of*-practice is *not* that practitioners' research provides all of the knowledge necessary to improve practice or that the knowledge generated by university-based researchers is of no use to teachers. Nor is it assumed here that using roughly the same strategies as university-based researchers, school-based teacher researchers add to the knowledge base a new body of generalizations based on their perspectives inside schools and classrooms. In other words, the assumption is not that expert teachers and others who are studying them (collaboratively or otherwise) generate a new or supplementary kind of formal knowledge about expert practices in teaching. But it is also not assumed that they generate and codify a new body of practical knowledge based on epistemic standards that are different from but derivative of those of formal knowledge. Rather, implicit in the idea of knowledge-*of*-practice is the assumption that, through inquiry, teachers across the professional life span—from very new to very experienced—make problematic their own knowledge and practice as well as the knowledge and practice of others and thus stand in a different relationship to knowledge. The third conception of teacher learning is not to be taken as a synthesis of the first and second conceptions.

Rather, it is based on fundamentally different ideas: that practice is more than practical, that inquiry is more than an artful rendering of teachers' practical knowledge, and that understanding the knowledge needs of teaching means transcending the idea that the formal-practical distinction captures the universe of knowledge types.

Images of Knowledge

The knowledge-*of*-practice conception turns on the assumption that the knowledge teachers need to teach well emanates from systematic inquiries about teaching, learners and learning, subject matter and curriculum, and schools and schooling. This knowledge is constructed collectively within local and broader communities. This image of knowledge has several iterations that grow out of different but somewhat related intellectual and educational movements. As we have suggested elsewhere (Cochran-Smith & Lytle, 1999), each of these movements constructs the role of teacher as knower and as agent in the classroom and in larger educational contexts, and most carry distinctly critical views of education and the power relations it entails. In his discussion of what constitutes knowledge, for example, Kincheloe (1991) asserts that, from a critical constructivist position, "there is no knowledge without a knower" and thus "it is impossible from [this] perspective to conceive knowledge without thinking of the knower" (p. 26). Linking knower and known is also part of the image of knowledge in the second conception of teacher learning, knowledge-*in*-practice. In this third conception, knowledge-*of*-practice, both knowers and knowledge are also connected to larger political and social agendas.[3]

In fact, some widely known advocates of action research regard constructing and reconstructing curriculum as central to the larger project of social change and the creation of a more just and democratic society (Anderson, Herr, & Nihlen, 1994; Carr & Kemmis, 1986; Noffke, 1991, 1997; Noffke & Brennan, 1997). From this perspective, the democratic impulse is paramount, as Noffke (1997) points out: Knowledge is constructed collaboratively by teachers, students, administrators, parents, and academics with the end of locally developed curriculum and more equitable social relations. The image of knowledge here is not narrow or technical, nor is the goal of inquiry taken to be production of "findings" but rather the raising of fundamental questions about curriculum, teachers' roles, and the ends as well as the means of schooling. Noffke argues that knowledge generation of this kind "embodies a critical stance toward the interests represented in all research forms. It seeks not additions to a knowledge base for teaching, but a transformation of educational theory and practice toward emancipatory ends" (p. 324).

A related but different image of knowledge in this third conception of teacher learning is represented in the work of school-based and university-based teachers and researchers committed to progressive education, the social responsibility of educators, and the construction of alternative ways of observing and understanding students' work, solving educational problems, and helping teachers uncover and clarify their implicit assumptions about teaching, learning, and schooling (Bussis, Chittenden, & Amarel, 1976; Carini, 1979, 1982, 1986; Duckworth, 1987; Goodman, 1985; Perrone, 1989; Strieb, 1985; Traugh et al., 1986). For example, the reflective practices of Carini and her colleagues at the Prospect School and Center are based on a phenomenological or descriptive epistemology (Himley, 1991) that privileges the understandings that emerge from "deep talk":

> Essentially this kind of talk asks participants to engage in a process of collaboratively generated meaning that takes place over a relatively long period of time . . . this reflective or descriptive process enables participants to see and re-see that shared focus of interest in view of an ever-enlarging web of comments, tensions, connections, connotations, differences, oppositions. This reading takes place within the permeable and interanimating border regions among writer, readers, language, and culture. Readers note emerging patterns and connections. They locate the topic within multiple contexts, widening the range of its correlatives, as they come to understand it more fully, both in its particularity and at the same time in its relatedness to other texts and contexts. (p. 59)

In work of this kind, the image of knowledge as collectively constructed is particularly striking; knowledge emerges from the conjoined understandings of teachers and others committed to long-term highly systematic observation and documentation of learners and their sense making. To generate knowledge that accounts for multiple layers of context and multiple meaning perspectives, teachers draw on a wide range of experiences and their whole intellectual histories in and out of schools.

A related image of knowledge grows out of work that links teacher education, qualitative research, and literacy studies. A central idea in this work is that knowledge of practice across the professional life span is generated by making classrooms and schools sites for research, working collaboratively in inquiry communities to understand the co-construction of curriculum, developing local knowledge, and taking critical perspectives on the theory and research of others (see, for example, Allen, Cary, & Delgado, 1995; Cochran-Smith & Lytle, 1993; Erickson, 1986; Fleischer, 1995; Florio-Ruane & Walsh, 1980; Hollingsworth et al., 1994; Ray, 1993; Stock, 1995; Vinz, 1996; Wells, 1994). From this perspective, Lytle and Cochran-Smith (1992) have characterized teacher research as a way of knowing about teaching locally that can also be useful to a more public educational community. They argue:

> Teacher research . . . makes visible the ways teachers and students negotiate power, authority, and knowledge in classrooms and schools. As a way of knowing, then, teacher research has the potential to alter profoundly the cultures of teaching—how teachers work with their students toward a more critical and democratic pedagogy, how they build intellectual communities of colleagues who are both educators and activists, and how they position themselves in relationship to school administrators, policy makers, and university-based experts as agents of systemic change. (p. 470)

Hargreaves (1996) also offers an image of knowledge as transformative. He argues for a new set of principles about knowledge development and use that would diversify what counts as knowledge, broaden the forms of discourse about knowledge, and widen the roles of teachers to include systematic inquiry and policy enactment.

Images of Teachers, Teaching, and Professional Practice

Implicit in the knowledge-*of*-practice conception of teacher learning is an image of professional practice as encompassing teachers' work within but also beyond immediate classroom action. As we have pointed out, the image of practice in the first conception, knowledge-*for*-practice, emphasizes how teachers use the knowledge base to solve problems, represent content, and make decisions about the daily work of the classroom. The image of practice in the second, knowledge-*in*-practice, emphasizes how teachers invent knowledge in the midst of action, making wise choices and creating rich learning opportunities for their students. Although different in important ways, both of these refer primarily to what teachers do within the boundaries of their roles as classroom managers, orchestrators, and planners. On the other hand, this third conception of teacher learning, knowledge-*of*-practice, emphasizes that teachers have a transformed and expanded view of what "practice" means. Teachers' roles as co-constructors of knowledge and creators of curriculum are informed by their stance as theorizers, activists, and school leaders. This image of practice entails expanded responsibilities to children and their families, transformed relationships with teachers and other professionals in the school setting, and deeper and altered connections to communities, community organizations, and school-university partnerships. We are not suggesting that an expanded view of practice results from *adding* teachers' activity outside the classroom to what they do inside but, rather, that what goes on inside the classroom is profoundly *altered* and ultimately transformed when teachers' frameworks for practice foreground the intellectual, social, and cultural contexts of teaching.

This third conception of teacher learning emphasizes images of teacher as agent and of teaching as agency in the classroom and in larger educational contexts. Although there are (and have been for some time) differing iterations of this idea, each carries with it a distinctly critical view of education and of knowledge and power relations within it. Each provides a critique—implicit or explicit—of prevailing concepts of the teacher as technician, consumer, receiver, transmitter, and implementor of other people's knowledge as well as a critique of many of the prevailing social and political arrangements of schools and schooling. Goswami and Stillman's (1987) volume, *Reclaiming the Classroom: Teacher Research as an Agency for Change,* suggests an image of practice transformed by teachers' research. They suggest that when teachers do research:

[they] become theorists, articulating their intentions, testing their assumptions, and finding connections with practice.... [Teachers] step up their use of resources; they form networks; and they become more active professionally.... They become rich resources who can provide the profession with information it simply doesn't have ... they become critical, responsive readers and users of current research ... they collaborate with their students to answer questions important to both, drawing on community resources in new and unexpected ways. The nature of classroom discourse changes when inquiry begins. (preface)

From this perspective, changing the curriculum, changing the nature of teachers' work, and changing the cultures of teaching and learning in and out of schools and classrooms are part of grass-roots efforts to reimagine the teaching of literacy and language through inquiry (Goswami & Stillman, 1987; Lytle, in press). From this perspective, the teacher's relationship to knowledge is quite different from that assumed in other conceptions of teacher learning.

The images of practice we have been describing as part of this third conception of teacher learning—critical, political, and intellectual—are implicit in the writing of student teachers and experienced teachers who work as researchers in their own schools and classrooms. Drawing on the writing of student teachers, for example, Cochran-Smith (1999) suggests that:

teaching for social justice is difficult and uncertain work . . . profoundly practical in that it is located in the dailiness of classroom decisions and actions—in teachers' interactions with their students and families, in their choices of materials and texts, in their utilization of formal and informal assessments . . . learning to teach for social justice is as much a matter of learning to construct particular practices as it is learning to theorize those practices.

In the writing of experienced teacher researchers (Ballenger, 1992; Fecho, 1998; Gallas, 1998; Resnick, 1996; Waff, 1994), there are elaborated and vivid images of what it means to construct pedagogies by challenging school and classroom practices, deliberating about what is regarded as expert knowledge, examining underlying assumptions, and making the lives of families and communities part of the curriculum. In the image of practice embedded in knowledge-*of*-practice, teaching for change is an across-the-professional-life-span project (Cochran-Smith & Lytle, 1992a).

Kincheloe (1991) has written explicitly about the critical nature of professional practice and of teacher research as a path to empowerment. He uses the word *critical* to refer specifically to critical European social and economic theory (with its roots in the Frankfurt School) and to the idea that teacher research is always "mindful of the relationship between teachers', students', and administrators' consciousness and the socio-historical contexts in which they operate" (p. 35). Images of practice as critical are also found in Freire's (1970) notion of liberatory pedagogy, Giroux's (1988) concept of the teacher as "transformative intellectual," and Kincheloe's (1993) elaboration of "critical constructivism."

Some of those who take the view that practice is critical suggest that there is a necessary link between critical social theory and critical educational practice. For example, Leistyna, Woodrum, and Sherblo (1996) argue:

Critical social theories thus function as both political and pedagogical practice. They should inspire the reconceptualization of different ways of knowing that rupture entrenched epistemologies, and they can equally help to foster participatory spaces for the sharing and production of knowledge, and the mobilization of agency to effect changes in the world. The very act of engaging one another and theorizing around the issues of oppression is inherently a form, if not the first seeds, of transformative practice. (p. 7)

Others, although acknowledging the potential of critical inquiry to alter the nature of practice and the role of teachers, do not assume a necessary relationship. Rather, there is the persistent worry that the power of action research/teacher research can be severely diminished if its "democratic edge is blunted" (Kincheloe, 1991, p. 83), if it is separated from "the political sphere" (Noffke, 1997, p. 306), or if its "generative nature" is allowed to "contribute to either its marginalization and trivialization, on the one hand, or its subtle co-optation or colonization, on the other" (Cochran-Smith & Lytle, 1998, p. 21).

Images of Teacher Learning and Teachers' Roles in Educational Change

As we indicated earlier, "new visions" of teacher education/professional development have emerged over the last several decades. From the perspective of knowledge-*of*-practice, these new visions have been informed by explorations of the cultures of schools and of teachers' work and workplaces. These suggest that what is needed in professional development are opportunities for teachers to explore and question their own and others' interpretations, ideologies, and practices (Grimmett & Neufeld, 1994; Hargreaves & Fullan, 1991; Lieberman & Miller, 1994; Little, 1993; Little & McLaughlin, 1993; McLaughlin, 1993). This means that teachers learn by challenging their own assumptions; identifying salient issues of practice; posing problems; studying their own students, classrooms, and schools; constructing and reconstructing curriculum; and taking on roles of leadership and activism in efforts to transform classrooms, schools, and societies.

Fundamental to this conception of teacher learning is the idea that teachers learn collaboratively, primarily in inquiry communities and/or networks (Lieberman, 1992) where participants struggle along with others to construct meaningful local knowledge and where inquiry is regarded as part of larger efforts to transform teaching, learning, and schooling. Over the last decade or so, a number of school- and university-based teachers and researchers have looked closely at the nature of teacher learning in inquiry communities (Allen, Cary, & Delgado, 1995; Banford et al., 1996; Cochran-Smith, 1991a, 1995a, 1995b, 1998; Cochran-Smith & Lytle, 1993; Evans, 1989; Gitlin et al., 1992; Goswami & Stillman, 1987; Grimmett & Neufeld, 1994; Hargreaves & Fullan, 1991; Hollingsworth & Sockett, 1994; Lytle, 1996; Lytle, Belzer, & Reumann, 1992, 1993; Lytle et al., 1994; Lytle & Fecho, 1991; McDonald, 1992; Meyer et al., 1998; Mohr & Maclean, 1987; Noffke & Stevenson, 1995; Wells, 1994). These communities often involve joint participation by teachers and researchers who are differently positioned from one another and who bring different kinds of knowledge and experience to bear on the collective enterprise. The key, however, is that all participants in these groups—whether beginning teachers, experienced teachers, teacher educators, or facilitators—function as fellow learners and researchers rather than experts. Although consultants and outside speakers as well as wide readings from multiple perspectives are often used as resources, the underlying conception is quite different from the idea of studying "the experts." Rather, new collaborative relationships are being crafted that replace the expert-novice relationship. These feature colleagues working together, bringing their perspectives to bear on inquiries into the complexities and messiness of teaching and learning.

In the knowledge-*of*-practice conception of teacher learning, the central image is of teachers and others working together to investigate their own assumptions, their own teaching and curriculum development, and the policies and practices of their own schools and communities. This means that teacher learning begins necessarily with identifying and critiquing one's own experiences, assumptions, and beliefs. This is related both to Freire's (1970) claim that it is critical for teachers to know their own knowledge and to Knoblauch and Brannon's (1988) notion that teacher researchers develop "knowledge of the making of knowledge" (p. 27).

Learning by engaging in systematic and intentional inquiry about practice (in the sense of the expanded notion of practice elaborated earlier) entails collaboratively reconsidering what is taken for granted, challenging school and classroom structures, deliberating about what it means to know and what is regarded as expert knowledge, rethinking educational categories, constructing and reconstructing interpretive frameworks, and attempting to uncover the values and interests served and not served by the arrangements of schooling. When work in communities is based on knowledge-*of*-practice—whether that work is referred to as teacher research, action research, or practitioner inquiry—the goal is not to do research or to produce "findings," as is often the case for university researchers. Rather, the goal is understanding, articulating, and ultimately altering practice and social relationships in order to bring about fundamental change in classrooms, schools, districts, programs, and professional organizations. At the base of this commitment is a deep and passionately enacted responsibility to students' learning and life chances and to transforming the policies and structures that limit students' access to these opportunities (Lytle & Cochran-Smith, 1994).

Teacher learning by constructing knowledge-*of*-practice—whether developing curriculum, understanding children's work, investigating how students and teachers together construct knowledge, or examining school policies and practices—always involves some kind of systematic collection, analysis, and interpretation of data sources. Of course, as Anderson, Herr, and Nihlen (1994) point out, what counts as data or as evidence in practitioner research is still being debated. Furthermore, teachers and other participants in inquiry communities have been inventing new forms and frameworks of analysis and interpretation. Some of these forms and frameworks may look quite unfamiliar to those who are accustomed to the traditional modes of data collection and analysis entailed in most university-based research. For example, one of the most striking images of learning by generating knowledge *of* practice is the image of teachers engaging in oral inquiry. Studying practice through oral inquiry is based on rich conversations about students' work, teachers' classroom observations and reflections, curriculum materials and practices, and classroom and school-related documents and artifacts. Although analyses of these data sources are primarily oral and constructed in the social interactions of a particular group, much of the documentation is in written form, as are group records. These enable teachers to revisit and reexamine their joint analyses.

Carini and her colleagues at the Prospect School and Center (Carini, 1975, 1986; Himley, 1991; Himley & Carini, 1991) provide the most elaborated accounts of what this kind of teacher learning through talk looks like. It is clear that what it does *not* look like is the casual chat of school hallways or lunchrooms. Nor, although relational, does it emphasize primarily the personal talk engaged in when offering moral support or empathizing. Rather, as Himley points out about the Prospect School in general, "'teacher talk'. . . is the central educational and epistemological activity" (p. 57):

What I call deep talk is based on the reflective practices developed by Carini and her colleagues at Prospect. . . . Essentially, this kind of talk asks participants to engage in a process of collaboratively generated meaning that takes place over a relatively long period of time. The purpose is to open up intellectual space, to understand more fully and richly a shared focus of interest—a drawing or written text, a child's school self, a keyword—through language and the power of collective thought. (p. 59)

Oral inquiries such as these represent teachers' self-conscious and often self-critical attempts to make sense of their daily work by talking about it in planned ways. In communities convened to explore issues and practices across contexts by examining particular cases, the primary outcomes are the enriched understandings of the participants.

Hollingsworth et al. (1994) and McDonald (1992) also use the metaphor of "talk" to describe teacher learning. Hollingsworth refers to "sustained conversation" wherein participants learn to articulate an "emerging feminist consciousness" (p. 7) as they explore the many relationships—classroom, school, and community—that bear on how they make sense of teaching and learning. McDonald describes teacher learning as a matter of "breaking professional silence" when teachers come together to think, discuss, write, and "read the texts" (p. 43) of teaching, in part by collaboratively commenting on the vignettes and commentaries of group members and in part by responding to and critiquing the research of others.

It is clear from the examples we have mentioned so far that there is a strong image of community in this third conception of teacher learning—that is, an image of teachers and other group members constructing knowledge by conjoining their understandings in face-to-face interactions with one another over time. In fact, the knowledge-*of*-practice relationship depends on the assumption that knowledge is socially constructed by teachers who work together and also by teachers and students as they mingle their previous experiences, their prior knowledge, their cultural and linguistic resources, and the textual resources and materials of the classroom. Cochran-Smith and Lytle (1993) focus on this idea explicitly. They argue that teacher research can be a powerful way for teachers to get at what is being socially constructed in and out of their classrooms—or the understandings they and their students are building as they "construct the curriculum" (p. 51) as well as the discrepancies that may exist between practices and theories of practice.

Teachers' development of deeper understandings of their own learning as socially constructed is often parallel to their efforts to construct inquiry-based curriculum and instruction with their students (Branscombe, Goswami, & Schwartz, 1992; Pappas & Zecker, 1998a, 1998b; Short, 1996; Wells, 1994). The parallelism between practitioners' inquiry and their construction with students of inquiry-based learning is no accident. When teachers who see teaching as learning and learning as teaching (Branscombe, Goswami, & Schwartz, 1992) work together in learning communities, they link what they learn about their own learning to new visions of what can happen in classrooms. Along these lines, Meyer (1998) characterizes teacher learning as a dialectic of composing and disrupting—composing a view of self, voice, relationships, and curriculum— while at the same time experiencing such elements as productively disruptive to many aspects of school life.

From the perspective of knowledge-*of*-practice, teacher learning is linked to larger change efforts—school reorganization, democratic schooling, and social justice—and to the expanded roles of teachers as leaders and activists. This image of teacher learning both invites and grows out of new kinds of collaborations among teachers and among teacher groups, schools, school systems, universities, and other organizations. For example, when teachers and teacher educators come together to construct and reconstruct curriculum (e.g., Hursh, 1997; Noffke, Mosher, & Maricle, 1994; Noffke & Stevenson, 1995), the goal is to unpack and remake the ideological underpinnings of the curriculum and reinvent their work along more ethical and democratic lines. The overarching agenda is political: to transform the relationships of the many stakeholders involved in the educational process and the traditional relations of power, voice, and participation. Noffke (1997) contrasts "a role for teachers in the collective production of knowledge leading to more democratic schools" (p. 319) with inquiry that focuses on the more narrow goal of individual development. Interestingly, Wells (1994) suggests that what "begins with the individual practitioner embarking on a personal inquiry" (p. 32) can evolve through more widespread collaboration into larger school change efforts. What may be important here is not the trade-off between an emphasis on individual development, on the one hand, and larger political agendas, on the other. Rather, what *is* important is whether or not and to what extent opportunities for individual learning and development are understood by the participants in learning communities to be *connected to* and carried out in the service of larger agendas for school and social change.

Clearly, there is a relationship between teacher learning in communities and larger efforts to change the cultures of schools and teaching. However, the exact nature of the relationship of the part to the whole is not so clear. Hargreaves (1994) suggests that in many cases it is impossible to change school cultures without first providing school structures that enhance opportunities for collaboration and collegiality among teachers. There are many initiatives related to teacher learning that grow out of the knowledge-*of*-practice conception of teacher learning and the idea of inquiry as reform. The complexity of the change process is clear in our discussion in the following section of some of these initiatives.

Current Initiatives in Teacher Learning

The knowledge-*of*-practice relationship is implicit in many of the projects related to the current wave of interest in teacher research and other forms of practitioner inquiry in the United States (Cochran-Smith & Lytle, 1999). The current U.S. movement, now a little more than a decade old,[4] involves a variety of local and national efforts to professionalize teaching and bring about educational change by enlarging the teacher's role—as decision maker, consultant, curriculum developer, analyst, activist, school leader. As we have pointed out elsewhere (Cochran-Smith & Lytle, 1998, in press), for example, the idea of teachers actively initiating and carrying out research in their own schools and classrooms is connected to programs of professional development and other strategies to professionalize teaching, to school and curricular improvement, to various school-based and school-system-wide restructuring and organizational changes, to challenges to the hegemony of a university-generated knowledge base for teaching, and to larger movements for social change and social justice.

In initiatives that are based on the knowledge-*of*-practice conception of teacher learning, the inquiry community is understood as the central context within which teacher learning occurs. Throughout this chapter, however, we have made it clear that the language and methods of "reflection," "cases," "coaching," and "mentoring" were not the defining characteristics of teacher learning initiatives based on the knowledge-*in*-practice relationship. Similarly, we want to make clear here that the language and methods of "teacher research," "action research," "networks," and "inquiry communities" do not define teacher learning initiatives based on the knowledge-*of*-practice relationship. Indeed, there are initiatives referred to as teacher study groups or action research projects or inquiry communities that are animated by each of the three conceptions of teacher learning outlined in this chapter. Some would argue that this is not possible—that an action research group based on the knowledge-*for*-practice relationship, for example, misunderstands the historical roots of action research and dilutes its necessarily political edge (e.g., Kincheloe, 1991; Noffke, 1997).

Historical roots notwithstanding, however, the fact is that terms like action research and teacher research have been widely appropriated and have come to mean many things as they are attached to various teacher learning initiatives and various educational purposes. Cochran-Smith and Lytle (1999), for example, suggest that teacher research has a protean shape, commenting that:

in this sense, the growth of the teacher research movement hinges on a paradox: as it is used in the service of more and more agendas and even institutionalized in certain contexts, it is in danger of becoming anything and everything. As we know, however, anything and everything often lead in the end to nothing of consequence or power.

We are suggesting here that sorting out the "anything and everything" of inquiry communities is a matter of understanding the larger educational purposes and the images of knowledge, practice, and change to which they are attached rather than the language used to describe them or the organizational innovations put into place. In teacher learning initiatives that derive from the knowledge-*of*-practice conception of learning, the point of action research groups or inquiry communities or teacher networks is to provide the social and intellectual contexts in which teachers at all points along the professional life span can take critical perspectives on their own assumptions as well as the theory and research of others and also jointly construct local knowledge that connects their work in schools to larger social and political issues.

The knowledge-*of*-practice conception of teacher learning is reflected in a number of efforts at the preservice level to make teacher learning more critical, including strategies that prompt prospective teachers to investigate their own autobiographies. Based on the assumption that teachers' conceptions of teaching are grounded in what Bullough and Gitlin (1995) call their "personal theories," a number of initiatives prompt students to think about who they are as teachers and students (e.g., Cochran-Smith, 1995a; Florio-Ruane, 1994; King & Ladson-Billings, 1990; Knowles, 1992; Knowles & Cole, 1996), particularly with regard to race, class, culture, ethnicity, language, and gender (e.g., Cochran-Smith, 1995a; Cochran-Smith & Lytle, 1992b; Florio-Ruane, 1994; Maher, 1991; Rosenberg, 1994; Sleeter, 1995; Zeichner, 1993).

A related initiative is the increasing use in preservice programs of critical reflections, ethnographies, teacher research, and action research (Adler, 1991; Beyer, 1988, 1991; Cochran-Smith, 1991b, 1994, 1995a, 1995b, in press; Cochran-Smith & Lytle, 1993; Goodman, 1991; Gore & Zeichner, 1991, 1995; Tabachnick & Zeichner, 1991). In most of these situations, student teachers are guided to connect their own experiences to critical social, cultural, political, and economic theories and studies. Usually the learning context is the student teaching seminar or university methods or foundations class. The point is to raise questions about the social conditions of schooling as well as teachers' and students' understandings of the subject matter and the students they teach.

These initiatives in the education of preservice teachers are parallel to some versions of "self-studies" at the higher education level (e.g., Albert et al., 1997, 1998; Cole & Knowles, 1998; Zeichner, 1998; Zollers, Albert, & Cochran-Smith, 1998) wherein teacher educators rethink their own assumptions, teaching strategies, and, in many cases, missed opportunities to clarify or connect with students (Cochran-Smith, 1995b; Zeichner, 1998). As Zeichner (1998) points out, self-study of this kind has the potential to move us "beyond the slogans of critical, multicultural and feminist pedagogies in teacher education and the uncritical glorification of methodologies such as case pedagogies and narrative" (p. 40) and toward interrogation and reconstruction of practice. Similarly, Cole and Knowles (1998) assert that self-study fundamentally challenges the status quo of the academy.

In some preservice initiatives, there are efforts to transform program and course contexts into communities of learners and to link the learning of preservice teachers with the learning of experienced teachers and teacher educators (Cochran-Smith, 1991a, 1994; Hursh, 1997; Zeichner & Miller, 1997). Cochran-Smith

(1994, 1998, 1999) refers to this initiative as "teacher education as inquiry," a term intended to highlight the importance of the inquiry community. A student teacher, Mary Kate Cipriani (cited in Cochran-Smith, 1999), makes the point best:

> My salvation became the teacher communities I [was part of]. . . . The term "communities" is used broadly. . . . It includes the mornings when [other student teachers] would come by my classroom to ask me questions. . . . It includes the ethnography paper group and the Sunday nights we spent beside [our professor's] fireplace wrenching and writhing over our journals and papers, looking for themes. It includes [my cooperating teacher] and me chatting about our students' academic behavior. . . . It includes dinners at [my supervisor's] house, classes at Penn, and special events like the Ethnography Forum and the AERA annual meeting . . . I am a teacher because we are a teacher community, and because we are a teacher community, I am a teacher.

In preservice initiatives that locate teacher learning inside communities, work is deliberately structured so that multiple viewpoints are represented, including reading research by school-based as well as university-based researchers and teachers. Time is allotted for groups to work together to hash out issues, write about their experiences, and share the data of their classrooms with one another. The key is that student teachers are socialized into teaching by becoming part of a community of researchers and learners who see questioning as part of the task of teaching across the life span.

Initiatives such as those just described are often located inside particular programs, or they may happen as the result of one or two teacher educators working closely with one or two school-based colleagues. Professional development schools, on the other hand, are part of a much larger initiative that links teacher learning at the preservice and in-service levels. Very loosely connected to one another, professional development schools are intended to provide new kinds of spaces for student teachers to learn along with experienced teachers as they construct knowledge of practice (Levine & Trachtman, 1997). The goal is in part the generation and dissemination of knowledge grounded in practice; in part to provide sites for the teaching, scholarship, and service of increasing numbers of regular university faculty; and in part to encourage school-based faculty to take on newly invented teaching roles at universities (Holmes Group, 1996) coupled with a larger role in policy decisions.

The establishment of professional development schools as major sites for teacher learning has enormous potential. Darling-Hammond (1994) asserts that

> professional development schools [PDSs] are creating entirely new frames for teacher learning— frames that provide opportunity for learning by teaching, learning by doing, and learning by collaborating. These enhance the learning of teacher educators, and veteran teachers as well as beginning teachers. . . . PDSs are creating possibilities for building entirely new ways of knowing and kinds of knowledge for the profession as a whole. (p. 10)

As we have argued throughout this chapter, however, simply because initiatives are characterized by the same language—here the language of professional development schools—does not mean that they are driven by the same conception of teacher learning. There have been some 250 professional development schools created at various locations across the country (Abdal-Haaq, cited in Levine & Trachtman, 1997). What happens inside each of them—the roles of teachers as leaders or organizers, the views of knowledge and practice that are reflected, and the changes that are actually made in terms of contexts for teacher learning— is not consistent. Zeichner and Miller (1997) rightly warn that "we must be very cautious at this early point in the evolution of Professional Development Schools about uncritically embracing the PDS as a panacea for the ills of teacher education" (p. 29). Despite a common rhetoric, there are professional development schools driven by each of the conceptions of teacher learning that we have outlined in this chapter, and thus this major initiative in teacher education takes many forms and has many different meanings.

Many current initiatives based on the knowledge-*of*-practice conception of teacher learning focus on the work of experienced teachers. Increasingly, these initiatives take the form of local, regional, or national networks, what Lieberman and Grolnick (1996) argue are "problematic but powerful third spaces [that] are becoming an important force for reform in American education" (p. 45). Networks vary in purpose and character but have in common the creation of contexts for teachers to direct their own learning and to do so in ways more congruent with their professional lives (Lieberman & Grolnick, 1996; McLaughlin & Talbert, 1993). Although not all teacher networks subscribe implicitly or explicitly to a knowledge-*of*-practice view of teacher learning, there are many that give inquiry-based professional development and the creation of teacher research teams or teacher inquiry communities primacy among their approaches to teacher learning.

The widespread activities of the National Writing Project, which some argue is the most successful large-scale professional development initiative ever, and the Breadloaf School of English are strong examples. Here the focus has been on writing, language, and literacy: Knowledge is constructed collaboratively, teacher to teacher, in institutes and on-line networks established to provide intellectual communities for exploring the social, cultural, and political dimensions of teaching and learning over time. Both the Breadloaf Rural Teachers Network and the National Writing Project teacher research groups place considerable emphasis on inquiry-based pedagogies and co-constructing knowledge with students. Many Breadloaf teacher researchers, for example, focus on teacher- and student-generated collaborative and community-based projects that combine action research, service, and advocacy. Writing project teachers also intentionally widen their inquiries to include other stakeholders in school change such as administrators, counselors, tutors, social workers, parents, and community members. Here and in other literacy-related teacher inquiry initiatives (e.g., Gallas, 1998; Wells, 1994), emphasis is placed on written documentation as a critical aspect of teachers' and students' inquiries as well as on the significance of disseminating knowledge beyond the local setting through presentation and publication.

Another set of initiatives features the efforts of teachers to improve their knowledge and practice by documenting children's learning in school contexts;

uncovering and clarifying their implicit assumptions about teaching, learning, and schooling; and solving a variety of school-based educational problems. Examples include the work of the North Dakota Study Group, the Prospect School teachers' institutes, and the Philadelphia Teachers' Learning Cooperative. As Carini (1986) points out, an important dimension of work of this kind has been the development of research and evaluation methods—primarily structured oral inquiry processes—that promote understanding of children's learning and both inform and are informed by teaching practices. Oral inquiry processes such as these represent teachers' self-conscious and often self-critical attempts to make sense of their daily work by talking about it in planned ways. The documentary processes developed by Carini and others at the Prospect School are theory-based, in that they emerge from a phenomenological view of knowledge and learning, as well as grounded theory, in that they provide a social context within which teachers together theorize their practice. The Prospect School Archive of Children's Work and its long-term records of teachers' deliberations serve as a living resource for the study of children's development and teacher learning over time.

The knowledge-*of*-practice conception of teacher learning is also evident in the rapidly increasing number of school- or district-based teacher inquiry communities that grow out of enduring school-university collaborative partnerships (Allen, Cary, & Delgado, 1995; Erickson & Christman, 1996; Hursh, 1997; Lytle et al., 1994; Lytle & Fecho, 1991; Michaels, 1998; Mohr & Maclean, 1987; Noffke et al., 1996; Wells, 1994). Describing the evolution of two elementary schools that "left the road most traveled," Allen, Cary, and Delgado (1995), for example, explore how teacher learning through inquiry is explicitly connected to the project of radically altering schools' discourse and decision-making processes related to teaching and learning. In many of these school-based initiatives, teacher learning occurs as a consequence of collegial efforts among teachers to identify critical school issues and to invent ecologically valid ways of collecting, analyzing, and interpreting site documents as well as interviews with colleagues, staff, parents, and students. Learning to use data for collaborative decision making is thus both a cause and a consequence of changing school culture.

A related set of initiatives for the learning of experienced teachers has been the result of efforts to create new and innovative research units, arrangements, or configurations either as expanded dimensions of university-school collaborations or as targeted efforts of foundations. Each of the eight specifically literacy-related national centers established in the last 10–15 years, for example, generated a unique program for teacher research reflecting that center's particular priorities and research programs (Lytle, in press). Another instance is the Santa Barbara Discourse Group (Green & Dixon, 1994), an unusual community of teachers, researchers, and graduate students who share a concern with "understanding how everyday life in classrooms is constructed by members through their interactions, verbal and other, and how these constructions influence what students have opportunities to access, accomplish, and thus, 'learn' in schools" (p. 231). Although its primary goal is the generation of knowledge about classroom and school life, the composition of this community and its program of research provide unique opportunities for school- and university-based researchers to learn from each other's contexts and to make their learnings available to other teachers and teacher groups through publication and presentation. In a growing number of cases, teacher learning as knowledge-*of*-practice also goes hand in hand with concerted efforts at "co-reform" (Allen, Cary, & Delgado, 1995) and the constructive disruption of school and university culture (Lytle & Cochran-Smith, 1994).

A particularly interesting initiative related to the knowledge-*of*-practice conception of teacher learning is the dissemination and funding of teachers' and other practitioners' research as well as studies of teachers' learning in inquiry communities and/or professional networks, as we have pointed out elsewhere (Cochran-Smith & Lytle, 1999). Although not entirely, most of these accounts and analyses stem from a knowledge-*of*-practice conception of teacher learning. In addition to Heinemann-Boynton/Cook, the National Council of Teachers of English, and other presses that have published teachers' writing for years, many prominent educational journals and yearbooks now include teachers' accounts of their own research. For example, the *Harvard Educational Review, Language Arts,* the *English Journal, Teaching and Change,* and the *National Writing Project Quarterly* publish research by teachers as well as articles about many aspects of teacher research. A recent yearbook of the National Society for the Study of Education (Hollingsworth & Sockett, 1994) was devoted entirely to teacher research and educational reform; a new journal, *Teacher Research: A Journal of Classroom Inquiry,* coedited by Brenda Power and Ruth Hubbard, has been published semiannually by the University of Maine since 1993; and a new series, *Practitioner Inquiry,* edited by Marilyn Cochran-Smith and Susan Lytle, has been published by Teachers College Press since 1996. In addition, several major research foundations, federal offices such as the Office of Educational Research Institute and the National Institute for Literacy, and professional organizations such as the National Council of Teachers of English and the International Reading Association support teacher research in various ways, including grants for teacher researchers and teacher research groups, as do some local school systems and public education funds. Among these, the Spencer Foundation has led the way by having as goals both supporting the work of inquiry communities and developing a body of research about teaching and learning that is grounded in practice. In addition, the MacArthur Foundation and the Spencer Foundation have together mounted a program of support for research on professional development. Many of these grants have been awarded for professional development initiatives that are based on a knowledge-*of*-practice conception of teacher learning.

In addition to increased funding for initiatives related to professional development, recent or forthcoming editions of major research handbooks include chapters that synthesize teacher research or practitioner inquiry efforts (see, for example, Burton, 1991; Henson, 1996; Lytle, in press; Zeichner & Noffke, in press). Finally, a growing number of national conferences focus exclusively on teacher research or include a significant number of teacher researchers as presenters. AERA, for example, has had an active special interest group focusing on teacher research since 1990. As mentioned previously, the Ethnography and Education Forum at the University of Pennsylvania has featured "Teacher Research Day" for more than a decade. An international conference on teacher research has been held annually at rotating sites in the United States for the last 7 years. And the National Council of Teachers of English has for many years included (and continues to include) a large number of teacher researchers in its annual national and regional programs. Finally, but not by any means less important, a large number of local and regional organizations both publish and feature teacher research at meetings and conferences.

DIRECTIONS FORWARD: INQUIRY AS STANCE

In the remainder of this chapter, we point to some of the significant issues about teacher learning raised by the conceptual framework suggested here. We do so by outlining the dimensions of a new construct that we have begun referring to as "inquiry as stance" (Cochran-Smith, 1998; Cochran-Smith & Lytle, 1998; Lytle, 1998).[5] This idea reflects our understanding and analysis of the three conceptions of teacher learning described in this chapter, particularly our efforts to contribute to and conceptualize the third, knowledge-*of*-practice. More specifically, the construct *inquiry as stance* emanates from a 3-year study of the relationships of inquiry, knowledge, and professional practice in urban inquiry communities. We offer a brief version of this construct in the final section of the chapter because we think it points to some of the most provocative questions related to teacher learning in communities as we move into the 21st century.

Inquiry as Stance: Beyond Certainty in Teacher Learning

The construct *inquiry as stance* is intended to offer a closer understanding of the knowledge generated in inquiry communities, how inquiry relates to practice, and what teachers learn from inquiry. In everyday language, "stance" is used to describe body postures, particularly with regard to the position of the feet, as in sports or dance, and also to describe political positions, particularly their consistency (or the lack thereof) over time. In the discourse of qualitative research, "stance" is used to make visible and problematic the various perspectives through which researchers frame their questions, observations, and interpretations of data. In our work, we offer the term *inquiry as stance* to describe the positions teachers and others who work together in inquiry communities take toward knowledge and its relationships to practice. We use the metaphor of stance to suggest both orientational and positional ideas, to carry allusions to the physical placing of the body as well as to intellectual activities and perspectives over time. In this sense, the metaphor is intended to capture the ways we stand, the ways we see, and the lenses we see through. Teaching is a complex activity that occurs within webs of social, historical, cultural, and political significance. Across the life span, we assert that an inquiry stance provides a kind of grounding within the changing cultures of school reform and competing political agendas.

Inquiry as stance is distinct from the more common notion of inquiry as time-bounded project or discrete activity within a teacher education course or professional development workshop. Teachers and student teachers who take an inquiry stance work within inquiry communities to generate local knowledge, envision and theorize their practice, and interpret and interrogate the theory and research of others. Fundamental to this notion is the idea that the work of inquiry communities is both social and political; that is, it involves making problematic the current arrangements of schooling; the ways knowledge is constructed, evaluated, and used; and teachers' individual and collective roles in bringing about change. *Inquiry as stance* as a construct for understanding teacher learning in communities relies on a richer conception of knowledge than that allowed by the traditional formal knowledge-practical knowledge distinction, a richer conception of practice than that suggested in the aphorism that practice is practical, a richer conception of learning across the professional life span than concepts of expertise that differentiate expert teachers from novices, and a richer conception of the cultures of communities and educational purposes than those implicit in many widespread school-wide reforms.

Against Dualisms: Limitations of the Formal Knowledge-Practical Knowledge Distinction

As we have pointed out, the knowledge-*for*-practice conception of teacher learning foregrounds formal knowledge as a base for improving practice, while the knowledge-*in*-practice relationship focuses on the importance of teachers' practical knowledge. Although these are strikingly different, both derive—or, as we have pointed out, are mistakenly taken to derive—from the distinction between formal and practical knowledge. As we have tried to show, while some of those who use the language of practical knowledge are calling for new epistemologies, others take as basic premises (a) that it is possible to delineate two kinds of knowledge for teaching, (b) that this distinction accounts for the universe of knowledge types in understanding teaching, and (c) that the practical knowledge concept adequately captures the work of teachers and the activity of teaching. This distinction works to maintain the hegemony of university-generated knowledge for teaching and carries with it the same power and status differentials associated with the disconnections of basic from applied research and theory from practice. It follows, then, that from the perspective of the formal knowledge-practical knowledge distinction, practical knowledge is in some senses low-status knowledge—bounded by the everyday, excessively local and particular, and possibly trivial. These implications serve to reify divisions that keep teachers "in their place"—the separation of practitioners from researchers, doers from thinkers, actors from analysts, and actions from ideas.

The formal knowledge-practical knowledge distinction is a dualism that has been part of epistemological discussions for years, although, we have shown, a number of scholars have called for "new epistemologies" that would better serve the knowledge needs of teachers and other practitioners and, in doing so, have contested the ideological, political, and social systems of the academy (e.g., Grimmett & Neufeld, 1994; Schon, 1995). This effort to break with the dominant epistemology has led to the development of some of the rich conceptions of practical knowledge described earlier. However, in many instances, scholars who claim to accept the possibility of "new epistemologies" have continued to impose on these new conceptions the distinctions and conventions of the old. As we have argued in more detail elsewhere (Cochran-Smith & Lytle, 1998), for example, Fenstermacher (1994) argues that it is essential to make very careful distinctions whenever the word *knowledge* is used to describe teachers' "mental states." He insists that if practical knowledge is to be considered real knowledge, then its epistemic claims (even in a new epistemology of practice) need to be born of a science "analogous to the science that yields formal knowledge" (p. 48). Along very similar lines, Huberman (1996) raises questions about the value of knowledge generated through inquiry or teacher research. He argues that if teacher researchers are not abiding by the established rules and not transcending the biases and perceptions of participants, then there is little possibility (and, Huberman would claim, little evidence) for the creation of a distinctive body of knowledge generated through inquiry. We think that part of what is happening in these critiques is what has often happened when new voices and modes of discourse push their way into existing conversations about ways of knowing, as Smith (1997) has skillfully pointed out in a discussion of the "stories researchers tell about themselves." Those located squarely inside the dominant epistemological and methodological paradigms use established terms, conventions, standards, and definitions to evaluate, and essentially dismiss, alternative ones (Cochran-Smith & Lytle, 1998). The concept *inquiry as stance* does not follow from the formal knowledge-practical knowledge distinction; rather, it emphasizes the importance of local knowledge that may also be useful to a more public educational community.

Teaching as Praxis: Beyond the Idea That Practice Is Practical

In teaching, the term *practice* has typically been used to refer to doing, acting, carrying out, and/or performing the work of the profession. Often this term is juxtaposed with the terms *theory* and *research* to suggest both relationships and disconnections—as in the common phrases putting theory into practice and translating research for practice and/or in the complaints that something is too theoretical, not practical enough, or, quite to the contrary, only practical and even anti-intellectual. These phrases seem to equate practice with that which is practical (Britzman, 1991), or useful, immediate, functional, and concerned with the everyday. From the perspective of *inquiry as stance,* however, neither the activity of teaching nor inquiry about teaching are captured by the notion that practice is practical. Rather, teaching and thus teacher learning are centrally about forming and re-forming frameworks for understanding practice: how students and their teachers construct the curriculum, co-mingling their experiences, their cultural and linguistic resources, and their interpretive frameworks; how teachers' actions are infused with complex and multilayered understandings of learners, culture, class, gender, literacies, social issues, institutions, histories, communities, materials, texts, and curricula; and how teachers work together to develop and alter their questions and interpretive frameworks informed not only by thoughtful consideration of the immediate situation and the particular students they teach and have taught but also by the multiple contexts within which they work.

Our idea of *inquiry as stance* is intended to capture some of the nature and extent to which those who teach and learn from teaching by engaging in inquiry interpret and theorize what they are doing. As we have pointed out (Cochran-Smith & Lytle, 1998), this problem is nicely explicated in the writing of McEwen (1991), who in turn draws on Carr's (1987) analysis of educational practice:

> Past efforts to understand the concept of practice within the field of education have tended to follow the natural sciences model in which theorizing is regarded as something distinct from the phenomena studied. In this view, practice is held to be, in itself, an atheoretical object—something theories are about rather than something that is inherently theoretical. The aim of theorizing according to the natural sciences model is to gain greater technical control over the phenomenal world. Thus, the concept of practice has become fixed in our minds as inhabiting the phenomenal world rather than the theoretical world. But to make such a division between theory and practice is to misunderstand the nature of practice. . . . By making the twin assumptions that all theory is non-practical and all practice is non-theoretical, this approach always underestimates the extent to which those engaged in educational practices have to reflect upon, and hence theorize, what, in general, they are trying to do. (pp. 13–14)

McEwen's commentary makes it clear that it is limiting to regard practice as primarily practical. A more generative conception is of "teaching as praxis," that is, the idea that teaching involves a dialectical relationship between critical theorizing and action (Britzman, 1991; Freire, 1970). The point here is that teachers theorize all the time, negotiating between their classrooms and school life as they struggle to make their daily work connect to larger movements for equity and social change.

Local Knowledge: Toward Constructing Interpretive Frameworks

We have suggested elsewhere that it is possible and indeed quite useful to talk about knowledge of teaching in ways that break with the traditional formal-practical knowledge distinction and that teachers' work in inquiry communities generates knowledge of teaching that is both local and public (Cochran-Smith & Lytle, 1998; Lytle & Cochran-Smith, 1992). Our local-public conception does not posit two kinds of knowledge analogous in any way to the distinction made between practical and formal knowledge. Rather, borrowing Geertz's (1983) term, we use *local knowledge* to signal both a way of knowing about teaching and what teachers and communities come to know when they build knowledge collaboratively. In his volume of essays on interpretive anthropology, Geertz talks about the difficulties involved in representing emic or insider knowledge and meaning perspectives. He suggests that ultimately anthropologists cannot really represent local knowledge, or what native inhabitants see, but only what they see through, that is, their interpretive perspectives on their own experiences.

What we are suggesting here is that representing teachers' local knowledge is similarly complicated. Using the phrase local knowledge, however, foregrounds the processes (not the products) of knowledge construction as they are expressed in and integrated with daily life in schools and classrooms and emphasizes the link of knower to that which is known and the context in which it is known. In this sense, constructing local knowledge is understood to be a process of building, interrogating, elaborating, and critiquing conceptual frameworks that link action and problem posing to the immediate context as well as to larger social, cultural, and political issues. Implicit in this process is a set of questions that function as lenses for seeing and making sense of practice broadly construed: Who am I as a teacher? What am I assuming about this child, this group, this community? What sense are my students making of what is going on in the classroom? How do the frameworks and research of others inform my own understandings? What are the underlying assumptions of these materials, texts, tests, curriculum frameworks, and school reporting documents? What am I trying to make happen here and why? How do my efforts as an individual teacher connect to the efforts of the community and to larger agendas for school and social change? When inquiry communities attempt to present and represent local knowledge of practice, their efforts invoke complex and provocative questions of ethics, access, and research methods that merit careful attention.

Learning Across the Life Span: Beyond the Expert-Novice Distinction

The knowledge-*for*-practice and the knowledge-*in*-practice conceptions of teacher learning pivot on a notion of expertise in teaching and the role of expertise in the improvement of practice. This notion reflects a methodological approach that is prominent in cognitive psychology and often used to study differences between expert and novice performances in a variety of areas. From the perspective of the knowledge-*for*-practice conception of teacher learning, the expert teacher is one with knowledge of the formal knowledge base generated or codified by university-based researchers. The expert teacher is expected constantly to update her or his knowledge of the knowledge base and adeptly follow the demonstrations and models of others. From the perspective of knowledge-*in*-practice, on the other hand, the expert teacher is defined as one who is able to articulate and make explicit the knowledge implicit in wise action and also to articulate this knowledge for novices or less accomplished teachers. Novice teachers, on the other hand, are expected to learn effective practices by imitating the strategies of their more competent colleagues. In each case, teacher learning is seen as a process of moving away from the status of novice to that of expert.

Implicit in the construct of *inquiry as stance* is a different conception of teacher learning across the professional life span than that implied by the expert-novice distinction. Learning from teaching through inquiry across the professional life span assumes that beginning and experienced teachers need to engage in similar intellectual work. Working together in communities, both new and more experienced teachers pose problems, identify discrepancies between theories and practices, challenge common routines, draw on the work of others for generative frameworks, and attempt to make visible much of that which is taken for granted about teaching and learning. From an inquiry stance, teachers search for significant questions as much as they engage in problem solving. They count on other teachers for alternative viewpoints on their work. In a very real sense, the usual connotation of "expertise" is inconsistent with the image of the teacher as lifelong learner and inquirer. Expertise implies certainty and state-of-the-art practice. Lifelong learning, on the other hand, implies tentativeness and practice that is sensitive to particular and local histories, cultures, and communities. The expert-novice distinction serves to maintain the individual in-the-head model of teacher learning that highlights individual differences among teachers. An across-the-life-span perspective on teacher learning is more relational—making salient the role of communities and intellectual projects of groups of teachers over time.

The Ends Question: Teacher Learning for What?

Inquiry as stance depends on the idea that knowing more and teaching better are inextricably linked to larger questions about the ends of teacher learning: What are or should be its purposes and consequences? Who makes decisions about these purposes and consequences? In what ways do particular initiatives for teacher learning challenge and/or sustain the status quo? What are the consequences of teachers' learning for students' learning? What part does teacher learning play in school reform? How is teacher learning connected to larger social, political, and intellectual movements? The most significant questions about the purposes and consequences of teacher learning are connected to teacher agency and ownership.

When wholesale participation in teacher learning initiatives is mandated at the school or school system level, or when teacher learning is scripted in certain ways, it becomes a substitute for grass-roots change efforts. In these instances, teacher learning becomes "simply" professional development—the production of a time- and place-bounded project or individual personal growth. When this happens, teacher learning functions as an end in itself. To the extent that teacher learning initiatives fit comfortably with a district's stated commitment to teacher leadership, site-based management, or curricular revision, for example, they can be regarded as at least compatible with, if not central to, ongoing efforts to improve schools. To the extent that teacher learning initiatives fit comfortably with a university or school district's institutional agenda for reflective practice, increased professionalism, and teacher accountability, they can be regarded as compatible with ongoing efforts toward professional development. But sometimes—if they work from an inquiry stance—teachers begin to challenge and then alter or dismantle fundamental practices such as tracking, teacher assignment, promotion and retention policies, testing and assessment, textbook selection, school-community-family relationships, administrator roles, personnel decisions, and school safety, not to mention raising questions about what counts as teaching and learning in classrooms. Sometimes teachers begin to reinvent their own job descriptions. They critique and seek to alter cultures of collegiality; ways that school or program structures promote or undermine collaboration; ratios of teacher autonomy to teacher responsibility; norms of teacher evaluation; relationships among student teachers, teachers, and their university colleagues; and the ways power is exercised in teacher-to-teacher, mentor-to-teacher, and school-university partnerships.

What this suggests to us is that there are starkly different kinds of teacher learning initiatives that feature what is referred to as inquiry—some that are readily integrated into the existing social and institutional arrangements of schools and school systems and others that are not. From the perspective of *inquiry as stance*, teacher learning is associated more with uncertainty than certainty, more with posing problems and dilemmas than with solving them, and also with the recognition that inquiry both stems from and generates questions. In many situations, ''questioning'' and ''challenging the system'' are rather difficult to explain as the consequences of inquiry-based teacher learning initiatives, and yet these may be precisely the kinds of consequences that are connected to more democratic schooling and to the formation of a more just society.

Inquiry as Agency: The Culture of Community

When teachers work in inquiry communities, they enter with others into ''a common search'' for meaning in their work lives (Westerhoff, 1987). The cultures of inquiry communities have several salient dimensions. Among them, time is one of the most critical. When groups of teachers come together as researchers, they need sufficient chunks of time in which to work and sufficient longevity as a group over time. When the pace of a community's work is unhurried and when members of the group make a commitment to work through complicated issues over time, ideas have a chance to incubate and develop, trust builds in the group, and participants feel comfortable raising sensitive issues and risking self-revelation. Over time, communities that support inquiry develop their own histories and in a certain sense their own culture—a common discourse, shared experiences that function as touchstones, and a set of procedures that provide structure and form for continued experience.

Another important dimension of the formation and maintenance of inquiry communities is the nature of the discourse—particular ways of describing, discussing, and debating teaching. In communities where inquiry is stance, groups of teachers and student teachers engage in joint construction of knowledge through conversation and other forms of collaborative analysis and interpretation. Through talk and writing, they make their tacit knowledge more visible, call into question assumptions about common practices, and generate data that make possible the consideration of alternatives. Part of the culture of inquiry communities is that rich descriptive talk and writing help make visible and accessible the day-to-day events, norms, and practices of teaching and learning and the ways different teachers, students, administrators, and families understand them. In this way, participants conjointly uncover relationships between concrete cases and more general issues and constructs. In addition, texts themselves play a critical role in forming and maintaining communities with an inquiry stance. Inquiry communities use a wide range of texts, not all of which are published or disseminated but are essential to teachers' individual and collective gathering, recording, and analyzing of data. These include reports and accounts of teacher researchers, action researchers, and other practitioners as well as selections from the extensive theoretical and research literatures in the many fields related to teaching, learning, and schooling.

The notion of *inquiry as stance* is intended to problematize the roles teachers play in designing and implementing initiatives for their own learning. When groups of teachers and others come together to learn, there are issues related to negotiating the agenda, sharing power and decision making, representing the work of the group, and dealing with the inevitable tensions of individual and collective purposes and viewpoints. These issues are seldom self-evident but always present. How and whether they are surfaced and dealt with indelibly shape the group and either circumscribe or open up its possibilities for productive work over time.

From an inquiry stance, teacher leadership and group membership look very different from what they look like when teachers are "trained" in workshops or staff development projects. Taking an inquiry stance on leadership means that teachers challenge the purposes and underlying assumptions of educational change efforts rather than simply helping to specify or carry out the most effective methods for predetermined ends. From the perspective of *inquiry as stance,* there is an activist aspect to teacher leadership that is closely linked to the expanded notion of practice we described in the third conception of teacher learning, knowledge-*of*-practice. From this perspective, inquiry communities exist to make consequential changes in the lives of teachers and, as important, in the lives of students and in the social and intellectual climate of schools and schooling.

It is our hope that the framework for understanding teacher learning presented in this chapter will support a different discourse about what it means when variously positioned reformers and policymakers advocate that teachers today need to know more to teach better. As we hope we have made clear, there are contrasting interpretations of what this relatively "simple" idea means. Beyond providing a sense of the range and variation of interpretations, however, a conceptual framework that interrogates underlying images of knowledge, practice, and their complex interrelationships exposes a number of provocative issues about the whole topic of teacher learning and the role of communities. These issues are at once subtle, in that very different meanings are often embedded beneath the surface of similar language and structures, and also striking, in that the differences are enormously significant for how teachers understand and position themselves in various initiatives for school improvement as well as how universities and other educational institutions position teachers and teacher learning in relation to change. The idea of *inquiry as stance* is intended to emphasize that teacher learning for the next century needs to be understood not primarily as individual professional accomplishment but as a long-term collective project with a democratic agenda.

NOTES

[1] A 3-year study of the relationships of inquiry to teachers' professional knowledge and practice across the professional teaching life span was supported by a Spencer Foundation grant to Marilyn Cochran-Smith and Susan L. Lytle. The study involved case studies of individual teacher researchers as well as teacher researcher groups, all of whom worked within the context of local and larger inquiry communities.

[2] See Cochran-Smith and Lytle (1998) for a lengthy discussion of these issues and a critique of the arguments offered by Fenstermacher and Huberman.

[3] This is also true of some teacher learning initiatives animated by the second conception that have become more or less subsumed by the third as the emphasis has shifted from the pedagogy of individual teachers to larger and more collaborative consideration of pedagogical and political contexts (P. Grimmett, personal communication, September 1998).

[4] We refer here only to the latest wave of interest in teacher research in the United States, which was marked roughly a decade ago by a number of key publications and events, rather than to the long history of the roots and relatives of teacher research in the United States and across the world.

[5] This concept is more fully described in our forthcoming book from Teachers College Press, *Inquiry as Stance*.

REFERENCES

Adler, S. (1991). The reflective practitioner and the curriculum of teacher education. *Journal of Education for Teaching, 17,* 139–150.

Albert, L. R., Cochran-Smith, M., DiMattia, P., Freedman, S., Jackson, R., Mooney, J., Neisler, O., Peck, A., & Zollers, N. P. (1997, April). *Seeking social justice: A teacher education faculty's self study, Year I.* Paper presented at the annual meeting of the American Educational Research Association, Chicago.

Albert, L., Cochran-Smith, M., DiMattia, P., Freedman, S., Jackson, R., Mooney, J., Neisler, O., Peck, A., & Zollers, N. (1998, April). *Seeking social justice: A teacher education faculty's self study, Year II.* Paper presented at the annual meeting of the American Educational Research Association, San Diego, CA.

Allen, J., Cary, M., & Delgado, L. (1995). *Exploring blue highways.* New York: Teachers College Press.

Anders, P. L., & Richardson, V. (1994). Launching a new form of staff development. In V. Richardson (Ed.), *Teacher change and the staff development process* (pp. 1–22). New York: Teachers College Press.

Anderson, G., Herr, K., & Nihlen, A. (1994). *Studying your own school: An educator's guide to qualitative practitioner research.* Thousand Oaks, CA: Corwin Press.

Ball, D. L. (1990, April). *Becoming a mathematics teacher through college-based and alternate routes.* Paper presented at the annual meeting of the American Educational Research Association, Boston.

Ballenger, C. (1992). Because you like us: The language of control. *Harvard Educational Review, 62,* 199–208.

Banford, H., Berkman, M., Chin, C., Cziko, C., Fecho, B., Jumpp, D., Miller, C., & Resnick, M. (1996). *Cityscapes: Eight views from the urban classroom.* Berkeley, CA: National Writing Project.

Banks, J. A. (1996). *Multicultural education, transformative knowledge and action: Historical and contemporary perspectives.* New York: Teachers College Press.

Barnes, H. (1989). Structuring knowledge for beginning teaching. In M. Reynolds (Ed.), *Knowledge base for the beginning teacher* (pp. 13–22). New York: Pergamon Press.

Berthoff, A. (1987). The teacher as researcher. In D. Goswami & P. Stillman (Eds.), *Reclaiming the classroom: Teacher research as an agency for change.* Upper Montclair, NJ: Boynton/Cook.

Beyer, L. (1988). *Knowing and acting: Inquiry, ideology, and educational studies.* London: Falmer Press.

Beyer, L. (1991). Teacher education, reflective inquiry, and moral action. In B. R. Tabachnick & K. M. Zeichner (Eds.), *Issues and practices in inquiry-oriented teacher education* (pp. 113–129). London: Falmer Press.

Branscombe, N. H., Goswami, D., & Schwartz, J. (1992). *Students teaching, teachers learning.* Portsmouth, NH: Boynton/Cook-Heinemann.

Britton, J. (1987). A quiet form of research. In D. Goswami & P. Stillman (Eds.), *Reclaiming the classroom: Teacher research as an agency for change.* Upper Montclair, NJ: Boynton/Cook.

Britzman, D. P. (1991). *Practice makes practice: A critical study of learning to teach.* New York: State University of New York Press.

Bullough, R. V., & Gitlin, A. (1995). *Becoming a student of teaching: Methodologies for exploring self and school context.* New York: Garland.

Burton, F. (1991). Teacher-researcher projects: An elementary school teacher's perspective. In J. Flood, J. N. Jensen, D. Lapp, & R. Squire (Eds.), *Handbook of research on teaching the English language arts.* New York: Macmillan.

Bussis, A. M., Chittenden, E. A., & Amarel, M. (1976). *Beyond surface curriculum.* Boulder, CO: Westview.

Carini, P. (1975). *Observation and description: An alternative methodology for the investigation of human phenomena.* Grand Forks: University of North Dakota Press.

Carini, P. (1979). *The art of seeing and the visibility of the person.* Grand Forks: North Dakota Study Group on Evaluation, University of North Dakota.

Carini, P. (1982). *The school lives of seven children: A five-year study.* Grand Forks: North Dakota Study Group on Evaluation.

Carini, P. (1986). *Prospect's documentary process.* Bennington, VT: Prospect School Center.

Carr, W. (1987). What is an educational practice? *Journal of Philosophy of Education, 21,* 163–175.

Carr, W., & Kemmis, S. (1986). *Becoming critical: Education, knowledge, and action research.* London: Falmer Press.

Carter, K. (1990). Teachers' knowledge and learning to teach. In W. Houston (Ed.), *Handbook of research on teacher education* (pp. 291–320). New York: Macmillan.

Christensen, D. (1996). The professional knowledge-research base for teacher education. In J. Sikula, T. Buttery, & E. Guyton (Eds.), *Handbook of research on teacher education* (2nd ed., pp. 38–52). New York: Macmillan.

Clandinin, D. (1986). *Classroom practice: Teacher images in action.* London: Falmer Press.

Clandinin, D., & Connelly, F. (1987). Teachers' personal knowledge: What counts as personal in studies of the personal. *Journal of Curriculum Studies, 19,* 487–500.

Clandinin, D., & Connelly, F. (1995). Teachers' professional knowledge landscapes: Secret, sacred, and cover stories. In F. Connelly & D. Clandinin (Eds.), *Teachers' professional knowledge landscapes* (pp. 1–15). New York: Teachers College Press.

Clark, C., & Peterson, P. (1986). Teachers' thought processes. In M. Wittrock (Ed.), *Handbook of research on teaching.* New York: Macmillan.

Clift, R., Houston, W. R., & Pugach, M. (Eds.). (1990). *Encouraging reflective practice in education: An analysis of issues and programs.* New York: Teachers College Press.

Cochran-Smith, M. (1991a). Learning to teach against the grain. *Harvard Educational Review, 51,* 279–310.

Cochran-Smith, M. (1991b). Reinventing student teaching. *Journal of Teacher Education, 42,* 104–118.

Cochran-Smith, M. (1994). The power of teacher research in teacher education. In S. Hollingsworth & H. Sockett (Eds.), *Teacher research and educational reform, yearbook of the NSSE.* Chicago: University of Chicago Press.

Cochran-Smith, M. (1995a). Color blindness and basket making are not the answers: Confronting the dilemmas of race, culture, and language diversity in teacher education. *American Educational Research Journal, 32,* 493–522.

Cochran-Smith, M. (1995b). Uncertain allies: Understanding the boundaries of race and teaching. *Harvard Educational Review, 65,* 541–570.

Cochran-Smith, M. (1998). Teaching for social change: Toward a grounded theory of teacher education. In A. Hargreaves, A. Lieberman, M. Fullan, & D. Hopkins (Eds.), *The international handbook of educational change.* Amsterdam: Kluwer Academic.

Cochran-Smith, M. (1999). Learning to teach for social justice. In G. Griffin (Ed.), *98th yearbook of NSSE: Teacher education for a new century: Emerging perspectives, promising practices, and future possibilities.* Chicago: University of Chicago Press.

Cochran-Smith, M., & Lytle, S. L. (1992a). Communities for teacher research: Fringe or forefront. *American Journal of Education, 100,* 298–323.

Cochran-Smith, M., & Lytle, S. L. (1992b). Interrogating cultural diversity: Inquiry and action. *Journal of Teacher Education, 43,* 104–115.

Cochran-Smith, M., & Lytle, S. (1993). *Inside/outside: Teacher research and knowledge.* New York: Teachers College Press.

Cochran-Smith, M., & Lytle, S. (1998). Teacher research: The question that persists. *International Journal of Leadership in Education, 1,* 19–36.

Cochran-Smith, M., & Lytle, S. (in press). The teacher research movement: A decade later. *Educational Researcher.*

Cohen, D. K., McLaughlin, M. W., & Talbert, J. E. (Eds.). (1993). *Teaching for understanding: Challenges for policy and practice.* San Francisco: Jossey-Bass.

Cole, A. L., & Knowles, J. G. (1998). The self-study of teacher education practices and the reform of teacher education. In M. L. Hamilton (Ed.), *Reconceptualizing teaching practice: Self-study in teacher education* (pp. 224–234). London: Falmer Press.

Colton, A., & Langer, G. (1994). Reflective decision making: The cornerstone of school reform. *Journal of Staff Development, 15,* 2–7.

Darling-Hammond, L. (1994). *Professional development schools: Schools for developing a profession.* New York: Teachers College Press.

Dewey, J. (1904). The relation of theory to practice in education. In C. A. McMurray (Ed.), *The third NSSE yearbook.* Chicago: University of Chicago Press.

Dewey, J. (1916). *Democracy and education: An introduction to the philosophy of education.* New York: Free Press.

Donmoyer, R. (1996). The concept of a knowledge base. In F. Murray (Ed.), *The teacher educator's handbook* (pp. 92–119). San Francisco: Jossey-Bass.

Duckworth, E. (1987). *The having of wonderful ideas.* New York: Teachers College Press.

Duckworth, E. (1997). *Teacher to teacher: Learning from each other.* New York: Teachers College Press.

Elbaz, F. (1983). *Teacher thinking: A study of practical knowledge.* London: Croom Helm.

Elbaz, F. (1990). Knowledge and discourse: The evolution of research on teacher thinking. In C. Day, M. Pope, & P. Denicolo (Eds.), *Insights into teachers' thinking and practice* (pp. 15–42). New York: Falmer Press.

Erickson, F. (1986). Qualitative methods on research on teaching. In M. Wittrock (Ed.), *Handbook of research on teaching* (3rd ed., pp. 119–161). New York: Macmillan.

Erickson, F., & Christman, J. B. (1996). Taking stock/making change: Stories of collaboration in local school reform. *Theory into Practice, 35,* 149–157.

Evans, C. (1989, April). *The educator's forum: Teacher-initiated research in progress.* Paper presented at the annual meeting of the American Educational Research Association, San Francisco.

Fashola, O. S., & Slavin, R. E. (1998). Schoolwide reform models: What works? *Phi Delta Kappan, 79,* 370–379.

Fecho, R. (1998). Cross boundaries of research in critical literacy classrooms. In D. Alverna (Ed.), *Reconceptualizing the literacies in adolescent lives.* Mahwah, NJ: Erlbaum.

Feiman-Nemser, S., & Beasley, K. (1997). Mentoring as assisted performance: A case of co-planning. In V. Richardson (Ed.), *Constructivist teacher education: Building new understandings* (pp. 108–126). Washington, DC: Falmer Press.

Feiman-Nemser, S., & Remillard, J. (1996). Perspectives on learning to teach. In F. Murray (Ed.), *The teacher educator's handbook* (pp. 63–91). San Francisco: Jossey-Bass.

Fenstermacher, G. (1986). Philosophy of research: Three aspects. In M. Wittrock (Ed.), *Handbook of research on teaching* (3rd ed., pp. 37–49). New York: Macmillan.

Fenstermacher, G. (1994). The knower and the known: The nature of knowledge in research on teaching. In L. Darling-Hammond (Ed.), *Review of research in education* (Vol. 20, pp. 3–56). Washington, DC: American Educational Research Association.

Fleischer, C. (1995). *Composing teacher-research: A prosaic history.* Albany: State University of New York Press.

Flood, J., Jensen, J. M., Lapp, D., & Squire, J. R. (Eds.). (1991). *Handbook of research on teaching the English language arts.* New York: Macmillan.

Florio-Ruane, S. (1994). Future teachers' autobiography club: Preparing educators to support literacy learning in culturally diverse classrooms. *English Education, 26,* 52–66.

Florio-Ruane, S., & Walsh, M. (1980). The teacher as colleague in classroom research. In H. Trueba, G. Guthrie, & K. Au (Eds.), *Culture in the bilingual classroom: Studies in classroom ethnography.* Rowley, MA: Newbury House.

Freire, P. (1970). *Pedagogy of the oppressed* (M. B. Ramos, Trans.). New York: Seabury Press.

Gallas, K. (1998). *Sometimes I can be anything.* New York: Teachers College Press.

Gardner, W. E. (1989). Preface. In M. C. Reynolds (Ed.), *Knowledge base for the beginning teacher* (pp. ix–xii). New York: Pergamon Press.

Geertz, C. (1983). Blurred genres: The refiguration of social thought. In C. Geertz (Ed.), *Local knowledge.* New York: Basic Books.

Giroux, H. (1988). *Teachers as intellectuals.* New York: Bergin & Garvey.

Gitlin, A., Bringhurst, K., Burns, M., Cooley, V., Myers, B., Price, K., Russell, R., & Tiess, P. (1992). *Teachers' voices for school change: An introduction to educative research.* New York: Teachers College Press.

Goodman, J. (1991). Using a methods course to promote reflection and inquiry among preservice teachers. In B. R. Tabachnick & K. Zeichner (Eds.), *Issues and practices in inquiry-oriented teacher education* (pp. 56–76). London: Falmer Press.

Goodman, Y. (1985). Kid watching: Observing in the classroom. In A. Jagger & M. Smith-Burke (Eds.), *Observing the language learner.* Newark, DE: International Reading Association.

Gore, J., & Zeichner, K. (1991). Action research and reflective teaching in preservice teacher education. *Teaching and Teacher Education, 7,* 119–136.

Gore, J., & Zeichner, K. (1995). Connecting action research to genuine teacher development. In J. Smyth (Ed.), *Critical discourses on teacher development* (pp. 203–214). London: Cassell.

Goswami, P., & Stillman, P. (1987). *Reclaiming the classroom: Teacher research as an agency for change.* Upper Montclair, NJ: Boynton/Cook.

Grant, C. A. (1997). Critical knowledge, skills, and experiences for the instruction of culturally diverse students: A perspective for the preparation of preservice teachers. In J. Jordan-Irvine (Ed.), *Critical knowledge for diverse teachers and learners* (pp. 1–26). Washington, DC: American Association of Colleges for Teacher Education.

Green, J., & Dixon, C. (1994). Talking knowledge into being: Discursive and social practices in classrooms. *Linguistics and Education, 5,* 231–239.

Griffin, G. (1989). Coda: The knowledge-driven school. In M. C. Reynolds (Ed.), *Knowledge base for the beginning teacher.* Oxford, England: Pergamon Press.

Grimmett, P. (1988). The nature of reflection and Schon's conception in perspective. In P. Grimmett & G. Erickson (Eds.), *Reflection in teacher education.* New York: Teachers College Press.

Grimmett, P. P., & Dockendorf, A. (1997). Exploring the labyrinth of researching teaching. In J. Loughran (Ed.), *Teaching about teaching.* London: Falmer Press.

Grimmett, P., & Erickson, G. (1988). *Reflection in teacher education.* New York: Teachers College Press.

Grimmett, P., & MacKinnon, A. (1992). Craft knowledge and the education of teachers. In G. Grant (Ed.), *Review of research in education* (Vol. 18, pp. 385–456). Washington, DC: American Educational Research Association.

Grimmett, P., MacKinnon, A., Erickson, G., & Riecken, T. (1990). Reflective practice in teacher education. In R. Clift, R. Houston, & M. Pugach (Eds.), *Encouraging reflective practice: An examination of issues and exemplars* (pp. 20–38). New York: Teachers College Press.

Grimmett, P. P., & Neufeld, J. (1994). *Teacher development and the struggle for authenticity: Professional growth and restructuring in the context of change.* New York: Teachers College Press.

Grossen, B. (1996, Fall). Making research serve the profession. *American Educator,* pp. 7–27.

Grossman, P. (Ed.). (1990). *The making of a teacher: Teacher knowledge and teacher education.* New York: Teachers College Press.

Hamilton, M. L., & Pinnegar, S. (1998a). Reconceptualizing teaching practice. In M. L. Hamilton (Ed.), *Reconceptualizing teaching practice: Self-study in teacher education* (pp. 1–4). London: Falmer Press.

Hamilton, M. L., & Pinnegar, S. (1998b). The value and the promise of self-study. In M. L. Hamilton (Ed.), *Reconceptualizing teaching practice: Self-study in teacher education* (pp. 235–246). London: Falmer Press.

Hargreaves, A. (1994). *Changing teachers, changing times: Teachers' work and culture in the postmodern age.* New York: Teachers College Press.

Hargreaves, A. (1996). Transforming knowledge: Blurring the boundaries between research, policy, and practice. *Educational Evaluation and Policy Analysis, 18,* 161–178.

Hargreaves, A., & Fullan, M. G. (1991). *Understanding teacher development.* London: Cassell.

Heaton, R. M., & Lampert, M. (1993). Learning to hear voices: Inventing a new pedagogy of teacher education. In D. K. Cohen, M. W. McLaughlin, & J. E. Talbert (Eds.), *Teaching for understanding: Challenges for policy and practice* (pp. 43–83). San Francisco: Jossey-Bass.

Henson, K. (1996). Teachers as researchers. In J. Sikula, T. Buttery, & E. Guyton (Eds.), *Handbook of research on teacher education* (2nd ed., pp. 53–64). New York: Macmillan.

Himley, M. (1991). *Shared territory: Understanding children's writing as works.* New York: Oxford University Press.

Himley, M., & Carini, P. (1991). The study of works: A phenomenological approach to understanding children as thinkers and learners. In M. Himley (Ed.), *Shared territory* (pp. 17–56). New York: Oxford University Press.

Hollingsworth, S., Cody, A., Davis-Smallwood, J., Dybdahl, M., Gallagher, P., Gallego, M., Maestre, T., Minarik, L., Raffel, L., Standerford, N. S., & Teel, K. (1994). *Teacher research and urban literacy education, lessons and conversations in a feminist key.* New York: Teachers College Press.

Hollingsworth, S., & Sockett, H. (Eds.). (1994). *Teacher research and educational reform: Yearbook of the NSSE.* Chicago: University of Chicago Press.

Holmes Group. (1996). *Tomorrow's schools of education.* East Lansing, MI.

Houston, W. R. (Ed.). (1990). *Handbook of research on teacher education.* New York: Macmillan.

Houston, W. R., & Clift, R. T. (1990). The potential for research contributions to reflective practice. In R. T. Clift, W. R. Houston, & M. C. Pugach (Eds.), *Encouraging reflective practice in education: An analysis of issues and programs* (pp. 208–224). New York: Teachers College Press.

Huberman, M. (1996). Moving mainstream: Taking a closer look at teacher research. *Language Arts, 73,* 124–140.

Hursh, D. (1997). Critical, collaborative action research in politically contested times. In S. Hollingsworth (Ed.), *International action research: A casebook for educational reform* (pp. 124–134). Washington, DC: Falmer Press.

Joyce, B., Showers, B., & Rohlheiser-Bennett, C. (1987). Staff development and student learning: A synthesis of research on models of teaching. *Educational Leadership, 45,* 77–87.

Kincheloe, J. (1991). *Teachers as researchers: Qualitative inquiry as a path to empowerment.* London: Falmer Press.

Kincheloe, J. L. (1993). *Toward a critical politics of teacher thinking: Mapping the postmodern.* Westport, CT: Bergin & Garvey.

King, J., & Ladson-Billings, G. (1990). The teacher education challenge in elite university settings: Developing critical perspectives for teaching in a democratic and multicultural society. *European Journal of Intercultural Studies, 1*(2), 15–30.

Knoblauch, C. H., & Brannon, L. (1988). Knowing our knowledge: A phenomenological basis for teacher research. In L. Z. Smith (Ed.), *Audits of meaning: A Festschrift in honor of Ann E. Berthoff.* Portsmouth, NH: Boynton/Cook-Heinemann.

Knowles, J. G. (1992). Models for understanding preservice and beginning teachers' biographies: Illustrations from case studies. In I. F. Goodson (Ed.), *Studying teachers' lives.* New York: Routledge & Kegan Paul.

Knowles, J. G., & Cole, A. L. (1996). Developing practice through field experience. In F. B. Murray (Ed.), *The teacher educator's handbook* (pp. 648–687). San Francisco: Jossey-Bass.

LaBoskey, V. K., Davies-Samway, K., & Garcia, S. (1998). Cross-institutional action research: A collaborative self-study. In M. L. Hamilton (Ed.), *Reconceptualizing teaching practice: Self-study in teacher education* (pp. 154–166). London: Falmer Press.

Lampert, M., & Ball, D. (1998). *Teaching, multimedia, and mathematics: Investigations of real practice.* New York: Teachers College Press.

Leinhardt, G. (1989). Capturing craft knowledge in teaching. *Educational Researcher, 19*(2), 18–25.

Leistyna, P., Woodrum, A., & Sherblo, S. A. (Eds.). (1996). *Breaking free: The transformative power of critical pedagogy.* Cambridge, MA: Harvard Educational Review.

Levine, M., & Trachtman, R. (Eds.). (1997). *Making professional development schools work: Politics, practice, and policy.* New York: Teachers College Press.

Lieberman, A. (1992). The meaning of scholarly activity and the building of community. *Educational Researcher, 21*(6), 5–12.

Lieberman, A., & Grolnick, M. (1996). Networks and reform in American education. *Teachers College Record, 98,* 6–45.

Lieberman, A., & Miller, L. (1991). Revisiting the social realities of teaching. In A. Lieberman & L. Miller (Eds.), *Staff development: New demands, new realities, new perspectives* (pp. 92–109). New York: Teachers College Press.

Lieberman, A., & Miller, L. (1994). Problems and possibilities of institutionalizing teacher research. In S. Hollingsworth & H. Socket (Eds.), *Teacher research and educational reform* (pp. 204–220). Chicago: University of Chicago Press.

Little, J. W. (1990). The persistence of privacy: Autonomy and initiative in teachers' professional relations. *Teachers College Record, 91,* 509–536.

Little, J. W. (1993). Teachers' professional development in a climate of educational reform. *Educational Evaluation and Policy Analysis, 15,* 129–151.

Little, J. W., & McLaughlin, M. (1993). *Teacher's work: Individuals, colleagues, and contexts.* New York: Teachers College Press.

Lytle, S. (1992). *Using ethnography for organizational development: Administrators learn about their students (and schools).* Unpublished manuscript.

Lytle, S. (1996). A wonderfully terrible place to be: Learning in practitioner inquiry communities. In P. A. Sissel (Ed.), *A community-based approach to literacy programs: Taking learners' lives into account.* San Francisco: Jossey-Bass.

Lytle, S. (1998, April). *Inquiry as a stance on teaching: The inservice case.* Paper presented at the annual meeting of the American Educational Research Association, San Diego, CA.

Lytle, S. (in press). Teacher research in the contact zone. In P. Kamil, P. Mosanthal, P. Pearson, & R. Barr (Eds.), *Handbook of reading research.* Mahwah, NJ: Erlbaum.

Lytle, S., Belzer, A., & Reumann, R. (1992). *Invitations to inquiry: Rethinking staff development in adult literacy education* (Tech. Rep. TR92-2). Philadelphia: National Center on Adult Literacy.

Lytle, S., Belzer, A., & Reumann, R. (1993). *Initiating practitioner inquiry: Adult literacy teachers, new teachers, and administrators respond to their practice* (Tech. Rep. TR93-11). Philadelphia: National Center on Adult Literacy.

Lytle, S., Christman, J., Cohen, J., Countryman, J., Fecho, R., Portnoy, D., & Sion, F. (1994). Learning in the afternoon: Teacher inquiry as school reform. In M. Fine (Ed.), *Charting urban school reform: Reflections on public high schools in the midst of change* (pp. 157–179). New York: Teachers College Press.

Lytle, S., & Cochran-Smith, M. (1992). Teacher research as a way of knowing. *Harvard Educational Review, 62,* 447–474.

Lytle, S., & Cochran-Smith, M. (1994). *Teacher research: Some questions that persist.* Paper presented at the Ethnography in Education Forum, Philadelphia.

Lytle, S., & Fecho, R. (1991). Meeting strangers in familiar places: Teacher collaboration by cross-visitation. *English Education, 23,* 5–28.

Maher, F. (1991). Gender, reflexivity, and teacher education. In B. R. Tabachnick & K. Zeichner (Eds.), *Issues and practices in inquiry-oriented teacher education* (pp. 22–34). London: Falmer Press.

McDiarmid, G. W. (1989). *Understanding history for teaching: A plan of study.* Unpublished manuscript, Michigan State University.

McDiarmid, G., & Ball, D. (1989). *The teacher education and learning to teach study: An occasion for developing a conception of teacher knowledge.* East Lansing: National Study for Research on Teacher Education, Michigan State University.

McDiarmid, G. W., Ball, D., & Anderson, C. W. (1989). Why staying one chapter ahead doesn't really work: Subject-specific pedagogy. In M. C. Reynolds (Ed.), *Knowledge base for the beginning teacher* (pp. 193–206). New York: Pergamon Press.

McDonald, J. P. (1992). *Teaching: Making sense of an uncertain craft.* New York: Teachers College Press.

McEwen, H. (1991, April). *Narrative understanding in the study of teaching.* Paper presented at the annual meeting of the American Educational Research Association, Chicago.

McLaughlin, M. (1993). What matters most in teachers' workplace context? In J. W. Little & M. McLaughlin (Eds.), *Teachers' work* (pp. 79–103). New York: Teachers College Press.

McLaughlin, M. W., & Talbert, J. E. (1993). Introduction: New visions of teaching. In D. K. Cohen, M. W. McLaughlin, & J. E. Talbert (Eds.), *Teaching for understanding: Challenges for policy and practice* (pp. 1–12). San Francisco: Jossey-Bass.

Merseth, K. K. (1996). Cases and case methods in teacher education. In J. Sikula, T. J. Buttery, & E. Guyton (Eds.), *Handbook of research on teacher education* (2nd ed., pp. 722–744). New York: Macmillan.

Meyer, R. (1998). *Composing a teacher study group.* Mahwah, NJ: Erlbaum.

Michaels, S. (1998). *Stories in contact: Teacher research in the academy.* Paper presented at the ADE, Lowell, MA.

Mohr, M. M., & Maclean, M. S. (1987). *Working together: A guide for teacher-researchers.* Urbana, IL: National Council of Teachers of English.

Munby, H. (1987). Metaphors and teachers' knowledge. *Research in the Teaching of English, 21,* 337–397.

Murray, F. B. (1989). Explanations in education. In M. C. Reynolds (Ed.), *Knowledge base for the beginning teacher* (pp. 1–12). New York: Pergamon Press.

Murray, F. B. (1996). Beyond natural teaching: The case for professional education. In F. Murray (Ed.), *The teacher educator's handbook* (pp. 3–13). San Francisco: Jossey-Bass.

National Council for Accreditation of Teacher Education. (1995). *Standards, procedures and policies for the accreditation of professional education units.* Washington, DC.

Noffke, S. (1991). Hearing the teacher's voice: Now what? *Curriculum Perspectives, 11*(4), 55–58.

Noffke, S. (1997). Professional, personal, and political dimensions of action research. In M. Apple (Ed.), *Review of research in education* (Vol. 22, pp. 305–343). Washington, DC: American Educational Research Association.

Noffke, S., & Brennan, M. (1997). Reconstructing the politics of action in action research. In S. Hollingsworth (Ed.), *International action research: A casebook for educational research.* Washington, DC: Falmer Press.

Noffke, S., Clark, B., Palmeri-Santiago, J., Sadler, J., & Shujaa, M. (1996). Conflict, learning, and change in a school/university partnership: Different worlds of sharing. *Theory into Practice, 35,* 165–172.

Noffke, S., Mosher, L., & Maricle, C. (1994). Curriculum research together: Writing our work. In S. Hollingsworth & H. Sockett (Eds.), *Teacher research and educational reform* (pp. 166–185). Chicago: University of Chicago Press.

Noffke, S., & Stevenson, R. (1995). *Educational action research: Becoming practically critical.* New York: Teachers College Press.

North, S. (1987). *The making of knowledge in composition: Portrait of an emerging field.* Upper Montclair, NJ: Boynton/Cook.

Pappas, C., & Zecker, Z. L. (1998a). *Working with teacher researchers in urban classrooms: Transforming literacy curriculum genres.* Mahwah, NJ: Erlbaum.

Pappas, C., & Zecker, Z. L. (Eds.). (1998b). *Teacher inquiries in literacy teaching-learning: Learning to collaborate in elementary urban classrooms.* Mahwah, NJ: Erlbaum.

Perrone, V. (1989). *Working papers: Reflections on teachers, schools, and communities.* New York: Teachers College Press.

Ray, R. (1993). *The practice of theory: Teacher research in composition.* Urbana, IL: National Council of Teachers of English.

Resnick, M. (1996). Making connections between families and schools. In H. Banford, M. Berkman, C. Chin, B. Fecho, D. Jumpp, C. Miller, & M. Resnick (Eds.), *Cityscapes: Eight views from the urban classroom.* Berkeley, CA: National Writing Project.

Reynolds, M. C. (Ed.). (1989). *Knowledge base for the beginning teacher.* New York: Pergamon Press.

Richardson, V. (1994a). Conducting research on practice. *Educational Researcher, 23*(5), 5–10.

Richardson, V. (1994b). Teacher inquiry as professional staff development. In S. Hollingsworth & H. Sockett (Eds.), *Teacher research and educational reform* (pp. 186–203). Chicago: University of Chicago Press.

Richardson, V. (Ed.). (1997). *Constructivist teacher education: Building new understandings.* Washington, DC: Falmer Press.

Richardson, V. (Ed.). (in press). *Handbook of research on teacher education* (4th ed.). New York: Teachers College Press.

Richardson, V., & Hamilton, M. (1995). Effects of the culture of two schools on the process and outcomes of staff development. *Elementary School Journal, 95,* 367–385.

Rosenberg, P. (1994, April). *Underground discourses: Exploring whiteness in teacher education.* Paper presented at the annual meeting of the American Educational Research Association, New Orleans.

Roth, R. A. (1996). Standards for certification, licensure, and accreditation. In J. Sikula, T. J. Buttery, & E. Guyton (Eds.), *Handbook of research on teacher education* (2nd ed., pp. 242–278). New York: Macmillan.

Russell, T. (1987). Research, practical knowledge, and the conduct of teacher education. *Educational Theory, 37,* 369–375.

Schon, D. A. (1983). *The reflective practitioner.* San Francisco: Jossey-Bass.

Schon, D. A. (1987). *Educating the reflective practitioner.* San Francisco: Jossey-Bass.

Schon, D. A. (1995, November/December). The new scholarship requires a new epistemology. *Change,* pp. 27–34.

Short, K. (1996). *Learning together through literacy: From Columbus to integrated curriculum.* York, ME: Stenhouse.

Shulman, J. H. (1992). *Case methods in teacher education.* New York: Teachers College Press.

Shulman, J. H., & Colbert, J. A. (1989). Cases as catalysts for cases: Inducing reflection in teacher education. *Action in Teacher Education, 11,* 44–52.

Shulman, L. S. (1986). Those who understand: Knowledge growth in teaching. *Educational Researcher, 5,* 4–14.

Shulman, L. S. (1987). Knowledge and teaching: Foundations of the new reform. *Harvard Educational Review, 51,* 1–22.

Shulman, L. S., & Grossman, P. L. (1987). *Final report to the Spencer Foundation* (Technical Report of the Knowledge Growth in Professional Research Project). Stanford, CA: Stanford University.

Sikula, J. (1996). Introduction. In J. Sikula, T. J. Buttery, & E. Guyton (Eds.), *Handbook of research on teacher education* (2nd ed., pp. xv–xxiv). New York: Macmillan.

Sleeter, C. E. (1995). Reflections on my use of multicultural and critical pedagogy when students are White. In C. E. Sleeter & P. L. McLaren (Eds.), *Multicultural education, critical pedagogy, and the politics of difference* (pp. 415–438). Albany: State University of New York Press.

Smith, J. (1997). The stories educational researchers tell about themselves. *Educational Researcher, 26*(5), 4–11.

Stock, P. (1995). *The dialogic curriculum: Teaching and learning in a multicultural society.* Portsmouth, NH: Boynton/Cook-Heinemann.

Strieb, L. (1985). *A (Philadelphia) teacher's journal.* Grand Forks: North Dakota Study Group, Center for Teaching and Learning.

Tabachnik, R., & Zeichner, K. (Eds.). (1991). *Issues and practices in inquiry-oriented teacher education.* London: Falmer Press.

Tom, A. R. (1985). Inquiring into inquiry-oriented teacher education. *Journal of Teacher Education, 36*(5), 35–44.

Tom, A. R., & Valli, L. (1990). Professional knowledge for teachers. In W. Houston (Ed.), *Handbook of research on teacher education* (pp. 373–392). New York: Macmillan.

Traugh, C., Kanevsky, R., Martin, A., Seletzky, A., Woolf, K., & Streib, L. (1986). *Speaking out: Teachers on teaching.* Grand Forks: University of North Dakota.

Vinz, R. (1996). *Composing a teaching life.* Portsmouth, NH: Boynton/Cook.

Waff, D. (1994). Romance in the classroom: Inviting discourse on gender and power. *The Voice, 3*(1), 7–14.

Wasserman, S. (1993). *Getting down to cases: Learning to teach with case studies.* New York: Teachers College Press.

Wells, G. (Ed.). (1994). *Changing schools from within: Creating communities of inquiry.* Portsmouth, NH: Heinemann.

Westerhoff, J. H. (1987). The teacher as pilgrim. In F. S. Bolin & J. M. Falk (Eds.), *Teacher renewal.* New York: Teachers College Press.

Wilson, S. (1994). *Is there a method in this madness?* East Lansing: National Center for Research on Teacher Learning, Michigan State University.

Wilson, S. M., Miller, C., & Yerkes, C. (1993). Deeply rooted change: A tale of learning to teach adventurously. In D. K. Cohen, M. W. McLaughlin, & J. E. Talbert (Eds.), *Teaching for understanding: Challenges for policy and practice* (pp. 84–129). San Francisco: Jossey-Bass.

Wilson, S. M., Shulman, L. S., & Richert, A. E. (1987). "150 different ways" of knowing: Representations of knowledge in teaching. In J. Calderhead (Ed.), *Exploring teachers' thinking* (pp. 104–124). London: Cassell.

Wittrock, M. C. (Ed.). (1986). *Handbook of research on teaching* (3rd ed.). New York: Macmillan.

Zeichner, K. M. (1993). *Educating teachers for cultural diversity.* East Lansing: Michigan State University.

Zeichner, K. M. (1998, April). *The new scholarship in teacher education.* Paper presented at the annual meeting of the American Educational Research Association, San Diego, CA.

Zeichner, K. M., & Miller, M. (1997). Learning to teach in professional development schools. In M. Levine & R. Trachtman (Eds.), *Making professional development schools work: Politics, practice, and policy.* New York: Teachers College Press.

Zeichner, K. M., & Noffke, S. (in press). Practitioner research. In V. Richardson (Ed.), *Teaching* (4th ed.). New York: Macmillan.

Zollers, N. J., Albert, L. R., & Cochran-Smith, M. (1998). *In pursuit of social justice: Collaborative research and practice in teacher education.* Unpublished manuscript, Boston College.

Manuscript received October 2, 1998
Accepted November 10, 1998

Chapter 9

Addressing the "Two Disciplines" Problem: Linking Theories of Cognition and Learning With Assessment and Instructional Practice

JAMES W. PELLEGRINO
Vanderbilt University

GAIL P. BAXTER
Educational Testing Service

ROBERT GLASER
University of Pittsburgh

On September 2, 1957, Lee Cronbach delivered his visionary presidential address to the American Psychological Association (APA), calling for the unification of differential and experimental psychology, the two disciplines of scientific psychology. He described the essential features of each approach to asking questions about human nature, and he strongly hinted at the benefits to be gained by unification. Cronbach was calling for linking theories and research on learning and instruction, especially the instructional treatments that logically and psychologically followed from such research, with the tradition of assessing individual differences in cognitive abilities. In his opinion, such work would probably yield information of profound educational relevance. In describing some illustrative examples, he stated, quite boldly, "Such findings ... when replicated and explained, will carry us into an educational psychology which measures readiness for different types of teaching and which invents teaching methods to fit different types of readiness" (p. 681). He subsequently went even further and argued that this work had broader theoretical impact and meaning. "Constructs originating in differential psychology are now being tied to experimental variables. As a result, the whole theoretical picture in such an area as human abilities is changing" (p. 682).

Preparation of this chapter was supported by the Learning Technology Center at Peabody College, Vanderbilt University; the K-12 Learning Consortium Project; the Learning Research and Development Center at the University of Pittsburgh; the National Center for Research on Evaluation, Standards, and Student Testing (CRESST); and the Educational Testing Service. The views expressed are solely those of the authors. We would like to express our appreciation to Dave Lohman, Lorrie Shepard, and Ali Iran-Nejad for their constructive comments on drafts of this chapter. We would also like to thank Dave Law for his assistance in assembling and reviewing some of the material discussed in this chapter, as well as his reactions to earlier versions. We dedicate this chapter to our departed colleague and friend Richard Snow, whose career was dedicated to seeking out answers to difficult questions about the nature of human abilities, constantly probing how such knowledge could be profitably used to enhance education. Many of our thoughts and insights draw heavily from his seminal works addressing the two disciplines issues highlighted in this chapter.

No doubt, Cronbach was overly optimistic about what would and could be accomplished at the practical instructional level and at the theoretical level. Much, however, has changed in the ensuing 40-plus years. Developments in cognitive psychology, together with changes in the goals and standards for instructional practice and heightened demands for educational assessments to both reform and inform education, collectively establish a new context for considering the confluence of cognitive science and psychometrics. Advances in cognitive science, learning, and human development provide new perspectives for the design, administration, and use of assessments of academic achievement. It is our contention that these perspectives are critical if contemporary education is to achieve the goal of helping all students succeed academically. To accomplish such a goal, assessment practices must be based on contemporary understandings and appropriate standards regarding the acquisition of proficiency and expertise in specific academic content domains. Assessment could then have a significant positive influence on what is learned in classrooms and on how knowledge and competence are demonstrated in various contexts of educational consequence, ranging from the classroom to state and national assessments of educational attainment.

In this chapter, we probe several issues of historical and conceptual significance that provide a foundation for negotiating a necessary and fruitful coordination of cognitive psychology and psychometrics, as originally envisioned by Cronbach (1957) and as further articulated over time by others (e.g., Anastasi, 1967; Glaser, 1981). The 40-year odyssey that we recount includes significant theoretical developments in cognitive psychology and changes in assessment practice that are coincident with the changing sociopolitical context of education. Explicit in our discussion are the consequent challenges to the research community to harness theoretical developments in ways that are responsive to demands for educational equity and accountability. A contemporary cognitive perspective on assessment can inform the larger educational debate about what types of learning matter most, and it can lead to improved educational practice at the place where learning and instruction occur. In presenting our case, we call attention to progress that has been made together with unresolved conceptual issues and divergent theoretical perspectives that affect any prospects for a truly successful integration of cognition, instruction, and assessment.

We begin with a historical account of how empirical and theoretical efforts in cognitive psychology were linked to and supported the study of individual differences in performance and learning. Our discussion starts with the 1960s and aptitude-treatment interaction (ATI) research of the type originally mentioned by Cronbach, and it continues through the 1970s and 1980s with a brief review of the substantial body of work on cognitive process analyses of aptitude and achievement. Despite intense activity in these lines of research and theory, neither one obtained the hoped-for objective of creating a measurement milieu that substantially contributed to the enabling conditions of a psychology of instruction. Subsequent efforts during the 1980s and 1990s to study competent performance and expertise were more relevant to this purpose. From such work a theory of cognition has developed that includes models of learning and performance in knowledge-rich domains, the type of theory needed to accomplish the goals of affecting instructional practice and improving educational attainment, including the "what" and "how" of educational assessment.

As we entered the 1990s, national standards in multiple curriculum areas, together with the formulation and adoption of national education goals, were a dominant force in shaping American educational policy, including assessment practices. We consider efforts to respond to these sociopolitical forces through changes in achievement testing that took into account developments in both cognitive and curricular theory. Multiple-choice tests were put under scrutiny, and their shortcomings forced the development of alternative forms of assessment. Performance-based assessments and multilevel scoring procedures were offered alongside traditional multiple-choice tests as part of a response to the expanded role of assessment in addressing issues of educational policy and practice. As progress was made in the development of alternative methods of assessment for various summative and formative purposes, the conceptual discrepancies between contemporary cognitive theory and extant psychometric models and methods became especially apparent. Resolution, of necessity, requires reconceptualizing psychometric theory to harness the theoretical developments in cognition in ways that are responsive to educational needs at multiple levels of practice and policy.

The implications of all that has gone before and the prospects for the future with regard to fully developing a cognitive approach to assessment are the subject of the final two sections of this chapter. We consider contemporary attempts to bridge the conceptual divide and tightly couple cognitive theories with psychometric models, including separate developments in the areas of aptitude and achievement assessment. It appears that more progress has been made in linking cognitive constructs with the design and assessment of cognitive aptitudes and that much remains to be done in the assessment of domains of academic achievement. We also consider the possibilities of bringing together cognitive theories of aptitude and achievement in the context of interactions with instructional treatments. This brings us full circle relative to Cronbach's original concerns. In the final section of the chapter, we reflect on the current state of knowledge with regard to unifying cognition and assessment and consider what still needs to be done for a rapprochement of the "two disciplines" that effectively serves the educational needs of an increasingly diverse population of students.

DEVELOPMENTS LINKING INDIVIDUAL DIFFERENCES ASSESSMENT WITH COGNITIVE THEORY AND RESEARCH

Despite the elegance of his logic, Cronbach's arguments and exhortations for unification of the two disciplines largely fell on deaf ears. Some might argue that this was because he was wrong about the utility of such an enterprise. We would argue instead that his fundamental premises were not flawed and that the rapprochement he sought remains important and desirable. Unfortunately,

Cronbach's problem was one of feasibility. What he could not foresee was that the necessary empirical and theoretical foundation on which to develop such a unified approach to understanding and assessing cognition was unavailable, nor could he have known that this state of affairs would remain so for quite some time.

In the intervening years, there has been a remarkable transformation in the study of learning and cognition (see, e.g., Bransford, Brown, & Cocking, 1999). As a result, the nature of the interaction between research and theory on cognition and instruction and research and theory on individual differences has changed significantly over the decades since Cronbach's address. The resultant state of knowledge and understanding renders it conceivable that some of what Cronbach wished for in 1957 might be attainable in the foreseeable future. To see how far we have come, as well as to appreciate what we have yet to do, we provide a recapitulation and analysis of some of the historical developments connecting research on learning and cognition with research on individual differences. We do so by selectively focusing on research in two broad areas: aptitude-treatment interactions and cognitive analyses of aptitude and expertise.

The Pursuit of Aptitude-Treatment Interactions

Cronbach's call to integrate differential and experimental psychology described the conflict between scientific traditions that originated in different conceptions of the natural world. Differential psychology, a "conservative" tradition, originated in the works of Darwin, Spencer, and Galton, whereas experimental psychology, a "liberal" tradition, originated in the works of Ward, James, and Dewey. Differential psychology attempted to identify the individual who would perform best in the environment, whereas experimental psychology tried to identify the environment that would work best for all individuals. In considering the future of these somewhat parallel lines of work for improving instruction, Cronbach (1957) concluded: "The greatest social benefit will come from applied psychology if we can find for each individual the treatment to which he can most easily adapt. This calls for the joint application of experimental and correlational methods" (p. 679).

Cronbach asked the two schools to pool their efforts in the combined evaluation of aptitudes and learning treatments with the expectation that some aptitudes would show strong interactions with educational treatments. For example, it was thought that using diagrams and figural materials would promote learning among individuals with high spatial ability. The effects of general aptitudes such as Spearman's *g*, however, were believed to effectively span all treatments and thus were expected to be less involved in ATIs. It was hoped that the combined study of aptitudes and educational treatments would form the basis of a new science benefiting both individuals and society as a whole (e.g., Cronbach & Gleser, 1957). By capitalizing on knowledge about specific ATIs, it would be possible for students lower in general aptitude to reach higher levels of achievement than were customary in the one-size-fits-all world of traditional education.

Almost 20 years later, Glaser framed the issues of assessment and learning in terms of a new "linking science." This psychology of instruction, argued Glaser (1976), would function prescriptively, turning knowledge gleaned from learning laboratories into instructional designs. As part of the prescription, individual learners would be matched by their initial states to optimal instructional treatments. Thus, the overall goal of the new science, and especially the combination of two of its components—describing the initial state of the learner and creating conditions that foster competence—was essentially an ATI design. To make this all possible would require the adoption of a new attitude toward assessment, namely, that it could be instrumental in providing information to improve instruction. This in turn would be facilitated by the development of new assessments of the specific cognitive processes and structures involved in academic learning and performance.

By 1975, two major research endeavors had begun that, at least in part, were based on the expectation that the study of ATIs would be useful in improving educational achievement. Nevertheless, in 1975, when Cronbach (p. 116) once again addressed the APA, he said, "the line of investigation that I advocated in 1957 no longer seems sufficient . . . complexity forces us to ask once again, Should social science aspire to reduce behavior to laws?" Essentially, evaluating ATIs turned out to be more complex than originally expected, as the effects of educational treatments and their interactions with student aptitudes were found to be highly contextualized. This created higher order interactions that were less generalizable than the first-order interactions envisioned in the original ATI proposal. Also, the confounding variables in the higher order interactions were often not part of the experimental design and were detected only post hoc in the context of a number of experiments providing similarly enigmatic results. Instructional implementation, teachers' perspectives and attitudes, and students' attitudes, maturation, and socioeconomic status were just a few among many variables that complicated the ATI picture. This is particularly problematic because higher order interactions, aside from being more difficult to interpret, are more difficult to show statistically as a result of the decrease in statistical power as the order of an interaction increases. Thus, statistically nonsignificant interactions became uninterpreted interactions, which in turn supported contradictory findings and precluded any general statement that could serve as a guide in instructional decisions.

Cronbach (1975) suggested that dealing with the problems of ATI research would require a more sophisticated approach that dealt with the combined challenges of complexity, statistical significance testing, and the ever-present factor of change. In particular, he was concerned with the practices of accepting the null hypothesis and reporting F statistics and associated significance levels without concern for practical significance. He suggested deemphasizing statistical significance testing in favor of using components of variance, effect sizes, and confidence intervals to evaluate the practical significance of variables and their interactions. Regarding complexity and change, Cronbach stressed that empirical relationships change with changes in time and place and the overall context in which research is conducted. Accordingly, researchers should attempt to observe and report the boundary conditions that limit generalizations of their findings. Apparently, this is what Cronbach meant when he questioned the utility of seeking psychological laws, which presumably would cover all persons at all times.

In 1977, Cronbach and Snow presented a book-length review of more than a decade's worth of ATI research. Among the conclusions they arrived at were the following: (a) ATIs do exist; (b) as yet, no ATI hypothesis had been sufficiently confirmed to serve as a basis for instructional practice; and (c) contrary to earlier predictions, general abilities enter into interactions more often than specific abilities. Snow (1989a, p. 21) noted it as an interesting aspect of the sociology of science that many cited the review as involving a negative conclusion, when "a thorough examination of it should lead to quite the opposite conclusion." Although they realized that there might be decades of research preceding an ultimate resolution, Cronbach and Snow remained generally optimistic regarding the potential utility of ATIs. Others, however, saw things somewhat differently:

> Even if one includes a general mental ability, which appears to interact relatively more often with certain instructional treatments than more specialized abilities, the overall conclusion regarding mental aptitude measures is that "no interactions are so well confirmed that they can be used as guides to instruction." In those occasional instances when positive results were obtained, no general principles emerged because the findings were rarely sustained when new subject matter tasks were used or when similar studies on the same tasks were undertaken. (Bond & Glaser, 1979, p. 139)

As implied in the preceding comments, the most consistent findings in ATI research are that general aptitudes interact with instruction (Cronbach & Snow, 1977; Snow, 1989a, 1994). This was surprising, because general aptitudes were not originally expected to be involved in ATIs but were expected to affect all treatments equally. Furthermore, general aptitudes were thought of as supporting a single rank ordering of individuals, and the ultimate goal of ATI research is to disrupt such rankings. However, in hindsight it becomes apparent that if one wants to disrupt a rank ordering, look first at what supports the ranking. In most cases, aptitude-treatment regressions involving general aptitudes are steeper in low-structure treatments, showing rapidly increasing benefit as aptitude increases, and shallower in high-structure treatments, providing potentially better outcomes for low-aptitude students. For example, elaborated materials tend to benefit low-aptitude students, whereas treatments that put the burden of organization on the learner tend to benefit high-aptitude students. Similarly, discovery learning tends to benefit high-aptitude students, whereas direct instruction tends to benefit low-aptitude students. Reversing the optimal treatment level for either group of students can also have detrimental effects. According to Snow (1989a, 1994), typical teaching is generally between the extremes of high and low structure but is probably closer to low structure than high. A number of personality traits or conative aptitudes also appear regularly in ATIs (see Snow, 1989b).

The failure of ATI research to prescribe assistance to instruction as was origi-nally intended suggested, among other things, that standardized tests may be inappropriate measures for this purpose. The assumption that the label of a particular aptitude measure had direct implications for instructional practice was generally false (e.g., pairing a spatial aptitude test with treatment procedures that deemphasized verbal content in instruction). The mere absence of words (diagrams, for example) by no means implies the presence of abilities required in such tests. When "off the shelf" aptitude measures were not available, investigators developed their own based on an analysis of what was sensible to measure, and, not surprisingly, the results were generally more informative. Although established tests of aptitude or general ability were reliable, they could not compete with information about learning processes afforded by tests specially constructed for experimental work (Bond & Glaser, 1979; Pellegrino & Glaser, 1979).

In short, there was a mismatch between the aptitude measures derived from a psychometric selection-oriented tradition and the processes of learning and performance under investigation in experimental and developmental psychology. The use of traditional psychometric instruments for fruitful ATI research requires a careful analysis of processes that relate aptitude, treatment, and the knowledge or skills being learned. Testable theories are required that describe competencies measured in the pretest, competencies required for task performance, and treatment procedures that connect the two (Snow, 1980). However, at the time of the initial ATI work, sufficient theories were not available to support those efforts.

For various reasons, including the developments considered next, enthusiasm for ATIs had waned considerably by the beginning of the 1980s, and this line of inquiry never emerged as a significant theoretical and empirical enterprise. Within the last decade, however, a small number of researchers have conducted what might be termed "second-generation" ATI research. This line of work carefully addresses some of the theoretical issues that plagued earlier work and has yielded some potentially interesting outcomes (e.g., Shute, 1993; Swanson, 1990). Further discussion of such work and its implications is presented in a later section.

Cognitive Analyses of Aptitude and Expertise

By the end of the 1960s and at the beginning of the 1970s, an emerging psychology of human cognition was focused on explicating the mental structures and processes underlying various simple and complex performances. The terminology of information processing, accompanied by the methodology of reaction time and protocol analyses, came to dominate the empirical and theoretical landscape. During the 1970s, it occurred to some resolute educational, cognitive, and developmental psychologists that it might be possible to accomplish part of what Cronbach originally suggested, that is, link individual differences in aptitude to constructs emanating from laboratory research on cognition. Because intelligence and aptitude tests are essentially measures of scholastic ability, it was also thought that one way to increase our understanding of academic achievement, and perhaps even improve it, would be to develop process-based performance models for intelligence and aptitude test items. From such knowledge, basic cognitive abilities might be identified that could then be influenced by instructional programs. Carroll (1978) described the situation as follows:

The performances required on many types of mental ability tests—tests of language competence, of ability to manipulate abstract concepts and relationships, of ability to apply knowledge to the solution of problems, and even of the ability to make simple and rapid comparisons of stimuli (as in a test of perceptual speed)—have great and obvious resemblances to performances required in school learning, and indeed in many other fields of human activity. If these performances are seen as based on learned, developed abilities of a rather generalized character, it would frequently be useful to assess the extent to which an individual has acquired these abilities. This could be for the purpose of determining the extent to which these abilities would need to be improved to prepare the individual for further experiences or learning activities, or determining what kinds and amounts of intervention might be required to effect such improvements. These determinations, however, would have to be based on more exact information than we now have concerning the effects of different types of learning experiences . . . on the improvements of these abilities. (pp. 93–94)

Extensive programs of research on the cognitive analysis of aptitude and intelligence began in the 1970s. Researchers pursued two complementary approaches to studying individual differences in cognitive abilities, termed the cognitive correlates approach and the cognitive components approach (Pellegrino & Glaser, 1979). The cognitive correlates approach consisted of assessing relationships between performances on psychometric ability tests with parameters derived from standard laboratory information-processing tasks. Typically, subjects were divided into high- and low-ability groups based on external aptitude test scores (e.g., Scholastic Aptitude Test [SAT] scores), and between-group analyses were conducted in which various parameters for basic information-processing operations, such as stimulus encoding and matching, memory search, and response execution, were used as dependent variables. Thus, the cognitive correlates approach attempted to explain differential performance on standard aptitude measures by using theory-based information-processing constructs. A significant mean difference between high- and low-ability groups suggested that the structure or process represented by the cognitive task parameter was instrumental in ability test performance. Overall, the cognitive correlates approach is best exemplified by the work of Hunt and his colleagues on verbal ability (Hunt, 1978; Hunt, Frost, & Lunnenborg, 1973; Hunt & Lansman, 1975) and is typified in the title of the article "What Does It Mean to Be High Verbal?" (Hunt, Lunnenborg, & Lewis, 1975). This approach was also used successfully to elucidate the varying nature of reading ability differences as represented in the extensive work done by Perfetti and his colleagues (see, e.g., Perfetti & Goldman, 1976; Perfetti & Hoagaboam, 1975; Perfetti & Lesgold, 1982).

The cognitive components (or task analytical) approach attempted to directly understand the components of performance underlying individuals' solution of items used to assess intelligence and aptitude. Working from detailed task analyses, the objective was to develop models of task performance and use these process models for analyzing individual differences. Information-processing parameters were then derived and used as the basis for explaining high and low scores. The cognitive components approach assessed performance strategies, executive routines, and also declarative and procedural knowledge that interacted with processing capabilities varying across individuals (Snow & Lohman, 1989). The componential approach has been highly influential in modeling performance in domains such as spatial transformation (e.g., Kyllonen, Lohman, & Woltz, 1984; Mumaw & Pellegrino, 1984; Pellegrino & Kail, 1982; Shepard & Cooper, 1983) and inductive and deductive reasoning (e.g., Goldman & Pellegrino, 1984; Kotovsky & Simon, 1973; Pellegrino & Glaser, 1982; Sternberg, 1977), domains that are primarily process based rather than knowledge based. The latter distinction became increasingly important as researchers pursued more complex domains of performance and more direct measures of learning within such domains.

Collectively, the cognitive correlates and cognitive components approaches provided substantial information regarding individual differences in performance on cognitive ability tests. Much of the work that has been done is both theoretically and methodologically elegant and, from a scientific standpoint, served to demonstrate how cognitive psychology could be effectively applied to analyzing important domains of human performance. Significant work in this vein continues, most notably in the study of individual differences in attentional processes, dynamic spatial reasoning (e.g., Law, Pellegrino, & Hunt, 1993; Pellegrino & Hunt, 1989), information coordination (Law, Morrin, & Pellegrino, 1995; Morrin, Law, & Pellegrino, 1994), and related instances of basic information processing (e.g., Kyllonen, 1993). Characteristic of this work is a focus on aspects of cognition that are largely structure and process oriented, and individual differences tend to be closely linked to limitations of the information-processing architecture such as working memory capacity and processing speed (e.g., Woltz, 1988; Woltz & Shute, 1993).

Despite the contributions of this line of cognitive research and theory, it has fallen short of its primary objective of developing measurement procedures that could inform teaching and learning. Lohman (1994) has suggested that there are at least two reasons for the apparent failure: (a) The assumption that psychometric tests would make good cognitive tasks, or vice versa, was generally false, and (b) cognitive performance does not decompose into components as neatly as was hypothesized. Lohman suggests that process analyses of individual performance are most useful when there are instructionally relevant differences in how subjects perform, and these kinds of differences are not likely to be found in psychometric test items designed and selected to produce homogeneous patterns of response. The regression slope, which is often the parameter of interest in componential models, is a product of the Person × Item interaction, and being a component of measurement error it is generally minimized in standardized ability tests. Furthermore, when heterogeneous performance does occur, it is likely to create problems for the regression model, and this is particularly true if the heterogeneity is within individuals.

Another fundamental problem with this entire approach is that many of the tasks and performances that have served as the focus of intensive study are very distal to the classroom learning environments and learning activities that one would ultimately hope to affect. A beginning identification of this problem can be discerned in the comments of Lauren Resnick (1979), who raised questions about the ultimate benefits of this approach to the study of individual differences at the time it was a burgeoning enterprise:

The assumption appears to be that these processes will be, in the main, the same ones called upon in performing important school tasks. I believe this assumption may be largely incorrect. Let me explain why. It seems probable that it is not *performance* on IQ tests that involves the same processes as learning in school. Rather it is *learning how* to perform well on IQ tests that involves the same processes. . . . I think it is highly unlikely that current IQ tests, even with the reinterpretation that is now proceeding, will be able to do this. Instead we will need tests that are more direct measures of the processes involved in *learning* to perform test and school tasks. I think these tests are likely to be actual samples of learning on tasks chosen to display the relevant processes as directly as possible. (Resnick, 1979, pp. 212–213)

Resnick's comments, although critical of the logic of the general approach, maintain a focus on the processes of cognition, an emphasis that was the dominant theoretical motif in cognitive psychology during the 1970s. The emphasis on process continued during the 1980s, although the nature of the tasks that were studied changed substantially as the field of cognitive psychology matured. In particular, researchers began to move beyond the study of processing in artificial or "toy" tasks and took on the serious and difficult task of modeling performance in complex domains of achievement in which knowledge as well as process was a significant hallmark of accomplishment and expertise.

Early examples of cognitive task analysis in school subjects (e.g., Klahr, 1977; Lesgold, Pellegrino, Fokkema, & Glaser, 1977) used information-processing concepts to describe various domains of achievement. Detailed models were developed and applied to the analysis of procedural knowledge components of the mathematics curriculum, including addition, subtraction, multiplication, and operations with fractions (Brown & Burton, 1978). Performance in a domain such as geometry required a more complicated set of models encompassing procedures and knowledge structures represented within a production system architecture, including cognitive mechanisms for setting goals and searching a problem space. In other complex domains of learning and performance, the modeling focused on conceptual knowledge, which was represented as semantic and propositional networks. Attention also turned to the analysis of forms of problem representation, the transfer of learning and problem solving to new situations, and ultimately to the characteristics of knowledge and performance that distinguish novice from expert performance.

The pioneering work of de Groot (1946/1978) on chess masters introduced the study of expertise, and a quarter century passed before the follow-up studies by Chase and Simon (1973) began to influence cognitive research and theory. Despite the seeming disconnection between chess and education, the paradigm of contrasting experts and novices both informed and stimulated the subsequent study of expertise in fields as diverse as physics (Chi, Feltovich, & Glaser, 1981), volleyball (Allard & Starkes, 1980), medicine (Lesgold et al., 1988; Patel & Groen, 1986), and writing (Bereiter & Scardamalia, 1987). A psychology of subject-matter expertise and complex learning slowly developed, and the study of individual differences became firmly embedded in domains of endeavor that were acquired over long periods of time.

Ultimately, the study of expertise and competence emerged as an alternative approach to the study of individual differences, one that was no longer linked to psychometrically defined constructs of aptitude or intelligence and their associated artifacts such as test item types. Rather, the study of individual differences focused on attained knowledge and related cognitive processes that are the object of deliberate instruction, practice, and learning. Verbal protocols and expert-novice comparisons provided the building blocks for a theory of expertise that described the acquisition and structure of declarative and procedural knowledge in various domains of human performance (Chi, Glaser, & Farr, 1988). In contrast to process-based aptitude performance, which was the focus of much of the research conducted in the 1970s, expertise is both knowledge based and process based; the primary process, and perhaps the characterizing feature of expertise (see, e.g., Bereiter & Scardamalia, 1993), is the continuous acquisition and restructuring of domain-based knowledge.

By the beginning of the 1990s, cognitive psychology and the study of individual differences had matured to the point where the groundwork was laid for fulfilling three of the four conditions necessary to achieve a psychology of instruction (Glaser, 1976). Analyses of competence and expertise were plentiful. Numerous descriptions existed of novice performance and misconceptions in multiple domains of achievement. There were even the beginnings of work focused on the design of conditions that foster the acquisition of competence taking into account theories of learning and expertise, including an extensive body of work on metacognitive monitoring (Brown & Palinscar, 1989), self-explanation (Chi, Bassock, Lewis, Reimann, & Glaser, 1989), and the deliberate employment of various strategies for text comprehension (Cote, Goldman, & Saul, 1998; Goldman, 1997). All of the work was firmly rooted in a rich psychology of cognition and cognitive development.

While it may have been overly optimistic, the argument was nonetheless made that the stage had been set for substantial changes in how issues of assessment could be approached.

Essential characteristics of proficient performance have been described in various domains and provide useful indices for assessment. We know that, at specific stages of learning, there exist different integrations of knowledge, different forms of skill, differences in access to knowledge, and differences in the efficiency of performance. These stages can define criteria for test design. We can now propose a set of candidate dimensions along which subject-matter competence can be assessed. As competence in a subject-matter grows, evidence of a knowledge base that is increasingly coherent, principled, useful and goal-oriented is displayed, and test items can be designed to capture such evidence. (Glaser, 1991, p. 26)

Such optimism about what was now known and about the possibilities for genuine change in assessment design and practice was reinforced more recently by Greeno,

Pearson, and Schoenfeld (1997) in the course of evaluating many of the cumulative results of cognitive science research on expertise and understanding in the domains of mathematics and literacy. Greeno et al. (1997) frame their discussion of what is now known squarely in the context of the opportunities, issues, and conundrums that such knowledge poses for an effective integration with assessment and instructional practice. We consider these issues further in the subsequent two sections after first discussing some aspects of the policy landscape that have profoundly shaped current assessment practice.

INTEGRATING COGNITIVE THEORY AND RESEARCH WITH ASSESSMENT AND INSTRUCTIONAL PRACTICES

While cognitive theory and research made substantial progress toward understanding and explicating individual differences in a wide array of cognitive performances, the worlds of assessment and instruction also underwent a number of important changes. Critical to these changes was a fundamental policy shift regarding the purpose and objectives of education, with increased demands for tests to simultaneously monitor and promote instructional changes. These changes, which set the stage and created an impetus for connecting cognitive and curricular theory with assessment practices, are briefly reviewed here. Subsequently, we recount efforts of the last two decades to align assessment with calls for curricular changes and conclude with the implications of this work for achievement testing.

An Impetus for Change

At the time of Cronbach's 1957 address, certain seminal changes in the world of assessment were already under way. For example, standardized, norm-referenced achievement test batteries had become an established part of educational practice, and their use was as prevalent as that of aptitude test batteries, if not more so. Questions about the condition of our schools and about levels of students' academic achievement received particular attention as the Soviets' launching of Sputnik fueled fears of a decrease in America's international dominance and a threat to future national security. Stemming from these and other events was a wave of educational reform with increased emphasis on mathematics and science preparation for the academically talented.

The post-Sputnik era of the 1960s also witnessed increased access to educational opportunity, particularly with respect to students with special educational needs. Federal legislation obliged the states to assume responsibility for the provision of equal educational opportunity. In 1965, the Elementary and Secondary Education Act (ESEA), Title I, called for financial assistance and special services for low-income students and districts and required performance data on students receiving assistance and evaluation data on outcomes of funded programs. As interest and enthusiasm grew for indicators that would measure progress toward the goal of providing all students with a good education, questions were raised about the quality and content of American education.

The federal government responded with two initiatives. The first was the Equality of Educational Opportunity Survey (EEOS), which provided information on the achievement of more than 600,000 children in elementary and secondary schools. The analysis of these data, the Coleman Report (Coleman et al., 1966), documented the enormous variation in achievement of 12th graders and showed that graduation rates revealed little about what graduates learned in school. More revealing forms of assessment seemed necessary.

The second federal initiative of the 1960s was the creation of the National Assessment of Educational Progress (NAEP). As the first of the successive waves of NAEP scores appeared, clear differences in the scores of various populations of students called into question the impact of reforms and brought to the forefront issues of educational equity and opportunity. Concerns about the achievements of American students have been amplified over time by numerous documents and reports using NAEP and other indicator data, including the 1983 publication of *A Nation at Risk* (National Commission for Educational Excellence, 1983). Issuance of the latter constituted a watershed in promoting public awareness of issues regarding American education.

Searching questions about the quality of education persist, and increasingly they have taken shape through debate focused on issues of accountability. Citizens, educators, and policymakers, at multiple levels from local school districts to the federal bureaucracy, want to know whether the investments that have been made in education in the ensuing decades are reaping rewards. Thus, efforts to devise useful assessment and accountability measures have proliferated along with separate state assessment programs. The federal initiative expanded so that the NAEP could provide state data and facilitate cross-state comparisons in a number of subject areas at specific grade levels. The first trial state assessments were administered in 1992, and through the NAEP program states can now compare the performance of their students with that of students in other states and the nation at large.

The 1990s also ushered in the standards-based reform movement (e.g., Bush, 1991; National Education Goals Panel, 1991), a broad national policy agenda involving content standards (i.e., what students should know), delivery standards (i.e., how schools will ensure that all students have a fair chance of achieving the standards), and performance standards (i.e., the level at which students should know the important content). Representative of such a trend is the May 1990 action of the National Assessment Governing Board in approving a document endorsing the establishment of three national levels of subject-matter achievement: basic, proficient, and advanced. These performance standards were then slated to be incorporated into reporting of the national assessment results. The generation, reporting, and validation of outcomes relative to such standards has become an issue of considerable study and debate within the NAEP assessment program (National Academy of Education, 1993, 1997; National Research Council, 1999). Various validity concerns have been raised, including the small numbers of students supposedly performing at the proficient level. In separate developments, recent results from the Third International Mathematics and Science Study

(TIMMS) have drawn attention to variations across Grades 4, 8, and 12 in the performance of American students relative to their counterparts in other countries. The TIMMS data have also highlighted differential curricular emphases and teaching practices across countries that may account for some of the observed performance differences.

Changing the Nature of Assessment Practice

The stage was thus set for changes in cognitive, curricular, and instructional theory to have an impact on assessment practice during the decade of the 1980s. In addition to the general influences noted earlier, two specific issues are worth mentioning as they propelled research to focus the assessment-instruction debate in ways that highlighted one over the other. The first was rooted in arguments concerning the pervasive negative influence of standardized tests on instructional practices. It was claimed that the content and format of typical achievement tests unduly influenced both the "what" and the "how" of teaching and learning. Standardized tests were seen as perpetuating a focus on memorization of isolated bits of factual knowledge and procedures that could be easily retrieved on tests composed largely of multiple-choice items (e.g., Fredericksen, 1984). Such an approach to assessment and instruction was largely a product of earlier behaviorist assumptions about the nature of knowledge and learning (see also Greeno et al., 1997). In contrast, important aspects of cognition and learning such as conceptual understanding, reasoning, and complex problem solving were often ignored, in part because they were more difficult to implement in the context of standardized assessments of achievement. As a consequence, these aspects of cognition and achievement were often neglected in the classroom learning milieu. The logic of the argument regarding negative consequences was that if important performances were not required on the tests, then they would not be the focus of work in the classroom.

In somewhat separate developments, the new curricular standards also fueled a desire to expand the scope of instructional practice to encompass broader goals for student learning (e.g., National Council of Teachers of Mathematics [NCTM], 1989; National Research Council, 1996). Work began on improving the content and process of classroom learning and largely deemphasized dominant assessment approaches. The latter were perceived as generally irrelevant to the types of teaching and learning that were desired. Much of the effort in this area was closely tied to emergent cognitive science understandings of the nature of reasoning and problem solving in knowledge-rich domains of achievement and the emergent efforts at curricular reform in mathematics and science.

In what follows, we first describe initial efforts to change the nature of assessment practice and the impact of these exploratory efforts on the current state of testing. We then provide examples of classroom assessment practices specifically designed to guide teaching and learning. Each approach highlights important considerations for the future of linking cognition and assessment.

Assessment-Driven Instruction

The perceived power of assessments to reform curriculum and instruction—and, as a consequence, improve teaching and learning—stimulated numerous development efforts in state and national testing programs (National Council on Education Standards and Testing, 1992). These large-scale testing efforts were influenced simultaneously by a cognitive perspective on thinking, reasoning, and problem solving in subject matters and traditional psychometric concerns for reliability and validity. With a goal toward influencing instructional practice (i.e., assessment-driven instruction), a number of significant changes were introduced to the design of assessments. First, the development process was informed by multiple perspectives, including cognitive psychologists, teachers, and subject-matter and measurement specialists. Second, the tasks generally consisted of open-ended prompts or exercises requiring students to write explanations, carry out a set of procedures, design investigations, or otherwise reason with targeted subject matter. Third, innovative multilevel scoring criteria or rubrics that gave consideration to procedures, strategies, and quality of response were favored over right/wrong scoring. Not surprisingly, given the state of the art, psychometric properties, particularly reliability, were of primary concern, as were practical considerations such as the time and cost of administration and scoring.

Connecticut and California provided models for other state testing programs, as they were among the first to develop and pilot new forms of assessment as part of statewide testing programs. Connecticut experimented with a variety of item or task forms, including extended performances involving groups of students, oral presentations, self-assessment, and model-based reasoning. California emphasized written explanations in mathematics and science and coordinated performance-based assessments tied to real-world situations such as recycling. Scoring rubrics were introduced as a way to judge the qualitative differences in student performance, and exemplars of various levels of understanding were provided for this purpose. Experienced teachers were recruited to develop various task forms in ways that were aligned with curricular frameworks for content and cognitive outcomes (e.g., application, inference). Furthermore, large numbers of teachers participated in the scoring of statewide samples of student responses to these new forms of assessment.

The application and use of rubrics to describe performance was viewed as a means to provide large-scale professional development in ways that would potentially affect classroom practice. Teachers, it was thought, would take from their scoring experiences innovative ideas for changing their own instructional practices, particularly an appreciation for observable qualitative differences in performance that signal relative understanding in a subject matter. The assumption that teachers will teach to the test rests on the notion that good tests will lead to good instruction. However, as we describe later, empirical support for the quality of the measures was not forthcoming for some time.

At about the time various states were experimenting with new forms of assessment, researchers in a number of disciplines began efforts to develop and articulate procedures for the design and evaluation of performance-based assessments that were predicated on constructive notions of teaching and learning (e.g., Baker, Freeman, & Clayton, 1991). Essentially, these exploratory efforts were subject specific, guided by a diverse range of participants (teachers, subject-matter and measurement specialists), and pursued under the broad umbrellas of cognitive psychology, curriculum reform, and traditional psychometric concerns for reliability and validity. Two examples follow, one in mathematics and one in science.

QUASAR (Quantitative Understanding: Amplifying Student Achievement and Reasoning), a national project, was designed to improve mathematics instruction for middle school students in economically disadvantaged communities (Silver & Stein, 1996). As part of this project, a set of open-ended assessment tasks was developed to monitor and evaluate the impact of the mathematics instructional program in participating schools. It is important to note that the tasks composing the QUASAR Cognitive Assessment Instrument (QCAI) were linked to important cross-program instructional goals, not within-school curriculum. Specifications for the QCAI were based on the construct domain of mathematics, as described in the *Curriculum and Evaluation Standards for School Mathematics* (NCTM, 1989), and included three components: cognitive processes (understanding mathematical concepts and procedures, problem solving, reasoning, creating mathematical arguments), mathematical content (number and operation, estimation, patterns, algebra, geometry and measurement, data analysis, probability and statistics), and modes of representation (pictorial, graphic, tabular, arithmetic and algebraic symbolic representations). A focused-holistic scoring rubric was developed for each task, and student performance was scored on a scale of 0 to 4, with each score level indicating a qualitatively different combination of mathematical knowledge, strategic knowledge, and communication skills (Lane, 1993).

In the area of science, Shavelson, Baxter, and Pine used a sampling theory approach to select tasks from a domain and then focus analysis on the extent to which students' performance on the sample of tasks was generalizable to the larger domain. Students were given a problem (e.g., determine the content of six boxes) and relevant equipment (batteries, bulbs, wires) and asked to document their answer and how they arrived at that answer (i.e., evidence). This task-based approach to assessment development was deliberately sensitive to the differential effectiveness of procedures or solution strategies as an essential criterion for evaluating performance (Baxter, Shavelson, Goldman, & Pine, 1992). For each of the developed assessments, student performance was scored in terms of the correctness of the answer and the quality of the procedures, strategies, or evidence used to support one's answer. Generalizability studies indicated that student performance was low and inconsistent across tasks and that assessment methods (e.g., hands on, computer, short answer) tapped different aspects of performance (Shavelson, Baxter, & Gao, 1993). Correlational evidence suggests that the performance-based measures are only moderately associated with standardized measures of aptitude and achievement. Furthermore, the performance of students with differing instructional histories was distinguishable on knowledge-based tasks and not on the tasks that required science-process skills with minimal demands for science content knowledge.

Initial efforts, such as those described, to develop alternative forms of assessment were of great interest to various audiences, and the outcomes of these efforts laid important groundwork for ensuing developments. Technical concerns, particularly the generalizability of performance across tasks, and practical concerns for cost of developing, administering, and scoring these new forms of assessment led to more complex assessment designs in which multiple methods were mixed. Content coverage could be accomplished through multiple-choice items, and cognitive concerns for thinking and reasoning might be more appropriately measured through a select number of constructed response or performance-based measures.

Their impact on large-scale testing (e.g., the NAEP program) notwithstanding, these efforts had minimal impact on instruction, in part because they were somewhat divorced from specific opportunities to learn. Rather, samples of tasks from curricular frameworks were administered and scored regardless of whether students had studied the topic or not. Typically, content coverage matters overrode cognitive considerations in task development, in part because there was no experience, guidelines, or models for how to do otherwise. More important, a number of studies suggested that the relatively poor performance of students was indicative of a lack of domain-specific knowledge, which imposed constraints on the ability of students to think and reason with their knowledge in differing contexts (Baxter, Elder, & Glaser, 1996; Baxter & Glaser, 1998; Hamilton, Nussbaum, & Snow, 1997; Magone, Cai, Silver, & Wang, 1994). The message emerging from this entire line of activity is that embedding assessments in the curriculum is essential if the goal is to use assessment innovations to influence and shape teaching and learning in ways consistent with instructional goals envisioned by reformers.

Validity and Effectiveness Concerns

As noted earlier, much of the assessment development effort in the 1980s through the early 1990s was guided by curricular frameworks that articulated in various forms the content and cognitive constructs to be assessed. Goals for assessing higher order thinking, problem solving, reasoning, and the like were stated prior to development of test items and tasks, but procedures for evaluating the extent to which these goals were achieved in the final assessment batteries were seldom undertaken. Nor were procedures or structures available to guide assessment development to ensure that goals were achieved. Linn, Baker, and Dunbar (1991), among others, cautioned that surface-level changes in assessments (e.g., constructed response, multiple scoring levels) were not sufficient to ensure that relevant cognitive processes were being tapped or that the tasks were any more complex than traditional forced-choice items. They suggested a set of "special" validity criteria to emphasize the unique characteristics of these "new" forms of assessment. These include consequences, fairness, transfer and generalizability, cognitive complexity, content quality, content coverage, meaningfulness, cost, and efficiency.

Techniques and methods for gathering and evaluating relevant evidence of these criteria have only begun to appear in the literature. Hamilton, Nussbaum, and Snow (1997) report on the use of interview procedures to supplement traditional psychometric analysis. Fifth-grade students were observed and interviewed while carrying out a science performance task. Six categories of cognitive demands were identified from the protocols: use of working memory, use of language and communication, metacognitive skills, application of prior knowledge and expectations, acquisition of new knowledge, and use of scientific processes. Analysis of a number of performance tasks led the authors to conclude that "interviews help in a new way to identify the actual cognitive demands and affordances of the test and the function in test performance of different kinds of content knowledge and reasoning for different students" (Hamilton, Nussbaum, & Snow, 1997, p. 199).

In a related effort, Baxter and Glaser (1998) subjected a variety of assessment tasks and scoring criteria to a cognitive analysis, using as a basis for their approach cognitive theories of expertise and competence. For this purpose, they developed an analytic framework that considers the nature of cognitive activity likely to be elicited by tasks with particular requirements for science content and science process skills. The cognitive activities, derived from studies on expertise, included problem representation, monitoring, strategy use, and explanation. As the subject-matter demands for content increase from lean to rich and the science process demands increase from constrained to open, consequent changes in opportunities for students to display each of these cognitive dimensions are afforded. For example, tasks that are content rich but process constrained permit opportunities for explanation but little else. In contrast, tasks that are content rich and process open provide opportunities for students to display knowledge-based differences in problem representation, monitoring, strategy use, and explanation.

Using this cognitive-content framework, Baxter and Glaser analyzed the extent to which alternative assessments are measuring cognitive capabilities that distinguish levels of competence. Examples from analyses of a diverse range of science assessments developed in state and district testing programs illustrate (a) matches and mismatches between the intentions of test developers (i.e., measure higher order thinking) and the nature and extent of cognitive activity elicited in an assessment situation and (b) the correspondence between the quality of observed cognitive activity and performance scores. In particular, a number of the tasks did not provide opportunities for students to display differential levels of understanding. In other situations, scoring systems were designed in ways that attended to the superficial aspects of performance—those that are easy to count, for example—rather than the quality of the thinking and reasoning underlying performance.

As this work demonstrates, changes in task format and scoring criteria did not always result in fundamental changes in what was being assessed. The problem, in part, stemmed from a lack of sufficient theory and technique to guide a more informed approach. In part, however, the problem stemmed from the context in which the assessments were designed and used (i.e., large-scale testing programs). As we describe in the following sections, the link between the instructional experiences of students and measures of learning is easier to forge within a classroom than across schools and districts in a state.

Integrating Assessments With Instructional Practice

During the 1990s, a body of work emerged that pursues a different route to improving learning outcomes by focusing directly on integrating assessment into classroom practice rather than attempting to change classroom practice indirectly through large-scale, externally administered assessments. An underlying premise behind this work is that the development and implementation of classroom-based assessment is fundamental to creating enhanced learning outcomes and opportunities for all students, especially when dealing with challenging subject matter and high expectations regarding conceptual understanding, reasoning, and transfer. As such, cognitive theories of knowledge and performance served as a basis for the design of learning environments and associated assessment practices to be used in diagnosing student understandings, monitoring the effects of instruction on learning, and promoting knowledge construction in these situations (e.g., Cognition and Technology Group at Vanderbilt [CTGV], 1997, 1998; Duschl & Gitomer, 1997; Hunt & Minstrell, 1994; Minstrell, 1992, 1999; White & Fredericksen, 1998).

Classroom-based formative assessment strategies have also been recognized as fundamental to implementing the new standards for instruction recommended by groups such as the National Research Council (1996) and the National Council of Teachers of Mathematics (1989). Such standards emphasize the importance of teaching in ways that promote deep understanding by students. To accomplish such ends for all students, teachers need to be more aware of the preconceptions that their students bring to new learning situations, to teach in ways that make students' thinking ''visible'' to themselves and other students, and to help students reflect on and reconcile their conceptions with those of others. Formative assessment thus becomes an essential part of the repertoire of effective teaching behaviors.

A recent review of classroom-based formative assessment by Black and Wiliam (1998) shows that such practices can have significant effects on overall student learning outcomes, with typical effect sizes of between .4 and .7. However, the same review reveals relatively sparse evidence of widespread deployment of such formative assessment practices. The Black and Wiliam findings are understandable, since the integration of formative assessment into classroom instructional practice can be a time- and information-intensive process. It must be managed, monitored, and used in environments with high levels of information flow and potential information overload. Thus, it is often difficult for teachers to instantiate and sustain serious formative assessment in environments that lack sophisticated data storage, manipulation, and feedback systems. It is not surprising, then, that various forms of technology have often proven useful in implementing successful formative assessment strategies at the classroom level. This is not to imply, however, that formative assessment integral to instructional practice is predicated on a technology infrastructure. What matters most is the careful probing and analysis of student understandings, which leads to sensitive student-specific adjustments in the overall learning environment, thereby influencing individual learning trajectories.

Two different sets of examples serve to illustrate work that has been undertaken on classroom-based formative assessment strategies. Common among these efforts is a focus on knowledge-rich domains, an emphasis on the development of conceptual understanding in a domain, and a view that assessment development should stem from an analysis of the various ways in which students conceptualize or explain situations or events. That is, an understanding of knowledge development in the domain serves as the guide for developing instruction and assessment. The assessment, in turn, provides feedback on instruction by calling attention to levels of student understanding at various times and in various contexts. Explicit attention to the iterative nature of teaching, learning, and assessment is the hallmark of the approaches described next. The differences lie primarily in the breadth of the subject matter that is the focus of this instruction-assessment cycle.

Mental Models and Misconceptions

Much of the cognitive research on mental models has been done in the domain of physical science, and research on classroom-embedded assessment draws heavily upon this work to support a process of cognitive diagnosis. The latter permits subsequent instructional contexts to be selected so as to challenge a student's conceptions of scientific phenomena and events and guide the student in the direction of increasingly sophisticated and complex conceptual understandings (e.g., Hunt & Minstrell, 1994; Minstrell, 1992; Minstrell & Stimpson, 1996; White & Fredericksen, 1998). Thus, the problems presented to students may not look substantially different from those found in a normal physical science curriculum. Rather, at the heart of the difference is how such problems are posed, how student responses are evaluated, and the role of each within an overall instructional system.

Minstrell and his colleagues (Hunt & Minstrell, 1994; Levidow, Hunt, & McKee, 1991) developed Diagnoser, a relatively simple computer program designed to evaluate the consistency of students' reasoning in particular situations. The system was designed from an analysis of students' understanding of physics problems and the categories or pieces of knowledge (termed facets) that students apply when solving these problems. "A facet is a convenient unit of thought, an understanding or reasoning, a piece of content knowledge or strategy seemingly used by the student in making sense of a particular situation" (Minstrell, 1992, p. 2). Facet clusters, such as the one shown in Table 1, are sets of related elements grouped around a physical situation (e.g., forces on interacting objects) or around

TABLE 1
Separating Fluid/Medium Effects From Gravitational Effects: Facets of Student
Understanding

310—pushes from above and below by a surrounding fluid medium lend a slight support
311—a mathematical formulaic approach (e.g., rho $\times$ g $\times$ h1 $-$ rho $\times$ g $\times$ h2 $=$ net buoyant pressure)
314—surrounding fluids don't exert any forces or pushes on objects
315—surrounding fluids exert equal pushes all around an object
316—whichever surface has greater amount of fluid above or below the object has the greater push by the fluid on the surface
317—fluid mediums exert an upward push only
318—surrounding fluid mediums exert a net downward push
319—weight of an object is directly proportional to medium pressure on it

some conceptual idea (e.g., meaning of average velocity). The individual facets of students' thinking refer to individual pieces, or constructions of a few pieces of knowledge and/or strategies of reasoning. Within a cluster, facets can be sequenced in an approximate order of development that ranges from appropriate, acceptable understandings for introductory physics to those that represent limited understandings or, in some cases, serious misunderstandings. Facets in the middle of this range frequently arise from formal instruction but may represent overgeneralizations or undergeneralizations in a student's knowledge structure.

Systematic knowledge of the levels at which students understand and represent physical concepts, principles, and/or situations is the starting point for developing highly informative assessment tasks. Figure 1 is an example of a constructed response item designed to probe levels of understanding from the facet cluster in Table 1. As discussed by Minstrell (1999), student responses to this item can be mapped to the facets in the cluster shown in Table 1 in a relatively straightforward manner. Students may be thinking that weight is due to the downward push by air (319), or they may believe that fluids (air or water) only push downward (318) or only push upward (317); that fluids push equally from above, below, and all around (315); that fluids do not push at all on objects in them (314); or that there is a differential in the push depending on how much fluid is above or below the object (316). If they do understand that there is a greater push from below than from above due to the greater pressure at greater depth, they may express it in a formulaic way (311) or with a rich conceptual description (310).

Single items such as that shown in Figure 1, even when coupled with qualitative evaluation frameworks such as the facet cluster in Table 1, seldom provide sufficient information to ascertain the specificity versus generality and appropriateness of a student's understanding. However, sets of items, or item families, can be constructed to assess the context specificity of a student's understanding. By considering the response patterns across pairs or sets of items such as those shown in Figures 1 and 2, an evaluation can be provided of how much a student's

FIGURE 1
Example Constructed-Response Item: Separating Fluid/Medium Effects From
Gravitational Effects

A solid cylinder is hung by a long string from a spring scale. The reading on the scale shows
that the cylinder weighs 1.0 lb.

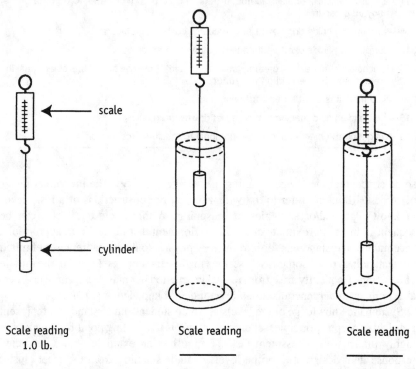

Scale reading
1.0 lb.

Scale reading
_____

Scale reading
_____

About how much will the scale read if the cylinder which weighs 1.0 lbs. is submerged just
below the surface of the water? What will it read when the cylinder is much deeper in the water?

Briefly explain how you decided.

Figure 1 is reprinted from *Grading the Nation's Report Card,* National Research Council, 1999; reprinted
with permission of the National Academy Press, Washington, DC.

understanding is tied to the specific surface situation described in a given problem.
For the conceptual domain illustrated, it is not uncommon for student understanding of the effects of a medium to achieve a more sophisticated level for the water
than air context. Minstrell (1999) has indicated that interpretable patterns of
responding across items can be obtained for various physical concepts and situations. It is also worth noting that many of the tasks and associated scoring rubrics
developed by Minstrell and others for use in a classroom setting can be used in
large-scale survey assessments as well (National Research Council, 1999).

FIGURE 2
Example Multiple-Choice Item: Separating Fluid/Medium Effects From Gravitational Effects

These pictures show three identical blocks attached to the spring scale. In one case the block is in the water, in another it is in air, and in the third the block is in a vacuum. In the air, the scale represents 10 lbs. to the nearest 0.1 lb.

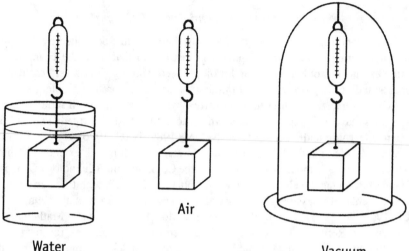

The scale readings would be

A.   about the same in all three environments.
B.   noticeably less in water but about the same in air and in a vacuum.
C.   noticeably less in air and in water.
D.   noticeably more in water and noticeably less in a vacuum.

Figure 2 is reprinted from *Grading the Nation's Report Card*, National Research Council, 1999; reprinted with permission of the National Academy Press, Washington, DC.

The Diagnoser computer program presents sets of problems such as the ones illustrated and records student responses and justifications as a means of identifying a student's understanding; then it provides instructional prescriptions when needed. The classroom instructor is also provided information about the range of student understanding for the class and thus can adjust lessons accordingly to assist students in developing a proper conceptual representation of the given problem domain. Minstrell (1999) has described how an integrated formative assessment and instruction system can produce significant changes in student achievement levels and conceptual understanding in various areas of the high school physics curriculum.

In similar work, White and Fredericksen (1998) direct their attention to learning and assessment environments that help young students acquire appropriate mental models for basic physical laws and their application across situations. Computer-based representations challenge students' existing conceptions and stimulate cross-student debates and experimentation to resolve discrepancies between what students think and what evidence from various inquiries seems to demonstrate. A cyclical sequence of hypothesize, test, generalize is promoted and supported by the software and the overall instructional design.

Support for Problem-Based Learning

The second set of examples differs from the work just described by focusing on larger units of scientific inquiry and instruction that have the character of more extended problem-based and project-based learning situations. Frequently, such situations engage students in individual and collaborative problem-solving activities organized around a complex real-world scenario. Such inquiry-based activities have been recommended in various standards for mathematics and science learning and teaching (e.g., NCTM, 1989; NRC, 1996).

An example of embedding assessment strategies within such extended inquiry activities can be found in work pursued by the Cognition and Technology Group at Vanderbilt on the development of a conceptual model for integrating curriculum, instruction, and assessment in science and mathematics (Barron et al., 1995, 1998; CTGV, 1994, 1997). The resultant SMART Model (Scientific and Mathematical Arenas for Refining Thinking) involves frequent opportunities for formative assessment by both students and teachers and includes an emphasis on self-assessment to help students develop the ability to monitor their own understanding and find resources to deepen it when necessary (Brown, Bransford, Ferrara, & Campione, 1983; Stiggins, 1994). The SMART Model involves the explicit design of multiple cycles of problem solving, self-assessment, and revision in an overall problem-based to project-based learning environment.

Activity in the problem-based learning portion of SMART typically begins with a video-based problem scenario such as the "Stones River Mystery" (SRM; Sherwood et al., 1995). SRM tells the story of a group of high school students who, in collaboration with a biologist and hydrologist, are monitoring the water in Stones River. The video shows the team visiting the river and conducting various water quality tests. Students in the classroom are asked to assess the water quality at a second site on the river. They are challenged to select tools that they can use to sample macroinvertebrates and test dissolved oxygen, to conduct these tests, and to interpret the data relative to previous data from the same site. Ultimately, they find that the river is polluted owing to illegal dumping of restaurant grease. Students then must decide how to clean up the pollution.

The problem-based learning activity includes three sequential modules: macro-invertebrate sampling, dissolved oxygen testing, and pollution cleanup. Each follows the same cycle of activities: initial selection of a method for testing or cleanup, feedback on the initial choice, revision of the choice, and a culminating task. The modules are preliminary to the project-based activity in which students conduct actual water quality testing at a local river. In executing the latter, they are provided with a set of criteria by which an external agency will evaluate written reports and accompanying videotaped presentations.

Within each activity module, selection, feedback, and revision make use of the SMART Web site, which organizes the overall process and supports three high-level functions. First, it provides individualized feedback to students and serves as a formative evaluation tool. The feedback suggests aspects of students' work that are in need of revision and classroom resources that students can use to help them revise. The feedback does not tell students the "right answer." Instead, it sets a course for independent inquiry by the student. The Web feedback is generated from data that individual students enter.

As an example, when students begin working on macroinvertebrates, they are given a catalog of sampling tools and instruments. Many of these are "bogus" and collect the wrong kind of sample; others are "legitimate" and will gather a representative sample of macroinvertebrates. The catalog items are specially designed to include contrasting cases that help students discover the need to know certain kinds of information. Students are asked to choose and justify their choice of tool. To help them make their choices, they are provided with resources, some of which are on-line, that they can use to find out about river ecosystems, macroinvertebrates, and water quality monitoring. Once students have made an initial set of choices, they use the SMART Web site. They enter their catalog choices and select justifications for their choices. Once students have submitted their catalog order on-line, the SMART Web site sends them individualized feedback. The catalog items and foils are designed to expose particular misconceptions. The feedback that students receive from the SMART Web site highlights why the selected tool is problematic and suggests helpful resources (sections of on-line and off-line resources, hands-on experiments, and peers). This form of feedback has been used in similar work on mathematics problem solving, and results suggest that it can be an effective stimulus for guided inquiry and revision by students.

The second function of the SMART Web site is to collect, organize, and display the data collected from multiple distributed classrooms ("SMART Lab"). Data displays are automatically updated as new data are submitted to the database by students. The data in SMART Lab consist of students' answers to problems and explanations for their answers. Each class's data can be displayed separately from the distributed classroom's data. This feature enables the teacher and her or his class to discuss different solution strategies and, in the process, address important concepts and misconceptions. These discussions provide a rich source of information for the teacher on how her or his students are thinking about a problem and are designed to stimulate further student reflection.

The third section of the SMART Web site consists of explanations by student-actors ("Kids Online"). The explanations are text based with audio narration, and they are errorful by design. Students are asked to critically evaluate the explanations and provide feedback to the student-actor. The errors seed thinking and discussion on concepts that are frequently misconceived by students. At the same time, students learn important critical evaluation skills.

The ability of students and teachers to make progress through the various cycles of work and revision and achieve an effective solution to the larger problem depends on a variety of resource materials carefully designed to assist the learning and assessment process. Students who use these resources and tools learn significantly more than students who go through the same instructional sequence for the same amount of time, but without the benefit of the tools and the embedded formative assessment activities, and their performance in a related project-based learning activity is significantly enhanced (Barron et al., 1995, 1998).

Incomplete Solutions and Unresolved Conceptual Problems

In the preceding discussion, we highlighted two general ways in which assessment practice has been connected with concepts arising from theories of cognition and learning. In the first set of examples, large-scale and largely summative assessment practices have been expanded with the goal of sampling a wider range of cognitive performances and affecting instructional practice at the classroom level. In the second set of examples, formative assessment tactics have been incorporated directly into teaching strategies for complex content with the goal of enhancing student learning outcomes. Both lines of work are important because they take the enhancement of classroom-based learning and instructional processes as the nexus for the connection between cognitive theory and assessment practice.

While much has been learned through these efforts, each approach has specific limitations. For example, we have described how significant attention to innovations in task format and concern for instructionally informative scoring criteria frequently conflicted with traditional concerns for reliability and validity (e.g., Dunbar, Koretz, & Hoover, 1991; Shavelson, Baxter, & Gao, 1993; Shavelson, Baxter, & Pine, 1991). Despite changes in task format and score emphasis, efforts to develop alternative assessments proceeded without a theory of assessment aligned with contemporary research on cognition and learning. Little attention was given to the underlying assumptions that "new" forms of assessment are direct measures of complex performances and that they can and do change classroom teaching and learning in positive ways. Indeed, procedures for evaluating the cognitive aspects of assessment situations, once developed, pointed to the difficulty in developing tasks and scoring systems consistent with goals for measuring thinking, reasoning, and problem solving (Baxter & Glaser, 1998; Hamilton et al., 1997).

It also appears to be the case that as assessment development and use moves away from the classroom teaching and learning situation, validity issues seem to take a back seat to issues of reliability and generalizability. In contrast, when assessments are integral parts of instructional practice, validity appears to be the primary issue and very often the major technical criterion by which assessments are judged. It is unfortunate that a better balance has yet to be achieved within and across approaches. By selectively focusing on a specific assessment purpose (summative vs. formative) as applied to a specific assessment context (large scale and high stakes vs. classroom based and low stakes), one or more critical issues of inference are largely ignored.

Available evidence also suggests that traditional methods for test design supplemented by cognitive analysis of content and process can usefully inform test development so that the stated goals may be more closely approximated than has generally been the case. However, layering new techniques on top of the old is but a temporary solution to the development of appropriate measures of subject-matter achievement. What is needed is a fundamentally different approach to assessment design, an approach that is grounded in theories of developing competence in specific subject matters and that is supported by relevant psychometric analyses. To inform educational practice, it is essential to define critical differences between successful and unsuccessful student performance and model these differences in a way that makes relevant cognitive activity apparent to teachers and students. Psychometric technology that has emerged in the context of selection and aptitude testing is not particularly appropriate for these purposes of achievement assessment. Clearly, no approach we have considered thus far attempts to fully confront the conceptual conflict between theories of cognition and learning and contemporary models and methods of psychometric technique. Before evaluating the effectiveness of attempts at more synthetic solutions, it is therefore important to examine the scope of the conceptual divide separating contemporary cognitive and psychometric theories.

As we have indicated, cognitive theory and research emphasize the knowledge structures and processes underlying understanding in various substantive performance domains. In considering such matters, the cognitive perspective also focuses on the ways in which such understandings are constructed by individuals. Such a perspective on the nature of knowledge and skill thus raises serious questions about what should be assessed and the manner of assessment. With regard to the latter, it has been argued that the assessment technologies currently in use to develop, select, and score test items and tasks, and thus to determine summary scores, treat content domains and cognition as consisting of separate pieces of information (e.g., facts, procedures, and definitions). This fragmentation of knowledge into discrete exercises and activities is the hallmark of "the associative learning and behavioral objectives traditions," which dominated American psychology for most of this century (Greeno et al., 1997). This "knowledge in pieces" view has dominated learning theory and instructional practice in America, as well as assessment and testing technology (Mislevy, 1993). Much of current testing technology is based on an underlying theory that allows tasks to be treated as independent, discrete entities that can be accumulated and aggregated in various ways to produce overall scores. Furthermore, test forms are compiled according to a simple substitution of one item for another or one exercise for another based on parameters of item difficulty. Mislevy (1996) captured part of the conceptual clash between a cognitively based approach to assessment and current psychometric methods.

To some extent in any assessment comprising multiple tasks, what is relatively hard for some students is relatively easy for others, depending on the degree to which the tasks relate to the knowledge structures that students have, each in their own way, constructed. From the trait-behavioral perspective, this is noise, or measurement error, that leads to: low reliability under classical test theory (CTT); low generalizability under generalizability theory; and low item discrimination parameters under item response theory (IRT). It obscures what one is interested in from that perspective, namely, locating people along a single dimension as to a general behavioral tendency as defined in terms of this particular domain of tasks. For inferences concerning overall proficiency in this sense, tasks that do not line people up in the same way are less informative than ones that do. (p. 392)

Standard test theory, that is, both classical true-score theory and item response theory, appears to be largely incompatible with the implications and findings of contemporary psychological theory and research. The former arose from the pressures to make selective decisions that required the ranking of students from high to low aptitude or achievement. Classical test theory (CTT) originated at the turn of the century in the work of Spearman (1904a, 1904b). Over time, the statistical tools available for analyses within the realm of CTT grew in both number and sophistication (e.g., Lord & Novick, 1968). However, the confounding of items (making up a test) with persons (taking the test) is a major shortcoming of CTT. There is no direct mechanism within CTT to compare test scores that are derived from different sets of items or obtained from groups of different ability levels.

Originating in the work of Lord (1952) and Rasch (1960), item response theory (IRT) was developed in response to these shortcomings. IRT proposes that an individual's performance is a product of his or her proficiency, and the probability of responding correctly to a given item is a function of his or her overall proficiency parameter and one or more item parameters (e.g., difficulty). As such, the item response rather than the overall test score becomes the object of measurement. When an IRT model can be supported, the scores on any two subsets of items can be compared on the same scale of measurement. Likewise, the scores of groups of different developmental or ability levels can be compared at one or multiple points in time.

Because of these features, IRT has facilitated contemporary practice in test design and analysis. For example, adaptive testing relies on estimates of which item would provide the most information given an individual's proficiency and responses to previous items. IRT has also had a major influence on large-scale educational assessment programs such as NAEP by making it possible to equate sets of items administered at different points in time and under different subject-matter frameworks. For example, multiple matrix sampling and IRT were used in developing a reading scale for the 1984 NAEP (Educational Testing Service, 1985) that allowed comparisons of reading scores across assessments conducted from 1971 to 1984 and across age cohorts of 9-, 13-, and 17-year-old students. Despite the technical and practical advantages of IRT methodology, characterizing test performance as the product of a unidimensional proficiency variable is at odds with current conceptions of achievement. Furthermore, there has been very little change in how understandings of the nature of developing subject-matter competence should influence the content, item types, or interpretation of tests.

Contemporary cognitive theorists would argue that inferences about the nature of a student's level of knowledge and achievement in a given domain should not focus on individual, disaggregated bits and pieces of information arrayed along a unidimensional item difficulty scale. More important than the questions students answer correctly is the overall pattern of responses that students generate across a set of items or tasks. The pattern of responses reflects the connectedness of the knowledge structure that underlies conceptual understanding and skill in a domain of academic competence. Thus, it is the pattern of performance over a set of items or tasks explicitly constructed to discriminate between alternative profiles of knowledge that should be the focus of assessment. The latter can be used to determine the level of a given student's understanding and competence within a given subject-matter domain. Such information is interpretive and diagnostic, highly informative, and potentially prescriptive. The examples provided earlier in this section for science learning (e.g., CTGV, 1997; Minstrell, 1992) illustrate just such an approach to assessment (see also National Research Council, 1999).

Two other features of subject-matter competence merit attention in designing assessments that are responsive to the changing educational environment. First, competence is defined, in part, by the extent to which knowledge and skills are transferable and applicable in a variety of tasks and circumstances. To know something is not simply to reproduce it but to be able to apply or transfer that knowledge in situations that are more or less similar to the originally acquired competence. Second, people's knowledge, understanding, and skill are reflected in their capacity to carry out significant, sustained performances both independently and in collaboration with others in a group. Especially important are group situations that emphasize distributed expertise and the sharing of knowledge across individuals to enable successful performance of a major task.

PURSUIT OF THEORY AND CONSTRUCT-DRIVEN ASSESSMENT

Efforts to develop alternative assessments aligned with highly sought after instructional changes, and advances in statistical method and technique for addressing important measurement problems, have for the most part proceeded with minimal attention to the developments in cognitive psychology. It is also clear that the task- or item-based approach to assessment design that relies on postdevelopment statistical criteria such as item difficulty to make decisions about the final test form has been influenced little by new developments. As noted by Mislevy (1993), "It is only a slight exaggeration to describe the test theory that dominates educational measurement today as the application of 20th century statistics to 19th century psychology" (p. 19). Thus, the problem we continue to face is how theory and research on cognition and instruction can allow us to go beyond current testing and assessment practices to achieve an understanding of an individual's underlying cognitive competence that can also be of benefit to instructional practice.

These problems are not new. The integration of assessment practices with advances in knowledge of cognition and human learning has been advocated for some time (Anastasi, 1967; Cronbach, 1957; Glaser, 1981; Nickerson, 1989; Resnick & Resnick, 1992). Nevertheless, efforts to articulate the rationale for such an approach through discussions of relevant cognitive research and its implications for assessment design were slow to develop (e.g., Glaser, 1986; Mislevy, 1993; Snow & Lohman, 1989, 1993; Sternberg, 1984; Wittrock & Baker, 1991). Furthermore, the discussion generally lacked the specificity necessary to effectively guide assessment design. The essence of the dilemma was well captured by Snow and Lohman (1989):

It seems clear to us, at least today, that cognitive psychology has no ready answers to the educational measurement problems of yesterday, today, or tomorrow. But it also seems clear to us that cognitive psychology has opened a spectrum of questions about what educational measurements do and do not represent and an equally large spectrum of methods for investigating such questions. (p. 320)

Theory and Construct-Driven Aptitude Assessment

After considering much of the work that has ensued on the cognitive analysis of aptitude, Snow and Lohman (1989, 1993) argued that developing a new generation of tests that seek to more accurately describe cognitive performance will require a new test theory, one that fully embodies a componential account of human information processing. Such an effort must be able to account for the various components of cognitive task performance such as stimulus encoding, feature comparison, rule induction, rule application, and response. In addition to explaining various cognitive components or processes, componential measurement theory will have to deal with the use of different strategies across individuals as well as shifting strategy use within individuals (e.g., Kyllonen, Lohman, & Woltz, 1984). Issues of learning and changing contributions of automatic and controlled processing must also be considered (e.g., Ackerman, 1987). Modeling and interpreting each of these dimensions, including the potential changes in these dimensions, may profit from a testing system that is adaptive (i.e., the succession of items for an individual will be based on substantive observations obtained during testing). Finally, a componential measurement theory will also have to deal with assessing the combined metrics of speed and accuracy so that their effects and interactions within and between individuals are accurately represented. Given such a complex, multifaceted model, the measurement of human performance can no longer be interpreted as representing a single dimension or trait.

Rather than develop an entirely new test theory, some have attempted to develop compound models that build on standard test theory and that include the cognitive variables believed to affect test performance. Faceted tests, proposed by Guttman (1970), are an early example of this kind of measurement application. More recent developments include hybrid approaches such as "tectonic plate" (Wilson, 1989), latent class (Haertel, 1984), and componential models (Embretson, 1984; Whitely, 1980).

A well-developed example of a hybrid approach is the incorporation of assumptions regarding cognitive complexity into Rasch models for certain types of aptitude test performance. Incorporating cognitive complexity into a Rasch model requires substituting a mathematical model of cognitive complexity for the item difficulty. An early example of such a model is Fisher's (1973) linear logistic latent trait model (LLTM), in which items are scored on factors affecting complexity. Embretson (1993) has used LLTM to model performance in two spatial ability tasks, the Space Relations Test from the Differential Aptitude Test (DAT) and the Spatial Learning Ability Test (SLAT; Embretson & Waxman, 1989). In doing so, she drew upon some of the earlier-mentioned cognitive components research on spatial ability and then demonstrated how LLTM can be used to (a) evaluate different processing models of test performance by comparing model fits, (b) evaluate the construct representation of a test using parameter estimates to determine the effect of cognitive variables that are represented by factors, and (c) select items for subsequent testing based on their cognitive representation, complexity, and difficulty.

One potential shortcoming of the LLTM method is that it requires a strong a priori model of task complexity and its relationship with difficulty. This was possible to some extent for the spatial aptitude items given considerable empirical analyses of cognitive processing factors in task performance (e.g., Kyllonen, Lohman, & Woltz, 1984; Mumaw & Pellegrino, 1984; Pellegrino & Kail, 1982; Shepard & Cooper, 1983). An alternative is the multicomponent latent trait model (MLTM; Embretson, 1983), which also requires an initial componential model but does not require the model to specify the relationships of stimulus features and complexity. To work without an a priori theory of difficulty, MLTM uses data from responses to standard items and responses to subtask items representing components of the standard item. Another latent trait model described by Embretson, the general component latent trait model (GLTM; Embretson, 1984), combines the LLTM and MLTM to create a more general model.

Embretson also has presented the multidimensional Rasch model for learning and change (MRMLC; Embretson, 1991), which treats change as a latent variable within a multidimensional item response model, thereby attempting to resolve a number of the problems and paradoxes associated with measuring change. The MRMLC, however, depends on a number of strong assumptions and requires adherence to a set design and complex administration conditions. More specifically, items are administered under successive conditions, with the first condition being the standard condition and the remaining conditions being the conditions of change, which can be either positive or negative (e.g., practice, instruction, or stress induction). Embretson (1993, p. 143) writes that MRMLC is "a dynamic, rather than a static, concept of ability" in which "performance is changing in both dimensionality and level, due to individual differences in modifiability."

Such merging of cognitive theories of performance with psychometric models and methods in the context of aptitude assessment represents a substantial advance in bridging the conceptual divide (see Fredericksen, Mislevy, & Bejar, 1993).

Work of this type clearly has significance for enhancing various aspects of selection testing and entrance exams such as the SAT and the Graduate Record Examination. Unfortunately, improvements in aptitude assessment design and development, despite their importance, provide little or no information to promote educational attainment in areas of academic achievement and instructional relevance. Furthermore, it is highly unlikely that the same merger of constructs that appear to work for certain domains of aptitude, albeit with complicated test administration and validation designs, can be productively extended to the assessment of achievement. Rather, the situation of achievement assessment is more complex, as described next.

Beyond Aptitude Assessment: Theory-Based Assessment of Achievement

While the gap between cognitive theory and assessment practice has narrowed somewhat in the world of aptitude testing, the gap has remained quite substantial in the world of achievement testing. As described earlier, achievement test developers, when faced with the challenge of developing alternative forms of assessment, generally adopted a task-centered approach as opposed to a construct-centered approach to generate assessments symmetric with instructional practice. In the intervening years, performance-based assessments and other alternatives to multiple-choice testing have come to play an increasingly central role in various state and national testing programs because of their perceived power to reform curriculum and instruction and, as a consequence, improve teaching and learning (National Council on Education Standards and Testing, 1992). In addition to their role as a political change agent, performance-based assessments are expected to measure student outcomes and provide standards for future performance, support comparisons across educational settings, and produce indices of change within and across these settings.

The perceived power of assessments to effect teaching and learning in optimal ways, although generally unsubstantiated, may be realized through the integration of assessment and learning as an interacting system. Heretofore, standardized assessment and the conditions of instruction and schooling have coexisted largely as decoupled systems. The move to standards-based assessment and reporting of performance in terms of achievement levels brings to the forefront the extent of the disconnection between the vision of reformers for equitable, sustained opportunities for acquiring knowledge and the experiences of students in various instructional settings. Given this disconnection between assessment and instruction, researchers and educators alike have called for changes that would result in test formats being more aligned with instructional tasks and test results being more useful for instructional decision making (Glaser, 1986; Linn, 1986; Nitko, 1989). Accomplishing this goal will require the integration of theories of knowledge and instruction with new psychometric models that describe acquired competence in subject-matter learning. Within this context, the theory-based constructs to be measured must be emphasized prior to test development and then used to generate item or task characteristics that are intended to influence the performance of more or less proficient students (National Research Council, 1999). In this way, assessments can be designed with predictable cognitive demands for specific groups of test takers (Nichols, 1994; Nichols, Chipman, & Brennan, 1995; Nichols & Sugrue, 1997). Messick summarized the approach as follows:

> A construct-centered approach would begin by asking what complex of knowledge, skills, or other attribute should be assessed, presumably because they are tied to explicit or implicit objectives of instruction or are otherwise valued by society. Next, what behaviors or performances should reveal those constructs, and what tasks or situations should elicit those behaviors? Thus, the nature of the construct guides the selection or construction of relevant tasks as well as the rational development of construct-based scoring criteria and rubrics. (1994, p. 17)

Mislevy and his colleagues have elaborated and extended Messick's "guiding questions" and formulated an assessment design theory centered around notions of evidence and inference. Broadly speaking, theories of learning and knowledge acquisition based in cognitive psychology provide the conceptual structure for formulating what constitutes evidence, and the statistical power of mathematical probability provides an empirical structure for drawing inferences from the attained evidence. The strength of this approach lies in its efforts to shift the focus of test design from items to substantive theory, that is, what is known about the display of differential competence in a domain, joined with the use of inferential reasoning for judging the evidence derived from the test situation. Examples of this approach to structure inferences about proportional reasoning, mixed-number subtraction, foreign-language learning, and accomplishment in a studio art program, among others, attest to the possibility for broad application in the future.

As described by Mislevy (1995, 1996), an iterative three-stage, assessment design process of necessity begins with a theory of performance in a domain, followed by generation of a set of tasks the responses to which can be analyzed/interpreted within that theory and then statistical comparisons of expected to observed performance to draw conclusions about level of student understanding within the targeted domain. Discrepancies between theoretical models of performance and patterns of observed performance in particular situations provide information for improving or changing the substantive theory underlying the initial design.

In designing assessments, one begins by characterizing differential competence or levels of knowing in a domain. For this purpose, a set of variables denotes relevant aspects of performance that signal differences in knowledge and skill (i.e., student models). These variables can take on any of a number of forms (e.g., quantitative, qualitative, or some combination) depending on the domain theory from which they are derived. The goal is to characterize performance in ways that capture the essential or critical distinctions between those with differing levels of knowledge and experience. In this regard, consideration of the key concepts in a domain, ways of understanding or misunderstanding them, and the common developmental trajectories through which learning progresses serves as an appropriate guide.

With the substantive theory of performance sufficiently delineated, tasks or situations are designed so as to provide an opportunity for students to display differential levels of understanding. Certainty of conclusions depends on the relevance of the obtained evidence to the domain of study and theory of performance. From theory and data, one posits probabilities for the ways that students with different configurations of knowledge, skills, or other distinguishing characteristics of performance (e.g., problem representation, strategy use) will solve problems, answer questions, and so on. Given a student's particular configuration of knowledge and skills, what is the probability that he or she will respond to a given task or situation in a particular way (e.g., right/wrong, quality of explanation)? These are initial performance expectations (conditional probabilities) based on expert opinion, theory, or pilot studies. These probabilities can be revised after performance is observed and inferences drawn about the appropriate or most likely level of competence or understanding as defined by the student model.

The essential thing is to define a space of "student models"—simplified characterizations of students' knowledge, skill, and/or strategies, indexed by variables that signify their key aspects (1995, p. 43). A properly structured statistical model embodies the salient qualitative patterns in the application at hand and spells out, within that framework, the relationships between conjectures and evidence. It overlays a substantive model for the situation with a model for our knowledge of the situation, so that we may characterize and communicate what we come to believe—as to both content and conviction—and why we believe it—as to our assumptions, our conjectures, our evidence, and the structure of reasoning. (Mislevy, 1996, p. 13)

The design just mentioned entails a myriad of complexities of practical application both theoretically and statistically. As efforts proceed in this direction, detailed examples of the design and decision-making process for creating assessments for school subjects will be necessary. Method and theory will also evolve, and techniques will need to be elaborated and refined as definitions of competence are extended. While much remains to be done at a practical level, an important cognitive-psychometric discourse has been established around achievement assessment, and a context has been established for bridging the conceptual divide in this critical domain of assessment and instructional practice.

Combining Aptitude and Achievement Assessment With Instruction: ATIs Reconsidered

The theoretical landscape now looks considerably different than it did in the 1960s and 1970s, when much of the ATI work reviewed by Cronbach and Snow (1977) was originally conducted. What can we now say about the logic and potential of such research in light of current understandings of cognition and assessment, especially with regard to the goal of using such knowledge to improve instructional and learning outcomes? This question can be approached by first examining two examples of second-generation ATI work and then considering whether the potential exists for building on such work and developing an expanded research agenda exploring AATIs: Aptitude × Achievement × Treatment interactions.

Shute's (1992, 1993) research using macroadaptive intelligent tutoring systems (ITS) can be characterized as second-generation ATI work because her hypotheses and assessments are derived from contemporary information-processing theories, particularly the ACT-R (Anderson, 1983, 1993) and four-sources (Kyllonen & Shute, 1989) theories. The ACT-R theory describes a three-stage process of cognitive skill acquisition involving structures and processes in working, declarative, and procedural memory, while the four-sources theory is a learning skills taxonomy that defines a four-dimensional space of subject matter, learning environment, desired learning outcomes, and learner attributes.

To evaluate the interaction of students' associative learning skills (AL) and different learning environments, Shute (1992) used an ITS designed to teach the basic principles of electricity, which could be operated in either of two modes, a rule-application environment or a rule-induction environment. The rule-application environment was a high-structure treatment in which each of the variables and their relationships in a problem were fully specified and explained. In the rule-induction treatment, which was a low-structure environment, the tutor identified the relevant variables in a problem, but the student was left to induce their relationships. In the criterion tasks, two types of knowledge were evaluated, with declarative assessments requiring students to answer factual questions and procedural assessments requiring students to apply Ohm's and Kirchhoff's laws in solving problems.

For declarative knowledge, Shute (1992) found that the rule-induction environment was optimal for high-AL students, whereas low-AL students acquired declarative knowledge better in the rule-application environment. For procedural knowledge, high-AL students performed better in the rule application environment and low-AL students did not perform well in either environment. Thus, there was a three-way interaction of AL, learning environment, and knowledge type. These results are best understood in terms of the overall match of the learning environment to the student's aptitude and the type of knowledge to be learned, consistent with the four-sources theory. In another ITS study that taught flight engineering, Shute (1993) found a three-way interaction of working memory capacity, general knowledge, and two types of problem sets. High-capacity/low-knowledge students performed better when assigned to an extended problem-set treatment, whereas low-capacity/high-knowledge students performed better in a constrained problem-set treatment.

Swanson's (1990) ATI work can also be characterized as second generation. His research shows the potentially dynamic nature of ATIs and how treatments may be adapted in dynamic situations to benefit the learner. Swanson employed two human tutors to teach optics to college students and trained the tutors to use three different tutoring approaches: high structure, low structure, and contingent. The latter method was based on principles such as Bruner's (1978) concept of scaffolding and Vygotsky's (1978) zone of proximal development. In contingent tutoring, learning is fostered by creating connections between what is to be learned and things that are already known, and students are given more or less support depending on the difficulty they are experiencing. Thus, the tutor switches between different levels of high- and low-structure treatment depending on how the student is performing the task. Across students varying in general aptitude, the contingent treatment was best for low-aptitude students and the low-structure treatment was best for high-aptitude students.

Swanson's study shows that students change as they develop knowledge and cognitive skills, as do the relationships of aptitudes, performance, and optimal treatments (see also Ackerman, 1988, 1989, 1996, 1997). Thus, ATIs are contextualized in the person-situation interaction, and these contexts change as learning progresses. Any research program that ignores this set of relationships not only will fall short of its potential to effect positive change but will probably find itself swamped in contradictory findings, the product of normal changes accompanying learning. Given the results and complexities of earlier ATI research, careful attention must be given to these issues; otherwise, there is the distinct possibility of history repeating itself!

The research of Shute (1992, 1993) and Swanson (1990) is informative and represents the beginning of a second generation of ATI research. For such research to have practical benefits, much more work remains to be done. The goal of such research should be to create a knowledge base that supports a system of instruction whereby individuals of mixed aptitudes can reach higher criterion levels of performance in various achievement domains. For this to come about, several points bear consideration. First and foremost, the assessments of aptitude and achievement, as well as the instructional treatments, should be based on detailed cognitive theories appropriate to each set of constructs. The ACT-R and four-sources theories provide a good starting point in terms of a substantive theory of cognitive aptitudes. Assessments based on ACT-R are likely to focus on the structures and processes of the working, declarative, and procedural memory systems. However, missing from the work of Shute and Swanson are detailed and integrated assessments of students' knowledge structures in the content domain to be learned (e.g., Mislevy, 1995, 1996; Tatsuoka, 1983).

As mentioned in the preceding discussion of achievement assessment, efforts to assess knowledge structures have begun to integrate traditional psychometric methods with new techniques such as Bayesian inference networks to create measurement models capable of assessing students' achievement relative to optimal and suboptimal domain performance models. Such models can be used to trace a student's progress through a given knowledge space and to adjust instruction accordingly. Since learning is a process of change, considerable focus should be on the changing relations of aptitudes, knowledge structures, and performance. Evaluating the changing relations of basic information-processing constructs such as working memory capacity and detailed knowledge-structure models can provide a more accurate depiction of the learning process than has previously been available. Given that knowledge structures represent levels of achievement, it may be heuristic to think of this type of investigation as an aptitude-achievement-treatment interaction (AATI) design.

One thing AATI research must emphasize relative to traditional ATI research is learning as a process of change. Historically, ATI designs involved an aptitude pretest, an educational treatment, and an achievement posttest. The posttest was then regressed on the pretest, and the interaction was assessed. If the interaction was significant, it could potentially serve as a guide to a macroadaptive treatment. In practice, however, this was rarely done, because unaccounted-for contextual effects such as change limited the generalizations that could be made from ATI results. One of the reasons for this is that change has been difficult to assess (see, e.g., Bereiter, 1963; Cronbach & Furby, 1970; Willet, 1988). However, developments in statistical techniques such as hierarchical linear modeling (Bryk & Raudenbush, 1992) and latent growth-curve modeling (Willet & Sayer, 1994) provide powerful new methods for describing change and incorporating this into the AATI design.

The optimal application of AATI findings will probably involve combined microadaptive and macroadaptive treatments that also take into account the situated nature of learning and encompass aspects of aptitude such as affect and conation (see, e.g., Snow, Corno, & Jackson, 1996). Given the complexities of microadaptation and human interaction, one possible environment for exploring and applying AATI findings is likely to be computer-based instructional and formative assessment systems that serve as an adjunct to classroom instruction. Ultimately, the goal of AATI research is to understand the development of knowledge and cognitive skill and provide optimal conditions for students with different aptitude profiles as they progress along a given learning trajectory. When this is finally done, AATI research may begin to play a truly constructive role in the educational process, in ways originally envisioned by Cronbach.

ACCOMPLISHMENTS AND ASPIRATIONS

In this chapter, we have tried to show how the relationships between the "two disciplines" of scientific psychology have changed over time since Cronbach's original plea for their unification. In so doing, we have looked at the initial atheoretical disconnection in the pursuit of Aptitude × Treatment interactions, which was followed by the cognitive analysis of aptitudes and the related cognitive analysis of performance in the study of expertise. With knowledge of the cognitive components of complex performance, the field then attempted more sophisticated and model-based understanding of the relationships between attained achievement and the conditions of learning. Assessment of performance and conditions of learning are now being studied as dynamically related events in experimental instructional situations. And efforts have been made to shift the focus of assessment design from items or tasks to important constructs derived from an understanding of the nature of competent performance in a domain and how it might be accessed, displayed, and scored in particular situations.

The historical path we have described shows continued effort to unite cognitive science with psychometrics in ways that benefited both psychology and education. The evidence is clear that we have accomplished much, even if the merger has been tentative and somewhat strained at times. Nevertheless, we remain quite removed from a theory and technology of assessment design that effectively meets the needs of various user communities and that is consistent with our current knowledge regarding the nature of expertise and achievement. Traditional disciplinary boundaries need to be redrawn and new disciplines defined in ways that focus a coordinated educational research and development agenda around the relationship between instruction and assessment. In this context, something more than the machinery of CTT and IRT is needed, and the sophistication of such an approach may well vary as a function of the aspects of cognition that are of primary concern as well as the types of inferences we wish to make and the purposes for which we make them.

In the future, test theory will have to account for differences among and within individuals in terms of knowledge structures such as schemas, mental models, and semantic and procedural networks. Relevant here are measures of current knowledge and skills as well as a means of characterizing change in the compilation and configuration of these structures as learning progresses. Given a student's particular constellation of cognitive processing efficiency, mental models, and position in a learning trajectory, what is the next step that will provide the student with optimal learning opportunities within a domain? This is not a new idea, particularly as regards individual variation among learners vis-à-vis the goals of testing and assessment in the schools.

Teachers and schools need information on individuals that is oriented toward instructional decision rather than prediction. Tests in a helping society are not mere indexes which predict that the individual child will adjust to the school or which relieve the school from assisting the student to achieve as much as possible. The test and the instructional decision should be an integral event. (Glaser, 1981, p. 924)

Creating conditions that support learning and foster subject-matter competence requires the adoption of new, more enlightened and productive attitudes toward assessment. Critical here is the notion that assessment can and should be instrumental in providing information to facilitate contemporary goals for instruction and inclusion rather than antiquated goals for ranking and selection. Competence will no longer be defined in terms of number of correct responses. Rather, emphasis will shift to characterizing the consistency, nature, and quality of performance under varying conditions. Given the complexity of knowledge and skills that are the focus of standards-based reforms, techniques and methods must be developed and sampled in ways that promote those aspects of subject-matter achievement that are most valued in particular contexts (e.g., school, workplace). Of necessity, attention will focus on the inferences that can be drawn regarding student learning and competence from meaningful combinations of evidence.

Certain conditions of assessment that are currently being advocated will certainly be pervasive in the future. One is socially situated assessment. Assessment will require performance in group efforts where students contribute to community tasks and assist others. Shared performance encourages and promotes a strong sense of community and an effective workforce, as learning becomes attuned to the constraints and resources of the environment. In this context, students develop and question their definitions of competence, observe how others reason, and receive feedback on their own problem-solving efforts. An important aspect of this social setting is that students develop facility in accepting help and stimulation from others.

A second issue is the display of competence. Advanced information technology will be used to openly display standards and criteria for competent performance to parents, teachers, and students. The performance criteria, by which the successful education of students is to be judged, must be as recognizable as possible so that they can motivate and direct learning and community expectations. This display particularly illustrates the relevance and utility of knowledge and skill that is being acquired for use and transfer to different life circumstances.

A third key issue is cognitive significance. Assessment will provide content coverage and not neglect significant processes of performance such as raising questions, representing and planning a problem prior to solution, and offering conceptual explanations. Constructing instructionally relevant assessment situations necessitates analyzing the cognitive requirements or demands of situations and designing related scoring procedures that attend to the differential complexity of the performances of more or less experienced learners.

With these criteria as a guide, the assessment of learning and achievement can be designed to provide useful information about content and skill that should be studied or taught in order to improve performance. For this purpose, testing must be an integral part of instruction so that assessment helps guide teachers and students toward the attainment of educational goals.

If assessments are occasional externally controlled events used primarily for aggregated measures of student achievement levels, they are unlikely to be constructed in ways that provide rich information about the processes of student learning and their individual, idiosyncratic approaches to different kinds of tasks and opportunities. Consequently, teachers will have little opportunity to use the results to understand the complex nuances of student learning in ways that support more successful instruction, and little information on which to act in trying to rethink their daily practices. (Darling-Hammond, 1994, p. 20)

Equally important is the utility of assessment information for increasing proficiency in students' ability to learn. The sheer amount of available and changing information will force curriculum and assessment to emphasize the utility of current learning and the organization of a student's knowledge to support future learning. Students will need to develop an attitude of attaining the knowledge and skill that is necessary for the intellectual activity of handling a large volume of information; they learn to take multiple perspectives, to generate key organizational concepts, and to make analogies to new situations. In essence, a part of their education focuses on generative abilities to update their knowledge-based competence and develop learning skills and strategies for efficiently accessing the resources for reasoned problem solving.

Thus, in the future, the assessment of achievement will encompass cognitive abilities, disciplinary performance objectives, measurement procedures, and instructional practices. "The consequent increase in complexity sometimes seems daunting, particularly because of the interdisciplinary nature of much of the discussion. Nonetheless, the effort is worthwhile because the ultimate goal is a body of theory and methods that should be immensely more valuable to the world of education" (Braun, 1993, p. 385). The effort begins by acknowledging assessment and instruction as integral systems that foster access to effective education and to the attainment of subject-matter competence and learning proficiencies. Research on one issue cannot proceed without cognizance of and integration of the other. Nor can either be effective without attention to the contributions of cognitive science to our understanding of the development and use of knowledge. Assessments of the specific cognitive processes and structures involved in learning and achievement can and should be subjected to empirical scrutiny that will challenge or support extant theories of learning and achievement. The success of this iterative endeavor is dependent on a shared agenda focused on the equitable improvement of educational opportunities and attainment. As recognized long ago by Cronbach, to keep such theoretical and empirical efforts separate is to ensure their respective inadequacy.

REFERENCES

Ackerman, P. L. (1986). Individual differences in information processing: An investigation of intellectual abilities and task performance during practice. *Intelligence, 10,* 101–139.

Ackerman, P. L. (1987). Individual differences in skill learning: An integration of psychometric and information processing perspectives. *Psychological Bulletin, 102,* 3–27.

Ackerman, P. L. (1988). Determinants of individual differences during skill acquisition: Cognitive abilities and information processing. *Journal of Experimental Psychology: General, 117,* 288–318.

Ackerman, P. L. (1989). Individual differences and skill acquisition. In P. L. Ackerman, R. J. Sternberg, & R. Glaser (Eds.), *Learning and individual differences* (pp. 164–217). New York: Freeman.

Allard, F., & Starkes, J. L. (1980). Perception in sport: Volleyball. *Journal of Sport Psychology, 2,* 22–33.

Anastasi, A. (1967). Psychology, psychologists, and psychological testing. *American Psychologist, 22,* 297–306.

Anderson, J. R. (1983). *The architecture of cognition.* Cambridge, MA: Harvard University Press.

Anderson, J. R. (1993). *Rules of the mind.* Hillsdale, NJ: Erlbaum.

Baker, E. L., Freeman, M., & Clayton, S. (1991). Cognitive assessment of history for large-scale testing. In M. C. Wittrock & E. L. Baker (Eds.), *Testing and cognition* (pp. 131–153). Englewood Cliffs, NJ: Prentice Hall.

Barron, B., Schwartz, D. L., Vye, N., Moore, A., Petrosino, A., Zech, L., Bransford, J. D., & the Cognition and Technology Group at Vanderbilt. (1998). Doing with understanding:

Lessons from research on problem and project-based learning. *Journal of Learning Sciences, 7,* 271–311.

Barron, B., Vye, N. J., Zech, L., Schwartz, D., Bransford, J. D., Goldman, S. R., Pellegrino, J., Morris, J., Garrison, S., & Kantor, R. (1995). Creating contexts for community-based problem solving: The Jasper Challenge Series. In C. Hedley, P. Antonacci, & M. Rabinowitz (Eds.), *Thinking and literacy: The mind at work* (pp. 47–71). Hillsdale, NJ: Erlbaum.

Baxter, G. P., Elder, A. D., & Glaser, R. (1996). Knowledge-based cognition and performance assessment in the science classroom. *Educational Psychologist, 31,* 133–140.

Baxter, G. P., & Glaser, R. (1998). The cognitive complexity of science performance assessments. *Educational Measurement: Issues and Practice, 17*(3), 37–45.

Baxter, G. P., Shavelson, R. J., Goldman, S. R., & Pine, J. (1992). Evaluation of procedure-based scoring for hands-on science assessment. *Journal of Educational Measurement, 29,* 1–17.

Bereiter, C. (1963). Some persisting dilemmas in the measurement of change. In C. W. Harris (Ed.), *Problems in measuring change* (pp. 3–20). Madison: University of Wisconsin Press.

Bereiter, C., & Scardamalia, M. (1987). *The psychology of written composition.* Hillsdale, NJ: Erlbaum.

Bereiter, C., & Scardamalia, M. (1993). *Surpassing ourselves: An inquiry into the nature and implications of expertise.* Chicago: Open Court.

Black, P., & Wiliam, D. (1998). Assessment and classroom learning. *Assessment in Education, Principles, Policy & Practice, 5*(1), 7–74.

Bond, L., & Glaser, R. (1979). ATI, mostly A and T and not much of I [Review of Aptitudes and instructional methods by L. J. Cronbach & R. E. Snow]. *Applied Psychological Measurement, 3,* 137–140.

Bransford, J. D., Brown, A., & Cocking, R. (1999). *How people learn: Brain, mind, experience and school.* Washington, DC: National Academy Press.

Braun, H. (1993). Comments on Chapters 11–14. In N. Fredericksen, R. J. Mislevy, & I. I. Bejar (Eds.), *Test theory for a new generation of tests* (pp. 385–390). Hillsdale, NJ: Erlbaum.

Brown, A. L., Bransford, J. D., Ferrara, R., & Campione, J. (1983). Learning, remembering and understanding. In J. H. Flavell & E. M. Markman (Eds.), *Handbook of child psychology: Vol. 3. Cognitive development* (4th ed., pp. 77–166). New York: Wiley.

Brown, A., & Palinscar, A. M. (1989). Guided, cooperative learning and individual knowledge acquisition. In L. B. Resnick (Ed.), *Knowing, learning, and instruction: Essays in honor of Robert Glaser* (pp. 393–451). Hillsdale, NJ: Erlbaum.

Brown, J. S., & Burton, R. R. (1978). Diagnostic models for procedural bugs in basic mathematical skills. *Cognitive Science, 2,* 155–192.

Bruner, J. S. (1978). The role of dialogue in language acquisition. In A. Sinclair, R. J. Jarvell, & W. J. M. Levelt (Eds.), *The child's conception of language* (pp. 241–256). New York: Springer.

Bryk, A. S., & Raudenbush, S. W. (1992). *Hierarchical linear models: Applications and data analysis methods.* Newbury Park, CA: Sage.

Bush, G. W. (1991). *America 2000: An educational strategy.* Washington, DC: U.S. Department of Education.

Carroll, J. B. (1976). Psychometric tests as cognitive tasks: A new "structure of intellect." In L. B. Resnick (Ed.), *The nature of intelligence* (pp. 27–56). Hillsdale, NJ: Erlbaum.

Carroll, J. B. (1978). How shall we study individual differences in cognitive abilities? Methodological and theoretical perspectives. *Intelligence, 2,* 87–115.

Chase, W. G., & Simon, H. A. (1973). Perception in chess. *Cognitive Psychology, 4,* 55–81.

Chi, M. T. H., Bassock, M., Lewis, M. W., Reimann, P., & Glaser, R. (1989). Self-explanations: How students study and use examples in learning to solve problems. *Cognitive Science, 13,* 145–182.

Chi, M. T. H., Feltovich, P., & Glaser, R. (1981). Categorization and representation of physics problems by experts and novices. *Cognitive Science, 5,* 121–152.

Chi, M. T. H., Glaser, R., & Farr, M. (Eds.). (1988). *The nature of expertise.* Hillsdale, NJ: Erlbaum.

Cognition and Technology Group at Vanderbilt. (1994). From visual word problems to learning communitites: Changing conceptions of cognitive research. In K. McGilly (Ed.), *Classroom lessons: Integrating cognitive theory and classroom practice* (pp. 157–200). Cambridge, MA: MIT Press/Bradford Books.

Cognition and Technology Group at Vanderbilt. (1997). *The Jasper Project: Lessons in curriculum, instruction, assessment, and professional development.* Mahwah, NJ: Erlbaum.

Cognition and Technology Group at Vanderbilt. (1998). Designing environments to reveal, support, and expand our children's potentials. In S. A. Soraci & W. McIlvane (Eds.), *Perspectives on fundamental processes in intellectual functioning* (Vol. 1, pp. 313–350). Greenwich, CT: Ablex.

Coleman, J. S., Campbell, E. Q., Hobson, C. J., McPartland, J., Mood, A. M., Weinfeld, F. D., & York, R. L. (1966). *Equality of educational opportunity.* Washington, DC: U.S. Government Printing Office.

Cote, N., Goldman, S. R., & Saul, E. (1998). Students making sense of informational text: Relations between processing and representation. *Discourse Processes, 25,* 1–53.

Cronbach, L. J. (1957). The two disciplines of scientific psychology. *American Psychologist, 12,* 671–684.

Cronbach, L. J. (1975). Beyond the two disciplines of scientific psychology. *American Psychologist, 30,* 116–127.

Cronbach, L. J., & Furby, L. (1970). How should we measure change—Or should we? *Psychological Bulletin, 74,* 68–80.

Cronbach, L. J., & Gleser, G. C. (1957). *Psychological tests and personnel decisions.* Urbana: University of Illinois Press.

Cronbach, L. J., & Snow, R. E. (1977). *Aptitudes and instructional methods: A handbook for research on interactions.* New York: Irvington.

Darling-Hammond, L. (1994). Performance-based assessment and educational equity. *Harvard Educational Review, 64,* 5–30.

de Groot, A. (1978). *Thought and choice in chess.* The Hague: Mouton. (Original work published 1946)

Dunbar, S. B., Koretz, D. M., & Hoover, H. D. (1991). Quality control in the development and use of performance assessments. *Applied Measurement in Education, 4,* 289–303.

Duschl, R. A., & Gitomer, D. H. (1997). Strategies and challenges to changing the focus of assessment and instruction in science classrooms. *Educational Assessment, 4,* 37–73.

Educational Testing Service. (1985). *The reading report card: Progress toward excellence in our schools. Trends in reading over four national assessments.* Princeton, NJ.

Embretson, S. E. (1983). Construct validity: Construct representation versus nomothetic span. *Psychological Bulletin, 93,* 179–197.

Embretson, S. E. (1984). A general latent trait model for response processes. *Psychometrica, 49,* 175–186.

Embretson, S. E. (Ed.). (1985). *Test design: Developments in psychology and psychometrics.* New York: Academic Press.

Embretson, S. E. (1991). A multidimensional item response model for learning processes. *Psychometrica, 56,* 495–515.

Embretson, S. E. (1993). Psychometric models for learning and cognitive processes. In N. Fredericksen, R. J. Mislevy, & I. I. Bejar (Eds.), *Test theory for a new generation of tests* (pp. 125–150). Hillsdale, NJ: Erlbaum.

Embretson, S. E., & Waxman, M. (1989). *Models for processing and individual differences in spatial folding.* Unpublished manuscript.

Fisher, G. (1973). Linear logistic test model as an instrument in educational research. *Psychologica, 37,* 359–374.

Fredericksen, N. (1984). The real test bias: Influences of testing on teaching and learning. *American Psychologist, 39,* 193–202.

Fredericksen, N., Mislevy, R. J., & Bejar, I. I. (Eds.). (1993). *Test theory for a new generation of tests.* Hillsdale, NJ: Erlbaum.

Glaser, R. (1976). Components of a psychology of instruction: Toward a science of design. *Review of Educational Research, 46,* 1–24.

Glaser, R. (1981). The future of testing: A research agenda for cognitive psychology and psychometrics. *American Psychologist, 36,* 923–936.

Glaser, R. (1986). A cognitive science perspective on selection and classification and on technical training. *Advances in Reading/Language Research, 4,* 253–268.

Glaser, R. (1991). Expertise and assessment. In M. C. Wittrock & E. L. Baker (Eds.), *Testing and cognition* (pp. 17–30). Englewood Cliffs, NJ: Prentice Hall.

Goldman, S. R. (1997). Learning from text: Reflections on the past and suggestions for the future. *Discourse Processes, 23,* 357–398.

Goldman, S. R., & Pellegrino, J. W. (1984). Deductions about induction: Analysis of developmental and individual differences. In R. J. Sternberg (Ed.), *Advances in the psychology of human intelligence* (Vol. 2, pp. 149–197). Hillsdale, NJ: Erlbaum.

Greeno, J. G., Pearson, P. D., & Schoenfeld, A. H. (1997). Implications for the National Assessment of Educational Progress of research on learning and cognition. In R. Glaser, R. Linn, & G. Bohrnstedt (Eds.), *Assessment in transition: Monitoring the nation's educational progress, background studies.* Stanford, CA: National Academy of Education.

Guttman, L. (1970). Integration of test design and analysis. In *Proceedings of the 1969 Invitational Conference on Testing Problems* (pp. 53–65). Princeton, NJ: Educational Testing Service.

Haertel, E. H. (1984). An application of latent class models to assessment data. *Applied Psychological Measurement, 8,* 333–346.

Hamilton, L. S., Nussbaum, E. M., & Snow, R. E. (1997). Interview procedures for validating science assessments. *Applied Measurement in Education, 10,* 181–200.

Hunt, E. (1978). Mechanics of verbal ability. *Psychological Review, 85,* 109–130.

Hunt, E., Frost, N., & Lunnenborg, C. (1973). Individual differences in cognition: A new approach to intelligence. In G. H. Bower (Ed.), *The psychology of learning and motivation* (Vol. 7, pp. 87–122). New York: Academic Press.

Hunt, E., & Lansman, M. (1975). Cognitive theory applied to individual differences. In W. K. Estes (Ed.), *Handbook of learning and cognitive processes: Introduction to concepts and issues* (Vol. 1). Hillsdale, NJ: Erlbaum.

Hunt, E., Lunnenborg, C., & Lewis, J. (1975). What does it mean to be high verbal? *Cognitive Psychology, 7,* 194–227.

Hunt, E., & Minstrell, J. (1994). A cognitive approach to teaching physics. In K. McGilly (Ed.), *Classroom lessons: Integrating cognitive theory and classroom practice* (pp. 51–74). Cambridge, MA: MIT Press/Bradford Books.

Klahr, D. (1976). *Cognition and instruction.* Hillsdale, NJ: Erlbaum.

Kotovsky, K., & Simon, H. A. (1973). Empirical tests of a theory of human acquisition of concepts for sequential events. *Cognitive Psychology, 4,* 399–424.

Kyllonen, P. C. (1993). Aptitude testing inspired by information processing: A test of the four-sources model. *Journal of General Psychology, 120,* 375–405.

Kyllonen, P. C., Lohman, D. F., & Woltz, D. J. (1984). Componential modeling of alternative strategies for performing spatial tasks. *Journal of Educational Psychology, 76*, 1325–1345.

Kyllonen, P. C., & Shute, V. J. (1989). A taxonomy of learning skills. In P. L. Ackerman, R. J. Sternberg, & R. Glaser (Eds), *Learning and individual differences* (pp. 117–163). New York: Freeman.

Lane, S. (1993). The conceptual framework for the development of a mathematics performance assessment instrument. *Educational Measurement: Issues and Practice, 12*, 16–23.

Larry P. v. Riles, 495 F. Supp. 926 (N.D. Cal. 1979).

Law, D. J., Morrin, K. A., & Pellegrino, J. W. (1995). Training effects and working memory contributions to skill acquisition in a complex coordination task. *Learning and Individual Differences, 7*, 207–234.

Law, D. J., Pellegrino, J. W., & Hunt, E. (1993). Comparing the tortoise and the hare: Gender differences in dynamic spatial reasoning tasks. *Psychological Science, 4*, 35–40.

Lesgold, A. M., Pellegrino, J. W., Fokkema, S. D., & Glaser, R. (Eds.). (1977). *Cognitive psychology and instruction* (NATO Conference Series III, Human Factors, Vol. 5). New York: Plenum.

Lesgold, A. M., Rubinson, H., Feltovich, P., Glaser, R., Klopfer, D., & Wang, Y. (1988). Expertise in a complex skill: Diagnosing X-ray pictures. In M. T. H. Chi, R. Glaser, & M. J. Farr (Eds.), *The nature of expertise* (pp. 311–342). Hillsdale, NJ: Erlbaum.

Levidow, B. B., Hunt, E., & McKee, C. (1991). The DIAGNOSER: A HyperCard tool for building theoretically based tutorials. *Behavior Research Methods, Instruments and Computers, 23*, 249–252.

Linn, R. L. (1986). Educational testing and assessment: Research needs and policy issues. *American Psychologist, 41*, 1153–1160.

Linn, R. L., Baker, E. L., & Dunbar, S. B. (1991). Complex, performance-based assessment: Expectations and validation criteria. *Educational Researcher, 20*, 5–21.

Lohman, D. F. (1994). Component scores as residual variation (or why the intercept correlates best). *Intelligence, 19*, 1–11.

Lord, F. M. (1952). A theory of test scores. *Psychometrica Monographs, 7*(4, Pt. 2).

Lord, F. M., & Novick, M. R. (1968). *Statistical theories of mental test scores.* Reading, MA: Addison-Wesley.

Magone, M. E., Cai, J., Silver, E. A., & Wang, N. (1994). Validating the cognitive complexity and content quality of a mathematics performance assessment. *International Journal of Educational Research, 21*, 317–340.

Messick, S. (1994). The interplay of evidence and consequences in the validation of performance assessments. *Educational Researcher, 23*(2), 13–23.

Minstrell, J. (1992, April). *Facets of students' knowledge: A practical view from the classroom.* Paper presented at the annual meeting of the American Educational Research Association, San Francisco.

Minstrell, J. (1999). Student thinking, instruction, and assessment in a facet-based learning environment. In J. W. Pellegrino, L. R. Jones, & K. J. Mitchell (Eds.), *Grading the nation's report card: Research from the evaluation of NAEP.* Washington, DC: National Academy Press.

Minstrell, J., & Stimpson, V. (1996). A classroom environment for learning: Guiding students' reconstruction of understanding and reasoning. In L. Schauble & R. Glaser (Eds.), *Innovations in learning: New environments for education* (pp. 175–202). Mahwah, NJ: Erlbaum.

Mislevy, R. J. (1993). Foundations of a new test theory. In N. Fredericksen, R. J. Mislevy, & I. I. Bejar (Eds.), *Test theory for a new generation of tests* (pp. 19–39). Hillsdale, NJ: Erlbaum.

Mislevy, R. J. (1995). Probability-based inference in cognitive diagnosis. In P. D. Nichols, S. F. Chipman, & R. L. Brennan (Eds.), *Cognitively diagnostic assessment* (pp. 43–71). Hillsdale, NJ: Erlbaum.

Mislevy, R. J. (1996). *Evidence and inference in educational assessment* (CSE Technical Report 414). Los Angeles: National Center for Research on Evaluation, Standards, and Student Testing, Graduate School of Education and Information Studies, University of California, Los Angeles.

Morrin, K. A., Law, D. J., & Pellegrino, J. W. (1994). Structural modeling of information coordination abilities: An evaluation and extension of the Yee, Hunt, and Pellegrino model. *Intelligence, 19,* 117–144.

Mumaw, R. J., & Pellegrino, J. W. (1984). Individual differences in complex spatial processing. *Journal of Educational Psychology, 76,* 920–939.

National Academy of Education. (1993). *The trial state assessment: Prospects and realities.* Stanford, CA.

National Academy of Education. (1997). *Assessment in transition: Monitoring the nation's educational progress.* Stanford, CA.

National Commission for Educational Excellence. (1983). *A nation at risk.* Washington, DC: U.S. Government Printing Office.

National Council of Teachers of Mathematics. (1989). *Curriculum and evaluation standards for school mathematics.* Reston, VA.

National Council on Education Standards and Testing. (1992). *Raising standards for American education.* Washington, DC.

National Educational Goals Panel. (1991). *Measuring progress toward the national educational goals: Potential indicators and measurement strategies.* Washington, DC: U.S. Government Printing Office.

National Research Council. (1996). *National science education standards.* Washington, DC: National Academy Press.

National Research Council. (1999). *Grading the nation's report card: Evaluating NAEP and transforming the assessment of educational progress.* Washington, DC: National Academy Press.

Nichols, P. D. (1994). A framework for developing cognitively diagnostic assessments. *Review of Educational Research, 64,* 575–603.

Nichols, P. D., Chipman, S. F., & Brennan, R. L. (Eds.). (1995). *Cognitively diagnostic assessment.* Hillsdale, NJ: Erlbaum.

Nichols, P. D., & Sugrue, B. (1997). *Construct-centered test development for NAEP's short forms.* Washington, DC: National Center for Education Statistics.

Nickerson, R. S. (Ed.). (1989). Special issue on educational assessment. *Educational Researcher, 18,* 3–33.

Nitko, A. J. (1989). Designing tests that are integrated with instruction. In R. L. Linn (Ed.), *Educational measurement* (3rd ed., pp. 447–474). New York: MacMillan.

Patel, V. L., & Groen, G. L. (1986). Knowledge based solution strategies in medical reasoning. *Cognitive Science, 10,* 91–116.

Pellegrino, J. W., & Glaser, R. (1979). Cognitive correlates and components in the analysis of individual differences. *Intelligence, 3,* 187–214.

Pellegrino, J. W., & Glaser, R. (1982). Analyzing aptitudes for learning: Inductive reasoning. In R. Glaser (Ed.), *Advances in instructional psychology* (Vol. 2, pp. 269–345). Hillsdale, NJ: Erlbaum.

Pellegrino, J. W., & Hunt, E. (1989). Computer controlled assessment of static and dynamic spatial reasoning. In R. F. Dillon & J. W. Pellegrino (Eds.), *Testing: Theoretical and applied perspectives* (pp. 174–198). New York: Praeger.

Pellegrino, J. W., & Kail, R. V. (1982). Process analyses of spatial aptitude. In R. J. Sternberg (Ed.), *Advances in the psychology of human intelligence* (Vol. 1, pp. 311–365). Hillsdale, NJ: Erlbaum.

Perfetti, C. A., & Goldman, S. R. (1976). Discourse memory and reading comprehension skill. *Journal of Verbal Learning and Verbal Behavior, 15,* 33–42.

Perfetti, C. A., & Hoagaboam, T. (1975). Relationship between simple word decoding and reading comprehension skill. *Journal of Educational Psychology, 67,* 461–469.

Perfetti, C. A., & Lesgold, A. M. (1982). *Reading ability.* Hillsdale, NJ: Erlbaum.

Rasch, G. (1960). *Probabilistic models for some intelligence and attainment tests.* Copenhagen: Danish Institute for Educational Research.

Resnick, L. B. (1979). The future of IQ testing. In R. J. Sternberg & D. K. Detterman (Eds.), *Human intelligence: Perspectives on its theory and measurement* (pp. 203–215). Norwood, NJ: Ablex.

Resnick, L. B., & Resnick, D. P. (1992). Assessing the thinking curriculum: New tools for educational reform. In B. R. Gifford & M. C. O'Connor (Eds.), *Changing assessments: Alternative views of aptitude, achievement, and instruction* (pp. 37–75). Boston: Kluwer.

Shavelson, R. J., Baxter, G. P., & Gao, X. (1993). Sampling variability of performance assessments. *Journal of Educational Measurement, 30,* 215–232.

Shavelson, R. J., Baxter, G. P., & Pine, J. (1992). Performance assessments: Political rhetoric and measurement reality. *Educational Researcher, 21*(4), 22–27.

Shepard, R. N., & Cooper, L. A. (1983). *Mental images and their transformations.* Cambridge, MA: MIT Press.

Sherwood, R. D., Petrosino, A. J., Lin, X., Lamon, M., & the Cognition and Technology Group at Vanderbilt. (1995). Problem-based macro contexts in science instruction: Theoretical basis, design issues, and the development of applications. In D. Lavoie (Ed.), *Towards a cognitive-science perspective for scientific problem solving* (pp. 191–214). Manhattan, KS: National Association for Research in Science Teaching.

Shute, V. J. (1992). Aptitude-treatment interactions and cognitive skill diagnosis. In W. J. Regian & V. J. Shute (Eds.), *Cognitive approaches to automated instruction* (pp. 15–43). Hillsdale, NJ: Erlbaum.

Shute, V. J. (1993). A macroadaptive approach to tutoring. *Journal of Artificial Intelligence in Education, 4,* 61–93.

Silver, E. A., & Stein, M. K. (1996). The QUASAR project: The "revolution of the possible" in mathematics instructional reform in urban middle schools. *Urban Education, 30,* 476–521.

Snow, R. E. (1980). Aptitude and achievement. *New Directions in Testing and Measurement, 5,* 39–59.

Snow, R. E. (1989a). Aptitude interactions as a framework for individual differences in learning. In P. L. Ackerman, R. J. Sternberg, & R. Glaser (Eds.), *Learning and individual differences: Advances in theory and research* (pp. 13–59). New York: Freeman.

Snow, R. E. (1989b). Cognitive-conative aptitude interactions in learning. In R. Kanfer, P. L. Ackerman, & R. Cudek (Eds.), *Abilities, motivation, and methodology: The Minnesota Symposium on Learning and Individual Differences* (pp. 435–474). Hillsdale, NJ: Erlbaum.

Snow, R. E. (1994). Abilities in academic tasks. In R. J. Sternberg & R. K. Wagner (Eds.), *Mind in context: Interactionist perspectives on human intelligence* (pp. 3–37). New York: Cambridge University Press.

Snow, R. E., Corno, L., & Jackson, D. (1996). Individual differences in affective and conative functions. In D. Berliner & R. Calfee (Eds.), *Handbook of research in educational psychology* (pp. 186–242). New York: Macmillan.

Snow, R. E., & Lohman, D. F. (1989). Implications of cognitive psychology for educational measurement. In R. L. Linn (Ed.), *Educational measurement* (pp. 263–331). New York: Macmillan.

Snow, R. E., & Lohman, D. F. (1993). Cognitive psychology, new test design, and new test theory: An introduction. In N. Fredericksen, R. J. Mislevy, & I. I. Bejar (Eds.), *Test theory for a new generation of tests* (pp. 1–17). Hillsdale, NJ: Erlbaum.

Spearman, C. (1904a). The proof and measurement of the correlation between two things. *American Journal of Psychology, 15,* 201–292.

Spearman, C. (1904b). "General intelligence" objectively determined and measured. *American Journal of Psychology, 18,* 161–169.

Sternberg, R. J. (1977). *Intelligence, information processing, and analogical reasoning: The componential analysis of human abilities.* Hillsdale, NJ: Erlbaum.

Sternberg, R. J. (1984). What cognitive psychology can (and cannot) do for test development. In B. S. Plake (Ed.), *Social and technical issues in testing: Implications for test construction and usage* (pp. 39–60). Hillsdale, NJ: Erlbaum.

Stiggins, R. (1994). *Student-centered classroom assessment.* New York: Merrill.

Swanson, J. H. (1990). One-to-one instruction: An experimental evaluation of effective tutoring strategies (Doctoral dissertation, Stanford University, 1990). *Dissertation Abstracts International, 50A,* 8.

Tatsuoka, K. K. (1983). Rule space: An approach for dealing with misconceptions based on item response theory. *Journal of Educational Measurement, 20,* 345–354.

Vygotsky, L. S. (1978). *Mind in society: The development of higher psychological processes.* Cambridge, MA: Harvard University Press.

White, B. Y., & Fredericksen, J. R. (1998). Inquiry, modeling, and metacognition: Making science accessible to all students. *Cognition and Instruction, 16,* 3–118.

Whitely, S. E. (1980). Multicomponent latent trait models for ability tests. *Psychometrica, 45,* 479–494.

Willet, J. B. (1988). Questions and answers in the measurement of change. In *Review of research in education* (Vol. 15, pp. 345–422). Washington, DC: American Educational Research Association.

Willet, J. B., & Sayer, A. G. (1994). Using covariance structure analysis to detect correlates and predictors of individual change over time. *Psychological Bulletin, 116,* 363–381.

Wilson, M. R. (1989). Saltus: A psychometric model of discontinuity in cognitive development. *Psychological Bulletin, 105,* 276–289.

Wittrock, M., & Baker, E. (1991). *Testing and cognition.* Englewood Cliffs, NJ: Prentice Hall.

Woltz, D. J. (1988). An investigation of the role of working memory in procedural skill acquisition. *Journal of Experimental Psychology: General, 117,* 319–331.

Woltz, D. J., & Shute, V. J. (1993). Individual differences in repetition priming and its relationship to declarative knowledge acquisition. *Intelligence, 17,* 333–359.

Manuscript received January 4, 1999
Accepted April 1, 1999

Chapter 10

Socio-Cultural Aspects of Assessment

CAROLINE GIPPS
Kingston University

This chapter reviews assessment from a socio-cultural perspective. Taking a broad sweep, I present a retrospective and prospective analysis of the role and functions of assessment in society, the school system, and the classroom. I begin with social and cultural issues at the level of the system macrostructure and gradually move the focus to social and cultural issues at the level of the classroom microstructure. The chapter is organized into four main sections. The first looks at the purposes assessment has served in society in the past as well as the role it plays today, driven largely by social, political, and economic forces. The second section describes developments in the conceptualization of forms of assessment over the last 20 years and seeks to explain these changes as being underpinned by changes in epistemology and views of learning. The third section focuses on assessment in the social world of the classroom, building on the developments articulated in the previous section to describe emerging practices. The final section explores some future directions.

I hope to show that, at all levels, assessment is a social activity and that we can understand it only by taking account of the social, cultural, economic, and political contexts in which it operates (Sutherland, 1996). Decisions about even apparently technical matters are influenced by political and ideological considerations. Similarly, the way students respond to assessment is subject to social and cultural influences. In the body of research and theory that builds on Vygotsky's work, *sociocultural* (generally unhyphenated) is used as a specific term embodying the roles of social interaction and cultural context in learning (Cobb, 1994) and identity formation (Penuel & Wertsch, 1995). That literature forms an important part of this chapter, but I take a wider focus, using the term socio-cultural in its broader sense.

There are two main themes that run through this chapter. The first is *power and control*, which are well understood at the system level but can also be used as analytical devices at the level of assessment in the classroom. The second is

I would like to thank Patricia Murphy, Patricia Broadfoot, Ingrid Lunt, Harry Torrance, and Geoff Whitty for their help and comments on the draft. Also, I would like to acknowledge the valuable contribution of my consulting editor, Carol Tittle, and the patience and forbearance of the editors, Ali Iran-Nejad and P. David Pearson. The responsibility for the final version of this chapter, the views and any shortcomings in it, is, of course, mine. Finally, my grateful thanks go to Kate Myronidis and Ann Doyle for their stalwart work in producing the manuscript.

the *interpretivist* paradigm underpinning many new developments in assessment. By combining interpretive and socio-cultural perspectives, we can begin to cast new light on the relationship and power dynamics between pupil and teacher in the context of assessment.

In this chapter, I use the term *assessment* as a general one. Assessment incorporates a wide range of methods for evaluating pupil performance and attainment, including formal testing and examinations, practical and oral assessment, and classroom-based assessment carried out by teachers. I use specific terms (e.g., standardized tests, portfolio assessment) where the discussion focuses on specific forms of assessment.

ASSESSMENT IN SOCIAL AND HISTORICAL PERSPECTIVE

Assessment for Selection and Certification

Assessment has a long history, and its role is a function of society's needs at the time. Selection has probably been the most pervasive role of assessment over the years (Glaser & Silver, 1994). Assessment for selection, which later became linked with certification, illustrates well the power and control aspects of assessment as well as its role in cultural and social reproduction.

There are, of course, a range of reasons for developing examination and testing systems. Eckstein and Noah (1993) offer the following purposes: reducing monopolies of birth and wealth, checking patronage and corruption, allocating scarce resources in higher education, and controlling curricula. The first three are linked with selection and certification, while the last (at an overt level) is a relatively new role for assessment. A historical model of the functions of national examination systems is put forward by Keeves (1994). In reviewing the national examination systems of 24 countries participating in the International Association for the Evaluation of Educational Achievement (IEA) Second Science Study in the mid-1980s, Keeves argues that the functions of national systems develop from a first stage of selection and certification to one of monitoring and, finally, one of exerting policy influence on curriculum and teaching.

Examinations were first developed in China under the Han dynasty (206 BC to AD 220) in order to select candidates for government service. The Jesuits introduced competitive examinations into their schools in the 17th century, possibly influenced by Jesuit travelers' experience in China. It was not until the late 18th century and early 19th century that examinations developed in northern Europe—in Prussia and then in France and England—again in order to select candidates for government. As Eckstein and Noah (1993) put it: "As modern states industrialized, improved communications, and evolved their large bureaucracies, the practice of selection by written, public examinations previously confined to China, became increasingly common" (p. 3). In China the exams were used only to select bureaucrats, with competition as the major characteristic. Certification emerged later in the European, and then American, exams as an important added purpose.

In Europe, as the industrial capitalist economy flourished, there was an increasing need for trained middle-class workers. Access to the professions had been determined, before the 19th century, by family history and patronage rather than by academic achievement or ability. Soon after the turn of the century, this picture began to change. The economy required more individuals in the professions and in managerial positions. Society, therefore, needed to encourage a wider range of individuals to take on these roles. The expanding middle classes realized that education was a means of acquiring social status, and they could see that it was in their children's interests to encourage them to aim for the professions. This was the first time that upward mobility became a practical proposition on a wide scale. Of course, there had to be some way of selecting those who were deemed suitable for training, as well as certifying those who were deemed to be competent. Thus, the professions began to control access to training and membership through examination. In Britain, it was the medical profession that, in 1815, first instituted qualifying exams. These exams were designed to determine competence and, therefore, limited access to membership of the profession (Broadfoot, 1979). Written exams for solicitors came in 1835, and exams for accountancy in 1880.

The universities were next to institute exams. The demand for entry from the middle classes increased, and in the 1850s Oxford and Cambridge set up examining boards, and London and Durham Universities introduced their own selective entry exams. It was still possible to buy one's way into a university, but before this, entry had been determined solely by family background. In 1855, entry exams were introduced as an alternative to patronage to select candidates for the rapidly expanding Civil Service. According to Trevelyan and Northcote (1853):

We are of the opinion that this examination should be in all cases a competing literary examination. This ought not to exclude careful previous inquiry into the age, health, and moral fitness of the candidates. Where character and bodily activity are chiefly required, more, comparatively, will depend upon the testimony of those to whom the candidate is well known; but the selection from among the candidates who have satisfied these preliminary inquiries should still be made by a competing examination. This may be so conducted as to test the intelligence, as well as the mere attainments of the candidates. We see no other mode by which (in the case of inferior no less than of superior offices) the double object can be attained of selecting the fittest person, and of avoiding the evils of patronage. (p. xxvii)

At the school level, in England, school leaving exams were formalized in the early part of the 20th century when the School Certificate was introduced as a standard school leaving and university entrance qualification (Broadfoot, 1979). This was necessary because of the increasing numbers completing secondary schooling. To obtain the school certificate required a pass in five or more academic subjects, with music and manual subjects being optional. The formal written examination of academic subjects was seen to be important because most of the early qualifying exams for entrance to the professions were written theoretical tests. Because written exams were associated with high-status professions, this type of exam became itself invested with high status.

In America, too, selection through examination for government jobs was instituted in order to curb political patronage. Eckstein and Noah (1993) point out that, at every level of government, examinations were instituted in the hope that this would check the pervasive practice of politicians favoring their supporters with jobs. In the early 1870s, exams were introduced for entry to the patent office, the census bureau, and the Indian office. From 1883, entry to the Civil Service required examination for all candidates except those at the highest level.

Thus, we can see that assessment for selection and certification has had a key social role to play in a range of countries. Such examinations were generally instituted to control patronage and to limit privileged access to specialized or higher education, the professions, and government posts. However, although the exams limited nepotism and corruption, they could not eliminate completely the advantages afforded by social status and wealth. In Britain, in the case of the Civil Service exams, it was still almost exclusively those who had received an appropriate fee-paying education who were able to pass (Eggleston, 1984). In Japan, examinations were used to select individuals for appointment to government positions from the mid-19th century, in an effort to remove the Samurai class from its dominant position in education and government. However, even by the start of the 20th century, sons from Samurai families (in this stage of history, we are talking largely about males) were far and away the majority in the various schools that allowed access to these examinations (Eckstein & Noah, 1993).

Assessment for selection has also been a key theme *within* the school system, with IQ testing playing a central role in both identifying those considered able enough for an academic secondary education and selecting out of the system those deemed ineducable. In 1905 Binet, a French psychologist, published the first intelligence test; this test was designed to identify children with special educational needs. His approach to the development of tests was a practical, even pragmatic, one: Items of an educational nature were chosen for their effectiveness in distinguishing between children who were judged by their teachers to be "bright" or "dull" (Wood, 1986).

At the same time, psychologists had been working on the theory of intelligence, and in 1904, a year before Binet's test appeared, Charles Spearman published a classic paper on general intelligence. Binet and Spearman were critical of each other's work, but the serendipitous timing of developments in the measurement and theory of intelligence gave IQ testing considerable appeal in the eyes of those responsible for the efficient functioning of the state education system (Thomson & Sharp, 1988). One of the reasons for this interest in IQ testing in England was that, as more and more children were brought into compulsory primary education, there was concern about the increasing numbers of children who were thought to be "subnormal" and therefore ineducable. Subnormality was, by the beginning of the 20th century, seen as being distinct from lunacy. Subnormal or "feebleminded" children needed to be sifted out from the rest of the child population so that they could attend special schools. Identifying these children accurately was clearly important, not only because of the stigma attached to attending a special school, but also because the special schools were more expensive to run. Binet's test was an ideal tool for identifying children for these special schools.

When free universal secondary education was introduced in England in 1944, there was pressure on placements for the highly selective, more academic grammar schools. Children were selected for these schools on the basis of their ability to benefit from this type of education. Assessments involved group IQ tests, math and English tests (the famous "11 +" examination), and teachers' reports. The White Paper of 1943, which outlined the 1944 legislation, suggested that allocation to secondary school should be primarily by teacher report, with the aid of intelligence tests if necessary. The minister of education, Ernest Bevin, complained that intelligence tests penalized the working class, whose children should have equal access opportunities. On the other hand, psychologist Cyril Burt claimed that selection by intelligence test only penalized the secondary schools, since children needed the right social background, as well as intelligence, to succeed there (Sutherland, 1984). As a result, both tests and teacher reports were used.

Thus, intelligence testing was introduced in England for selecting children in response to particular needs. The tests were used to identify subnormal children and take them out of the "normal" school system, as well as to allocate normal children to different types of secondary school.

In America, selection tests within the school system were used for differential placement of students to schools and in ability groups. This became an increasingly important way of managing the system when, in the first quarter of the 20th century, large numbers of immigrants came from southern and eastern Europe and put pressure on the school system. As with the use of IQ tests in England, there were two purposes: identifying students who had special educational needs to remove them from "normal" schooling and grouping students of similar ability for instructional purposes (Glaser & Silver, 1994).

Early Work: Criticisms and Controversies

Selection on the basis of academic merit has a firm philosophical foundation in terms of equity. Equity was the driving force behind the development of "objective" tests. By "objective" I am referring to multiple-choice tests and others that require no judgment in scoring. Such tests have highly replicable and reliable scoring—hence the name objective. However, subjective judgment enters into the writing of such tests, through the selection of material and answer choices. The development of objective tests for sorting and selecting students was seen, on both sides of the Atlantic, as a scientific, even progressive, activity. However, later critiques of IQ tests, and of examinations, as tools of equity questioned this view.

An early assumption of the concept of intelligence was that IQ scores should remain fairly constant throughout life. However, during the 1920s and 1930s, some researchers began to discover that substantial shifts in children's measured IQ, both upward and downward, could result from major environmental changes in their lives. Studies reviewed in the mid-1940s indicated not only that measured IQ was not constant, as was generally believed at the time, but also that IQ development was closely related to factors in the social environment (Husen & Tuijnman, 1991). Thus, the equity argument for selection by IQ test was threatened. In the United States, Gould (1981) argued that Binet's test was "highjacked" by American psychologists who espoused a hereditarian theory of intelligence. These psychologists took Binet's scores as measures of an entity called intelligence, assumed that intelligence was largely inherited, confused cultural and environmental differences with innate properties, and believed that inherited IQ marked people and groups for life and assigned individuals to an inevitable station. In England during the 1950s and 1960s, evidence grew that the 11+ selection procedure (which by then almost universally involved group IQ tests of verbal or nonverbal reasoning ability) was biased in favor of children from middle-class backgrounds, was amenable to coaching, and therefore was not a measure of pure "talent" (Yates & Pidgeon, 1957).

Another assumption, and part of the attraction of IQ tests, was that nonverbal tests were independent of culture. Evidence to contradict this belief began to emerge in the 1950s (Torrance, 1981), and there now seems to be a fairly clear understanding that IQ tests are biased in favor of individuals from the dominant culture who designed the tests. In the United Kingdom and the United States, this meant those from a White, male, middle-class background (Gipps & Murphy, 1994). In the United States, the 1979 watershed case of "Larry P" resulted in the banning of the use of IQ tests in California to allocate children to classes for the educable mentally retarded on the grounds that they discriminated against Blacks and other minority groups. A second case in Chicago the following year was not upheld (Wigdor & Garner, 1982), but nevertheless, the whole issue of the use of IQ tests for the placement of children of minority status came to the fore. In both the United States and the United Kingdom, the use of IQ tests is now greatly constrained.

Broadfoot (1996), a sociologist, argues that assessment in developed societies with mass education systems, whether for selection or certification, has a single underlying rationale: to control mass education and the nature of its goals and rewards. It operates to distribute, in a justifiable way, social roles that are not all equally desirable. Individuals are allowed to compete on an equal basis to demonstrate their competence. The provision of an apparently fair competition allows those who are not successful to accept their own failure (thus controlling resentment among the least privileged) and acquiesce in the legitimacy of the prevailing social order. Broadfoot cites IQ testing as a means of social control "unsurpassed in teaching the doomed majority that their failure was the result of their own inbuilt inadequacy" (Broadfoot, 1979, p. 44). The argument in this case is that intelligence testing obscures the perpetuation of social inequalities because it legitimates them: Tests designed by White, male, majority psychologists will tend to reflect the values, culture, and experience of the authors. It is not that the White middle classes are more intelligent or better able to acquire intelligence; rather, intelligence is defined by them and measured according to their characteristics.

In the case of examinations, the critique has essentially similar underpinnings. Performance at school may be affected by social and cultural background factors. Among these factors are poverty, poor resources at home and/or at school, absenteeism owing to work or domestic duties, mismatch between the language and culture of the home and the school, gender bias, and ethnic discrimination. As a result, examinations may be biased, and furthermore, because of their role in certification, they may institutionalize and legitimate social stratification.

Bourdieu and Passeron (1976) argue that the middle classes, unable to perpetuate their status through capital alone at the beginning of this century, were able to fall back on a second line of defense: a school system that, although apparently allowing equal opportunity, was, in fact, geared to the culture of the ruling class. The system allowed them to perpetuate their privileged position by giving them a better chance of educational success. Thus, we have the notion of "cultural capital" as opposed to financial or material capital. The cultural capital argument is that children from lower social groups are not less intelligent or less academically capable, but children from middle-class homes are better able to do well at school because of the correspondence of cultural factors between home and school. As a result, examinations have a legitimating role in that they allow the ruling classes to legitimate the power and prestige they already have. According to Connell (1993), "In Western school systems, and Western-style school systems elsewhere in the world, a particular assessment regime is hegemonic. This means both that it is culturally dominant, connected with the society's central structures of power; and that it functions to maintain the social power and prestige of dominant groups" (p. 75).

In reviewing the role of schooling in social reproduction, Jules Henry, an American anthropologist, claimed that schools are—and have to be—conservative places. If the schools trained students to be truly creative or to engage in interrogation of the culture, the culture would fall apart. "American classrooms, like educational institutions anywhere, express the values, preoccupations, and fears found in the culture as a whole. School has no choice; it must train the children to fit the culture as it is" (Henry, 1963, p. 287).

Foucault (1977) argued that assessment is one of the most significant disciplinary mechanisms of society. Foucault's work focuses on power relations in social interactions, and he argues that all types of social relationships are relationships of power. One of Foucault's themes was the use of surveillance as a form of social control, and here he implicated assessment. Surveillance uses a special microtechnology—the examination—that combines the "deployment of force and the establishment of truth" (1977, p. 184). Foucault also wrote about "normalizing judgment," which involves the concept of a norm that acts as a basis for categorization, and this, together with the act of surveillance, makes educational examinations one of the most powerful instruments for locating each individual's place in society. Here we see the articulation between control and power in assessment.

Bernstein (1977), too, sees the education system as a major determinant of the social order: It regulates the kind of worker produced and which individuals will reach positions of power and privilege. It does this by controlling the forms of knowledge taught, and, while allowing the education system to respond to new social and economic conditions, it always works in the interests of particular dominant class groups. "How a society selects, classifies, distributes, transmits and evaluates the educational knowledge it considers to be public, reflects both the distribution of power and the principles of social control" (p. 55). Much of Bernstein's early work focused on his two "message systems" of curriculum and pedagogy. A focus on his third "message system," evaluation, came later (Bernstein, 1982, 1996), when he gave an explicit role to evaluation as part of the pedagogic device. In this he acknowledges the growing role and importance of assessment today.

In summary, Bernstein argued that there has been a change of emphasis from overt to covert assessment and from specific to diffuse evaluation criteria. Overt assessment, or "objective" evaluation, is based on specific criteria, precise measurement, and standardization, which allows for comparison between schools and for an apparently objective evaluation of a pupil's progress. "This very objectivity, this recourse to scientific rationality, lends to the assessment a legitimacy which makes it hard to refute" (Broadfoot, 1996, p. 85). In informal or progressive pedagogy, evaluation procedures, Bernstein argues, are more diffuse, and assessment is covert and not so apparently precise, making direct comparison of pupils and schools more difficult. Because of the nature of informal or progressive pedagogy, there are few traditional criteria for evaluation, since there is little standardization of curriculum or pedagogy across schools. In such a pedagogic system, informal classroom-based assessment, while seeming benign, actually gives more control over performance and success to the teacher. Such assessments, Bernstein argues, are potentially controlling rather than progressive and liberating. Thus, following Foucault, some critique informal, continuous pupil assessment, which is loosely defined and therefore pervasive, as acting as an instrument of surveillance (Hargreaves, 1986).

Broadfoot builds on the general theoretical perspectives of Bernstein and Foucault to argue that

> because assessment procedures are so closely bound up with the legitimization of particular educational practices, because they are the overt means of communication from schools to society and . . . the covert means of that society's response in the form of control, assessment may be the most important of the three message systems. Assessment procedures may well be the system that determines curriculum and pedagogy and, hence, social reproduction. (Broadfoot, 1996, pp. 87–88)

Thus, it seems that it would be difficult to underestimate the power of assessment in the school system.

To summarize, although IQ testing, objective testing, and external examinations were seen originally as equitable tools for selection and certification purposes, a sociological critique calls this into question. Assessment, in its various forms, has a key role to play in cultural reproduction and social stratification. The power of assessment, and its role in control, is well acknowledged in relation to external assessment. However, the work of Henry, Foucault, Bernstein, and Broadfoot makes it clear that informal assessment carried out in the classroom can be seen in a similar framework. I analyze this issue more closely in the third section of the chapter.

Recent Trends: Assessment for Curriculum Control

More recent trends show assessment being used to control and drive curriculum and teaching. This is the final stage of Keeves's (1994) historical model following on from selection, certification, and monitoring. Here the issue is control, through centralization of curriculum and/or assessment. The driving force behind these developments is essentially economic.

Following trends in the globalization of world markets and an emphasis on measuring outputs, a number of countries are using assessment to gear up their education systems. Introducing a national curriculum or a national assessment program (or both) is a common response to global demands (Connell, 1993). In the United States, New Zealand, Australia, and the United Kingdom, governments have linked economic growth to educational performance and are using assessment to help determine curriculum, to impose high "standards" of performance, and to encourage competition among schools. Technological developments demand better educated as well as more thoughtful and flexible workers across the labor market, to strengthen a country's technological base and foster a spirit of enterprise and initiative (Brown & Lauder, 1996). The apparent mismatch between the output of the schools and the needs of the labor market in the 1980s, as indicated by the number of unqualified school leavers and by the number of young unemployed citizens, suggested that education had departed from the "real world" of work, and the result has been to seek to recouple education with the economy (Neave, 1988). An Organization for Economic Co-operation and Development (OECD) study looking at international patterns of assessment in 1995–1996 noted that nearly every OECD country was reexamining its curriculum and redefining the outcomes, usually in terms of competencies (Stevenson, 1996).

On the back of globalization, the performance of key nations is of interest to all. A fascination with performance indicators and international comparisons of performance encourages governments not only to use assessment to drive and control their curricula and teaching but also to invest large sums of money in international surveys of educational achievement. Unwelcome findings from these studies trigger national debate (ignoring warnings about sampling bias and curricular focus; e.g., Stedman, 1997) and much soul searching, as evidenced by the U.S. National Commission on Excellence in Education (NCEE) report in 1983. The NCEE report concluded:

If an unfriendly foreign power had attempted to impose on America the mediocre educational performance that exists today, we might well have viewed it as an act of war. As it stands, we have allowed this to happen to ourselves. . . . We have, in effect, been committing an act of unthinking, unilateral educational disarmament. (NCEE, 1983, p. 5)

Countries that consistently do well on comparisons of standards in education and training (Germany, France, Japan, and, more recently, Singapore, and not the United States and Britain) have in common in their societies a great emphasis on educational achievement, fostering high educational aspirations among individual learners (Green, 1997). Alongside this are centralized national curricula and standardized assessment procedures. In these countries, "At the end of compulsory schooling there are appropriate examinations or awards for all children in whichever type of institution or stream" (Green, 1997, p. 120). Educational and vocational qualifications in these systems tend to be well understood by the society and either afford entry to higher education or have genuine currency in the labor market.

Such centralization and control sits uneasily with traditionally liberal education systems such as those of the United States and Britain. On the other hand, evidence is mounting that unregulated curricular and assessment regimes increase variability of practice across schools and therefore standards of performance, enhancing the spread of attainment within age cohorts. That this spread of attainment is linked to social class underlines the equity argument for having common, centralized expectations and standards. Indeed, the strongly centralized French system was essentially designed to promote equality in an education system that aims to treat all pupils the same.

In the United States, too, there has been increased activity and interest in using assessment as a policy tool to drive the school system. Standardized commercial testing has been part of the educational system in America since the 1920s, but in the last two decades there has been vigorous growth in the market for testing (Madaus & Raczek, 1996). Indeed, Weiss (1987) argues that standardized tests and exams have become the nation's cradle to grave arbiter of social mobility. It is a highly lucrative business (with a revenue of between one-half and three-quarter billion dollars annually for the sales, scoring, and reporting of elementary and secondary school tests) and essentially unregulated. Haney et al. (1993) estimated the indirect costs of state and district testing in the 1980s to be at least $311 million (in 1988 dollars). By adding in teacher and student time, their highest estimate is $22.7 billion per year, which was more than double the total federal expenditure on secondary and elementary education in 1987–1988 (Madaus & Raczek, 1996, p. 163).

Airasian (1988) takes the view that the growth of "high stakes" testing programs in the United States has much to do with exerting symbolic control over the education system in the absence of a national curriculum. A high stakes test is one with results that are significant for the pupil, the teacher, or the school. Airasian argues that the legitimacy of these assessment programs derives not from empirical evidence of their probable effectiveness but from the perceptions they evoke and the symbol of order and control they represent. They offer educational outcomes in traditional terms of certification and exam passes and are linked with traditional moral values. Because of this symbolism, they strike a responsive chord with the public at large, which helps to explain the widespread and speedy adoption of this form of innovation.

TABLE 1
Curriculum and Assessment Questions in Relation to Equity

Curricular questions	Assessment questions
Whose knowledge is taught?	What knowledge is assessed and equated with achievement?
Why is it taught in a particular way to this particular group?	Are the form, content, and mode of assessment appropriate for different groups and individuals?
How do we enable the histories and cultures of people of color, and of women, to be taught in responsible and responsive ways?	Is this range of cultural knowledge reflected in definitions of achievement? How does cultural knowledge mediate individuals' responses to assessments in ways that alter the construct being assessed?

After Apple (1989) and Gipps and Murphy (1994).

Airasian's argument about the moral element of particular forms of testing programs is particularly interesting in relation to developments in England in the late 1980s, when a return to traditional teaching and traditional examination was, in the view of the extreme right, linked to reasserting traditional moral values. Tests, Airasian concludes, are socially valued and respected symbols of a broad range of administrative, academic, and moral virtues in society. With the added feature of central control, together with sanctions for poor performance, symbolic importance is increased. The argument goes that, as well as the actual impact that such high stakes tests have on pupils, teachers, or the curriculum, there is likely to be an important perceptual impact on the public at large. Airasian (1988) points out that "this perceptual impact underlies the social consensus, or social validation that provides the legitimization of testing as a workable and desired reform strategy" (p. 312).

Apple (1993) writes about the politics of schooling and knowledge and the links that exist between a national curriculum and the control of school knowledge. This indicates that new curricula and any linked assessments need to be evaluated for equity implications every bit as much as IQ tests and selection examinations. For example, tremendous arguments were waged in Britain over the content of the national curriculum introduced in the 1980s, particularly in relation to history and English literature. This curriculum, which determined what a generation of pupils saw as their historical and literary heritage, largely ignored the contribution of women and that of people from minority ethnic groups. Apple (1989) argues that attention must be focused on important curricular questions in relation to equity, to which Gipps and Murphy (1994) add assessment questions (see Table 1).

What the questions in Table 1 are getting at is how a subject is defined in the curriculum and how achievement within the curriculum is construed; the way in which achievement is defined and assessed reflects the value judgments of powerful groups in society. People outside those groups who are subject to different values and experiences will be disadvantaged by assessments based on such perspectives. It is not realistic to imagine a time in the future when differential values and power positions will be removed; they will no doubt change, but differences in values will continue. Hence, for fairness in assessment, interpretations of students' performance should be set in the explicit context of what is or is not being valued. This requires that there be an explicit account of the constructs being assessed and of the criteria for assessment, which should be available to both teachers and students.

For a society such as the United States that values individual achievement and wishes to ensure that benefits are distributed on the basis of merit, there is, of course, a powerful argument for using tests that are deemed "objective." As changes are made to year 2000 goals, testing will continue to be an instrument of educational reform in the United States. In the process, the struggle will be over who controls the voluntary national tests and the actual content of the test exercises.

From a comparative education perspective, Eckstein (1996) poses the following question: Why are nations now so interested in the instruments of assessment and in the management of examinations? The reason, he concludes—apart from pedagogical considerations such as enhancing student learning and policy issues such as improving school management—is that examinations are a means of exerting power over individuals and groups. Nations are more aware than ever before that their fortunes in the world depend on the educational levels of their populations. Following the sociologists' argument, the "owners" of examinations, whether ministries of education, boards of examiners, or private agencies, possess power over important resources and decisions. Moreover, the results have economic as well as social value to the individual. Poor examination results may deny students access to certain levels and forms of advanced schooling and thus close the doors to social, political, and economic advancement.

Equity is clearly an important theme in this use of assessment. On the one hand, centralized, common curricula and common standards or benchmarks are seen as important for an equitable society (although there is an argument, too, that treating everyone the same is inequitable). On the other hand, such policies exert great power over the education system and individuals' lives. Therefore, the content of both curriculum and assessment needs to be evaluated in terms of fairness, bias, and inclusion of minority group cultural knowledge.

In summary, external assessment has had a historical role in selection and certification, and the sociological critique indicates the role of assessment in cultural and social reproduction. At the system level, assessment is now being used in many countries for curriculum control. These roles for assessment, while often proposed in order to allocate fairly educational opportunities, or to offer equal access to curriculum, tend to be driven by political and economic demands. This may imperil the equity impact.

CHANGES IN THE PRACTICE AND PHILOSOPHY OF ASSESSMENT

I now move to more recent trends in design. There have been considerable developments in the nature and conceptualization of assessment over the last

15–20 years, as any student, or user, of assessment will know. Many of the current developments, including performance assessments, portfolios, and "authentic" assessments, have a rather different approach from traditional standardized tests or examinations. Put simply, the focus has shifted toward a broader assessment of learning, enhancement of learning for the individual, engagement with the student during assessment, and involvement of teachers in the assessment process. The purpose of these assessments, in the main, is not that of selection or certification, and this different purpose allows greater flexibility in style of assessment. But these developments do not result simply from a change in purpose; the practice and philosophy of assessment has undergone a change in the last two decades. This change in assessment, which some describe as a paradigm shift, is illustrated by the title of this chapter: Fifteen years ago, it would not have been considered relevant to have a chapter on the socio-cultural aspects of assessment. Testing (and examining in the United Kingdom) was seen as a technological activity based in psychometric theory with its emphasis on replicability and generalizability. Measurement did not permit an engagement with the individual being tested or an understanding of the cultural nature of tests (Broadfoot, 1994; Gipps, 1994a; Wolf et al., 1991).

Psychometric theory developed originally from work on intelligence and intelligence testing. The underlying notion was that intelligence was innate and fixed in the way that other inherited characteristics are, such as skin color. Intelligence could therefore be measured (since, like other characteristics, it was observable), and, on the basis of the outcome, individuals could be assigned to streams, groups, or schools that were appropriate to their intelligence (or "ability," as it came to be seen). Lohman (1997) and others would argue that much of the early work in this field has been caricatured, inaccurately, and that the developers of intelligence tests were not as narrow-minded as they are made out to be. But the traditional psychometric testing model was essentially one of limitation: The aim was to measure attributes that were a property of the individual and were thought to be fixed. This notion of limitation is now seen to be a major disadvantage of the classical psychometric approach (Goldstein, 1993).

Along with psychometric theory, its formulas and quantification, came an aura of objectivity; such testing is "scientific," and therefore the figures it produces must be accurate and meaningful. The measurements that individuals amass via such testing (e.g., IQ scores, reading ages, rankings) come to have a powerful labeling potential. As Lohman (1997) points out, the political and social climate at the time was a culture that viewed sorting children as a progressive reform and intelligence tests as the fairest measure to determine the ability levels of all pupils, regardless of their racial, cultural, and language background. By the 1970s, however, in a very different social climate, these same tests were viewed as biased in regard to gender, ethnicity, and social class—and thus unfair.

With the psychometric model comes an assumption of the primacy of technical issues, notably standardization and reliability (Goldstein, 1996). If individuals are to be compared with one another, then we need to be certain that the test or assessment was carried out in the same way for all individuals, that it was scored in the same way, and that the scores were interpreted in the same way. Within this model, standardization is vital to support the technical reliability of the test. However, these requirements can have a negative effect on the construct validity and curricular impact of the test, since only some material and certain tasks are amenable to this type of testing.

These new developments in assessment—performance assessment, "authentic" assessment, portfolio assessment, and so forth—are part of a move to design assessment that supports learning and provides more detailed information about students (Wolf et al., 1991). This move was initiated in the late 1950s (around the time of the publication of Bloom's taxonomy of educational objectives) as educators began to articulate a need for assessment that was designed specifically for educational purposes and could be used in the cycle of planning, instruction, learning, and evaluation. Wood (1986) cites Glaser's 1963 article on criterion-referenced testing as a watershed in the development of a new type of assessment, which moved away from classical testing based on psychometric theory. Glaser's article made the point that norm-referenced testing developed from psychometric work that focused on aptitude, selection, and prediction. Educational assessment, by contrast, aims to devise tests that look at the individual as an individual, rather than in relation to other individuals, and to use measurement to identify strengths and weaknesses individuals might have so as to aid their educational progress.

Such an aim is, of course, laudable, but this newer approach is possible only for certain assessment purposes. The interrelationship between purpose and design is well illustrated here. For external assessment at the system level and for high stakes purposes, forms of standardization that lead to high reliability are of key importance. For assessment used in the classroom and for diagnostic or formative purposes, such attention to reliability is less relevant, and the main focus is on construct validity and use of results at the class/school level. Thus, it is important to consider the most appropriate balance between reliability and validity in assessments for different purposes. Harlen (1994) suggests we deal with this tension by considering the quality of a test, which she sees as requiring the maximum level of reliability appropriate for a test's purpose while maintaining high levels of construct and content validity.

This is not the place for a detailed account of the current thinking on reliability and validity. These issues are addressed elsewhere, and the interested reader is referred to Cronbach (1988), Messick (1989), Tittle (1989), Linn (1993), Shepard (1993), Gipps (1994a), and Moss (1994). However, what is important for this chapter is to point out the issues around the design of assessment for different purposes and the need to continue to develop our interpretations of these key concepts. In this vein, Moss (1994) argues for a dialogue between psychometric and hermeneutic approaches to warranting knowledge claims:

Ultimately, the purpose of educational assessment is to improve teaching and learning. . . .|Current conceptions of reliability and validity in educational measurement constrain the kinds of assessment practices that are likely to find favor, and these in turn constrain educational opportunities for teachers

FIGURE 1
CRESST Conceptual Model

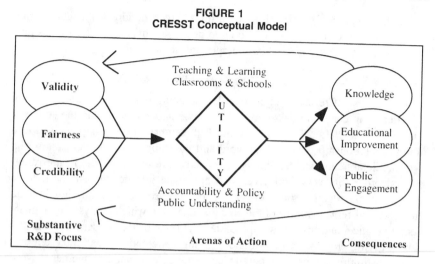

and students. A more hermeneutic approach to assessment would lend theoretical support to new directions in assessment and accountability that honor the purposes and lived experiences of students and the professional, collaborative judgements of teachers. Exploring the dialectic between hermeneutics and psychometrics should provoke and inform a much needed debate among those who develop and use assessments about why particular methods of validity inquiry are privileged and what the effects of that privileging are on the community. (p. 10)

The question is, To what extent and for which assessment purposes should we be concerned with standardization, replicability, and generalization? For some purposes, would we not be better off focusing on the quality of the performance and fairness in scoring? By the same token, in some cases would it not be preferable to credit a specific accomplishment in and of itself without the assumption of generalizability or prediction?

An example of the changing conception of assessment, broadened from a technical activity, is given by the conceptual model guiding research on assessment being carried out by CRESST (the National Center for Research on Evaluation, Standards, and Student Testing) at the University of California, Los Angeles (see Figure 1). In this model, what is required for a good assessment is ''an expanded view of validity, including attention to intended purposes and consequences; heightened concerns for inclusion of and fairness to all students; and recognition of the importance of public credibility'' (Land, 1997, p. 4). ''Based in cognitive theory, the CRESST models focus on core types of learning that recur across the curriculum: conceptual understanding, knowledge representation, problem solving, communication, and team work'' (p. 6). Such a broad model illustrates a very different conception of assessment and different requirements for design, both of which stem from a changed philosophy of assessment.

Some of the most innovative thinking around assessment at the level of the teacher and student in the classroom comes from the work of sociocultural theorists. Because of its significance for this chapter, I address this work in more detail in the third section. Now I go on to describe why such a change has taken place in assessment and what is underpinning it.

Changing Epistemologies

The process of reform and change that is taking place in education, and that is reflected in changes in assessment, has to be understood within the context of our era. In the classical age, before the 17th century, there was perceived to be a direct relationship between the word and the thing it represented; knowledge was predictable and stable, and symbols and representations simply mirrored a natural order that was God given and not to be questioned. The shift to the enlightenment began in the 17th century, moving from a classical view in which the word was representative of the object to a view in which analysis of language, social practice, and history was possible. The hope of the modern age was that, through tying progress to reason and bringing systematic human intervention to social institutions, more democratic and equitable social arrangements would be created.

The world in which we now find ourselves, characterized as postmodern, suggests that our old ways of understanding and questioning the world need adjusting if we are to influence it (Greene, 1994). Knowledge does not exist objectively out there, independent of the knower; the categories of "truth" and "knowledge" are seen to be not only hugely complex and subjective but politically saturated. In this paradigm, there is no grand narrative, no great conceptual framework (Lather, 1992). This has created a crisis of confidence in Western conceptual systems born out of a realization of the limits of enlightenment rationality. Together with paradigm shifts in the philosophy of science, this crisis of confidence has produced a body of criticism of the notion of scientific method as "transhistorical, culture-free, disinterested, replicable, testable, empirical substantiation of theory" (Lather, 1992, p. 3).

In the postmodern world view, assessment, as is the case with other activities, is seen to be value laden and socially constructed. To see assessment as a scientific, objective activity is mistaken; assessment is not an exact science (Broadfoot, 1994; Wolf et al., 1991). There have been debates about the subjective nature of knowledge, particularly in science, for more than a century; however, this change in view is seen as part of the postmodern condition. The modernist view is that it is possible to be a disinterested observer, while the postmodernist view is that such detachment is not possible. We are social beings who construe the world according to our values and perceptions; thus, our biographies are central to what we see and how we interpret it. Similarly in assessment, performance is not "objective"; rather, it is construed according to the perspectives and values of the assessor, whether the assessor is the one who designs the assessment and its "objective" marking scheme or the one who grades open-ended performances.

Alongside the shift away from a world view characterized by scientific certainty is the development of an epistemology (or theory of knowledge) based on an interpretivist stance. Claims about what exists in the world imply claims about how what exists may be known. Many of the newer developments in assessment are rooted in an interpretivist perspective. The interpretive approach focuses on participants' own perspectives in conceptualizing and reconstructing their experiences and world view. The interpretive paradigm brings out the importance of understanding a learner's response in relation to the learner's expectations of and assumptions about the classroom process, interpretation of the task demand, and the criteria for success (Aikenhead, 1997). It would also place subjects' and users' interpretation of generalizability at the forefront in any evaluation of a test's validity (Moss, 1992). Moss (1996) argues that bringing an interpretive conception of social science to bear on assessment will support the development of assessment theory and practice. She draws on hermeneutics (an epistemology that deals with interpretation) as a philosophy that is useful in thinking about assessment. Moss (1994) argues that a hermeneutic approach to assessment involves holistic, integrated interpretations of performances that aim at contextualized understanding of real attainments. She notes that

most hermeneutic philosophers share a holistic and integrative approach to interpretation of human phenomena that seeks to understand the whole in light of its parts, repeatedly testing interpretations against the available evidence until each of the parts can be accounted for in a coherent interpretation of the whole. (p. 7)

Ryan (1988) draws on Habermas's three paradigms to develop a framework for conceptualizing assessment and evaluation. The *empirical-analytic* (a technical rationalist, logical positivist orientation) relates to traditional standardized measurement-based approaches to assessment. The *interpretive* (an orientation that aims to understand things from the student's point of view) includes "alternative" methods of assessment such as portfolios and concept mapping. The *critical-theoretic* (an orientation based on eliminating oppression in human relationships) would include student self-evaluation and collaboratively developed assessment rubrics.

The same broad interpretive approach can be seen in naturalistic approaches to evaluation of programs and curricula (Eisner, 1993). Guba and Lincoln (1989) argue for a reconceptualization of the traditional program evaluation criteria of reliability, validity, and generalizability to look instead at qualities such as trustworthiness and authenticity, with "thick description" of context and participants playing a key role. Trustworthiness, according to Guba and Lincoln, is based on credibility, transferability, and dependability, and all of these terms can be articulated in relation to assessment of pupils (Gipps, 1994a). Authenticity in assessment can be seen as having to do with the extent to which the relevant constructs are fairly and adequately covered in an assessment. Fairness suggests that *all* groups' constructs are included rather than just the test developer's (Gipps & Murphy, 1994).

Tittle (1994) proposes a framework for an educational psychology of assessment that has three dimensions: the epistemology and theories involved (both general and in relation to subject matter); the interpreter and user, whose presence, characteristics, needs, and values must be brought into the frame; and the characteristics of the assessment itself. Such a model, while different from that proposed by CRESST, shares with it the understanding that assessment is a social activity that has a range of values and valences.

Changing Views of Learning and the Implications for Assessment

A significant shift has also occurred in our understanding of how learning takes place. Work in constructivist psychology shows learning in terms of an organic process of reorganizing and restructuring as the student learns, suggesting that learning is a process of knowledge construction (Driver et al., 1985; von-Glasersfeld, 1987). Learning occurs not by recording information but by interpreting it, so instruction must be seen not as direct transfer of knowledge but as an intervention in an ongoing knowledge construction process (Resnick, 1989). Thus, in constructivist learning theory, students learn by actively making sense of new knowledge, making meaning from it (Iran-Nejad, 1995), and mapping it into their existing knowledge map or schema. Shepard (1991) notes that "contemporary cognitive psychology has built on the very old idea that things are easier to learn if they make sense" (p. 8). Isolated facts, if learned, quickly disappear from the memory because they have no meaning and do not fit into the learner's conceptual map. Knowledge learned in this way is of limited use because it is difficult for it to be applied, generalized, or retrieved. According to Shepard (1992), "Meaning makes learning easier, because the learner knows where to put things in her mental framework, and meaning makes knowledge useful because likely purposes and applications are already part of the understanding" (p. 319).

The theoretical basis to constructivist views of learning is essentially epistemological, an explanation of how knowledge is created (Airasian & Walsh, 1997; Cobb, 1994). Epistemology and theories of learning are linked, since it is likely that one's views of the nature of knowledge and the acquisition of knowledge will be congruent. Thus, interpretivism and constructivism are related. As with interpretive approaches, the constructivist paradigm does not accept that reality is fixed and independent of the observer; rather, there are multiple constructions of reality. Airasian and Walsh (1997) ask why constructivism has become so popular as a learning theory and link it with this changing epistemology: As the observer constructs reality, the learner constructs his or her own knowledge. In addition, constructivist theory makes the implicit assumption that all students can and will learn, and thus, Airasian and Walsh argue, constructivism symbolizes emancipation. As Wolf et al. (1991) put it, constructivism emphasizes a notion of mindfulness that is open to all: "Across ages and classes, all learners construct (rather than merely absorb) knowledge, because inference, observation, rule generation and theory building are open to all" (p. 48).

Incorporating Piaget's concepts of assimilation and accommodation, constructivists argue that learning is characterized as a process of self-organization in which the subject reorganizes his or her activity to eliminate perturbations, such as those arising from new or conflicting pieces of evidence, so that the learner has knowledge that is viable in his or her experience (von Glasersfeld, 1989). Thus, Piagetian constructivists analyze learning within the individual, giving priority to pupils' sensory-motor and conceptual activity. Social constructivists, however, tend to emphasize the socially situated nature of much learning (Driver et al., 1994; Pollard, 1990) and focus on the individual acquiring knowledge in social action. In Pollard's (1990) social-constructivist model of the teaching/ learning process, he stresses the importance of the teacher as a "reflective agent." This role is dependent on sensitive and accurate assessment of a child's needs and places a premium on formative teacher assessment of pupil understanding.

The approach of Vygotskyan *sociocultural* theorists is different again. According to Wertsch (1991): "The basic goal of a sociocultural approach to mind is to create an account of human mental processes that recognizes the essential relationship between these processes and their cultural, historical and institutional settings" (p. 6). Like constructivists, socioculturalists assume human agency in the process of coming to know, but socioculturalists further argue that meaning derived from interactions is not exclusively a product of the person acting. They view the individual engaged in relational activities with others. Building on Vygotsky's arguments about the importance of interaction with more knowledgeable others and the role of society in providing a framework for the child's learning, sociocultural theorists thus describe learning in terms of apprenticeship (e.g., Brown et al., 1993; Glaser, 1990; Rogoff, 1990), legitimate peripheral participation (Lave & Wenger, 1991), or negotiation of meaning in the construction zone (Newman, Griffin, & Cole, 1989). As Bruner and Haste (1987) put it, through "social life, the child acquires a framework for interpreting experience and learns how to negotiate meaning in a manner congruent with the requirements of the culture. 'Making sense' is a social process; it is an activity that is always situated in a cultural and historical context" (p. 1). Also, "the child's development depends upon her using, so to speak, the tool kit of the culture to express the powers of mind" (p. 5). Newman, Griffin, and Cole (1989) describe the teacher's role in helping to develop cognitive systems in the process of construction in the classic Vygotskyan zone of proximal development. They thus write about "the changing functional system which is the interactive construction zone" (p. 76).

Rogoff (1990) argues that cognitive development is an apprenticeship that occurs through guided participation in social activities with "companions" who support and stretch children's understanding of a skill in using the tools of culture. "The particular skills and orientations that children develop are rooted in the specific historical and cultural activities of the community in which children and their companions interact" (p. vii). Lave and Wenger (1991) also situate learning in certain forms of social (co)participation but go on to argue that it is mediated by the differences of perspective among the co-participants. Learning does not take place only in the learner; rather, it is distributed among the co-participants, although the apprentice is likely to be the one most dramatically transformed.

Lave and Wenger characterize learning not as the acquisition of knowledge but as increasing access to participating roles in expert performances; their "legitimate peripheral participation" is a way of acting in the world, and learning is not a way of coming to know about the social world but, rather, a way of being in it.

While both social constructivists and socioculturalists focus on the individual's learning within the social setting of the classroom, most constructivists (including social constructivists) and sociocultural theorists approach research on learning in different ways. Significantly, they disagree over whether "mind is located in the head or in the individual-in-social-action" (Cobb, 1994, p. 13). The constructivist perspective focuses on what children learn and the processes by which they do so, while the sociocultural perspective focuses on the conditions for the possibility of learning. The two schools do, however, have two elements in common: They both emphasize the crucial role of activity in learning, and both focus on the processes of learning.

I have spent some time on new understandings of learning, since theories of learning have implications for assessment design. In the traditional model of teaching and learning, the curriculum is seen as a distinct body of information, specified in detail, that can be transmitted to the learner. Assessment here consists of checking whether the information has been received. Standardized achievement tests evaluate students' abilities to recall and apply facts learnt routinely. Even items that are designed to assess higher level activities often require no more than the ability to recall the appropriate formula and to make substitutions to obtain the correct answer. Students who conceive of knowledge as collections of facts will use learning strategies that are aimed at successful memorization (Entwistle, 1992; Marton & Saljo, 1984) rather than engaging in deep learning.

Good learners tend to have good metacognitive strategies. Metacognition is a general term that refers to a second-order form of thinking: thinking about thinking. It includes a variety of self-awareness processes to help plan, monitor, orchestrate, and control one's own learning. To do this, learners use particular strategies that hinge on self-questioning in order to make the purpose of learning clear, searching for connections and conflicts with what is already known, and judging whether understanding of the material is sufficient for the task. An essential aspect of metacognition is that learners appraise and regulate their own learning by self-assessment or self-evaluation. If pupils are to become competent assessors of their own work, they need sustained experience in ways of questioning and improving the quality of their work and supported experience in self-assessment, which includes understanding what counts as the standard expected and the criteria on which they will be assessed (Sadler, 1989).

Constructivist models of learning, which see learning as a process of personal knowledge construction and meaning making, describe a complex and diverse process and therefore require assessment to be diverse, examining in more depth the structure and quality of students' learning and understanding. While, for example, standardized multiple-choice or short answer tests are efficient at sampling the acquisition of specific knowledge gained from teachers, more intense, even interactive assessment (e.g., essays and performance assessments, small-group tasks and projects) is needed to assess the processes of learning and understanding, and to encourage a deeper level of learning.

The implications of sociocultural approaches to learning for assessment practice are not easy to unpack. Put most simply, the requirement is to assess process as well as product; the conception must be dynamic rather than static (Lunt, 1994), and attention must be paid to the social and cultural context of both learning and assessment. I address this in more detail in the next section.

In summary, changes in assessment practice and design reflect changes in world view, a resulting change in epistemology, and new understandings of learning. These have powerful messages for how we construe, design, and evaluate assessment.

ASSESSMENT IN THE SOCIAL WORLD OF THE CLASSROOM

I now want to bring the focus down to assessment as played out in the classroom. This is important since, as pointed out at the start of the previous section, many of the new developments in assessment are designed for use by teachers at the classroom level. First, I address the implications of Vygotskyan sociocultural theory for assessment. Second, I look at the assessment relationship between teacher and pupil from an interpretive perspective and in relation to power and control. As Bernstein and Foucault warn us, informal classroom assessment can be a mechanism of control in the same way that external and/or high stakes assessment can.

Assessment in Sociocultural Theory

For insight into assessment in the sociocultural model, I turn again to the work of Vygotsky. Vygotsky pointed to the importance of tools and aids in human learning. The use of external supports is a key element in the development of mental functions. Assessment in the traditional examination and psychometric model, which denies the pupil the use of external tools, reduces its usefulness and ecological validity. Following Vygotsky's ideas, we should develop assessment that allows the use of auxiliary tools (including adults) and thus produces best performance rather than typical performance. Such assessment may be interactive and is termed dynamic assessment. As Lunt (1994) explains:

Dynamic assessment procedures . . . involve a dynamic interactional exploration of a learner's learning and thinking process and aim to investigate a learner's strategies for learning and ways in which these may be extended or enhanced. Since it offers individuals an opportunity to learn, dynamic assessment has the potential to show important information about individual strategies and processes of learning and, therefore, to offer potentially useful suggestions about teaching. (p. 152)

Looking for best performance (i.e., using assessment that elicits elaborated performance or tests at the upper rather than lower thresholds of performance) resonates with Vygotsky's *zone of proximal development* (Vygotsky, 1978). In this process, assessor and pupil collaborate to produce the best performance of which the pupil is capable. Giving help, in order to obtain best performance, is the rule in this model; by contrast, help is withheld in standardized tests and produces "typical" performance.

When learning is considered as much a social as an individual process, evaluation of progress in learning takes on a different form. Rather than assessing an individual's performance on a task at one point in time, in dynamic assessment the social system of the teacher and pupil is assessed. However, even in dynamic assessment, help is at some point withheld and an evaluation of performance made. As Newman, Griffin, and Cole (1989) put it:

> Dynamic assessment, then, shares a feature in common with the traditional testing method of assessment in that it requires putting the child "on her own." Support has to be removed until the child begins to falter. One difference between the two approaches lies in the fact that dynamic assessment achieves a finer-grained idea of the child's level of "independent ability." (p. 79)

Such interactive assessment can reduce anxiety in the test situation and thus encourage best performance (Nuttall, 1987). It may be particularly beneficial for children from minority groups, who might be disadvantaged in the standardized situation. The experience of the early national assessment program in England showed (Gipps, 1994b) that, in comparison with standardized tests, interactive, classroom-based standard assessment tasks, despite a heavy reliance on language, offered minority group children a better opportunity to show what they knew, understood, and could do.

Rogoff (1990) argues that there are cultural values involved in definitions of intelligence and valued behavior and that these values affect understandings of assessment. For example, the characteristics of a good narrative vary across cultures, as do indigenous concepts of intelligence. According to Rogoff (1990), "Cultural variation appears in value judgements about the desirability of speed, abstraction and memory skills, and the separability of social from cognitive skills and knowledge from action . . . performance in cognitive tasks is inseparable from values about appropriate social relationships in such situations" (pp. 58–59). Reliance on others for help in problem-solving situations varies according to the cultural setting. In traditional American and British school settings, relying on a companion for help in assessment is likely to be considered cheating, whereas in other settings in everyday situations *not* to use a companion's assistance may be regarded as inappropriate.

Some researchers in the sociocultural perspective, which focuses on situated learning, suggest that assessment is not necessary, while others suggest that individuals must be assessed as part of a group. For example, Lave and Wenger (1991) argue that, in the apprenticeship system, testing is not necessary since increasing participation has its own use value; in settings such as schools, however, learning becomes commoditized, and exchange value, demonstrated through testing, replaces use value:

The commoditization of learning engenders a fundamental contradiction between the use and exchange values of the outcome of learning, which manifests itself in conflicts between learning to know and learning to display knowledge for evaluation. Testing in schools and trade schools (unnecessary in situations of apprenticeship learning) is perhaps the most pervasive and salient example of a way of establishing the exchange value of knowledge. Test taking then becomes a new parasitic practice, the goal of which is to increase the exchange value of learning independently of its use value. (p. 112)

The requirement, in the sociocultural perspective, to assess the processes of learning and to assess learning in the social setting can be met in a number of ways. Portfolios can be used to reflect the processes of learning and their development over time. Portfolios, of course, take many forms: They may contain items selected at intervals by the teacher or "best" pieces of work chosen by the pupil; work in the portfolio may be assessed in a more or less standardized way (Koretz et al., 1993). To support the sociocultural model of learning, they need in some way to reflect or articulate the social setting in which the learning took place. Commentary by the teacher and the pupil can describe the social situation of learning. For example, student and teacher commentaries are part of the final portfolio in the PROPEL project (Wolf et al., 1991). These commentaries are focused on the process of learning and developing achievement, and they encourage reflection on the part of both pupil and teacher. The process, Wolf (1989) argues, is difficult because portfolios "demand intimate and often frighteningly subjective talk with students" (p. 37). Pupils may be unwilling to engage in the intellectual process, while teachers may be unable to give up control of the discussion. But when it works, she argues, it is well worth the effort.

Assessment within a social situation can be afforded by assessing students in collaborative group activities in which they contribute to a task and help others. "In such assessment, as in instruction using group approaches, the student can observe how others reason and can receive feedback on his or her own efforts. In this context, not only performance, but also the facility with which a student adapts to help and guidance, can be assessed" (Glaser & Silver, 1994, pp. 412–413). Such socially situated collaborative assessment also has the advantage of encouraging students to develop and question their definitions of competence. Brown and colleagues analyze collaborative assessment environments and compare them with collaborative teaching environments. In their view (Brown et al., 1992), the crucial difference between the two is that in the teaching environment aid is opportunistic, while in the assessment environment aid is in the form of "standardized hints."

Lampert (1990) describes a project in the teaching of mathematics in which the roles and responsibilities of teachers and students within classroom discourse were altered. Sometimes the teacher consciously held back from commenting on answers given by students, and so the class developed discussion around the problems and tasks, made hypotheses about solutions, and took risks in the way that the mathematical community would. The teacher, standing back, refused to be the intellectual authority in the way that is normally the case in school mathematics. This approach to learning in a classroom community entails a

different view of assessment of pupil attainment, one based very much on understanding:

The questions I expected them to answer went beyond simply determining whether they could get
the solutions. I also expected them to answer questions about mathematical assumptions and the
legitimacy of their strategies. Answers to problems were given by students, but I did not interpret
them to be the primary indication of whether they knew mathematics. (p. 38)

The emphasis was on the analysis of the students' language, their assertions, and
their ability to demonstrate that their strategies were valid. In such a group/community
learning situation, assessment may be focused as much on the group as on individuals:
"By the end of the lesson, 14 of the 18 students present in the class had had
something mathematically substantial to say about exponents" (p. 52).

Cobb and Bowers (1998), too, talk about assessment (using the term *evaluation*)
within the group. Within their cognitive and situated perspective on learning,
performance is socially situated. Therefore, the teacher should evaluate the
group's changing beliefs and reasoning, and the individual should be evaluated
in relation to the group. The issue for Cobb and Bowers is how one views
individuals whose (mathematical) reasoning is less effective than others in the
group. They describe such students as those who have less sophisticated ways
of participating in particular classroom practices. Since performance is socially
situated, the performance resides not just in the student but in the relationship
between the teacher and the individual. They treat academic success/failure as
the exclusive property neither of individual students nor of the instruction they
receive. They see it as a "relation" between individual students and the practices
that they and the teacher construct. So, pupil assessment in this model focuses
on the individual as part of the group, and the key issue becomes how or whether
one interprets the evidence of performance of individuals.

Assessment within the framework of sociocultural theory is seen as interactive,
dynamic, and collaborative. Rather than an external and formalized activity,
assessment is integral to the teaching process and embedded in the social and
cultural life of the classroom. Such an approach is seen as constructive—because
of its focus on assessing the process of learning, the attempt to elicit elaborated
performance, and the emphasis on collaborative activity (whether the collaboration is with the teacher or a group of peers). Much of the work in this field is
still at the level of research, however, and a number of issues remain to be
clarified. For example, such assessment is often time consuming and demands
particular skills of the teacher/assessor. The procedures, being unstandardized,
do not meet traditional reliability criteria, and this has an impact on the purposes
for which the assessment can or should be used. There are many issues to be
resolved around the evaluation of individuals within group performance. A key
issue, too, is the relationship between teacher/assessor and pupil.

The Assessment Relationship

In traditional assessment, the relationship between teacher and student is a
hierarchical one. The teacher sets and defines the task and determines its evaluation. The student's role is to be the object of this activity and, through the

completion of a range of tests, to be graded. However, if one uses an interpretive approach, there are other ways of seeing this relationship. In newer forms of assessment, such as negotiated assessment and self-assessment, the student has a role in discussing and negotiating the terms and outcomes of the assessment, although in reality such a practice may be rare. The thesis behind such a nontraditional approach (critical-theoretic in Habermas's framework) is that students need to become involved in the assessment process so that they are encouraged to monitor and reflect on their own performance in order to become self-monitoring and self-regulating learners (Broadfoot, 1996; Wittrock & Baker, 1991; Wolf et al., 1991). A key element of the interpretive paradigm is the need to understand a learner's response. In relation to informal assessment, this includes the learner's expectations, assumptions, and interpretations of the classroom culture, task demands, and criteria for success (Aikenhead, 1997). Sadler (1998), developing this line of argument further, points out that teachers commonly bring with them to the assessment setting a more elaborate and extensive knowledge base, a set of attitudes or dispositions toward teaching as an activity, skill in devising assessments, a deep knowledge of criteria and standards appropriate to the assessment task, evaluative skills in making judgements about student performance, and expertise in framing feedback statements. Sadler argues that an appreciation of these resources and skills is important because eventually the teacher must share them with the student in order to pass them on.

Ultimately the intention of most educational systems is to help students not only grow in knowledge and expertise, but also to become progressively independent of the teacher for lifelong learning. Hence if teacher-supplied feedback is to give way to self assessment and self monitoring, some of what the teacher brings to the assessment act must itself become part of the curriculum for the student, not an accidental or inconsequential adjunct to it. (Sadler, 1998, p. 82)

Taylor et al. (1997), discussing the communicative relationships of pupils and teachers, also draw on the work of Habermas, to develop the notion of *open discourse*. In open discourse, communication is oriented toward understanding and respecting the perspectives of others. According to Taylor et al. (1997):

Open discourse gives rise to opportunities for students to (1) negotiate with the teacher about the nature of their learning activities (2) participate in the determination of assessment criteria and undertake self-assessment and peer-assessment (3) engage in collaborative and open-ended enquiry with fellow students and (4) participate in reconstructing the social norms of the classroom. (p. 295)

Taylor and colleagues do not articulate how such a communicative climate might be set up, but they have developed a questionnaire to evaluate the learning environment on five key dimensions, including shared control and student negotiation.

Torrance and Pryor (1998) argue that informal assessment in the classroom can be construed as a key arena for the negotiation of classroom relationships. They use the example of assessment of 5-year-old children on entry to school, which is widely encouraged in England and Wales. Termed baseline assessment, it involves the teacher in a one-to-one assessment with the child. Part of the requirement for this assessment is that it be used to measure progress of the individual by age 7 and to analyze school performance. Torrance and Pryor describe an observation of such an assessment event, indicating that it is by no means a transparent technical activity but part of the child's earliest initiation into the rituals of schooling. This early assessment is a crucial initial context in which the struggle for classroom power between teachers and pupils is manifested. Here definitions of what it is to be a teacher and pupil are first set in play. While the teacher attempts to encourage the pupil's responses (through praise, smiles, etc.), she is also determined to exercise control over the pupil in order to accomplish her agenda. Torrance and Pryor are not suggesting that power should not be exercised; rather, they are suggesting that its operation is an inevitable feature of classroom life. They point out that the process of question and answer on which much classroom assessment is based can be problematic, since much of what appears to be simple information gathering has more of a classroom management function than a cognitive one.

In Torrance and Pryor's view, we need to recognize the tension between the assessment requirements of prescribed curricula and the assessment needs of individual pupils who are struggling to make sense of the ideas with which they are confronted. Indeed, in a sociocultural perspective, the task is, in a sense, constructed by the student, not the teacher/assessor. The situatedness of the individual determines what sense is made of what the assessor provides (Cooper & Dunne, 1998). There should be opportunities when criteria are discussed and negotiated with the pupil, and assessment thus becomes a more collaborative enterprise. Such a situation would allow more opportunities for establishing a teacher-pupil relationship based on *power with* the pupil as opposed to *power over* the pupil.

However, developing such a relationship is not straightforward. In an analysis of teachers' informal assessment of pupils in Switzerland, Perrenoud (1991) claims that, since many pupils are content to do what is minimally required in order to "get by," attempts by teachers to engage them more deeply in learning and sharing power through self-assessment will require a shift in the established equilibrium. "Every teacher who wants to practise formative assessment must reconstruct the teaching contracts so as to counteract the habits acquired by his pupils. Moreover, some of the children and adolescents with whom he is dealing are imprisoned in the identity of a bad pupil and an opponent" (Perrenoud, 1991, p. 92). Similarly, in an early evaluation of records of achievement in England, a profiling portfolio scheme that involved pupil self-assessment and negotiation of target setting, Broadfoot et al. (1988) found that secondary pupils viewed self-assessment as difficult, partly because they were not used to it and partly because the assessment criteria were unclear. Pupils' perceptions of teacher expectations, their views on what was socially acceptable, and their anxiety not to lose face affected their self-evaluation. Furthermore, there were gender and ethnic group differences in approach to the process of self-assessment and "negotiation" with teachers. Boys tended to be more likely to challenge a teacher's assessment and to have a keen sense of the audience for the final record, while girls tended to enter into a discussion and to negotiate more fully. In instances in which pupils and teachers do not share a common cultural group, pupils may be disadvantaged by teachers not recognizing fully their achievements. Thus, it appears that, if self-assessment of their work is to be empowering to pupils, considerable development will be required of teachers as well as preparation of the pupils.

Feedback from the teacher to the student, which is a key link between assessment and learning, can also be analyzed in terms of the power relationship between teacher and student. In informal classroom-based assessment, formative assessment is the process of appraising, judging, or evaluating students' work or performance and using this to shape and improve their competence. This refers to teachers using their judgments of children's knowledge or understanding to feed back into the teaching process. Sadler's detailed discussion (1989) of the nature of qualitative assessment gives feedback a crucial role in learning; he identifies the way in which feedback should be used by teachers to unpack the notion of excellence, which is part of their "guild knowledge," so that students are able to acquire understanding of standards for themselves.

Research conducted by Tunstall and Gipps (1996) to describe and classify feedback from teachers to young pupils as part of informal assessment suggests that such feedback can be categorized as evaluative or descriptive. Evaluative feedback is judgmental, with implicit or explicit use of norms. Descriptive feedback is task related, making specific reference to the child's actual achievement or competence. Tunstall and Gipps identified two types of descriptive feedback associated with formative assessment. One, *specifying attainment* and *specifying improvement*, shows a mastery-oriented approach to formative assessment. It involves teachers' acknowledgment of specific attainment, the use of models by teachers for work and behavior, diagnosis using specific criteria, and correcting or checking procedures. The other, *constructing achievement* and *constructing the way forward*, involves teachers' use of both sharp and "fuzzy" criteria, teacher-child assessment of work, discussion of the way forward, and the use of strategies for self-regulation.

The feedback categorized as *specifying* is that in which teachers retain control and power. They tell pupils whether or in what way their work is good and what needs to be done to improve on the task. In *constructing*, the teacher is sharing power and responsibility with the pupil. Teachers using the latter type of feedback conveyed a sense of work in progress, heightening awareness of what was being undertaken and reflecting on it; thus, the effect was one of bestowing importance on the work. Teachers' use of this feedback shifted the emphasis more to the child's own role in learning, through approaches that passed control to the child. There was more a feel of teacher as "facilitator" than "provider" or "judge" and more of "teacher with the child" than "teacher to the child." This type of feedback encouraged children to assess their own work and provided them with strategies that they could adopt to develop their work. Teachers, in this approach, were involving learners in the process of assessment as well as demonstrating power with—rather than power over—them.

Another tool that plays a key role in informal assessment is questioning. However, it must be acknowledged that questioning in the classroom setting is not straightforward. Where teachers' questioning has always been restricted to "lower order skills," students may well see questions about understanding or application as unfair, illegitimate, or even meaningless (Schoenfeld, 1985). And, as Rogoff (1990) argues, there are cultural differences in how individuals respond to questioning.

For example, schooled people are familiar with an interview or a testing situation in which a high-status adult, who already knows the answer to a question, requests information from a lower-status person, such as a child. In some cultural settings, however, the appropriate behaviour may be to show respect to the questioner or to avoid being made a fool of by giving the obvious answer to a question that must be a trick question whose answer is not the obvious one (otherwise why would a knowledgeable person be asking it?). (p. 59)

It has to be said that Rogoff addresses quite extreme cultural variance in her work. Cultural and social differences *within* a classroom are likely to be less extreme, but nonetheless, they will be significant and indeed potentially more subtle and complex in their effects.

Another reason why classroom questioning is not straightforward is that much teacher questioning is "closed." Pupils may develop strategies to discover the answer the teacher wants before actually committing themselves to it (Edwards & Mercer, 1989; Pollard, 1985). In such a climate, attempts by the teacher to engage in detailed diagnostic questioning may be misinterpreted (Torrance, 1993). As Edwards and Mercer (1989) point out: "Repeated questions imply wrong answers" (p. 45), and the pupil may change tack in order to give the "correct" answer and stop the questioning process rather than become engaged in an interactive process with the teacher. Opening up of questioning by the teacher may be seen as sharing power and control, and indeed what counts as acceptable knowledge, with the pupils.

As Black and Wiliam (1998) argue, the "opening moves" of teachers and students in the negotiation of classroom contracts will be determined by the epistemological, psychological, and pedagogical beliefs of both teachers and pupils. When a teacher questions a student, the teacher's beliefs will influence both the questions asked and the way answers are interpreted (Tittle, 1994). In turn, the student's responses to questioning will depend on a host of factors. For example, whether the student believes ability to be incremental or fixed will have a strong influence on how the student sees a question: as an opportunity to learn or as a threat to self-esteem (Dweck, 1986). Even where the student has a "learning" as opposed to "performance" orientation, the student's belief about what counts as "academic work" (Doyle, 1988) will have a profound impact on the "mindfulness" with which that student responds to questions.

Because of the public nature of much questioning and feedback, and the power dynamic in the teacher-student relationship, assessment plays a key role in identity formation. The language of assessment and evaluation is one of the defining elements through which young persons form their identity, for school purposes at least. The role of assessment as a social process has to be acknowledged in this sphere: Identity is socially bestowed, socially sustained, and socially transformed (Berger, 1963). Penuel and Wertsch (1995) argue that

identity formation must be viewed as shaped by and shaping forms of action, involving a complex interplay among cultural tools employed in the action, the sociocultural and institutional context of the action, and the purposes embedded in the action. Taking human action as the focus of analysis, we are able to provide a more coherent account of identity, not as a static, inflexible structure of the self, but as a dynamic dimension or moment in action, . . . identity formation is a moment of rhetorical action, concerned with using language in significant interpersonal contexts to form identities. (pp. 84–85)

If identity is conceived as concerned with persuading others and oneself about who one is, the judgment of others is crucial. Simultaneously reflecting and observing, the individual evaluates himself or herself "in the light of what he [or she] perceives to be [the] way in which others judge him [or her] in comparison to themselves and to a typology significant to them" (Erikson, 1968, p. 22). Indeed, following Bernstein's argument about the pervasiveness of covert, informal assessment, it may be that the teacher's regular classroom-based assessment of the pupil has more impact on identity formation than the results of standardized tests and formal examinations or report cards. Ames's (1992) work, too, shows how the classroom assessment climate can affect students' views of themselves. Classrooms in which assessment focuses on comparison and competition with others can lead to negative affect in children who compare unfavorably. Ames argues that students' perceptions of their ability are particularly sensitive to social comparison information. Children's evaluations of their ability and feelings toward themselves are more negative when the classroom climate is focused on winning, outperforming one another, or surpassing some normative standard than when children focus on trying hard, improving their performance, or just participating.

In summary, it is clear that social and cultural issues are just as significant in assessment at the classroom level as they are in external assessment at the system or societal level. What we look for in our students and whether we assess performance of the individual or the group are culturally determined. Newer conceptions of assessment, emanating from the sociocultural school and the interpretive tradition, require us to rethink some of our society's traditional assumptions about assessment. As a result, some new approaches offer assistance in the assessment task to see how the process of learning is developing, make assessments in the social setting of the group, open up the traditional relationship between teacher and student in order to recognize the learner's perspective, and give the student an understanding of the assessment process and evaluation criteria. In the latter case, the role of the teacher is not being diminished by passing responsibility for assessment to the student. Rather, this is an additional responsibility the teacher must take on in order to develop the students as self-monitoring learners.

Airasian and Walsh (1997) claim that constructivism is a theory about learning that has not been articulated for teaching. One could make the same claim about the sociocultural theory of learning, while the implications of neither theory have been fully unpacked for assessment purposes. As Dwyer (1998) notes, new models are sought of assessment of the learning process and the social context in which both learning and assessment take place, but much of this work remains at a theoretical level. What is still often overlooked, however, is the power in the relationship between student and teacher in the assessment act; this is a key factor that must come into the frame. There are cultural and gender overtones here indicating that, again, we need to consider equity implications.

CONCLUSIONS AND LOOKING FORWARD

Where does this review of the social and cultural influences on assessment (at both the system and classroom level) leave us, and where does it point? What should be clear from the first section of the chapter is that formal examining and assessment have been used to control access to higher levels of education and the professions. In doing this, they have contributed to cultural and social reproduction. Testing is now being used to control curriculum and teaching. Assessment is therefore a powerful device. There is also growing interest in assessment outcomes as performance indicators, as well as national and political pressure for highly reliable "objective" assessment in order to be able to rank order and grade the performance of individuals and schools (and even countries). At the same time, as the third section shows, developments in cognition and learning are telling us to assess more broadly, in context, and in depth. This requires methods of assessment that do not lend themselves readily to traditional reliability, highlighting the tension between types and purposes of assessment. Is this a tension that is resolvable? Experience in England shows that it is possible to run a national assessment program that includes high-quality examinations and some performance assessment (see Stobart & Gipps, 1997). It is possible to design an assessment program with different features and purposes at different levels of the school system (see James & Gipps, 1998). In both cases, some reliability is sacrificed for enhanced validity and the assessment of higher order cognitive/thinking skills. However, acceptance of such an assessment system by any society will be determined by cultural values and political imperatives. There is evidence that there may be a move away from narrow high stakes testing and examining in some countries as nations realize the importance of producing individuals who can work collaboratively and demonstrate higher order skills. For example, the Singapore government announced in early 1998 that there will be more project work, more collaborative and independent inquiry, and some open book exams to encourage thinking and discovery rather than regurgitation of inert ideas (MacBeath, 1998).

A concern with equity was originally behind the introduction of formal examining and the use of IQ testing. Similarly, new approaches to assessment have been held out as being able to redress previous inequities and biases in assessment

(Garcia & Pearson, 1991). According to Wolf et al. (1991), "There is a considerable hope that new modes of assessment . . . will provide one means for exposing the abilities of less traditionally skilled students by giving a place to world knowledge, social processes, and a great variety of excellence" (p. 60). Neill (1995) argues that performance assessment and evaluation of culturally sensitive classroom-based learning have the potential to foster multicultural inclusion and facilitate enhanced learning. Others sound a note of caution: Performance assessment on its own will not enhance equity. Consideration must still be given to students' opportunity to learn (Linn, 1993), the knowledge and language demands of the task (Baker & O'Neil, 1995), and the criteria used for scoring (Linn, Baker, & Dunbar, 1991). Clearly, as with traditional forms of assessment, questions of fairness arise in the selection of tasks and in the scoring of responses. Furthermore, the more informal and open-ended such assessment becomes, the greater the reliance on the judgment of the teacher/assessor. Here we come again to the issue of power and control, a theme of this chapter. Alternative forms of assessment do not, of themselves, alter power relationships and cultural dominance in the classroom.

However, a broadening of assessment approach will offer pupils alternative opportunities to demonstrate achievement if they are disadvantaged by any one particular assessment in a program. According to Linn (1992), "Multiple indicators are essential so that those who are disadvantaged on one assessment have an opportunity to offer alternative evidence of their expertise" (p. 44). The best defense against inequitable assessment is openness. Openness about design, constructs, and scoring will bring out into the open the values and biases of the test design process, offer an opportunity for debate about cultural and social influences, and open up the relationship between assessor and learner. These developments are possible, but they require political will. As Garcia and Pearson (1994) reluctantly conclude, assessment is a political act.

A second theme of the chapter is the developing interpretivist approach in assessment. From an interpretivist viewpoint, it is important to acknowledge the complexity of interactions among students, teachers, and assessment. Factors such as students' perceptions of how testing affects them (Herman et al., 1997), student and teacher confidence in the veracity of test results, and differences in student and teacher perceptions of the goals of assessment all need to be considered. Tittle's (1994) framework is one of the broadest so far articulated in this vein. Tittle proposes evaluation of both student and teacher perspectives using questionnaires to assess student feelings and thought in doing mathematical problems. Teachers review these responses using a think aloud procedure, and this information aids the use of assessment for teaching. The assessment result itself is only one piece of information the teacher will draw on in making inferences and determining subsequent steps; the other pieces of information are the pupil's personal and learning history, the realities and constraints of the class or group setting, and the type of assessment information (whether it is detailed or a single figure, criterion referenced or a standardized score, etc.). Teachers' interpretation of the test score is dependent on other knowledge they have, including how the pupil responded to the tasks that made up the assessment and how he or she will respond to the follow-up tasks and activities. Tittle's argument (1989) is that we need to extend validity inquiry to include the teacher's and student's perspective in the validation of what test scores mean and whether they are useful to teachers and learners, since we cannot assume that the teacher shares the same frame of reference as the test developer.

The interpretivist approach has implications for how we see the student-teacher relationship. The didactic relationship between teacher and student is traditionally a hierarchical one and the assessment relationship one of judgment or surveillance. If we are serious about taking an interpretive approach and bringing the student into some ownership of the assessment process (and hence into self-evaluation), teachers must share power with students rather than exerting power over them. We must help teachers to reconstruct their relationships, in both learning and assessment, as they shift responsibility to the students. This does not mean the teacher giving up responsibility for student learning and progress; rather, it means involving the learner more as a partner.

The contribution of researchers such as Cobb and Lampert indicates one way forward: In their classroom mathematical practice, the teacher sets up discipline-focused, process-thinking-oriented interactions in classroom discourse and activities. Assessment here can be seen not as teacher centered and covert (in Bernstein's terms) but as group centered and between peers, with shared standards and definitions of mathematical thinking. The classroom then becomes in effect a self-evaluating (self-assessing) organization, not unlike the self-evaluating school or business. In classes where the teacher has socialized students into such a culture, assessment is shared among teacher and students (although they are clearly not equal partners, since the teacher is an expert in mathematical understanding). Furthermore, students who have self-evaluation skills may use them with other teachers who do not operate in this way.

The theoretical debate about whether learning is a cognitive or a social process must seem overly esoteric to many practitioners. The responses of Cobb, Greeno, and Resnick and Nelson-Le Gall are helpful here. While coming from slightly different theoretical backgrounds, they argue that the tension between individual construction and enculturation is not resolvable; rather, we need to develop both perspectives (Greeno, 1997). Resnick and Nelson-Le Gall (1997) believe that intelligence (or "being smart") has as much to do with how individuals construe themselves and their action-in-the-world as with the specific skills they possess at any given moment. Cobb (1994) concludes that "learning is a process of both self-organization and a process of enculturation that occurs while participating in cultural practices, frequently while interacting with others" (p. 18). Indeed, Cobb and Bowers (1998) argue that there is an ethical requirement to study the diversity of student reasoning while at the same time seeing that diversity as socially situated. In a similar vein, Lunt (1994) argues that, at the classroom level, the task for the future is to develop assessment procedures that "combine the strengths of qualitative descriptions of processes of learning with quantitative information on individual differences. . . . Such assessment will need to take into account both the social and contextual factors surrounding individual learning and the interactions involved in instruction and the way that these affect an individual's learning'' (p. 167).

It seems clear that whatever happens with external, imposed assessment, whether for selection and certification or in national schemes to control and drive curriculum and teaching, a key direction for the future lies in the development of teachers' classroom assessment skills. It is evident from this chapter that some teachers are operating in collaborative, constructivist ways supported by portfolio work, for example, or as evidenced by their feedback to learners. Such practice is not common but clearly can become part of the teacher's repertoire. This implies the continued development of new assessment strategies for use by teachers, involving group and interactive assessment and interview and portfolio approaches. It will involve extending teachers' skills in observation and questioning while making them aware of social and cultural influences on the assessment process. We need to bring out into the open the nature of the power relationship in teaching and assessment and point out the possibility of reconstructing this relationship. Perhaps most important, we need to encourage teachers to bring pupils into the process of assessment, in order to recognize their social and cultural background, and into self-assessment, in order to develop their evaluative and metacognitive skills. All of these acts are, on the basis of this review, both possible and necessary if assessment is to be more equitable and fulfill its promise to aid and support high-quality learning.

REFERENCES

Aikenhead, C. (1997). A framework for reflecting on assessment and evaluation. In *Globalization of science education—Papers for the Seoul International Conference* (pp. 195–199). Seoul: Korean Educational Development Institute.

Airasian, P. W. (1988, Winter). Measurement driven instruction: A closer look. *Educational Measurement: Issues and Practice*, pp. 6–11.

Airasian, P., & Walsh, M. (1997, February). Constructivist cautions. *Phi Delta Kappan*, pp. 444–449.

Ames, C. (1992). Classrooms: Goals, structures and student motivation. *Journal of Educational Psychology, 84*, 261–271.

Apple, M. W. (1989). How equality has been redefined in the conservative restoration. In W. Secada (Ed.), *Equity and education*. New York: Falmer Press.

Apple, M. (1993). The politics of official knowledge: Does a national curriculum make sense? *Teachers College Record, 95*, 222–241.

Baker, E., & O'Neil, H. (1995). Diversity, assessment, and equity in educational reform. In M. Nettles & A. Nettles (Eds.), *Equity and excellence in educational testing and assessment* (pp. 69–87). Boston: Kluwer.

Berger, P. (1963). *Invitation to sociology*. New York: Penguin Books.

Bernstein, B. (1977). *Class codes and control* (Vol. 3). London: Routledge & Kegan Paul.

Bernstein, B. (1982). Codes, modalities and the process of cultural reproduction: A model. In M. Apple (Ed.), *Cultural and economic reproduction in education*. London: Routledge & Kegan Paul.

Bernstein, B. (1996). *Pedagogy, symbolic control and identity.* London: Taylor & Francis.

Black, P., & Wiliam, D. (1998). Assessment and classroom learning. *Assessment in Education, 5,* 7–74.

Bourdieu, P., & Passeron, J. (1976). *Reproduction in education, society and culture.* London: Sage.

Broadfoot, P. (1979). *Assessment, schools and society.* London: Methuen.

Broadfoot, P. (1994). *Educational assessment: The myth of measurement.* Bristol, England: University of Bristol.

Broadfoot, P. (1996). *Education, assessment and society.* Buckingham, England: Open University Press.

Broadfoot, P., James, M., McMeeking, S., Nuttall, D., & Stierer, S. (1988). *Records of achievement: Report of the National Evaluation of Pilot Schemes (PRAISE).* London: Her Majesty's Stationery Office.

Brown, A., Ash, D., Rutherford, M., Nakagawa, K., Gordon, A., & Campione, J. (1993). Distributed expertise in the classroom. In G. Salomon (Ed.), *Distributed cognitions.* New York: Cambridge University Press.

Brown, A., Campione, J., Webber, L., & McGilly, K. (1992). Interactive learning environments: A new look at assessment and instruction. In B. Gifford & M. O'Connor (Eds.), *Changing assessments: Alternative views of aptitude, achievement and instruction.* Boston: Kluwer Academic.

Brown, P., & Lauder, H. (1996). Education, globalization and economic development. *Journal of Education Policy, 11,* 1–25.

Bruner, J., & Haste, H. (1987). *Making sense: The child's construction of the world.* New York: Routledge.

Cobb, P. (1994). Where is the mind? *Educational Researcher, 23*(7), 13–20.

Cobb, P., & Bowers, J. (in press). Cognitive and situated learning perspectives in theory and practice. *Educational Researcher.*

Connell, R. (1993). *Schools and social justice.* Toronto: Our Schools/Our Selves Education Foundation.

Cooper, B., & Dunne, M. (1998). Anyone for tennis? Social class differences in children's responses to national curriculum mathematics testing. *Sociological Review, 46,* 115–148.

Cronbach, L. (1988). Five perspectives on validity argument. In H. Weiner & H. Braun (Eds.), *Test validity.* Hillsdale, NJ: Erlbaum.

Doyle, W. (1988). Work in mathematics classes: The context of students' thinking during instruction, *Educational Psychologist, 23,* 167–180.

Driver, R., Asoko, H., Leach, J., Mortimer, E., & Scott, P. (1994). Constructing scientific knowledge in the classroom. *Educational Researcher, 23*(7), 5–12.

Driver, R., Guesne, E., & Tiberghien, A. (1985). *Children's ideas in science.* Buckingham, England: Open University Press.

Dweck, C. S. (1986). Motivational processes affecting learning. *American Psychologist, 41,* 1040–1048.

Dwyer, C. (1998). Assessment for classroom learning: Theory and practice. *Assessment in Education, 5,* 131–138.

Eckstein, M. (1996). A comparative assessment of assessment. *Assessment in Education, 3,* 233–240.

Eckstein, M., & Noah, H. (1993). *Secondary school examinations: International perspectives on policies and practice.* New Haven, CT: Yale University Press.

Edwards, D., & Mercer, N. (1989). *Common knowledge.* London: Routledge.

Eggleston, J. (1984). School examinations—Some sociological issues. In P. Broadfoot (Ed.), *Selection, certification and control.* Lewes, England: Falmer Press.

Eisner, E. (1993). Reshaping assessment in education: Some criteria in search of practice. *Journal of Curriculum Studies, 25,* 219–233.

Entwistle, N. (1992). *The impact of teaching in learning outcomes in higher education.* Sheffield, England: CVCP Staff Development Unit.

Erikson, E. (1968). *Identity: Youth and crisis.* New York: Norton.

Foucault, M. (1977). *Discipline and punishment* (A. Sheridan, Trans.). London: Allen Lane.

Garcia, G., & Pearson, P. (1991). The role of assessment in a diverse society. In E. Herbert (Ed.), *Literacy for a diverse society* (pp. 253–278). New York: Teachers College Press.

Garcia, G., & Pearson, P. (1994). Assessment and diversity. In L. Darling-Hammond (Ed.), *Review of research in education* (Vol. 20, pp. 337–391). Washington, DC: American Educational Research Association.

Gipps, C. (1994a). *Beyond testing: Towards a theory of educational assessment.* London: Falmer Press.

Gipps, C. (1994b). Developments in educational assessment or what makes a good test? *Assessment in Education, 1,* 283–291.

Gipps, C., & Murphy, P. (1994). *A fair test? Assessment, achievement and equity.* Buckingham, England: Open University Press.

Glaser, R. (1963). Instructional technology and the measurement of learning outcomes: Some questions. *American Psychologist, 18,* 519–521.

Glaser, R. (1990). Toward new models for assessment. *International Journal of Educational Research, 14,* 475–483.

Glaser, R., & Silver, E. (1994). Assessment, testing, and instruction: Retrospect and prospect. In L. Darling-Hammond (Ed.), *Review of research in education* (Vol. 20, pp. 393–421). Washington, DC: American Educational Research Association.

Goldstein, H. (1993). Assessing group differences. *Oxford Review of Education, 19,* 141–150.

Goldstein, H. (1996). Statistical and psychometric models for assessment. In H. Goldstein & T. Lewis (Eds.), *Assessment: Problems, developments and statistical issues.* Chichester, England: Wiley.

Gould, S. (1981). *The mismeasure of man.* New York: Norton.

Green, A. (1997). *Education, globalisation and the nation state.* London: Macmillan.

Greene, M. (1994). Epistemology and educational research: The influence of recent approaches to knowledge. In L. Darling-Hammond (Ed.), *Review of research in education* (Vol. 20, pp. 423–464). Washington, DC: American Educational Research Association.

Greeno, J. (1997). On claims that answer the wrong questions. *Educational Researcher, 26*(1), 5–17.

Guba, E., & Lincoln, Y. (1989). *Fourth generation evaluation.* London: Sage.

Haney, W., Madaus, G., & Lyons, R. (1993). *The fractured marketplace for standardized testing.* London: Kluwer Academic.

Hargreaves, A. (1986). Record breakers? In P. Broadfoot (Ed.), *Profiles and records of achievement.* London: Holt, Rinehart & Winston.

Harlen, W. (Ed.). (1994). *Enhancing quality in assessment.* London: Chapman.

Henry, J. (1963). *Culture against man.* New York: Random House.

Herman, J., Klein, D., & Wakai, S. (1997). American students' perspectives on alternative assessment: Do they know it's different? *Assessment in Education, 4,* 339–352.

Husen, T., & Tuijnman, A. (1991). The contribution of formal schooling to the increase in intellectual capital. *Educational Researcher, 20,* 10–25.

Iran-Nejad, A. (1995). Constructivism as substitute for memorization in learning: Meaning is created by learner. *Education, 116,* 16–31.

James, M., & Gipps, C. (1998). Broadening the basis of assessment to prevent the narrowing of learning. *The Curriculum Journal, 9,* 285–297.

Keeves, J. P. (1994). *National examinations: Design, procedures and reporting* (Fundamentals of Educational Planning No. 50). Paris: UNESCO.

Koretz, D., McCaffrey, D., Klein, S., Bell, R., & Stecher, B. (1993). *The reliability of scores from the Vermont Portfolio Assessment Program* (CSE Technical Report 355). Los Angeles: University of California, Los Angeles.

Lampert, M. (1990). When the problem is not the question and the solution is not the answer: Mathematical knowing and teaching. *American Educational Research Journal, 27,* 29–63.

Land, R. (1997). Moving up to complex assessment systems. *Evaluation Comment, 7,* 3.

Lather, P. (1992). Critical frames in education research: Feminist and poststructural perspectives. *Theory into Practice, 31,* 2–13.

Lave, J., & Wenger, E. (1991). *Situated learning: Legitimate peripheral participation.* Cambridge, England: Cambridge University Press.

Linn, M. C. (1992). *Gender differences in educational achievement, sex equity in educational opportunity, achievement and testing.* Princeton, NJ: Educational Testing Service.

Linn, R. L. (1993). Educational assessment: Expanded expectations and challenges. *Educational Evaluation and Policy Analysis, 15,* 1–16.

Linn, R., Baker, E., & Dunbar, S. (1991). Complex, performance-based assessment: Expectations and validation criteria. *Educational Researcher, 20*(8), 15–20.

Lohman, D. (1997). Lessons from the history of intelligence testing. *International Journal of Educational Research, 27,* 359–377.

Lunt, I. (1994). The practice of assessment. In H. Daniels (Ed.), *Charting the agenda.* New York: Routledge.

MacBeath, J. (1998, April 10). Just think about it. *Times Educational Supplement,* p. 13.

Madaus, G., & Raczek, A. (1996). The extent and growth of educational testing in the United States: 1956–1994. In H. Goldstein & T. Lewis (Eds.), *Assessment: Problems, developments and statistical issues.* Chichester, England: Wiley.

Marton, F., & Saljo, R. (1984). Approaches to learning. In F. Marton, D. Hounsell, & N. Entwistle (Eds.), *The experience of learning.* Edinburgh: Scottish Academic Press.

Messick, S. (1989). Validity. In R. Linn (Ed.), *Educational measurement* (3rd ed.). Washington, DC: American Council on Education.

Moss, P. A. (1992). Shifting conceptions of validity in educational measurement: Implications for performance assessment. *Review of Educational Research, 62,* 229–258.

Moss, P. A. (1994). Can there be validity without reliability? *Educational Researcher, 23*(2), 5–12.

Moss, P. (1996). Enlarging the dialogue in educational measurement: Voices from interpretive research traditions. *Educational Researcher, 25*(1), 20–28.

National Commission on Excellence in Education. (1983). *A nation at risk: The imperative for educational reform.* Washington, DC: U.S. Government Printing Office.

Neave, G. (1988). Education and social policy: Demise of an ethic or change of values? *Oxford Review of Education, 14,* 273–283.

Neill, M. (1995). Some prerequisites for the establishment of equitable, inclusive multicultural assessment systems. In M. Nettles & A. Nettles (Eds.), *Equity and excellence in educational testing and assessment* (pp. 115–157). Boston: Kluwer.

Newman, D., Griffin, P., & Cole, M. (1989). *The construction zone: Working for cognitive change in school.* Cambridge, England: Cambridge University Press.

Nuttall, D. (1987). The validity of assessments. *European Journal of Psychology of Education, 11,* 108–118.

Penuel, W., & Wertsch, J. (1995). Vygotsky and identity formation: A sociocultural approach. *Educational Psychologist, 30,* 83–92.

Perrenoud, P. (1991). Towards a pragmatic approach to formative evaluation. In P. Weston (Ed.), *Assessment of pupils' achievement: Motivation and school success* (pp. 77–101). Amsterdam: Swets & Zeitlinger.

Pollard, A. (1985). *The social world of the primary school.* London: Holt, Rinehart & Winston.

Pollard, A. (1990). Towards a sociology of learning in primary school. *British Journal of Sociology of Education, 11*, 241–256.

Resnick, L. (1989). Introduction. In L. Resnick (Ed.), *Knowing, learning and instruction: Essays in honor of R. Glaser.* Hillsdale, NJ: Erlbaum.

Resnick, L., & Nelson-Le Gall, S. (1997). Socializing intelligence. In L. Smith, J. Dockrell, & P. Tomlinson (Eds.), *Piaget, Vygotsky and beyond.* New York: Routledge.

Rogoff, B. (1990). *Apprenticeship in thinking: Cognitive development in social context.* Oxford, England: Oxford University Press.

Ryan, A. (1988). Program evaluation within the paradigm: Mapping the territory. *Knowledge: Creation, Diffusion, Utilization, 10*, 25–47.

Sadler, R. (1989). Formative assessment and the design of instructional systems. *Instructional Science, 18*, 119–144.

Sadler, R. (1998). Formative assessment: Revisiting the territory. *Assessment in Education, 5*, 77–84.

Schoenfeld, A. (1985). *Mathematical problem-solving.* New York: Academic Press.

Shepard, L. (1991). Psychometricians' beliefs about learning. *Educational Researcher, 20*(7), 2–16.

Shepard, L. (1992). What policy makers who mandate tests should know about the new psychology of intellectual ability and learning. In B. Gifford & M. O'Connor (Eds.), *Changing assessments: Alternative views of aptitude, achievement and instruction.* London: Kluwer Academic.

Shepard, L. (1993). Evaluating test validity. In L. Darling-Hammond (Ed.), *Review of research in education* (Vol. 19, pp. 405–450). Washington, DC: American Educational Research Association.

Stedman, L. C. (1997). International achievement differences: An assessment of a new perspective. *Educational Researcher, 26*(3), 4–15.

Stevenson, D. (1996, April). *International patterns of assessment: Policy change.* Paper presented at the annual meeting of the American Educational Research Association, New York.

Stobart, G., & Gipps, C. (1997). *Assessment: A teachers' guide to the issues.* London: Hodder & Stoughton.

Sutherland, G. (1984). *Ability, merit and measurement: Mental testing and English education, 1880–1940.* New York: Oxford University Press.

Sutherland, G. (1996). Assessment: Some historical perspectives. In H. Goldstein & T. Lewis (Eds.), *Assessment: Problems, developments and statistical issues.* Chichester, England: Wiley.

Taylor, P., Fraser, B., & Fisher, D. (1997). Monitoring constructivist classroom learning environments. *International Journal of Educational Research, 27*, 293–301.

Thomson, G., & Sharp, S. (1988). History of mental testing. In J. Keeves (Ed.), *Educational research methodology and measurement: An international handbook.* Oxford, England: Pergamon Press.

Tittle, C. (1989). Validity: Whose construction is it in the teaching and learning context? *Educational Measurement: Issues and Practice, 8*, 5–13.

Tittle, C. (1994). Toward an educational-psychology of assessment for teaching and learning—Theories, contexts, and validation arguments. *Educational Psychologist, 29*, 149–162.

Torrance, H. (1981). The origins and development of mental testing in England and the United States. *British Journal of Sociology of Education, 2*, 45–59.

Torrance, H. (1993). Formative assessment: Some theoretical problems and empirical questions. *Cambridge Journal of Education, 23*, 333–343.

Torrance, H., & Pryor, J. (1998). *Investigating formative assessment: Teaching, learning and assessment in the classroom.* Buckingham, England: Open University Press.

Trevelyan, S. C., & Northcote, S. S. (1853). *Report on the organisation of the permanent civil service.* London: Parliamentary Proceedings.

Tunstall, P., & Gipps, C. (1996). Teacher feedback to young children in formative assessment: A typology. *British Educational Research Journal, 22,* 389–404.

von Glasersfeld, E. (1987). Learning as a constructive activity. In C. Janvier (Ed.), *Problems of representation in the teaching and learning of mathematics* (pp. 3–18). Hillsdale, NJ: Erlbaum.

von Glasersfeld, E. (1989). Cognition, construction of knowledge, and teaching. *Synthese, 80,* 121–140.

Vygotsky, L. (1978). *Mind in society.* London: Harvard University Press.

Weiss, J. (1987). The golden rule bias reduction principle: A practical reform. *Educational Measurement: Issues and Practice, 6.*

Wertsch, J. V. (1991). *Voices of the mind: A sociocultural approach to mediated action.* Cambridge, MA: Harvard University Press.

Wigdor, A., & Garner, W. (1982). *Ability testing: Uses, consequences and controversies, Part 1.* Washington, DC: National Academy Press.

Wittrock, M. C., & Baker, E. L. (1991). *Testing and cognition.* Englewood Cliffs, NJ: Prentice Hall.

Wolf, D. (1989). Portfolio assessment: Sampling student work. *Educational Leadership, 46*(7), 35–39.

Wolf, D., Bixby, J., Glenn, J., & Gardner, H. (1991). To use their minds well: Investigating new forms of student assessment. In *Review of research in education* (Vol. 17, pp. 31–74). Washington, DC: American Educational Research Association.

Wood, R. (1986). The agenda for educational measurement. In D. L. Nuttall (Ed.), *Assessing educational achievement.* London: Falmer.

Yates, A., & Pidgeon, D. A. (1957). *Admission to grammar schools.* London: NFER/Newnes Educational.

Manuscript received February 2, 1998
Accepted November 15, 1998

Chapter 11

Persistent Methodological Questions in Educational Testing

JOHN HATTIE
University of Auckland

RICHARD M. JAEGER AND LLOYD BOND
University of North Carolina at Greensboro

The topic of this chapter—persistent methodological issues in educational testing—could readily fill several volumes. In fact, entire volumes have been written solely on the historical underpinnings of educational testing (Sutherland, 1984; Ward, Stoker, & Murray-Ward, 1996a, 1996b, 1996c; Woolf, 1961), and an aperiodic updating of the field has been provided in three editions of *Educational Measurement* (Lindquist, 1951; Linn, 1989; Thorndike, 1971). In a single chapter, therefore, it is necessary to be selective, to highlight some issues entirely to the detriment of others. Our selection and consideration of issues was framed by two desires. The first was to place the plethora of measurement issues in a coherent framework. The second was to convey, for each issue addressed, a sense of its historical underpinnings, its current status, and how we reasonably see it developing in the future.

We view educational testing as a cyclic process: through the continual conception, construction, administration, use, and evaluation of educational testing programs in the short term and through the continuing evolution of educational testing and measurement as a field in the long term. As illustrated in Figure 1, educational testing often begins with specification of conceptual models of measurement. Conceptions of measurement were initially quite simple ("assigning numbers to the results of an observation") but later became both clearer and more complex, as in the Jones (1971, pp. 336–337) formulation:

Measurement, then, is a purposive acquisition of information about the object, organism, or event measured by the person doing the measuring. It is determination of the magnitude of a specified attribute of the object, organism, or event in terms of a unit of measurement. The result of measurement is expressed by a numeral. The classification of attributes, either qualitative or quantitative, is distinguished from the measurement of attributes, which must be quantitative.

More recent conceptions of measurement (Hambleton, Swaminathan, & Rogers, 1991; Messick, 1989, 1994; Snow & Lohman, 1989) have paid far closer

We thank our consulting editors, Robert Linn and Ed Haertel for their thoughtful insights on our chapter.

FIGURE 1
Testing Issues and Topics Addressed

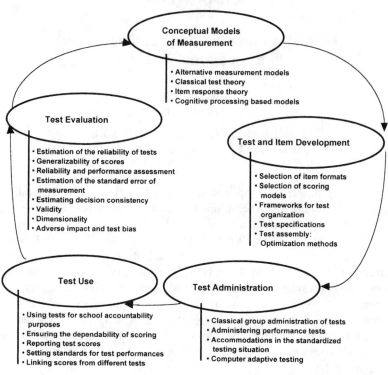

attention to the conceptual and theoretical structures of the attributes to be measured and to the relationship between those theoretical structures and their numerical representation when measurement takes place. It is a far cry from merely specifying the result of an examinee encountering a test item as correct (typically scored 1) or incorrect (typically scored 0) to modern statistical models of the relationship between an examinee's standing on some latent variable and the probability that his or her encounter with a test item will lead to a successful solution (Birnbaum, 1968; Hambleton, Swaminathan, & Rogers, 1991; Lord & Novick, 1968; Rasch, 1960, 1961).

There are many models of measurement. ''Classical test theory'' defines the examinee's standing as the expected value of the observed score over parallel forms and/or repeated administrations of a specific, intact test. An alternative model is one in which the score is referenced to an item domain rather than a specific test and attempts are made to rigorously define what an item is. This model treats the test score as a domain score estimate, or the proportion of all items in the domain that an examinee could answer correctly (one example could be generalizability theory). A third model is a latent trait concept that also is referenced to an item domain but defines an examinee's score as a location on a latent continuum. A fourth model is a set of more sophisticated sampling conceptions that attend to cognitive structures underlying the performance of the item (see Embretson, 1995a, 1995b, 1997; Snow & Lohman, 1989). For example, Mislevy (1986) has described a Bayesian inference networks model that shares with item response models the idea that individual responses and task parameters result in probabilities of specified response outcomes. This model relies, however, more heavily on cognitive analysis to construct a framework and refine estimates. When considering these conceptual models of measurement, which are often combined in various ways, we address three issues: alternative models of measurement, methods for estimating the quantities that characterize the statistical properties of test items and the abilities of examinees, and (under the heading "scale invariance") the property of measurement that permits comparison of the abilities of two individuals even though they have performed completely different sets of tasks.

Once a conceptual model of measurement has been adopted, there begins the task of constructing the instruments through which the magnitude of the attribute to be measured will be made manifest. We address a series of topics in describing advances in the development and assembly of tests. These topics include the selection of the formats in which tasks (typically termed test items) will be presented to examinees; the selection of scoring models or the rules by which examinees' performances on test items will be assigned numeric values; how test developers specify the boundaries and organization of the domain of knowledge, skills, or abilities to be measured; and models for assembling tests so as to satisfy these boundaries and organizational specifications while maximizing desirable measurement properties.

The manner under which tests are administered has become a persistent methodological question, primarily because of the tensions between the desire to provide standardized conditions under which the test or measure is administered (to ensure more comparability of scores) and the desire for representativeness or authenticity in the testing condition (to ensure more meaning in inferring from the score). Under the heading of "test administration," we address the classical group administration of tests (the prototypical procedure since the development of the Army Alpha Test during World War I), the recent return to performance testing and the related notion of authentic assessment, accommodations in the standardized testing situation to involve all examinees, and the comparatively recent use of computers not only for administration of tests but for adaptive selection of test items on the basis of an examinee's responses to items that have already been presented. These issues are important to ensure that there is the least possible contamination of measurement (a condition in which the outcomes of measurement might be attributed to an examinee's standing on the attribute to be measured or to a plethora of other causes, such as conditions that interfered with the examinee's performance) and that all possible examinees are included in the testing situation.

As Jones (1971) noted, an important characteristic of measurement is that it is purposive. That is, tests are administered not simply to satisfy the curiosity of testing professionals but because the results of testing are to be used. Common uses of educational testing affect school districts, schools, school personnel, and students. In this section of the chapter, we begin by examining those uses and the pitfalls associated with them. We then describe the development and maintenance of the ongoing testing programs that are the bulwark of formal testing activity in the United States today. We consider once again the ways in which students' performances on tests can be scored, here addressing the practicalities of scoring rather than the conceptual issues underlying selection of a scoring model. The results of testing typically are reported in a number of ways, and we consider the alternatives and their common uses. A common tension arises from reporting results for diagnostic or accountability reasons. We then address the specialized issue of setting standards for test performance. This issue is of increasing importance in educational testing, as test results are used to make critical selection and classification decisions about students and teachers. Finally, there are persistent issues relating to using different tests for the same purpose. Consider, for example, a college permitting applicants to submit either Scholastic Aptitude Test (SAT) or American College Testing Assessment (ACT) scores, which leads to critical issues of equating, calibration, projection, and moderation.

We conclude with a discussion of the critical issues relating to test evaluation. These issues include reliability (especially reliability of performance assessments), generalizability of scores, estimation of standard errors, estimation of decision consistency, the concept and methods of validation, the dimensions that the test purportedly assesses, and adverse effects and bias. Evaluation leads to action—sometimes a return to the conceptual models underlying measurement and other times a return to modification of the myriad operational decisions that define an ongoing testing program. In either case, the unifying desire is to improve the quality of measurement.

In Figure 1, we have represented educational testing as a cyclic process both to symbolize its ongoing evolution and to convey the idea that testing does not end when scores have assigned or when the reliability of a test has been estimated. It is likely that test developers, users, and evaluators may begin at different places in this circle, and this has often led to much variability in the emphases placed on different measurement topics. Furthermore, it is rare to note that all aspects of the cycle are addressed with respect to any one use of scores and score interpretations. These five major parts of the cycle have been debated since the beginnings of measurement; hence, we contend that they remain among the most persistent methodological questions in educational testing.

CONCEPTUAL MODELS OF MEASUREMENT

Mathematical models of psychological and educational measurement trace their conceptual origin to two venerable traditions in American academic psychology: trait psychology and behaviorism. Traits are more or less enduring dispositions to behave in certain ways across diverse situations. The notion that persons can be described by the relative degree to which they possess certain traits is still the predominant popular (and scientific) view, and it underlies even modern measurement philosophy. Thus, early test theorists conceived of test performance and its measurement as reflecting an individual's position on a scale that mirrored more or less of a given "trait."

Test performance may also be viewed as a sampling of an individual's behavior over a variety of related situations. Thus, test performance can be modeled from the perspective of behavioral psychology as a summary statement about "a behavioral tendency in a class of stimulus situations" (Mislevy, 1995, p. 44). One can imagine a theoretically infinite domain of tasks (or, in measurement terminology, items) from which a representative sample is administered to individuals. The notion of trait is, in this view, replaced by the notion of a consistent tendency to behave in a certain way under specified stimulus conditions.

These two psychological traditions have served test theorists well as paradigms from which to model cognitive achievement, personality variables, and attitudes. But the past century has witnessed major advances in psychological theories of knowledge, achievement, and attitude development. Trait psychology, associationism, and behavior modification have been largely replaced by paradigms that emphasize how knowledge is acquired, how it is organized and accessed in long-term memory, and how information is processed during problem solving. Psychological and educational measurement theory, it must be admitted, has largely ignored these developments. Although the measurement profession has long been aware of this, only recently have the dimensions of the problem been fully described (Mislevy, 1995). We return to this point later.

Alternative Measurement Models

We noted earlier that there are at least four major models of measurement, and often there have been further models based on interactions of these more fundamental models. For example, the National Assessment of Educational Progress (NAEP) reporting benchmark scales are based on a latent trait conception by drawing upon a more sophisticated version of the item domain model to help communicate score meaning.

Gulliksen's (1950) classic text provides the most complete introduction to classical test theory. Thorough advanced treatment can be found in Lord and Novick (1968). Excellent introductions to both classical test theory and item response theory can be found in Allen and Yen (1979) and Crocker and Algina (1986). Baker (1992); Lord (1980); Hambleton, Swaminathan, and Rogers (1991); and van der Linden and Hambleton (1997) provide thorough introductions to item response theory.

Classical Test Theory

Some 100 years ago, Edgeworth (1888, 1892) and Spearman (1904, 1907) advanced what has come to be known as classical test theory. This measurement model has been the workhorse of educational and psychological measurement for much of this century. The model is simple, elegant, and surprisingly durable. It states that an individual's observed, measured status on an attribute, x, is a function of two independent and additive components: a "true" score, t, and a random or error score, e: $x = t + e$.

Although the model has also gone under the name classical true score theory, it is actually a theory about errors of measurement. The true score component is assumed to be fixed over some reasonable interval of time. In the spirit of trait psychology noted earlier, a person's vocabulary, attitude toward communism, and quantitative reasoning ability, for example, do not change markedly from day to day or week to week but remain relatively constant over moderate to extended intervals of time.

If a person is administered two "parallel tests" on successive days, it is highly unlikely that he or she will have identical scores on both tests. The vagaries of sampling items from the theoretically infinite number of possible items in a domain, variations in examinee attention, clerical errors, and so forth virtually guarantee that scores on parallel or equivalent tests will not be identical. Such errors are assumed to be completely random. Whether an individual's true score is at the mean of some distribution, two standard deviations above, or two standard deviations below, the variance of errors around his or her true score is assumed to be the same. That is, the standard deviation of errors of measurement ("the standard error of measurement") is assumed to be the same for all examinees.

The importance of the assumptions that errors of measurement are random and that the variances of such errors are the same for all examinees should not be lost on the reader, for the entire superstructure of classical test theory rests on their validity. To be sure, the assumptions are only approximately true (and are patently false in some applications), but the wide applicability and durability of the classical test theory model attests to their usefulness in many applied situations. The preceding three assumptions (the constancy of t, the randomness of e, and the equality of error variances), along with the definition of parallel tests as two tests (1 and 2) for which $t_{i1} = t_{i2}$ for all individuals i and for which $\sigma^2(e_1) = \sigma^2(e_2)$, constitute the foundation of the classical test theory model. All of the familiar measurement concepts used to evaluate and analyze tests (test reliability, correction for attenuation, effect of test length on reliability, etc.) can be derived from these four basic postulates.

The measurement profession has known from the very beginning that the classical model, despite its popularity and durability, has serious shortcomings. Under the classical model, for example, our estimate of the difficulty of an item on a test of cognitive ability will vary depending on the sample of examinees to which it is administered. It follows that a given individual will appear quite able relative to one sample of test takers but much less so relative to another. Thus, an examinee's characteristics and test characteristics cannot be separated, such that under the classical model an examinee's score is defined only with respect to a class of (typically hypothetical) parallel tests as opposed to being defined in terms of a latent trait continuum that also affords a metric for item parameters.

Our estimate of Johnny's mathematical aptitude should not depend on the specific test he happens to take or the sample of students who happen to take the test with him. This situation has been described by Hambleton, Swaminathan, and Rogers (1991):

Perhaps the most important shortcoming [of classical test theory] is that examinee characteristics and test characteristics cannot be separated: each can be interpreted only in the context of the other. . . . An examinee's ability is defined only in terms of a particular test. When the test is "hard," the examinee will appear to have low ability; when the test is "easy," the examinee will appear to have higher ability. . . . Whether an item is hard or easy depends on the ability of the examinees being measured, and the ability of the examinees being measured depends on whether the test is hard or easy!. . . Hence it is very difficult to compare examinees who take different tests and very difficult to compare items whose characteristics change as the test context changes.

Item Response Theory

Item response theory (IRT) is an elegant and powerful model of test performance that obviates virtually all of the shortcomings of classical test theory just described. The model, which originally went under the rather stilted title "latent trait theory," is more than a half-century old (Lawley, 1943; Lazarsfeld, 1950; Lord, 1952; Tucker, 1946). Because of the daunting calculations involved, the model did not become practical until the advent of high-speed computers in the late 1960s and early 1970s. Although the classical model still dominates the limited volume test market and tests designed for specific research purposes (Conoley & Impara, 1995; Goldman, Mitchell, & Egelson, 1997), IRT has all but supplanted classical test theory in large-scale testing programs.

As the name implies, item response theory attempts to model (in probabilistic terms) the response of an examinee to an individual test item. An examinee's ability, θ, and an item's inherent difficulty, b, are scaled along the same horizontal dimension. To the extent that the examinee's ability "exceeds" the item's difficulty along the dimension, the examinee is said to have an increasingly better than 50-50 chance of getting the item right. If the examinee's ability falls "below" (i.e., to the left of) the item's difficulty, then the examinee is said to have a less than 50-50 chance of getting the item right. When the two parameters coincide, the probability of the examinee getting the item correct is one half. Thus, item response theory attempts to model, in probabilistic terms, the difference ($\theta - b$) between θ and b. In order to scale this difference so that it is a probability function with a range from 0 to 1, it is first necessary to carry ($\theta - b$) into an exponent. By convention, the base of the exponent is the number e (the base of natural logarithms). The resulting exponential expression, $e^{(\theta - b)}$, when divided by the scaling constant, $[1 + e^{(\theta - b)}]$, gives the desired result, the logistic function $p(u = 1|\theta) = e^{(\theta - b)}/[1 + e^{(\theta - b)}]$. According to the preceding, the probability of an examinee with ability θ getting an item correct, $p(u = 1)$, follows the familiar logistic function, an S-shaped function quite similar to the normal ogive.

The difficulty parameter b in item response theory is one of three parameters that characterize any given item. Items differ not only in their difficulty but also in their ability to discriminate between examinees who are high on the attribute and those who are low on the attribute. The discrimination parameter a indexes the ability of the item to discriminate between examinees of differing ability. For multiple-choice tests of cognitive ability and achievement, even persons very low on the construct being measured have a nonzero chance of getting the item correct by guessing. The so-called "guessing parameter" c indexes the probability that an examinee with very low ability will get the item right by chance alone. The full three-parameter item response model is therefore $p(u = 1|\theta) = c + (1 - c)(e^{a(\theta - b)}/(1 + e^{a(\theta - b)}))$.

Cognitive-Processing-Based Models

It should be clearly noted that neither the classical model nor the IRT model of test performance attempts to model the actual *processes* underlying performance. Nor do they have much to say about the *nature* of skilled performance per se. The user must examine the test in question for him- or herself and deduce, from a cognitive analysis of the items at various points along the proficiency scale, to understand what a given score "means." It is in this sense that formal mathematical models of test performance have largely ignored information-processing advances in our understanding of proficiency and achievement. This point is well stated by Snow and Lohman (1989):

Summary test scores, and factors based on them, have often been thought of as "signs" indicating the presence of underlying, latent traits. . . . An alternative interpretation of test scores as samples of cognitive processes and contents, and of correlations as indicating the similarity or overlap of this sampling, is equally justifiable and could be theoretically more useful. The evidence from cognitive psychology suggests that test performances are comprised of complex assemblies of component information-processing actions that are adapted to task requirements during performance. The implication is that sign-trait interpretations of test scores and their intercorrelations are superficial summaries at best. At worst, they have misled scientists, and the public, into thinking of fundamental, fixed entities, measured in amounts. Whatever their practical value as summaries, for selection, classification, certification, or program evaluation, the cognitive psychological view is that such interpretations no longer suffice as scientific explanations of aptitude and achievement constructs. (p. 317)

A signal challenge for measurement theory in the coming century is the development of models of test performance that reflect new understandings of the nature of aptitude and proficiency. In a series of recent papers, Mislevy (1996a) has adapted IRT models to complex cognitive models of document literacy, mixed number subtraction, and, even more ambitiously, advanced placement studio art portfolios. His is, admittedly, only a start, and considerably more work in these areas is needed. Other models include Embretson's multicomponent model (1995a, 1997), Fischer's (1997) linear logistic Rasch model, and Mislevy and Gitomer's (1996) hybrid latent class and latent trait models.

Comments on the Models

It is fascinating to recall that, in 1904, Spearman laid the foundations for common factor analysis and true score theory as alternative explanations for the same data set (see Traub, 1997, for more of this history). He argued that the conditional independence of observable test scores, given an unobservable true score variable, implies particular patterns of relationships among those observable scores (deriving from his findings of the disappearance of tetrad differences among correlations). This led to the pursuance of inferring in terms of unobservable variables and thus underscores the similarities between item response models and factor analysis.

McDonald (1985a) has elaborated and advanced the evolution of these differences. While the concepts of latent trait and common factor are similar, he noted that the latent trait model is a stronger counterpart of the common factor model in that a limited number of common factors explain the correlations between observed variables "in the sense that for any fixed values of the factors these correlations vanish. . . . Because it is possible for two variables to be uncorrelated and yet not entirely statistically independent" (now known as the principle of local independence), the principles underlying the latent trait model are different from the common factor model and more stringent (McDonald, 1985a, p. 203). Although the estimation procedures that were developed to estimate the various parameters of the classical model were based on linearity, there is no requirement for this (and nonlinear factor analysis has been available for some decades but rarely used in this context; Etezadi-Amoli & McDonald, 1983; McDonald, 1967).

It is likely that factor analysis and item response models will be reunited, and this promises rich possibilities for moving forward to develop more comprehensive theories. Muraki and Carlson (1995), for example, have developed full information factor analysis for polytomous item responses and have demonstrated relationships between factor loadings and multidimensional parameters similar to those developed in the item response models (Bock, Gibbons, & Muraki, 1988; Luecht & Miller, 1992; Reckase, 1985; Reckase & McKinley, 1991). McDonald (1985a, 1997) has developed the normal ogive harmonic analysis robust method (NOHARM), which permits estimation of parameters in both exploratory and confirmatory multidimensional models (Fraser, 1988).

Given that earlier writings clearly related the parameters in factor analysis and item response models (Lawley & Maxwell, 1971; Lord, 1980; McDonald, 1967, 1985a), it is surprising that it took so long to appreciate the importance of this relationship for developing multidimensional item response models. Advances by Muthén (1978), Bock and Aitkin (1981), and Reckase (1985, 1997; Reckase & McKinley, 1991) have provided more evidence of the advantages of considering item response models and factor analysis as complementary procedures to investigate the interactions between items and people. Connections among goodness-of-fit statistics (Elias, Hattie, & Douglas, 1998), polytomous items (Nandakumar, Yu, Li, & Stout, 1998), item linking (Reckase, Carlson, Ackerman, & Spray, 1987), and multidimensional score interpretation (Ackerman, 1992; Reckase, 1985, 1997) will ultimately lead to a deeper understanding of responses on performance items, since it is inevitable that these items are inherently multidimensional (Yen, 1994).

A major advantage of the item response model derives from the promise of invariance; that is, the model provides information (or, conversely, the standard error of ability estimates) for any given set of items at each point along the ability scale. There are no assumptions of normal distribution, and the IRT model "permits the interpretation of a test score in terms of what that score implies about the examinee's ability to perform. Given an appropriately chosen set of calibrated benchmark items, this means that true criterion referencing of test scores is possible" (Burket, 1984, p. 15). As Linn (1990) has noted, this criterion referencing has been used extensively with the IRT-based scales of the NAEP, which has benchmark scores that show the kinds of problems that students at a given scale score have a high probability of answering correctly. Linn, however, continues by raising some concerns (such as scale shrinkage) about using IRT-based scores on achievement tests.

A more recent concern has been the comparability of performance assessments (Shavelson, Baxter, & Gao, 1993; Shavelson, Gao, & Baxter, 1996). There are many possible threats in linking and placing such items on some common and understood scale. Haertel and Linn (1996) identified threats such as small number of items, administration in groups and classrooms, appropriate and inappropriate collaboration or coaching, high or low stakes, test security, effects of scoring training, social effects on scoring groups negotiating meanings and consensus about the interpretation of scoring, effects of construct-irrelevant variance in test scores, dependence on reading and writing, differences in student motivation to performance exercises, students' previous experience with similar tasks, and effects of language and culture. They concluded that "imprecision could be reduced and that the remaining imprecision could be evaluated more accurately if content specifications for performance exercises were prepared in greater detail and tests were constructed as purposively weighted collections of tasks sampled from narrow content domains" (pp. 74–75).

TEST AND ITEM DEVELOPMENT

Selection of Item Formats

The past 100 years have been dominated by the multiple-choice item and a technology to develop such items to form "best" tests. There have been numerous suggestions for creating dichotomous items (see Haladyna & Downing, 1989a, 1989b; Roid & Haladyna, 1982) and a concerted but largely unrewarding effort to devise more informative scoring models to capitalize on information at the item level (Frary, 1989; Stanley & Wang, 1970). Maximizing information at the item level adds little in comparison with merely adding a few extra items. The item response model weights items according to their "information," and users of the classical model typically choose items that have the highest discrimination. These methods, however, do not overcome the problems associated with guessing. Obtaining a correct answer by guessing has an expectancy of 25% with a four-option multiple-choice item, although such guesses have a merit of zero. Although many test companies, by effectively writing good items, can reduce the amount of guessing that takes place, the problem still remains. Furthermore, there are alternative methods that have evolved for responding to guessing issues (e.g., Cloze tests, fill in the blank, selection/identification, reordering/rearrangement, substitution/correction, performance exercises). Developers of achievement tests intended for large-scale use have shown a recent resurgence of interest in performance exercises. An alluring appeal of such performance measures is that there is much information in each item, and guessing appears to be minimized.

A persistent problem in test theory relates to whether the same dimensions are being assessed when the same item is administered via different formats. Traub (1993) provides an excellent review of the research relating to the equivalence of the traits assessed by multiple-choice and constructed tests. This author found little sound evidence of such equivalence or the nature of what it is that is different, if anything, about the characteristics measured by the two item formats (see also Bennett & Ward, 1993). Shavelson, Baxter, and Pine (1992) compared student performances on hands-on science tasks with computer simulations, short-answer questions, and multiple-choice questions. They found that computer simulations were fairly close approximations for hands-on tasks but not short-answer or multiple-choice questions. They suggested that the hands-on and computer simulations shared much in common with the innovative science instruction that preceded the testing, whereas the written methods were more influenced by ability requirements that may have less to do with the instruction and more to do with general proficiencies.

Selection of Scoring Models

Rather than considering the format of the test as the best source of distinguishing tests, it may be more advantageous to consider the scoring models. There are many lens through which to view scoring models, such as the model underlying the score of the item (e.g., 0–1 dichotomous or $0-n$ polytomous scoring) or the basis for scoring the responses (e.g., analytic or holistic). The appeal of dichotomous scoring is obvious not only because it is inexpensive and efficient but also because it appears parsimonious. The price, however, relates to the loss of information resulting from having only two options per item (e.g., 0 or 1) and the problems associated with linearity. The alternative is to use polytomous scoring, in which there are graded responses to the item/performance. These scoring models provide much more information, involve fewer problems with nonlinearity, and are appealing to the test taker and developer. Certainly, as more performance assessments are used, there will be a continued need for polytomous models that provide more item/test information.

Recently, van der Linden and Hambleton (1997) classified procedures based on polytomous item formats into six types. The first is based on unidimensional logistic models, a method pioneered by Samejima (1997). This type includes nominal response models and scoring multiple-choice responses instead of just the correct response and all other incorrect choices (Bock, 1997). The second refers to models based on items for which response time or number of successful attempts are of interest. The third type is multidimensional IRT models (McDonald, 1985b, 1997; Reckase, 1985, 1997) and multicomponent response models, which aim to provide a deeper understanding of examinee performance when performance involves completing many small steps (Embretson, 1995b, 1997). The fourth type involves models based not so much on the parameter structure of the items as on the shape of the functions (Mokken, 1997). The fifth type is models based on nonmonotone functions (the probability of passing does not necessarily increase as people have more of the underlying proficiency; Andrich, 1997, Hoijtink, 1990). Finally, the sixth type is models that account for special properties of the response process, such as accounting for groups rather than individuals as the unit of analysis (Bock, 1997), and models that handle local dependence (Jannarone, 1986), which may become particularly important with the scoring of performance assessments.

There has been a persistent debate about the benefits of scoring essays or performance assessments using analytical versus holistic or global scoring. In the analytic method, the ideal answer is broken down into specific parts, with points assigned to each part; in the holistic method, the rater forms a single overall judgment of the quality of the answer (often then referenced to an ''ideal'' answer). The more critical question involves the information provided to raters, and as recent experiences with performance assessment have demonstrated, the quality of the scoring rubric and the appropriate training of the raters are more critical than whether the scoring is analytic or holistic.

Frameworks for Test Organization: Test Specifications

There are two levels of debate relating to choosing the frameworks for test organization. At one level, the issues pertain to the appropriate and defensible standards that the resulting test is aimed to measure. Typically, a group of experts meet to determine the most defensible set of standards. Surprisingly, there are few guidelines for determining the validity of these processes (Hattie, 1996; Linn, Baker, & Dunbar, 1991). A major consideration is the relevance and representativeness of test content to the applied domain (Messick, 1995, p. 20), which may derive from a number of sources, including ''evidence that the test validity reflects processes, or constructs judged to be important in domain functioning, or significant test correlations with criterion measures of domain performance.''

Perhaps the starting point for determining content standards is a job analysis. Licensed practitioners are asked to identify and then place job tasks in priority order. The knowledge and skills needed to perform the job tasks safely and effectively are inferred and become the content standards that guide item and test development. When such analyses are not possible (e.g., when there are no credentialed workers), an alternative procedure involves seeking advice from the major professional groups with a stake in determining those to be certified/ licensed by the consequent assessment. Smith, Greenberg, and Muenzen (1993) reviewed procedures employed by various licensure and certification agencies in defining content standards and concluded that "there is no single correct process for developing content specifications. Combinations of approaches may be appropriate depending on the purpose, scope, and financial and personal resources available to the credentialing organization" (p. 11). The agencies they reviewed implemented one of two overall strategies. "The first approach emphasizes the contribution of a relatively small, but select group of subject-matter experts who are responsible for the development of the content specifications. The composition of the expert panel typically includes academics and practitioners" (p. 12). The second approach supplements the work of the subject-matter experts by a survey of credentialed practitioners as a verification check on the accuracy and completeness of the initial delineation.

The second level of debate for determining test frameworks refers to the taxonomies that supposedly underlie the best development of items to ensure coverage of the domain. The best known is Bloom's taxonomy (Bloom, Engelhart, Furst, Hill, & Krathwohl, 1956). This taxonomy is more than 40 years old and has dominated advice as to how items should be specified and evaluated. Bloom's taxonomy proposes six levels—knowledge, comprehension, application, analysis, synthesis, and evaluation—and the typical advice for test planning is to devise a two-way table of subject content along one dimension and these six levels along the other. After specifying how many items are desired within each cell, item developers then ensure that there are sufficient items to meet these specifications, and evaluators of the subsequent tests check to ensure that the responses are attuned with the specifications.

There have been many criticisms of this taxonomy: There is no evidence for the invariance of the stages; the taxonomy is not based on any known theory of learning or teaching; it presupposes that there is a necessary relationship between the questions asked and the responses to be elicited; it separates "knowledge" from the intellectual abilities or processes that operate on this "knowledge"; it is not accompanied by criteria for judging the outcome of the activity; and there is little evidence supporting the invariance and hierarchical nature of the six levels (Calder, 1983; Ennis, 1985; Furst, 1981; Hill & McGaw, 1981; Kropp, Stoker, & Bashaw, 1966; Kunen, Cohen, & Solman, 1981; Miller, Snowman, & O'Hara, 1979; Schrag, 1989; Seddon, 1978).

Anderson (1994, 1997) has proposed a revised version of Bloom's taxonomy to address many of these criticisms. The new proposal involves adding a second dimension to the present six categories. Knowledge is not only "what is recalled" (the content) but also the ability to recall (the process of knowing). This permits the "crossing" of each type of knowledge (remembering, understanding, applying, analyzing, synthesizing, and evaluating) with each cognitive process (declarative, conceptual, procedural, and metacognitive), leading to 24 cells in the revised model. In contrast to the original, the revised taxonomy recognizes a broader range of contextual factors that influence the learning and use of cognitive processes. Two primary examples are the knowledge, abilities, attitudes, and interests brought by the student to the learning situation (collectively known as the history of the learner) and the conditions under which the learning is expected to occur (e.g., the activities in which students are expected to engage, the ways in which the material to be learned is represented to learners).

A more defensible model needs to be derived from cognitive psychology, one that acknowledges that "we interpret experience and solve problems by mapping them to internal models; these internal models must be constructed; and the constructed models result in situated knowledge that is gradually extended and decontextualized to interpret other structurally similar situations" (Mislevy, 1996a, p. 389). Thus, we need measurement models that acknowledge that different knowledge structures can lead to the same behavior, where observed behavior constitutes indirect evidence about cognitive structure, and we need to assess the degree or depth to which students understand or process.

A model that can meet these requirements is Biggs and Collis's SOLO (structure of the observed learning outcome) taxonomy. Biggs and Collis (1982, 1989) developed their model from a study of learning outcomes in various school subjects and found that students learn quite diverse material in stages of ascending structural complexity that display a similar sequence across tasks. This led to the formulation of the SOLO taxonomy. The taxonomy makes it possible, in the course of learning a subject, to identify in broad terms the stage at which a student is currently operating. In this consistent sequence, or cycle, the following stages occur.

1. Prestructural: There is preliminary preparation, but the task itself is not attacked in an appropriate way.
2. Unistructural: One aspect of a task is picked up or understood, and there is no relationship of facts or ideas.
3. Multistructural: Two or more aspects of a task are picked up or understood serially but are not interrelated.
4. Relational: Several aspects are integrated so that the whole has a coherent structure and meaning.
5. Extended abstract: The coherent whole is generalized to a higher level of abstraction.

The unistructural and multistructural stages are at the surface or reproducing levels, which depend on an intention that is extrinsic to the real purpose of the task, and thus they usually require investing minimal time and effort consistent with appearing to meet requirements, invoking already-understood information, and rarely going beyond the surface of the content. These approaches can increase one's knowledge and involve memorization and reproducing as well as the application of facts and processes in different contexts. The relational and extended abstract stages are at the transforming or deep level, which reflects an intention to gain understanding by relating to the task in a way that is personally meaningful or that links with existing knowledge. The aim is to understand, see something in a different way, change as a person, or process surface learning in a deep manner (Biggs, 1987; Marton & Säljö, 1976, 1984).

The SOLO taxonomy can readily be used to devise test items (see Hattie & Purdie, 1998), and several procedures for the analysis of SOLO-based test items have been suggested. Wilson (1989) recommended using the one-parameter partial credit model to analyze SOLO items, and he demonstrated how fit statistics could be used to ascertain which items students are not completing to the expected level of their learning capabilities (see also Wilson & Masters, 1993). Wilson and Adams (1993) introduced the ordered partition model for analyses of SOLO items, in which item responses are categorized and then scored in ordered levels (see also Biggs, 1990; Lam & Foong, 1996; Wilson & Iventosch, 1988).

Given the earlier discussion about the integration of the more static models (e.g., item response theory) and the more cognitive processing models, it is likely that this may lead to more item taxonomic models, like SOLO, to create more optimal items. Consider, for example, the finding of Fennema, Carpenter, Jacobs, Franke, and Levi (1998) that there were no gender differences in solving number fact, addition/subtraction, or nonroutine problems throughout the 3 years of their study. Each year, however, "there were strong and consistent gender differences in the strategies used to solve problems, with girls tending to use more concrete strategies like modeling and counting and boys tending to use more abstract strategies that reflected conceptual understanding" (p. 11). Such findings will lead to more attention to developing items that assess both the content and the cognitive processes that students use as they are learning. The more recent attempts to create cross-national assessments may also underline the importance not only of content specification but also of assessing strategies that students use to determine their answers.

Test Assembly: Optimization Methods

These problems of developing new measures of processing and achievement are forcing measurement specialists to reinvestigate test assembly methods. The most common methods involve assessing the contributions of items to the test (via some modification of item-total correlations) and item difficulty levels. Using IRT methods, Lord (1977) recommended a procedure involving selecting a target information curve for the test and then choosing items with information curves to fill the target information curve. These methods need to be considered along with the critical issues relating to item content and dimensionality. The content specifications (perhaps via Bloom or SOLO) are of primary importance, as is the choosing of item domains sufficiently unidimensional that the resulting scores are interpretable along a meaningful scale (Haertel, 1985; Mislevy, 1988; Snow & Lohman, 1989; Traub & Wolfe, 1981).

van der Linden (1996; van der Linden & Luecht, 1996) has emphasized the importance of considering that item development (particularly within computerized adaptive testing, but also in general) involves designing a test that is optimal in some of its attributes while simultaneously requiring that the test assumes certain prespecified levels of values for a set of other attributes. Formally, this involves a test assembly process as an instance of constrained optimization and, thus, involves linear programming methods to choose items that maximize the specification of some objective function while satisfying various constraints placed on the desired test. Objective functions include maximizing test reliability, minimizing number of items in a test, maximizing information at a given cut point, matching a test characteristic function to a target function, minimizing items with explicitly gender or content orientation, and ensuring minimal items on various subdimensions. Examples of constraints include setting the number of items at some value, setting the number of items in the total tests on a particular topic to some value, setting the mean item difficulty at some value, ensuring that certain items appear on the test, ensuring that certain items do not appear simultaneously on the test, and setting the total length of the tests to some number of lines.

TEST ADMINISTRATION

The manner under which tests are administered has become a persistent methodological question, primarily because of the tensions between the desire to provide standardized conditions under which the test or measure is administered (to ensure more comparability of scores) and the desire for representativeness or authenticity in the testing condition (to ensure more meaning in inferring from the score). These issues are important to ensure that there is the least possible contamination of the meaning of the resultant test scores and that all possible examinees are included in the testing situation. Thus, issues of standardization are closely tied to questions of construct validity, comparability, and fairness.

Classical Group Administration of Tests

Given that the history of testing grew from mass testing, particularly in the military, it is not surprising that there are still entreaties to "follow the manual" when administering tests. While such standardization may assist in ensuring some dependability in scoring, attention has moved beyond such appeals to more concern about the interpretations of the scores, of which administration issues are but one issue in the interpretation. Furthermore, the advent of computerized scoring has meant that even the order of administering test items may not need to be standardized, although the full implications of the importance of the order of test items remain unresolved (Leary & Dorans, 1985). The increase in high-stakes statewide testing, particularly performance testing, has led to more discussion about preventing and detecting cheating, about the ways to handle "cooperative" projects in which more than one student is expected to cooperate in producing the performance, and about how to assign scores to individuals (Wollack & Cohen, 1998).

Administering Performance Tests

Exercises in performance assessments tend to be less standardized than multiple-choice tests, have fewer items sampling the content domain, can involve more student choice and local adaptation of assessment, and have less standardization in scoring. There has been an upsurge in performance testing formats such as interviews, constructed responses, exhibitions, direct observations, and portfolios (although the latter method seems more of a "catchall" phrase than a format). Many schools have long used these methods, and now statewide, national, and international assessments have incorporated performance assessments into their programs. It has only been in the past decade that the technical feasibility of large-scale performance assessments has become systematically a topic of study. The recent monograph by Phillips (1996) recognizes the major issues such as validity, generalizability, comparability, and performance standards and fairness. Many of these issues are discussed in the present chapter.

Accommodations in the Standardized Testing Situation

With the expansion of statewide and related high-stakes testing, many states are holding all students to the "same expectations." Given the high-stakes nature of many of these assessments, there is a temptation to exclude more students with disabilities or limited English proficiency so that they will not count in overall summaries, to discourage these students from participating in courses that are assessed (or to drop out completely), or to concentrate instruction on the students nearer the cut score and provide much less for those unlikely to reach the "standard." This has led to a resurgence of interest in the effects of accommodations to the testing process, particularly the testing medium, time limits, and test content. An important question is the following: "What would this examinee's score have been under standardized testing conditions had she or he not been handicapped?" (Burns, 1998; Nester, 1993).

Computer Adaptive Testing

In the early days of the development of measurement models, there was much emphasis on the performance of students on various tasks. When developing his intelligence scales, Binet (1911), for example, was interested in tasks that demonstrated the "best possible adaptation of the individual to his environment" (p. 172), and when he died he was working on adding adaptive, inventive responses about "attitudes in action" to address the question "How shall we measure the richness of intelligence, the sureness of judgment, the subtlety of the mind?" particularly accounting for how they vary across national and socioeconomic conditions. As Binet's biographer has commented (Wolf, 1973, p. 217), it is fascinating to note how measurement specialists still have to urge "that the development, use, and interpretation of tests should be reunited with the mainstream of psychology."

Binet developed an adaptive testing procedure that still underlies the administration and scoring of the Stanford-Binet intelligence tests. The child does not receive all items in the Stanford-Binet; rather, an estimate is made of the starting item, a series of items supposedly graded in difficulty is then administered, and items are administered until the examinee gets a series of items (within a year group) incorrect.

There were developments for sequential administering of items (e.g., Cronbach & Gleser, 1965), but it was the advent of more readily available computers that led to the resurgence of interest in adaptive testing. Unlike traditional testing, in computer adaptive testing (CAT) all examinees do not complete the same items. Rather, the computer selects successive items depending on an examinee's response to prior items. An examinee who answers the first item (usually an item of medium difficulty) correctly is presented with a more difficult item. If he or she answers the second item correctly, a still more difficult item is presented. The reverse is true if the examinee answers the first two items incorrectly. The result is a much more efficient measurement; less proficient examinees do not spend a lot of time on difficult items that they cannot answer correctly, and more proficient individuals do not waste time on items that are trivially easy for them. The result is that it takes approximately 40% fewer items to obtain the same level of measurement precision that would be obtained were all items administered to all examinees.

The early promises of adapting or tailoring test administration to most efficiently select items to estimate individual examinees' proficiencies were enticing. Using different items for different people with computer adaptive testing permits more efficient estimation of proficiency, the possibility that tests results can be rapidly communicated to the examinee, the possibility of measuring a broader range of skills in an efficient manner, the opportunity to implement more open-ended and alternative item formats (e.g., ordering tasks, marking parts of passages that support an inference, text editing, and listening comprehension), the immediate facility to assess and adjust for differential item response latencies among subgroups of test takers (Bloxom, 1985; Luce, 1986; Mislevy, Wingersky, Irvine, & Dann, 1991; Wainer, 1977), the administration of secure tests on more testing dates and at more testing sites, and the opportunity to provide more automated test information and diagnostics to the examinee. The methods for accomplishing this have been well documented (Wainer, 1990).

The lessons learned from the practical implementation of CAT, however, have led to a series of new problems. Large item banks are needed to ensure sufficient items for various levels of proficiency, multiple paths through the items at the beginning of the CAT are necessary to avoid violations of test security (it is relatively easier than first imagined for examinees to pass on their "memory" of the first few items and thus give advantage, particularly if a fixed number of items are administered; this problem led the Educational Testing Service to temporarily suspend the CAT for the Graduate Record Examination program), and there are issues relating to test disclosure laws.

These CAT problems are forcing measurement specialists to reinvestigate test assembly methods. For example, van der Linden (1996; van der Linden & Luecht, 1996) has emphasized the importance when developing the best test (particularly within CAT, but also in general) of designing a test that is optimal in some of its attributes while simultaneously requiring that the test involves certain prespecified levels of values for a set of other attributes (as noted earlier).

TEST USE

Tests are administered primarily because someone had a desire to use the scores. It has became more prevalent that those who wish to use the scores are not necessarily those who administer the tests or those who will interpret the results. Politicians, usually at the behest of taxpayer calls for accountability, have insisted on tests being administered so that the test scores can be used to "monitor" the status of schools.

Using Tests for School Accountability Purposes

Dorn (1998, p. 16) has argued that, "over the past twenty years, the dominant method of discussing the worth of schools in general has been the public reporting of aggregate standardized test score results. Popular news sources typically distort and oversimplify such findings (see also Berliner & Biddle, 1995; Darling-Hammond, 1992, 1994; Koretz, 1992a, 1992b; Koretz & Deibert, 1993; Shepard, 1991). The recent public debate over schools is not rich, reliant on multiple sources, or nuanced." Dorn argues that accountability through test scores encourages oversimplification rather than a more extensive public discussion, separates student performance from classroom practice, tends to make the interests of all children common, and can divide the interests of schools and communities through competition for prestige and resources. Of most concern is whether tests used for these purposes have satisfactory and convincing validity arguments for the interpretation of scores in the manner that accountability advocates proclaim.

There is a plethora of evidence demonstrating the effects of high-stakes testing in schools (see Shepard et al., 1996). For example, in a recent review of 578 studies investigating the effects of testing on classroom learning, Black and Wiliam (1998, p. 59) concluded that "the tests seldom inform teachers of previously unrecognized student talents and seldom identify deficits in a way that directs remedial instruction" (see also Crooks, 1988). Significant positive effects have been that such testing has concentrated teachers' minds on the state curriculum, there is more attention to a broad coverage of the total curricula that may be assessed in the tests, and there is more debate about the comparability information on the performances of students (although it is not clear that the test reports assist in ensuring that such comparability is meaningful). The negative effects include a diminution of attention to the skills of learning and deep processing, increased dropout by students, more difficult conditions for teachers to turn students into lifelong learners, decreased confidence by the public in the education system (as attention concentrates on low-performing schools), and greater incentives for excellent teachers to abandon the classroom. Smith and Rottenberg (1991), for example, documented the major implications of testing:

1. External testing reduces the time available for instruction. This time includes time for testing, test preparation (while elective, the time reflects the degree of pressure felt by teachers to raise the test scores and the importance they perceive the scores to have for administrators and the public), and recovery from testing.

2. Schools neglect material that external tests exclude. Subjects not tested are neglected; reading real books, writing in authentic contexts, solving problems that require more than rote recognition, creative and divergent thinking, longer term integrative projects, and the like were gradually squeezed out of instruction. The focus is on teaching "basic skills"; students have less to read, write, or think about and fewer avenues of interest such as those provided by science and social studies. Focusing instruction on test materials also slights the breadth, complexity, and form within reading, math, and language.

3. External testing encourages use of instructional methods that resemble tests. As stakes rise, teaching becomes more like the tests.

4. External testing encourages narrow forms of school organization. Test scores influence decisions to place students in homogeneous groups and tracks and lead to blaming of the students.

5. External testing negatively affects teachers. Teachers are aware of the variability of test scores, the importance of considering standard error, and the effects of factors other than their own teaching, and they are kept off balance in the face of the "numbers." They become autonomous professionals. "They redefine problem solving as the operations necessary to solve word problems on tests, they neglect social studies and science, integration of knowledge, production of discourse on novel problems, critical thinking, civic participation, cultural knowledge" (Smith & Rottenberg, 1991, p. 11).

A rise in test scores is not necessarily an indicator that these high-stakes assessments have had a positive effect on student learning, as it may be more related to teaching more narrowly to a particular test.

Tests and measures are part of the process of instruction; they are rarely used to measure outcomes alone (Brookhart, 1994). Crooks (1988) and Black and Wiliam (1998) have detailed the actual use of tests in classrooms, and we have argued that teachers' major interest in using tests relates to the amount of information and feedback it provides to them (Hattie & Jaeger, 1998).

Ensuring the Dependability of Scoring

The recent emphasis on performance assessments has served to highlight the critical importance of different methods for scoring. As noted earlier, there has been a resurgence of effort in developing scoring rubrics and training raters in using these rubrics (often including the use of anchor and benchmark papers). Haertel and Linn (1996) describe a typical process:

Raters are organized into small groups ("tables") each with a more experienced "table leader" who can answer specific questions as they arise. Some previously scored papers are seeded throughout those being scored for the first time so that each rater's accuracy can be monitored continually. If an individual rater appears to be performing below standard, the table leader may "read behind" that rater, monitoring his or her performance more closely until the problem is corrected. (p. 62)

This attention to scoring, along with detailed training in scoring, can lead to high levels of rater consistency (Dunbar, Koretz, & Hoover, 1991). Furthermore, it has been realized that such scoring is a social process in negotiating meanings, and this can lead to problems of replicating the quality of scoring on later occasions (although this can be addressed by seeding papers from different administrations into the new scoring).

Many researchers have proposed computer-automated scoring methods (Bejar, 1991; Bennett et al., 1990; Bennett, Steffen, Singley, Morley, & Jacquemin, 1997; Braun, Bennett, Frye, & Solway, 1990; Clauser, Margolis, Clyman, & Ross, 1997; Clauser et al., 1995; Page & Petersen, 1995). For example, Clauser et al's. (1995) procedure involves scoring open-ended responses to a vignette describing a patient's condition. The computer scoring recognizes approximately 9,000 terms represented in more than 2,000 different tests, examinations, treatments, consultations, and so on. The condition of the patient changes on the basis of the underlying disease and the examinee's actions. Scoring can be achieved through a regression-based approach (experts achieve consensus decisions in categorizing all actions into three levels), and the mean serves as the dependent measure. The seven independent measures are the counts of actions ordered by the examinee within the three most beneficial and three riskiest actions and the time interval in which the examinee completed the most essential beneficial actions.

Reporting Test Scores

One of the continuing dilemmas in educational testing concerns the reporting of results. Although valid interpretation and use of test results depend critically on the effectiveness with which they are reported, relatively little research on the validity of test score interpretation or on the relative effectiveness of various reporting alternatives has been conducted. Graphing methods have rarely been used to assist in interpreting test information, and, with the increasing power of computing, it is likely that there will be a renewed interest in novel and powerful graph reporting. Wainer (1992, 1996, 1997) illustrates a number of ways in which tabular and graphical data displays can be formatted so as to emphasize important results and eliminate unimportant ones. For example, Wainer has advocated the use of tri-linear plots, which portray three variables expressed in the form of components of a total. An example could be the relative performance of two states, say North Carolina and Washington, and the nation as a whole on an NAEP assessment (see also Ramsey, 1993; Tukey, 1977).

In terms of reporting results, NAEP has received more attention than most other testing programs. Student achievement results from NAEP have been summarized in a variety of ways (Phillips et al., 1993). In the original conception of NAEP, results were reported in terms of students' collective performances, exercise by exercise. The proportion of tested students who completed an exercise correctly (called a *p* value) was reported for each NAEP exercise, overall, and for major subgroups, including those classified by region, gender, size and type of community, education level of the students' parents, and race/ethnicity. This approach to reporting is consistent with the vision held for NAEP by its principal architect. Although reporting results by item embodies an appealing simplicity and clarity, the sheer volume of reported statistics made it difficult for users to integrate and understand students' achievement in a comprehensive way.

Subsequent reporting involved IRT scaled scores (Beaton & Johnson, 1992; Martinez & Mead, 1988; Mullis, Oldefendt, & Phillips, 1977); item mapping, which identified, for a large number of NAEP items, the scale score at which 80% of students answered the item correctly (Phillips et al., 1993); scale anchoring, which described the meaning of students' knowledge and skills at designated positions on the NAEP scale (Beaton & Allen, 1992; Mullis, Dossey, Owen, & Phillips, 1993); designated achievement levels, such as "basic," "proficient," and "advanced," for each tested grade (Hambleton & Slater, 1995; Jaeger, 1996); and the "market basket" approach (Forsyth, Hambleton, Linn, Mislevy, & Yen, 1996; Mislevy, 1996b). With the market basket approach, NAEP performance reports include the release of a representative sample of the items and exercises used in an assessment, together with their scoring rubrics. For example, the released items would be one of a number of psychometrically parallel collections actually administered to individual students. The advantage of this definition of a market basket is the possibility of reporting students' performances in an observed-score metric that would avoid the need for the kinds of sophisticated statistical manipulations of data required by the current IRT scaling. For example, it would be possible to simply report the percentage of available score points earned by the average student in a population or subpopulation. Seeing the collection of items referenced by the percentage, the hope is that users could more readily understand the meaning and the limitations of NAEP scores. This market basket approach to reporting would make clear precisely the kinds of skills NAEP assessed as well as the skills it did not assess under a particular label (e.g., mathematics achievement).

Numerous writers have noted the remarkable errors related to differing methods of reporting, and it is perhaps surprising that there is not more systematic study on more effective methods of score reporting (Hambleton & Slater, 1995; Hawkins, 1995; Jaeger, 1996; Koretz & Deibert. 1993). We particularly note an excellent source of future study relating to schools reporting student performance to parents (Jaeger, Gorney, Johnson, Putnam, & Williamson, 1993).

Setting Standards for Test Performance

The claim is often made that standards are judgments (Glass, 1978; Zieky, 1995) and that different methods for setting standards lead to different results (Jaeger, 1989). This should not imply that evidence to support the choice of method and evidence of the quality of uses and interpretations of standards are not essential. It is important that the standard-setting method reflect the nature of the decision process, that it be replicable (Brennan, 1995), and that there is evidence to support the intended interpretations and to refute competing interpretations (Kane, 1992; Shepard, 1993).

Most of the standard-setting methods in popular use apply solely to tests composed of traditionally scored, selected-response items (Angoff, 1971; Ebel, 1972; Jaeger, 1982; Nedelsky, 1954). These methods assume unidimensional, summative scoring of tests and apply solely to dichotomously scored test items. Mills and Melican (1988) divided these methods into two categories: normative methods based on an individual's ranking within a group and absolute methods based on evaluation of examinees or tests. We believe that standard-setting procedures that pay attention to the cognitive models of both the judges (those who set the standards) and the participants (those for whom the standards are set) are more likely to lead to defensible cut scores.

Setting performance standards is a process of eliciting reasoned judgments from experts who are knowledgeable about the demands of the test or assessment for which a standard is to be set, who understand the meaning of scores at various levels on the scale or scales used to summarize examinees' performances, and who fully comprehend the definitions of ability associated with the performance standard or standards they have been asked to establish. As assessments and their scoring become increasingly complex and multidimensional, the task of setting a reasoned performance standard becomes ever more difficult and demanding. Setting performance standards is an example of a larger class of problems identified in the psychological literature as judgment or decision-making tasks (Pitz & Sachs, 1984). A judgment or decision-making task is characterized by uncertainty of information or outcome or by an outcome dependent on personal preferences, or both. If judges are to provide reasoned recommendations on an appropriate performance standard, the process through which they consider alternatives and come to a judgment must help to resolve their uncertainties. Jaeger (1994) has argued that resolution of uncertainty occurs through an iterative process that incorporates initial judgments, information on the consequences of initial judgments, the opportunity to learn about the rationales underlying fellow judges' judgments, and opportunities to reconsider initial judgments in light of the information gained from these sources.

Hambleton and Plake (1995) evaluated a modified Angoff approach to setting a cut score across a series of performance assessments. This involved reading descriptions of the target competencies and then proceeding through a series of structured tasks whereby they provided sets of relative weights for the various dimensions to be scored for the "just barely certifiable candidate" as well as their confidence level in the relative weights. They did this for each of the five performance exercises and then completed a similar exercise that led to weights for summing across the five exercises. Berk (1995) placed this method in the context of many alternative methods for setting a cut score and reiterated a series of characteristics related to setting cut scores, including the importance of influence of judges in group feedback and discussion and the political, economic, social, and/or educational consequences of decisions. Jaeger, Mullis, Bourque, and Shakrani (1996) have detailed the methods used in a variety of major performance systems, such as NAEP, the National Board for Professional Teaching Standards, the Maryland Statewide Assessment, and the Kentucky Instructional Results Information System.

There is also the issue of setting standards for profiles across discrete tasks, a situation common in credentialing of complex performances (such as teacher performance). Consider two alternative standard-setting procedures based on harnessing cognitive processing judgments rather than only final recommendations. The *dominant profile judgment* method, described by Plake, Hambleton, and Jaeger (1997), requires panels of standard-setting judges to specify the lowest profile of performance on the exercises that compose an assessment that should result in examinees receiving a "passing mark." All examinees with profiles of performance that dominated the specified minimum (in the sense of having score values equal to or greater than the minimum) also would be certified. This approach to standard setting, however, often leads to substantially reduced measurement reliability and, in particular, dramatically increased probabilities of false-negative errors of examinee classification. The reason is the partially conjunctive nature of the standards. Whenever classification of examinees as passing an assessment depends on their performance on a single assessment exercise, as with a standard that prohibits earning a score below some threshold on any given exercise, resulting reliability will be low. Regardless of the method used to derive them, conjunctive standard-setting rules—that is, rules that invoke multiple hurdles to achieve certification—should be avoided for this reason.

An alternative method is *judgmental policy capturing* (Jaeger, 1994, 1995a, 1995b; Jaeger, Hambleton, & Plake, 1995). This method involves judges studying exercises and tests, learning about the meaning of each possible score on each exercise, reading and discussing benchmark responses to each exercise that received scores within specified ranges, discussing how each exercise scoring rubric was applied to each response, and why each response was an exemplar of performance for a given score range. Judges are then shown profiles of scores that examinees might earn on the various exercises and are asked to consider each profile of scores as though it (a) represented the score profile of an actual examinee and (b) was the sole basis for judging the performance classification (e.g., pass/fail) of the examinee. Judges work independently as they classify each profile of scores on the exercises into one of the scoring categories. An ordinary-least-squares multiple regression analysis is then used to fit a compensatory model (Coombs, 1954) to each judge's recommendation. This analytic model is used to "capture" the judgment policy of each judge who classifies examinees' profiles of performance.

Judgmental policy capturing provides a consistent mapping function that uses judgment data to develop a monotone relationship between a multidimensional profile of scores on individual exercises and a holistic judgment scale. When analyzed, the mapping function reveals two essential elements of the relationship. The first is the leniency or severity of the judge in classifying an entire profile of scores (e.g., What scores on the exercises must be earned in order to be classified at a given level on the holistic judgment scale?). The second is that the process reveals the relative weights a judge accords each of the scores in a profile when classifications on the holistic judgment scale are made.

The method can be improved by providing judges with feedback on the results of their first round of judgmental policy capturing, together with instruction on how to interpret that feedback. This information allows the judges to examine and understand the severity or leniency of their classifications of profiles and, particularly, the overall levels of profiles that led them to distinguish between examinees whose performances on the exercises warranted "passing" and those that warranted "failing." This could lead to further rounds of policy capturing.

Linking Scores From Different Tests

There are many situations in which it is necessary to compare the performance of examinees who have taken different tests. When a school district changes from one test developer to another, for the first year after the transition, teachers, administrators, and the public would like to know how to interpret scores on the new test in terms of the old in order to monitor student trends. In college admissions, it is necessary to compare students who have taken different forms of the SAT or ACT. Also, it is critical that cut scores in professional licensure and certification testing represent the same level of proficiency from year to year.

In the preceding situations and many more like them, a way must be found to transform scores on one test to scores on the other, that is, to "link" scores from different tests. Transforming temperatures from the Celsius scale to the Fahrenheit scale is a simple, although not exact, analogy. The well-known formula for doing this is $Fo = (9/5)Co + 32$. Thus, a temperature of 10 degrees Celsius, when inserted into the formula, gives a temperature of 50 degrees Fahrenheit. Note that the transformation is strictly symmetric. If we insert 50 degrees Fahrenheit into the formula for converting the Fahrenheit scale to the Celsius scale [$Co = (5/9)Fo - 17.78$], we obtain 10 degrees Celsius. Symmetry is an essential condition for an adequate linking.

The most rigorous and strongest kind of linking, and the one with the most technical support, is "equating" (Feuer, Holland, Bertenthal, Hemphill, & Green, 1998). This form of linking is possible if certain specific conditions such as test content, format, difficulty, and reliability are equivalent. Such is approximately the case, for example, with different forms of the SAT and ACT. Although exact equality of test difficulty and reliability is never strictly met, minor differences present no serious problems for a sound and useful score equating. The two tests to be equated must be administered to the same group of examinees or to large random samples from the same population. In linear equating, the raw scores corresponding to the Z scores on the two tests to be linked are said to be "equated." Thus, if a score of 83 on text X corresponds to a Z score of 1.20, and a score of 89 on test Y corresponds to a Z score of 1.20, then 83 on test X and 89 on test Y are interpreted to represent the same proficiency, knowledge, or skill. A similar logic applies to equipercentile equating. Here, raw scores on the two tests corresponding to the same percentile in the group of examinees are said to be equated. In anchor equating, a more efficient although somewhat less exact procedure, a smaller set of items common to both tests, or administered as a separate section of each test, is used to link the two tests. The IRT model provides an elegant and robust alternative to linear and equipercentile equating that involves not so much "equating" two tests as placing them on a common scale by calibrating individual items to the underlying construct.

It should be obvious that an essential condition for equating tests is that they measure the same construct or constructs. There is no sense in which a test of analogical reasoning and a typing test can be "equated." Nor can a test of reading and a test of mathematics be equated. The reason for this can be seen in Lord's (1980) definition of equated tests: Two tests are equated if it is a matter of indifference to examinees which test they take. For unequally reliable tests of some proficiency or skill, examinees high on the construct would prefer the reliable test; examinees low on the construct would prefer the unreliable test.

Equating may be thought of as one end of a continuum of linking stringency (Feuer et al., 1998), and there are many possible designs for equating scores, such as anchor, linear, equipercentile, kernel, and IRT methods (Holland & Rubin, 1982; Holland & Thayer, 1989; Kolen & Brennan, 1995; Petersen, Kolen, & Hoover, 1989). Other methods of linking contain increasingly more "noise" or errors in the transformations. When the conditions for strict equating are not met, as, for example, when two tests or assessments are constructed for different purposes or developed from different content frameworks, test scores from the two tests may still be placed on the same scale. Such scores are said to be "comparable" or "calibrated" and typically result in linked scores that are less consistent across different populations. Often, it is acknowledged up front that two tests measure different but related constructs. In these situations, linear regression can be used to predict or "project" scores on one test from scores on another. Note that the symmetry characteristic of equating tests does not obtain for projected scores. The weakest form of linking, moderation, is used when tests have been developed from different content frameworks and administered to different, nonequivalent groups of examinees, possibly for different purposes. Statistical moderation matches scores based on the two test distributions; social moderation depends on matching distributions based on human judgments about comparable performance. Moderation is the least consistent of the various linking procedures and allows only very general comparisons (Linn, 1995; Mislevy, 1992).

A difficult technical challenge facing the measurement profession in the coming century will be to develop better ways to link tests designed for different purposes, under different administration conditions, with different frameworks, and so forth. Increasingly, school districts and states would like to know how their students compare with those in other school districts, other states, and even other countries. International competition and the global economy have occasioned an intense interest in international comparisons of students' academic proficiency.

The technical and practical challenges confronting attempts to link diverse tests have been well documented by Feuer et al. (1998). In addition to differences in when particular test content is introduced into a particular state or district's curriculum, issues of differential motivation also complicate linking. A high-stakes test in one state (e.g., a graduation test), when linked to a low-stakes test in another, will give misleading results because of the substantial differences in student motivation. Feuer et al. (1998), in their review of attempts to link various state tests to NAEP and to one another through the development of a single scale, gloomily concluded that it was not feasible. Theirs is a considered judgment, but the pressure to provide ways of linking student performance on diverse measures of educational achievement will doubtless continue into the 21st century and will remain a signal challenge to the measurement profession.

TEST EVALUATION

There are a plethora of topics that relate to the evaluation of tests, and we highlight four: estimation of the reliability of tests, test validation, adverse impact and test bias, and ensuring that scores reflect the desired underlying dimensionality.

Estimation of the Reliability of Tests

Characterization and estimation of the reliability of measurements have enjoyed a rich methodological history that now spans nearly a century. Early conceptions of measurement reliability were reviewed briefly in Stanley's classic chapter on reliability theory (1971; see also Feldt & Brennan, 1989) and were described in some detail by Traub (1997). Writing on the origins of classical test theory, Traub cited the development of the correlation coefficient by Pearson (1896), pioneering work on correlational indicators of measurement reliability by Spearman (1904, 1910), and reactions to the application of reliability estimates in adjusting correlation coefficients by Pearson (1904). Traub noted:

Classical test theory [in which the concept of reliability plays a central role] is an emanation of the early 20th century. It was born of a ferment the ingredients of which included three remarkable achievements of the previous 150 years: A recognition of the presence of errors in measurements, a conception of that error as a random variable, and a conception of correlation and how to index it. Then in 1904 Charles Spearman showed us how to correct a correlation coefficient for attenuation due to measurement error and how to obtain the index of reliability needed in making the correction. Spearman's demonstration marked the beginning, as I see it, of classical test theory. (p. 8)

Spearman identified as a ''reliability coefficient'' the ''average correlation between one and another of . . . several independently obtained series of values for p'' (1904, p. 90), and in 1910 he updated that definition to ''the coefficient between one half and the other half of several measures of the same thing'' (p. 281). Despite the popularity of such relatively modern alternatives to a single indicator of measurement reliability, such as generalizability theory (Brennan, 1992; Cronbach, Rajaratnum, & Gleser, 1963; Cronbach, Gleser, Nanda, & Rajaratnum, 1971; Shavelson & Webb, 1991) and various indexes of measurement precision derived from item response theory (Birnbaum, 1967; Hambleton, Swaminathan, & Rogers, 1991; Lord, 1965, 1980; Lord & Novick, 1968; Rasch, 1961), it is the norm rather than the exception to find the reliability of a test summarized in terms of a single coefficient that can, theoretically, assume a value between zero and one. Thus, Spearman's pioneering work is today present throughout a range of applied work in educational testing and measurement despite a host of more sophisticated developments.

Spearman's approach was grounded in the idea that the rank order of a group of examinees on some measured ability or other characteristic should remain relatively stable were they to be measured a second time. The measurement procedure was deemed to be reliable only to the degree that the relative ordering of examinees produced by the initial administration of a measurement device could be reproduced on retesting.

The formulation of classical test theory gave rise to a host of designs and strategies for collecting reliability information and for analyzing it. To compute the degree of correlation between two measures of a characteristic, consistent with Spearman's definition of reliability, it was initially necessary to observe that characteristic on two separate occasions. In many practical circumstances, collecting two distinct sets of measurements was infeasible, inconsistent with the definition of the characteristic to be measured, or too costly. For some characteristics, the mere act of measurement is likely to change an examinee's true score (which must be assumed to be constant for a given examinee if Spearman's notion of consistency of rank order as an indicator of reliability is to make sense). An example of such a characteristic is the tendency to be more, or less, anxious at a given moment. Although psychologists have regarded one component of anxiety (termed "trait anxiety" by Spielberger, 1980) as a reasonably stable personality component, they have characterized another component, termed "state anxiety," as more transitory in nature. The act of measuring state anxiety is likely to induce a change in its value by heightening examinees' awareness of their current emotional state.

The cost and infeasibility of administering two separate measures led to the development of designs and equations for estimating reliability on the basis of a single measurement, provided that it could be decomposed into separate parts. One simple approach was based on correlating examinees' scores on the even items on a test with their scores on the odd items (Brown, 1910). After many seminal contributions, Cronbach introduced coefficient alpha, which is still widely used as an index of measurement reliability (Cronbach, 1951; Guttman, 1945; Kuder & Richardson, 1937). It is critical to note, however, that this estimate of reliability is sample dependent and thus shares the problems outlined earlier relating to the classical test model.

Generalizability of Scores

In 1963, Cronbach, Gleser, and Rajaratnum introduced the then-revolutionary idea that error of measurement was not merely an amorphous, indeterminate, randomly determined inevitability of every measurement procedure. They proposed that measurement error could be analyzed and estimated in terms of the conditions that gave rise to its presence. Fundamental to their formulation—

since termed "generalizability theory"—was the idea that in conducting a measurement procedure, a researcher had in mind some universe of conditions across which the results of that measurement were to be generalized. Elements of that universe might include such facets as a range of occasions on which measurement might take place, a range of forms of the measurement instrument, and a range of persons who might evaluate and score an examinee's performance on the measurement instrument. Any single measurement is regarded in generalizability theory as a sample from the desired universe of generalization. To the degree that a measurement procedure is reliable, the sample of performance will generalize well over the facets that define the universe of interest.

Generalizability theory is central to current research on measurement reliability. In the 35 years since its introduction, a substantial body of literature has resulted in its further exposition (Brennan, 1992; Cronbach, Gleser, Nanda, & Rajaratnum, 1971; Shavelson & Webb, 1991) and its extension to a host of measurement strategies and situations in which measurement takes place (e.g., see Brennan, 1994; Cronbach, Linn, Brennan, & Haertel, 1997).

The increasing reliance on generalizability theory and the current focus on estimation of the magnitude of the standard error of measurement are to some degree stimulated by the movement beyond selected-response items in educational testing. Even in such large-scale testing programs as NAEP, students complete test items and exercises that require them to provide written responses, to perform some task (such as conducting experiments), and to explain the reasoning behind their answers by preparing brief written essays. Such performance exercises, or "extended constructed response exercises," as they are termed in NAEP, must be scored by hand and are typically read by more than one rater; thus, errors that are attributed to judges and examinees (and their interactions) can be estimated.

The time required to administer a performance exercise is usually substantially greater than the time required to administer a selected-response test item. Since testing time is always limited, it becomes important to determine the minimum number of performance exercises needed to ensure adequately reliable measurement. Several components of error variation play a major role when a test is composed of relatively few performance exercises.

First, it is difficult to construct equally difficult test items. When a test is composed of, say, 50 multiple-choice items, it matters little whether some are a bit more difficult and others are a bit easier. With careful item writing, it is possible to construct two 50-item multiple-choice tests so that their *average* difficulty is quite similar. In contrast, when a test of expository writing consists of a single 30-minute essay (as is true of the writing tests used in a number of states' uniform statewide assessments), it is difficult to construct two writing prompts that present examinees with equally difficult tasks. Thus, one source of error variance in a writing test, or any other test composed of very few tasks, is variance due to selection of prompts or exercises.

Even if two essay prompts present examinees with tasks that are equally difficult, on average, it is likely that one of the prompts will be relatively easier for some examinees and the other will be easier for other examinees. Thus, the rank ordering of examinees is likely to be different across the two prompts. This kind of examinee-exercise interaction is another component of error variation in measurement.

When raters judge the performances of examinees on tasks such as writing an essay, some raters are inevitably more lenient than others. On average, Rater 1 might be a "softie," giving most examinees high scores, whereas Rater 2 might be a classic "scrooge," assigning low scores to all but the very best performances. When different raters score the performances of different examinees, such variation in the tendency of one or another rater to assign higher or lower scores becomes a source of error variance. The score earned by a given examinee is a function not merely of her or his ability but of the rater(s) who happened to judge the examinee's performance as well.

In addition to the tendency of some raters to be generally more stringent and others to be generally more lenient in their scoring, there is the possibility that some raters will be more stringent or more lenient than others when judging the performance of a particular examinee. That is, there might be an interaction effect between the particular characteristics of a given examinee's response to an exercise and the propensity of some judges to be attracted to, or repelled by, those characteristics. One judge might be attracted to the use of polysyllabic words, while another might be a stickler for simplicity, apart from their tendencies to be harsh or lenient in their general scoring. A writer whose native language is German and whose second language is English would therefore probably be advantaged by the assignment of a judge with a penchant for conjoint vocabulary and disadvantaged by the assignment of a judge who was weaned on Strunk and White (1979). This kind of rater-by-examinee interaction is another source of error variance that can be examined through generalizability theory.

The list goes on. A relatively simple generalizability design in which a number of examinees are assessed via several exercises, with each response scored by several raters, gives rise to no less than seven sources of variation in scored performance: main effects due to sampling of examinees, exercises, and raters; so-called two-way interactions between examinees and exercises, examinees and raters, and exercises and raters; and, finally, a three-way interaction among examinees, exercises, and raters, the magnitude of which cannot generally be estimated separately from that of additional sources of error variance (such as differences in the conditions of administration of the exercises). The magnitude of variation in examinees' scores ascribable to each of these sources can be estimated by using generalizability theory. These estimates, in turn, can be used to determine how many exercises must be administered and how many raters must score the performances of each examinee to reduce error variation to an acceptable level or, equivalently, to increase measurement reliability (generalizability) to an acceptable level. Cronbach, Linn, Brennan, and Haertel (1997) provide an excellent hypothetical example of the use of generalizability theory for this purpose, in the context of a performance assessment.

Reliability and Performance Assessment

Increased use of performance exercises in large-scale educational assessments has been accompanied by the use of such assessments as a basis for making important decisions about individual students, such as the instruction and rewards they will be provided or the sanctions that will be imposed on them. This movement toward test-based accountability in public education shows no sign of abating, and we expect it to increase in the coming years.

When tests are used within an accountability framework, students are classified on the basis of their test scores. In some settings, such as the NAEP, the test scores of individual students are not released, so the classification of a student as "below basic," "basic," "proficient," or "advanced" (the designators used with NAEP) is not consequential. (In NAEP, "plausible value" estimates of the ability of individual examinees are computed solely for the purpose of compiling distributions of such estimates for populations and subpopulations of interest. Neither test scores for individuals nor assignments of individuals to the NAEP achievement-level categories are reported.) In other contexts, however, including a multitude of statewide educational assessments, students whose test performances result in their assignment to a "below proficient" category are retained in their grade, are required to attend school during the summer, or are denied a high school diploma despite completion of all required courses with passing grades.

When tests are used to make these kinds of "high-stakes" decisions for individual examinees, measurement reliability is particularly salient. The lower the reliability of a test or assessment, the greater its standard error of measurement. The greater its standard error of measurement, in turn, the greater the likelihood that individual examinees will be classified erroneously, simply as a result of error of measurement. We predict, therefore, increasing emphasis on estimation of measurement error and on estimation of probabilities of misclassification of examinees as a result of measurement error. We conclude this section by illustrating some recent approaches to estimating measurement error and classification errors in the context of high-stakes assessments. The continued use of performance assessments in high-stakes contexts will only serve to increase the importance of these approaches and, we would predict, stimulate the development of more effective strategies for estimating these parameters.

Estimation of the Standard Error of Measurement

Cronbach (personal communication, 1995) suggested an appropriate strategy for estimating the standard error of measurement and, from that statistic, the reliability of a performance assessment composed of a small number of discrete exercises that are administered only once. His idea was to conduct a series of multiple regression analyses wherein examinees' scores on each performance exercise are used as measures of a dependent variable. This dependent variable is regressed on examinees' scores on all of the other performance exercises in the assessment. The standard error of estimate from the regression analysis with scores on a given exercise as the dependent variable is used as an estimate of the standard error of measurement of that exercise. Thus, with a set of k performance exercises, k multiple regression analyses would be conducted, with scores on each exercise regressed on examinees' scores on the remaining $(k - 1)$ exercises.

This approach to reliability estimation assumes that the variance of scores on any one exercise that is not predictable from scores on the other exercises is attributable to error of measurement. When performance exercises are used to assess examinees within a broad, multifaceted domain, the attribution to error of all variance of scores on a given exercise that cannot be predicted from scores on other exercises might not be reasonable. That is, some unpredictable variation more reasonably might be attributed to the multidimensionality of the domain than to error variance. To account for this possibility, when exercises can be allocated to subdomains on some substantive basis quite apart from the performance data at hand, the reliability of the overall assessment might more reasonably be estimated via a stratified version of Cronbach's alpha coefficient.

Estimating Decision Consistency

When assessments are used for selection purposes, it is of interest to estimate the consistency with which examinees are classified into the same category, regardless of the judges who score their performances on individual exercises. Traub, Haertel, and Shavelson (1996) developed an approach that assumes that each examinee has completed k exercises and that the examinee's responses to each exercise have been scored independently by two judges. Traub et al. noted that the pairs of scores assigned to the k exercises could be portrayed in terms of 2^k profiles of scores, of which 2^{k-1} could be used to form distinct pairs of profiles. They assumed that each examinee would be assigned a score on the entire assessment that was a weighted sum of his or her exercise scores.

When the scores awarded to the examinee by the judges listed in any profile are weighted and summed, this either results in an overall performance score that is above some predetermined performance standard (in which case the examinee would be passed) or results in an overall performance score that is below the performance standard (in which case the examinee would be failed). For any distinct pair of profiles, then, we have two decisions for an examinee. These decisions will either be consistent (e.g., pass/pass or fail/fail) or inconsistent (e.g., pass/fail or fail/pass). An index of decision consistency for an individual examinee, denoted by p_{Cj}, is the proportion of the $2^k - 1$ distinct profile pairs that result in consistent decisions. An overall index of decision consistency, denoted by p_C, can be defined as the average of the indices of decision consistency for individual examinees. This average is merely the proportion of profile pairs that result in consistent pass or consistent fail decisions, averaged across all examinees.

Several features of this index of consistency of scoring are worth noting. First, it is highly sensitive to the placement of the performance standard in relation to the distribution of examinees' overall performances. If the performance standard is extreme—either at a very small or at a very large percentile of the overall score distribution—most examinees' overall performance scores will be far above or far below the performance standard. In that case, most examinees would be failed (if the performance standard is high) or would be passed (if the performance standard is low). In either of these cases, the index of decision consistency would be high, merely as a consequence of the marginal distribution of scores of the examinees. This possibility suggests that the index of decision consistency should be compared with the proportion of consistent decisions that would be expected by chance, were examinees to be assigned randomly to the pass and fail categories in the proportions dictated by the placement of the performance standard within the examinees' distribution of overall performance (e.g., by using an index such as Cohen's kappa).

Conditional Decision Consistency

Since we would expect more consistent classification of examinees whose overall performance scores were well above or well below the passing standard, it might be of interest to estimate the decision consistency index conditionally, depending on the distance of an examinee's overall performance score from the performance standard. In light of the definition of the decision consistency index for an individual examinee, p_{Cj}, it is possible to calculate an average consistency index for examinees with overall performance scores within any specified subset of the observed performance-score distribution. These values can then be plotted as a function of overall performance score to learn how quickly classification of examinees becomes consistent as their performances differ to a greater degree from the performance standard.

Conditional Probability of Passing an Assessment

An alternative indicator of the precision of an assessment is the probability that an examinee with a true score a given distance above (or below) the performance standard would be passed. If an assessment measured examinees' abilities with perfect precision, all examinees with true scores less than the performance standard would be failed and all those with true scores greater than or equal to the performance standard would be passed. In that case, a plot of the probability of passing, as a function of true score, would be a step function taking on a value of zero or one with no intermediate values.

In reality, since assessments are always errorful to some degree, the probability of passing will be some continuous function of the difference between an examinee's true overall score on the assessment and the performance standard. The higher the reliability of the assessment, the smaller the standard error of measurement, and the more steeply the plot of the probability of passing will increase from the region where examinees' true scores are below the performance standard to the region where their true scores are above the performance standard.

Probabilities of Erroneous Classification of Examinees

When an assessment is used for purposes of selection, it becomes important to determine the probability that an examinee whose true overall performance is equal to or greater than the performance standard will, nonetheless, be classified as failing the assessment. This is known as the probability of a false-negative error. Likewise, it is important to determine the probability of a false-positive error of classification—the probability that an examinee whose true overall performance is below the performance standard will, nonetheless, be classified as passing the assessment. Livingston and Lewis (1995) developed a method for estimating these probabilities for performance assessments.

The Livingston and Lewis method requires an estimate of the reliability of the assessment, a distribution of overall performance scores on the assessment, knowledge of the minimum and maximum possible overall performance scores that could be earned on the assessment, and specification of a performance standard on the scale of the overall performance score. Their procedure is a multistep method that is computationally intensive but yields a number of useful indicators of precision, including (a) the "effective length" of the assessment, (b) the probability of a false-negative error of classification, (c) the probability of a false-positive error of classification, (d) the expected number of false-negative errors of classification in a given sample of examinees, (e) the expected number of false-positive errors of classification in a given sample of examinees, (f) the expected number of erroneous classifications in a given sample of examinees, (g) the probability that examinees would be consistently classified on the basis of two independent administrations of the assessment, and (h) an estimate of Cohen's kappa for two independent administrations of the assessment.

It should be noted that the Livingston and Lewis method yields an index of decision consistency and a kappa value that reflect sources of measurement error in addition to inter-assessor inconsistency. These estimates take into consideration such contributions to error of assessment as scoring errors, the interaction between examinees and individual assessment exercises, and variation due to repeated, independent administration of the assessment (assumed to occur with no changes in examinees' true scores). Thus, the decision consistency index and kappa values provided by the Livingston and Lewis method should more accurately reflect the precision of an assessment than will the values that result from the Traub et al. (1996) method of estimating inter-assessor consistency.

We anticipate increasing attention to these alternative indicators of measurement precision in the future, as tests and assessments are used in ways that have important consequences for examinees. We would also expect measurement research to focus increasingly on models and strategies for characterizing the precision of assessments and on the fidelity of decisions that are based on their use in selection and classification of examinees. More inclusive generalizability models, of the type illustrated in Cronbach et al. (1997), will help to pinpoint major contributors to imprecision in measurement, while consequential indicators will be used to determine whether measurement procedures are up to the task of making important decisions about individual examinees.

Validity

There has been a renewed emphasis on validating the interpretation of scores, and an excellent discussion of the critical issues can be found in Shepard (1993).

Messick (1989, 1994, 1995) has been most forceful in providing a "unified though faceted" approach to the notion of validity. He commenced by stating:

Validity is an integrated evaluative judgment of the degree to which empirical evidence and theoretical rationales support the "adequacy" and "appropriateness" of "inferences" and "actions" based on test scores or other modes of assessment. As will be delineated shortly, the term test score is used generically here in its broadest sense to mean any observed consistency, not just on tests as ordinarily conceived, but on any means of observing or documenting consistent behaviors or attributes. Broadly speaking, then, validity is an inductive summary of both existing evidence for and the potential consequences of score interpretation and use. Hence what is to be validated is not the test or observation device as such but the inferences derived from test scores or other indicators—inferences about score meaning or interpretation and about the implications for action that the interpretation entails. (p. 13)

He then considers four facets of validity. Although Messick presents these facets in a 2 × 2 table (Functions or Outcomes of Testing × Sources of Justification), it is easier to consider his arguments if they are presented in a series of four categories (Shepard, 1993), with each one adding the validity evidence from the previous one. Shepard noted that it is not necessary to commence from construct validity and move forward, since there can be instances in which it is more appropriate to start from other bases of evidence.

evidential basis of test interpretation	construct validity
evidential basis of test use	+ relevance and utility
consequential basis of test interpretation	+ value implications
consequential basis of test use	+ social consequences

While most affirm the primacy of validity, this has not always been followed in actions (see Gipps, 1994; Linn, 1994). There has been little debate about the importance of the first two or three of Messick's bases for validity; most debate has concerned the appropriateness of including the fourth level as part of test validity. As Maguire, Hattie, and Haig (1994) have claimed, an emphasis on consequential validity has led to an overemphasis on (a) the role of the developer of large-scale standardized tests, although such tests occupy a small place in the testing lives of students; (b) large-scale, systematic, and planned assessments; (c) test score use rather than test development; and (d) protecting part of the test community from increased litigation.

Instead, Maguire et al. separate the link from construct to indicator (the response elicited by an item, observation) and from indicator to score. Tests and scoring procedures are "*mediating empirical operations* to make constructs into numbers. If the things that we do with these numbers (make decisions, conduct research, etc.) are to have any validity, then we must take great care in developing the tests and scoring procedures. It is not obvious that the common practice of administering large numbers of items and computing number correct, or weighted aggregates, retains the representational link between scores and constructs" (p. 123).

The increased use of performance measures will increase the attention to this link between scores and constructs. Linn and Miller (1968) made the following important comments about validity:

> It is widely agreed that validity is the most important consideration in the evaluation of the use of a test. Validity is always a matter of degree. It is not a single all-or-none concept. Rather the concern is with the degree to which the accumulated evidence supports a particular test use. Many forms of evidence may be relevant in evaluating the validity of a particular test use, and it is not possible to give a simple prescription for the forms or adequacy of the evidence in the abstract. Professional judgment is required to determine the forms of evidence that are most appropriate in a given situation and to judge the adequacy of the support for the intended purpose. (p. 47)

There is thus no simple formula for determining the kinds of validity evidence that will be sufficient when tests or assessments are used for any purpose, and particularly when they are used for making the kinds of high-stakes decisions that are becoming increasingly frequent in modern applications of educational testing.

Consistent with the emphasis on the validity of score interpretations, the traditional validity trinity of content, criterion, and construct validity can be interpreted as providing a series of procedures to assess the validation arguments. That is, the following can be conceived as possible (depending on the purpose) arguments that can be used to defend particular score interpretations: duplicative construction (Cronbach, 1971, 1988), expert weighting of items, relating scores to a criterion, factor analysis, known-groups methods (Hattie & Cooksey, 1984), multitrait-multimethod techniquess, and meta-analysis (Schmidt, Hunter, Pearlman, & Hirsch, 1985). These are all part of the never-ending process of collecting and evaluating evidence that supports the use of the test scores for making particular decisions.

Traditional claims to the validity of instruments used for professional certification and licensure are grounded in the requirements of the *Uniform Guidelines on Employee Selection Procedures* (1978), the *Principles for the Validation and Use of Personnel Selection Procedures* (Society for Industrial and Organizational Psychology, 1987), and the *Standards for Educational and Psychological Testing* (American Psychological Association, American Educational Research Association, & National Council on Measurement in Education, 1985). The forms of validity evidence recognized in these sources include evidence that the content of a certification or licensure test or assessment is appropriate to its use, evidence that the test or assessment predicts some valued outcome (such as performance in an occupation or a profession), and evidence that scores earned on the test exhibit relationships that are consistent with theory concerning the abilities that the test or assessment is claimed to measure.

Given the emphasis on validity as argument, Crooks, Kane, and Cohen (1996) outlined a set of validation criteria threats to each of eight linked stages of inferences and assumptions underlying performances and interpretations of scores. For each linked stage, they identified validity threats. Their eight stages (and threats) are (a) administration of assessment tasks to students (low motivation, anxiety, inappropriate assessment conditions), (b) scoring of the performances on tasks (undue emphasis on some criteria, low interrater or intrarater consistency), (c) aggregation of scores on individual tasks to produce combined scores (tasks too diverse, inappropriate weighting, overrepresentation of the domain), (d) generalization from the particular tasks included in a combined score to the entire domain of similar tasks (conditions of assessment too variable, inconsistency of scoring criteria for different tasks), (e) extrapolation from the assessed domain to a target domain containing all tasks relevant to the proposed interpretation (conditions of assessment too constrained, underrepresentation of domain), (f) evaluation of the student's performance to form judgments (inadequately supported construct interpretation, biased explanation), (g) decision on actions to be taken in light of the judgments (inappropriate standards, poor action decisions), and (h) impact on the student and other participants arising from the assessment processes, interpretations, and decisions (positive consequences not achieved, serious negative impact).

Crooks et al. noted the importance of all links in their chain and that the strength of a chain depends on its weakest link, although we suggest that Wittgenstein's (1953) claim is more appropriate: "The strength of the chain lies not in one fiber running throughout the entire length, but in the overlapping of many fibers" (p. 149). The nature of the decision to be made would determine where more attention should be focused, and Crooks et al. concluded usefully by claiming that "examining each link and looking for weaknesses in the chain of inference, including those arising from common specific threats, provides a systematic approach to validation" (p. 284).

Dimensionality

A critical concern underlying the claims for validity argument relates to ensuring appropriate representation of the construct to be assessed. There is a need to ensure that the construct is neither overrepresented nor underrepresented and that the fundamental classical and item response test theory assumption of unidimensionality is not violated. This assumption specifies that a score can have meaning only if the set of items measures only one attribute. If the measuring instrument has a number of items that measure differing dimensions, it is difficult to interpret a total score from a set of items, to make psychological sense when relating variables, or to make comments about individual differences. The concept of unidimensionality is a specific instance of the principle of local independence, that is, the existence of one latent trait underlying the data (Hattie, 1984, 1985).

The principle of local independence requires that responses to different items are uncorrelated when θ (the person's ability) is fixed, although it does not require that items be uncorrelated over groups in which θ varies. Lord and Novick (1968) gave the definition of local independence more substantive meaning:

An individual's performance depends on a single underlying trait if, given his value on that trait, nothing further can be learned from him that can contribute to the explanation of his performance. The proposition is that the latent trait is the only important factor and, once a person's value on the trait is determined, the behavior is random, in the sense of statistical independence. (p. 538)

As many have demonstrated, the statement of the principle of local independence contains the mathematical definition of latent traits (e.g., see McDonald, 1981). That is, $\theta_1, \ldots, \theta_k$ are latent traits if and only if they are quantities characterizing examinees such that, in a subpopulation in which they are fixed, the ability scores of the examinees are mutually statistically independent. Thus, a latent trait can be interpreted as a quantity that the items measure in common, since it serves to explain all mutual statistical dependencies among the items. Since it is possible for two items to be uncorrelated and yet not be entirely statistically independent, the principle is more stringent than the factor-analytic principle that their residuals be uncorrelated. If the principle of local independence is rejected in favor of some less restrictive principle, then it is not possible to retain the definition of latent traits, since it is by that principle that latent traits are defined. It is possible to reject or modify assumptions as to the number and distributions of the latent traits and the form of the regression function (e.g., make it nonlinear instead of linear) without changing the definition of latent traits.

A set of items can be said to be unidimensional when it is possible to find a vector of values $\theta = (\theta_i)$ such that the probability of correctly answering an item k is $\pi_{ik} = f_k(\theta_i)$ and local independence holds for each value of θ. This definition is not equating unidimensionality with local independence, because it can further require that the conditioning involve only one θ dimension and that the probabilities p_{ik} be expressed in terms of only one θ dimension.

McDonald (1981) outlined ways in which it is possible to weaken the strong principle, in his terminology, of local independence. The strong principle implies that not only are the partial correlations of the test items zero when the latent traits are partialed out, but also the distinct items are then mutually statistically independent and their higher joint moments are products of their univariate moments. A weaker form is to ignore moments beyond the second order and test the dimensionality of test scores by assessing whether the residual covariances are zero (see also Lord & Novick, 1968, pp. 225, 544–545). Under the assumption of multivariate normality, the weaker form of the principle implies the strong form, and vice versa. McDonald (1979, 1981) argued that this weakening of the principle does not create any important change in anything that can be said about the latent traits, although strictly it weakens their definition.

Stout (1987, 1990) also used this weaker form to develop his arguments for "essential unidimensionality." He devised a statistical index based on the fundamental principle that local independence should hold *approximately* when sampling from a subpopulation of examinees of *approximately equal ability*. He defined essential unidimensionality as follows: A test $(U_1, \ldots, U_N)$ of length N is said to be essentially unidimensional if there exists a latent variable θ such that, for all values of θ,

$$\frac{1}{N(N-1)} \sum_{1 < i \neq j < N} |Cov(U_i, U_j|\theta)| \approx 0.$$

That is, *on average*, the conditional covariances over all item pairs must be small in magnitude (for more detail regarding theoretical developments, see Junker, 1990, 1991, 1992; Nandakumar, 1994; Nandakumar & Stout, 1993; Stout, 1990). Essential unidimensionality thus replaces local independence and is based on assessing only the dominant dimensions.

Stout then developed an empirical notion of unidimensionality to match his weaker form. Either a subjective analysis of item content or an exploratory factor analysis is used to develop a core set of items, and this set is termed by Stout the assessment subtest. The remaining set of items, termed the partitioning subtest, is used to partition examinees into groups for a stratified analysis. When the total set of items is unidimensional, the assessment and partitioning sets are both unidimensional; when the dimensionality is greater than one, however, "the partitioning subtest will contain many items that load heavily on at least one other dimension not measured by the assessment subtest" (pp. 591–592).

There are many applications of Stout's procedures (Nandakumar, 1993) and simulation studies that have supported the value of his statistic (Hattie, Krakowski, Rogers, & Swaminathan, 1996). Zhang and Stout (1997) have generalized the Stout procedure via the DETECT method (Dimensionality Evaluation to Enumerate Contributing Traits). This method simultaneously assesses the latent dimensionality structure and determines the degrees of multidimensionality present in test data. This procedure has been extended by Kim (1994) to identify the partition P of the available k items into disjoint and exhaustive subsets that best represents the underlying dimensionality structure. The best partition is detected by $DETECT_{max}$, and thus it is a measure of the amount of departure from unidimensionality. The methods have been generalized to polytomous items (Nandakumar et al., 1998).

It is critical to note that the assumption of unidimensionality does not necessarily imply that only the most simple of tasks can be assessed by these measurement models. We routinely use scores that represent purposively weighted composites of several variables (e.g., SAT verbal, IQ scores, self-concept). The critical issue relates to the (often implicit) weighting of distinct but related components. These may be specified by tables of test specifications (such as Bloom or SOLO) or by judgmental analyses of how a score is to be weighted (see earlier discussion relating to judgmental decision making). Given that these Stout indices are based on factor and cluster analysis methods, there may be much to gain from cross fertilizing item response and factor theory and developing goodness-of-fit indices that demonstrate fit at various parts of the total model (at the item and person levels, for example). This could lead to better understandings of the performances of examinees on items (on the basis of how examinees cognitively process the demand of the item) and the performance of the item relative to other information (see Elias, Hattie, & Douglas, 1998).

Adverse Impact and Test Bias

It is important to keep in mind the distinction between *adverse impact*, on the one hand, and *bias*, on the other. An assessment is said to exhibit adverse impact with respect to examinee race, for example, if the rate at which African-American examinees are certified is substantially below the certification rate of White, non-Hispanic examinees. The differential certification rate alone is sufficient for adverse impact to exist. The reason or reasons for the differential certification rate are not relevant to a determination of adverse impact. Differential certification rates may result from assessor biases, from biases in the conceptualization of the domain to be assessed, from characteristics of the scoring scheme as it was applied to certain examinees, or from differential access to professional or collegial help in preparing for the test or assessment, to name just a few potential sources. But the content of the exercises and the procedures used to administer and score the exercises may be totally free of these deficiencies. Determining whether adverse impact, to the extent that it exists, results from genuine differences between the performances of groups or is an artifact of deficiencies in the assessment system requires additional study and investigation.

By contrast, an assessment is said to exhibit bias if significant, systematic differences in performance among subgroups in the examinee population can be ascribed to actual flaws or deficiencies in one or more aspects of the assessment system itself that have the effect of disadvantaging members of a specific group. Such deficiencies may be due to "construct-irrelevant" factors in the assessment. For example, in the assessment of mathematical proficiency, if the intent is to assess proficiency in mathematics as "purely" as possible without confounding the measurement with linguistic ability, it would be important to keep the required level of competence in the language in which the test is written to a minimum. If the examination includes word problems, then the vocabulary and linguistic demands of the problems should be as simple as possible. Otherwise, persons less proficient in the language of the test, such as those for whom the language is a second language or those who speak specific dialects within the general population, may be unfairly penalized because of purely linguistic, as distinct from mathematical, considerations.

It is also important to note that biases may enter the assessment even when the assessment does not contain construct-irrelevant factors. For example, exercises may contain only the knowledge, skills, and abilities specified in the content domain, but these may be sampled in a nonrepresentative way so that some abilities and skills (e.g., writing) are overemphasized and others (e.g., vocabulary) are underemphasized. To the extent that subgroups of the examinee population differ in these abilities, the assessment will penalize some examinees (see Bond, Moss, & Carr, 1996).

Differential item functioning (DIF) is present when examinees of the same ability but belonging to different groups have differing probabilities of success on an item. Thus, DIF procedures based on this condition of "the same ability" are most credible, with some methods being based on the latent ability (Thissen, Steinberg, & Wainer, 1988) but most based on the observed score such as the Mantel-Haenszel method (Holland & Thayer, 1988), parametric item response theory procedures (Raju, van der Linden, & Fleer, 1995), and logistic regression methods (Swaminathan & Rogers, 1990).

The logistic regression method is preferred because it can detect both uniform (where there is no interaction between ability level and group membership) and nonuniform (where there is interaction) DIF and because it allows multiple dimensions to be treated explicitly within the model (see Mazor, Kanjee, & Clauser, 1998; see also Ackerman, 1992; Ackerman & Evans, 1993; and Zwick & Ercikan, 1989, for similar but more cumbersome procedures based on the Mantel-Haenszel method). A more recent development has led to investigation of how several individually biased items can combine to exhibit a major and biasing influence at the test level. Shealy and Stout (1993) have proposed a simultaneous item bias procedure (SIBTEST) for both dichotomous and polytomous items (Chang, Mazzeo, & Roussos, 1996) and for unidimensional and multidimensional tests (Stout, Li, Nandakumar, & Bolt, 1997).

CONCLUDING COMMENTS

During the past century there have been major advances in our theories about knowledge, achievement, and attitude development. There have been major landmarks moving from the associationists and behavior modifiers through to the current emphasis on cognitive processing and constructivism. Many of our measurement models have not kept apace with these changes, and, as we move into new areas of measurement theory, there is a rich legacy on which to build better test models that capture the complexity and richness of achievement, learning, and attitudes. To fully optimize the advantages of this heritage, it will be necessary in the immediate future to modify our testing models by readdressing the implications of performance assessments and reassessing the learning models underlying the present measurement models. Given the improvements in modern technology, we are likely to see an emphasis on reporting using more fascinating and informative methods and on using more effective ways to communicate the complex information that is becoming the norm when reporting test results.

The underlying assumptions of our present major measurement models (classical and item response) seem to be grounded on Bloom's first one or two levels of knowledge and comprehension; they are more capable of modeling these two levels and less capable of modeling the higher order processing proficiencies. One implication of the current trend to use performance assessments is that we may need to expand our models to include higher order or deeper conceptions of learning and knowing. This may lead us to return to our roots in measurement and consider item specification procedures, developing and defending innovative scoring methods, and a return to issues of decision consistency, along with the familiar refrain as to the importance of defending arguments about the appropriate interpretations of test scores.

Test scores are often referred to as indicators of the presence of underlying latent traits, whereas they could also be conceived as elicitors of cognitive processes and samples of content. "The evidence from cognitive psychology suggests that test performances are comprised of complex assemblies of component information-processing actions that are adapted to task requirements during performances'' (Snow & Lohman, 1989, p. 317). Both the classical test theory model and many of the item response models are premised on the notion of latent traits that are ''relatively stable characteristic[s] of a person—an attitude, enduring process, or disposition—which is consistently magnified to some degree when relevant, despite considerable variation in the range of settings and circumstances'' (Messick, 1989, p. 15).

Mislevy (1996a) has argued that the ''standard mental measurement paradigm attends to the problem stimulus strictly from the assessor's point of view, administering the same tasks to all examinees and recording outcomes in terms of behavior categories applied in the same way for all examinees'' (p. 391). With performance assessments, there are many more indirect sources of evidence that the assessor would want to examine, particularly the cognitive processes and depth of processing that the individual deploys in attacking and solving the problem and in recording the performance.

For example, teachers are expected to have knowledge proficiencies about the content they teach; about how to use this knowledge of content; about errors, misconceptions, and preconceptions; about how to use other resources to teach; and about reflection on their teaching. Teachers are not merely the repositories of knowledge, however; to know something is not just to have received information but to have interpreted it and related it to knowledge one already has. In addition, it is critical that teachers know how to perform the tasks of teaching, know when to perform, and know how to adapt that performance to incoming information and to new situations. Successful teaching also requires dispositions (e.g., enthusiasm, commitment, inclusion) to appropriately perform in the art of teaching such that teachers can enhance and engage elementary students in learning and achievement.

During the past decade, there has been a return to performance assessment. Although this has many seductive ''face'' validity properties, the psychometrics underlying these forms of assessment are still being developed (Phillips, 1996). Many of the more recent advances in psychometrics have been related to performance assessments, including developing new cognitive processing models, an emphasis on writing excellent items, developing and defending innovative scoring methods, and a return to issues of decision consistency and standard errors when assessing reliability.

Thus, we suggest that the past can provide directions for the future. We need to return to the basics to build new models. These models will involve better item/test writing specifications to maximize the information available, more attention to writing items that capture higher order or deep processing, more attention to ensuring fairness, closer relationships between proficiencies and cognitive processing, and a need to directly relate the uses and consequences of test score interpretations. van der Linden and Hambleton (1997) predict that IRT may adopt a new identity ''as an enthusiastic provider of psychological models for cognitive processes,'' and they regard this as an unexpected bonus, one that may ''help to better integrate measurement and substantive research—areas that to date have lived too apart from each other'' (p. 22). We concur.

REFERENCES

Ackerman, T. A. (1992). A didactic explanation of item bias, item impact, and item validity from a multidimensional perspective. *Journal of Educational Measurement, 29*, 67–91.

Ackerman, T. A., & Evans, J. A. (1993). The influence of conditioning scores in performing DIF analysis. *Applied Psychological Measurement, 18*, 329–342.

Allen, M. J., & Yen, W. M. (1979). *Introduction to measurement theory*. Monterey, CA: Brooks/Cole.

American Psychological Association, American Educational Research Association, and National Council on Measurement in Education. (1985). *Standards for educational and psychological testing*. Washington, DC: American Psychological Association.

Anderson, L. W. (1994). Research on teaching and teacher education. In L. W. Anderson & L. A. Sosniak (Eds.), *Bloom's taxonomy: A forty-year retrospective. Ninety-third yearbook of the National Society for the Study of Education: Part II* (pp. 126–145). Chicago: University of Chicago Press.

Anderson, L. W. (1997, March). *Rethinking Bloom's taxonomy: Implications for testing and assessment*. Paper presented at the Fourth European Electronic Conference on Assessment and Evaluation.

Andrich, D. (1997). An hyperbolic cosine IRT model for unfolding direct responses of persons to items. In W. J. van der Linden & R. K. Hambleton (Eds.), *Handbook of modern item response theory* (pp. 399–414). New York: Springer-Verlag.

Angoff, W. H. (1971). Scales, norms, and equivalent scores. In R. L. Thorndike (Ed.), *Educational measurement* (2nd ed., pp. 508–600). Washington, DC: American Council on Education.

Baker, F. B. (1992). *Item response theory: Parameter estimation techniques*. New York: Marcel Dekker.

Beaton, A. E., & Allen, N. L. (1992). Interpreting scales through scale anchoring. *Journal of Educational Statistics, 17*, 191–204.

Beaton, A. E., & Johnson, E. G. (1992). Overview of the scaling methodology used in the National Assessment. *Journal of Educational Measurement, 29*, 163–175.

Bejar, I. I. (1991). A methodology for scoring open-ended architectural design problems. *Journal of Applied Psychology, 76*, 522–532.

Bennett, R. E., Gong, B., Kershaw, R. C., Rock, D. A., Soloway, E., & Macalalad, A. (1990). Assessment of an expert system's ability to grade and diagnose automatically students' constructed responses to computer science problems. In R. O. Freedle (Ed.), *Artificial intelligence and the future of testing* (pp. 293–320). Hillsdale, NJ: Erlbaum.

Bennett, R. E., Steffen, M., Singley, M. K., Morley, M., & Jacquemin, D. (1997). Evaluating an automatically scoring, open-ended response type for measuring mathematical reasoning in computer-adaptive tests. *Journal of Educational Measurement, 34*, 162–176.

Bennett, R. E., & Ward, W. C. (1993). *Construction versus choice in cognitive measurement: Issues in constructed response, performance testing, and portfolio assessment*. Hillsdale, NJ: Erlbaum.

Berk, R. A. (1995). Something old, something new, something borrowed, a lot to do. *Applied Measurement in Education, 8*, 99–109.

Berliner, D. C., & Biddle, B. J. (1995). *The manufactured crisis: Myths, fraud, and the attack on America's public schools*. Reading, MA: Addison-Wesley.

Biggs, J. B. (1987). *Student approaches to learning and studying*. Hawthorn, Victoria: Australian Council for Educational Research.

Biggs, J. B. (1990). Asian students' approaches to learning: Implications for teaching overseas students. In M. Kratzing (Ed.), *Eighth Australian learning and language conference* (pp. 1–51). Brisbane: Queensland University Technology Counselling Services.

Biggs, J. B., & Collis, K. F. (1982). *Evaluating the quality of learning: The SOLO taxonomy (Structure of the Observed Learning Outcome)*. New York: Academic Press.

Biggs, J. B., & Collis, K. F. (1989). Toward a model of school-based curriculum development and assessment using the SOLO taxonomy. *Australian Journal of Education, 33,* 151–163.

Binet, A. (1911). Nouveles reserches sur la mesure du niveau intellectual chezles enfants d'ecole. *L'Anee Psychologique, 17,* 145–201.

Birnbaum, A. (1967). *Statistical theory for logistic mental test models with a prior distribution of ability* (Research Bulletin No. 67-12). Princeton, NJ: Educational Testing Service.

Birnbaum, A. (1968). Some latent trait models and their use in inferring an examinee's ability. In F. M. Lord & M. R. Novick (Eds.), *Statistical theories of mental test scores* (pp. 397–479). Reading, MA: Addison-Wesley.

Black, P., & Wiliam, D. (1998). Assessment and classroom learning. *Assessment in Education, 5,* 7–74.

Bloom, B. S., Engelhart, M. D., Furst, E. J., Hill, W. H., & Krathwohl, D. (1956). *Taxonomy of educational objectives: The cognitive domain*. New York: McKay.

Bloxom, B. (1985). Considerations in psychometric modeling of response time. *Psychometrika, 50,* 383–397.

Bock, R. D. (1997). The nominal categories model. In W. J. van der Linden & R. K. Hambleton (Eds.), *Handbook of modern item response theory* (pp. 33–49). New York: Springer-Verlag.

Bock, R. D., & Aitkin, M. (1981). Marginal maximum likelihood estimation of item parameters: An application of an EM algorithm. *Psychometrika, 46,* 443–459.

Bock, R. D., Gibbons, R., & Muraki, E. (1988). Full information item factor analysis. *Applied Psychological Measurement, 12,* 261–280.

Bond, L., Moss, P., & Carr, P. (1996). Fairness in large-scale performance assessment. In G. W. Phillips (Ed.), *Technical issues in large-scale performance assessment* (pp. 117–140). Washington, DC: U.S. Government Printing Office.

Braun, H. I., Bennett, R. E., Frye, D., & Solway, E. (1990). Scoring constructed responses using expert systems. *Journal of Educational Measurement, 27,* 93–108.

Brennan, R. L. (1992). *Elements of generalizability theory* (rev. ed.). Iowa City, IA: American College Testing.

Brennan, R. L. (1994). Variance components in generalizability theory. In C. R. Reynolds (Ed.), *Cognitive assessment: A multidisciplinary perspective* (pp. 175–207). New York: Plenum.

Brennan, R. L. (1995). The conventional wisdom about group mean scores. *Journal of Educational Measurement, 14,* 385–396.

Brookhart, S. M. (1994). Teachers' grading: Practice and theory. *Applied Measurement in Education, 7,* 279–302.

Brown, W. (1910). Some experimental results in the correlation of mental abilities. *British Journal of Psychology, 3,* 296–322.

Burket, G. (1984). Response to Hoover. *Educational Measurement: Issues and Practice, 3*(4), 15–16.

Burns, E. (1998). *Test accommodations for students with disabilities*. Springfield, IL: Charles C Thomas.

Calder, J. R. (1983). In the cells of Bloom's taxonomy. *Journal of Curriculum Studies, 15,* 291–302.

Chang, H. H., Mazzeo, J., & Roussos, L. (1996). Detecting DIF for polytomous scored items: An adaptation of the SIBTEST procedure. *Journal of Educational Measurement, 33,* 333–353.

Clauser, B. E., Margolis, M. J., Clyman, S. G., & Ross, L. P. (1997). Development of automated scoring algorithms for complex performance assessments: A comparison of two approaches. *Journal of Educational Measurement, 34,* 141–161.

Clauser, B. E., Subhiyah, R. G., Nungester, R. J., Ripkey, D. R., Clyman, S. G., & McKinley, D. (1995). Scoring a performance-based assessment by modeling the judgements of experts. *Journal of Educational Measurement, 32,* 397–415.

Conoley, J. C., & Impara, J. C. (Eds.). (1995). *The twelfth mental measurements yearbook.* Lincoln, NE: Buros Institute of Mental Measurements.

Coombs, C. H. (1954). *A theory of data.* New York: Wiley.

Crocker, L., & Algina, J. (1986). *Introduction to classical and modern test theory.* New York: CBS College Publishing.

Cronbach, L. J. (1951). Coefficient alpha and the internal structure of tests. *Psychometrika, 16,* 297–334.

Cronbach, L. J. (1971). Test validation. In R. L. Thorndike (Ed.), *Educational measurement* (2nd ed.). Washington, DC: American Council on Education.

Cronbach, L. J. (1988). Five perspectives on validation argument. In H. Wainer & H. Braun (Eds.), *Test validity* (pp. 3–17). Hillsdale, NJ: Erlbaum.

Cronbach, L. J., & Gleser, G. C. (1965). *Psychological tests and personnel decisions* (2nd ed.). Urbana: University of Illinois Press.

Cronbach, L. J., Gleser, G. C., Nanda, H., & Rajaratnum, N. (1971). *The dependability of behavioral measurements: Theory of generalizability for scores and profiles.* New York: Wiley.

Cronbach, L. J., Linn, R. L., Brennan, R. L., & Haertel, E. (1997). Generalizability analysis for performance assessments of student achievement or school effectiveness. *Educational and Psychological Measurement, 57,* 373–399.

Cronbach, L. J., Rajaratnum, N., & Gleser, G. C. (1963). Theory of generalizability: A liberalization of reliability theory. *British Journal of Statistical Psychology, 16,* 137–163.

Crooks, T. J. (1988). The impact of classroom evaluation practice on students. *Review of Educational Research, 38,* 438–481.

Crooks, T. J., Kane, M. T., & Cohen, A. S. (1996). Threats to the valid use of assessments. *Assessment in Education, 3,* 265–285.

Darling-Hammond, L. (1992). Educational indicators and enlightened policy. *Educational Policy, 6,* 235–265.

Darling-Hammond, L. (1994). Performance-based assessment and educational equity. *Harvard Educational Research, 85,* 438–481.

Dorn, S. (1998). The political legacy of school accountability systems. *Educational Policy Analysis, 6* [On-line serial]. Available: http://olam.ed.asu.edu/epaa/v6n1.html

Dunbar, S. B., Koretz, D. M., & Hoover, H. D. (1991). Quality control in the development and use of performance assessments. *Applied Measurement in Education, 4,* 289–303.

Ebel, R. L. (1972). *Essentials of educational measurement* (2nd ed.). Englewood Cliffs, NJ: Prentice Hall.

Edgeworth, F. Y. (1888). The statistics of examinations. *Journal of the Royal Statistical Society, 51,* 599–635.

Edgeworth, F. Y. (1892). Correlated averages. *Philosophical Magazine, 34,* 190–204.

Elias, S., Hattie, J. A., & Douglas, G. (1998, March). *An assessment of various IRT and SEM fit indices to detect unidimensionality.* Paper presented at the annual conference of the National Council for Measurement in Education, San Diego, CA.

Embretson, S. E. (1995a). A measurement model for linking individual learning to processes and knowledge: Application and mathematical reasoning. *Journal of Educational Measurement, 32,* 277–294.

Embretson, S. E. (1995b). Working memory capacity versus general control processes in abstract reasoning. *Intelligence, 20,* 169–189.

Embretson, S. E. (1997). Multicomponent response models. In W. J. van der Linden & R. K. Hambleton (Eds.), *Handbook of modern item response theory* (pp. 305–321). New York: Springer-Verlag.

Ennis, R. H. (1985). A logical basis for measuring critical thinking skills. *Educational Leadership*, pp. 45–48.

Etezadi-Amoli, J., & McDonald, R. P. (1983). A second generation nonlinear factor analysis. *Psychometrika, 48*, 315–342.

Feldt, L. S., & Brennan, R. L. (1989). Reliability. In R. L. Linn (Ed.), *Educational measurement* (3rd ed., pp. 105–146). Washington, DC: American Council on Education.

Fennema, E., Carpenter, T. P., Jacobs, V. R., Franke, M. L., & Levi, L. W. (1998). A longitudinal study of gender differences in young children's mathematical thinking. *Educational Researcher, 27*(5), 6–11.

Feuer, M. J., Holland, P. W., Bertenthal, M. W., Hemphill, F. C., & Green, B. F. (1998). *Equivalency and linkage of educational tests.* Washington, DC: National Academy Press.

Fischer, G. H. (1997). Unidimensional linear logistic Rasch models: The nominal categories model. In W. J. van der Linden & R. K. Hambleton (Eds.), *Handbook of modern item response theory* (pp. 225–243). New York: Springer-Verlag.

Forsyth, R., Hambleton, R. K., Linn, R. L., Mislevy, R., & Yen, W. (1996). *Design feasibility team: Report to the National Assessment Governing Board.* Washington, DC: National Assessment Governing Board.

Frary, R. B. (1989). Partial-credit scoring methods for multiple-choice tests. *Applied Measurement in Education, 2*, 79–96.

Fraser, C. (1988). *NOHARMII. A Fortran program for fitting unidimensional and multidimensional normal ogive models of latent trait theory.* Armidale, Australia: University of New England.

Furst, E. J. (1981). Bloom's taxonomy of educational objectives for the cognitive domain: Philosophical and educational issues. *Review of Educational Research, 51*, 441–453.

Gipps, C. V. (1994). *Beyond testing: Toward a theory of educational assessment.* London: Falmer Press.

Glass, G. V. (1978). Standards and criteria. *Journal of Educational Measurement, 15*, 237–261.

Goldman, B. A., Mitchell, D. F., & Egelson, P. E. (1997). *Directory of unpublished experimental mental measures.* Washington, DC: American Psychological Association.

Gulliksen, H. (1950). *Theory of mental tests.* New York: Wiley.

Guttman, L. (1945). A basis for analyzing test-retest reliability. *Psychometrika, 10*, 255–282.

Haertel, E. (1985). Construct validity and criterion-referenced testing. *Review of Educational Research, 55*, 23–46.

Haertel, E., & Linn, R. L. (1996). Comparability. In G. W. Phillips (Ed.), *Technical issues in large-scale performance assessment* (pp. 59–78). Washington, DC: U.S. Government Printing Office.

Haladyna, T. M., & Downing, S. M. (1989a). A taxonomy of multiple-choice item-writing rules. *Applied Measurement in Education, 2*, 37–50.

Haladyna, T. M., & Downing, S. M. (1989b). Validity of a taxonomy of multiple-choice item-writing rules. *Applied Measurement in Education, 2*, 51–78.

Hambleton, R. K., & Plake, B. S. (1995). Using an extended Angoff procedure to set standards on complex performance assessments. *Applied Measurement in Education, 8*, 41–56.

Hambleton, R. K., & Slater, S. C. (1995). *Are NAEP executive summary reports understandable to policy makers and educators?* Amherst, MA: National Center for Education Statistics.

Hambleton, R. K., Swaminathan, H., & Rogers, H. J. (1991). *Fundamentals of item response theory.* Newbury Park, CA: Sage.

Hattie, J. A. (1984). Decision criteria for assessing unidimensionality: An empirical study. *Multivariate Behavioral Research, 19,* 49–78.

Hattie, J. A. (1985). Methodology review: Assessing unidimensionality of tests and items. *Applied Psychological Measurement, 9,* 139–164.

Hattie, J. A. (1996, April). *Validating the specification of a complex content domain.* Paper presented at the annual conference of the American Association for Research in Education, New York.

Hattie, J. A., & Cooksey, R. W. (1984). Procedures for assessing the validity of tests using the "known groups" method. *Applied Psychological Measurement, 6,* 295–305.

Hattie, J. A., & Jaeger, R. M. (1998). Assessment and classroom learning: A deductive approach. *Assessment in Education, 5,* 111–122.

Hattie, J. A., Krakowski, K., Rogers, H. J., & Swaminathan, H. (1996). An assessment of Stout's index of essential unidimensionality. *Applied Psychological Measurement, 20,* 1–14.

Hattie, J. A., & Purdie, N. (1998). The SOLO model: Addressing fundamental measurement issues. In B. Dart & G. Boulton-Lewis (Eds.), *Teaching and learning in higher education* (pp. 145–176). Melbourne: Australian Council for Educational Research.

Hawkins, E. (1995). Impact of the 1992 National Assessment of Educational Progress trial state assessment. In R. Glaser, R. L. Linn, & G. Bohrnstedt (Eds.), *Quality and utility: The 1994 trial state assessment in reading, background studies* (pp. 403–427). Stanford, CA: National Academy of Education.

Hill, P. W., & McGaw, B. (1981). Testing the simplex assumption underlying Bloom's taxonomy. *American Educational Research Journal, 18,* 93–101.

Hoijtink, H. (1990). A latent trait model for dichotomous choice data. *Psychometrika, 55,* 641–656.

Holland, P. W., & Rubin, D. B. (1982). *Test equating.* New York: Academic Press.

Holland, P. W., & Thayer, D. T. (1988). Differential item performance and the Mantel-Haenszel procedure. In H. Wainer & H. I. Braun (Eds.), *Test validity* (pp. 129–145). Hillsdale, NJ: Erlbaum.

Holland, P. W., & Thayer, D. T. (1989). *The kernel method of equating score distributions* (Program Statistics Technical Rep. No. 89-94). Princeton, NJ: Educational Testing Service.

Jaeger, R. M. (1982). An iterative structure judgement process for establishing standards on competency tests: Theory and application. *Educational Evaluation and Policy Analysis, 4,* 461–475.

Jaeger, R. M. (1989). Certification of student competence. In R. L. Linn (Ed.), *Educational measurement* (3rd ed., pp. 485–514). New York: American Council on Education.

Jaeger, R. M. (1994, October). *On the cognitive construction of standard-setting judgements: The case of configural scoring.* Paper presented at the NCES/NAGB conference on standard-setting methodology, Washington, DC.

Jaeger, R. M. (1995a). Setting performance standards through two-stage judgemental policy capturing. *Applied Measurement in Education, 8,* 15–40.

Jaeger, R. M. (1995b). Setting standards for complex performances: An iterative, judgemental policy capturing strategy. *Educational Measurement: Issues and Practice, 14,* 16–20.

Jaeger, R. M. (1996, April). *Reporting large-scale assessment results for public consumption: Some propositions and palliatives.* Paper presented at the annual meeting of the National Council on Measurement in Education, New York.

Jaeger, R. M., Gorney, B., Johnson, R. L., Putnam, S. E., & Williamson, G. (1993). *Designing and developing effective school report cards: A research synthesis.* Kalamazoo: Center for Research on Education Accountability and Teacher Evaluation, Western Michigan University.

Jaeger, R. M., Hambleton, R. K., & Plake, B. S. (1995, April). *Eliciting configural performance standards through a sequenced application of complementary methods.* Paper presented at the annual meetings of the American Educational Research Association and the National Council on Measurement in Education, San Francisco.

Jaeger, R. M., Mullis, I. V. S., Bourque, M. L., & Shakrani, S. (1996). Setting performance standards for performance assessments: Some fundamental issues, current practice, and technical dilemmas. In G. W. Phillips (Ed.), *Technical issues in large-scale performance assessment* (pp. 79–115). Washington, DC: U.S. Government Printing Office.

Jannarone, R. J. (1986). Conjunctive item response theory kernels. *Psychometrika, 51,* 357–373.

Jones, L. V. (1971). The nature of measurement. In R. L. Thorndike (Ed.), *Educational measurement* (2nd ed., pp. 336–373). Washington, DC: American Council on Education.

Junker, B. W. (1990). *Progress in characterizing strictly unidimensional IRT representations* (Tech. Rep. No. 498). Pittsburgh, PA: Carnegie Mellon University.

Junker, B. W. (1991). Essential independence and likelihood-based ability estimation for polytomous items. *Psychometrika, 56,* 255–278.

Junker, B. (1992, April). *Ability estimation in unidimensional models when more than one trait is present.* Paper presented at the annual meeting of the American Educational Research Association, San Francisco.

Kane, M. T. (1992). A sampling model for validity. *Applied Psychological Measurement, 6,* 125–160.

Kim, H. R. (1994). New techniques for the dimensionality assessment of standardized test data (Doctoral dissertation, University of Illinois at Urbana-Champaign). *Dissertation Abstracts International, 55,* 5598.

Kolen, M. J., & Brennan, R. L. (1995). *Test equating.* New York: Springer-Verlag.

Koretz, D. (1992a). *National educational standards and testing: A response to the recommendations of the National Council on Education Standards and Testing.* (ERIC Document Reproduction Service No. ED 351 386)

Koretz, D. (1992b). What happened to test scores, and why? *Educational Measurement: Issues and Practice, 11,* 7–11.

Koretz, D., & Deibert, E. (1993). *Interpretations of National Assessment of Educational Progress (NAEP) anchor points and achievement levels by the print media in 1991.* Santa Monica, CA: Rand. (ERIC Document Reproduction Service No. ED 367 683)

Kropp, R. P., Stoker, H. W., & Bashaw, W. L. (1966). The validation of the taxonomy of educational objectives. *Journal of Experimental Education, 34,* 69–76.

Kuder, G. F., & Richardson, M. W. (1937). The theory of estimation of test reliability. *Psychometrika, 2,* 151–160.

Kunen, S., Cohen, R., & Solman, R. (1981). A levels-of-processing analysis of Bloom's taxonomy. *Journal of Educational Psychology, 73,* 202–211.

Lam, R., & Foong, Y. Y. (1996). *Rasch analysis of math SOLO taxonomy levels using hierarchical items in testlets.* (ERIC Document Reproduction Service No. ED 398 271)

Lawley, D. N. (1943). On problems connected with item selection and test construction. *Proceedings of the Royal Society of Edinburgh, 61,* 273–287.

Lawley, D. N., & Maxwell, A. E. (1971). *Factor analysis as a statistical method.* London: Butterworths.

Lazarsfeld, P. F. (1950). The logical and mathematical foundation of latent-structure analysis. In S. A. Stouffer (Ed.), *Measurement and prediction.* Princeton, NJ: Princeton University Press.

Leary, L. F., & Dorans, N. J. (1985). Implications for alternating the context in which test items appear: A historical perspective on an immediate concern. *Review of Educational Research, 55,* 387–413.

Lindquist, E. F. (Ed.). (1951). *Educational measurement.* Washington, DC: American Council on Education.

Linn, R. L. (Ed.). (1989). *Educational measurement* (3rd ed.). New York: American Council on Education.

Linn, R. L. (1990). Has item response theory increased the validity of achievement test scores? *Applied Measurement in Education, 3,* 115–141.

Linn, R. L. (1994). Performance assessment: Policy promises and technical measurement standards. *Educational Research, 23,* 4–14.

Linn, R. L. (1995). Linking statewide tests to the National Assessment of Educational Progress: Stability of results. *Applied Measurement in Education, 9,* 135–156.

Linn, R. L., Baker, E. L., & Dunbar, S. B. (1991). Complex, performance-based assessment: Expectations and validation criteria. *Educational Research, 20,* 15–21.

Linn, R. L., & Miller, M. D. (1968). Review of test validation procedures and results. In R. M. Jaeger, J. C. Busch, L. Bond, R. L. Linn, M. D. Miller, J. Millman, R. G. O'Sullivan, & R. Traub (Eds.), *An evaluation of the Georgia teacher certification testing program.* Greensboro: Center for Educational Research and Evaluation, University of North Carolina, Greensboro.

Livingston, S. A., & Lewis, C. (1995). Estimating the consistency and accuracy of classifications based on test scores. *Journal of Educational Measurement, 32,* 179–197.

Lord, F. M. (1952). A theory of test scores. *Psychometric Monographs, No. 7.*

Lord, F. M. (1965). A strong true-score theory, with applications. *Psychometrika, 30,* 239–270.

Lord, F. M. (1977). Practical applications of item characteristic curve theory. *Journal of Educational Measurement, 14,* 117–138.

Lord, F. M. (1980). *Applications of item response theory to practical testing problems.* Hillsdale, NJ: Erlbaum.

Lord, F. M., & Novick, M. R. (1968). *Statistical theories of mental test scores.* Reading, MA: Addison-Wesley.

Luce, R. D. (1986). *Response times: Their role in inferring elementary mental organization.* New York: Oxford University Press.

Luecht, R., & Miller, T. R. (1992). Unidimensional calibrations and interpretations of composite traits for multidimensional tests. *Applied Psychological Measurement, 16,* 279–293.

Maguire, T. O., Hattie, J. A., & Haig, B. (1994). Construct validity and achievement assessment. *Alberta Journal of Educational Psychology, 40,* 109–126.

Martinez, M. E., & Mead, N. A. (1988). *Computer competence: The first national assessment.* Princeton, NJ: Educational Testing Service.

Marton, F., & Säljö, R. (1976). On qualitative differences in learning: I. Outcome and process. *British Journal of Educational Psychology, 46,* 4–11.

Marton, F., & Säljö, R. (1984). Approaches to learning. In F. Marton, D. Hounsell, & N. Entwistle (Eds.), *The experience of learning* (pp. 36–55). Edinburgh: Scottish Academic Press.

Mazor, K., Kanjee, A., & Clauser, B. E. (1998). Using logistic regression and the Mantel-Haenszel with multiple ability estimates to detect differential item functioning. *Journal of Educational Measurement, 32,* 131–144.

McDonald, R. P. (1967). Nonlinear factor analysis. *Psychometric Monographs, No. 15.*

McDonald, R. P. (1979). The structural analysis of multivariate data: A sketch of general theory. *Multivariate Behavioural Psychology, 14,* 21–38.

McDonald, R. P. (1981). The dimensionality of tests and items. *British Journal of Mathematical Statistical Psychology, 34,* 100–117.

McDonald, R. P. (1985a). *Factor analyses and related methods.* Hillsdale, NJ: Erlbaum.

McDonald, R. P. (1985b). Unidimensional and multidimensional models for item response theory. In D. J. Weiss (Ed.), *Proceedings of the 1982 Item Response Theory and Computer Adaptive Testing Conference.* Minneapolis: University of Minnesota.

McDonald, R. P. (1997). Normal-ogive multidimensional model. In W. J. van der Linden & R. K. Hambleton (Eds.), *Handbook of modern item response theory* (pp. 258–269). New York: Springer-Verlag.

Messick, S. (1989). Validity. In R. L. Linn (Ed.), *Educational measurement* (3rd ed., pp. 13–103). New York: American Council on Education.

Messick, S. (1994). The interplay of evidence and consequences in the validation of performance assessments. *Educational Research, 23,* 13–23.

Messick, S. (1995). Standards of validity and validity of standards in performance assessment. *Educational Measurement: Issues and Practice, 14,* 5–8.

Miller, H. G., Snowman, J., & O'Hara, T. (1979). Application of alternative statistical techniques to examine the hierarchical ordering in Bloom's taxonomy. *American Educational Research Journal, 16,* 241–248.

Mills, C. N., & Melican, G. J. (1988). Estimating and adjusting cutoff scores: Features of selected methods. *Applied Measurement in Education, 1,* 261–275.

Mislevy, R. L. (1986). Bayes modal estimation in item response theory. *Psychometrika, 51,* 177–195.

Mislevy, R. J. (1988). Scaling procedures. In A. E. Beaton (Ed.), *Expanding the new design: The NAEP 1985–86 technical report* (pp. 177–204). Princeton, NJ: Educational Testing Service.

Mislevy, R. J. (1992). *Linking educational assessments: Concepts, issues, methods, and prospects.* Princeton, NJ: Educational Testing Service.

Mislevy, R. J. (1995). Probability-based inference in cognitive diagnosis. In P. Nichols, S. Chipman, & R. Brennan (Eds.), *Cognitively diagnostic assessment* (pp. 43–71). Hillsdale, NJ: Erlbaum.

Mislevy, R. J. (1996a). Test theory reconceived. *Journal of Educational Measurement, 33,* 379–416.

Mislevy, R. J. (1996b, December). *Implications of market-basket reporting for achievement level setting.* Paper presented at the Setting Consensus Goals for Academic Achievement workshop, Washington, DC.

Mislevy, R. J., & Gitomer, D. H. (1996). The role of probability-based inference in an intelligent tutoring system. *User Modeling and User-Adapted Interaction, 5,* 252–282.

Mislevy, R. J., Wingersky, M. S., Irvine, S. H., & Dann, P. L. (1991). Resolving mixtures of strategies in spatial visualisation tasks. *British Journal of Mathematical and Statistical Psychology, 44,* 265–288.

Mokken, R. J. (1997). Nonparametric models for dichotomous responses. In W. J. van der Linden & R. K. Hambleton (Eds.), *Handbook of modern item response theory* (pp. 351–367). New York: Springer-Verlag.

Mullis, I. V. S., Dossey, J. A., Owen, E. H., & Phillips, G. W. (1993). *The 1992 mathematics report card.* Washington, DC: U.S. Department of Education.

Mullis, I. V. S., Oldefendt, S. J., & Phillips, D. L. (1977). *What students know and can do: Profiles of three age groups.* Denver, CO: National Assessment of Educational Progress.

Muraki, E., & Carlson, J. E. (1995). Full-information factor analysis for polytomous item responses. *Applied Psychological Measurement, 19,* 73–90.

Muthén, B. (1978). Contributions to factor analysis of dichotomous items. *Psychometrika, 30,* 419–440.

Nandakumar, R. (1993). Assessing essential unidimensionality of real data. *Applied Psychological Measurement, 17,* 29–38.

Nandakumar, R. (1994). Assessing dimensionality of a set of items—Comparison of different approaches. *Journal of Educational Measurement, 31,* 17–35.

Nandakumar, R., & Stout, W. (1993). Refinements of Stout's procedure for assessing latent trait unidimensionality. *Journal of Educational Statistics, 18,* 41–68.

Nandakumar, R., Yu, F., Li, H., & Stout, W. (1998). Assessing unidimensionality of polytomous data. *Applied Psychological Measurement, 22,* 99-115.

Nedelsky, L. (1954). Absolute grading standards for objective tests. *Educational and Psychological Measurement, 14,* 3–19.

Nester, M. A. (1993). Psychometric testing and reasonable accommodation for persons with disabilities. *Rehabilitation Psychology, 38,* 75–85.

Page, E. B., & Petersen, N. S. (1995). The computer moves into essay grading. *Phi Delta Kappan, 76,* 561–565.

Pearson, K. (1896). Mathematical contributions to the theory of evolution: III. Regression, heredity and panmixia. *Philosophical Transactions, A, 187,* 253–318.

Pearson, K. (1904). On the laws of inheritance in man. II. On the inheritance of the mental and moral characters in man, and its comparison with the inheritance of physical characters. *Biometrika, 3,* 131–190.

Petersen, N. S., Kolen, M. J., & Hoover, H. D. (1989). Scaling, norming, and equating. In R. L. Linn (Ed.), *Educational measurement* (3rd ed., pp. 221–262). New York: Macmillan.

Phillips, G. W. (Ed.). (1996). *Technical issues in large-scale performance assessment.* Washington, DC: U.S. Government Printing Office.

Phillips, G. W., Mullis, I. V. S., Bourque, M. L., Williams, P. L., Hambleton, R. K., Owen, E. H., & Barton, P. E. (1993). *Interpreting NAEP scales.* Washington, DC: National Center for Education Statistics.

Pitz, G. F., & Sachs, N. J. (1984). Judgment and decision: Theory and application. *Annual Review of Psychology, 35,* 139–163.

Plake, B. S., Hambleton, R. K., & Jaeger, R. M. (1997). A new standard-setting method for performance assessments: The dominant profile judgement method and some field-test results. *Educational and Psychological Measurement, 57,* 400–411.

Raju, N., van der Linden, W., & Fleer, P. (1995). IRT-based internal measures of differential functioning of items and tests. *Applied Psychological Measurement, 19,* 353–368.

Ramsey, J. O. (1993). *TESTGRAF: A program for the graphical analysis of multiple-choice test and questionnaire data.* Unpublished technical manual, McGill University, Montreal, Quebec, Canada.

Rasch, G. (1960). *Probabilistic models for some intelligence and attainment tests.* Copenhagen: Danish Institute for Educational Research.

Rasch, G. (1961). On general laws and the meaning of measurement in psychology. *Proceedings of the Fourth Berkeley Symposium on Mathematical Statistics and Probability, 4,* 321–324.

Reckase, M. D. (1985). The difficulty of test items that measure more than one ability. *Applied Psychological Measurement, 9,* 401–412.

Reckase, M. D. (1997). A linear logistic multidimensional model for dichotomous item response data. In W. J. van der Linden & R. K. Hambleton (Eds.), *Handbook of modern item response theory* (pp. 271–286). New York: Springer-Verlag.

Reckase, M. D., Carlson, J. E., Ackerman, T. A., & Spray, J. A. (1987). *The interpretation of unidimensional IRT parameters when estimated from multidimensional data.* Paper presented at the annual meeting of the Psychometric Society, Toronto.

Reckase, M. D., & McKinley, R. J. (1991). The discriminating power of items that measure more than one dimension. *Applied Psychological Measurement, 15,* 361–373.

Roid, G. H., & Haladyna, T. M. (1982). *A technology for test-writing technology.* New York: Academic Press.

Samejima, F. (1997). Graded response model. In W. J. van der Linden & R. K. Hambleton (Eds.), *Handbook of modern item response theory* (pp. 85–100). New York: Springer-Verlag.

Schmidt, F. L., Hunter, J. E., Pearlman, K., & Hirsch, H. R. (1985). Forty questions about validity generalization and meta-analysis. *Personnel Psychology, 32,* 697–698.

Schrag, F. (1989). Are there levels of thinking? *Teachers College Record, 90,* 529–533.

Seddon, G. M. (1978). The properties of Bloom's taxonomy of educational objectives for the cognitive domain. *Review of Educational Research, 48,* 303–323.

Shavelson, R. J., Baxter, G. P., & Gao, X. (1993). Sampling variability of performance assessments. *Journal of Educational Measurement, 30,* 215–232.

Shavelson, R. J., Baxter, G. P., & Pine, J. (1992). Performance assessments: Political rhetoric and measurement reality. *Educational Measurement, 21,* 22–27.

Shavelson, R. J., Gao, X., & Baxter, G. P. (1996). On the content validity of performance assessments: Centrality of domain specification. In M. Birenbaum & F. J. R. C. Dochy (Eds.), *Alternatives in assessment of achievements, learning processes, and prior knowledge* (pp. 131–141). Boston: Kluwer Academic.

Shavelson, R. J., & Webb, N. M. (1991). *Generalizability theory: A primer.* Newbury Park, CA: Sage.

Shealy, R., & Stout, W. (1993). A model-based standardization approach that separates true bias/DIF from group ability differences and detects test bias/DIF as well as item bias/DIF. *Psychometrika, 58,* 159–194.

Shepard, L. A. (1991). Will national tests improve student learning? *Phi Delta Kappan, 73,* 232–238.

Shepard, L. A. (1993). Evaluating test validity. In L. Darling-Hammond (Ed.), *Review of research in education* (Vol. 19, pp. 405–450). Washington, DC: American Educational Research Association.

Shepard, L. A., Flexner, R. J., Hiebert, E. H., Marion, S. F., Mayfield, V., & Weston, T. J. (1996). Effects of introducing classroom assessments on student learning. *Educational Measurement: Issues and Practice, 15,* 7–18.

Smith, I. L., Greenberg, S., & Muenzen, P. M. (1993). *Procedures employed by selected licensure and certification agencies in defining content standards: A report to the technical advisory group.* Greensboro: Center for Educational Research and Evaluation, University of North Carolina, Greensboro.

Smith, M. L., & Rottenberg, C. (1991). Unintended consequences of external testing in elementary schools. *Educational Measurement: Issues and Practice, 10,* 7–11.

Snow, R. E., & Lohman, D. F. (1989). Implications of cognitive psychology for educational measurement. In R. L. Linn (Ed.), *Educational measurement* (3rd ed., pp. 263–331). New York: Macmillan.

Society for Industrial and Organizational Psychology. (1987). *Principles for the validation and use of personnel selection procedures.* Washington, DC.

Spearman, C. (1904). The proof and measurement of association between two things. *American Journal of Psychology, 15,* 72–101.

Spearman, C. (1907). Demonstration of formulae for true measurement of correlation. *American Journal of Psychology, 18,* 161–169.

Spearman, C. (1910). Correlation calculated from faulty data. *British Journal of Psychology, 3,* 271–295.

Spielberger, C. D. (1980). *Preliminary professional manual for the Test-Anxiety Inventory.* Palo Alto, CA: Consulting Psychologists Press.

Stanley, J. C. (1971). Reliability. In R. L. Thorndike (Ed.), *Educational measurement* (2nd ed., pp. 356–442). Washington, DC: American Council on Education.

Stanley, J. C., & Wang, M. D. (1970). Weighting test items and test-item options, an overview of the analytical and empirical literature. *Educational and Psychological Measurement, 30,* 21–35.

Stout, W. F. (1987). A nonparametric approach for assessing latent trait unidimensionality. *Psychometrika, 52,* 589–617.

Stout, W. F. (1990). A new item response theory modelling approach and applications to unidimensionality assessment and ability estimation. *Psychometrika, 55,* 293–325.

Stout, W. F., Li, H. H., Nandakumar, R., & Bolt, D. (1997). Multisib: A procedure to investigate DIF when a test is intentionally two-dimensional. *Applied Psychological Measurement, 21,* 195–213.

Strunk, D., & White, E. B. (1979). *The elements of style.* New York: Macmillan.

Sutherland, G. (1984). *Ability, merit, and measurement: Mental testing and English education 1880–1940.* Oxford, England: Clarendon.

Swaminathan, H., & Rogers, H. J. (1990). Detecting differential item functioning using logistic regression procedures. *Journal of Educational Measurement, 27,* 361–370.

Thissen, D., Steinberg, L., & Wainer, H. (1988). Detection of differential item functioning using the parameters of item response models. In P. W. Holland & H. Wainer (Eds.), *Differential item functioning* (pp. 67–113). Hillsdale, NJ: Erlbaum.

Thorndike, R. L. (Ed.). (1971). *Educational measurement* (2nd ed.). New York: American Council on Education.

Traub, R. E. (1993). On the equivalence of the traits assessed by multiple-choice and constructed-response tests. In R. E. Bennett & W. C. Ward (Eds.), *Construction versus choice in cognitive measurement: Issues in constructed response, performance testing, and portfolio assessment* (pp. 29–44). Hillsdale, NJ: Erlbaum.

Traub, R. E. (1997). Classical test theory in historical perspective. *Educational Measurement: Issues and Practice, 16,* 8–14.

Traub, R. E., Haertel, E. H., & Shavelson, R. J. (1996, April). *The effects of measurement error on the trustworthiness of examinee classifications.* Paper presented at the annual meeting of the American Educational Research Association, New York.

Traub, R. E., & Wolfe, R. G. (1981). Latent trait theories and the assessment of educational achievement. In D. C. Berliner (Ed.), *Review of research in education* (Vol. 9, pp. 377–435). Washington, DC: American Educational Research Association.

Tucker, L. R. (1946). Maximum validity of a test with equivalent items. *Psychometrika, 11,* 1–13.

Tukey, J. W. (1977). *Exploratory data analysis.* Reading, MA: Addison-Wesley.

U.S. Department of Justice. (1978). *Uniform guidelines on employee selection procedures.* Washington, DC.

van der Linden, W. J. (1996). Assembling tests for the measurement of multiple traits. *Applied Psychological Measurement, 20,* 373–388.

van der Linden, W. J., & Hambleton, R. K. (1997). Item response theory: Brief history, common models, and extensions. In W. J. van der Linden & R. K. Hambleton (Eds.), *Handbook of modern item response theory* (pp. 1–28). New York: Springer-Verlag.

van der Linden, W. J., & Luecht, R. M. (1996). An optimization model for test assembly to match observed-score distributions. In G. Engelhard & M. Wilson (Eds.), *Objective measurement: Theory into practice* (Vol. 3, pp. 405–418). Norwood, NJ: Ablex.

Wainer, H. (1977). Speed vs. reaction time as a measure of cognitive performance. *Memory and Cognition, 5,* 278–280.

Wainer, H. (Ed.). (1990). *Computerized adaptive testing: A primer.* Hillsdale, NJ: Erlbaum.

Wainer, H. (1992). Understanding graphs and tables. *Educational Researcher, 21*(1), 14–23.

Wainer, H. (1996). Using trilinear plots for NAEP state data. *Journal of Educational Measurement, 33,* 41–55.

Wainer, H. (1997). Improving tabular display, with NAEP tables as examples and inspirations. *Journal of Educational and Behavioral Statistics, 22,* 1–30.

Ward, A., Stoker, H. W., & Murray-Ward, M. (Eds.). (1996a). *Educational measurement: Origins, theories and explications: Basic concepts and theories.* New York: University Press of America.

Ward, A., Stoker, H. W., & Murray-Ward, M. (Eds.). (1996b). *Educational measurement: Origins, theories and explications: Theories and applications.* New York: University Press of America.

Ward, A., Stoker, H. W., & Murray-Ward, M. (Eds.). (1996c). *Educational measurement: Origins, theories and explications: Theories and applications* (Vol. 2). New York: University Press of America.

Wilson, M. (1989). A comparison of deterministic and probabilistic approaches to measuring learning structures. *Australian Journal of Education, 33,* 127–140.

Wilson, M., & Adams, R. J. (1993). Marginal maximum-likelihood estimation for the ordered partition model. *Journal of Educational Statistics, 18,* 69–90.

Wilson, M., & Iventosch, L. (1988). Using the partial credit model to investigate responses to structural sub-tests. *Applied Psychological Measurement, 1,* 319–334.

Wilson, M., & Masters, G. N. (1993). The partial credit model and null categories. *Psychometrika, 58,* 87–99.

Wittgenstein, L. (1953). *Philosophical investigations.* Oxford, England: Basil Blackwell.

Wolf, T. H. (1973). *Alfred Binet.* Chicago: University of Chicago Press.

Wollack, J. A., & Cohen, A. S. (1998). Detection of answer coping with unknown item and trait parameters. *Applied Psychological Measurement, 22,* 144–152.

Woolf, H. (1961). *Quantification: A history of the meaning of measurement in the natural and social sciences.* Indianapolis, IN: Bobbs-Merrill.

Yen, W. M. (1994). Effects of local item dependence on the fit and equating performance of the three-parameter logistic model. *Applied Psychological Measurement, 8,* 125–145.

Zhang, J., & Stout, W. (1997). On Holland's Dutch identity conjecture. *Psychometrika, 62,* 375–392.

Zieky, M. J. (1995). A historical perspective on setting standards. In *Proceedings of the Joint Conference on Standard Setting for Large Scale Assessments* (pp. 1–38). Washington, DC: National Assessment Governing Board and National Center for Education Statistics.

Zwick, R., & Ercikan, K. (1989). Analysis of differential item functioning in the NAEP history assessment. *Journal of Educational Measurement, 26,* 55–66.

Manuscript received August 15, 1998
Accepted December 15, 1998